Seventy years have passed since the Second World War, yet the books and articles still keep coming in a never-ending stream – discussing the question of what role the deliveries of arms and materials by Soviet Allies played in the victory of the Red Army. In Russia, the American Bell P-39 Airacobra fighter – along with the Studebaker US6 truck and canned stewed meat – became the symbols of Allied help to the USSR during the Second World War. Other aircraft which arrived to the country under the Lend-Lease program are less known, but also made a valuable contribution to the victory.

The author of this book has, for the first time, assembled a huge volume of information relating to the delivery of aviation equipment from the UK and the USA. Based on documents from Russian and foreign archives, museums and also veterans' recollections, the author has made a qualitative and quantitative appraisal of the influence of these deliveries upon the Soviet war effort and airpower during the conflict. The book details the routes of the aircraft deliveries to Russia, the modifications which were done in order to suit the demands of the Russian climate, and the specifics of their frontline use, as well as the process of the new aircraft being mastered by the units of the Red Army Air Force.

The first foreign aircraft arrived in the Soviet Union with No.151 Wing RAF in 1941 and their use expanded rapidly: they took part in the counter-offensive near Moscow, the battles for Stalingrad and the Kursk salient, and operations of the war up to the battle for Berlin and the capitulation of Japanese forces in the North China.

The author includes the results of the combat assessments of the aircraft, which were done at the Scientific Testing Institute of the Air Force, as well as reports from frontline regiments and multiple combat episodes – detailing the views of the Soviet designers and pilots on the British and American aircraft. A separate chapter provides information about the aircraft which were not officially delivered, but appeared in the Soviet Union accidentally.

For the first time, an attempt has been made to assess the influence of the deliveries of material and equipment upon the Soviet aviation industry and war effort. The author's impressive text is supported by nearly 700 color and black and white photographs, 100 color aircraft profiles, plus maps and charts.

Vladimir Kotelnikov was born in Moscow on 9 December 1951. He graduated from the Moscow Aviation Institute (University) in 1975 and was engaged in research and development in the area of high-temperature strength. Vladimir obtained the academic degree of Candidate of Science in 1981 and read lectures on aircraft piston engine design at the Moscow Aviation Institute.

Since the 1980s, Vladimir has conducted archive researches on the history of Russian aviation of the interwar and Second World War period. In addition, he paid specific attention to the history of foreign aircraft testing and operations in Russia. As a result of his work, he has had several hundred articles and dozens of books published across Russia, the Ukraine, Poland, the UK, France, Germany, Spain and the US – among them *Americans in Russia*, *Russian Piston Aero Engines*, *Early Russian Jet Engines*, *Air War Over Khalkhin Gol* and *Le Petlyakov Pe-2*.

Being an aviation historian, he received a diploma of a professor of the Academy of Aviation and Aeronautics Science, and currently acts as a consultant on piston aero engines design to Russian aviation museums, as well as to different aircraft restoration groups.

Since 2003, Vladimir has held the post of editor of the *Aviakollektsiya* aviation history magazine, which is published in Moscow.

LEND-LEASE AND SOVIET AVIATION IN THE SECOND WORLD WAR

Vladimir Kotelnikov

Helion & Company

Helion & Company Limited
Unit 8 Amherst Business Centre
Budbrooke Road
Warwick
CV34 5WE
England
Tel. 01926 499619
Email: info@helion.co.uk
Website: www.helion.co.uk
Twitter: @helionbooks
blog.helion.co.uk/

Published by Helion & Company 2017. Reprinted in paperback 2021
Designed and typeset by Mach 3 Solutions Ltd, (www.mach3solutions.co.uk)
Cover designed by Paul Hewitt, Battlefield Design (www.battlefield-design.co.uk)

ISBN 978-1-914059-59-9

British Library Cataloguing-in-Publication Data.
A catalogue record for this book is available from the British Library.

Contents

Acknowledgments

The author has spent more than 20 years on this historical research. The first variant of the book, though not published, was ready in 1995. During these years, many of the ones who helped to collect the research material have passed away and, among them, the direct participants of the described events: pilots, engineers, technicians and workers. The author would like to extend his sincerest thanks for the help he received in the preparation of this book to the following persons (in Russian alphabetical order): V.Ya. Andreev, E.N. Arsenyev, A.A. Artemyev, V.A. Bakursky, M.N. Blinov, N.O. Valouev, F.I. Vasilyev, V.S. Vakhlamov, M.L. Gallay, P.P. Gamov, K. Geust, A.B. Grigoryev, M.I. Grigoryev, N. Eastaway, A.A. Zhdanov, K.P. Ikonnikov, S.M. Kaminsky, A.V. Kanevsky, A.A. Kasyanov, L.B. Kachorovsky, A.Yu. Kotlyarov, A.V. Kuzhelev, I.P. Lebedev, O.Yu. Leiko, M.A. Maslov, A.A. Matveev, A.N. Medved, P.N. Navarnov, S.N. Nakoryakov, B.L. Osetinsky, T.N. Pekov, S.V. Pelin, V.I. Perov, V.M. Perov, G.F. Petrov, I.A. Platonov, G.F. Priymuk, O.V. Rastrenin, V.M. Ratkin, V.G. Rigmant, Yu.V. Rybin, R. Wray, G.O. Sloutskiy, A.I. Smolyarov, S.Ya. Tatushin, I.M. Filippov, D.B. Khazanov and S.A. Yakovenko.

Photo Sources

Russian State Military Archive
Russian State Archive of Economics
Scientific-Memorial Museum of N.E. Zhukovsky
Museum of the Russian Air Force
Central House of Aviation and Cosmonautics
Museum of Vnukovo Airport
Krasnoyarsk Regional Museum
Russian Aviation Research Trust
Finnish Wartime Photograph Archive

The private archives of the following persons (in Russian alphabetical order): E.N. Arsenyev, A.A. Artemyev, O. Belaveychuk, V.S. Vakhlamov, M. Gosudarkin, A. Ezhov, A.A. Zhdanov, P.V. Zaika, V. Zolotov, V. Ivanov, O. Ilyushenko, A.V. Kanevsky, A. Kirindas, M. Kolomiets, A.Yu. Kotlyarov, A.V. Kuzhelev, Yu. Kuzmin, I.P. Lebedev, O.Yu. Leiko, M.A. Maslov, I. Moshchanskiy, S. Nakoryakov, I. Negenblya, M. Orlov, B.L. Osetinsky, V.I. Perov, V. Petrov, G.F. Petrov, E. Potanina, O.V. Rastrenin, V.G. Rigmant, Yu.V. Rybin, G.O. Sloutskiy, A.I. Smolyarov, D.A. Sobolev, V. Fitsev, M. Chirkin, A.A. Yurgenson and N.V. Yakubovich.

List of Russian Abbreviations

GUGK	Chief Administration of Geodetic Surveying and Cartography (*Glavnoe Upravlenie Geodezii i Kartografii*)
GUGMS	Chief Administration of Hydrometeorological Service (*Glavnoe Upravlenie Gidrometeosluzhby*)
GULGMP	Chief Administration of Mining and Smelting Industry Camps (*Glavnoe Upravlenie Lagerey Metallurgicheskoy Promyshlennosty*)
GUSMP	Chief Administration of the Northern Maritime Route (*Glavnoe Upravlenie Severnogo Morskogo Puti*)
LII	Flight Testing Institute (*Lyotno-Ispytatelniy Institut*)
NAMI	Scientific Automotive Engine Institute (*Nauchniy Avtomotorniy Institut*)
NII GVF	Scientific Research Institute of the Civil Air Fleet (*Nauchno-Issledovatelskiy Institut Grazhdanskogo Vozdushnogo Flota*)
NII VVS	Scientific Testing Institute of the Air Force (*Nauchno Ispytatelniy Institut Voenno-Vozdushnykh Sil*)
NIPAV	Scientific Research Range of Aviation Armament (*Nauchno-Issledovatelsky Poligon Aviatsionnogo Vooruzheniya*)
NKAP	People's Commissariat of Aviation Industry (*Narodnyy Komissariat Aviatsionnoy Promyshlennosti*)
NKVD	People's Commissariat of Internal Affairs (*Narodnyy Komissariat Vnutrennikh Del*)
OELID TsAGI	Department for Flight Tests and Refining of the Central Aerohydrodynamic Institute (*Otdel Letnykh Ispytaniy i Dovodok Tsentralnogo Aerogydrodynamicheskogo Instituta*)
OKB	Experimental Design Bureau (*Opytnoye Konstruktorskoye Byuro*)
TsAGI	Central Aerohydrodynamic Institute (*Tsentralnyy Aerogydrodynamicheskiy Institut*)
TsIAM	Central Institute of Aviation Engine-Building (*Tsentralny Institut Aviatsionnogo Motorostroeniya*)
UMVL	Department of International Airlines (*Upravlenie Mezhdunarodnykh Vozdushnykh Liniy*)

Introduction

Seventy years have passed since the Second World War, yet the books and articles keep coming in a never-ending stream – discussing the question of what role the deliveries of arms, military vehicles, equipment and materials by Soviet Allies really played in the victory of the Red Army…

In this book, only a single aspect of the problem will be reviewed, which is the influence of the Allies' assistance on Soviet aviation. Aviation was a sphere where the deliveries from the USA, Great Britain and Canada had the most significant impact. Aircraft were among the major military assets received by the Soviet Union. The share of imported aviation materiel in the Red Army was much greater than that of tanks, ordnance and small arms – and this, accordingly, had a greater influence both on the course of military operations during the Second World War, and on the post-war development of aviation.

Unfortunately, the subject of the use of British and American materiel by the Red Army Air Force has been poorly studied in Russia. The military and technical evaluation of the Lend-Lease role in aviation can be found mostly in articles, periodicals and, to some extent, in memoirs. Furthermore, such an evaluation is rather superficial and sketchy, and gives an account only of the most general quantitative and qualitative features. At the Soviet time, it used to be reduced to a single, standard phrase – stating that such a role was 'of no particular significance'. For a long time, the topic was diligently avoided – especially where the adoption of the Western experience by Soviet engineers and designers was concerned – thus, for many years, a veil was cast over the case of reverse-engineering the B-29 bomber, which was turned into the Soviet Tu-4.

In the mid-1980s, the situation changed dramatically when some statements appeared in which the Allies' assistance was overestimated. To some extent, this was connected with the advent of a lot of young people becoming aware of TV and journalistic spheres, but whose education was insufficient and whose knowledge of history was based on Hollywood movies. Through their efforts, Lend-Lease was then depicted as a crucial factor that had enabled the 'barbarous Russia' to conquer the strongest European power, but it has not been until the recent decade that serious, thorough and balanced works appeared that analyzed the influence of the British and American assistance on the Soviet Air Force, and on the industry and economics of the USSR in general.

It should be noted that the American Lend-Lease program is only a portion (albeit the essential one) of the total assistance rendered to the Soviet Union by the Allies throughout the Second World War. Still, in this work, the other components of such assistance will be covered as well.

This topic has been studied in Western countries for years, with many books and articles testifying to that fact; however, foreign publications often fail to provide comprehensive information and even contain gross mistakes that are brought about by both deep-rooted ideological clichés and a lack of access (for foreigners) to many archival and literature-based sources.

During the Second World War, the British deliveries to the Soviet Union included the Hawker Hurricane and Supermarine Spitfire fighters, Handley Page Hampden torpedo bombers, Armstrong Whitworth Albemarle transport aircraft and American-built airplanes such as the Bell P-39 Airacobra fighters (in the USA, this export version was referred to as P-400), Curtiss Tomahawk and Kittyhawk fighters (both of which were versions of the same P-40 aircraft type), North American Mustang fighters (known in America as P-51) and Douglas Boston two-engine bombers (Douglas A-20 Havoc in the American aviation). The Soviet Union was also provided (for familiarization purposes) with single examples of the De Havilland Mosquito bomber, the Short Stirling bomber and the Hawker Typhoon fighter-bomber.

Deliveries from the USA included fighter aircraft (Bell P-39 Airacobra, Bell P-63 Kingcobra, Curtiss P-40 Warhawk and Republic P-47 Thunderbolt); bombers (Douglas A-20 Havoc and North American B-25 Mitchell); the Douglas C-47 Skytrain transport aircraft; the PBN-1 Nomad flying boat; the Consolidated PBY-6A Catalina amphibious aircraft; the Vought OS2U Kingfisher catapult-launched observation floatplanes; and the North American AT-6 Texan trainer aircraft. The Curtiss C-46A Commando was supplied in a single example, and the Consolidated B-24 Liberator, which was abandoned by the American crew after a crash landing in Yakutsk, is also reckoned to be among the aircraft delivered under Lend-Lease.

The list above includes only the officially delivered airplanes, yet in fact, the Soviet Union had at its disposal aircraft of approximately 15 types – all of which had been obtained by the country in different ways (e.g. abandoned by their crews after forced landings, interned under the Russo-Japanese Treaty of Neutrality, or re-captured – originally by the Germans – and then taken by Soviet troops from the Germans).

It should be noted that the airplanes delivered during the war by the Allies were, by no means, the first aircraft of British or American origin in Russia.

1

The Past Experience

It would be incorrect to say that before the Second World War, Soviet pilots and engineers were unfamiliar with British and American aircraft; on the contrary, they had, by that time, already acquired considerable experience in this respect.

The first British and American airplanes arrived in Russia as early as before the First World War – and the very first proposal of the delivery of airplanes to the Russian Military Ministry came from America. In spring 1906, the Wright brothers sent to St Petersburg a letter containing the appropriate enquiry, but the proposal went almost unnoticed.

In 1909, Russian generals resolved upon purchasing the Wright biplanes; however, the seller in the transaction was France instead of the USA. France had been quick to become the leader in the world of aviation, and that was where the best aircraft and the best engines were manufactured. Therefore, it was no wonder that France, of all countries, became Russia's major and long-term partner in the sphere of aviation. It is from France that most of the equipment for land-based military aviation was imported. Engines and flight instruments were purchased in France, and the first Russian pilots were trained in France as well. Aircraft factories in Russia commenced operations under licenses granted by French companies; the French established branch offices (which specialized mostly in engine manufacture) in Russia. British aviation, at the time, was lagging behind French aviation both in terms of quantity and quality. Accordingly, purchases from Great Britain were minor. Only a small batch of the Bristol Boxkite trainer biplanes (which, by the way, were, essentially, replicas of the French Farman aircraft) was imported from Great Britain in 1911.

Before the beginning of the First World War, the Russian fleet purchased a batch (albeit a small one) of the Curtiss floatplanes. At the time, Russian aviation was almost entirely under the French influence and the share of aircraft purchased in Great Britain or the USA was negligible. Consequently, the British and American aircraft had almost no influence on the aircraft industry in Russia.

During the First World War, Russia took sides with the Entente. The front had a strong demand for aircraft; the demand was greater than the capacity of the still poorly-developed Russian factories. Purchases from America rocketed; however, the majority of the selected aircraft types turned out to be unsuccessful, and found almost no use in military activities. Deliveries from Great Britain started in 1916, so therefore, the Russian Army had been using at the front mostly aircraft of French origin.

British airplanes came in much less quantities than French ones and none of the British types happened to be widely used in Russian aviation. At the front, RAF FE.2b reconnaissance aircraft and the RAF BE.2e spotter reconnaissance airplane found limited application. Russian factories built mostly aircraft of French designs (Nieuports, Farmans and Voisins), and these constituted most of the aircraft in frontline air detachments and groups.

The only British aircraft that saw extensive service with the Russian aviation was the Sopwith 1½ Strutter. This efficient airplane was delivered to Russia from both Great Britain and France, where it was license-built. The Sopwith became an illustrative demonstration of the advanced level of

British aircraft industry. By that time, new airplanes were thrown into battle at the Western Front as well – among them reconnaissance aircraft, bombers and fighters. British designers had graded up, in terms of their level, to French ones, and even began to outclass the latter in certain aspects. It was not by chance, then, that French factories also began manufacturing the 1½ Strutter.

Large batches of British airplanes came to Russia as late as after the abdication of Tsar Nicolas II in February 1917, which was at the time of the Interim Government. They had been carried by sea via Archangelsk and Murmansk. A comparatively small number of British reconnaissance and fighter aircraft had had the time to get to the front lines before the Bolsheviks took power in October. Out of the Sopwith Triplanes that arrived in autumn that year, only several aircraft were used. By that time, the factories in Petrograd and Moscow had been preparing for the license-manufacturing of the Sopwith 1½ Strutter and the De Havilland DH.4. An almost complete set of documentation had (luckily) been received for the former, whereas for the latter, the factories had to work with only a partial set of documents. Commencement of production of the British aircraft undermined the theretofore nearly monopolistic positions of the French manufacturers in the Russian market. In summer 1917, the Interim Government started negotiations on the delivery of warplanes from the USA; however, there turned out to be not enough time to complete the negotiations.

Soon after the October Revolution, the Civil War blazed up. The Red Army was fighting with the White Army; meanwhile, Great Britain was actively supporting the latter, both by sending troops and making deliveries of materiel and armament, as well as providing military advisers and instructors. Squadrons of the Royal Air Force engaged in battles in the north and in the south to support the White Guards' units. In autumn 1919, the British Government decided to evacuate the troops; however, assistance to the White Armies (first of all, to that under the command of General Denikin and his successor, Baron Wrangel) continued. The Americans took part in the intervention in the north and in the Far East; however, the scale of the American intervention was much lower, and the US military aviation was not involved in operations in Russia.

In total, several hundred British aircraft were delivered to the White Army. The airplanes provided to the White Army were more advanced than those sold to Russia before October 1917. The White Guards received a considerable quantity of the De Havilland DH.4 and DH.9; the RAF RE.8 reconnaissance/light bomber aircraft; the Sopwith Camel; and the RAF SE.5 fighters, which had already shown themselves to good advantage at the Western Front. The quantities of the supplied Bristol F.2B, Sopwith Pup and Sopwith Snipe fighters were much less. The leaving British troops left behind the Fairey III and the Short Type 184 seaplanes. In the White Armies' aviation, British aircraft were already prevailing over French ones. American deliveries were limited to 28 unarmed LWF V biplanes, which had been acquired by the Czechoslovak Corps and were later taken by Admiral Kolchak.

The Red Army took a considerable portion of the Russian Army's aircraft and the greater part of logistic storage facilities. The latter accommodated many of the 1½ Strutters, which became one of the most extensively used types in the Workers' and Peasants' Red Air Fleet in the beginning of the Civil War. Later, various British aircraft were captured by the Red Army as trophies. Throughout the Civil War, both sides frequently used the same types of airplanes to combat each other.

Upon termination of the Civil War, the Red Air Fleet turned out to be in a critical state. The Russian factories were, to a considerable extent, crippled by the economic dislocation and many of them were idle. Consequently, aircraft were manufactured in much less quantities than during the reign of the Tsar.

The airplanes still in service represented a medley of machines of Russian and foreign manufacture, some of which had survived in a single example. Most of them were obsolete, or in a state of extreme wear, and had seen multiple repairs.

Since no hopes were to be laid on the prompt launching of domestic manufacture, the country had to resort to purchases from abroad – and there was some fertile ground for that. After the termination of the First World War, huge orders to aircraft manufacturers were canceled at once. The warehouses were stuffed with large quantities of unclaimed products, which the manufacturers were ready to sell very cheaply. Foreign aircraft manufacturers were ready to take any orders so as to load the production facilities with work. The Soviet Government started buying aircraft from Italy, France, the Netherlands and, some time later, from Germany; however, the largest quantity of aircraft was purchased (strangely enough) from Great Britain, in spite of the rather strained relations between this country and Soviet Russia, yet business is business. First, the purchases were made through intermediaries in Sweden; then directly as well. The acquisitions were carried out via the Anglo-Russian Cooperative Society (ARCOS).

In the early 1920s, the Workers' and Peasants' Red Air Fleet (later renamed the Workers' and Peasants' Red Army Air Force) accepted into service the Martinsyde F.4 fighters and the De Havilland DH.4 and DH.9 reconnaissance aircraft. The two latter types became rather widely spread. Apart from being imported as complete aircraft, they were purchased in the form of disassembled airframes, which were then assembled at Soviet factories and fitted with engines of various types. Later, manufacture of the De Havilland DH.9 aircraft version was launched in Soviet Russia under the designation of R-1. The aircraft were fitted with the M-5 engine (a copy of the American Liberty engine). The R-1s remained the Workers' and Peasants' Red Army Air Force's most extensively used aircraft for a long time.

Similarly, manufacture of the Avro 504K biplane was launched in Petrograd. The Soviet version was designated U-1. The aircraft were fitted with the M-2 engine (a copy of the French Le Rhone Jb). Before the beginning of the 1930s, these aircraft were used in all flying schools of Soviet Russia. A small number of the MF-4 fighters, which were, essentially, somewhat degraded Martinsydes, were also manufactured in Moscow.

British companies offered other types of aircraft to the Soviet Government as well – thus, in 1922, the Board of Vickers Limited sent a letter to Moscow stating the company's willingness to sell a batch of five two-engine Virginia bombers (albeit unarmed). The suggested availability date was set at six months after the execution of the contract; however, the agreement was never concluded. Perhaps it was the rather high price that turned out to be the discouraging factor.

In April 1924, Vickers Limited suggested setting up the production of its aircraft in Russia. Rolls-Royce joined the project, with the intent to launch the manufacture of the necessary engines. The British offered loans for 60 percent of the total cost of the orders, and the Soviet party was granted the right to select aircraft and engine types. It was assumed that the Soviet Government would provide a factory, which was to be further re-equipped by the British party. The negotiations lasted until November 1924 and the variants discussed included the creation of a joint venture (with Vickers to invest two thirds of the money) and the leasing of the factory under concession terms. It was expected that for the first several years, the aircraft would be assembled from imported parts, and then independent manufacture would begin; however, the parties failed to reach an agreement (preference was given to Germany's Junkers Company).

In summer 1925, the Gloster Aircraft Company offered the Grebe III fighters with Jupiter engines. On 22 July 1925, the offer was discussed by the Science Committee of the Air Force Administration, which recommended declining it.

The aircraft bought in Great Britain constituted an appreciable portion of the air force fleet during the first half of the 1920s. As for aircraft manufactured by Soviet factories – by means of reverse-engineering British designs – they played an important role for a much longer time. The U-1s and (especially) the R-1s remained in service for many years. The latter was manufactured in large quantities until 1932 and operated by flying schools until 1935, when it was finally superseded by the R-5, which was designed by N.N. Polikarpov.

By the end of the 1920s, almost all aircraft in service with the Workers' and Peasants' Red Army Air Force were of domestic manufacture, notwithstanding the fact that in many cases, both aircraft and engines were, essentially, copies of the foreign types. The foreign-manufactured aircraft that remained in service were very few, and in the first half of the 1930s, all of them were superseded by original Soviet models.

Along with the above-mentioned aircraft types, several British airplanes were purchased in the early 1920s as samples for examination. Among them were the Norman-Thompson NT.2b flying boat; the Vickers Viking IV amphibian; the Avro Baby and De Havilland DH.53 light aircraft; the Vickers Vernon and De Havilland DH.34 cargo/passenger airplanes; and the Handley Page Hanley I torpedo bombers. Some of them, after the examination, saw short-term service with the air force units, while the torpedo bombers were used for experiments with the first Soviet aerial torpedoes.

After the 'ARCOS case' and the break of diplomatic relations in 1928, purchases of aircraft in Great Britain were ceased for some time. As for the USA, in the 1920s, Soviet Russia was not buying any aircraft from this country at all, with only aircraft engines and accessories, instruments and some other equipment being imported from the USA. Such a situation existed until the early 1930s, when the USSR initiated a rapid development of its military and civil aviation.

Starting from the early 1930s, Soviet factories were manufacturing, on a large scale, aircraft of original designs that did not bear the impress of replication (which had been the case before). From 1930-1940, the USSR received quite a limited number of British aircraft, which were intended to be used solely to study the experience of British designers. After the examination and testing, some individual assemblies and the most efficient design solutions – but not aircraft as a whole – were reverse-engineered.

In early 1932, the Chief Administration of the Civil Air Fleet suggested purchasing examples of passenger aircraft abroad. A list was prepared, which included aircraft from the USA, Great Britain, France and Czechoslovakia. It was planned that the Blackburn Nile three-engine flying boat and the De Havilland Moth light airplane would be purchased in England; however, for reasons of financial saving, the entire list was rejected.

A much greater attention was paid to interests of military agencies. The Soviet administration concluded that licenses for modern engines and examples of the high-speed fighters should be purchased abroad to accelerate modernization of the Soviet fighter airplanes. Purchases were intended to be made in the USA, Great Britain and France, and 1.5 million rubles were allocated from the budget for this purpose. It was ordered that the imported examples should be subjected to comprehensive tests, and all useful new features found should be implemented in the design of new Soviet fighters.

On 22 April 1932, a meeting held by the Deputy Chief of Air Force Administration S.A. Mezheninov issued a recommended list of aircraft to be purchased. The top position was given to British aircraft manufactured by Hawker Aircraft Limited – namely the Hawker Fury single-seater and the Hawker Hart two-seat heavy fighter. It was suggested that two examples of each aircraft should be acquired. In addition, a single example of the Vickers Jockey monoplane fighter was on the list. In case Hawker refused to sell its aircraft, or if the British Government opposed the idea, the meeting recommended ordering aircraft from the Fairey Aviation Company (a rival to Hawker). The intention was to order, from Fairey, the Firefly single-seater and the Fox two-seater (also in the fighter version).

The draft resolution by the Defense Committee restricted the choice (perhaps for reasons of saving) to the Firefly, the Fox and the Hart (in two examples each). Finally, a commission appointed to review the matter and chaired by the Red Army Arms Materiel Supervisor, Army Commander M.N. Tukhachevsky, resolved that only the Firefly and the Hart should be bought.

Hawker refused to sell the Hart in a single example – fearing that the Soviets would reverse-engineer the aircraft and start manufacturing it without a license. Better success was achieved with the Firefly: in 1932, the fighter arrived in Moscow and was subjected to an entire set of tests.

From early 1932, the command of the Workers' and Peasants' Red Army Air Force began to take an interest in foreign-manufactured autogiros. Finally, it led to the purchase (in 1935) of an example of the Avro Cierva C.30A wingless autogiro, which was tested and examined in the Department for Flight Tests and Refining of the Central Aerohydrodynamic Institute (*Otdel Letnykh Ispytaniy i Dovodok Tsentralnogo Aerogydrodynamicheskogo Instituta*, or OELID TsAGI) and in the Scientific Testing Institute of the Air Force (*Nauchno Ispytatelniy Institut Voenno-Vozdushnykh Sil*, or NII VVS).

In 1930, another Fairey fighter came to the Soviet Union: it was a Fairey Fantome all-metal biplane, which had been designed under the order of the Belgian Government, but had never been accepted for service in Belgium. Two such aircraft were ordered by Soviet representatives in December 1935. The aircraft arrived trouble-free in Leningrad in autumn the following year, and were thoroughly studied at NII VVS.

In 1936, Aeroflot began operations on its first international route from Moscow to Prague; however, the Chief Administration of the Civil Air Fleet had no up-to-date passenger aircraft in its fleet. The outdated Tupolev ANT-9 was, at the time, performing the function of the 'flagship' aircraft in the Soviet civil aviation. Aeroflot management suggested to the government that some aircraft should be bought in England; however, this idea faced severe criticism for reasons of the country's image – thus, for example, Air Force Commander Y.I. Alksnis wrote: 'We should fly aircraft of our own; buying aircraft in England for such purposes is a shame that our enemies will not hesitate to use against us'. Finally, it was decided that the operations on the route would be performed by the already mentioned ANT-9. On 31 August 1936, it made its first and only flight to Prague. No other flights to the capital of Czechoslovakia were made that year. The real operations on the route began only in 1937, with the flights performed by a Douglas DC-2 which had been bought in the USA.

During the Spanish Civil War, a De Havilland Dragon two-engine wooden biplane was captured from the nationalists. Together, with captured German and Italian aircraft, it was taken to the USSR and subjected to studies at NII VVS. The airplane was highly marked and recommended as an example for designing medical evacuation aircraft in the Soviet Union.

Soviet delegations visited England on a regular basis to attend air shows in Hendon. They also visited research and development organizations, design offices and factories.

In autumn 1937, Fairey representatives showed at their factory airfield the new P.4/34 light bomber to the Soviet delegation, which included P.V. Rychagov, S.P. Suprun and Air Attaché in London Cherniy. The aircraft was demonstrated both on the ground and in flight. The delegation expressed a favorable opinion of the aircraft and provided a recommendation to the Soviet Government that one such aircraft should be purchased for examination purposes. The possibility of purchasing the airplane was explored via the Trade Representation; however, the idea was rejected, with a ban imposed by the Air Ministry invoked as the reason for such rejection. Consequently, in July 1938, Fairey themselves approached the Soviet Embassy with a proposal to sell the license for 62,000 UK pounds. The Material-Technical Support Department of the Workers' and Peasants' Red Army Air Force objected – explaining: 'The power unit is the only interesting item in the P-4… we would like to buy just one aircraft, two as a maximum'; however, the British totally declined the idea of selling the P.4/34 'in kind', since the only available aircraft was essentially a prototype. In July 1939, the Engineering Department of the Trade Representation provided information that Fairey had offered three options: (i) a license for 50,000 UK pounds; (ii) one example of the Battle for 13,500 UK pounds; or (iii) a license and a Battle for 62,000 UK pounds. None of the options suited the Russians.

The Soviet Union was also interested in another British type – namely the Blenheim high-speed bomber. In 1939, the Soviet Trade Representation in London approached the Bristol Airplane Company with a proposal to buy an example aircraft 'of the 1938 type' (apparently the Blenheim IV); however, the company refused to sell the airplane. In a letter dated 23 August, the Bristol Airplane Company made a counterproposal – stating that they were ready to deliver a batch of 20 aircraft for 30,000 UK pounds each. Since the Soviets wanted to purchase the aircraft solely for familiarization purposes, such a quantity of the Blenheims was simply not needed and the deal fell through – thus, in fact, before the end of the 1930s, only two Fairey fighters, the C.30A autogiro and the Hawk Trainer were received by the Soviet Union. The latter airplane, after thorough testing, was enlisted to the personal flight of the air force commander.

During the same period, the Soviets began expressing a keen interest in the status of aircraft industry in the USA, which was quickly gaining the leading position in the world. It had taken the American aircraft companies a lot of time to enter the Soviet market due to political restrictions imposed by the government. The USA did not recognize Soviet Russia, with the formal reason consisting of the Soviet Government's refusal to repay the debts of the pre-Revolution period; however, the Americans kept trading with the USSR, since they were unwilling to lose the rather large Soviet market.

In May 1924, the Amtorg Trading Corporation was registered in the USA. It was deemed an American corporation, but, in fact, belonged to the USSR and performed the functions of a trade representation. Via Amtorg, raw materials were sold, and machinery and equipment (including those for the aircraft industry) were purchased.

American aviation in the 1920s was still lagging behind the advanced European countries. For this reason, the purchasing of aircraft equipment in the USA was confined to Liberty engines (new and used), their parts and accessories (to be used in the manufacture of the M-5 engine, which was essentially a Soviet copy of the Liberty engine), units for oil and fuel supply systems, and examples of instruments and equipment.

The late 1920s was marked by the growing Soviet interest in original American aircraft and aviation engine designs, the aircraft industry's organizational structure, new technologies, and operating practices in military and civil aviation. In return, various American companies started offering their products both for civil and military purposes; however, such mutually beneficial contacts provoked severe opposition on the part of the US Department of State and the administration of President H. Hoover in general. The latter strongly objected to any communication with 'godless Bolsheviks' and, specifically, in such an important area as aviation. An especially severe reaction was caused by attempts to buy any military materiel. Such deals were usually made by the Soviet party via intermediaries, which were often under the cover of bogus buying companies.

All initial attempts to acquire military aircraft in the USA ended in failure. The Glenn L. Martin Company case gave rise to an enormous row. In winter 1929, the Martin Company suggested delivering to the Workers' and Peasants' Red Army Air Force a batch of two-engine flying boats – short-range maritime reconnaissance aircraft. The project was prepared by the Martin designers and updated to meet technical requirements provided by Moscow. In terms of flight performance, the all-metal American seaplane exceeded, to a certain extent, the Savoia-Marchetti S.62bis wooden biplane offered by the rival company from Italy. The aircraft was expected to have a higher payload and better seaworthiness. A draft agreement was prepared for the purchase of 20 flying boats (at the cost of 55,000 US dollars each) and a license for their manufacture in the USSR; however, when in July 1930 the company made an informal enquiry to the Department of State regarding the possibility to obtain an export permit, it faced a rebuff. The reaction was: "Military aircraft for Soviet Russia? In no case will this happen!" Fearing undesired publicity, the Martin Company and Amtorg set about denying the fact of negotiations altogether. The Russian archives still keep a whole file of plans for 'covering the tracks' of this deal. Nevertheless, the story 'leaked through' to newspapers. The case reached President Hoover, who was a sheer anti-communist and he expressly vetoed the fulfilment of the order. The only party that profited from the entire matter was the Italians. They sold to the Red Army Air Force the flying boats, a license for their manufacture and a large batch of aviation engines.

Perhaps, for the very same reasons, the negotiations held in the USA in January 1930 by Chief of the Air Force Administration P.I. Baranov himself failed as well. Baranov tried to come to an agreement on creating in the USSR a mixed-capital joint-stock company to manufacture Curtiss aircraft and engines, and on purchasing the Keystone-Loening Commuter amphibious aircraft.

The constant tension in relations with the Department of State resulted in a considerable drop in goods turnover between the Soviet Union and the USA. Things went so far that on 7 September 1931, the Soviet Government issued a resolution prohibiting the placing of orders in America. The resolution evidently remained in effect for a rather short time; however, it undoubtedly affected the contacts between the countries in all areas – including the aviation industry.

As was already noted, in early 1932, the Chief Administration of the Civil Air Fleet attempted to obtain fund allocations for purchasing examples of modern passenger aircraft abroad. There were intentions to buy a Pilgrim 100 ten-seater and a Lockheed Orion high-speed monoplane in the USA; however, the money for this purpose was never allocated.

In April 1932, the above-mentioned commission – chaired by M.N. Tukhachevsky – suggested ordering in America, for examination purposes, examples of the Boeing P-12F and Lockheed YP-24 fighters (two examples of each aircraft). For the Boeing fighter, a letter with an offer was received from the Boeing Company; however, in spite of the fact that the purchase was approved by a resolution of the Soviet Defense Committee, the American fighters were not purchased at the time.

It was only after F. Roosevelt's win of the presidential elections in 1933 that the situation took a turn for the better. Diplomatic relations were established with the USSR and export limitations were gradually removed. The only prohibition was in respect of purchasing any aircraft or equipment that was supplied to the US military forces.

The range of items bought in the USA grew to include flying instruments, life vests and inflatable life boats, refueling trucks, hydraulic jacks and oxygen units. In 1934, examples of lubricating oils were brought to Moscow from America. These were analyzed, and the results were used to prepare specifications for new oils of domestic manufacture.

Soon the American airplanes again appeared in the Russian sky. The first of such aircraft was probably brought by the US Embassy. It was even entered in the Soviet civil aircraft register under a quite rare designation – beginning with the Russian letter 'Ч' (transliterated to English as 'Ch'). The aircraft was designated 'Ч-2', where 'Ч' stood for *Chastny* – meaning 'private'. That was a disarmed Douglas O-38 observation aircraft, which was owned by Deputy Military Attaché of the USA T. White. On 24 June 1934, in the course of the Moscow-Leningrad flight, the aircraft engine failed, with White landing on swampy ground. The hard braking before a drainage ditch caused the aircraft to stand on its nose; the pilot, however, was not hurt in the accident.

The first American aircraft that became Soviet property were two Consolidated Fleetster monoplanes. Their purchase was brought about by emergency circumstances, rather than by the purchase schedule. The steamship *Chelyuskin*, which had been making a voyage along the northern maritime route with a research expedition on board, was crushed by icepacks and sank near the Chukotka Peninsula shore. Aircraft pilots were entrusted with the mission of rescuing the crew who had escaped onto drift ice. To be on the safe side, it was decided that apart from Soviet aircraft, American ones should also be bought in Alaska and ferried across the Bering Strait – thus, the Fleetsters played their intended part in the rescue operations.

In the 1930s, delegations of Soviet aircraft manufacturers became frequent visitors in America. After a visit of A.N. Tupolev's group in 1935, an order was made for examples of the Northrop 2E attack aircraft and the Douglas DC-2 passenger aircraft. These airplanes provided for the Soviet specialists an opportunity to familiarize themselves, for the first time, with welded fuel tanks, automatic riveting and many other technical innovations.

In spring 1936, a Vultee V-1A aircraft was purchased from the Vultee Aircraft Corporation for the renowned pilot A.A. Levanevsky, who made a flight from Los Angeles to Moscow in it. A year later, three modern seaplanes – including two Douglas DF flying boats and a Sikorsky S-43A amphibian – were imported from the USA to operate along large rivers of Siberia.

In May-September 1936, a team of air force executives – headed by Chief of the Material-Technical Support Department Brigade Commander B.I. Bazenkov – came to the USA. The team made a tour of factories and airfields, and visited the American colleagues at Wright Field air base, where the Americans demonstrated laboratories, test rigs and some of the airplanes being tested – including the Martin B-12 and the Douglas B-18 bombers; the Seversky P-35 fighter; and the Douglas and Lockheed passenger aircraft. On returning to Moscow, Bazenkov suggested implementing (in the domestic aircraft industry) many of the innovations that he had seen in America. In particular, he recommended purchasing licenses and technical aids for flight instruments, as well as special varnishes and paints.

The next step forward consisted in the purchase (in 1936-1937) of licenses for several American military and civil aircraft. Two points of view came to a collision: senior executives of the Chief Administration of Aircraft Industry of the People's Commissariat of Heavy Industry – headed by M.M. Kaganovich – had, from the very beginning, been standing for the purchase of aircraft examples and their further reverse-engineering. The Workers' and Peasants' Red Army Air Force Command – including Air Force Commander Y.I. Alksnis – believed that the purchase of technical aids would considerably expedite the development process, whereas excessive economy might lead to mass manufacture of already outdated aircraft types. Originally, the list of aircraft discussed in terms of purchase possibilities included the Vultee V-11 light attack bomber; the Martin 139; the Douglas DB-1 (B-18) and Boeing 299 (B-17) bombers; and the Douglas DC-2 transport plane. On Kaganovich's initiative, the Consolidated 28 (PBY-1) was added to the list. Later on, the list was supplemented with the Seversky 2PA two-seat fighter and the Martin 156 large flying boat. Licenses were purchased under a resolution of the Council for Labor and Defense, which was dated 11 April 1936.

In fact, five licenses were bought – including those for the Vultee V-11; the Consolidated 28; the Seversky 2PA; the Martin 156; and the Douglas DC-3 (which was a development of the DC-2). Of those, three were put into production – namely the Vultee V-11 (Soviet designations BSh-1 and PS-43); the Consolidated (Soviet designation GST); and the Douglas DC-3 (Soviet designation PS-84, but later Li-2). Only the latter saw real mass production. Manufacture of all three aircraft was mastered as late as 1939. The Martin 139WR bomber was acquired in the single example for study purposes.

All American aircraft featured elaborated technology, fitness for mass manufacture and proper attention given to maintainability. As part of the preproduction process, Soviet factories mastered the advanced mold-loft template production technique. Implementation of the American examples made the related industries considerably improve their techniques as well. Nearly all license contracts provided for the purchase of equipment in complete sets and the mastering of unfamiliar manufacturing processes. Furthermore, the contracts stipulated the training of specialists; the provision of materials; the description of calculation and test methods (along with specific designs); prospective modifications; and even new aircraft projects – thus, for example, the Vultee Aircraft Corporation provided conceptual designs of several attack aircraft and light bombers (including a ship-based one).

In 1937, two more aircraft were bought in the USA in an emergency. To search for S.A. Levanevsky's crew, which became missing en route from Moscow to America, a Consolidated

PBY-1 flying boat (and then a Lockheed L-10E two-engine transport aircraft) were promptly purchased. The crew of the renowned polar explorer H. Wilkins used those aircraft for flights in the north of Canada. Later, they were transported to the Soviet Union and put in service with the Polar Aviation.

Since the mass manufacture of the PS-84 aircraft was somewhat delayed, the Soviet administration, without further waiting, set about purchasing the Douglas DC-3s in America. That was the only American aircraft type that was bought in the 1930s in noticeable quantities.

Concurrently, licenses for (and examples of) advanced aircraft equipment were purchased. The first Soviet variable-pitch propellers – VISh-2, VISh-3 and VISh-5 – were manufactured under a license granted by the American Hamilton Company. The variable-pitch propellers were installed to the Tupolev ANT-40 (SB) high-speed bombers and the Ilyushin DB-3 long-range bombers. The AVP-12 hydraulic autopilot, which was accepted into service with the Workers' and Peasants' Red Army Air Force in 1939, was a replica of the Sperry autopilot (the 1934 type). The Ilyushin TsKB-30 'Moscow', which was used by V.K. Kokkinaki and M.Kh. Gordienko to fly across the Atlantic Ocean, was fitted with an American Fairchild radio compass.

A batch of MN-12 radio compasses was purchased from the Bendix Corporation. These were accepted in March 1939 in the USA by the Soviet commission, which was headed by I.S. Mitsner. Envisaging further orders, the Americans demonstrated a newer and much more advanced design under the designation MN-26. Later, these were delivered to the Soviet Union under the Lend-Lease program. The purchased instruments were loaded to the *Chelyuskinets* steamship, but unfortunately, they were damaged during transportation.

In the second half of the 1930s, the USSR began to place orders with American companies for increasingly large research and development projects in the aircraft industry. The Radio Corporation of America received an order for the development of a special television station to be arranged on board an aircraft. Soviet strategists assumed that a television reconnaissance aircraft so equipped would translate the picture of the battlefield, or the troops on the march, directly to the military unit's headquarters. The station was designed and manufactured; it weighed 270kg and could transmit images over a distance of up to 25km. In October 1937, the new station was tested on an Ilyushin TB-3. By that time, the Research and Development Institute No.8 (NII-8) of the People's Commissariat of Defense Industry had already reverse-engineered the American example and had started developing a more compact version for the DB-3; however, the tests demonstrated that the efficiency of observations using the TV station was unsatisfactory. The screen was only 12cmx17cm in size, and the TB-3 'hanging' above the battlefield was much too vulnerable.

In May 1937, an agreement was concluded for the design of a 'substratospheric bomber' for the Workers' and Peasants' Red Army Air Force. A certain (unrenowned) Jackson & Moreland firm was named as a contractor; however, most probably, it was only an intermediary covering some large aircraft company. A heavy four-engine bomber (with Wright Cyclone G100 or G102A engines) was expected to have a take-off weight of 27,000kg and a maximum speed of 600km/h at the specified altitude. The mission flight range was 4,800km. The pressurized cabin ensured long-time crew operations at a high altitude.

The design was successfully completed. In October 1936, a dummy aircraft was subjected to wind-tunnel tests at the facilities of the Massachusetts Institute of Technology. The documentation package – including 55 sheets of drawings, collected data, calculations, an explanatory note and appendices thereto, and a model of the fuselage – were handed over to Amtorg in February 1939. On 4 March, the entire package arrived in Moscow. In April, translation of the documents to Russian was commenced; concurrently, an acceptance committee was being formed to include representatives of the Air Force Command, NII VVS and the People's Commissariat of Aviation Industry. Unfortunately, the future destiny of the project's materials is obscure.

A joint project with the Douglas Aircraft Company might have become the acme of the Soviet-American cooperation. A team, with the participation of Soviet specialists, was preparing the creation of a new two-engine dive bomber. The decision to make an appropriate contract with Douglas was approved by the Defense Committee on 10 September 1939. The specifications that were prepared in Moscow described an ultra-modern aircraft with pressurized cabins, tricycle landing gear, internal bomb carriers, and the ultimate automation of aircraft controls and power plant controls.

Along with the above, the continuous importing of different technical literature and documentation to Russia should be mentioned. The publications delivered and translated included manuals and handbooks for aircraft designers; training aids for personnel of the US Army Corps; technical requirements for the acceptance of aircraft, engines, equipment, fuel, oil and lubricants; and descriptions of instruments and mechanisms. All such publications were obtained using both official and non-official channels.

In 1938-1939, the topic of purchasing examples of up-to-date American military aircraft for the further mastering of their production in the USSR re-emerged. Again, the Douglas B-18 was considered; it was, however, rejected as an outdated model. Instead, a lot of fruitless efforts were made to get some 10 advanced Douglas A-20 bombers.

Some of the suggested aircraft were rejected by the Soviet party – thus, for example, in December 1938, Beechcraft sent a letter stating their willingness to sell a batch of the AT-18 or BT-18D two-engine trainer aircraft. The negotiations lasted for almost a year; however, the Soviet party found the suggested price of 56,650 to 59,695 US dollars for each aircraft too high and refused to buy even examples.

In November 1939, the war with Finland began and on 2 December 1939, the President of the USA declared a 'moral embargo' for aircraft deliveries to the Soviet Union. American companies, one by one, started terminating contracts with Russia and all the official channels became paralyzed, yet unofficial channels survived. The intelligence kept 'drawing' technical documentation in the same way as it used to do it before. On 21 September 1938, NII VVS received (from the Intelligence Section of the General Staff) documentation for the Lockheed Hudson bomber – including secret drawings of the British Air Ministry.

In March 1940, a gradual restoration of communication began. The Chief Administration of Aviation Procurements again raised the issue of purchasing examples of modern military aircraft in the USA for study purposes. On 14 March, a list of the most interesting aircraft was approved; it included the Lockheed XP-38 and Curtiss XP-40 fighters, and the Stearman X-100 bomber. The latter went no farther than the single prototype and never came to the USSR; as for the former two aircraft, the Soviet specialists got a chance to study them as soon as during the war with Germany. In general, however, the amount of Soviet-American communication decreased in 1940, but was then restored to the previous level in June 1941 and then increased manifold later on.

Some of the aircraft that were purchased abroad in the second half of the 1930s (or captured in Poland or in the Baltic States) continued in service throughout the war years. This was the case, primarily, with the American Douglas DC-3 airliners, which were in both military and civil service. The Soviet Union operated approximately 20 such aircraft. The Civil Air Fleet also had at its disposal single examples of the Lockheed L-10 and L-14 passenger aircraft. The Vultee V-11GB attack aircraft, which had been bought as an example for mass manufacture in the USSR, served in the disarmed condition as a high-speed liaison aircraft in the departmental aviation of the People's Commissariat of Air Industry. The last of the two aircraft of this type were written off after a crash in October 1943. The Consolidated PBY-1 and Douglas DF flying boats and a Sikorsky S-43A amphibian were in service with the Polar Aviation.

Aircraft that had been manufactured in the USSR under American licenses were available in much greater quantities. The PS-84 (in 1942, designated Lisunov Li-2) was the most up-to-date passenger aircraft in the USSR at the time. Throughout the war, it was used both as a transport aircraft and as a long-range night bomber. It was the most mass-produced type – a combination of American design and Soviet manufacture. The single-engine PS-43 mail planes were available in much lesser quantities. These were, essentially, the disarmed BSh-1 bombers which had been manufactured under the Vultee V-11GB license, but never saw service with the air force. They were taken by the Chief Administration of the Civil Air Fleet and used to carry mail. During the war, these aircraft were placed in service with the 3rd Liaison Air Division and carried couriers with important documents to the front lines and back. The GST flying boats (essentially a version of the famous Consolidated PBY Catalina) were in operation with the Black Sea Fleet, the Northern Fleet and the Polar Aviation Administration. The Far East Department of the Civil Air Fleet operated the only Martin 156 four-engine flying boat that was at the Soviets' disposal (designated PS-130 in the USSR).

As for British aircraft, there was, at first, only a small quantity of them. Only a few civil aircraft of British manufacture were performing flights along the rear routes in the European portion of the Soviet Union. Those were the De Havilland Dragon Rapid and the Percival Q.6 Petrel aircraft, which had theretofore belonged to Baltic airlines. In August 1941, during the Anglo-Soviet invasion of Iran, several Iran-assembled Hawker Audax biplanes were captured, which were mistakenly referred to as Harts in the documents of the Chief Administration of the Civil Air Fleet.

Throughout the Second World War, thousands of aircraft delivered to USSR by the Allies joined the Soviet fleet of foreign-manufactured aircraft.

A rather 'rare bird' in Russia: the British-built Vickers Bullet fighter.

Sopwith triplane fighters arrived in Russia shortly before the October Revolution and were not extensively used in the hostilities.

The Sopwith 1½ Strutter was manufactured in Russia by the former Lebedev Factory. It was operated in June 1921 by the 39th 'Iron' Reconnaissance Air Detachment.

The US-built LWF V biplane was captured by the Red Army. Such aircraft were used during the course of the Russian Civil War by Kolchak's army and by the Czecho-Slovak Corps.

Technicians working on a DH.9A of the *Ilyich* Air Detachment. The aircraft bears the inscription *Luganskiy Krasnoznamyonets*, or the Lugansk Red Banner Carrier, Kharkov airfield, 1924.

The Avro 504 biplane during tests at the Scientific and Experimental airfield in Moscow.

The British-built Martinsyde F.4 Buzzard, which was in service with the Workers' and Peasants' Red Army Air Force in the 1920s.

The Norman Thompson NT.2b flying boat, Oranienbaum hydroaviation base, 1923.

The Vickers Viking amphibian in Petrograd.

The Soviet-made Polikarpov R-1 reconnaissance aircraft had a similar appearance to the DH.9A, but it was not an exact copy of the latter. This photo shows an aircraft manufactured by Taganrog Factory No.31 in 1931.

The British-built Fairey Firefly IIM fighter was purchased for familiarization purposes in 1932.

The Cierva C-30A autogyro during tests at NII VVS in 1935.

The Miles Hawk trainer during tests at NII VVS in 1937. Later, the aircraft was included in the personal flight of the Chief of the Red Army Air Force.

One of two Consolidated 17AF Fleetster monoplanes in the original American paint scheme, which were obtained in the USA for the rescue operation of the *Chelyuskin* steamer crew and its passengers.

The Soviet aviation delegation, which was led by A.N. Tupolev, during a visit to the USA.

The BSh-1 attack aircraft (a licensed copy of the Vultee V-11GB) was built in a series, but was never adopted for service with the Red Army Air Force. The BSh-1s were handed over to civil aviation as high-speed mail carrier aircraft under the PS-43 designation. At the time of the war, they were in service with the 3rd Liaison Air Division.

The US-built Vultee V-11GB ground attack aircraft/light bomber during tests at NII VVS in 1937.

The Model 28-2 flying boat during test flights in the USA.

A Soviet DC-2 at an airfield in Prague.

The Vultee V-1A, which was flown in 1936 by S.A. Levanevsky from Los Angeles to Moscow.

Soviet specialists planned to modify the huge Martin 156 flying boat into an 'ocean bomber', but these plans never materialized.

An S-43 amphibian in service with the GUSMP at a beaching area.

One of two Douglas DF flying boats operated by the Soviet Union at a polar pilots' base in Zakharkovo in 1937.

The US-built two-seater Seversky 2PA-L Convoy Fighter during tests at NII VVS in 1938.

The Lockheed L-10E Electra two-engined aircraft, which was bought in 1937 to search for S.A. Levanevsky's crew when they became lost during a transpolar flight.

The DC-3 for the Soviet Union being assembled in California.

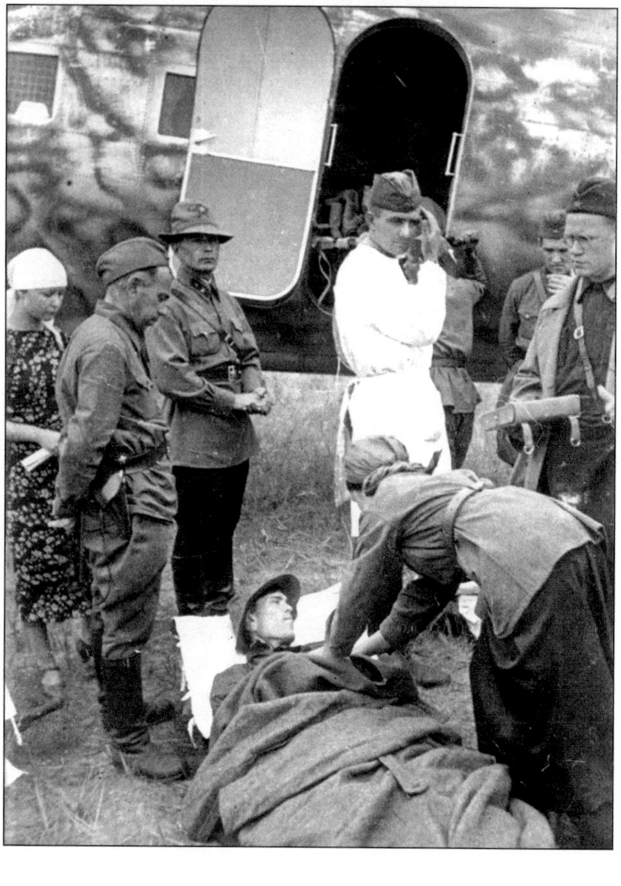

The majority of the purchased DC-3s were handed over to the air force units. This photo shows the wounded being picked up from a field area during the Battle of Khalkhyn Gol in 1939.

This DC-3 was operated by the Soviet Department of International Airlines.

A crew of the Soviet DC-3 upon arrival in Berlin.

A Li-2, which was manufactured in 1943. Its primary differences from the original DC-3 consisted mostly of the presence of armament, and in the arrangement of the cargo door on the left side of the fuselage.

This wartime photo shows two aircraft of US origin that were built in the Soviet Union: the PS-84 (Li-2) on the left and the PS-43 on the right.

2

What is 'Lend-Lease'?

Deliveries of British and American arms materiel at the time of the war are usually referred to in Russia as 'Lend-Lease', but this is not quite correct. The reception of military weaponry and munitions by the Soviet Union from the USA under the Lend-Lease Act, as passed by the US Congress on 11 March 1941, covered only a portion (albeit the major one) of the entire assistance rendered by the Allies during the Second World War.

Under the mentioned Act (Bill), the US Government was entitled to 'transfer title to, exchange, lease, lend, or otherwise dispose of' any military materials or military information to the government of any country if such country's defense against aggression was vital for defense of the United States. This was far from an act of altruism. The Second World War had, by that time, been in full swing and was quite likely to reach the USA (and that was exactly what eventually happened). The Americans understood that it was more beneficial to arm and equip the required belligerent than to have to wage a war themselves.

Thanks to President F. Roosevelt's far-sightedness, the USSR had been from the very beginning on the list of potential assistance recipients under the mentioned Bill. At the time, that looked far from obviously justified. After the signing of the treaty with Germany, Stalin had been treated like an ally of Hitler's. Relations between the Soviet Union and Western countries deteriorated after the beginning of the Winter War in November 1939. America imposed a 'moral embargo' on deliveries of anything that could be used for military purposes, and this primarily affected equipment deliveries and technical cooperation. The provision of documentation under license contracts was suspended. Meanwhile, England and France set about working out a plan of an air attack on the Baku area; the Soviet Union, in return, was preparing to make air strikes on British and French bases in the Middle East and even intended to put the Suez Canal out of operation. The Germans were, at the very least, suspecting it because reconnaissance information regarding the strike targets had been requested from them. The situation could have ended up in the USSR being on a different side during the Second World War – thus, Roosevelt's considerations were rather far from obvious; the history, though, proved that he had been right.

The beginning of actual deliveries under the Lend-Lease program was declared by the President's Directives. Directive 1 covered Great Britain, and Directive 2 concerned Greece; the subsequent Directives dealt with Yugoslavia and China.

On the morning of 22 June 1941, the troops of Germany and their allies crossed the Soviet border; German aircraft started strafing the near-border areas. The war began over a huge front – spreading from the Barents Sea to the Black Sea. As the old proverb has it, 'your enemy's enemy is your friend'. The Prime Minister of the United Kingdom, Winston Churchill, had a cordial dislike for Bolsheviks, but he was a man of wisdom and promptly concluded that an additional ally would surely do no harm to Great Britain. In his speech, he declared support to the Soviet Union during the war against Germany and a willingness to provide the required assistance to Russia. Soviet and British diplomats, as well as military men, started discussing the mechanisms of such assistance.

America also expressed its willingness to render the required support. The first declaration to that effect was made in President Roosevelt's speech of 24 June, when he said that the USA would provide "all the necessary support to the Soviet Union." Practical steps followed the declaration. On that very day, the Soviet accounts with the banks, which had theretofore been frozen, were released. From 26 June onwards, the Neutrality Act ceased to be in effect in respect of the Soviet Union; this cleared the way for buying arms in the USA on a cash-and-carry basis, with payments made in cash and transportation carried out by Soviet vessels. On 30 June, a list of cargoes that the Soviet Union needed was handed over to H. Wallace, who was, at the time, the acting Secretary of State; the list, however, looked unrealistic in many aspects. The Soviets wanted to receive everything at once, and without being adequately aware of the American industry's capacities – thus, for example, the list included 3,000 fighters and 3,000 bombers. To fulfil such an order, the USA would have had to completely cut off exports to other countries (including Great Britain) and to curtail deliveries to its own air force. As for money for such extensive purchases, there was an intention to raise it by obtaining a five-year loan from the USA and by complementing the credit facility funds with barter deliveries of raw materials.

There was an intention to carry out purchases via the already mentioned Amtorg, which was headed at the time by K.I. Lukashev. The responsibility rested with Amtorg's Engineering Department, in spite of the fact that its headcount did not exceed four persons. An interesting fact is that since Amtorg was deemed an American company, it received commission fees from the People's Commissariat of Foreign Trade and paid taxes to the US budget.

On 27 July, a Soviet military mission – headed by General F.I. Golikov – arrived in Washington. The mission personnel included future Air Force Chief Engineer A.K. Repin, Head of the Military Factories Department L.L. Raikov and Engineer P.I. Barabanshchikov. Repin was appointed Deputy Chairman for Amtorg. More specialists were transferred to Amtorg staff later – including 10 aviation specialists. The military mission was supplemented by some of the specialists from the team of the famous test pilot M.M. Gromov (who had been Head of the Flight Test Institute of the People's Commissariat of Aviation Industry before the war), who had arrived via Alaska to become familiar with American aircraft.

In July, the Russian section of the Office of Lend-Lease Administration was established, with Colonel Philip Faymonville (the former US Military Attaché in Moscow) as the Head of the Section. In late July to early August, Hopkins – a representative of the US President – visited the Soviet capital to verify the needs of the country's armed forces. Hopkins had a talk with I.V. Stalin who, inter alia, pointed out the Soviet Union's wish to receive medium bombers and fighters.

On 1 August, Secretary of War H. Stimson authorized the sale of 200 P-40 fighters to the Soviet Union. On the following day, a license for the export of arms to Russia was drawn up, with a permit to use American merchant vessels for the transportation of any exported arms.

The aircraft were purchased in America and the shipments started in September. The Soviet Union immediately purchased 59 aircraft, a number of trucks, various chemicals, petroleum products, explosives and considerable quantities of industrial equipment. Deliveries by sea to the Soviet Union totaled 166,000 tons. Aviation, in particular, received engines, propellers, 10,500 bombs and 407,900 shells; however those were not yet part of the Lend-Lease program. According to what Lend-Lease Administrator E. Stettinius wrote in his memoirs, throughout October 1941, the Russians had been paying for all deliveries received by the Soviet Union. Before 30 October, the Soviet Union spent 92 million US dollars on those purchases. According to American data, 10 million US dollars out of the above amount were settled in gold, and 50 million US dollars were set off with counter-deliveries of valuable raw materials. The gold was delivered on board *Dneprostroy* and *Azerbaijan* vessels in October-November 1941.

On 12 September, the Defense Supplies Corporation of the USA and Amtorg signed an agreement on the purchase of manganese, chrome ore, asbestos, platinum and other raw materials from the Soviet Union for a sum total of 100 million US dollars. The Americans made upfront payments for these shipments for a sum of 50 million US dollars in tranches of five million each, with the rest to be paid upon delivery of cargoes. It is probable that this 50 million constituted the amount reckoned in by the Americans. Further deliveries were made under Lend-Lease.

On 1 October, the first of the tripartite (with the USA, the United Kingdom and the Soviet Union as parties) Lend-Lease protocols was signed in Moscow to determine further scope and due dates of deliveries. The Allies undertook to deliver 400 aircraft (300 fighters and 100 bombers) each on a monthly basis.

In practice, the Lend-Lease Act application to the Soviet Union was initiated on 28 October and followed (two days later) by an interest-free loan of one billion US dollars granted by the USA for the purchase of materiel and raw materials. On the very same day, the President informed Stalin thereof. Roosevelt's Directive – proclaiming the USSR's defense as being vital for America – was solemnly promulgated on 7 November. This can be regarded as the official date of the Soviet Union joining Lend-Lease.

After the Japanese attack on Pearl Harbor, a certain interruption followed. On 13 December, the American Government requisitioned (for the needs of the US' own armed forces) part of the materiel that had been manufactured for foreign customers. Among others, all Soviet orders for arms were blocked. In ports, unloading of the already loaded cargoes began. On 17 December, however, a decision was made that the shipments which had already been prepared for loading should not be suspended. As soon as 28 December, President Roosevelt ordered that the previously agreed scopes of deliveries be restored – beginning from 1 January 1942. Furthermore, on 17 March, he declared assistance to the USSR a top priority. Later, another credit line of 1 trillion US dollars was opened for the USSR. In addition to that, direct purchases of different equipment and munitions for currency and gold continued; these, however, were considerably less in amount than the Lend-Lease deliveries.

So how did Lend-Lease actually work? Various materiel, arms, equipment and materials were bought from the manufacturers at the expense of funds allocated by the US Congress for each financial year. It was stipulated that outward shipments should include only the items that were exportable in terms of secrecy considerations (this stipulation was primarily applicable to various aircraft and aviation equipment) and that satisfying the needs of the United States' own armed forces should be the overriding priority (for that reason, the most advanced aircraft were not exported or, otherwise, were delivered in limited quantities).

The purchased materiel was, from a legal point of view, the property of the American armed forces – thus, for example, aircraft (depending on their functionality) belonged to the US Army Air Force or to the US Navy. Acceptance of such aircraft was performed by the US military inspection. The tails always bore military inventory numbers, and these numbers were never changed, nor repeated; all the appropriate documentation was prepared with a reference to them. In the Soviet Union, these numbers were usually not painted over, since claim reports (when drawn up) referred to nothing else but such numbers. All aircraft types supplied under Lend-Lease (regardless of whether they were in service with the US armed forces, or were manufactured solely for export purposes) had American military designations – thus, for example, the Martin 187 Baltimore bomber, which was manufactured only under British orders, was referred to as A-22 in American documents.

It was intended that all the military materiel would be provided by the Allies for the duration of the war. After the end of the war, the surviving materiel would have to be returned to the USA (if required by the latter), or paid for; this was envisaged by Article V of the Soviet-American agreement on mutual assistance of 11 June 1942. Payments were to commence five years after the war, and would stretch over 10 years. The mentioned agreement was the principal document which laid the legal foundation for shipments of American materiel and equipment to the Soviet Union.

In the USSR, the reception of American assistance was the responsibility of the People's Commissariat of Foreign Trade, which was headed by A.I. Mikoyan. Specialists and military men who were involved in the acceptance of the materiel were attached to the Commissariat. They were not, however, included in the staff of the People's Commissariat of Foreign Trade, and regular employees of the Commissariat tended to 'look down' on them. The somewhat inferior status of the acceptance personnel was, by the way, reflected in their salaries.

In practice, the system worked as follows: the Soviet General Staff, together with the Air Force Staff, determined the total demand of foreign aircraft and the required aviation equipment and supplies. The requests for equipment, tools, raw materials and transport were submitted to the People's Commissariat of Aviation Industry. All of this was discussed with the Allies within the scope of the effective annual agreement, and decisions were made as to who would supply what and in which amount (per categories or, for aircraft, per classes). The decisions constituted the basis for annual Protocols. Protocol I (also referred to as the 'Moscow Protocol') covered the period up to 30 June 1942; the subsequent three Protocols were, in effect, exactly for one year each (from 1 July through to 30 June). This was accounted for by the fact that the US Congress allocated money per financial year, and a financial year covered exactly the said period.

The last Protocol – Protocol IV – expired on 1 July 1945; however, for the Allies, the war was still going on, with military activities against the Japanese still continuing. Stalin undertook to take part in the defeating of Japan and, consequently, the Soviet Union needed additional assistance in the form of arms, materiel and various military materials to strengthen the Soviet forces in the Far East. Deliveries made for this purpose were included in the special 'Annex III'.

As soon as the parties' obligations were determined by a Protocol, the next step was to detail the structure of deliveries. The Soviet party enquired of the Allies about the possibility to deliver certain types of aircraft, equipment or arms. Information for this purpose was collected by military attachés, acceptance inspectors and the intelligence. The Soviet Government Procurement Commission, which was headed by General Lieutenant V.I. Belyaev (replaced in December 1943 by General Lieutenant P.G. Rudenko), worked in the USA from 24 February 1942. This allowed avoiding, to a considerable extent, Amtorg's brokerage.

At first, the Soviet administration (apparently) was not quite aware of what was manufactured where and in what quantities – thus, they attempted to order certain aircraft that had never been mass-manufactured (for example, the Supermarine Spitfire Mk III), or to buy the Avro Manchester bombers (which were obviously far from successful) in Great Britain – and the case with the ordering of the A.W.41 Albemarle bombers in 1942, which is described in detail below, testifies to a poor awareness of Soviet officials in respect of properties of foreign aircraft. On other occasions, the Allies were requested to deliver certain aircraft in a quantity exceeding the total manufacture of the type in question. The former Chairman of the Council of Ministers N.I. Ryzhkov, in his book on Lend-Lease, straight-up admitted: 'It would be fair to attribute a considerable portion of complaints to the Soviet military acceptance inspection'. I, for my part, believe that the phrase is true not only in regard to acceptance inspection, but to authorities at all levels.

Not everything that was desired could be obtained. In turn, the Allies offered something else and such situations resulted in a trade-off. Within the limits of the funds allocated by the US Government, orders were placed with different companies for aircraft, equipment, spare parts, engines, arms and ammunition. The ordered items conformed to technical requirements as adopted by the US armed forces, and were checked by American military inspectors, with participation of Soviet inspectors from time to time.

From the middle of the war, the Soviet Union started sending to the USA requirements to modify the materiel in certain aspects. Some of the requirements were accepted (for example, those relating to aircraft painting): the Douglas A-20 bombers underwent even more serious modifications; in a special modification center in Tulsa, they were customized to accommodate a crew of four persons, as was adopted in the USSR. The aircraft spares were brought to special bases, where they were put in batches and accompanied with specifications in the Russian language; then the aircraft were transported, in one way or another, to a location where the acceptance/handover took place. That was where the Soviet mission – including representatives of the People's Commissariat of Foreign Trade and military men – was arranged. The procedure included an aircraft inspection, with checks for completeness and the rectification of any detected defects, as well as a test flight. Within the scope of the same procedure, the aircraft insignia were usually changed by the means of applying red stars. The accepted aircraft were registered and further transported as Soviet ones.

Any materiel that was lost during transportation – and before acceptance by the Soviet representatives – was made up for by additional shipments. For any aircraft that crashed in Soviet territory during its ferried journey to the front, the Allies were not liable.

Military assistance from Great Britain, which had actually started earlier than the Americans' assistance, was based on similar principles. The agreement on joint actions was signed in London, on behalf of the Soviet Union, by General F.I. Golikov in early July 1941 on the way to the USA. The use of Lend-Lease principles as a basis was decided upon in the course of correspondence between I.V. Stalin and W. Churchill in September 1941. In his letter Stalin wrote: '... Please accept my gratitude for the promise... to sell 200 more fighters to the Soviet Union'. The reply of the British Prime Minister was: '...You have used the word 'sell'. We do not regard the matter from this point of view and have never been thinking of any payment... all assistance has rested on the same basis... as the American Lend-Lease Bill, i.e. without any official cash settlements'. Legally, it was formalized later in the Treaty of Alliance in the War of 26 July 1942.

The logistic principles of British shipments were somewhat different from the Americans' principles, as the British differentiated between military shipments (arms, materiel, special-purpose transport vehicles, communication equipment etc.) and non-military shipments (industrial equipment, tools, raw materials and semi-finished products). The former were made as per the Lend-Lease procedure, beginning from 6 September 1941, whereas the latter were based on the principle that the difference between the cost of shipments from Great Britain to the USSR and back was deemed sold against a five-year credit line at an interest of three percent per annum. The Americans used no such differentiation, and the entire credit line was deemed an interest-free one. Similarly (to what was the case with the USA, before the creation of the required legal base), the Soviet party had been placing orders with British companies using its own funds.

The British were responsible not only for themselves, but also for the then huge British Empire – thus, for example, shipments from Canada (which were rather impressive in their amount) were not initially separated from the total British obligations. The key factor was that diplomatic relations between the USSR and Canada were established as late as 12 June 1942.

In July 1941, the Soviet mission, which was headed by Rear Admiral N.M. Kharlamov, settled in London. In particular, among its members were Colonel N.N. Pugachev, Colonel V.M. Dragun, Major A.F. Sizov and Captain II Rank P.I. Baranov. The mission interacted with the Trade Representation Engineering Department, which supervised the aircraft shipments. In October, 14 aviation specialists joined the department (although it later turned out that none of them spoke English); later, a special Air Department was established as part of the Engineering Administration, into which the Engineering Department was developed.

To begin with, Prime Minister W. Churchill suggested to his Cabinet that aircraft of American manufacture should be shipped first. This discharged the British party from aircraft quality liability and shifted the spare parts provision responsibilities onto the USA.

The aircraft shipped from England included those which had already seen service with the Royal Air Force, but were not much needed by the latter, and those which had been delivered to Great Britain and forwarded directly to the USSR without having been operated by the British. Among such aircraft were both ones that had been purchased in the USA before the creation of the

Lend-Lease system, and ones delivered under Lend-Lease. Later, direct shipments of aircraft which had been ordered by the British in the USA started coming directly from the USA. They quite often came in a special export version, as agreed upon with the customer. Hence, the American aircraft delivered against the US' obligations should be differentiated from those sent by Great Britain.

An interesting fact is that the aircraft which came as gifts from organizations and individuals were included among the total deliveries. These aircraft, although given as presents to the Soviet people, were also regarded as American property. Cases are known when aircraft abandoned in the Soviet territory (because of various malfunctions) were listed among those delivered under Lend-Lease; however, in most cases, such aircraft were written off by the owner and were officially deemed lost by the latter, in spite of being actually operated by Soviet aviation. Still, such 'side channels' constitute only a fraction of a percent of the entire quantity of aircraft handed over to Soviet Union.

Deliveries under Protocol I were fulfilled (on the whole, approximately 80 percent) and the Soviet Union planned to receive, in total, 3,600 aircraft. In practice, the USA sent 1,311 aircraft (1,239 of which arrived by sea) and 1,822 aircraft came from Great Britain. The total cost of aircraft and different aviation equipment was estimated at 176 million US dollars. The lagging behind the target figures was accounted for, inter alia, by delays in taking the already accepted cargoes out of the ports. The Soviet merchant fleet was far from large; the Soviet Union had to charter foreign vessels in conditions of the constantly increasing demand for transportation services. The Americans even threatened the reduction of assistance, since the aid (not infrequently) became 'hung up' in the ports. At the time, the American Government had no reliable information at its disposal as to how tight the situation was in overloaded Soviet ports.

The deliveries under Protocol II (Washington) were shaken, to a considerable extent, by the destruction of Convoy PQ 17 in July 1942, after which the northern route ceased to be operative until autumn that year. Thirty vessels en route to Archangelsk and Murmansk were returned and unloaded in British ports. This (perhaps) accounts for the fact that the Protocol was signed 'retroactively' on 6 October 1942 and, on 30 October, Roosevelt established a Special Board to coordinate all activities relating to assistance to the USSR. The President's Directive of 9 January 1943 demanded that maximum quantities of cargoes be delivered to the Soviet ports.

An attempt was first made to use the Pacific route instead of the northern one. Fifty-three American merchant ships and six tankers staying in the ports of the East Coast hoisted red flags and were entered in the Soviet register with newly drawn-up documents. This allowed passing through the combat operations zone under the Soviet-Japanese Neutrality Pact. All kinds of items were allowed to be delivered in this manner except for military materiel and ammunition. The role of the principal route at the time was given to the 'Persian Corridor', which is described in detail below. It was a route beginning in the ports of Iran and Iraq, and it was also used to carry bombers that were ferried there across the South Atlantic. The ALSIB route (Alaska-Siberia route, but also known as the Krasnoyarsk route) came into operation in September 1942 and gradually became the primary route for aircraft ferry and express transportation of highly valuable cargoes. The USA performed their obligations under Protocol II in full. Throughout the term of the Protocol, the USA delivered to the Soviet Union 3,816 aircraft – including 995 aircraft against Great Britain's obligations. The latter figure is also included by the British in the total number of aircraft delivered against their obligations (2,195 aircraft). Throughout the period, the Americans – in excess of their obligations under the Protocol – delivered 30 Beechcraft AT-6 trainer aircraft. Furthermore, a number of aircraft from the subsequent Protocol (including 63 Douglas A-20s, 13 North American B-25s and 50 Bell P-39s) were delivered in advance. The total cost of American aircraft and aviation equipment was estimated at 358 million US dollars. The British supplemented the specified shipments with an additional 150 Supermarine Spitfires, 32 Handley Page Hampdens, 14 A.W.41 Albemarles and 16 Hawker Hurricanes.

Protocol III (London) was distinctive in that it was signed (along with the original parties) by Canada, which acted as an equal participant and whose obligations were described separately. In the preceding two documents, it had been regarded as a part of the British Empire and that the responsibility for cargoes shipped from Canada had rested with the British Government. In June 1943, Soviet representatives started negotiations with the Canadians on shipments of De Havilland Mosquitoes and Supermarine Spitfires. The latter were not made in Canada (the Mosquitoes, on the contrary, were manufactured in large quantities); however, the negotiations failed (most probably on account of considerable orders from the 'mother country', or in respect of the long-range reconnaissance version, which was also from the USA).

The total amount of American shipments to the USSR throughout the term of the London Protocol exceeded the specified limits by nearly one third. The USA delivered 5,735 aircraft – including 1,732 aircraft against Great Britain's obligations. Notably, the Soviet demand had originally exceeded the figure almost twice (the Soviet Union had requested as many as 8,160 aircraft). Deliveries of oil products became an important component during the period, with approximately 900,000 tons shipped from the USA and an additional 160,000 tons sent from British oil refineries in Iran.

Protocol IV (Ottawa) took a long time to be signed (as late as 17 April 1945), with the reason being the USSR's requests for the delivery of complete sets of industrial equipment in large quantities – including four oil refineries. The Americans believed that such equipment would no longer be needed for war purposes, and the American Department of War insisted that attention be focused on transfers of nothing else but military materiel. In this respect, Washington exerted pressure on London too. The Soviet party, on the other hand, was willing to give up tanks and aircraft in favor of industrial machines and tools. The parties, however, managed to reach a compromise, although it should be noted that the deliveries had been going on quite smoothly without a formal document. The peculiarity of this period consisted of the opportunity to operate (from autumn 1944) the Black Sea ports, which started accommodating the Allies' vessels – thus partially lessening the load on the 'Persian Corridor'; however, aircraft were not delivered via this route. Protocol IV was suspended on 8 May 1945, following the capitulation of Germany. On 12 May, the US President declared that the only help to be provided thenceforward would have to be that required for military operations in the Far East. Before 12 May, 2,983 aircraft had been shipped to the Soviet Union – including 178 on behalf of the British. An interesting fact is that for the majority of aircraft types, the total result of Protocol IV exceeded the Soviet demand – thus, for example, 346 North American B-25 bombers were shipped instead of the 306 requested, and 272 Douglas C-47 transport aircraft instead of 241.

Further shipments were made within the scope of the already mentioned 'Annex III', and deliveries of equipment shipped in complete sets continued as well. Assistance from the Allies was terminated altogether no sooner than when Japan capitulated.

An English wartime poster in Russian, which says: 'From the British people. To the Victory! We are with you'.

Members of M.M. Gromov's team – after familiarization with the B-25 bomber – in Spokane.

Aerocobras and Kingcobras on the assembly line of the Bell Factory in Niagara Falls.

Bell pilots flying Kingcobras over the picturesque Niagara Falls.

3

The Long Ways

There were several ways to deliver aircraft from Great Britain or the USA, but the northern route (by sea to Murmansk and Archangelsk) was the first to start functioning. The aircraft arrived with the very first Convoy PQ 0 ("Dervish"), which reached Archangelsk on 31 August 1941. Its six merchant ships were escorted by the HMS *Argus* aircraft carrier, two cruisers, two destroyers, four patrol ships and three minesweepers. The aircraft were carried both on the deck of the HMS *Argus* and in boxes on merchant ships. In total, Convoy 0 brought 64 aircraft. The next convoy, PQ 1, brought 193 fighters. Altogether throughout 1941, seven convoys (in total, 53 merchant ships) came to Archangelsk (as for Murmansk, it was too close to the front lines, and ships were not unloaded there at the time). The seven convoys brought 484 Hawker Hurricane fighters, 216 P-40s and eleven P-39s. Of those, 125 aircraft arrived from the USA; the rest comprised British deliveries. At the time, that was the only route to deliver military assistance to the Soviet Union.

From January 1942, Murmansk was opened for the convoys. The Soviet steamship *Dekabrist*, whose cargo included American bombers, was the first to moor there on 20 December 1941. On 11 January, the first British convoy of nine transport ships arrived. The aircraft allocated for local air units were assembled in situ; the rest were usually sent by railway to inland locations. Boxes from the vessels were unloaded directly onto railway platforms. From Murmansk, the aircraft were usually shipped via the Kirovsk railway, and then further operated by units of the Karelian Front and the Leningrad Front. From the ports of the Archangelsk node (Archangelsk proper, Bakaritsa and Severodvinsk), the aircraft were carried to an assembly site near Archangelsk; then by air to the Vologda suburbs (or later, to the same location directly via the railway, to Sokol station).

Aircraft were coming with each of the Allies' convoys – thus, for example, Convoy PQ 12 arrived at Murmansk on 12 March, with a cargo of 200 aircraft. The next, Convoy PQ 13, reached Russia on 3 April. Its vessels brought 159 fighters and bombers. Before June 1942, 1,903 aircraft were delivered via the northern ports; however, deliveries via the northern route were irregular, with peculiarities of the convoys' navigation accounting for this fact. As the polar night was turning into polar day, navigation became increasingly dangerous. The Arctic convoys had to face bad weather, icepacks and German U-boats. The latter, jointly with the enemy aviation, which was concentrated in Norway, inflicted increasingly severe losses on the convoys on their way to Russia's northern ports. Convoy PQ 17, which was destroyed by the Germans in early July 1942, suffered the most terrible fate: on the order of the British Admiralty, the majority of escorts left the merchant ships and the latter thus became prey for U-boats, bombers and torpedo bombers. Of 32 merchant ships, 21 were lost; 122,000 tons of valuable cargo – including 210 aircraft – went down. After the loss of PQ 17, navigation of the convoys was suspended until autumn, with the idea being that the following polar night would impede the enemy's operations. The next convoy, PQ 18, whose cargo included 270 aircraft, sailed only in September; its ships arrived on 17 September. A similar situation took place in 1943, with navigation suspended for the entire period of the polar day.

The northern route was the shortest one, with the sea passage from England taking only 10-14 days; however, it was the most dangerous route as well. Beginning from spring 1942, German aircraft, U-boats and surface ships started the persistent hunting for the ships of the Allies' convoys. The losses on the northern route were also the greatest ones.

As the convoys' escorts and air cover improved, and the German 'war machine' was gradually becoming weaker, the losses lessened. Throughout 1944 and the first half of 1945, the convoys delivered 1,345 aircraft to Murmansk and Archangelsk.

The last convoy, JW 67, arrived at Kola Inlet on 20 May 1945 after the capitulation of Germany. Single vessels carrying aircraft from England came to Soviet northern ports in summer the same year.

In total, 4,790 aircraft were brought via the northern ports. The importance of the northern route for aircraft deliveries was gradually decreasing: versus the 2,532 aircraft which arrived via the northern route in 1941 through to 1942, only 804 aircraft were delivered in 1943, 766 in 1944 and 688 in 1945.

The long southern route – referred to in the West as 'the Persian Corridor' – was suggested as an alternative to the dangerous northern route. In early 1942, preparations for aircraft shipments via Iraq and Iran had started (the latter had, from August 1941, been invaded by Soviet and British troops). Fighters and light bombers were usually delivered to Basra by sea. From Basra, they were taken to British air bases in Iraq and assembled there. At first, Margil airfield was used for the purpose, with the aircraft acceptance performed by the Soviet inspection. Veterans of the route remembered that before the dispatch from Moscow, all the military personnel (even the sergeants) had been ordered to change to clothes made from high-quality woolen cloth, and had also received new high boots. On arrival, the military men had to face a heat of over 30°C! The British colleagues came to help and shared some of their tropical outfits with the Soviets – and the result was beyond description! At the airfield, one could see almost knee-length Soviet service shirts in combination with pith helmets, undershirts, briefs and high boots… Due to the peculiarities of the situation, there was almost no fault-finding in respect of clothing; only the higher management had to suffer from sweating in their outfits.

The 'Persian Corridor' was safer, but took more time. Delivery by sea from the USA encircling Africa alone took approximately three months.

In May 1942, the assembly facilities were shifted to a larger base in Shuaiba, at a distance of 20 miles from Basra. The Soviet inspection personnel also moved there. An interesting fact is that in April 1940, Shuaiba airfield was on the list of targets to be bombed in case of a conflict with England and France. From Shuaiba, the aircraft were ferried by British pilots to Abadan in Iran. In Abadan, the aircraft were subjected to final acceptance by the Soviet personnel. The Soviet base in Abadan was headed by Colonel I.D. Muravyov, who was superseded by Major General I.V. Obraztsov. The procedure was as follows: the aircraft was subjected to a thorough inspection, and if it was found to be fit for flight, a British pilot was the first to test-fly it; then the same was repeated by the Englishman's Soviet colleague. If no objections were expressed, the aircraft was prepared for the ferry; otherwise, it was returned in order to have the objections rectified. By autumn 1943, 165 Soviet specialists had been involved in inspection activities in Abadan.

It was only in 1944 that Spitfire IX fighters were assembled in Shuaiba and Soviet ferry pilots of the 71st Fighter Ferry Air Regiment were taking them away directly after assembly. From Abadan, the aircraft were ferried to Tehran, and then to Ajikabul airfield in Azerbaijan. These ferry operations were performed by flight personnel of the 6th Ferry Air Regiment, which was under the command of Major Mishchenko. They had to fly over mountains and deserts, and sometimes, the aircraft in Tehran were handed over directly to pilots of combat regiments. In this manner, for example, the 16th Guards Fighter Air Regiment was provided with Airacobras.

Concurrently with the operations described above, the Douglas Aircraft Company (USA) started building assembly facilities in Abadan. The ships carrying the aircraft were thus unloaded in Iranian ports, from where the boxes were carried by motor trucks to Abadan; in Abadan, the aircraft were assembled and test-flied. The acceptance procedure was the same as with the British. Sometimes, the aircraft were returned to the assembly factory to have the defects rectified (for example, a batch of Airacobras was rejected on account of the secondary shaft whipping).

The British also started carrying a portion of the Spitfires, as unloaded in Basra to Abadan, and to assemble them there. By May 1943, approximately 200 Britons and 350 Americans had been working at the aircraft assembly facility in Abadan; however, the factory only dealt with aircraft of American manufacture (and not even all of them). The North American B-25 bombers, which featured high-range performance, made flights on the route from the USA to Brazil; then to the Western Coast of Africa; to the Middle East; and finally, to Iran. Air ferrying of the bombers from Florida to Iraq somewhat expedited the process. When the Americans built an intermediate base on Ascension Island, they started ferrying the A-20s by air as well. Throughout 1942, 900 aircraft were ferried in this manner.

Small batches of aircraft were carried in boxes by motor trucks to the Iranian port of Pehlevi on the Caspian Sea, from where they were shipped by steamships to Baku or Krasnovodsk, but their share was negligible. According to Soviet documents, only 23 aircraft were carried in such a manner – including 22 aircraft in 1942 and just one aircraft in 1944.

The majority of aircraft arrived in Azerbaijan by air. Hurricanes, Spitfires, P-39s, P-40s, P-47s, A-20s, B-25s and AT-6s were carried via Iran. Before 1 April 1943, Abadan received 1,025 aircraft; before 30 June 1944, this number grew by 2,900 aircraft more. In total, 5,648 aircraft were ferried – including 680 aircraft in 1942, 3,016 aircraft in 1943 and 1,938 aircraft in 1944. The Soviet mission in Basra was in operation until October 1944. On 15 October, the camp in Shuaiba was wound up, whereas assembly of the aircraft had been terminated as early as September. The last aircraft from Iran (three Republic P-47D fighters) were ferried to the USSR in February 1945. In total, 14 aircraft were ferried via the southern route throughout 1945.

Both the Americans and the Soviets were seeking a route that would be both safe and rather short. The fact that the two countries are separated by the Bering Strait, which is easily traversable by aircraft, contributed to the search. In early June 1942, the Americans suggested ferrying the aircraft directly from Alaska to Chukotka. On 17 June, US President F. Roosevelt wrote to I.V. Stalin: 'Ambassador Litvinov notified me of your approval of the ferry of American aircraft via Alaska and Northern Siberia to the Western Front, and I am glad to know it'. The new scheme offered time-saving prospects and provided opportunities even for the ferry of short-range aircraft (in particular, fighters which were not capable of a trans-oceanic flight).

On 1 July, Stalin informed Roosevelt: '... The Soviet Government has already given the required orders to complete as soon as possible the activities now going on in Siberia for preparation to reception of the aircraft...' The activities had indeed been under way for a rather long time. As early as July 1941, the State Defense Committee adopted a resolution on surveying the route of the future airway to establish a shortcut connection between the USSR and the USA.

Regular air communication was not available in the north of Eastern Siberia at the time. More or less acceptable (but unpaved) airfields were only in Magadan, Yakutsk and Petropavlovsk-Kamchatsky. Airfields in general were a rare thing, and they were designed mostly for light aircraft such as the Polikarpov U-2 or R-5, which used skis in winter. The locality was sparsely populated and poorly known, with the greater portion of it covered with dense taiga. Mountain ranges were in the way and the winters brought heavy frosts.

The air route had to be created anew – including the construction of airfields (which involved bringing people, construction materials and vehicles to hard-to-reach areas); establishing a fuel supply system; setting up the weather service and communications; and installing homing radio beacons.

Three variants of the route were considered: the first one passed along the northern maritime route, where the Chief Administration of the northern maritime route had established a network of small stations and posts that were used by the Polar Aviation; in winter, however, the polar night reigned in the locality. The second route ran across Kamchatka and Northern Sakhalin to Komsomolsk-on-Amur. This was dangerously close to the bases of the Japanese, who had already been at war with the USA and could become the USSR's enemy as well at any time. The third variant, which was deemed the most advantageous, ran via Chukotka and Yakutia to Krasnoyarsk. Here, some of the existing airfields could be used. As a result, the Soviet Government approved the route from Uelkal via Seymchan, Yakutsk and Kirensk to Krasnoyarsk.

The construction of the Soviet portion of the route started in accordance with the Resolution of the State Defense Committee of 9 October 1941, with experienced engineer D.E. Chusov in charge. A large number of people were involved in the construction activities, and people were taken from all populated areas along the future route. These were supplemented by Civil Air Fleet personnel and military personnel, as well as prisoners of *Dalstroy* prison camps, who were supervised by the People's Commissariat of Internal Affairs (*Narodnyy Komissariat Vnutrennikh Del*, or NKVD). A dense network of camps was covering Chukotka and Kolyma at the time; however, there was a shortage of manpower – thus, school studies were suspended in Markovo and even children aged 12 or 13 joined the workforce as auxiliary workers. To some of the selected sites, no roads existed at all, so seaplanes were used to transport people and all the required materials. There were still more remote locations, where people went by deer-drawn or dog-drawn sledges, used skis or simply walked.

Before June 1942, construction of the main airfields was complete. Over the entire length of the more than 6,000km-long route, about 15 principal and alternate airfields were reconstructed or constructed anew. They even appeared in such 'wild' areas as Khandyga, Chaibukha and Uelkal – thus, in Uelkal, the airfield was arranged on a pebble spit in the Bay of Krest. A decision was made to make the airfield from wooden battens reinforced with clay. Chukotka is a tundra place; there are no forests, and all wood is of imported origin. In September 1942, the battens were brought by sea from Vladivostok, but the waters were too shallow for the ships to reach land. The battens were thrown overboard and washed ashore, so the few representatives of the local population and the camp prisoners who were involved in the work had to collect the battens and carry them to the construction site. A metal cabin and several plywood-wall *yarangas* (skin tents) – faced on the outside, with snow bricks to contain heat – were erected for the personnel. Wooden plank-beds covered with deerskin functioned as sleeping accommodation. Later, several prefabricated houses were delivered from Canada by air.

The airfield in Kirensk was built by human force – using spades and pickaxes. Soil was carried by horses and tamped using manual tampers.

The responsibility for operations pertaining to the creation and maintenance of the route rested with several authorities: the Chief Civil Air Fleet Administration was in charge of the construction of airfields and further maintenance of the route. Military personnel and the NKVD had to render assistance by means of providing working personnel. The People's Commissariat of Foreign Trade was documenting the reception of materiel from the American party. Acceptance was ensured by the air force, which delegated engineers and technicians to the USA. The air force also provided part of the flight crews to ferry the aircraft to Krasnoyarsk. Other authorities were entrusted with the task to supply the route with all necessary things. General supervision over the Krasnoyarsk route was carried out by the Chief Air Force Administration; then, for a short period of time, it was under the control of Long-Range Aviation and, from 15 June 1943, under the control of the Chief Civil Air Fleet Administration.

It was assumed that the Americans would deliver the aircraft to Alaska to prepare them for further ferrying. First, the American party intended to choose Marks Field in Nome as the main base, yet the Americans feared a possible airstrike by the Japanese aviation from the Aleutian Islands, so they opted for Ladd Field near Fairbanks. The Soviet military mission and the ferry crews' base was arranged there. The Soviet crews were supposed to ferry the aircraft from Ladd Field to Krasnoyarsk.

As previously mentioned, the Americans referred to the route as the ALSIB route, but in the Soviet Union, it was officially referred to as the Krasnoyarsk route, since its terminal point was Krasnoyarsk. In some Soviet documents, it is also mentioned as the northern air route.

A special team of ferry pilots was formed into the 6th Backup Air Brigade in Ivanovo. Seven ferry regiments and the 8th Transport Air Regiment were to be formed for the route's maintenance purposes. The tendency was to take pilots from combat regiments which had already had a chance to fly foreign aircraft in military operations, or from among ferry pilots who had worked on the southern route from Iran; however, some of the pilots for the new regiments came directly from flying schools. To gain experience in operating foreign aircraft, the pilots were trained to fly the Bell P-39s, the Curtiss P-40s and the North American Mustang I fighters. In Ivanovo, training flights were conducted using fighters; in Undol (the Gorky region), bombers were utilized for training. The training was supervised by Colonel N.K. Romanov and special attention was paid to take-off and landing techniques on aircraft with a nose wheel, which was not encountered on aircraft of Soviet manufacture at the time.

Rather strict criteria were used to select the flight personnel, with three serious errors leading to the rejection of the candidate. As a result, only the best were accepted; from among the pilots who arrived in Ivanovo, only one in five was enrolled in the ferry regiments.

The 8th Transport Air Regiment was manned by experienced Civil Air Fleet and Polar Aviation crews, and the PS-84 (Li-2) transport aircraft for the regiment were taken from the Civil Air Fleet and Polar Aviation as well.

In early August 1942, Commander of the Northern Fleet 2nd Air Group I.P. Mazuruk, who was an experienced polar pilot and held the rank of Colonel, received an order to vacate command of the group and depart for Moscow as soon as possible. To get to Moscow, he flew a disarmed SB bomber which had been requisitioned in the beginning of the war from the Polar Aviation. In Moscow, Mazuruk attended a Kremlin meeting on the preparation of the ALSIB route, and had a talk with Stalin. Mazuruk left the meeting holding the post of Route Supervisor.

Mazuruk visited Ivanovo, where the training of flight crews had, by that time, been completed. A decision had been made not to create the 6th and 7th Ferry Air Regiments, and to restrict the number of ferry regiments to five. Each regiment had two fighter squadrons and two bomber squadrons, which specialized in the ferrying of specific aircraft types. Nevertheless, the Transport Air Regiment retained the number '8th'. All of the regiments were grouped into the 1st Ferry Air Division, with Mazuruk deemed its commander as well.

The ferry over the territory of the USSR was arranged in the relay pattern. The 1st Ferry Air Regiment, which was under the command of Lieutenant Colonel P.V. Nedosekin (later Lieutenant Colonel N.S. Vasin), was based in Alaska at Ladd Field and ferried the aircraft to Uelkal in Chukotka. It was done in two stages: first, the aircraft flew along the Yukon; then they made an intermediate landing in Nome, on the Bering Strait Coast. Marks Field in Nome accommodated a small contingent of Soviet mechanics and engineers. Half-way between Fairbanks and Nome, there was the alternate airfield of Galena, which could be used in bad weather. After refueling, the aircraft flew over the strait and the eastern part of Chukotka and landed in Uelkal, or on alternate airfields in Anadyr or Markovo. There, the 2nd Air Regiment 'picked up the baton' and the pilots who had arrived from Alaska went back by the Li-2 transport aircraft.

The 2nd Ferry Air Regiment was based in Uelkal and was under the command of Lieutenant Colonel A.N. Melnikov (from June 1944, it was under the command of Major M. Pavlenkov). The 2nd Air Regiment had to deal with a difficult route via the central portion of Chukotka and the Kolyma Range to Seymchan. Furthermore, the aircraft were ferried by pilots of the 3rd Ferry Air Regiment, which was under the command of Lieutenant Colonel N. Tverdokhlebov (but later, Major B. Frolov). That was the most dangerous portion of the route, with 1,180km between Seymchan and Yakutsk. The air road passed over the high-mountain terrain of the Chersky Range and the Verkhoyansk Range via the 'cold pole' in Oymyakon. The pilots, who flew the aircraft at high altitudes, had to wear oxygen masks. In Seymchan in winter, the thermometer went down to -60ºC; in Oymyakon, it went down to -70ºC. Because of the severe winter cold, the aircraft would sometimes make a detour to bypass Oymyakon and an intermediate landing was made in Magadan or Zyryanka.

Yakutsk accommodated the 4th Ferry Air Regiment, which was under the command of Major P.E. Smolyakov (later, he was superseded by Major Dmitriev, and then by Major S. Vlasov). The 8th Transport Air Regiment, which was under the command of Lieutenant Colonel V.A. Pushchinsky, was based at the same airfield. The 4th Air Regiment flew the segment from Yakutsk to Kirensk. At this segment of the route, the aircraft flew along the Lena River and (at a portion of the segment) over taiga. Pilots of the 5th Air Regiment, which was under the command of Colonel M. Matyushin (and later, Major I. Pronyushkin), had to deal with the final segment, which was from Kirensk to Krasnoyarsk. The transportation of flight personnel in early November 1942 ended in a crash. Soon after departure from Krasnoyarsk, a Lisunov Li-2 – with two squadrons of fighter pilots on board – crashed into the ground. Nobody survived.

Mazuruk arranged his headquarters in Yakutsk and it accommodated all principal services, workshop units and a replacement training unit.

Aircraft fuel and oil for the route under construction were shipped by sea from the USA; the rest of what was required (foodstuffs, fuel for motor vehicles and electric generators, construction materials etc.) was brought from the south by sea or by rivers.

On 4 September, two Li-2s carrying the Soviet mission personnel landed at Fairbanks airfield. The mission included 50 engineers and technicians, whose task was to accept American aircraft, and also a young interpretress; all of them had earlier worked at the Iranian route. Colonel M.G. Machin, who was recalled from the Voronezh Front, where he had been the commander of the 207th Fighter Air Division, became chief of the mission.

By that time, the first aircraft to be handed over to the USSR had already arrived at Fairbanks. On the American side, the responsibility for the delivery of aircraft from factories to Alaska rested with the 7th Ferrying Group of the US Air Force Air Transport Command Alaska Wing. It was under the command of Brigadier General D. Gaffney (and, from September 1944, Colonel R. Killer) and its headquarters was located in Great Falls, Montana, near the international boundary. That was the junction of the routes from different manufacturer factories and the place where the northbound way via Canada to Alaska began. Women's Air Force service personnel also took part in the ferrying of aircraft over the territory of the USA.

American pilots ferried the aircraft northward along the Pacific Coast. They utilized a 'through' ferrying system, with one and the same crew flying from Great Falls to Fairbanks. The first aircraft for the USSR – five A-20B bombers – were delivered to Ladd Field on 3 September. Eight days later, Lieutenant Anderson brought a group of twenty-two P-40 fighters to the same location.

In-situ maintenance, required repairs and the handover of aircraft to the Soviet mission was the responsibility of the 348th Airfield Service Squadron. Ladd Field was a rather well-equipped location: there was all the required service spaces, as well as accommodation facilities, a canteen, a mess and a large hangar, which could hold 30 fighters or 20 bombers at a time. All of the buildings were arranged in a circle and connected by a heat-insulated underground passage, which proved to be very convenient in the conditions of a northern winter.

For the USAAF, large-scale operations in the Far North's conditions turned out to be quite difficult at first. Mechanics encountered difficulties with engines starting at low temperatures, so warm-air furnaces and heaters of various types had to be brought. The hydraulic fluid thickened, and oil and grease on moving elements froze, so American scientists urgently set about developing fluids and oils that would be operable in the cold. Instruments on aircraft which were kept outdoors froze. Therefore, small, removable electrical heaters were manufactured to be attached to instrument panels. Both American and (sometime later) Soviet pilots used wheeled landing gear all year round, and without changing it to skis. In conditions of severe frost, wheels of parked aircraft tended to freeze down to snow. To avoid this, the personnel positioned the aircraft on wooden boards.

As soon as 14 September, specialists of the Soviet mission accepted the first batch of A-20 bombers; then the P-40K fighters and the B-25 bombers followed. Information on detected defects was written in chalk directly on the aircraft hulls.

On 24 September, four Lisunov Li-2s carrying the flight crews of the 1st Ferry Air Regiment landed in Fairbanks. On 29 September, training flights on the A-20s were conducted; as soon as the following day, a dozen of the A-20s in V-formation headed for Nome. Major P.V. Nedosekin piloted the lead bomber. The aircraft landed safely in Nome, yet bad weather prevented them from any further flying. Only as late as 7 October would the bombers continue on their way westward. In Markovo, the aircraft were handed over to crews of the 2nd Air Regiment; then on 11 October, the first group of P-40K fighters took the way. Two days later, and already in the Soviet territory, it suffered its first losses. Before Uelkal, an A-20 was the lead aircraft, but later, a Li-2 took over the lead; however, the transport aircraft – and a rather worn one, too – flew at a much lower speed than the fighters. Furthermore, its crew had no experience in flying a lead aircraft. In thick clouds, the formation disintegrated. The fighters – one by one, or in twos – returned to Uelkal. Two P-40Ks perished together with their pilots. During subsequent ferry operations, only the A-20 or B-25 bombers were used as the lead aircraft.

In spite of all difficulties, the first batch of fighters kept moving towards Krasnoyarsk. On 27 October, the aircraft reached Yakutsk; in early November, they arrived in Krasnoyarsk. According to the Krasnoyarsk route report, the number of aircraft ferried by the end of October included (in total) twenty-eight P-40 fighters, fourteen A-20 Havoc bombers and ten C-47 Skytrain transport aircraft.

The next batch of P-40Ks started on their way on 3 November, and the ferrying of the third batch began in December. One of the fighters of this batch made a forced belly landing onto the thin ice on the Lena. The pilot managed to escape from the cockpit before the aircraft broke the ice and sank, which was accompanied by the howling of the alarm horn, which had become activated automatically during the landing, with the landing gear up.

Throughout the three autumn months, the Americans delivered to Alaska 129 aircraft – including the first batch of the North American B-25 Mitchell bombers. On 28 October, a Soviet crew under the command of Captain P.P. Gamov made the first training flight on a B-25; on 3 November, the crew was sent westward to fly the lead aircraft in a group of the P-40s. Nearly every day in November (weather permitting), batches of aircraft departed toward Krasnoyarsk and, for the first time, they included the Bell P-39 Airacobra fighters. Throughout November, nine B-25s, thirty A-20s, twelve P-39s and fourteen P-40s were ferried.

During the first months of the route operation and, on some occasions, afterwards – when the inflow of aircraft to be ferried was too large – both Soviet and American pilots worked concurrently at the segment before Nome.

Fighters were usually ferried in groups of eight to 12 aircraft and accompanied by a lead bomber, with more advanced navigation aids, and a navigator on board. The bomber took off first and waited for the rest of the group to gather. The fighters adopted the V-formation, with the lead aircraft at the vertex, while another bomber followed the formation as the trailing aircraft (it watched for stragglers). In case of a forced landing, the trailing bomber had to precisely determine its location and call for help. The A-20 and B-25 bombers usually departed as the lead aircraft to accompany fighter groups; sometimes though, they might fly independently in small groups, which was just the same as the C-47 transport aircraft.

Before the end of 1942, the Soviet mission accepted 148 aircraft, and among them were forty-eight P-40Ks (P-40K-1s and P-40K-10s) and ten B-25s. The aircraft delivered to Krasnoyarsk included ten C-47s, ten B-25s, fifty-six A-20s, twelve P-39s and forty-three P-40s. Quite a number of aircraft were lost in incidents and crashes, and among the written-off aircraft were a B-25, ten A-20s, an Airacobra and four P-40s – thus, for example, on 20 November 1942, Captain Kovylin (because of a technical failure) had to make a forced landing to a tiny patch of land 100km to the north from the settlement of Berelekh. The A-20 bomber was broken down, and there was no possibility to evacuate even the intact assemblies of the aircraft; luckily, the entire crew survived.

In autumn 1942, American pilots were ferrying seven Douglas A-20s to Nome; however, the bad weather made two aircraft perform emergency landings. One of those aircraft landed in the mountains, and the other one on the Bering Strait Coast. The former was broken down and, therefore, written off; for the latter, a decision was made to restore it. A team of American mechanics arrived at the location and, for nearly two months, they were repairing the badly damaged bomber. A small airstrip was arranged on the pebbles along the coast; however, the attempt to take off from the airstrip failed (the crosswind was drifting the aircraft to the sea). Fortunately, a smooth ice floe (approximately 600m long) was found nearby. A road was laid in the snow using a Jeep; via the road, the A-20 taxied out to the ice. Captain Gamov then managed to take off from the ice floe and ferried the bomber to Nome.

The Soviet side of the ALSIB had to face approximately the same problems as the American side, with the only difference being that winters in Yakutia were even colder than in Alaska. Motor oil and hydraulic fluid at such temperatures solidified, while rubber became embrittled. At many locations, there were no hangars at all; all procedures were performed outdoors. In such conditions, it was often found out that aircraft designers had not considered winter operation peculiarities. Some of the access holes were so small that one could not reach inside them even with a hand clad in a warm glove, which is to say nothing of a fur mitten. Before departure, personnel had to heat oil tanks and engines using blow lamps and primus stoves; some makeshift heaters were also made, which worked on firewood. Pilot V.M. Perov remembers that during the first winter of the route's operation, snow at parking areas where American aircraft were located was red because of the hydraulic fluid that leaked through cold-frozen sealants. Coolant and the anti-freezing agent in the cooling system were replaced with more cold-resistant Soviet ones.

A lot of problems were connected with clearing the airfields from snow. Special-purpose vehicles were scarce, so personnel had to use spades mostly. In the middle of winter, lines of huge snow piles flanked the airstrips.

December 1942 brought the first death of a Soviet citizen on the route. Engineer B.V. Kiselnikov died in a crash, together with American pilot Captain Glass and his engineer during the test flight of a B-25C in Fairbanks.

From the beginning of 1943, the amount of work on the route started growing and the number of aircraft was increasing. The once prevailing P-40 fighters had almost disappeared by spring 1943, and the last three Kittyhawks were handed over in Krasnoyarsk in April. Instead, a mass inflow of Airacobras began. The number of Airacobras that departed from Fairbanks was 29 in January, 59 in February and 55 in March. This aircraft type became the principal one for the ferry pilots of the Krasnoyarsk route for a long time. In February, the number of B-25 bombers grew abruptly: first, only the C versions were delivered; then, the D version also appeared.

The warm season relieved the ferry pilots of certain wintertime problems, yet new difficulties arose. Fog above airfields, low clouds and myriads of mosquitoes and gnats complicated the situation for aviators, and frequent wild fires covered large spaces with dense smoke. During the first five months of the ALSIB operation, 45 crashes occurred. Further on, the accident rate was continuously decreasing.

The peak number of aircraft en route in 1943 was achieved in June. Nearly 300 aircraft – including 195 P-39s – were ferried to Krasnoyarsk.

In 1943, an attempt was made to ferry the aircraft without the relay pattern; it meant that a single crew was intended to fly from Uelkal to Krasnoyarsk. For this purpose, the 7th Ferry Air Regiment was created; however, the idea fell short of expectations. The regiment lasted for only three months and was then disbanded.

The construction of all kinds of buildings was actively going on, and among the buildings were barracks, hotels, hangars and service facilities. The existing aircraft were expanded and new ones were created. From 1944, demountable metal coverings imported from America were used for this purpose, and the number of homing radio stations was increasing. Route Construction Supervisor Chusov was awarded the Order of the Red Star, but was then removed from office for 'bad management'.

The increasing amount of aircraft delivered via the route brought about the reorganization of its operation. The Route Command was separated from the Ferry Air Division Command. Mazuruk retained his post of Division Commander, whereas Major General I.S. Semyonov became Route Supervisor (in August 1944, he was superseded by Lieutenant General M.I. Shevelev, who had earlier been Chief of Staff for Long-Range Aviation). Above these, a 'superstructure' appeared in the form of the Moscow to Uelkal Air Road Administration, which was headed by Major General A.A. Avseevich. He was not a pilot, but a *chekist* (common name in Soviet Union explaining a person serving for a State security organization, which originated from *CheKa, chrezvychay-naya komissiya*, or the Emergency Committee established in 1917) who had, some time before, completed a course of training in a flying club. The 1st Air Regiment was withdrawn from the division and placed under the command of the Soviet mission in Fairbanks.

At first, no regulated system existed for the handover of aircraft, which were delivered via the route to air force units. The responsibility for acceptance in Krasnoyarsk was imposed upon the 45th Backup Air Regiment, which was under the command of Major Vlasov. The unit did not have enough resources to arrange further transportation of the large quantities of aircraft. As a result, by early July 1943, more than 250 aircraft which were to be sent to the front had been accumulated in Krasnoyarsk; however, some of them were unserviceable after the long ferry journey. To carry out their further shipment, the 15th Air Base was arranged under the command of Major V.I. Shibailo (later, Major E.Kh. Khoroshilov and Major Nazarov). The base was located at Yemelyanovo airfield, where the inbound American aircraft from Alaska landed. The base personnel totaled approximately 300 persons.

The majority of the aircraft were shipped from Krasnoyarsk via railway. For this purpose, they were ferried from Yemelyanovo to another airfield in Barmakoi, which was near the railway station in Bugach. From the Barmakoi parking apron, the aircraft were towed to the station and disassembled, preserved and mounted on wooden supports on platforms. The supports were made in situ from pinewood and cedarwood; the pines and cedars were cut nearby. All of these procedures were performed in any weather, and at temperatures down to -50°C. In winter, the soldiers received ('in connection with the cold season', similarly to those in the lines) 100g of vodka per head. Every 10 days, the base sent 30-32 aircraft westward, which was a quantity sufficient enough to equip an air regiment; shipments per month amounted to a park for an entire division. In such a manner, approximately two thirds of Airacobras were shipped to the front.

Other aircraft were ferried by air, and this was the responsibility of the 9th Ferry Air Regiment, which was subordinate to the 15th Air Base. Identical in structure to the ALSIB ferry regiments, the 9th Air Regiment included two fighter squadrons and two bomber squadrons. The regiment was under the command of Major P.P. Loginov, but later Major Tabanchuk.

Aircraft ferried via the Krasnoyarsk route were of various types: the Curtiss P-40K Kittyhawks were shipped only during the first months of the route operation. In total, 43 Kittyhawks reached Krasnoyarsk; their ferry was terminated in March 1943. For a long time, the Bell P-39 Airacobra was the most mass-shipped aircraft on the route. The total quantity of Airacobras accepted in Alaska was 2,618; of these, 1,592 aircraft were reckoned among the shipments under Great Britain's obligations, and 27 aircraft were a replacement of shipment losses. A total of 2,593 Airacobras reached Krasnoyarsk. Aircraft of versions D, K, M, N and Q were consecutively shipped from Fairbanks, and the Airacobras were ferried in two or three batches at a time. They took off one after the other and adopted V-formations, each with its own lead aircraft. In such cases, the first lead aircraft was usually piloted by the regiment commander; he controlled the entire aircraft group over the radio. The last five P-39Qs were accepted and ferried to the Soviet Union in winter 1945.

As for bombers, the Douglas A-20 Havoc was the most popular one on the ALSIB route, and all modifications of the aircraft went through the Soviet acceptance in Alaska. Before the beginning of 1943, the A-20Bs prevailed; then they became gradually superseded by the A-20Cs. In summer 1943, the Americans brought the first A-20G-1 attack aircraft to Fairbanks, and later, other versions of this modification were delivered. In spring 1944, the A-20Js appeared on the route; some time later, the K- and H-type aircraft also came, but in comparatively small quantities. The manufacture of the A-20s at the time began to wound down gradually. In total, 1,363 bombers of this type were accepted in Fairbanks, with 1,330 of them reaching Krasnoyarsk.

Among the en-route wrecks, there happened to be the A-20G, which was a gift to the Soviet pilots by Hollywood comedian R. Skelton. In terms of propaganda, the situation was awkward; then Mazuruk ordered that the 'We dood it!' slogan, which had been emblazoned on the gift, be painted on another aircraft of exactly the same type. Duly painted, the aircraft was sent further and, finally, it was modified into a torpedo bomber – seeing service with one of the crews of the Baltic Fleet Air Force 51st Mine-and-Torpedo Air Regiment.

The B-25 bombers came in considerably smaller quantities. The number of such aircraft accepted in Alaska totaled 733 (of those, the greatest quantity (396) was accepted in 1944), but only 725 of them reached the destination point. Before 1944, C and D versions were shipped; later, the J version became the prevailing one. In 1944, four B-25Gs, which were equipped with 75mm cannons, were ferried, while the last of the B-25Js flew the route in summer 1945.

The ferrying of the Douglas C-47 Skytrains started in mid-October 1942. The first of the Skytrains were placed in service with the 8th Transport Air Regiment, which then scrapped the most worn PS-84s. All of the C-47s that were shipped by the USA to the Soviet Union came via Alaska and Chukotka. The shipped modifications included the C-47s, C-47As and C-47Bs. Of the 707 aircraft of this type which were accepted in Fairbanks, only two aircraft crashed en route. The most intensive ferrying took place in April and May 1945. Of all the others, the C-47 became the last heavy aircraft that flew via the ALSIB route before the air road was closed in September 1945. On 8 September, a C-47 piloted by Captain Gamov's crew departed from Fairbanks and finally landed in Yakutsk.

In early summer 1944, the Americans ferried the first Bell P-63 Kingcobra fighters to Alaska. As soon as late 1944, these aircraft were prevailing over Airacobras; from early 1945, they exceeded (in quantity) all of the other aircraft types combined. Initially, the P-63s were ferried via the usual route to Krasnoyarsk; however, in summer, the flow changed its direction. The change was brought about by the end of the war in Europe and in preparation for warfare against Japan. The aircraft from Markovo were conveyed to Petropavlovsk-Kamchatsky (Yelizovo airfield), where the 128th Composite Air Division was being rearmed.

From the end of June, the route from Krasnoyarsk was extended via Chita to Ukkurey for the needs of the Zabaykalye Front. Some of the aircraft were ferried there directly from Yakutsk. Later, a route from Ukkurey to Khabarovsk was flown; for time-saving reasons, a decision was made to fly directly across the territory of Manchuria. The Japanese did not even attempt to attack the airspace violators, which flew in large groups and close formations.

In total, the Soviet mission in Fairbanks accepted 2,397 P-63s of the A and C modifications. According to the Krasnoyarsk route report, the number of ferried and handed-over aircraft is 2,340. The last aircraft arrived as late as after the capitulation of Japan, and one of the very last P-63s arrived in Kamchatka on 29 September 1945. That was (perhaps) the last of all the aircraft that had been ferried by the 1st Ferry Air Division. The quantities of Kingcobras that had been accumulated in Krasnoyarsk and Ukkurey by the end of September were so large that they were distributed over combat units until September the following year.

In spring 1945, the Americans allocated 54 North American AT-6F Texans. The first batch took to the road in early June without the customary lead aircraft. The issue was that the Texans were too slow speed-wise to be escorted by the A-20s or the B-25s. Changes had to be made to the route as well. At the segment assigned to the 3rd Air Regiment, an intermediate landing was made in Omolon for refueling purposes (otherwise, the aircraft would not have had enough fuel to fly to Seymchan). The low operating ceiling made ferrying across the Verkhoyansk Range impossible. Therefore, the route was shifted northward, with the aircraft flying to Oymyakon, and then to Yakutsk along the crest line of the Verkhoyansk Range and the Suntar-Khayata Range. Sometimes, on the way from Oymyakon, the group of AT-6s made a refueling stop in Khandyga.

There were aircraft which were ferried in just a few examples (e.g. three Republic P-47D-10 Thunderbolt fighters and a single Curtiss C-46A Commando).

The route was also used to convey valuable cargoes, and these were carried on board the C-47s being ferried. The cargoes included spare parts for aircraft, technical documentation, special tools, flight clothing, motion-picture film, chemicals, radioactive preparations (for phosphorescent paint) and medicines that were not produced in the USSR at the time; however, there were some occasions when the aircraft carried expensive writing paper and even almost 500 kg of lipstick. Mail for American POWs in Japan was carried via the Soviet Union as well. Sometimes, in Magadan, the aircraft were additionally loaded with gold from local goldfields.

Mazuruk was in command of the division until June 1944; then the command was taken over by Colonel Melnikov, who was soon promoted to the rank of Major General.

The route was in intensive service until the capitulation of Japan. From among the 39 aircraft which were accepted in August 1945, 20 aircraft were returned to the Americans; then the Soviet mission in Fairbanks was closed. The last acceptance personnel were taken away by air on 29 September 1945; then, in October, the 1st Ferry Air Division was disbanded.

The toll taken by incidents and crashes along the American segment of the ALSIB route totaled 133 aircraft – including two P-40s, two C-47s, four B-25s, seventy-one P-39s and thirty-three A-20s. Of them, 75 aircraft were lost in the territory of the USA proper, and 59 aircraft were lost in Canada and Alaska. According to the official report, 8,094 aircraft were ferried via the Krasnoyarsk route. The total number of written-off aircraft was 81; of these, the majority was written off in 1942 and during the first half of 1943. On the other hand, according to the American statistics, only 7,925 aircraft were handed over in Fairbanks. The reason for such a discrepancy still remains unclear.

Some of the ferried aircraft were handed over at intermediate points of the route – thus, for example, the civil aviation performed the acceptance of C-47s in Yakutsk. The aircraft flew further with other crews and were not reckoned in the route reports. The number of aircraft that went through the 15th Air Base totaled 5,583.

Throughout the operation period of the Krasnoyarsk route, its pilots' aggregate flying hours totaled 252,796 and each of the pilots ferried 150-200 aircraft. For example, Captain P.P. Gamov's 'ferrying score' amounted to 340 aircraft, whereas that of Captain G.V. Sorokin's was 360.

Throughout the same time, however (according to I.Y. Negenblya's estimate), losses in incidents and crashes totaled 44 aircraft and 115 people. This is no surprise, given the peculiarities of the route, as described by Mazuruk: "Geographically, the route is so difficult that a 'forced landing' in the meaning attributed to this term in the European portion of the USSR is not possible here. A forced landing beyond an airfield means a catastrophe."

Nonetheless, some pilots who suffered a crash in thick taiga managed to survive after going through amazing adventures – thus, Senior Sergeant I. Dyakov made an emergency landing in an unpopulated area near the Verkhoyansk Range. There was not even the smallest field that would be fit to land an aircraft. On the following day, a B-25 came and dropped foodstuffs, the required outfit and a sub-machine gun. In this manner, Dyakov was provided with the required supplies for five weeks; thirty-four days later, a Yakut, who had (for a remuneration in the form of a barrel of alcohol) undertaken to find and bring back the pilot, broke through to Dyakov's location on a deer-drawn sledge.

In autumn 1943, at the same segment of the route, the engine of pilot A. Terentyev's P-39 Airacobra failed. The pilot managed to perform a ditching to a small river in a ravine between the mountains. For two days, Terentyev was staying near his aircraft, but nobody came; then the pilot took the box with the emergency ration and went down the river. He was lucky to find, after several days of walking, a hut left by geologists. According to the taiga custom, the geologists had left a reserve of food there. Terentyev walked further and met some Evenki hunters, and they helped him get to the nearest settlement.

Some of the pilots were reported missing and, many years afterwards, people found wrecked aircraft and the remains of the crew members in them. The body of Lieutenant V.I. Kovalyov, who was reported missing between Seymchan and Yakutsk in March 1943, was found by hunters only two years later. At the same segment of the route, an A-20 bomber piloted by Senior Lieutenant I.L. Grozdnensky's crew was lost; the wreckage was found only in 1973. Another A-20, which crashed on 21 May 1943, was found in October 1980.

The bulk of the aircraft delivered to us by the Allies came via the three major routes (that is, the northern, southern and eastern ones); however, there were other routes, via which comparatively small batches were conveyed.

Some aircraft came disassembled from the US Western Coast ports to Vladivostok; however, after the beginning of the war in the Pacific in December 1941, only the Soviet ships could carry the aircraft. The Japanese, at that, kept stopping and detaining the ships under various pretexts and, furthermore, some of the ships were sent to the bottom. As has already been discussed, the transportation of military materiel and ammunition was prohibited by the Japanese. For all that, according to Soviet summary reports, 17 aircraft were somehow brought by sea to Vladivostok in 1943; however, their types remain unknown. American documents do not confirm any shipment of aircraft via the mentioned route.

In 1942, an attempt was made to set up the ferrying of transport aircraft from Scotland by air. For this purpose, a team of Soviet pilots, navigators, a radio operator and mechanics was carried to Errol air base. They completed a course of training to fly the Armstrong Whitworth Albemarle aircraft. That was an extremely risky operation, since the aircraft being ferried had to fly across the North Sea, Denmark, Norway, Sweden, the Baltic Sea and further over a territory occupied by the Germans. The aircraft were only protected from enemy fighters and anti-aircraft fire by the darkness of the night and by clouds; however, on the other hand, such conditions made navigation difficult. In this manner, more than 10 aircraft were ferried. The further shortening of darkness hours made ferry flights much more dangerous, and the Albemarle flights were canceled. A single De Havilland Mosquito bomber, which was provided by the British, was also flown over this route.

Alternative routes for aircraft ferrying from Great Britain – bypassing the Iberian Peninsula and along the North Africa Coast, and further via Iran and Iraq – were considered; however, these were never put into practice.

Several routes (depending on the destination point) were used for the ferrying of the Consolidated PBY Catalina flying boats. All of the routes started on the US Coast, where the aircraft were accepted and the Soviet crews were trained. The aircraft allocated for the Northern Fleet and the White Sea Flotilla were flown via Iceland and Great Britain, in detour of Norway, which was occupied by the Germans. Flying boats for the Black Sea Fleet were ferried via approximately the same route as the B-25 bombers, with landings in Puerto Rico, Trinidad, Brazil, Senegal, Cairo, Baghdad and, finally, in Sevastopol. A segment of the route passed over a desert, where a seaplane could make a belly landing, but could hardly take off. In ferrying these two groups of Catalinas, the Soviet crews were assisted by British pilots and radio operators. Aircraft for the Pacific Fleet were delivered by American pilots to Alaska; then Soviet pilots ferried them via the Bering Strait and further still via Anadyr, Magadan and Nikolaevsk-on-Amur to Vladivostok.

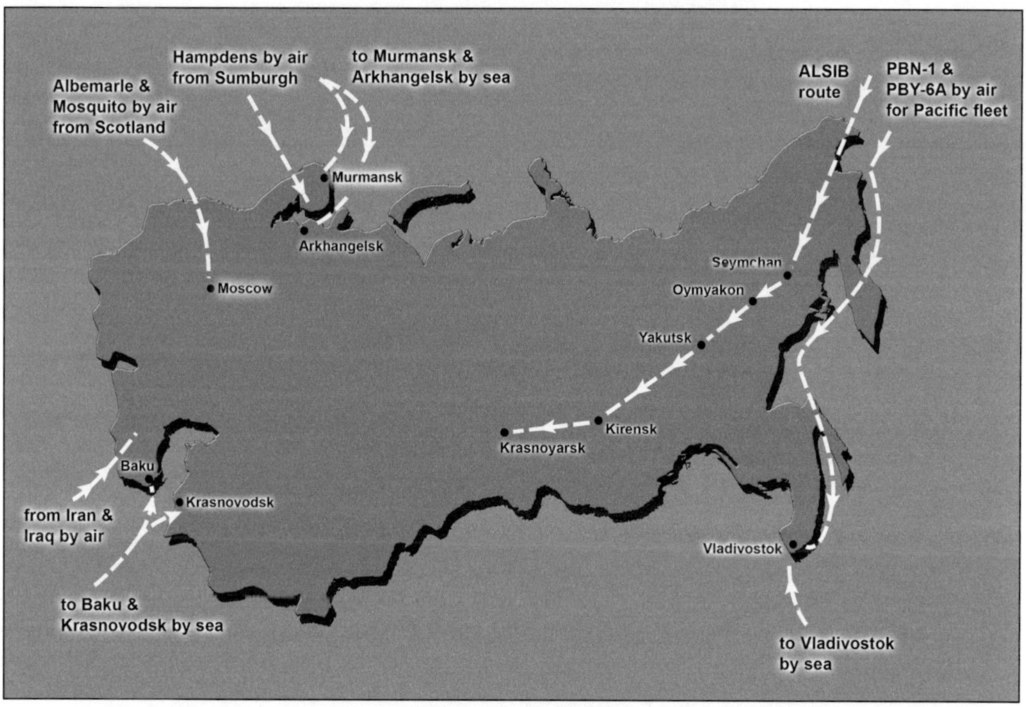

A map showing the routes via which the Allies' aircraft were delivered to the USSR during the Great Patriotic War.

Containers with the Hurricanes being loaded onto a British port in 1941.

The ship deck accommodates a semi-disassembled A-20 bomber. The cover protecting the joint in the fuselage tail bears the marking '*NKVT — USSR*', where 'NKVT' means 'People's Commissariat of the Foreign Trade'.

An American ship with A-20 bombers on board in the port of Murmansk during early 1942.

Spitfire VB fighters being prepared for handover to Soviet representatives.

Adjustment of the Spitfire armament; note the red stars on the fuselage and wing.

A British technician painting a red star on a Spitfire.

The arrival of the first group of Soviet ferry pilots in Abadan.

The American fighters wait to be uncrated at one of the hangars in Abadan for further assembly and, ultimately, delivery to Russia.

A-20B bombers at the airfield in Abadan.

A-20G-1s waiting to be ferried to the USSR at the airfield in Abadan.

AT-6C trainers at the parking area in Abadan.

The arrival of the Soviet mission in Nome on 3 September 1942.

General H. Arnold is greeting the head of the Soviet mission, Colonel M.G. Machin (to the left), and Chief Acceptance Engineer P. Kiselev.

The Command of the 1st Ferry Air Division at their headquarters. From left to right: A.S. Pushkarsky, A.G. Melnikov, I.P. Mazuruk and I.Y. Pryanishnikov.

These P-40 fighters have been prepared for ferrying to the USSR, and are awaiting departure in Alaska.

The signing of the Acceptance Act on 14 September 1942, which facilitated the first batch of A-20B bombers being delivered via Alaska.

Soviet acceptance officers G. Smirnov and N. Borovikov studying technical documentation of the A-20B. In the center is the representative of the Douglas Aircraft Company and interpreter E. Makarova.

The American instructor Captain de Tolli, along with Colonel Machin and the interpreter Serebrennikov, near an A-20B bomber.

A large hangar at Ladd Field, where aircraft repairs were carried out.

The nose of a B-25 bomber (in the foreground) bears chalk markings made by Soviet acceptance personnel.

Soviet acceptance officer Captain Pokrovsky inspecting the cockpit of an A-20 bomber.

A Bell P-39 Airacobra in flight and carrying an external semi-drop-shaped fuel tank.

Two B-25s standing side by side, and featuring both Soviet and American insignias.

A P-39Q-15 fighter being warmed up before take-off at Ladd Field.

The A-20Gs on a snow-covered airfield.

A command post at Yakutsk airfield in 1944.

Division Commander Melnikov and Flag Navigator Lieutenant Colonel Tuzhik verifying the route with pilots of the 2nd Ferry Air Regiment in summer 1944.

The P-39 Airacobras were fitted with radio compasses in the USA; note the loop aerial visible under the rear fuselage.

Lieutenant Pelageychenko accepting from his American colleague a P-39, which was bought with money collected by female school students from the city of Buffalo.

The Russians and the Americans having a joint photo taken prior to the ferrying of the first batch of Kingcobras to the Soviet Union.

A typical group formation: leading is a B-25, followed by P-39 fighters and a trailing A-20. Smoke caused by fires in the taiga can be seen below, summer 1943.

Colonel Machin preparing for getting into the cockpit of a P-63 fighter.

A group of P-63s, with a leading B-25, flying above the Verkhoyansk Range.

Technical personnel rotate the engine on an A-20 bomber.

Lieutenant Colonel Melnikov analysing the recent ferry flight with pilots of the 2nd Ferry Air Regiment in 1944.

Personnel of the 1st Transport Air Division, who took part in ferrying the Albemarles from Britain.

A ferry crew near a PBN-1 flying boat on Kodiak Island in 1944.

4

A Few Words about Figures

As of today, the issue of quantitative amounts of the Allies' shipments has already been studied well enough. The figure of 18,700 aircraft (sometimes the quantity of 18,865 is specified) agrees well with Soviet and foreign sources, both on the whole and as far as the calculations of data on specific aircraft types is concerned.

Seemingly, everything is simple enough. One would think that England and the USA should have been thoroughly recording what they were shipping. In fact, that was not quite the case. First, not all of the aircraft reached their final destination: some of them sank together with the ships which carried them, while others crashed during ferrying.

Second, there is certain confusion with documents. There were cases when instead of an aircraft, which had been badly damaged during transportation to the Soviet acceptance commission location, another aircraft – of the same type and modification, but bearing a different number – was handed over to the commission. In England, disputes are still going on as to which Stirling was handed over to the Soviets in Tehran. A wrecked Hampden which was found relatively recently in the Kola Peninsula had two registration numbers instead of one! It turned out that during the overhaul (which had been conducted in England), the tail of one aircraft had been attached to the fuselage of the other aircraft. There were cases when, in the Middle East, the aircraft which had already been shipped were recalled to replenish the fleet of the British Air Force unit and flown to the front. The Americans, for their part, after the Japanese fleet's attack on Pearl Harbor, requisitioned part of the Airacobras from the British order that had been handed over by the British to the Soviet Union, and sent them to take part in military activities in New Guinea. Churchill once wheedled out of Stalin 40 Boston bombers which had, by that time, already been unloaded in Basra – promising to provide Spitfires in return (and he kept his promise).

Third, the Soviet Air Force employed the practice of using group spare part sets which were intended for a specific number of the manufactured aircraft, whereas the British spare parts came in bulk only. Therefore, instead of spare part sets, the British sent to the USSR additional aircraft – and usually defective ones, which were intended to be dismantled, but the Soviet acceptance inspectors counted such aircraft as good ones! As a result, the documented number of the Hurricane fighters accepted exceeds the number of such fighters handed over, but these are but minute fractions which do not affect, in any material respect, the general picture – thus, let us stay with the figure of 18,700. Should it be deemed a large or a small quantity? The total share of imported materiel in the Soviet aviation throughout the Second World War is usually estimated to be equal to 12 percent, yet the calculation of such figure includes (in respect of the number of aircraft made in the Soviet Union) the entire manufacture for the years 1941 and 1945, which is incorrect.

Warplanes comprised the principal share of the total aviation materiel shipped by the Allies. According to the already mentioned official data, the number of combat planes manufactured in the USSR throughout the war totals 112,100 (however, this figure is currently believed to be overstated too). Accordingly, 700 transport aircraft and 74 trainer aircraft should be subtracted from the total imports. The result will be approximately 18,000-112,100 (i.e. some 16 percent of the domestic manufacture), which is, generally speaking, not a large share as well; then there should be considered proportions per different aircraft classes. Fighters constituted the majority of imported materiel, and some sources provide a figure of 12,200 aircraft of this class; however, such an estimate is inconsistent with the sum total of quantities per aircraft types, with the latter adding up to approximately 13,500 aircraft. This is the figure which will be used as the basis for the calculations.

Throughout the Second World War, the Soviet Union manufactured more than 57,000 fighters – thus, the share of imported fighters totals approximately 19 percent of this quantity (i.e. every sixth fighter received by the air force was an imported one). It is true that not all of them took part in the war – thus, for example, of the 2,400 American Bell P-63 Kingcobra fighters, only 400 were used in warfare against Japan in August 1945, yet considerable quantities of Soviet-manufactured aircraft were staying in the rear as well!

The total number of shipped bombers amounted to 4,000 against the Soviet manufacture of 17,800. The resultant share is also slightly below 19 percent.

There were categories where the role of Lend-Lease shipments was considerably higher – thus, for example, the only up-to-date heavy transport aircraft in the Soviet aviation at the time was the Lisunov Li-2 (PS-84). The number of such aircraft, as manufactured throughout the years of war, totaled 2,258, but the American factories added to this amount 907 Douglas C-47s, which were, essentially, a development of the same Douglas DC-3 that had been modified into the Li-2.

As for hydroaviation, the picture there was much more vivid. Throughout the war, almost no Soviet seaplanes were manufactured. Given this, 165 Consolidated PBY Catalinas, which were shipped from the USA, turned out to be a considerable help.

Another fact not to be omitted is that the Soviet Union manufactured 37,000 armored attack aircraft, with none shipped from abroad, and that reason being that no such aircraft were made by the Allies.

All of the above figures calculated are average ones. In fact, the Allies' shipments were distributed over time in a rather non-uniform manner. The 'lion's share' fell within 1944-1945, whereas in the beginning of the war, the shipments were coming literally by driblets. In 1941-1942, the agreed volumes of aircraft shipments were often not complied with. The USA in 1941 fulfilled, on average, only one fourth of their obligations. From 1 October 1941 through to 30 June 1942, the Soviet Union received from the Americans 267 bombers and 278 fighters, which constituted 29.7 percent and 30.9 percent respectively of the quantities specified in the agreement. On the whole, throughout the first two years of war, approximately 4,300 American aircraft arrived in the USSR. The situation normalized in the second half of 1943; later on, a steady growth of shipments followed. At the time, the growth of importing was considerably outrunning the growth of domestic manufacture. In 1943, the number of aircraft manufactured by the USSR was 1.3 times greater than in 1942, whereas imports throughout the same time period increased 2.5 times. In 1944-1945, shipments from abroad grew approximately twofold against 1941-1943.

At the time, the Soviet Union itself was rendering assistance in the restoration and strengthening of aviation in the countries of Eastern Europe by supplying (in total) more than 2,300 aircraft, which is comparable with Great Britain's shipments throughout the same period. In should be mentioned though that the shipments from the Soviet Union included (inter alia) captured German aircraft and imported American ones.

The assistance rendered to the Soviet aviation by the Allies could be compared with American shipments to Great Britain. Throughout the Second World War, the British imported from America 33,700 aircraft, whereas their own factories manufactured 94,600 warplanes. If one was to leave out from the transoceanic shipments 500 North American T-6 Texan trainer aircraft and 1,900 transport aircraft (including C-47s, C-53s, C-54s and C-87s), the result would show that approximately 26,800 combat planes came from the USA to Great Britain – thus, the share of imported materiel in the military assets of the British aviation would be approximately 22 percent. It should be mentioned though that the 'mother country' shared some of the shipped aircraft with its dominions. The picture would become still more vivid if one considered the numerical strength of Great Britain's aviation. The maximum number of aircraft over the entire range of armed forces throughout the war in the Soviet Union was 15,818 versus 8,395 (i.e. nearly twice as little) in Great Britain. Hence, it may be concluded that the British aviation was much better provided with aircraft then the Soviet aviation (to a considerable extent) thanks to the Americans' assistance. Furthermore, the British also received aircraft built by factories in Canada. It is no wonder then that after 1943, the Royal Air Force managed to establish a large reserve of materiel, which had some indirect effect both on the quantity and quality of shipments to the USSR.

Great Britain's priority in receiving assistance under Lend-Lease was stipulated from the very beginning by President F. Roosevelt in his speech at a press conference on 24 June 1941. Advocates of such an approach felt that the Soviet Union would not be able to make use of American aircraft with sufficient efficiency. Indeed, the British and the Americans had much more in common both in approaches to strategic and tactical application of aviation, and in techniques and traditions of operation and maintenance, as well as personnel training and many other things. In England and its dominions, there were branches of American companies; this facilitated repair and maintenance. Soviet mechanics were astounded to find in the manuals an instruction to call (in case of a failure) the London office and to make a request for a service team visit. The Soviet Allies had also much in common in terms of aviation combat operation support procedures and, finally, even before the creation of Lend-Lease, the British had been using a large number of American aircraft. It should be admitted that the general British culture of aircraft operation (which was often achieved due to less severe combat operation conditions) was considerably higher than that of the Soviet Air Force. Nevertheless, the British, from time to time, did some juggling – thus, for example, they overstated the losses of imported aircraft in reports for the USA.

Let us now consider British and American shipments. In total, the USSR received 14,759 aircraft of American types, regardless of the source of shipment. The rest were of British types, although some of those were manufactured in Canada. In fact, it is difficult to clearly distinguish between British, American and Canadian shipments. As has already been discussed above, American aircraft could come both directly from the USA and via Great Britain. On the other hand, among the aircraft shipped from the USA, there were those equipped to both American and British standards, with different equipment and weapons (which were sometimes of British manufacture). The aircraft that came from Britain included (among others) the American aircraft which had been bought before Lend-Lease, or shipped under Lend-Lease; ones which had been re-equipped or modified in England; and ones which had not. There were aircraft which had already seen service with the Royal Air Force and had undergone overhauls (one or more), and there were almost brand-new ones – thus, for example, among the handed-over Boston bombers, there were old DB-7Bs, which had, years before, been bought in the USA; the DB-7Cs, which had been ordered by Dutch and later seized by the British, following the occupation of the Netherlands; and the Boston III and IIIA types, with 7.69mm British guns. Furthermore, there were also aircraft shipped to the USSR directly from the USA.

Deliveries from Canada, as has already been mentioned, were not discussed separately until Protocol III; instead, they were included into Great Britain's obligations. Even British sources, rather than stating the number of Hawker Hurricane fighters of modifications X, XI and XII, chose to include them among the similar Hurricane IIBs; the total number of them received by the USSR was 1,557.

All of the above figures refer to aircraft which actually arrived in the USSR; the number of shipped ones was, of course, higher, but how much higher was it? Here is some data per specific aircraft types: the number of aircraft which reached the Soviet Union totaled 862 out of 870 North American B-25 bombers, 4,952 out of 5,065 Bell P-39 fighters, 196 out of 203 Republic P-47 Thunderbolts and 2,917 out of 3,125 Douglas A-20 bombers.

At the beginning, the 'losses in transit' were not high. Of the 103 vessels constituting the first 12 convoys, only one failed to reach the Soviet ports. This does not mean though that the entire cargo was delivered in an intact condition, and it sometimes took two or three months to deliver an aircraft from an American factory to the terminal in Archangelsk. Containers were exposed to salty seawater and icing; they were knocked about by storms and damaged during multiple handling operations. As a result, some of the arriving aircraft were discarded on arrival as unfit for restoration. German efforts against the Arctic convoys was gradually increasing, and sometimes the losses were exorbitant: of 297 bombers carried by Convoy PQ 17, 210 sank. In 1943, 12 percent of aircraft, on average, were lost in transit.

The above losses only include the ones suffered in transit beyond the USSR territory, so to them, there should be added the aircraft crashed during further ferry and transportation operations. Some of them were destroyed by German aviation on railways and airfields, while others were wrecked in the course of pilots' training (including conversion training), but this is a different issue, which will be touched upon later.

Taking all of this into consideration, what percentage of the fleet, as shipped to us, actually took part in combat activities and how large was its share in the forefront? By the beginning of the Battle of Moscow, in which air units fitted with imported aircraft participated, there had been less than one percent of British and American aircraft at the front. In total, throughout 1941, 740 imported aircraft were received. In 1943, the share of imported aircraft in the forefront was 11 percent; at the end of the war, it reached 20 percent (i.e. each fifth aircraft in the front was of foreign origin).

The share of aircraft of foreign manufacture in the combat army in April 1943 was equal to approximately one fourth, and this figure quite agrees with N.I. Ryzhkov's estimate. The largest number of such aircraft was in Karelia (225 aircraft), Transcaucasia (251) and the Moscow region (207). The air force of the Northern Fleet included 182 aircraft of foreign manufacture, and the 4th Air Army had 119 such aircraft.

Locally, the share of imported aircraft could be much larger – thus, for example, at the end of 1941 in the Karelian Front, the foreign fighters constituted 65 percent of the entire fleet, whereas their share in the air force of the Northern Fleet was nearly half. In February 1942, the ratios shifted further in favor of the imported aircraft; in Karelia, there were 190 imported fighters versus 44 of Soviet manufacture.

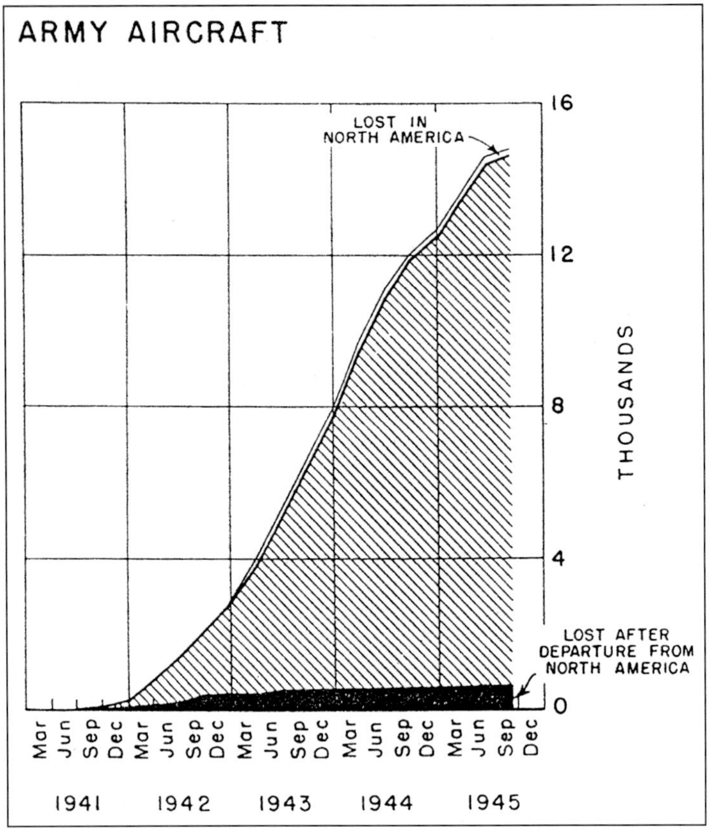

Aircraft shipments from the USA (seaplanes not included) and losses at the American territory – and beyond it – before their transfer to the Soviet side.

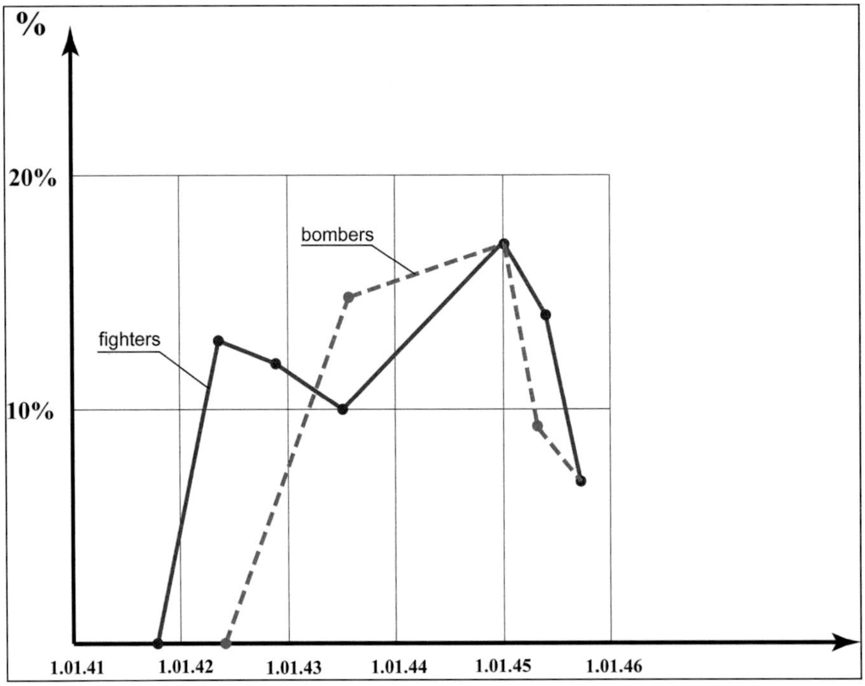

The share of imported aircraft at the Soviet-German Front.

5

Specific Peculiarities of Imported Aircraft, their Modifications and Conversions

The use of imported aircraft in the USSR had certain specific peculiarities which often impaired the efficiency of the application of British and American aircraft, and sometimes brought about the need to modify them to Soviet requirements. Therefore, this is worth being dwelt upon in more detail.

Air combat operations in the Soviet-German Front were considerably different from those conducted by British and American pilots in Europe, Africa and the Pacific Ocean. Both war conditions and application techniques were different there. The Allies' primary striking force in Europe consisted of several-thousand-strong heavy bomber units and supporting forces for their operations; the latter included reconnaissance aircraft and heavy escort fighters. Smaller aircraft, before reaching targets in Germany (or in the territories occupied by the Germans), also had to fly a long way. The large amount of combat operations above the sea in the Atlantic Ocean and in the Pacific Ocean brought about the large-scale development of hydroplanes and carrier-based aviation, as well as the appearance of a new class of aircraft, with the latter being wheeled long-range aircraft for patrolling the vast ocean spaces. In the Pacific theater of operations, the belligerents were usually separated by large distances and made attacks from one island on another. That was the war to whose requirements the Allies' warplanes were adapted. Requirements to them included a long flying range, proper navigation and radio equipment, high altitude performance etc.

The specifics of war-making in the Soviet-German Front was different. Combat operations mainly took place on the land; aircraft had to operate almost exclusively in the near-front zone (the share of strategic strikes by the long-range aviation was extremely small). Air battles usually occurred at altitudes below 5,000m, which meant that pilots had to deal with low-range and low-altitude flying. The vast majority of ground targets were pinpoint targets, or small-sized area-type ones. Therefore, the main aircraft groups in the USSR comprised comparatively light and maneuverable fighters, whose primary task was to carry out aerial combat against the enemy fighters and bombers; armored attack aircraft, who were to assault targets directly on the battlefield or nearby; and, finally, front-line bombers (including dive bombers), who were to hit targets beyond the front line.

As for attack aircraft, everything was clear: there was no way of receiving them from any source, because no other country (except the Soviet Union and Germany) manufactured such aircraft. In respect of fighters and bombers though, the Soviet Union counted on the Allies' assistance. In a talk with H. Hopkins in late July 1941, I.V. Stalin stated, among the top-priority needs, that the Soviet Union would like to receive from the USA medium bombers with an operating radius of 600-1,100km, as well as fighters. The priority was given to bombers, with a ratio of three to one. The reason, apparently, was rooted in the fact that the overloaded Soviet industry was unable to quickly increase the manufacture of bombers.

These were the aircraft categories which constituted the majority of the Allies' shipments; however, the aircraft received by the Soviet Union had been designed many years before, and nobody had ever expected that they would be used by the Soviet Union – thus, they had been intended for application (as has already been discussed) in quite different war-making conditions. Such an approach originated from the technical assignments, by means of which air force staff determined the trends for their aviation. Those aircraft had been created to suit their 'own needs' and, furthermore, it sometimes turned out that the aircraft were no longer meeting even the requirements of its own armed forces because time was moving on, and conditions and concepts were changing.

Let us consider, for example, altitude performance. Foreign fighters usually offered good performance at altitudes of 6,000-8,000m (often better than that of their Soviet 'contemporaries') and a higher service ceiling. This was determined (mostly) by the design altitudes of the engines installed on such aircraft; however, at lower altitudes, their performance dropped. A vivid example is the Supermarine Spitfire V, which was, on the whole, an undoubtedly successful aircraft, yet the altitude performance of its Merlin engines was considered excessive by Soviet specialists.

All of the American fighters had a greater size and a considerably greater weight than the Soviet ones, and these parameters affected their maneuverability. The Soviet fighters of the time had a take-off weight of 2,600-3,300kg, whereas the American ones weighed 3,700-9,500kg (with the lower limit represented by the Airacobra, which became 'well-naturalized' in Soviet aviation). The situation looked quite natural, given that the Soviet aircraft had a range of 600-900km, whereas the American ones offered 1,000-3,500km. Instrumentation and radio equipment was beyond comparison as well. The outfit of the Soviet fighters of the time were referred to in the West as being 'Spartan'; some of the aircraft were not even fitted with a radio receiver, let alone a transmitter. The same was true for the navigation equipment, yet all such devices constituted additional weight; however, in conditions of a land-based low-altitude air war, the value of such equipment dropped because one could fly at daytime, for example, using visual landmarks, plus the time in flight was not long. To improve flight performance, certain 'superfluous equipment' (in particular, oxygen bottles, fire extinguishers and even 'excessive' armor and weapons (e.g. as the case was with the P-39Q)) was sometimes removed from aircraft in the Soviet Union.

British fighters were closer to the Soviet ones in terms of size and weight characteristics, but also tended to have larger parameters, especially as regards size.

The aircraft that showed themselves to the best advantage in the Soviet Union were exactly those which, in terms of their performance, were closest to the Soviet-manufactured ones – and thus, were the optimum aircraft for the Soviet-German Front conditions. That was the case, for example, with the Airacobras and the Bostons, which represented medium-altitude and low-altitude aircraft with a low (according to American standards) operational range, which was pronouncedly intended for tactical purposes. It is the dissimilarity in criteria that brings about the huge difference in opinion in respect of the same aircraft in Russia and in Western countries. A vivid example of this is the Bell P-39 Airacobra fighter, which was considered 'a remnant of isolationism' in the USA and found absolutely unfit for combat application in England, yet the aircraft showed itself to good advantage in the Soviet-German Front.

The efficiency of foreign aircraft was considerably impaired, especially during the early years of the war, by their 'exactingness' in respect of operating conditions. They required good fuel and quality oil – thus, for example, the Rolls-Royce Merlin engine installed on the Hurricanes and Spitfires, as well as the American Allison V-1710 engine (which was used on the P-40s, P-39s, P-63s and Mustangs in 1941), ran on fuel with an octane rating of 87. As early as before the war, such a level was reached both by the USA and by all principal European countries. The powerful Twin Wasp engines, which were mounted on the B-25 bombers, consumed fuel of an even higher quality, with an octane rating of 95-100. By the end of the Second World War, many other engines had been using fuel of such a rating. Meanwhile, the Soviet Union mostly utilized B-70 and B-78 aviation fuel (with the figure in the designation standing for the octane number). The Soviet factories simply possessed no technology to produce fuel of a higher grade, so new engines, which featured high compression and high boost, were protected against detonation by means of adding tetraethyl lead (either the Soviet 'Product R-9', or the imported American one) to such low-grade fuel. Furthermore, Soviet fuel was rather impure and often contained water. This was brought about by the low transportation, storage and fueling standards.

Attempts to operate imported aircraft with Soviet fuel resulted in a loss of power and engine failures. This brought about a necessity to import greater amounts of high-octane fuel – thus, for example, under Protocol III, the British undertook to deliver 100,000t of aviation fuel from Iran. Besides, isooctane and alkyl benzene were imported from the USA; these, on a par with the quality imported fuel, were mixed with low-grade Soviet fuel to obtain 'something in between' – thus, the B-78 fuel at the time was, essentially, a mixture of the B-74 grade with the American alkyl benzene.

Furthermore, Soviet fuel contained excessive aromatic hydrocarbons. They produced a detrimental effect on the soft tanks which were used on American aircraft. The uncured tread rubber layer (whose purpose was to swell, and thus seal puncture holes) suffered especially severe erosion under the influence of the Soviet fuel. Lumps of decomposed tread material were sometimes found in the tanks, and the ingress of such a lump into the fuel intake system brought about fuel feed cut-off and a dead engine.

Beginning from the middle of the war, efforts were made to operate the foreign aircraft with only good fuel, so often, it was pure imported fuel. A conversion to Soviet fuel was considered undesirable; in such cases, the engine boost was restricted and some engine power settings were prohibited to use. Gradually, the fueling techniques were improved to provide protection against the ingress of dirt and water-based condensation. Severe penalties were imposed for violations of such techniques, especially if they resulted in a crash. Of course, in critical situations, any fuel that was ready at hand was used; however, this always affected the engine life.

According to the standards of the year 1944, the American V-1710 engines ran on 4B-78, 1B-95 and B-100 fuel grades, with the latter being the preferable one; early versions of the R-2600 engines consumed 3B-74 and 2B-78 grades, later versions of the R-2600 engines utilized the 4B-74 grade, and the latest versions of the R-2600 engines ran on 4B-78 and B-100 grades. The first figure before 'B' in the designations stood for the number of cubic centimeters of the R-9 product per one kilogram of fuel. It was allowable to replace the 4B-78 grade with captured Astra Romania fuel, to which 20 percent of isooctane and tetraethyl lead were added. The British Merlin 66 engine ran on 4B-78 or B-100 fuel.

Experience of the 6th Fighter Corps showed that the V-1710 engine, when running on pure imported B-100 fuel, could operate for 240 hours or more without any problem, whereas with 4B-78, it began to lose power and to consume increased amounts of oil after 180 or 200 hours, and then constantly suffered from various breakdowns.

The situation was similar with lubricating oils. British and American engines required their 'habitual' oils; with Soviet ones, they demonstrated overheating and the jamming of movable parts. In the 1930s, the Soviet Union was exporting aviation oils, and even the British Royal Air Force utilized the Soviet oils for some time. The only nuance was that before use, such oils were subjected to purification. Soviet grades contained several undesirable admixtures. They did not affect bearing inserts in Soviet engines; however, the coating of bearing inserts in foreign engines differed from that in Soviet ones. The admixtures washed out certain components from them, with an abrupt increase in friction being the result. In particular, the Allison engine, with its silver bearings, demanded oil of high purity and high viscosity. With Soviet oils, the inserts quickly wore out; the engines' operating time failed to reach even a half of their assigned life. Gradually, suitable combinations of Soviet oils were developed for foreign aircraft, and this helped to solve the problem to some extent. Importing lubricating oils from abroad was established as well. Furthermore, and similar to the situation with fuels, procedures for preparation, additional purification and filling were optimized. According to the already mentioned standards of the year 1944, the R-2600 engines ran exclusively on imported oils, whereas in respect of the Allison and Merlin engines, a conversion to Soviet MS and MK grades was allowed if foreign oils were not available.

All British and American engines with a liquid cooling system were, at the time, utilizing ethylene glycol-based liquids. The British used glycol liquid, and the Americans had Preston liquid at their disposal. These liquids provided more efficient cooling and prevented the danger of radiators freezing in the winter, since such liquids were, essentially, anti-freeze agents. In the Soviet Union, flights all year round were made using water, which was either distilled or bichromate-softened. Anti-freeze agents were used only in conditions of severe frost, mostly in Siberia. Ethylene glycol was produced by the Soviet industry in quite modest amounts. Alcohol-glycerol anti-freeze agents did not freeze, yet their thermal efficiency was lower than that of water.

A lack of special mixtures led to some attempts to operate foreign aircraft using water, such as Soviet ones. Such attempts brought about the need to modify the cooling system, since water had a different density, different thermal conductivity, different thermal capacity, different boiling temperature and different vapor pressure. This caused a lot of problems, whereas the results were unimpressive: in summer, engines tended to overheat; in winter, water draining was a vexation, since the design of many imported engines did not provide for complete draining.

The Soviet Union started importing British and American cooling liquids as well. Here, another problem emerged: such liquids were not intended to withstand Russian frost; however, a way out was found: glycol and Preston liquid were usually shipped in the form of concentrates – thus, the Soviet personnel had learned to dilute them in different ratios. For example, the Merlin XX engine, as mounted on the Hawker Hurricane fighter, usually ran on a mixture of 30 percent glycol and 70 percent distilled water; however, the Soviet personnel utilized the fifty-fifty ratio. Raw materials to produce Soviet anti-freeze agents were also imported. Soviet fluids were intended for lower freezing temperatures and proved to be more efficient.

Due to the intensity of aviation-related activities, which was considerably higher in the Soviet-German Front than in the West and in the Pacific, maintenance schedules and prescribed operating regimes were often not complied with. This also affected the technical condition of the aircraft (and Soviet ones too).

In the beginning of the war, a lack of ammunition for foreign weapons manifested itself. Soviet specialists attempted to modify weapons so as to make them usable with Soviet shells or, vice versa, to re-design shells to make them fit for use with foreign guns. Later, on the contrary, ammunition shipments became unreasonably large to the extent that sometimes, there was no other choice but to destroy ammunition soon after unloading in the Soviet territory! At first, there was a lack of spare parts and engines, but such problems were mostly settled by way of mass importing.

Aircraft which were coming from abroad had been designed to suit the needs of national armed forces, yet not infrequently, they had to deal with different problems under different conditions. In their choice of the most efficient areas for application of the aircraft received from England and from the USA, Soviet specialists tried to use their positive features to the best advantage, while compensating for shortcomings. This involved certain changes in the original functionality of some aircraft – thus, for example, the North American B-25 aircraft, which had been a frontline bomber in the USA (but whose performance was more similar to the Soviet Ilyushin Il-4) – after a relatively short period of time in the forefront – was turned into a long-range night bomber. On the other hand, the Douglas A-20G was designed as a heavy attack aircraft, but failed to meet the competition with the Ilyushin Il-2. From attack aircraft, the A-20Gs were converted into reconnaissance aircraft, torpedo bombers, heavy night fighters and frontline bombers (after modifications). Of course, there were some failures – thus, there were attempts to use the tank-buster

Hawker Hurricane IID (which was, in terms of combat survivability, considerably behind the Ilyushin Il-2, with its 37mm guns) in air defense forces, but altogether, without success.

To better adapt foreign aircraft to conditions of a different theater of military operations, many of them were subjected to certain modifications. The latter may be categorized into six groups.

The first group included modifications in order to adapt foreign aircraft to winter operations. As is known, the Russian climate is different, and winters in Great Britain are much warmer. The Canada-United States border lies somewhere in the Poltava latitude. Hence, one can draw appropriate conclusions. The Allies had simply no need to make any serious preparations for aircraft operations in conditions of severe cold. The Americans do have Alaska, yet during the pre-war period, almost no air force units were deployed there.

In the USSR, on the other hand, in late 1941, the aviation personnel had to face ruptures in radiators and pipelines caused by freezing, the thickening of oil and hydraulic fluids, and the freezing of propeller hubs. Landing gear failed to extend, or to be locked down; propeller blades ceased to change their pitch; and engines became overheated (in conditions of frost!) because of clogged oil pipelines. Warmth-keeping procedures (in respect of vulnerable pipelines and assemblies) were started: first on the initiative of individual mechanics and engineers, and later in a well-organized manner (and on a wider scale) – thus, for example, aircraft arriving from Iran were subjected to mandatory warmth-keeping treatment in backup regiments in Transcaucasia. A.P. Golubkov's Design Bureau was developing special modification procedures and designing additional protections, such as engine cowling front shields with adjustable louvers (similar devices were used on Soviet aircraft). Later, additional modifications were carried out, which consisted of the replacement of anti-freeze agents and hydraulic fluids with more efficient (in conditions of severe cold) Soviet grades.

Beginning from 1943, aircraft shipped from the USA via the ALSIB route were subjected to 'winterization'. The aircraft underwent additional warmth-keeping treatment: cold-resistant rubber was used for gaskets and hoses, and wheels were fitted with special-purpose winter tires; heating devices were also installed.

The winter operation procedures also included the use of skis for foreign aircraft. Specialists in the Soviet Air Force could not arrive, for a long time, at a final decision as to whether warplanes needed skis or not. Initially, the issue was resolved unambiguously: in summer, flights were performed with wheels; in winter, skis were used. Seaplanes were also fitted with skis as soon as water became covered with ice; however, flight performance was slightly affected by such modifications because the winter landing gear was heavier and created a higher drag. The difference grew still greater after a conversion to retractable landing gear. Furthermore, the skis proved to cause more difficulties during retraction than wheels. For a rather long time, Soviet combat aircraft had retractable wheeled landing gear for the summer season and fixed skis for the winter season. During the war against Finland, different variants were tried. Wheels were replaced by skis and vice versa, but finally, a conclusion was drawn that the most advantageous solution was to tramp and pack snow with wheels (and, therefore, to make flights from snowed areas using wheels), yet during the first half-year of the Great Patriotic War, the retreat was so fast that there was no time for preparing airfields. Into the bargain, a considerable amount of ground service equipment was lost or abandoned during the retreat, so there was no other choice left but to return to the use of skis. With skis, one could land on a completely unprepared airfield (sometimes, even covered with deep snow), or take off from it. The Petlyakov Pe-2s, Ilyushin Il-2s and other aircraft types were then also fitted with retractable skis. In 1942-1943, ski landing gear variants were also designed for the Airacobras and Hurricanes; however, this approach did not gain much popularity and was soon forgotten beyond recall.

The second group of modifications included forced modifications which were brought about by a lack of spare parts or consumables. Usually, these were confined to the installation of suitable assemblies and sub-assemblies of Soviet manufacture. The replacement of engines on the P-39 and P-40 fighters with Soviet M-105 engines (which were fitted with appropriate propellers) may be considered the most complex among such modifications. Modifications to fit Soviet assemblies always brought a lot of trouble, and it was not 'just for fun' that such modifications were implemented. There was, as already mentioned, attempts to modify the fighters' cooling system to run on water because of the unavailability of suitable anti-freeze agents. Such alterations were characteristic of the first half of the war, but as shipments of spare parts became more regular and complete, the need for such alterations vanished; however, after the termination of the war, a necessity of replacing engines on the Consolidated PBY Catalinas and Douglas C-47 Skytrains with ones of domestic manufacture arose again.

Modifications of the third group were aimed to enhance defense capacity and combat survivability, and to increase combat efficiency. The first task was usually accomplished by way of installing Soviet weapons. Soviet cannons and machine guns offered the advantage of a high rate of fire and a high muzzle velocity. Furthermore, the conversion to Soviet weapons helped to simplify ammunition supplies due to a reduction in the number of the required shell types. The Hurricanes and Bostons were rearmed on a mass scale; similar projects were considered for the Tomahawks, Albemarles and C-47s.

To enhance combat survivability, imported aircraft were fitted with armor and provided with an inert gas system, which had shown itself to good advantage in the USSR, but was relatively rarely encountered in the West.

Efforts to increase combat efficiency consisted of attempts to make greater use of aircraft capabilities – thus, for example, the Douglas A-20 could carry a heavier load than the one which its bomb racks were designed for. Considering the possibility of carrying different types of ammunition, the aircraft turned out to be considerably underloaded. In response, a scheme for the replacement of existing bomb armaments with examples of Soviet manufacture was worked out, which allowed eliminating the shortcomings to a considerable extent.

For other aircraft, the range of bomb load variants was complemented with Soviet types – thus achieving greater flexibility in the performance of combat missions, and (similarly to the case with guns and cannons) simplifying the supplies.

An interesting aspect is connected with the implementation of chemical armaments on foreign aircraft, which initially, had not been fitted with armaments of this kind. Before the war, such armaments in the Soviet Air Force were deemed mandatory for almost all aircraft classes. Therefore, the decision was made to fit the Hurricanes and Bostons with chemical spray tanks. Thankfully, no use was ever made of them.

The fourth group of modifications included those for the enhancement of flight performance. These generally consisted of the lightening of aircraft by way of removing certain equipment which was considered superfluous for the Soviet-German Front. The removed items usually included parts of armor, oxygen equipment and (in respect of the P-39Q) under-wing guns.

The fifth group dealt with airframe reinforcements to meet Soviet structural strength standards, which were higher than the Western standards. These modifications were mostly conducted in respect of the P-39 and P-63 fighters, which were subjected (on a mass scale) to a reinforcement of the primary structure in the tail portion of the fuselage. The procedure for such a modification was worked out by the Air Force Central Scientific and Experimental Base, and was distributed to air units and workshops in the form of a package of documentation, complete with drawings.

Finally, the sixth group included modifications to change aircraft functionality. These varied from relatively simple ones (such as the installation of radio compasses to the Supermarine Spitfires and P-40s in Air Defense Regiments), to rather complex ones (for example, the conversion of the Douglas A-20G into a torpedo bomber – including the creation of the navigator's compartment – and the installation of torpedo bridges and additional fuel tanks).

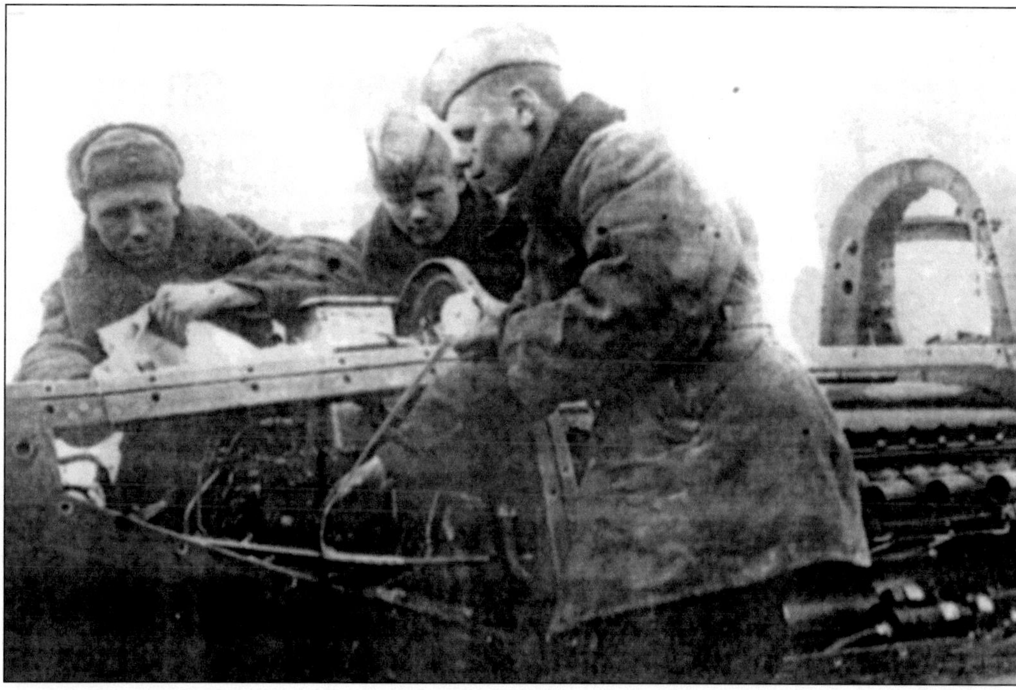

Pipelines of the P-39 Airacobra power plant being protected with heat-insulating materials; the 11th Backup Air Regiment, Kirovabad, 1943.

A Soviet crew in front of their A-20B bomber; note the protective winter front shield on the engine cowling.

An A-20G aircraft which has been modified into a torpedo bomber, with the navigator's cabin arranged in the fuselage nose; the 51st Mine-and-Torpedo Air Regiment of the Baltic Fleet Air Force.

This P-40EF photo reconnaissance aircraft was modified from the P-40 Kittyhawk fighter.

In the USSR, the armament of the early versions of the Hurricane was found to be inefficient and was replaced with Soviet cannons and machine guns. This photo shows a modified Canadian-built Hurricane X, which was tested at NII VVS as a fighter-bomber.

The Hurricane IID anti-tank aircraft found no efficient application in the USSR

6

Mastering the Imported Aircraft

The British Hawker Hurricane fighters were the Allies' first aircraft to arrive in the USSR. At the time of their handover to the Northern Fleet Air Force, the training of Soviet personnel was conducted by flight and ground crews of the Royal Air Force 151 Wing. The task of familiarization and training was set from the very beginning among the top-priority ones; it was being accomplished concurrently with combat operations, and was gradually taking more and more time. Both British and Soviet interpreters were engaged in the effort.

A small group of Soviet pilots completed conversion training at the 10th Kilometer airfield, near Archangelsk. The runway there was made from wood; both the runway and airfield structures had been expeditiously built by prisoners. At this airfield, under the supervision of two American instructors (note that the USA had not yet joined the war at this time) H. Zemke and J. Allison, Soviet pilots learned to fly the P-40 fighters. Later, the same pilots were involved in the ferrying of aircraft which were assembled at the 10th Kilometer airfield to the Vologda region.

Later still, the task of converting to imported aircraft was entrusted to backup air regiments and brigades. On 9 October 1941, the People's Commissariat of Defense published the Order on Arrangement of Acceptance, Assembly and Study of Foreign Aircraft. The Order appointed two backup regiments (the 22nd Backup Air Regiment and the 27th Backup Air Regiment) for the aforementioned purpose. The 22nd Backup Air Regiment had already been established; its formation had begun as early as mid-September at an airfield near Kineshma. Colonel Y.I. Shumov was in command of the unit, and the headquarters was based in Kineshma. In autumn 1941, 22 British military men – including engineers, technicians and instructor pilots – arrived at the unit's facilities. The Soviet party delegated a number of officers from the Foreign Department of the Air Force Chief Administration who could speak English, and who were also familiar with foreign aircraft. The 27th Backup Air Regiment was established at the facilities of the Vologda Training Center at Kadnikov airfield, at a distance of 50km to the north-east from Vologda, near Sokol station. V.I. Panteleev became the first commander of the regiment.

The specific feature of the backup regiments comprised the presence of assembly teams among their personnel – thus, the 22nd Backup Air Regiment had four assembly teams. The majority of aircraft arrived at the regiments' facilities via railway in containers, and were assembled in situ.

The Order of 9 October demanded that the preparation of the two backup regiments be completed before 15 October; in general, the date was met. It was intended that the air units to be sent for conversion training would leave the old aircraft in the front, and the crews would be carried to the backup regiments without aircraft. There, new recruits and veterans returning from hospitals would join the crews. Upon completion of the training course, the regiments would immediately receive a set of new aircraft and go back to the forefront.

That was how the system started working. As early as in late autumn, the first regiments operating the Hurricane and Tomahawk fighters joined battles at the approaches to Moscow.

In spring 1942, principal activities relating to conversion training for foreign aircraft were shifted in the southern direction, to the vicinity of Ivanovo. In March, the 22nd Backup Air

Regiment was moved to Ivanovo-Yuzhny airfield. There, the regiment consisted of three squadrons, which specialized in individual fighter types: the 1st Squadron flew the Hurricanes; the 2nd Squadron used the P-40s; and the 3rd Squadron specialized in the P-39s. In May 1942, the 14th Backup Air Regiment, which had been formed in November the previous year in Rybinsk under the command of Major N.I. Bocharov, joined the mastering of foreign aircraft. On 16 May, the 22nd Backup Air Regiment and the 14th Backup Air Regiment were combined to form the 6th Backup Air Brigade, with the headquarters in Ivanovo. In November, the 14th Air Regiment was also relocated to Ivanovo-Yuzhny airfield.

After the beginning of aircraft deliveries via Iraq and Iran, a similar training center was created in the south, in Transcaucasia. Initially, it accommodated two regiments (the 11th Air Regiment and the 25th Air Regiment), and these units had been formed as early as summer 1941; originally, they had been specializing in fighter pilots' training on the LaGG-3 aircraft. The 11th Backup Air Regiment had been deployed near Rostov-on-Don, whereas the 25th Backup Air Regiment was positioned in Vaziani. In 1942, the former was moved to Kirovabad and, from March 1942, the 11th Air Regiment carried out training on the A-20 bombers; fighter regiments on the P-39s were passing through the 25th Air Regiment. Later, the 26th Backup Air Regiment was established, where it was deployed at the airfield near Sandary station and was engaged in the training of flight and maintenance crews on the LaGG-3s and P-39s. The unit also carried out the acceptance and shipments of the LaGG-3 fighters which were coming from Factory No.31 in Tbilisi. All of these regiments were considered to be separate from one another, and were subordinated directly to the Transcaucasian Front Air Force Commander.

After the defeat of Convoy PQ 17, shipments of aircraft via the northern route were temporarily ceased. As a result, in November 1942, the 27th Backup Air Regiment was disbanded. Instead, however, the 45th Backup Air Regiment, which was under the command of Major Vlasov, joined intensive operations in Krasnoyarsk, which became a place for the arrival of aircraft coming via the Bering Strait.

On 5 October 1943, the first special train carrying the command of Colonel N.K. Kretov's 4th Backup Air Brigade arrived in Kirovabad, and the 11th, 25th and 26th Backup Air Regiments became subordinated to the brigade. On 10 November, a special Kirovabad-based technical regiment, whose purpose was to carry out repairs and modifications on imported aircraft, joined the brigade. Due to poorly developed communications, it turned out to be rather difficult to coordinate (from Kirovabad) the regiments, which were scattered over more than 300km. Therefore, before 10 December 1943, command of the brigade moved to Tbilisi. The 11th Backup Air Regiment had three airfields (Kirovabad Central, Ali Bayramli and Alabashly), and the 25th Backup Air Regiment and the 26th Backup Air Regiment utilized two airfields each (the former, Vaziani and Sartichala; the latter, Sandar and Koda). The Brigade Command was based at Navtlug airfield, near Tbilisi.

At first, training activities were focused on the training and formation of regiments coming from the front and from the rear; however, at a later time, the focus was shifted to the training of 'march regiments', which were further used as replacements for the operating units and formations. Later still, individual pilots and technicians were trained.

Before September 1943, the 11th Backup Air Regiment specialized solely in the Douglas A-20 bombers; later, the P-39 fighters also appeared there. The 25th and 26th Backup Air Regiments dealt only with fighters (the P-39s, P-40s, Hawker Hurricanes and Supermarine Spitfires in the 25th Air Regiment, and the P-39s and LaGG-3s in the 26th Air Regiment). Therefore, the 25th and 26th Backup Air Regiments are referred to in some documents as 'Backup Fighter Air Regiments'. Throughout 1943, units of the 4th Backup Air Brigade trained 12 bomber regiments, 23 fighter regiments and a reconnaissance squadron.

In May 1944, the 22nd Backup Air Regiment (at the time, under the command of Major N.I. Bocharov) was moved to Kubinka, in the Moscow region. Another regiment of the 4th Backup

Air Brigade (i.e. the 14th Backup Air Regiment) was, during the summer of the same year, moved to the Tula suburbs.

Over the course of time, training regiments for naval aviation also appeared, whose units conducted training on both British and American aircraft. In particular, the Northern Fleet had the 3rd Training Air Regiment, with approximately 20 imported aircraft at its disposal.

Concurrently with the training in backup regiments, flight crews were not infrequently mastering foreign aircraft on their own, sometimes directly at the front or in the near-front service area.

The training of flight and technical crews to operate British and American aircraft involved a number of difficulties: at first, there was a tangible lack of various manuals, instructions, descriptions and drawings. Even the documents that did come were published in English, which only a few had any command of, and all of the placards on the aircraft were in English too.

Tables, instructions on board and instrument scale calibrations were rendered in miles, feet and gallons, to which the Soviet personnel was not accustomed. Speed was presented in miles, flight altitude in feet and the take-off/landing run in yards (just the same as runway lengths). These units were not decimal ones, so it was not easy converting them to the metric system. As for gallons, there were two types – American gallons and British imperial gallons – and both could be used in the documentation for aircraft of the same type, depending on the source of shipment. Personnel had to memorize English words; to draw conversion tables and charts; and to paste them onto instrument panels of trainer aircraft.

Different countries had different standards. On Soviet aircraft, the arrangement of instruments conformed to the instructions of the NII VVS and was, approximately, uniform. This facilitated the training, with the pilot habitually looking at the required instrument. The Allies had their standards as well, yet their standards varied. The same was the case with the aircraft control stick and pedals: the shape of the control stick was different; the trigger switches were arranged in a different manner; and the wheel brakes were operated in a different way. On the Hurricanes, for example, the control stick was of a 'broken' type, which was quite unusual for Soviet pilots.

Imported aircraft were designed to utilize different operation and maintenance procedures – thus, for example, the British preferred carbon dioxide to compressed air, with the former being safer in terms of fire hazards, but the Soviet Air Force had no equipment to obtain carbon dioxide at airfields.

Specialists of NII VVS and the Scientific Research Institute of the Civil Air Fleet (*Nauchno-Issledovatelskiy Institut Grazhdanskogo Vozdushnogo Flota*, or NII GVF), as well as professors of Zhukovsky Air Force Academy, were involved in work. As early as 1942, they prepared the required documentation – including instructions, descriptions and schedules. Specialists began looking for Soviet substitutes for scarce foreign oils, coolants and hydraulic liquids, which had theretofore been tried by air units on an experimental basis (the result being that the equipment in question would either work or become broken).

Beginning from 1943, the USA started supplying (together with aircraft) excellent American descriptions and manuals, which were translated into Russian (thankfully, there were quite a lot of Russian-speaking emigrant engineers) and published to an excellent quality in the USA. They replicated the original documents, which were prepared for the US Army Air Force, to the very last detail. There were a lot of excellent art-type illustrations, as well as diagrams and photographs (complete with explanations). The somewhat boring text was interleaved with comic pictures, which caricatured various operational stages, or the consequences of violating the manual's requirements. People said that the comic sketches were made by artists at Walt Disney's studio.

'Comic strips' of a kind (essentially, manuals for the repair of certain assemblies in the form of sketches) were prepared for technicians. They illustrated step by step which tool one should use and what one should open, loosen or remove, and how one should reassemble everything after the repair; sometimes, however, the meticulous American adherence to the original documentation perplexed the minds of the Soviet personnel. What should one actually do if the maintenance instructions read that in case of a hydraulic accumulator failure, one should call London over the phone and request that the accumulator be replaced, or for a repair team to be sent? (The original manual was for the export aircraft for the British.) The nearest phone was a field telephone in the headquarters, so was it possible to use it to call London? And what would the security officer think of it?

As for the maintenance manual for the Consolidated PBY-6A Catalina flying boat, it has amused immensely even the author of this book: the 'Check-up Procedures' section states that the pilot should personally check for the availability of toilet paper on board the aircraft! Perhaps the members of the Soviet Political Bureau knew at the time what 'toilet paper' was, yet a lad who had got enlisted from a village – and had been hastily trained in a flying school during wartime – could hardly know that. Consequently, documentation that was published in the USA at a later time was usually subjected to editing by some of the Soviet military specialists who worked in America.

Before the beginning of 1943, a clear-cut system for the training of flight and maintenance crews had already become established, and there were training programs and instructors who had thoroughly mastered foreign aircraft. The Air Force Engineering-Technical Service was monitoring the operational experience with British and American aircraft, as well as the changes that were being made to them by manufacturers. Gradually, the supply system developed – bringing the operating conditions closer to the Western standards.

Until the end of the war, the system was constantly improving and its working conditions were becoming more and more favorable.

British Flight Lieutenant J. Ross is briefing Lieutenant Maksimovich of the 72nd Combined Air Regiment before the latter's first sortie in a Hurricane; Vaenga airfield, autumn 1941.

A Soviet tractor tows a partly assembled Hurricane of the 22nd Backup Air Regiment during late 1941.

A P-40E being refueled at Ivanovo airfield in 1942.

A P-40E understudy at the 6th Backup Air Brigade in 1942.

An A-20 Boston is prepared for a training flight.

Maintenance personnel of the 26th Backup Air Regiment studying the P-39 Airacobra in 1943.

The refueling of a P-39 fighter; the 26th Backup Air Regiment, 1943.

Replenishing the 37mm cannon ammunition of the Airacobra; the 11th Backup Air Regiment, Kirovabad.

Crews of a backup brigade discussing the Hurricane's piloting techniques.

Pilots receive instructions on the A-20's flying specifics in Central Asia.

7

Lend-Lease Aircraft

The 'lion's share' of imported aircraft comprised eight aircraft types: the British-built Supermarine Spitfire and Hawker Hurricane fighters; the US-built Bell P-39 Airacobra, Curtiss's P-40 Warhawk (Tomahawk and Kittyhawk) and Bell P-63 Kingcobra fighters; the (also American) Douglas A-20 Havoc (in the Soviet Union, it was better known by its British name, 'Boston') and North American B-25 Mitchell bombers; and, finally, the Douglas C-47 Skytrain transport aircraft. The Republic P-47 Thunderbolt fighters and the seaplanes of the Consolidated PBY Catalina family came in considerably less quantities.

Four of the above-mentioned main types were manufactured throughout the war. Production of the Bostons, Hurricanes, Airacobras and Warhawks was ceased in 1944, and all of these aircraft were in service with the air forces of their countries of manufacture, as well as with the air forces of other Allies. To what extent did such types correspond to what was 'state of the art' at the time? None of these aircraft was a novelty as of the time of shipment to the USSR, except for the P-63. The Hurricanes and Spitfires had been in production for four or five years, while others had been in production for two or three years; all of them had been well-mastered by the factories and in service. On the whole, only the Hurricanes and Tomahawks could be described as 'outdated', so the remaining types were quite up to date; however, it is the former two aircraft that constituted the majority of deliveries in 1941 and in the first half of 1942. For example, only these fighter types were coming from Great Britain; the USA was mostly shipping the P-40s of earlier versions.

In terms of a general assessment of the aviation shipments' structure, it may be safely said that the shipped materiel only included the aircraft, which the Allies could comparatively (and easily) do without. This is true both for the breakdown of the arriving aircraft per classes, and for their qualitative level. From among the US Army Air Force's aircraft as mentioned above, the ones that saw extensive service throughout the war were the North American B-25s, Republic P-47s, Douglas C-47s and (in the naval aviation) the Consolidated PBY Catalinas. These constituted approximately 15 percent of American assistance to the Soviet Union; however, the Soviet Union received only a small share of the manufactured aircraft (less than 10 percent of the total manufacture of the B-25s, and less than one percent of the total manufacture of the P-47s). The P-40 (in different modifications) saw quite extensive use with the USAAF throughout the war; nevertheless, from approximately 1943, it was 'ousted' to perform the function of a bomber fighter and ground attack aircraft, and was superseded by the more advanced North American P-51 Mustang. In spite of this fact, its manufacture continued (mostly for export purposes) on account of the well-developed production process. The Airacobras and Bostons were manufactured by the Americans primarily for Lend-Lease shipments, and the number of such aircraft in Soviet aviation was (by far) greater than that in the USAAF. This was accounted for by differences in war conditions and strategies between the USSR and the Allies. The Airacobras and Bostons found no 'ecological niche' for themselves in their own armed forces, yet they turned out to be well suited to the conditions of the Soviet-German Front; here, however, the 'leftover principle' manifested itself too. According to the American historian J. Mesco, the majority of the A-20Bs: '… were sent to Russia under the

Lend-Lease Agreement. This decision was due to two main deficiencies [*sic*] in design: the lack of self-sealing fuel tanks and poor armor protection'.

The Hurricanes had, by 1941, undoubtedly been obsolete. After the Battle of Britain, they were gradually transferred to secondary theaters of military operations and superseded by the Spitfires. The majority of the Hurricanes as received by the Soviet Union in the beginning were those handed over by British units being re-armed – and it was a similar situation with the Spitfires. The first Spitfires (the VB modification), which were delivered to the Caucasus in early 1943, were 'second-hand' ones as well. The situation later recurred with the Spitfire IXs, but without any prejudice to their combat advantages.

Of course, in 1941-1942, the Soviet Government could not afford to be too choosy. A general shortage of aircraft due to huge losses at the front; the shutdown of many factories that happened to be located at territories occupied by the Germans; and the evacuation of production facilities to the east (in December 1941, the total aircraft manufacture amounted to a meager 600 aircraft) brought about the need to send to the front line anything that could become of use (even to the least possible extent). In comparison to the I-5 biplanes (which were retrieved from trainer units, or reconstructed from the already scrapped junk), or to the I-15bis (which, though less ancient, were rapidly becoming obsolete), the Hurricane was a truly serious combat aircraft. In terms of performance, it excelled (in many aspects) the I-16s and I-153s, which constituted the majority of the Soviet fighter fleet. The Tomahawk, in turn, looked to advantage against the background of the Hurricane. As the Soviet Air Force was becoming 'saturated' with up-to-date aircraft, the Hurricanes and Tomahawks were gradually transferred to handle secondary tasks.

Foreign aircraft were successfully used by Soviet pilots. There is no need to dwell much on the efficient use of the Airacobras, since 59 victories won by A.I. Pokryshkin (48 of which were achieved in the P-39s) speak for themselves. Naval aviation made successful use of the A-20s – employing the latter among the principal types of torpedo bombers. A Kittyhawk was successfully flown by the Northern Fleet ace B.F. Safonov.

On the whole, the share of foreign aircraft in the forefront was undoubtedly conspicuous, though not decisive; however, there were areas where their role turned out to be of great importance.

First of all, it was the fighter aviation of the air defense forces. Of 10,000 aircraft received by the air defense forces throughout the war, approximately 7,000 aircraft were of a foreign type. This was due to the excellent altitude performance of many British and American fighters, their powerful weapons and good radio equipment and instrumentation – thus, for example, the air defense forces received all of the Spitfire IXs that were shipped to the Soviet Union. Finally, by the end of the war, of the 81 fighter defense aviation regiments, 40 regiments had been flying foreign aircraft. Heavy night fighters fitted with radars were, at the time, part of long-range aviation rather than defensive aviation; however, such fighters performed well-defined functions. Furthermore, it should be noted that the only division of such aircraft that existed at the time in the Soviet Union flew the American A-20Gs.

Second, it was hydroaviation. During the war, the Soviet Union's manufacture of seaplanes was almost zero. As of early 1944, only 52 aircraft of this type (mostly single-engine ones) remained in service. The aircraft shipped from the USA, which amounted to 136 flying boats and 48 amphibians, not only helped to restore the country's combat hydroaviation, but also raised it to an entirely new level by considerably enhancing its capabilities, since the PBN-1s and the PBY-6As (which were shipped under Lend-Lease) outperformed not only the archaic MBR-2s, but also the few surviving GSTs. As of the end of the war, imported seaplanes constituted 73 percent of the air force equipment in three Western fleets.

Third, it was transport aviation. During the war, only one up-to-date transport aircraft type was manufactured in the USSR – namely the PS-84 (aka Lisunov Li-2), which was, essentially, a license-built version of the American Douglas DC-3 (the version from 1935). The more advanced

Douglas C-47s of different versions, which were shipped from the USA via the Bering Strait in a quantity of 707, provided considerable help in intensive transportation operations at the final stage of the Soviet Union's war against Germany.

Fourth (and finally), it was mine and torpedo aviation. Throughout 1942-1945, the navy received 68 percent of imported torpedo bombers. With the exception of 20 Handley Page Hampdens in service with the Northern Fleet, those were the American Douglas A-20s of different modifications. By the end of the war, the A-20 had become the most common torpedo bomber and skip bomber type with the Baltic Fleet, Black Sea Fleet, Northern Fleet and, during the first post-war years, also in the Pacific.

Now that you, dear reader, are familiar with the general features of the aircraft as shipped by the Allies – and the peculiarities of their operation and combat applications – it is time to proceed with a detailed description of those aircrafts' fate in the Soviet Union, and they will be presented in the order in which the aircraft were shipped:

7.1 Hawker Hurricane

In 1932, the design office of Hawker Aircraft Ltd. commenced work on a new monoplane fighter, which was intended as a high-speed interceptor. Chief Designer S. Camm was in charge of the design process, and the mass-manufactured Fury biplane was used as the prototype; all principal features of its design were preserved, except that the new aircraft was designed with only one wing and a closed cockpit. Similar to the Fury, the fuselage was based on a tube truss, which bore a light frame made from metal alloys and wood; the frame was covered with a metal sheet in the forward portion, and with fabric in the aft. The wing had a metal frame and fabric covering as well. In terms of design and production technology, the fighter represented a kind of an intermediate stage on the way to aircraft with load-bearing skin.

With the advance of the design process, the aircraft's appearance was changing. The designers abandoned the idea of steam cooling for the engine; the Goshawk engine was replaced with the newest Merlin one (at the time, referred to simply as 'PV.12'); and provisions were made for landing gear retraction in flight. At first, the aircraft was fitted with four guns (two of them in the fuselage); then with six guns and, finally, with eight guns – and all of them in the wing.

The prototype of the future Hurricane made its maiden flight on 10 October 1935. The initial information regarding the new British monoplane fighter created by Hawker designers came to the Soviet Union nearly as soon as the aircraft reached the stage of factory tests. The aircraft aroused interest: in January 1936, it was included in the list of aircraft as approved by the Council of Labor and Defense in order to purchase their examples abroad. A large amount of currency was allocated for the purchase, and negotiations with Hawker were initiated via the Soviet Trade Representation in London; however, the company refused to sell the aircraft at the time – invoking secrecy as the reason for refusal.

In July 1937, the prototype Hurricane was displayed at the traditional exhibition in Hendon. Division Commander N.N. Bazhanov, who was, at the time, the head of NII VVS and a member of the Soviet delegation in Hendon, wrote telegraphically in his report: 'Hawker Hurricane; With Merlin; Was not demonstrated in flight; The aircraft with the 1,065hp engine can provide over 500km/h'. The latter was, at the time, quite impressive.

Mass manufacture of the fighters was launched in September that year; beginning from December, the aircraft were placed in service with the Royal Air Force. At the time, the Hurricane was, by right, deemed one of the best fighters in the world. The Hurricanes were manufactured in large quantities, since the aircraft was simple in terms of the production process, as well as being rather cheap and fit for use by an inexperienced pilot, which was good, given that lots of pilots of this level appeared within the extensively expanding British aviation.

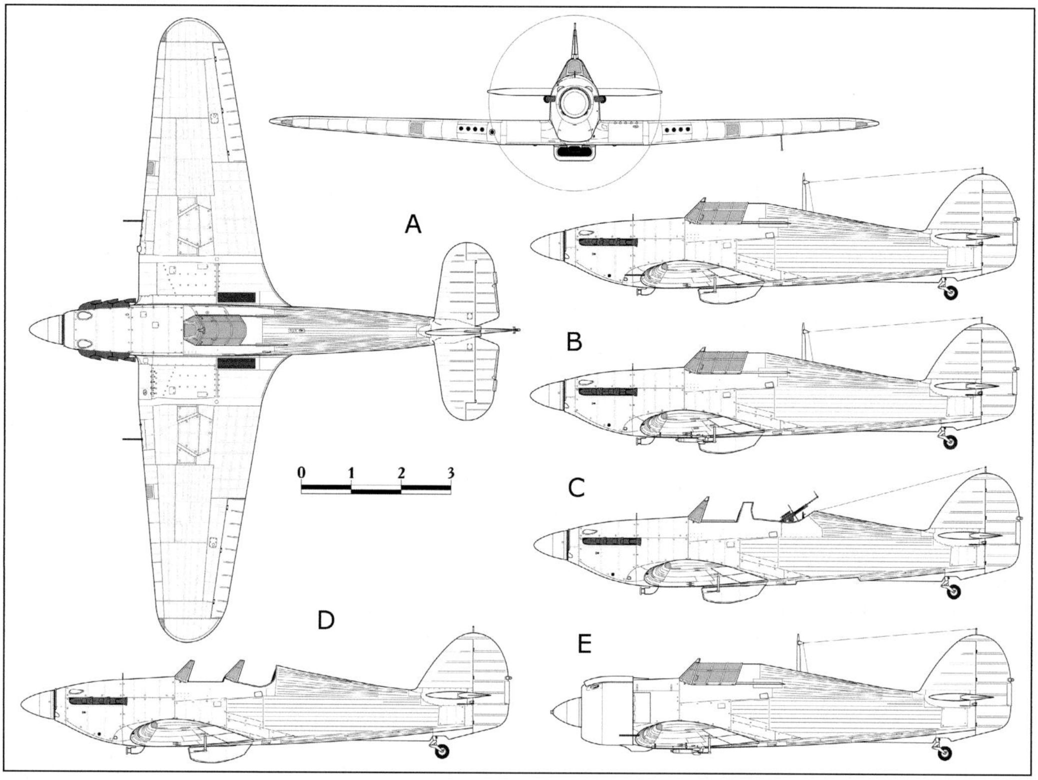

Hurricane IIB

A Three-view of the Hurricane IIB, with two ShVAK cannons and two UBK machine guns.
B Hurricane IIB, with four UBK machine guns and six RO-82 rail launchers for RS-82 rocket projectiles.
C Hurricane IIB modification into a two-seat artillery spotter plane.
D Hurricane IIB modification into a two-seat trainer by the 39th Workshops of the Northern Fleet Air Force, 1942.
E Variant of the Hurricane IIB powered by the M-82 engine, which was proposed by Factory No.81.

In the beginning of the Second World War, the Hurricane was the principal fighter type in Great Britain. The Hurricanes were fighting in France and in Norway, and made an immense contribution to the Battle of Britain. By that time, the aircraft had received a three-blade variable-pitch propeller and a metal-skin wing; in September 1940, the manufacture of the Hurricane II modification, with a 1,185hp Merlin XX engine, was started. Such aircraft were manufactured in version A (with eight 7.69mm guns), version B (with 12 guns) and version C (with four 20mm cannons).

An opportunity for Soviet specialists to become properly familiar with the British fighter was opened up, surprisingly, in Germany, where a captured Hurricane was demonstrated to the Soviet aviation delegation in March 1941; however, in comparison to a Supermarine Spitfire (which was standing nearby), the Hurricane was assessed as an almost obsolete aircraft.

The situation, however, changed again, as Germany turned into an enemy instead of a potential ally. In late June 1941, the Soviet Union requested as many as 3,000 fighters from Great Britain as part of its military assistance. In reply, a single example was offered. On 18 July, another request was sent in – suggesting that if the British could not give their own aircraft, they might share the ones shipped from America. In two days, Prime Minister Churchill agreed and promised to ship 200 Tomahawks; on 18 August, 200 Hurricanes were added to them.

On 21 July 1941, in his letter to I.V. Stalin, Churchill wrote that the British Administration was considering (as a further step) the possibility to base several British fighter squadrons in Murmansk. For the practical implementation of the suggestion, No.151 Wing RAF was formed on 12 August at Leconsfield airfield under the command of Wing Commander H. Ramsbottom-Isherwood. The wing included two new squadrons (No.81 Squadron and No.134 Squadron), and the remaining squadrons were manned with rather experienced personnel from other air units which had passed through military operations in the skies of France and Great Britain. Among the pilots there were quite a number of Battle of Britain participants: in particular, Flight A from No.504 Squadron, whose operational record had been opened as early as 1939 in France, joined (in its entirety) No.81 Squadron. The pilots thought that they would be sent to Africa, but they understood their mistake no sooner than they had started to receive cold weather outfits. The wing was intended to fight not in a hot desert, but beyond the Arctic Circle in the Kola Peninsula.

No.151 Wing set out for Murmansk with the first convoy of ships, which was going from England to the Soviet northern ports. Twenty-four Hurricane IIB fighters were loaded on board HMS *Argus*, and 15 more were disassembled and packed into containers for delivery by merchant ships. The personnel (more than 500 persons) were placed on board HMS *Argus*, merchant ships and escorting destroyers. On 28 August, HMS *Argus* arrived in Murmansk, but only as late as 7 September did the fighters take off from the ship and land at Vaenga airfield, which was operated by the Northern Fleet Air Force.

The merchant ships were unloaded in Archangelsk, and there was a task of assembling 15 fighters. A team of 38 persons, with the engineer Gittins as a team leader, was accommodated on an old paddle-wheel steamer. The Soviet party delegated that a Soviet engineer and several Red Army men render their assistance to the British. The steamer's derrick booms and hand winches were made use of, and trestles and building slipways were nailed together by the team personnel themselves from planks and bars, which were delivered to the site.

Days in the autumn were short; a typical day lasted a maximum of 6.5 hours. Therefore, work was started and ended in artificial light, and occupied 12-13 hours per day. Three fighters were assembled during the first day, and the delivery of the assembled aircraft to the shore turned out to be the most difficult job, as none of the derrick booms was designed to carry more than a ton. Consequently, an intricate suspension system was developed. The hoisting of the first three assembled aircraft – including all preparation procedures – took five days. On the ninth day, all 15 fighters were taken to Kegostrov airfield, from where they departed for Murmansk. The assembly team was also taken to Murmansk on board a passenger PS-84.

Crews of 151 Wing were charged with three tasks – namely to demonstrate support of the USSR's military effort by the Allies; to strengthen the air grouping near Murmansk (i.e. the northern flank of the Leningrad Front and the Air Force of the Northern Fleet); and to ensure the familiarization of Soviet aviators with British aircraft. All three tasks were rather important: No.151 Wing was the Allies' first military unit to arrive on Soviet land. The irony of fate consisted of the fact that the pilots of the Royal Air Force, who had been opponents to the pilots of the Red Army air detachments at the same location (in the north of Russia) during the Civil War, were the first to lend a helping hand to their Soviet colleagues.

The arrival of the 39 Hurricanes resulted in an almost twofold increase of the numerical strength of the Northern Fleet's fighter aviation, under whose operational command the British wing was placed. Notwithstanding the fact that the Hurricane IIB (as of autumn 1941) had been far from a novelty, and its performance was, in many aspects, lower than that of the principal German fighters and the newest Soviet fighters, it considerably exceeded the obsolete I-15bis, I-153s and I-16s which constituted the majority of fighters in the Northern Fleet. The appearance of British aircraft near Murmansk considerably facilitated the enhancement of air protection for this Soviet port, which was the closest one to Great Britain. Ramsbottom-Isherwood's wing was also intended to become a kind of conversion training center for Soviet pilots and technicians prior to the commencement of aircraft shipments from Great Britain and the USA.

Near Murmansk, the British crews encountered uncustomary food. They learned to eat *borsch* and *schi* (Russian types of soup), and tea was (surprisingly) served with no milk, in ribbed glasses and strangely accompanied with brown bread on which butter was spread, which was 'pale like lard'. On the other hand, wine, which was served at dinner (and without limitations), met general approval. The British never found out what kind of wine it was, and Russian waitresses in the canteen referred to it simply as 'wine'. According to pilots' reminiscences, it was something not dissimilar to port wine.

There were complaints about the presence of bedbugs in the barracks and, as a result, an overall disinfection was carried out, but the most 'exotic' thing was (probably) the outdoor lavatory, which one could especially 'appreciate' in the cold weather. Meanwhile, it was getting far from hot in the airfield, given a typical mid-September in the polar region.

On 11 September, the British pilots made their first patrolling flight near the front line, but met no other aircraft in the air. On the following day, three Hurricanes of No.134 Squadron were the first to take off from the airfield. They noticed several German bombers, but failed to intercept them. A pair from No.81 Squadron became airborne after the first three aircraft and encountered an enemy Bf 110 two-engine fighter; they attacked it by fire, but failed to bring it down. Later, on the same day, two Hurricane trios performed the escorting of Soviet bombers. The first victories were won during the fifth flight of the day. A German Hs 126B observation aircraft, which flew with an escort of five Messerschmitts, was attacked by five Hurricanes of No.81 Squadron, and the 'surprise factor' was made use of to the full extent: three German fighters were left to burn down in the tundra; the damaged observation aircraft turned back; and the British lost one of the Hurricanes, whose pilot sergeant, N. Smith, was killed. That was the only aircraft of No.151 Wing to be shot down by the Germans throughout one and a half months of military operations conducted by British pilots in the polar region.

At the end of the same day, five other British fighters intercepted three enemy bombers which were heading for Archangelsk. Four Bf 109s, which were escorting the bombers, declined battle. The Hurricanes made the enemy aircraft drop their bombs at random locations and then turn back.

On the same day, the enemy's reconnaissance spotted the British fighters. The reconnaissance determined the number of aircraft (rather precisely) 'from a squadron to a wing'; then, five days of bad weather followed. It was only on 17 September that British aircraft took off and engaged at once. The battle turned out to be a success for them: with no losses suffered, they brought down three Messerschmitts; one more Messerschmitt was reported 'probably shot down'.

It started snowing as early as 22 September; then the personnel had to constantly clean the aircraft from snow and frequently warm up the engines, lest oil should freeze up. Fuel and oil were of Soviet origin, but the British were not quite happy with them, and so made efforts to filter fuel as frequently as possible to avoid pipelines clogging and carburetor contamination.

Wheeled landing gear was used to make flights from the snowed airstrip; for this purpose, snow was tamped and rolled. On the snow-covered airfield, the landing run increased; as for wheel brakes, one had to exercise utmost care when using them.

On the same day (22 September), Northern Fleet Air Force Commander Major General A.A. Kuznetsov paid a visit to the British. The general decided to learn to fly the Hurricane himself, so he brought with him a teacher of English as an interpretress. Together, they drew an instrument panel on paper and translated the instruments' purpose and units of measure; then Kuznetsov, as an exemplary student, began answering the 'What is this?' question over and over again. After several training sessions with British pilots, the general himself got the aircraft off the ground (there were no dual control aircraft), and later, he used a Hurricane for a rather long time as his personal aircraft. Afterwards, the aircraft was transferred to the 72nd Fighter Air Regiment (later renamed to the 2nd Guards Fighter Air Regiment). In 1942, Lieutenant P.P. Markov, who was, at the time, flying the aircraft, was hit by German fighters and made a forced landing on a frozen lake at a distance of 4km to the west from Murmansk. There was no time to remove the aircraft; when the ice thawed, the aircraft sank. The Hurricane stayed at the bottom of the lake for nearly 70 years; then, in October 2004, it was recovered and sent for restoration.

Now let us continue with combat operations of 151 Wing: on 24 September, the British pilots (for the first time) went on the mission of escorting the new Petlyakov Pe-2 bombers (earlier, they had performed the escorting of the SB bombers). It turned out that the Hurricanes had difficulties keeping up with the Pe-2s; the former had to constantly fly at full speed – especially on the way back to the base – with the bombers carrying no bombs.

By 30 September, the British pilots had already shot down a dozen enemy planes. The Soviet party suggested paying bonuses of 1,000 rubles per victory to the pilots. The conversion to British pounds was made at the official exchange rate. Therefore, the amount was quite substantial (240 UK pounds), given that the salary of a flight lieutenant in the RAF was, at the time, equal to 20 UK pounds; however, the Wing's Command declined the suggestion – stating that the acceptance of such payments would impair the pilots' professional honor.

On 6 October, the Germans were strafing Vaenga. On one of the Hurricanes, splinters broke the canopy window and punctured the tires. With the bombing still going on, British fighters began to take off. A bomb exploded in front of pilot S. Edmison's aircraft and the plane's engine shut down. The pilot jumped out of the cabin and onto the wing, but the blast of another bomb flung him to the ground; however, he escaped unhurt.

Two more German Ju 88 bombers and a Messerschmitt were brought down during the air battle; three more Junkers aircraft were categorized as 'probably shot down'; and six were reported damaged. The British suffered no casualties.

In pursuit of the enemy, Flight Lieutenant M. Rook (the No.134 Squadron Leader's brother) happened to become separated from the rest of his patrol; then he noticed a group of fighters. Having mistaken them for his fellow Hurricanes, he joined the formation, but suddenly saw the German crosses. It was just in time that he saw them, because one of the Germans had already opened fire on him by then. Rook dodged and, in turn, responded with a salvo of all 12 guns. The German fighter exploded in flight. In the midst of the commotion, the British pilot managed to shirk away and return to Vaenga.

By that time, training had become the key activity for the Wing. The famous ace Major B.F. Safonov was the second Soviet pilot to master the Hurricane, and this took place on 8 October. Captain Kukharenko and Captain Yakovenko were the next to complete conversion training. By 16 October, as many as 10 Soviet pilots had completed the training.

Before 20 October, RAF pilots had made 365 sorties; the number of claimed German aircraft varied (according to different sources) from 12-16. The British pilots provided air cover to the troops near the front line and the city of Murmansk, as well as intercepting German bombers and escorting Soviet bombers. More than 30 escort missions were flown, with a zero tally of bombers shot down by the Germans.

It was already real winter time; the frost was below -30°C. The polar night was approaching… a typical day during which one could fly lasted a meager two or three hours. The personnel were having a hard time shoveling the snow away from the aircraft.

In late October (upon completion of the training of a relief from among the Soviet naval aviation personnel), the British handed over 28 aircraft to the Northern Fleet Air Force (one of the fighters had crashed earlier, on 27 September). The aircraft were used to form the 78th Fighter Air Regiment, which was under the command of B.F. Safonov. The Soviet Command recognized the contribution of the British aviators: four of them (Wing Commander Ramsbottom-Isherwood, Squadron Leaders A.H. Rook and A.G. Miller, and Flight Sergeant Ch. Haw) were awarded the Order of Lenin. They, by the way, were the only four British servicemen to hold this Soviet award. The last party of specialists from among the men of 151 Wing returned home on board the *Kenya* cruiser in early October 1941.

The first bunch of Hurricanes was followed by an intense inflow of aircraft of the type, which were manufactured at British and Canadian factories. Ships of the northern convoys kept bringing containers with new Hurricanes. Later, the fighters began to arrive along the southern route via Iran. In total, throughout 1941-1944, the Soviet Union accepted 3,082 aircraft of this type (of those, the military aviation received 2,834 aircraft). At least 210 of the shipped aircraft were of the IIA type; besides, there were 1,557 aircraft of the IIB type and similar Canadian versions (X, XI and XII), 1,009 Type IIC fighters, 60 Type IID aircraft and 30 Type IV airplanes. Some of the Hurricane IIAs were, in fact, remakes of the old Type I aircraft, with the remaking having been performed by Rolls-Royce. In autumn 1942, there also appeared a Sea Hurricane, which was launched from the *Empire Morn* CAM (Catapult Aircraft Merchant) ship sailing as part of Convoy PQ 18. Flying Officer Burr, who was piloting the Sea Hurricane, destroyed a German torpedo bomber, landed in Archangelsk and left the aircraft there.

It is noteworthy that according to official British data, the number of aircraft shipped to the USSR was considerably lower, and amounted to 2,952 fighters. The difference is due to the fact that instead of group spare-part sets (which were, in the Soviet Air Force, intended for a specific number of aircraft of the same type), the British shipped additional fighters that were often incomplete or damaged. The Soviet party, nevertheless, counted such shipments among the aircraft, rather than the spare parts.

The fact that during the first years of the war, Great Britain was shipping only the Hurricanes to the Soviet Union can (strange though it may seem), to a considerable extent, be 'credited' to Comrade Stalin. As has already been mentioned, in September 1941, a conference was held in Moscow to discuss the system of the Allies' aircraft shipments to the Soviet Union. The conference issues included (inter alia) determining aircraft types and quantities. The British delegation was painstakingly 'promoting' the Hurricanes, whereas the Soviet party resisted and demanded the Spitfires. Finally, the British suggested a 'fifty-fifty' option: that is, equal quantities of the Spitfires and the Hurricanes; it looked like the Russians agreed. Member of the British delegation Lord Beaverbrook (who was, at the time, Minister of Aircraft Production) even sent a wire to the appropriate effect to London. Here, however, Stalin interposed; the shorthand records of the negotiations unambiguously testify to such a fact. The Soviet leader realized that the only thing the two aircraft had in common was the engine, and was anxious lest the concurrent mastering of the two unfamiliar aircraft should present considerable difficulties for the air force. Stalin asked Beaverbrook whether Great Britain could cover the entire amount of shipments with the Spitfires, and the answer was in the negative. To the question as to whether the same could be done with the Hurricanes, the answer was: "Yes." People's Commissar of Aviation Industry Shakhurin tried to dissuade Stalin from such a decision, but failed. As a result, the Soviet party agreed to the Hurricanes.

Twenty-eight Hurricane IIBs of 151 Wing were officially handed over to the Northern Fleet Air Force on 21 December. Much earlier, on 22 September, the Commission of NII VVS, which was chaired by Colonel K.A. Gruzdev, accepted the first 'directly shipped' Hurricane (s/n Z2899). The commission's opinion was based solely on the results of a visual inspection of the aircraft, since the operating manual and the description were sent from England to the USSR only on the following day. The report states that the aircraft was far from new, was rather worn and that the starting lever, clock and ammunition package were missing. The case was no exception; on the contrary, it was quite normal for the first batches of the Hurricanes. It should be noted, however, that it was later found out that the Hurricane in question had been supplied as a set of spare parts, rather than as a complete fighter aircraft.

Specialists who were involved in the acceptance of British aircraft noted that many fighters (unlike those coming from the USA) were incomplete and needed repairing. There were aircraft which had, by that time, flown more than a hundred hours.

In charge of the pilots' conversion training and equipping air units with the Hurricanes were several backup regiments and training units. The 22nd Backup Air Regiment, which was stationed in Kineshma, became the first to handle the task.

The introduction of the Hurricanes started from the north. The 72nd and 78th Air Regiments of the Northern Fleet Air Force started to use this type in combat in November-December 1941, as well as the 152nd and the 760th Air Regiments of the Leningrad (later Karelian) Front aviation. These regiments mastered the new type either with the help of British pilots, or on their own.

The first air units that 'graduated' from the backup brigades and regiments were the 4th Fighter Air Regiment and the 28th Fighter Air Regiment, which completed their conversion training in early December 1941. The 4th Fighter Air Regiment was withdrawn from the front in November – having lost the majority of its MiG-3 fighters. By 1 December, all pilots of the regiment had mastered the Hurricanes, and in January, the regiment joined the Yaroslavl-Rybinsk region's air defense forces. In total, throughout 1941, the USSR received 484 Hurricanes.

To Russian pilots, the British fighter looked extraordinarily large. The Soviet Yak-1, LaGG-3 and MiG-3 were much smaller; as for the I-16 and I-153, they looked like fleas against the Hurricane.

The very first cases of operational use of the Hurricanes at the front revealed numerous disadvantages: weapons aroused most of the objections, as eight to twelve 7.69mm guns could not inflict any significant damage on well-armored (and rather 'viable') German combat planes. Here is a characteristic example of that: in January 1942, three Hurricanes of the 191st Fighter Air Regiment were chasing a Junkers Ju 88 reconnaissance aircraft for 10 minutes and peppering it with incessant fire, yet they failed to bring it down. Furthermore, weapons had poor reliability. In cold weather, the locks of the guns (which were arranged in the wing) often froze up – making the aircraft combat-ineffective. An insufficient efficiency of weapons sometimes made the pilots resort to ram attacks.

On 31 May 1942, the afterwards famous ace Amet-Khan Sultan – having shot away all ammunition – ram-attacked a Ju 88 with his aircraft. The fighter struck the German bomber from below; the enemy aircraft wing crushed the Hurricane's canopy, and the pilot found himself clenched in the cockpit. The aircraft 'grappled' with each other, but Amet-Khan managed to push his fighter away from the enemy aircraft using his hands, and bailed out of the deformed aircraft.

The flight performance of the Hurricanes did not arouse much enthusiasm as well. NII VVS received (for study purposes) a Hurricane IIA with eight guns and an additional 'tropical' air filter. Tests that were promptly carried out by NII VVS showed that in terms of speed, the aircraft was somewhere between the I-16 and the Yak-1. To its principal opponent in the north – the German Bf 109E – it was inferior in speed at low and medium altitudes (by 40-50km/h) and in rate of climb. It was only at the altitudes of 6,500-7,000m that their performance became approximately equal. The maximum speed obtained during the tests was 522km/h. In a dive, the clumsy Hurricane 'pancaked'; this prevented it from accelerating quickly. On the other hand, among its advantages was the low turn radius, which was due to the low load on the wing – allowing it to carry out successful dogfights in horizontals.

The landing gear (from the Soviet point of view) had a rather poor design. In spite of the fact that the aircraft's center of gravity was, to a sufficient extent, in the aft portion, its nose-over angle was only 24° (taking into account deceleration), whereas the minimum required value established by NII VVS was 26.5°. As the aircraft ran out of fuel and ammunition, the nose-over angle became still less. Therefore, landings on the uneven ground of field airfields were fraught with a high probability of nosing-over. This resulted, first of all, in damage to the wooden blades of the Rotol propellers; unlike metal ones, they were nearly non-repairable.

The Hurricane was also susceptible to nosing-over during taxiing. The aircraft had a disagreeable propensity for raising its tail with the engine running (the Soviet Yakovlev aircraft featured similar behavior), so to prevent aircraft damage, one or two technicians were often seated in the aft portion of the fuselage. Sometimes they failed to jump off in time, and became 'airborne' against their will. In 151 Wing, such a situation resulted in an aircraft crash, with two mechanics killed and the pilot injured.

The Hurricanes' combat efficiency was further impaired by a shortage of spare parts, and Rotol propellers were especially scarce. Along with breakages caused by nosing-over and cracks brought about by bullets, they also suffered damage from stones which were drawn in at take-off. Sometimes, up to half of the shipped aircraft remained grounded because of the unavailability of propellers. In March through to April 1942, the Soviet Union managed to set up the production of spare blades for the British propellers.

At times, a loss of combat efficiency by the Hurricanes reached an enormous level. In spring 1942, due to a lack of certain parts and assemblies, only two aircraft out of the 18 at the disposal of the 488th Fighter Air Regiment were able to fly. In November the same year, the 122nd Fighter Air Division (which provided air cover for Murmansk) could count on only three combat-ready fighters out of its 69 Hurricanes.

Pilot I.N. Stepanenko of the 4th Fighter Air Regiment commented on the Hurricane: "The aircraft is heavy, and is more of an attack aircraft than a fighter." The answer of Commander of the 485th Fighter Air Regiment G.V. Zimin as regards the result of a simulated battle with the American P-39 during training in Ivanovo was: "Alas, I might as well have been trying to fight the Airacobra while riding a pterodactyl." In the 769th Fighter Air Regiment, they went farther still and dubbed the British fighter a 'Flying Cow'; however, the Hurricane should not be painted entirely black, as pilots found quite definite merits of the fighter as well. In spite of being somewhat clumsy, the aircraft proved manageable and easy to fly. The control stick required little effort, and the rudder and elevator trim tabs were efficient. The Hurricane performed various maneuvers easily and in a stable manner, and was fit for use by pilots of medium skill, which was not insignificant in wartime conditions. Pilots also liked the spacious cockpit, which had a good field of view. The fact that all of the shipped Hurricanes were fitted with radio communication equipment was a considerable advantage, as it should be borne in mind that for Soviet fighters of the time, standards prescribed installing radio transmitters on one aircraft in three; in fact, even this was not fulfilled. Pilot I.A. Kaberov remembered: "The radio is working excellently; there is neither noise, nor clacking." Unfortunately, British radio sets were powered from dedicated battery cells (in spite of the fact that the aircraft was fitted with a storage battery) and, in winter – especially in the north – the charge sufficed only for one-and-a-half to two hours of operation, no matter how the mechanics might have tried to wrap the radio sets in warmth-keeping material, but even given all of the advantages, the result was unambiguous. At the end of 1941, the Hurricane was considerably inferior to enemy fighters. Therefore, as soon as the Hurricanes were received, Soviet specialists commenced making alterations to them in an effort to rectify or, where rectification was not possible, at least mitigate the principal disadvantages of the British fighter.

As soon as autumn 1941, the 78th Fighter Air Regiment (at the suggestion of its leader, B.F. Safonov) carried out the reworkings of the received aircraft to make them suited to carry Soviet weapons. The four Browning machine guns were replaced with two 12.7mm BK machine guns, with a stock of 100 rounds per gun; two bomb racks for 50kg bombs were added. Firepower was also enhanced by two RS-82 rocket projectiles. In January 1942, N.F. Kuznetsov's aircraft in the

191st Fighter Air Regiment was fitted with two 20mm ShVAK cannons. Similar work was also carried out in other air units, with the installation of four to six rocket projectiles being a common modification.

Poor armor protection of the Hurricane gave rise to objections as well. Therefore, standard armor backrests were often removed and replaced with Soviet ones. At first, such work was performed directly in the regiments (thus, for example, on the already mentioned aircraft of Kuznetsov's, the protection plate from a crashed I-16 was installed), but later, the same was done in factory conditions as part of the rearmament, which will be explained below.

By winter 1941/1942, a rather large number of Hurricanes had been operating at the front. The Northern Fleet Air Force alone had at its disposal 70 such aircraft as of December 1941. In early 1942, three fighter regiments (Nos.67, 429 and 488) were raised near Moscow, in addition to the regiments that were operating in the north. The Moscow counter-offensive was the first large-scale operation in which the 'Soviet' Hurricanes took part. They acted dynamically at the front to provide air cover for the troops in the forefront. At daytime, the aircraft performed air cover missions in small groups – thus, for example, on 18 March 1942, fighters of the 67th and the 429th Fighter Air Regiments departed from Monino airfield to cover the troops at the segment between Krasny Kholm and Baryatinskaya. Flight Lead Senior Lieutenant A.N. Chemodanov directed the aircraft to a flight of Ju 88 bombers. Chemodanov himself downed one of the Junkers aircraft. The Hurricanes, in turn, were attacked by German Bf 109 fighters. In the course of the battle, they damaged pilot Parmenov's aircraft. Lieutenant Shlyakhov came to Parmenov's help and set about escorting the latter to the home airfield. Another Hurricane of the 67th Fighter Air Regiment joined the two. In the heat of the battle, Lieutenant Spiridonov found himself separated from Flight Lead Chemodanov and followed the trio – thus, unexpectedly, Chemodanov remained alone. He spotted two fighters and thought them to be his subordinates. Chemodanov caught up with them, but only to find out that those were Messerschmitts. The senior lieutenant attacked one of them head-on, and then applied fire from behind. As a result, the German aircraft wing dropped and the Messerschmitt went down, but the second opponent set the Hurricane on fire. Chemodanov had no other choice but to bail out.

The winter of 1941/1942 brought a lot of troubles to the regiments which had the British fighters in operation. Aircraft troubles included the clogging of pneumatic system charging connections with dirt and ice (on some of the aircraft, such connections were arranged in the wheel hub); ruptures or clogging of hoses and pipes; failures of air compressors; and damage to carburetor throttles due to frozen oil.

Oil system problems were persistent. For example, on 16 November 1942, Junior Lieutenant Chistyakov of the 287th Fighter Air Regiment was patrolling the Khimky — Kryukovo segment when he noticed an oil pressure drop. This was followed by gray smoke emitting from the exhaust pipes. Chistyakov shut down the engine and started gliding onto a snow-covered field at a distance of 2km from Khimki. As a result of the belly landing, the propeller was broken; the propeller spinner and the lower portion of the engine cowling collapsed; the radiator was torn off; and the right wing and several stringers on the right side of the fuselage were damaged. Later, it was discovered that the oil tank vent system had frozen through; during the warming-up, the tank burst and the oil leaked. Regiment Commander Lieutenant Colonel Dodonov ordered that warmth-keeping procedures be exercised in respect of oil tanks, and vent systems be cleaned every day before departure.

The cold caused weapons and components of aircraft equipment to freeze. To avoid this, additional drain taps were fitted into pipelines to ensure the complete drainage of coolant and oil from aircraft on the ground; pipelines, electric accumulators and storage batteries were protected using winter operation materials. Rotol propellers were prone to freeze through on the ground at a low pitch (due to oil freezing); in fact, two hours were enough for propeller hubs to become completely seized. As a counteraction step, hubs under propeller spinners were protected with felt caps. At temperatures below -20°C, wooden blades were becoming loose in their attachment sockets and had to be additionally secured by screws. There was a practice of stuffing the radiators on the ground with special cushions; to ensure radiator protection in flight, a portion of the radiator was blocked with an ordinary board (the size of which had to be determined 'experimentally').

Certain difficulties were connected with attempts to operate the Hurricane with water in the cooling system instead of the glycol-based mixture. For this purpose, the system was subjected to several modifications – including the removal of the thermostatic regulator, which had been calibrated to operate with glycol and did not let any fluid with a temperature lower than 85°C to pass into the radiator; the removal of the bypass tube; and the removal of several secondary lines (e.g. the carburetor heating line). Later, the conversion to more frost-resistant anti-freezing agents of Soviet manufacture was implemented. A.P. Golubkov's design office carried out dedicated activities for adapting the British fighter to conditions of the Russian winter.

A mass appearance of Hurricanes at the Soviet-German Front took place in spring/summer 1942 – thus, on 26 March 1942, the raising of the 814th Fighter Air Regiment began. July can be deemed the peak time, as during that month, as many as eight Hurricane-flying regiments were sent out to the forefront. The Hurricanes were in service with the naval aviation of the Northern Fleet and the Baltic Fleet, with air force regiments operating in the Karelian Front, Kalinin Front, North-Western Front and the Voronezh Front, and with air defense forces units in various regions of the country. In total, throughout 1941-1942, 29 regiments fitted with the British fighters were sent to the front.

The disadvantages of the Hurricanes proved costly for Soviet pilots. Losses were very high – thus, for example, in March 1942 in the North-Western Front, two regiments which had been flying the British fighters were depleted by the Germans in less than a week of battles. Insufficient speed and a poor vertical maneuvering performance brought about a need to make formations as close as possible and to conduct only horizontal combats with fighters. There were situations when, with German fighters in view, the Hurricanes adopted a defensive circular formation, with no attempt to attack. During the hard year of 1942, the Hurricanes' share among the aircraft lost by the Soviet Air Force was equal to approximately eight percent, which exceeded their share in the overall aircraft fleet; however, in the hands of experienced pilots, these aircraft also achieved considerable combat success, even in conditions of the enemy's numerical superiority. For example, in April 1942, four Hurricanes of the 485th Fighter Air Regiment – under the command of Lieutenant Bezverkhny – courageously engaged ten Bf 109s. As a result of the combat, three German aircraft and two Hurricanes were shot down. On 19 June, seven fighters of the same regiment – led by Regiment Commander G.V. Zimin – attacked twelve Junkers Ju 87 dive bombers which were being escorted by 15 Messerschmitts over the 'Ramushevsky Corridor'. Ten German aircraft and one Soviet aircraft were brought down.

According to the historian N.G. Bodrikhin's estimate, the 'victory record' is held by Captain I.I. Zabegailo of the 1st Guards Fighter Air Regiment, who, flying a Hurricane, destroyed 12 German aircraft; however, the pilots' skill and heroism were not enough. As early as September 1941, the question of modernizing the weapons of the British fighter was brought up. The reason consisted (apart from the already mentioned insufficient efficiency of the fighter) of a shortage of 7.69mm rounds; tracers and incendiary rounds were the scarcest. On 20 November, the Air Force Chief Administration made a request to the People's Commissariat of Aviation Industry to organize the rearmament of the Hurricanes. The work was entrusted to *Opytnoye Konstruktorskoye Byuro* (Experimental Design Bureau) No.15 (known as OKB-15), which was headed by B.G. Shpitalny. The design bureau considered three modification options for the Hurricane: a version with four 20mm ShVAK cannons; a version with two ShVAK cannons and two BK large-caliber machine guns; and finally, a version with four BK machine guns. The latter option provided for a saving in weight, but was not approved; such an outcome may be attributed to a shortage of large-caliber machine guns at the time.

OKB-15 prepared drawings for the modification of the fighter in two versions. One of the versions included two ShVAK cannons (with a stock of 120 rounds each), two BK machine guns (with a stock of 120 rounds each as well) and six RO-82 rail launchers for RS-82 rocket projectiles. An interesting fact is that the machine guns and the cannons were arranged asymmetrically. They had a slight (approximately 50mm) shift to the right-hand side. In a similar manner, the first (closest to the fuselage) pair of rocket projectiles was installed, with the only difference being that the distance from the aircraft centerline was larger (approximately 100mm). The rest of the RS-82s were suspended symmetrically. This version allowed retaining the four Browning machine guns in the wing (with a stock of 300 rounds each), or replacing them with ShKAS machine guns of Soviet manufacture.

The other version provided for the installation of four ShVAK cannons (with the same stock of 120 rounds each) and six RO-82 rail launchers. This allowed retaining two Browning machine guns, or installing two ShKAS instead of them (with 300 rounds per gun). Accordingly, in December 1941, two prototypes were made at Factory No.115 and they were subjected to range field tests. The second version demonstrated higher destructive potential, but the aircraft had become heavier. With two ShVAK cannons and two BK machine guns, the fighter's weight was a little lower than that of the standard Hurricane IIB. Accordingly, flight performance improved a bit; however, certain disadvantages in the feeding of the BK machine guns were revealed.

At first, the version combining the ShVAK and the BK was declared disqualified. Nevertheless, it was later deemed preferable. Furthermore, it was prescribed that the aircraft so armed (with certain slight modifications) be regarded as the 'reference' aircraft.

Initially, it was planned that the modification of the Hurricanes would be carried out directly at the facilities of combat units, but later, there appeared an idea to perform the work in a centralized manner at Factory No.21 in Gorky; however, this factory was manufacturing (at full capacity) Lavochkin fighters. Therefore, the modification of the Hurricanes to make them able to carry Soviet weapons was entrusted to Factory No.81 and an appropriate order was issued on 21 February 1942. It was planned that by 20 April, 400 fighters would have been rearmed; there was an intention to gradually withdraw them from different air units for modification purposes. Equipment and workers who were intended to carry out the modification of the Hurricanes were deployed in the vacant shops of Factory No.39 (near Moscow Central airfield), which had been evacuated from Moscow. Documentation and the 'reference aircraft' were also brought there.

According to the schedule, the first 60 fighters were to have been rearmed by 15 March; however, from the very beginning, the production personnel encountered a number of hindrances: first, discrepancies were detected between the drawings and the 'reference aircraft'; second, the manufacture of the BK machine guns had been discontinued, and production of the more advanced UB machine guns had been launched instead. On 12 March, a decision was made to fit the aircraft with UBT machine guns (the UB version for the turret). These were available in a sufficient quantity and, furthermore, their reloading mechanism was better suited to the Hurricane in terms of the required effort. Therefore, the round-feeding system and the case ejection chute had to be modified; however, the UBT machine guns were not available at the factory warehouse as well. Instead, there was a batch of ShVAK cannons. Production specialists made use of the drawings for the previously rejected, but better developed version, and the first aircraft left the factory with a set of four cannons each. All of these troubles brought about delays in the performance of the schedule, so by 18 April, only 32 finished fighters had been put into service, in spite of the achieved output rate of seven aircraft per day; however, by early May, all 400 Hurricanes had been rearmed and the factory received an order for the modification of another batch of 400 fighters, followed by an additional 200. Both aircraft, which had just arrived from Great Britain, and those which had already been at the front were subjected to modification. Teams from Factory No.81 performed the modification procedure at the Moscow Region airfields in Kubinka, Khimki, Monino and Yegoryevsk as well. These bases of the 6th Fighter Air Regiment were used to rearm aircraft which could not be ferried to the factory because of various malfunctions. By the end of 1942, 925 Hurricanes with Soviet cannons and machine guns had been placed in service. The modification of each aircraft had cost approximately 13,000 rubles, but on the other hand, the new powerful weapons expanded the aircraft capabilities both in air battles and in ground-target operations. It should be noted that a slight change in the center-of-gravity position brought about a certain lag in any one fighter's ability to recover from the spin, and caused a transformation of the spin condition to a flat one; this, however, posed no great hazard.

In June 1942, one of the modified Hurricanes was tested by NII VVS. It was fitted with two ShVAK cannons (with a combat stock of 120 rounds each) and two UBT machine guns (with 100 rounds each). The aircraft carried no rifle-caliber machine guns. Provisions were made for the mounting of six RS-82 rocket projectiles under the wing and, in such a configuration, the take-off weight totaled 3,352kg.

There were also provisions for carrying (under the wing) two bombs (100kg each) or VAP-6m chemical spray tanks – and the latter was an innovation. In England, the Hurricanes sometimes carried smoke generators under the wing to create smokescreens, whereas fitting this aircraft with any offensive chemical weapons had never been considered. The VAP-6m chemical spray tank was, essentially, a streamlined tank filled with a solution of a toxic agent. Standard toxic agents at the time were yperite and lewisite, with kerosene used as the solvent. Fluid was displaced from the tank by ram air and sprayed via the nozzle. Spray tanks were used to make strafing attacks on marching or stationed troops, or on baggage trains moving along the roads.

Weapons and combat stock added 171kg to the Hurricane's weight. The aircraft aerodynamics was slightly impaired because of the protruding rails for rocket projectiles, bomb racks and barrels of Soviet cannons and machine guns. On the Hurricane IIB, Browning machine gun barrels were originally hidden inside the wing; holes in the wing's leading edge were papered over before firing.

Test aircraft were flown by Captain Golofastov and Major Khomyakov, and the flying time totalled 22 hours and 15 minutes. Of course, the increased weight and impaired aerodynamics affected the flight performance. The maximum speed dropped to 498km/h (and to 490km/h, according to another document), and the take-off run and maneuverability became slightly worse as well. The mounting of rocket projectiles 'cost' the aircraft 9km/h; the bombs 'ate away' 16km/h; and the clumsy chemical spray tanks 'devoured' 19km/h. This is comparable to the influence of a closed cockpit canopy, which brought about a difference of 13km/h. After the modification, the aircraft's center of gravity shifted forward – thus causing a slight worsening in its spinning performance; however, this was deemed non-hazardous.

In the USSR, the Hurricane was often used as a fighter-bomber and, to some extent, as an attack aircraft. With the Soviet weapons and two FAB-100 bombs, the aircraft was easily controllable; there was only a slight deterioration in take-off performance, and a reduction in speed by 42km/h. The aircraft was viable: once, the aircraft piloted by A.L. Kozhevnikov of the 438th Fighter Air Regiment suffered 162 puncture holes, but nevertheless, the pilot managed to land safely on the home airfield.

From time to time, successful bomb attacks were delivered by the Hurricanes. In summer 1942, an aircraft of the 191st Fighter Air Regiment (fitted with Soviet weapons) used their cannons and rockets to smash a German motor convoy to pieces near Novy Oskol. In August 1943, the Hurricanes, together with the Ilyushin Il-2s, bomb-destroyed the German airfield near Luostari; the enemy's casualties comprised 11 fighters and a Ju 52/3m transport. For such operations, fighter regiments of the air force were often made use of; however, at some locations, regiments of a pure attack purpose had the Hurricanes at their disposal (e.g. the 65th Air Regiment in the north).

In August 1942, the 3rd Guards Fighter Air Regiment began operating within the Baltic Fleet. It was fully fitted with the British fighters which had been rearmed to carry ShVAK cannons and UB machine guns (in total, there were 23 aircraft). Beginning from 14 August, the regiment was providing air cover for the Oranienbaum foothold. Pilots of the regiment were successfully fighting enemy bombers and, at the same time – realizing the inferiority of the Hurricane's flight performance to that of the Bf 109 – they adopted solely defensive tactics. At first, head-on attacks were attempted, but with little success, so later, the 'merry-go-round' arrangement was implemented. The aircraft adopted a circular formation and then climbed helically inside a circle of the Messerschmitts, which had a greater turning radius. The higher they managed to climb, the less the enemy's advantage became; then the Hurricanes made attempts to attack from above. Finally, a decision was made to stay with the simple defensive circle, with each pilot within the circle covering the tail of the aircraft flying ahead of him. The circle then drifted (little by little) to the friendly territory.

In spite of the fact that nearly all battles were fought in conditions of the enemy's numerical superiority (by 1.5 times, on average), sometimes the pilots of the 3rd Guards Fighter Air Regiment managed to achieve quite creditable results. On 17 August, eight Hurricanes conducted a battle against six fighters, which was described as: "D.XXI with retractable landing gear." It is probable that these were the Finnish G.50s. The Hurricanes shot down two of them, with no losses on their part. On 11 September, a flight of eight Soviet aircraft encountered the same number of Bf 109Fs near Pervy Gorodok. As a result, three Messerschmitts and a Hurricane were shot down. In total, from 14 August through to 22 September, the regiment destroyed 51 enemy aircraft, whereas its own casualties totaled 14 aircraft.

The participation in battles on the Don River – and later, at the distant approaches to Stalingrad – proved a serious challenge for the Hurricanes. In the north, the Germans often made use of obsolete materiel; by contrast, in summer 1942 they flung (to the south) all the best that they had. It was there that the 235th Fighter Air Division, which was under the command of Lieutenant Colonel I.D. Podgorny, was urgently moved. Initially, the division included the 191st, 436th and 46th Fighter Air Regiments; later, the 180th Fighter Air Regiment joined it. All of the regiments flew the Hurricanes only. In early June, the division was ready for combat operations; reports of the Political Department, however, stated a certain 'lack of confidence in the Hurricanes on the part of the flight crews'.

The Soviet aviation was acting in extremely severe conditions, with the enemy commanding the air. Throughout the first five days in July, the Hurricanes – in spite of constant redeployments and a shortage of fuel and spare parts – destroyed 29 enemy aircraft. Senior Political Instructor Kh.M. Ibatulin achieved a particular success: on 1 July, he personally shot down two enemy aircraft and refused to disengage, in spite of the torn-off engine cowling on his Hurricane. To a certain extent, the success of the British aircraft was brought about by their smooth interaction with modern fighters of Soviet manufacture, and the sufficient competence of the pilots who flew them. Throughout July, the division lost 17 Hurricanes, whereas the enemy's casualties totaled at least twice as many combat planes. Gradually, both belligerents improved the quality of the aircraft being flung into the battle. The most up-to-date versions of the Yakovlev and the Lavochkin aircraft appeared in the skies of Stalingrad. On account of the absence of replacements, the British fighters (little by little) disappeared from the fleet of the 8th Air Army. As of 1 August, there were only 11 of them left – and of those, only three were battle-worthy.

This phenomenon was a common, rather than a local one. As of 1 July, the air force had 202 Hurricanes at its disposal; in November, there were only 130 left. They kept playing an important part only at the northern segments of the Soviet-German Front.

Convoy PQ 18 (September 1942) included SS *Empire Morn*. At the very end of the voyage, Flying Officer J. Burr took off from the ship to hold off an attack by the He 111Hs. He 'pressed' one of the bombers to the water; then, in an attempt to make a turn, the Heinkel ran into the waves, but Burr kept firing. When the Ju 88s appeared instead of the He 111Hs, he simulated attacks to misguide the opponents. Having estimated the fuel reserve, the pilot headed for the shore and, in a few hours, Burr landed on Kegostrov.

In total, throughout 1942, the Soviet Union received 932 Hurricanes, which was a considerable quantity; however, the British fighters' lagging behind the demands of the time was becoming more and more obvious. On 25 November, First Deputy Air Force Commander G.A. Vorozheikin reported to Stalin: "At the front, the Hurricanes have shown themselves to disadvantage." A gradual 'saturation' of the frontline aviation with more advanced aircraft entailed a step-up in the Soviet requirements to shipments from Great Britain. On 5 November, People's Commissar of Trade A.I. Mikoyan ordered that the Trade Representation in London should accept only new aircraft, or those who had (by the time of shipment) flown 30 hours or less. The 'major-caliber artillery' joined the 'struggle' against shipments of 'second-hand' fighters to the Soviet Union as well. The notice from the air force's headquarters to Mikoyan read: 'On 13 November 1942, Comrade Stalin personally indicated that such aircraft should not be accepted'.

In autumn 1942, it was requested that the quantity of the Hurricane shipments be reduced to one fourth of the total fighter shipments from Great Britain, and that only the C modification (fitted with cannons) be shipped. Furthermore, from 1 January 1943, the Soviet party wished to receive only the Spitfires, but the British objected to the idea; however, the share of the Hurricanes in the shipments soon began to dwindle indeed.

As soon as a considerable quantity of up-to-date aircraft was received, the Hurricanes gradually ceased to operate at the front in the capacity of fighters. A small number of the Hurricanes were used as short-range reconnaissance aircraft. The conversion of such Hurricanes was carried out directly at the facilities of the respective air units and, similar to their British counterparts, they carried a vertical aerial camera (usually the AFA-I) in the fuselage behind the pilot's seat. Such aircraft were at the disposal of both special reconnaissance regiments (e.g. the 118th Independent Reconnaissance Air Regiment of the Northern Fleet) and ordinary fighter regiments (e.g. the 3rd Guards Fighter Air Regiment of the Baltic Fleet). Spotter reconnaissance squadrons had such aircraft as well, but their total number was not more than 20. They operated in the Leningrad Front, Volkhov Front and the Kalinin Front.

In the Saratov Higher Aviation/Glider School, the Hurricanes were fitted with special locks in order to convert them into towing airplanes for the A-7 and G-11 combat gliders. With the gliders, the Hurricanes made several sorties to partisans.

During 1944, the air force was gradually discarding the Hurricanes which were still present in different air units. Throughout the year, 249 aircraft were written off; of those, 215 were discarded by reason of being worn. The extent of combat activity throughout the period can easily be determined if the casualties are considered: during the year, 15 aircraft were reported missing in action for unknown reasons; five were brought down by anti-aircraft gunners, but none were lost in aerial battles. As of 1 May 1945, the combat army had, at its disposal, only eight Hurricanes; thirty-four more Hurricanes remained in the rear military districts.

Air defense forces became the principal sphere of application for these British fighters in the second half of the war. As has already been mentioned, defensive air units began to receive the Hurricanes in December 1941 – thus, for example, in early October 1942, the 26th Fighter Air Regiment, which was under the command of Major G.G. Petrov in Ivanovo, received 20 fighters of the IIB type. The aircraft were immediately ferried to Moscow for rearmament, and all of them were fitted with ShVAK cannons, UB machine guns and rocket projectiles. As soon as the rearmament was complete, the Hurricanes were ferried in two batches (10 aircraft per batch) to Levashovo airfield, near Leningrad. Two of the regiment's three squadrons were provided with the British fighters; the third squadron flew the MiG-3s and the I-16s.

In November 1942, the Germans resumed night raids on the city – thus, the Hurricanes found application as night fighters. On 30 (or, according to other documents, 29) November, Major N.G. Molteninov was patrolling at an altitude of 5,000m when he spotted the enemy's He 111 bomber. The fighter approached it from the rear to a distance of 50m, and started firing; the Heinkel then fell near Krasny Bor.

Beginning from late 1942, the process of the fighter defense aviation's 'saturation' with Hurricanes gathered pace dramatically. This was due to the arrival of the aircraft of the IIC modification from England. The first of them was (supposedly) the fighter which bore s/n BN428. At the time, none of the Soviet fighters were fitted with weapons as powerful as the four 20mm cannons, but on the other hand, the results of the Hurricane IIC tests at NII VVS showed that it was still slower than the IIB because of a higher weight. It was totally unfit for anti-fighter operations, yet it could, nevertheless, pose much of a threat for enemy bombers. It is no wonder then, that the majority of aircraft of this type that were shipped to the USSR went to air defense regiments. For example, they were placed in service with the 964th Fighter Air Regiment, which in 1943-1944, provided air cover for Tikhvin and the Ladoga route. As of 1 July 1943, the air defense forces had at their disposal 495 Hurricanes; by 1 June 1944, their number had reached 711. They were in service there throughout the entire war, with 252 enemy aircraft credited to them. The reinforcement of the air defense forces with the British aircraft allowed redeploying (closer to the front line) more combat-effective regiments which operated Soviet aircraft or the American Airacobras.

The British aircraft found a rather efficient application with the air defense forces. Since all of the British fighters were fitted with radio communication equipment, reliable guidance could be carried out over the radio in accordance with radar data, or with the forward ground observation posts' data – thus, on 24 March 1942, a flight of Hurricanes from the 796th Fighter Regiment was directed to a group of eight Ju 87s and ten Bf 109s, which were heading for Murmansk. Two Junkers aircraft were shot down, while others released their bombs randomly to the hills westward of the city and fled.

The period was marked by several occasions of the Hurricane IICs' spin stalls. Sometimes the IIBs entered an unintentional stall as well, but such cases were comparatively rare – thus, for example, on 1 February 1942, during a mock air combat, Senior Lieutenant Bukshtanovich of the 67th Fighter Air Regiment, who was flying a Hurricane IIB, entered an unintentional spin at an altitude of 2,500m. After three turns, the spin became flat; Bukshtanovich was unable to recover. The aircraft crashed into the ground – killing the pilot. The Investigation Commission later found out that the fighter's rudder balance had become partially detached.

As for the Hurricane IICs, they experienced such a situation not infrequently due to a certain forward shift of the center of gravity in comparison to the previous modification. The descriptions of accidents and crashes are all alike and, in all cases, there were several turns of an ordinary spin, which were then followed by the flat spin condition; then the spinning of the aircraft down to the ground – thus, on 3 July 1943, Flight Leader Senior Lieutenant Sukhanov entered an unintentional spin when performing a barrel roll. On 7 August, Junior Lieutenant Potaskaev got into a spin after a combat turn. Sergeant Seregin managed to recover from a spin, but the altitude was too low to enter a level flight; the aircraft crashed into the ground and the pilot was killed.

There were cases of aircraft tuck-under as well. Senior Sergeant Krimenko got into a dive after a right turn and pulled out too abruptly. The overload caused the landing gear to unlock and the wheels moved to the opposite direction – damaging the landing gear wells and the wing skin. The sergeant had to make a forced belly landing.

Concerned about the recurring accidents, Western Front Air Defensive Force Commander Major General S.A. Pestov twice applied to NII VVS in August 1943 with a request to investigate into the issue and provide recommendations. Indeed, NII VVS conducted additional spin tests of the Hurricane and determined the conditions to be avoided.

In 1944, some of the Hurricanes were used by the air defensive forces as lamplighter aircraft in repelling the night attacks. Usually, an aircraft of this type carried two SAB-100 illuminating bombs and dropped them at an altitude of 2,000-2,500m above the enemy bombers; then an assault team delivered an attack. Different air defense forces regiments had at their disposal two to four Hurricanes for such purpose.

In 1944, even German reconnaissance aircraft ceased penetrating deep to the inland territory of the Soviet Union; however, in Kalmykia, the last combat sortie was flown by the Hurricanes as late as 23 May 1944. Four pilots of the 933rd Fighter Air Regiment were entrusted with the task of finding and destroying the German Focke-Wulf FW 200C transport aircraft which was carrying a group of agents to the deep rear, and made a refueling stopover in the steppes. Having flown a distance of approximately 270km, the fighters spotted the four-engine transport aircraft and set it on fire; after that, they provided fire support for an NKVD unit, which captured the crew and passengers.

As of 1 May 1945, the air defense forces had 731 Hurricanes at their disposal. The overwhelming majority of the Hurricanes were of the IIC modification; there were 570 of them.

In the naval aviation – in the Northern Fleet – the Hurricanes also stayed longer than in the air force. During that period, they (to some extent) made up for the shortage of bombers and attack aircraft. Among the Hurricanes' principal inland targets were the airfields of Hebugten, Luostari, Salmiyarvi and Svartnes, where the aircraft of the German Luftflotte 5 were concentrated. In the north, the Hurricanes were also test-operated in the capacity of night bombers. In February 1943, they made nuisance raids on Luostari and Hebugten. One by one, they flew over the target (with an interval of 10-20 minutes) and dropped bombs onto grounded aircraft from an altitude of 400-800m.

The Hurricanes also took part in operations at sea lanes against small vessels. In certain cases, bombs were not needed to sink a motor boat or a similar craft; cannon fire was quite enough. Here, the Hurricane IIC proved efficient. On 2 June 1943, even a small merchant ship with a displacement of 800 tons was sent to the bottom in this manner (in the Syltefjord). Of course, the pilots' skills played an important part here – thus, for example, a flight of eight Hurricanes used up 540 rounds on 4 June to sink a motor boat south-east of Varde before it went down.

In combat maneuver units of the Northern Fleet Air Force, the Hurricanes were used until October 1944 when the last regiment (the 27th Fighter Air Regiment) was fitted with more advanced aircraft. As of 1 January 1945, there were only five aircraft of this type on the list – and all of them in auxiliary units. In the Baltic Fleet, the Hurricanes disappeared much earlier (in October 1942). The 3rd Guards Fighter Air Regiment, which was operating there, received the LaGG-3 fighters instead.

The anti-tank Hurricane IIDs with two 40mm cannons each, which had been quite successful in Africa and in the Far East, found no efficient application in the USSR. The first batch of such aircraft was shipped from Iraq to the 11th Backup Air Regiment in Kirovabad in August 1943. All of them were fitted with Merlin XX engines and Vickers S cannons. In early 1944, a total quantity of 46 aircraft of the IID type came to the Soviet Union, but sometime later, several tens of similar Hurricane IVs with Merlin 24 engines were shipped by Great Britain. Their principal difference consisted of the multi-purpose mount, which allowed the attachment of (under the wing) 40mm cannons, guiding rails for rocket projectiles, bomb racks or smoke generators.

In November 1943, two Hurricane IIDs were brought to NII VVS and they were test-flown until 23 December. In February 1944, one of the aircraft was handed over to the Scientific Research Range of Aviation Armament (*Nauchno-Issledovatelsky Poligon Aviatsionnogo Vooruzheniya*, or NIPAV), whose specialists were interested (first and foremost) in the aircraft cannons. The tests showed that the Hurricane IID was of little use as an attack aircraft, since it was poorly armored and had no bombing armament. The Ilyushin Il-2 could do much better anything the Hurricane IID was able to do. Furthermore, 40mm high-explosive rocket projectiles and armor-piercing incendiary rocket projectiles were not manufactured in the USSR; one could only rely on shipments from England, and this, of course, reduced the aircraft value. A decision was made to use the Hurricane IIDs in the air defense forces of the rear military regions against enemy low-speed bombers. At the end of 1943, the 441st Fighter Air Regiment of the 106th Air Defense Forces Division, which was stationed near Bologoe station, was equipped with aircraft of the IID and IV types – and there they were operated during 1943-1944. The Hurricanes took off to intercept enemy aircraft several times; however, there were no cases reported of any combat encounter with the enemy. The regiment commander requested more than once that the heavy and clumsy Hurricanes be taken away and replaced with the Yakovlev Yak-9, which were in service with other regiments of the division; finally, he achieved his purpose.

Nevertheless, some of these aircraft got to the front line. Before the opinion of NII VVS was received, the 246th Fighter Air Regiment began conversion training on the Hurricane IIDs from the first batches in November 1943 in Ajikabul. As late as June 1944, the regiment was sent to the front in the vicinity of Bobruysk; this unit, however, saw almost no combat service as well. In September, the Hurricanes were entirely replaced with the Yak-1s.

Some individual Hurricanes were subjected to interesting modifications: several aircraft were modified into two-seat trainers. They were manufactured at different locations, and almost all of them differed from each other. For example, the version created in Aviation Workshop 30 of the Northern Fleet had the second cockpit in place of the former fuselage fairing. The instructor was protected from the wind only by means of a bent plexiglass visor. To improve the field of view, the canopy of the forward cockpit (where the trainee sat) was also removed. Such aircraft were manufactured beginning from summer 1943 in Aviation Workshop 55 in Ivanovo, under the supervision of S.E. Yefimov. The prototype aircraft was test-flown in the second half of July. A version with a rear mobile gun unit is also known; it was tested at NII VVS as a spotter aircraft. In 1943, prototypes of cargo-carrying and ambulance Hurricanes were manufactured.

There were attempts to fit the British fighters with skis to allow for the Russian winter conditions. In the already mentioned Saratov Higher Aviation/Glider School, one of the aircraft was equipped with non-retractable skis, and it was test-flown by A.E. Augul. In early 1942, at the facilities of Factory No.81, one of the fighters from the 736th Fighter Air Regiment which had been delivered for repair was fitted with ski landing gear, which was retractable in flight. The aircraft was tested during the period from 5-15 February at Central airfield. The tests flights were performed by V.A. Stepanchonok of NII VVS and by pilots of the 10th Guards Fighter Air Regiment and the 736th Fighter Air Regiment; however, other fighters were not subjected to such a modification and the Hurricanes continued to make take-off and landing runs over tramped snow in winter conditions using their wheels.

A shortage of spare Merlin engines in the first half of the war – and the desire to enhance the fighters' performance by means of power plant modifications – gave rise to several projects involving the fitting of the Hurricanes with Soviet M-105, AM-37A, M-88B and M-82A engines. The former two engines were, like the Merlin, 12-cylinder liquid-cooled engines. With the M-105 engine, which was inferior to its British equivalent in terms of power, efficiency and altitude parameters, the aircraft performance degraded. The AM-37 was considerably heavier; with this engine installed, the center of gravity was shifted forward – thus making the landing more hazardous than with the standard engine. The M-88B was inferior to the Merlin in terms of power as well. Furthermore, its double-row configuration brought about the need to modify the fuselage with side extensions similar to those on the La-5 (which was based on the LaGG-3). The removal of the liquid cooling system caused the center of gravity to move forward, so this had to be counterbalanced by the rearrangement of equipment. The M-82A had a similar configuration, but provided a higher thrust – thus offering prospects of performance improvement (especially at low and medium altitudes); however, the installation of this engine entailed the same troubles as with the M-88B. None of the projects saw practical implementation.

On account of a shortage of spare parts, British radio stations on aircraft of the 4th Backup Air Brigade were replaced with RSI-4 radio stations of Soviet manufacture.

In total, throughout the war, the Soviet Air Force and fighter air defense forces lost 1,813 Hurricanes. Of these, approximately 14 percent were written off after accidents or crashes; it was the highest percentage for fighters in the Soviet aviation, with the La-5s ranking second (12.5 percent). As of summer 1945, there remained quite a number of British aircraft in service; however, after the victory over Germany, they quickly disappeared from the strength of the Soviet aviation – having been entirely replaced with more advanced Soviet and imported fighters. The Hurricanes did not take part in the brief campaign against the Japanese Kwantung Army in China; the three air armies in the Far East had no Hurricanes at all at their disposal.

The Resolution of the Council of Ministers of the USSR dated 22 March 1946 prescribed that 421 Hurricanes be written off. These constituted nearly the entire number of aircraft of this type which stayed at that time in the Soviet Union and were able to fly. After the post-war reduction in armed forces, military units actually ceased to operate the Hurricanes; in 1946-1947, the majority of the fighters were scrapped; however, for some of the aircraft, a 'new job' was found: the disarmed Hurricanes were converted into weather reconnaissance aircraft. Such aircraft were used by the departmental aviation of the Chief Administration of Hydrometeorological Service. Its Hurricanes bore registration numbers beginning with the letter M. The Chief Administration of Hydrometeorological Service received, in total, more than 150 aircraft, and they flew from the western frontiers to Yakutia as part of various air detachments. The meteorological Hurricanes carried out the vertical sounding of atmosphere, cloud photography and various measurements. For this purpose, they were fitted with special instruments. To facilitate cloud flying, some of the aircraft were equipped with radio compasses – thus, for example, aircraft reg/n M-324 was equipped with an American MN-26 radio compass which had been removed from a Kingcobra. Photographing was usually done from two-seat aircraft (the former trainer aircraft).

Before the end of 1947, the fleet of the weather reconnaissance Hurricanes was dwindling mostly due to accidents. Throughout 1946, four aircraft were written off after crashes; two more were written off for the same reason in 1947. In 1948, two Hurricanes were lost. On 14 February 1948, aircraft reg/n M-309 of the Kiev Air Detachment suffered an engine-connecting rod failure. Pilot A.G. Olkhovenko made a forced landing, but without much success. The pilot was not injured, but the aircraft was discarded. On 4 December, aircraft reg/n M-292 of the Tashkent Air Detachment disappeared without a trace. Neither the fighter wreckage, nor pilot Matrenko was found in the course of the search.

As of 1 October 1947, the Chief Administration of Hydrometeorological Service had 104 Hurricanes at its disposal – including 81 serviceable ones; however, the wear and shortage of spare parts began to manifest themselves. As of 1 July 1948, the administration's fleet comprised only 50 British aircraft; by 1 January 1949, the number had decreased to 48. In the beginning of 1949, preparations for the total decommissioning of aircraft of this type were started. According to the respective order, the operation of the Hurricanes was to be discontinued from 1 January 1950 'upon expiry of service lives'. In fact, the meteorological service had 10 aircraft of this type at its disposal; of those, only five aircraft were able to fly. All of them were written off before 1 April – and it is at this point that the history of the Soviet Hurricanes terminates.

Currently, the Hurricanes are exhibited in Russia at the Vadim Zadorozhny Museum in Archangelskoye (Moscow region), and on display in the Museum of the Great Patriotic War in Moscow. One more Hurricane (model IIC Trop.) is placed on a monument in the town of Revda.

The Hurricanes of RAF No.151 Wing at Vaenga airfield in autumn 1941.

Soviet and British servicemen unload a Hurricane container from a flatcar.

The Hurricanes of RAF No.151 Wing at Vaenga airfield.

A break between the sorties.

A Hurricane at Vaenga airfield; note the Soviet SB bomber in the background.

Major General A.A. Kuznetsov getting into the Hurricane cockpit before his first flight.

The personal Hurricane (tactical number '01') of Major General A.A. Kuznetsov, who was the Northern Fleet Air Force Commander.

The Soviet ace B. Safonov before his first flight in a Hurricane.

A Soviet pilot receives pre-flight instructions before a training sortie on a Hurricane.

Commander of the 78th Fighter Air Regiment and Hero of Soviet Union Major B. Safonov near a Hurricane.

The first Hurricane delivered to the USSR (s/n Z2899).

A team which conducted the Hurricane testing at NII VVS.

A Soviet technician repairs a Hurricane propeller; the 128th Fighter Air Regiment, Moscow area, 1941.

A damaged Hurricane after a forced landing near Archangelsk.

A formation of Hurricanes flying for a mission.

Captain Dizhevsky and Senior Lieutenant Doroshin after a mission; the Northern Fleet Air Force, 1942.

Senior Lieutenant P.G. Sgibnev dons his parachute before departing on a mission in April 1942.

The Hurricanes in the sky, above the Kola Peninsula.

Northern Fleet fighter ace P.G. Sgibnev (in the middle), with the regiment's pilots.

The wreckage of a Hurricane flown by General Kuznetsov was lifted from the bottom of a lake.

A still from video footage of a Hurricane of the 78th Fighter Air Regiment during landing at Vaenga airfield in spring 1942.

Filling ammunition boxes of the Hurricane's wing-mounted machine guns in 1942.

Commander of the 17th Guards Attack Air Regiment Lieutenant Colonel V. Belousov pinning an order to one of the regiment pilots, Karelian Front, summer 1942.

Pilots of the 3rd Guards Fighter Air Regiment of the Baltic Fleet Air Force studying the Hurricane's cockpit in summer 1942.

The Hurricane IIB of the 1st Squadron, 609th Fighter Air Regiment, which made a forced landing in the Finnish territory (near Rukajärvi) in April 1942. Pilot Junior Lieutenant N. Beletsky was taken as a prisoner of war. The Finns tried to assemble a serviceable Hurricane from two damaged airplanes, but later abandoned the idea.

Back home in triumph: a Soviet pilot returning from a mission stands on his Hurricane.

Soviet pilots standing in front of a Hurricane; note the engine cowl of the parked aircraft, which is protected by a quilted cover against overcooling.

The Hurricanes of the Northern Fleet Air Force at an airfield in early summer 1942.

A Hurricane in a temporary winter camouflage.

A German soldier inspecting a shot-down Soviet Hurricane.

A Soviet soldier guarding a Hurricane at an airfield.

Pilots of the 1st Squadron, 609th Fighter Air Regiment standing in front of a Hurricane in 1942.

A Hurricane after a forced landing at the Kalinin Front in 1942.

Finnish soldiers evacuate a Hurricane after a forced landing near Tikkisyarvi on 6 April 1942. The fighter pilot Junior Lieutenant Vavyakin of the 609th Fighter Air Regiment was hiding in the woods for five days, but was then taken as a prisoner of war. The Finns attempted to restore the aircraft to flying condition, but did not succeed.

The cockpit of the Hurricane which was captured by Finnish forces.

This Soviet Hurricane bears an inscription, which translates as: 'Learn how to fight the skunk in Safonov's style'.

B.G. Shpitalny (second from left) and his colleagues near a re-armed Hurricane.

This Hurricane was modified at Factory No.115 with the Soviet armament (two ShVAK cannons and two BK machine guns) in December 1941.

This Hurricane version, modified by Factory No.115, was fitted with four ShVAK cannons in December 1941.

This modified Hurricane received attachment points for six PS-82 rocket projectiles.

Two ShVAK cannons in the Hurricane's left-wing panel, together with an easily removable 3ROB-82 battery of three rail launchers, with PS-82 rocket projectiles.

ShKAS machine guns being prepared for mounting on a Hurricane.

Armament technicians working on a ShVAK cannon which has been installed on a Hurricane.

This Hurricane was equipped with Soviet armament, North-Western Front, 1942.

A Hurricane which has just returned from a mission, South-Western Front, 1942.

A Hurricane carrying six RS-82 rocket projectiles is taxiing to take-off, Don Front, 1942.

A Hurricane with Soviet armament getting ready for take-off.

Soviet technicians assembling a Hurricane in one of the air force units.

Hurricanes equipped with Soviet armament, Karelian Front, 1943.

Soviet ground crew in front of a Hurricane; the 7th Air Army, 1943.

A Hurricane in the frontline unit; note the Lavochkin and Yakolev fighters in the background.

The Hurricane IIC/Trop during tests at NII VVS.

The Hurricane IIC/Trop fitted with external fuel tanks.

The Hurricane IID during tests at NII VVS in December 1943.

The 40mm Vickers Class S cannon in a fairing under the wing of a Hurricane IID.

A two-seat Hurricane trainer in the 136th Stationary Aircraft Repair Shop of the 7th Air Army.

This two-seat Hurricane was used as an artillery observation aircraft; note the ShKAS machine gun mounted in the rear cabin.

Partly disassembled Hurricanes in the course of transportation by rail (probably to be disposed of) at the end of the war.

A Hurricane IIC/ Trop exhibited as a monument in Revda.

The Hurricane IIB exhibited in the Technical Museum of Vadim Zadorozhny in Archangelskoe (Moscow region).

A Hurricane on display in the Museum of the Great Patriotic War at Poklonnaya Hill. Unfortunately, the aircraft armament was restored incorrectly and the cockpit canopy looks different from the original one.

The restored Hurricane in the museum at Verkhnyaya Pyshma in the Urals in 2017. The aircraft is painted in the colors of the famous pilot P.G. Sgibnev.

7.2 Supermarine Spitfire

After the war, the German fighter ace Günther Rall remembered: "I shot down my first Spitfire in Russia. That was near the village of Krymskaya. When I reported that I had shot down a Spitfire, everybody was stunned; however, on the following day, we saw quite a number of them." Rall was not mistaken: in the battles over the Kuban, the Soviet Air Force indeed made use of Spitfires.

The Supermarine Spitfire descended from the 'Type 224' monoplane fighter, which was developed in 1933 by a design team of Supermarine Aviation, which was led by R. Mitchell. The Type 224 was quite unlike the graceful Spitfire; however, the aircraft gradually acquired new features. By early 1935, the fighter – then referred to as 'Type 300' – had already looked much alike the customary appearance. It had the distinctive elliptical wing, a retractable undercarriage, the powerful Merlin engine, an enclosed cockpit, an ejector-type radiator and armament comprising six to eight 7.69mm machine guns. The all-metal aircraft featured an advanced design, with load-bearing skin and excellent aerodynamics. The prototype Spitfire flew for the first time on 6 March 1936.

In July the same year, the aircraft was displayed at the air show in London, and there it was noticed by a group of Soviet specialists who had arrived in England to carry out the acceptance of a newly-purchased Fairey Fantome fighter.

Class 1 Military Engineer Grebenev wrote in his report:

> The aircraft is a monoplane; it has a wooden fabric-covered propeller; the fuselage is probably made from duralumin; the rudder, the elevator, and the ailerons are covered with fabric. The wing is covered with plywood [Author's note: the engineer was misled by the putty and polish, like on the Rolls-Royce]. On the wing surface, there are dents between the stringers. This testifies to either inadequate thickness or to the insufficient mastering of the technology for manufacture of such wings. The radiator is arranged under the right wing; the oil cooler is under the left wing. In flight, the engine cut off twice. I gather the fuel supply system is not perfect yet…

Arrangements of the aircraft production took a lot of time. For manufacture of the fighter, a lot of special-purpose equipment and tooling was required. Furthermore, the aircraft was supposed to be built jointly by several companies manufacturing different assemblies. Afterwards, such an approach quickly allowed boosting the output; however, the first-production Spitfire was flown as late as 15 May 1938. By the end of the year, the Royal Air Force had received only 49 aircraft.

After the onset of the Second World War, a decision was made not to send the Spitfires across the English Channel; they were saved for the British air defense forces. The number of Spitfires grew, and they were able to cope with the German Messerschmitts much better than the Hurricanes; however, the Germans shot down the Spitfires and took them as trophies as well. In March 1941, a captured Spitfire IA was demonstrated in Germany to the Soviet aviation delegation led by I.F. Petrov; moreover, test pilot S.P. Suprun was offered an opportunity to fly the aircraft. Suprun made two flights in the Spitfire, and the aircraft produced a superb impression. The pilot noted the excellent stability, controllability and the ease in performance of maneuvers, take-off and landing. The commission's report read: 'The best of the observed aircraft… is the British Spitfire single-seat fighter'. Among the drawbacks, the Soviet specialists at the time mentioned the small fuel reserve and the absence of cannons and large-caliber machine guns among the armaments.

The aircraft was being gradually improved. It was fitted with an automatic propeller, armor backrests, an armament heating system and a collimator sight. Some of the fighters were manufactured with 20mm cannons and the Mk I was superseded by the Mk II with a more powerful engine, self-sealing fuel tanks and an armored glass in the windshield.

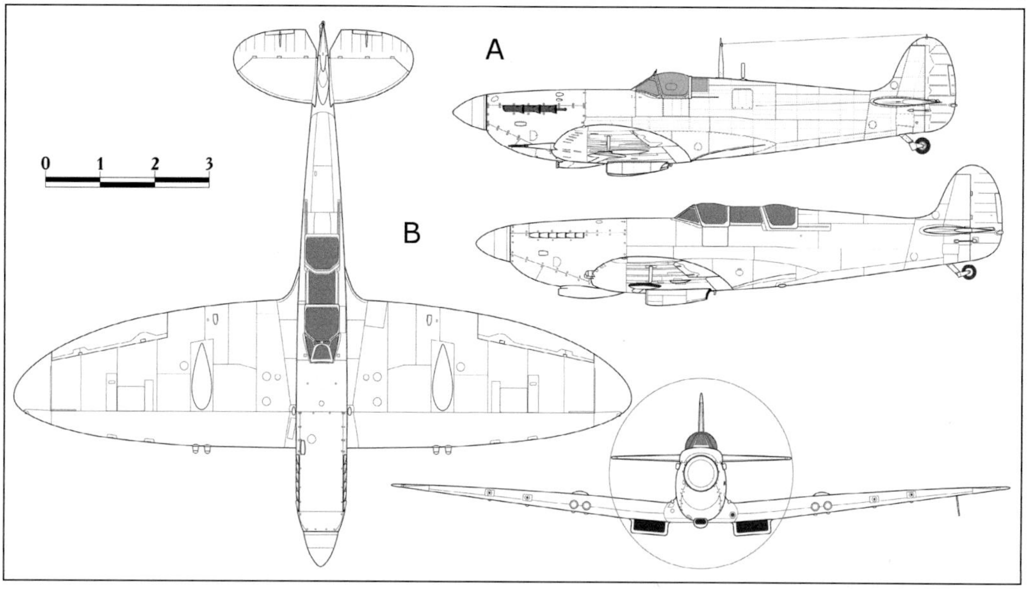

Spitfire

A Spitfire VB, with an RPK-10M radio compass.

B Three-view of the Spitfire IX UTI two-seat trainer, which was modified by the 1st Aircraft Repair Base.

Subsequent to the German invasion of the USSR, at the time when Allied relationships began to be established following Churchill's speech, the Spitfire was demonstrated in August 1941 (among other aircraft) at the Duxford base to a group of Soviet aviators. On 20 August, one of the pilots from the group even made a familiarization flight – and it was not by chance. In just two months, during the negotiations in Moscow, the fighter was offered for shipment to the Soviet Union; however, as was already discussed in the previous chapter, Stalin – being concerned about the possible difficulties with the concurrent mastering of two British fighter types – declined the offer at that time.

Beginning from February 1942, British factories were building the new Mk V with a Merlin 45 engine (1,470hp). The two-stage, gear-driven centrifugal-type supercharger ensured an excellent altitude performance by the engine. Later, other versions of the engine were used as well. The Mk V was built in Version A (with 12 machine guns), Version B (with two cannons and four machine guns) and Version C (which could carry four cannons or the same armament as Version B, but with a larger ammunition stock). Concurrently, armed and unarmed photographic reconnaissance aircraft were built on the basis of various modifications.

At the time, only single examples of the Spitfire were getting to the USSR; they came beyond the scope of official shipments. Those were no other than the reconnaissance aircraft, which were operated from the bases in the Soviet territory by the RAF units, and were left in Russia upon termination of the work period. In September 1942, three Spitfire PR IV aircraft arrived at the Afrikanda settlement in the Kola Peninsula. The small reconnaissance unit, which was under the command of Lieutenant Fairhurst, was part of the composite group (led by Group Captain Hopps) that was expected to take part in providing air cover for Convoy PQ 18 (Operation 'Orator'). The Mk IV was based on the Mk V fighter, but carried no armament; its wing's leading edge accommodated integral fuel tanks.

From Vaenga airfield, near Murmansk, the British aircraft flew to take photographs of German ships in Northern Norway. On 9 September, one of the photo reconnaissance aircraft was damaged by bomb blast fragmentation during an enemy air raid; a replacement aircraft promptly arrived. On 27 September, pilot Walker's aircraft did not return from a photographing mission in Altafjord. Upon completion of the operation, the British refused to carry out the dangerous ferrying back of the Spitfires and handed them over as a present for the Northern Fleet Air Force. In the opinion of British mechanics, two of the aircraft were quite airworthy, whereas the third one was rather a collection of spare parts than an aircraft. On 20 October 1942, all three reconnaissance aircraft were formally accepted by the Soviet party.

In spring 1943, three more Spitfire PR IVs arrived at Vaenga from the Shetland Islands, and they were led by No.543 Squadron Leader Robinson. This time, their mission was to collect intelligence for the preparation of Operation 'Source', which was, essentially, a raid by midget submarines to neutralize the battleship *Tirpitz*, which was moored in Altafjord. On 11 November, the flight and ground crews of the British units boarded a destroyer, but the aircraft were again left in Vaenga.

For the last time, the photo reconnaissance Spitfires came to the Kola Peninsula in March 1944 and worked there until the end of May. Of the three aircraft which were sent out from Sumburgh, one was lost on the way to Murmansk. Due to engine troubles, No.542 Squadron Leader Furniss was flying at too low an altitude and was initially attacked by German anti-aircraft gunners and then by Soviet ones. The latter damaged his aircraft tail assembly and the pilot had to bail out; Furniss reached Murmansk by train. Another Spitfire was discarded after an emergency landing on 19 April. On 31 May, the crew of No.542 Squadron's unit was recalled to their home country, and their last aircraft was handed over to the Northern Fleet.

Thus, in total, the Northern Fleet Air Force came into possession of seven Spitfire PR IVs. The fleet's documents provide a figure of 10 aircraft, which takes into account the entire number of Spitfires ferried to the Soviet territory – including those lost while still being under the British jurisdiction. Apparently, the photo reconnaissance aircraft which was fit for spare parts only was also restored.

All of the PR IVs were handed over to the 28th Independent Reconnaissance Air Squadron, which later joined the 118th Independent Reconnaissance Air Regiment. As of 1 January 1943, the squadron had at its disposal three Spitfires, two Tupolev SB bombers and four Petlyakov Pe-3 heavy fighters. After being handed over to Soviet pilots, the aircraft were not repainted. They retained their peculiar color scheme and all the insignias, and only the numbers on the tails was added. As for red stars instead of the British roundels, they were painted on the aircraft immediately upon arrival at Vaenga. Both British and Soviet pilots flew with the red stars; for the British, it was part of the local exotic environment.

Formations of the squadron (and later, the regiment) never included more than three or four Spitfires. They were not assigned to individual pilots, with the reason being that there were locations which only a Spitfire could reach. The criteria for the selection of flight crews were exacting. The Northern Fleet Spitfires were flown by proficient pilots who had gained their competence during pre-war time, and had considerable flight experience and an excellent piloting technique; often these were former flight school instructors.

Pilots had a high opinion of the British aircraft: it offered high speed and maneuverability, and was easy and comfortable to fly. At a high altitude, it easily evaded all German and Soviet fighters which were used in the north. The ability to fly at high speeds and altitudes made up for poor armaments, as the pilot's sole weapon was the PPSh sub-machine gun, which lied behind the back of the seat and was to be used in case of an emergency landing. The aircraft more than once demonstrated its combat survivability as well: once, Captain I.A. Platonov safely came back from a reconnaissance mission with a hole in the wing "through which one could see ground." At first, the only trouble consisted of a shortage of spare parts which were not shipped from England, so mechanics had to work wonders of resourcefulness – thus, for example, Lieutenant Manochkin fitted a Spitfire with wheels from a MiG-3.

The Spitfire was deemed the best single-engine reconnaissance aircraft in comparison to the modified (for purposes of photographic survey missions) Yak-1s, LaGG-3s, Hurricanes, Airacobras and Kittyhawks which were operated by the regiment at different times. Finally, of the single-engine aircraft, only the Spitfires and the Kittyhawks remained in service with the regiment.

Since the 118th Air Regiment belonged to the naval aviation, its principal photo survey objectives included naval stations and airfields in Northern Norway. Often the Spitfires, which were flown by Soviet and British pilots, took turns in making photos of the same targets. Altafjord and the ships that were moored there, with the dreadful *Tirpitz* in the lead, was the top-priority target for the reconnaissance aircraft. On 7 May 1943, a Soviet Spitfire managed to take photos of the battleship *Scharnhorst*; the heavy cruiser *Admiral Scheer*; two cruisers; a depot ship; and four destroyers in Altafjord.

On 12 September 1943, British pilots twice attempted to break through to the battleship's mooring location; however, the weather disrupted their plans. One of the reconnaissance officers of the Northern Fleet, Captain L.I. Yelkin (later a Hero of the Soviet Union), made his way to the German base in thick clouds. He made his first passage in the rain at an altitude of approximately 50m. The pilot waited for half an hour, and the visibility became slightly better; then he made three passages over the German base and took photographs of everything that was worthy of attention. After a six-hour flight, his Spitfire landed safely and Yelkin went on to be awarded the Order of the British Empire. On 1 April 1944, before the attack of the British ship-based aircraft on *Tirpitz*, Altafjord was photographed by two Soviet Spitfire PR IVs and a Petlyakov Pe-3.

In the 118th Independent Reconnaissance Air Regiment, the Spitfires were operated rather intensively. Pilots brought valuable information regarding the status of the enemy's forces and the layout of the enemy's ships and aircraft – thus, for example, Captain I.A. Platonov, who has already been mentioned above, discovered in March 1945 a new airfield in Bardufoss which the Germans had been successfully concealing since autumn the previous year. The navy's photo reconnaissance aircraft carried out missions for the benefit of land-based troops as well.

Among naval aviators, the Spitfire gained the reputation of a reliable and robust aircraft. None of the Spitfires was ever written off due to an accident; they either fell victims to enemy fighters, or were just reported 'missing in action' (MIA). The aircraft which Yelkin was flying before going MIA on 29 February 1944 (while he was making a voyage to Narvik) was found in Norway as late as 1993. This Spitfire's rudder is now on display in one of the Norwegian museums. In total, out of seven Soviet Spitfires, six were lost throughout the war.

Of all the received Spitfires, only two aircraft remained in service as of February 1945. A year later, one of them was handed over to the Northern Fleet Museum in Murmansk. Its further fate is unknown.

One of the Spitfire VBs which was received at a later stage of the war was, in 1943, converted into a reconnaissance aircraft similar to a PR IV. For this purpose, the VB was disarmed and fitted with a camera, and its fuel reserve was increased. In May the same year, the aircraft was tested at NII VVS and won appreciation on the part of the Institute's experts.

The Spitfires in the fighter version appeared in the Soviet Union much later than the reconnaissance aircraft did. Having had enough trouble with the Hurricanes, which were considerably inferior to the German Messerschmitt Bf 109Fs in terms of combat qualities, the Red Army Air Force Command began to insist (in an increasingly perseverant manner) that the more advanced Spitfires be shipped. On 25 September 1942, First Deputy Air Force Commander G.A. Vorozheikin expressed in his letter to Stalin a wish that before the end of the year, the Spitfires should constitute three fourths of the fighters as shipped from Great Britain and, after the beginning of 1943, the shipments should include the Spitfires only. On 4 October, the USSR Ambassador in London

I.M. Maisky officially addressed the British Government with an enquiry regarding the possibility to ship fighters of this type. In five days, Churchill returned an answer stating the readiness to furnish 150 complete aircraft, plus 50 aircraft for spare parts. The latter was brought about by the fact that the Soviet aviation (as has already been discussed above) practiced the arrangement of spare parts into individual (per single aircraft) or group (per batch of aircraft) spare part kits. The British, on the other hand, were in the habit of shipping additional fighters (usually worn ones, which were subject to dismantling) instead of group spare part kits. The pliability of the British Prime Minister was, to some extent, displayed in exchange for Stalin's consent to hand over to the British a portion of the bombers which had been brought by the Americans for the USSR to the Persian Gulf ports. Shipment of the Spitfires to the Soviet Union constituted the first case of an official handover of these aircraft to a foreign State, except for a single aircraft which was given as a present to the French in 1940. The fighters were ferried to the USSR along the southern route via Iraq and Iran.

On 10 January 1943, the ship *City of Derby* brought 35 Spitfire VBs to Basra. The rest arrived before the end of March. Some of the aircraft were damaged during transportation (including five aircraft damaged on board the *City of Lille* steamship), or were transferred to British or American units in the Middle East.

All of these aircraft had already seen service, but had been repaired in the UK before shipment. During the course of repairs, the aircraft of different series and years of manufacture had been modified to a common standard. In certain cases, such modifications resulted in the narrowing-down of the fighters' combat capabilities – thus, for example, underwing fuel tanks were removed from aircraft of later makes. Modern TR 1133 VHF radio stations were replaced with older TR 9D models (though, according to Soviet standards, the latter were quite good too).

By 1 March 1943, 150 aircraft had come from England; eighty-seven of them arrived in Basra, and were then taken to Shuaiba airfield to be assembled. For acceptance, the aircraft were sent to Abadan and, from there, the fighters – already with red stars painted on them – flew to Transcaucasia. As of the already mentioned 1 March, 15 aircraft were accepted; of them, only five flew away. In total, the Soviet party accepted 143 Spitfire Mk VBs.

In the 25th Backup Air Regiment in Transcaucasia, the conversion training of pilots from combat regiments was conducted. The 57th Guards Fighter Air Regiment, which was led by Lieutenant Colonel A.A. Osipov, was the first to master the new aircraft. In early February 1943, the regiment handed over the last four I-16s and departed for conversion training. At first, only one Spitfire was provided to the regiments; the pilots studied it diligently, but did not have the heart to fly it, for want of a flight manual. The regiment commander was the first to have a go at getting off the ground, and the task turned out to be surprisingly easy, as the Spitfire proved much simpler to fly than the extremely austere I-16. The rest of the pilots followed Osipov in mastering the new aircraft.

A team of pilots made six flights to ferry aircraft for the regiment from Tehran. On 23 April, the fighters landed in Krasnodar, and the regiment joined the 9th Guards Fighter Air Division of the 4th Air Army. Soviet troops were preparing for a new offensive, and the village of Krymskaya, which was the Germans' principal center of resistance, was to be taken first. On 28 April, combat sorties began. At first, the Spitfires were not infrequently subjected to fire from Soviet anti-aircraft units and fighters. Therefore, the regiment had to 'make a tour' of neighboring regiments in order to demonstrate the aircraft both on the ground and in flight.

On 29 April, the regiment made 28 sorties to escort bombers and attack aircraft, and 23 sorties to provide air cover for the troops. Four air battles occurred throughout the day. During the first days, bad luck pursued the 57th Air Regiment. Its failures were, for the most part, connected with the obsolete tactics of conducting horizontal combats, whereas the Spitfire was particularly good at vertical maneuvering (in the opinion of A.L. Ivanov, who fought in the 57th Air Regiment, the

Spitfire exceeded (in these aspects) both the Yak-1 and the La-5). The enemy was not to be underestimated either: the Soviet Guards had to fight against the elite Luftwaffe fighter units JG 3 and JG 52. It was, at that time, that Rall shot down a Spitfire; however, not only the Soviet aircraft were burning…

As soon as new tactics were adopted, the efficiency of combat operations grew. On 3 May, four Spitfires led by Senior Lieutenant V.E. Soldatov attacked a group of He 111 bombers near the village of Neberdzheevskaya. Soldatov shot down one of them; the rest released their bombs at random and then fled. On the same day, a battle occurred, with four Spitfires opposing 18 German bombers and 12 German fighters; one of the latter was shot down. In the twilight, another major combat took place: escorted by ten Messerschmitts, eighteen He 111s were heading for the front line. Eight aircraft of the 57th Air Regiment engaged the escorting group, while two were attacking the bombers. One of the He 111s left with a trail of smoke behind it; another exploded in mid-air. In total, in 52 combat sorties made during the day, the regiment destroyed nine German aircraft.

Battles near Krymskaya were remarkable for the high intensity of air operations, as the fighters carried out four or five combat sorties per day. During the short period of 3-8 May, pilots of the 57th Air Regiment shot down 26 enemy aircraft of various types.

The exploits of Lieutenant S.S. Azarov on 8 May 1943 became rather widely known: a flight of four Spitfires led by Senior Lieutenant V.E. Soldatov was assigned the task of covering the Il-2 attack aircraft during a raid on an airfield near the village of Krymskaya; however, on the way to the point of rendezvous with the attack aircraft (west of Abinskaya), the Spitfires were attacked by six Bf 109s; later, two more German aircraft engaged. In the unequal battle, the Soviet pilots shot down one (according to other sources, two) of the German fighters. The Soviet party lost the Spitfire which had been piloted by Lieutenant Martynov. Azarov, who had run short of ammunition, used his aircraft to cover Soldatov's Spitfire, which was being attacked by two Germans. Azarov bailed out of the burning fighter; he was burning while descending with the parachute. Later, he died from burn-related injuries. Azarov was posthumously awarded the title of Hero of the Soviet Union.

On 15 May, the regiment was redeployed to Slavyanskaya and, from there, the fighters kept flying to the front line; warfare intensity remained unabated. On 28 May, as early as 10 o'clock, pilots of the regiment claimed six aerial victories.

The regiment, however, suffered considerable losses as well: on average, there were 32 sorties per each shot-down Spitfire. Combat-worthiness also decreased due to the wear of the materiel. There was a shortage of spare engines, so mechanics had to put makeshift gaskets made from tin cans on piston rings so that the engines would continue to operate. In late June, an order was issued which prescribed that the regiment hand over the remaining Spitfires and withdraw to the rear for re-equipment purposes. Only one flight stayed at the front; its activity consisted mainly in the 'hunting' of the German FW 189 spotter reconnaissance aircraft from 'ambush' sites. On 14 June, these Spitfires were also handed over. Later, the regiment was fitted with the American P-39s.

In early August, another Spitfire regiment appeared at the front: it was the 821st Fighter Air Regiment, which was under the command of Major V.M. Chalov. As of 4 August, it had 29 fighters at its disposal. The regiment was stationed in Shakhty and Chapaevka, and fought in the ranks of the 8th Air Army near the Molochnaya River and the Mius River. Its aircraft were primarily used to provide air cover for troops near the front line, since their rather worn engines often failed. For this reason, the pilots (not infrequently) had to make forced landings. Nevertheless, only one Spitfire was written off due to non-combat reasons. Before 26 August, pilots of the 821st Fighter Air Regiment shot down five Bf 109s, three FW 189s, an FW 190 and a Ju 87. Also, a German reconnaissance aircraft was destroyed by means of a ram attack.

On 9 August, Junior Lieutenant Lobachev ran out of ammunition in a battle with two Messerschmitts. On the way back to the home airfield, he spotted an FW 189. Lobachev hit the enemy aircraft with his fighter's wing and chopped off the opponent's tail; its crew was taken prisoner.

The regiment's own losses were not large, and totaled only nine aircraft (including the one wrecked in an accident). Taking into account the replacements, which came from the 25th Backup Air Regiment, there were more combat-worthy fighters at the end of August than there had been at the beginning of the operation; however, the same as in the 57th Air Regiment, keeping the aircraft combat-worthy proved a hard task. Spare parts were scarce and none of the promised additional Spitfires had arrived. One of the fighters had to be fitted with wheels from a LaGG-3; on another one, a Soviet RSI-4 radio station was installed. Also, there were problems with the emergency landing gear extension. The system utilized compressed carbon dioxide, which was not in use with Soviet aviation, so therefore the system had to be modified to operate from compressed air.

On 26 August, the regiment was withdrawn for reorganization and its pilots never flew the Spitfires anymore – thus, the application of the Spitfire VBs at the forefront was of a local and rather brief nature. Throughout all of 1943, 28 aircraft of this type were lost in battles. Causes of such a situation are rooted in the peculiarities of the combat application of fighters over the Soviet-German Front, and in the specific features of the Spitfire as identified in the course of State tests conducted on one of the VB aircraft by NII VVS in May-June 1943. Contrary to the common practice, the tests were carried out 'retroactively'; at the time of the tests, the British aircraft had already been fighting over the Kuban. Conclusions made by the examiners coincided, in general, with the opinion of combat pilots.

It was noted that the aircraft was simple and comfortable to fly, and fit for use by pilots of even lower-than-average skills. The Merlin 46 engine developed a power of 1,165hp at an altitude of 5,800m, whereas the principal Soviet engine (M-105PA), which was installed to fighters in 1941-1942, could scarcely produce 1,050hp at 4,000m. With a gross weight approximately equal to that of the Yakovlev Yak-1, the Spitfire offered a better altitude performance and a higher ceiling.

In terms of armament, the Spitfire exceeded all Soviet fighters which existed during the first half of 1943. The weight of fire as provided by the two cannons and four machine guns amounted to 3.54kg/s. It was only later that this value was outperformed by the Yak-9T, with 3.78kg/s. Since (unlike the Hurricane) the Spitfire was used in the Soviet Union as a 'pure' fighter only, it was not fitted with either bomb racks or launching rails for rocket projectiles.

At the same time, however, the British aircraft undercarriage was not fit for operation from bumpy, grass-covered airfields. Because of the narrow track, the fighter was reeling at taxiing, and often short of touching the ground with its wing. The small 'anti-nose-over' angle sometimes caused the Spitfire to 'nuzzle' into the ground. I.F. Isayenko remembered after the war that the aircraft: "…all the time was about to plunge its nose into the ground…"

At low and medium altitude, the VB type was inferior to the up-to-date Soviet and German fighters in many aspects. Furthermore, by 1943, the Spitfire VB had become considerably obsolete; besides, the aircraft which were shipped to the Soviet Union were far from new, and could hardly demonstrate all of their capabilities. Also, a number of unpleasant drawbacks were revealed, such as the unreliability of the emergency canopy releasing system. Weapons were widely spaced over the wing in a pattern (which seemed strange to Soviet pilots), and were adjusted to distances which were inconsistent with Soviet standards.

On the other hand, the Spitfires' principal virtue consisted of good altitude performance; in this aspect, they exceeded Soviet aircraft. Therefore, the British fighters found application in the air defense forces. In 1943, the first 20 Spitfire VBs were handed over to defensive air units. First and foremost, the aircraft were sent to the Moscow region. In August 1943, they were received by the 16th Fighter Air Regiment in Lyubertsy and, sometime later, by the 67th Fighter Air Regiment.

In July 1942, the Germans began using Ju 86R high-altitude aircraft for day reconnaissance operations in the skies of the Soviet capital. At altitudes of 12,000-13,000m, they were beyond the reach of anti-aircraft artillery and the fighters which were at the disposal of the Soviet Air Force in the Moscow region.

A pair of Spitfires from the 16th Fighter Air Regiment, together with 13 other fighters of various types, took off on 22 August 1943 to intercept a Ju 86R which had already been loitering above Moscow for an hour and a half. Awaiting no threat, the German pilot made three passages above the center of the city. This was the sixth time when the Germans had demonstrated such audacity. Only one fighter – a Spitfire flown by pilot A. Semyonov – managed to get close to the German aircraft. Having climbed to 11,500m (the top limit for a Spitfire), the pilot spotted the enemy 500m above and ahead of his aircraft. Semyonov fired at the German aircraft from a nose-up position; however, the weapons froze up and failed after several shots.

Senior Lieutenant Zernov, who was of the same regiment, was not successful in attacking a Junkers either. On 6 September, he pursued a German reconnaissance aircraft until his oxygen reserve was completely used up, but to no effect.

Three (according to other data, two) Spitfire VBs in June-July 1943 were placed in service with the 2nd Guards Fighter Air Corps, which provided air cover for Leningrad. For some time, they were in operation with the 26th Guards Fighter Air Regiment.

It is probably for the purposes of the air defense forces that a suggestion was made in May 1943 that the weight of the Mk VB should be reduced by means of removing machine guns from it. The idea was approved by Chief Engineer of the Air Force A.K. Repin, and there was an intention to start with modifying one aircraft and testing it at NII VVS; however, there is no information on whether it was actually done.

In the capacity of an air defense fighter, the Spitfire's disadvantage consisted of an absence of radio navigation equipment; this made its use in adverse weather conditions and at night difficult. In Leningrad, one of the aircraft was fitted with the Soviet radio compass RPK-10M. In the air defense forces regiments, the Mk VBs remained in service until the end of the war. As of the end of 1945, the defensive air units still had 12 aircraft of this type at their disposal.

Seventeen Spitfire VBs were allocated to the naval aviation, and almost all of them were handed over to the Black Sea Fleet Air Force. In particular, they went to the 3rd Squadron of the 7th Fighter Air Regiment, whose mission was to provide air cover for naval stations on the Caucasian Coast. The regiment's multifarious materiel included the MiG-3s, P-40Es and even the I-15bis. The Spitfires were in service with the regiment until the end of 1944 and, as of 1 November, there were 10 of them.

There was an intention to use the Spitfires as catapult-launched fighters to protect large warships (in the same manner as the British Sea Hurricanes or, rather, the Italian Re 2000 Catapultabiles). The British aircraft was chosen due to their high structural strength and low weight. In late 1943, at the Kirov Lifting and Transporting Equipment Factory in Leningrad, design work was started to adapt Soviet catapults to the aircraft. In 1944, the conversion of the catapult on the *Molotov* light cruiser of the Black Sea Fleet began.

In June the same year, nine fighters of the 7th Fighter Air Regiment were handed over to the specially formed 24th Squadron of Shipboard Aviation, which was led by Major Vinogradov and stationed at Mikha-Tskhakaya airfield. Along with the fighters which were intended to be catapult-launched, the unit included a flight of Be-4 (KOR-2) reconnaissance aircraft (also launched from ship-based catapults) and a detachment of target towing airplanes which were used for the training of anti-aircraft gunners to fire on the targets towed by them.

The Spitfires which were intended to be carrier-based underwent modifications. Sockets for catapult grips were mounted under wing fillets, and part of the equipment and all cannons – together with ammunition load – were removed for weight-saving purposes.

In late august 1944, the squadron was transferred to Gelendzhik. In September, four fighters were loaded on board a barge; they were accompanied by three pilots (Senior Lieutenant A.A. Pilyuk, Lieutenant I.I. Shevchenko and Junior Lieutenant G.M. Vorobyov). The aircraft were carried to the *Molotov* cruiser. First, the fighter pilots were 'trained' on the Be-4s, which were flown by pilot Sokolov – thus, they were given a chance to feel what it was like to be catapult-launched.

At the next stage, the catapult-launching of the Spitfires began. The fighters were lifted (one by one) from the barge to the cruiser and positioned on the catapult platform. At the start, the control stick and the throttle quadrant were interlocked. Pilyuk was the first one to be 'launched'; his aircraft dropped down on 5-6m in the beginning, but then started climbing. The fighter landed successfully on a coastal airfield in Gelendzhik. Shevchenko was the second to make the flight, and Vorobyov was the third. The idea remained confined to the tests; in 1946, the 24th Squadron was disbanded.

For shipments under Protocol III, the Soviet Union requested as many as 1,200 Spitfires. Great Britain agreed to deliver 1,050 aircraft (this time, Mk IXs). The earlier Mk IX was, essentially, the same as the Mk V, but with the Merlin Series 60 engine. Its power was in excess of 1,500hp. Depending on the engine version, the Spitfire IXs were manufactured in either the configuration LF (for low altitudes), F (for medium altitudes) or HF (for high altitudes). The wing could be standard or shortened (with reduced wing tips, this allowed for increasing the rate of roll and enhancing maneuverability). In the course of mass manufacture, the aircraft was fitted with a new rudder; a retractable tailwheel; a Type E wing carrying two 20mm cannons and two 12.7mm machine guns; an additional fuel tank in the fuselage; and – at the final stages of mass production – a reduced fuselage dorsal fairing and a bubble-type round-view canopy.

The first six aircraft arrived in Basra on the *City of Eastbourne* merchant ship. Those were old aircraft which had already seen repair, and they were shipped via Iraq and Iran. A little bit later, deliveries via the northern ports began; then, brand-new fighters (just from the factories) started arriving.

Shipments of the Spitfires ended after the termination of the war in Europe. The *Sannytian* ship arrived as late as 12 June 1945 in Molotovsk (Severodvinsk) – carrying 53 fighters on board.

In total, the Soviet Union received 1,185 Spitfire IXs; of those, 1,183 were of type LF IX and two of type HF IX.

The Spitfire IXs of various versions were thoroughly studied at NII VVS. The first of them (type LF IX) was tested there in September 1944. The tests showed that the aircraft, with a powerful altitude engine, boasted a much greater service ceiling than that of any mass-manufactured Soviet fighter; it climbed steadily to 12,500m. Furthermore, an HF IX, which was tested in May through to August 1945, could climb to 13,100m. This exceeded the service ceiling of the Yak-9U by 2,450m, and that of the La-7 by 2,350m. The British fighter also exceeded them in terms of climbing ability and power of armament. The equipment which was installed on the Spitfire distinguished it to its advantage as well; however, at low and medium altitudes, the LF IX was considerably behind the up-to-date Soviet fighters – thus, for example, in terms of speed near the ground, it lost as much as 100km/h to the La-7. Therefore, the use of Spitfires at the front line was found to be inexpedient and all of them were transferred to the air defense forces' regiments.

Throughout 1944, the air defense forces received 297 aircraft. Beginning from summer, the LF IXCs and LF IXEs were handed over to the 26th and 27th Guards Fighter Air Regiments near Leningrad; the 16th and 177th Fighter Air Regiments in the Moscow region; the 767th Fighter Air Regiment near Murmansk; and also to others. For example, the 19th Fighter Air Regiment of the air defense forces was stationed at Yagodnik airfield, near Archangelsk; two of its squadrons were fitted with fighters with an ordinary wing, whereas the third squadron flew aircraft with a shortened wing. The British aircraft was welcomed in the air force units. L.B. Kocharovsky, who served in the 767th Fighter Air Regiment, remembered that in terms of piloting technique, the

Spitfire was as simple as the Yak-1, but was more inert in maneuvering, in spite of the shortened wing tips. Restrictions in respect of take-off and landing at a stiff crosswind were also a nuisance.

Of course, accidents occurred in the course of mastering the new aircraft – thus, for example, in the 177th Fighter Air Regiment, Junior Lieutenant Ivanov (during his first solo flight on 22 January 1945) broke the left landing gear leg at landing. There were worse situations as well: two days later, in the 67th Fighter Air Regiment, two fighters collided in mid-air during an attack on a target which was being towed by a target-towing airplane. Both pilots (Lieutenant M.M. Bodrov and Lieutenant P.G. Fedorov) were killed. On 18 May, in the 767th Fighter Air Regiment, Lieutenant Babonin: "… chopped off Lieutenant Semyonov's tail…" What were the consequences of the 'tail-chopping'? The author has not managed to find out yet. In most cases, however, the situations were much plainer and included omissions at landing, landings with the undercarriage retracted (young pilots tend to forget, you know…) and nose-overs on the snow. There were also cases of equipment failure – thus, on 13 June 1945, Lieutenant I.T. Zakharenkov of the 767th Fighter Air Regiment, 1st Squadron had to perform an emergency landing in a forest. The aircraft wing and part of the empennage were torn off; the pilot was killed by the trunk of a tree, which fell on the cabin.

By the end of the hostilities in Europe, 26 out of the existing 81 air defense forces regiments had been flying the Spitfires. In May 1945, the number of Spitfires as in service with the air force – including the air defense forces – totaled 859; of those, 26 were in transit. The 'lion's share' of the British fighters (826) were in use with the air defense forces' units – including 11 Mk Vs. In the combat army, the latter were almost not found at all, and the figures of the casualties looked accordingly: from among the Spitfire Vs which had been intensively used at the front line, the land-based aviation's losses throughout the war totaled 112 aircraft, whereas for the LF IXs (which had been mostly staying in the rear), the losses amounted to only 18.

The majority of the air defense forces' regiments which were fitted with the British fighters stayed rather far from the front. The exception was the Leningrad region, which was still visited by German reconnaissance aircraft. There, combat encounters between the Spitfire LF IXs and the enemy occurred. On 20 October 1944, twice Hero of the Soviet Union Major A.T. Karpov of the 27th Guards Fighter Air Regiment took off to perform an intercept mission. In climb, the pilot lost consciousness due to a failure of the oxygen system and died in the crash. The British oxygen regulator, whose tubes tended to freeze up in severe cold, was unreliable and, for this reason, was often replaced with the Soviet KPA-3 regulator.

On 8 March 1945 near Leningrad, pilots V.F. Rybin and I.M. Fedotov of the 11th and the 102nd Guards Fighter Air Regiment respectively (on the LF IXs) intercepted and shot down a German Ju 88S reconnaissance aircraft which was flying at a high altitude. Two pairs of the Spitfires took off to intercept it in accordance with radar data. Fedotov was the first to find the target, which was above the Koporsky Bay and at an altitude of 9,000m. He first performed a frontal attack and then approached the enemy from the rear; then Senior Lieutenant Rybin engaged. Together, the Soviet fighters damaged also the second engine of the reconnaissance aircraft. The Germans made a forced landing near the village of Zhuravov Konets and were taken as prisoners of war.

As already discussed, one of the Spitfire's disadvantages as an interceptor was the absence of the means of navigation and target detection in poor visibility conditions. In view of this fact, some of the aircraft were fitted with the Soviet RPK-10 radio compasses; for this purpose, the radio compasses had to be converted to be able to operate from a 12v electrical power supply system (at that time, the standard voltage in the USSR was 24v). The loop aerial was installed on the fuselage, behind the radio mast. On fighters fitted with the KPA-3 oxygen regulator, the indicator was arranged on the instrument panel in place of the British oxygen regulator; on non-modified aircraft, it was installed on a separate panel. In the 1st Fighter Army of the air defense forces, the mass installation of the RPK-10 began from 26 June 1945 under the orders of the chief engineer.

At the end of the war, two aircraft of the 26th Guards Fighter Air Regiment of the air defense forces were fitted with the RD-1 television system. Images from a ground radar station tube, with a map applied to it, was sent to the aircraft system display. The airplanes were flown by Regiment Commander Lieutenant Colonel V.A. Matsievich and Captain N.G. Shcherbina; however, no opportunity to carry out an interception and attack presented itself during the tests.

Of the two HF IXs, one was left at NII VVS and the other was probably handed over to the 16th Fighter Air Regiment; in November 1944, a certain 'Spitfire 9G' was listed in the regiment's books among other aircraft. No major modifications were carried out on the aircraft in the air defense forces, although sometimes, oxygen masks were replaced with Soviet ones and SCh-3 IFF transponders were also installed. The Spitfire-operating regiments of the air defense forces were regarded as the most battle-worthy of all regiments fitted with imported aircraft.

Initially, the Resolution of the Council of Ministers of 22 March 1946 prescribed (as part of the post-war reduction in force) that 1,139 Spitfires be written off; however, the Resolution was not complied with. The Spitfires remained for several more years in service with the Soviet aviation until 1947-1948 and, at some locations, even until 1951, which was when the conversion to jet-propelled aircraft began. For example, the 177th Fighter Air Regiment was converted to the Yak-17s in 1948 in Yaroslavl. The 19th Fighter Air Regiment, which was stationed at Vaskovo airfield in Archangelsk, began receiving the La-9s in autumn 1949.

The Spitfire was much appreciated by pilots (first and foremost) on account of its ease of piloting. The LF IX modification retained several 'inherited vices' from its predecessors (e.g. the low anti-nose-over angle; the unstable narrow-track landing gear; and the poor rearward view); however, the pilots eventually got used to them and learned to compensate for them. The Spitfire played an important role during the post-war years as a high-altitude training fighter. Pilots practiced high-altitude flying in the Spitfires before the conversion to jet fighters.

For training purposes, several aircraft were modified into the two-seater Spitfire IXUTI (sometimes also referred to as 9U, or Sp 9U) with an enclosed cockpit. Such aircraft were at the disposal of different regiments, and they were made in the air force aircraft repair shops.

On 25 September, test parachute-jumper V.G. Romanyuk made a jump from a two-seater Spitfire's cockpit at an altitude of 13,108.5m. He was falling for 107 seconds without drawing the parachute, but then he landed safely. The Spitfire in this flight was piloted by A. Proshakov; however, the triumph of having achieved the world record was marred: on the same day, at Podolsk airfield, N.A. Amitaev was killed in a high-altitude jump from an aircraft of the same type because of a rupture in the tube of the oxygen regulator.

Thus, in spite of the fact that the battle achievements of the Spitfire at the Soviet-German Front were rather modest, this aircraft left a remarkable imprint in the history of Soviet aviation; however, none of the Russian museums has a Spitfire on display. An Mk IX, which was found near Murmansk, was taken to the Isle of Wight to be restored.

A Spitfire VB ready for ferrying to the USSR at Hapmat airfield in Iraq.

Spitfires that have been prepared for handover to Soviet representatives. The aircraft in the foreground (s/n EP465) was later flown by Junior Lieutenant Egorov of the 821st Fighter Air Regiment. He flew four combat sorties in it and was killed on 9 August 1943 in an air combat above Krymskaya village.

The Spitfire VB, which was modified in the USSR in a similar vein to the PR Mk IV reconnaissance version, during tests at NII VVS in 1943.

The Spitfire camera lens in the side camera window.

A Spitfire VB during test at NII VVS in May 1943.

A Spitfire VB of the 57th Guards Fighter Air Regiment, Kuban, 1943.

A Spitfire VB of a service regiment.

This Spitfire VB of the 2nd Guards Fighter Air Corps of Air Defense Forces was equipped with an RPK-10M radio compass, Leningrad, 1945.

The lightened Spitfire VB of the 24th Squadron of Naval Aviation on the catapult of the *Molotov* light cruiser of the Black Sea Fleet, September 1944.

A Spitfire on a catapult carriage; note the removed cannons.

The Spitfire V of the 2nd Guards Fighter Air Corps of Air Defense Forces, Leningrad, 1945.

A Spitfire LF IX with shortened wing tips during tests at NII VVS in September 1944.

A Spitfire HF IX during tests at NII VVS in May 1945; note the incorrect orientation of the fuselage star – indicating that the insignias were applied in the UK.

Hero of the Soviet Union Lieutenant Colonel V.A. Matsievich (Commander of the 26th Guards Fighter Air Regiment) in front of a Spitfire LF IX.

Pilot Mayboroda of the 26th Guards Fighter Air Regiment near his Spitfire.

The Spitfire LF IX in flight.

An unknown pilot on the wing of a Spitfire LF IX.

Pilots and technicians of the 2nd Guards Fighter Air Corps at an airfield near Leningrad in 1945.

Pilots of a fighter regiment in front of the Spitfire LF IX.

A meeting of the 26th Guards Fighter Air Regiment at an airfield near Leningrad in 1945.

A formation of the 26th Guards Fighter Air Regiment personnel near their aircraft in 1945.

Pilot V.F. Rybin of the 11th Guards Fighter Air Regiment, who took part in an air combat on 8 March 1945, in which a Ju 88S German reconnaissance aircraft was shot down.

The crash of a Spitfire of the 1st Squadron, the 767th Fighter Air Regiment on 13 June 1945. Pilot Lieutenant Zakharenkov perished in the crash.

A commanding officer visiting one of the air defense regiments equipped with Spitfires.

Lieutenant L.B. Kachorovsky getting out of the cockpit of his Spitfire LF IX; the 767th Fighter Air Regiment, 1947.

A post-war group photo of maintenance personnel near a Spitfire IX.

A Spitfire IX being prepared for the next mission.

A group of pilots in front of a Yakovlev Yak-9; note the Spitfire IX in the background.

The installation of a loop aerial of the RPK-10M radio compass on the fuselage of a Spitfire LF IX.

The installation of a radio compass control panel on the right wall of the cockpit.

A Spitfire IX UTI two-seat trainer, which has been modified by the 1st Aviation Repair Base, Leningrad, summer 1945.

Commander of the 26th Guards Fighter Air Regiment of Air Defense Forces Lieutenant Colonel Matsievich during a briefing near a Spitfire IX UTI in 1945.

7.3 Curtiss P-40 Tomahawk/Kittyhawk

Fighters of the P-40 family (known in the Soviet Union under their British names 'Tomahawk' and 'Kittyhawk') are ranked third in the Soviet aviation throughout the Great Patriotic War in terms of quantities – being behind only the Airacobras and the Hurricanes – and they were the first American aircraft shipped to the USSR under the military assistance program.

When Germany invaded the USSR, and Great Britain – represented by Prime Minister Churchill – declared its willingness to render military assistance, the issue of choosing the aircraft types to be shipped arose. On 18 July, the Soviet Ambassador addressed the British Government on the issue and, two days later, the British Air Ministry decided to allocate 200 Tomahawks. These included both the aircraft already delivered to Great Britain, and the ones which were still staying in the USA. In the documents of the British Government (which were published later), the following rationale for such a decision was provided: aircraft of this type were not in use with the British aviation in Europe; they were about to be withdrawn from service in the Middle East; and they were of American origin. Therefore, the British were not responsible for their quality and supply of spare parts. On 25 July, Churchill (in his letter) informed Stalin of the decision.

A day earlier, the US Undersecretary of State advised Soviet Ambassador K.A. Umansky of the Americans' readiness to soon provide at least a squadron of the P-40s. The documents brought to Moscow by A. Harriman – the representative of the US President – contained a more precise figure of 900 fighters to be shipped before June 1942. It should be noted that Chief of the US Army Air Force H. Arnold intended to give to the USSR mostly the P-40s for the reason that it was the only mass-produced American land-based fighter.

The Curtiss Hawk 81A (that was its original name) was designed under the direction of D.R. Berlin in the middle of 1938 and was, essentially, a combination of the airframe of the P-36A (Hawk 75) fighter (version of the year 1935) and the new Allison V-1710 liquid-cooled row engine. The name 'Hawk' was traditionally given to all Curtiss fighters, with the project number added to it. In January 1939, the prototype XP-40 outperformed both the future Airacobra and the Lightning. This brought to Curtiss a very large (at that time) contract for 524 aircraft, with its total cost being approximately 13 million US dollars. As soon as May 1940, the US Army Air Force began acceptance of the first mass-manufactured P-40s.

It could hardly be said that the P-40's flight performance was exceptionally impressive: the armament consisted of two 12.7mm machine guns arranged under the engine cowling; however, the aircraft was rather easy as regards operation and piloting, and was based on a design that was well known to production personnel, as well as being quite fit for mass manufacture. That was exactly what the American military aviation (which was then on the upswing) needed; then the company received large orders from Great Britain and France. Taking into account the wishes of new customers (who had, already, acquired a certain battle experience), the company gradually introduced armor; installed self-sealing fuel tanks; and made the armaments more powerful. First, two 7.62mm machine guns were added in the wings (on the P-40B); then, two more machine guns were installed (on the P-40C and its export version, the H.81A-1 for France), but the French had suffered a defeat earlier than they had received at least one fighter. The entire batch went to the British, and they named the aircraft 'Tomahawk I'. The Royal Air Force considered the aircraft unfit for combat application. Their flight performance parameters were not high, whereas vulnerability was considerable (at that time, they had neither the armor, nor the sealing protector in the tanks). Therefore, they were used as trainer aircraft.

The next large batch (ordered by the British themselves) was designated 'Tomahawk II'. Those aircraft had both armor and a layer of protective rubber in the tanks; however, by that time, the Battle of Britain had been won, the manufacture of the Spitfires and the Hurricanes was successfully growing, and the RAF Command had become more selective.

The British agreed to provide a hundred of the Tomahawk IIs to China (these aircraft were later flown by the famous *Flying Tigers*); two-hundred were to go to the Soviet Union. On 1 September 1941, an Allies' convoy arrived in the port of Archangelsk with the first 48 fighters (the Hurricanes and the Tomahawks from England) on board. The assembly work was started at the wooden airfield named 'The 10th Kilometer', which had been hurriedly constructed by camp prisoners. To provide assistance in the assembly and mastering of the aircraft, a team of mechanics and engineers arrived from Great Britain; earlier (in late June), Lieutenant Alison (a specialist for the P-40) and Instructor Pilot Zemke had come from the USA. The aircraft turned out easy to fly: it took Military Acceptance Specialist Major N.I. Khramov several hours to learn piloting the Tomahawk; then, he took off and performed a series of complex aerobatic maneuvers in it.

In the second half of September, pilots of NII VVS ferried six Tomahawks from the Archangelsk region to the 27th Backup Air Regiment in Kadnikov, as it was intended that the conversion training of flight and ground crews should be started there. Assembly facilities were shifted to the Sokol settlement at a distance of 15km from Kadnikov. There, workshops were arranged under the direction of Engineer Chasovikov, who was assisted by four British specialists. The fighters were coming in boxes via railway.

In late September 1941, instructors of the 27th Backup Air Regiment were assigned a combat mission which consisted of the escorting of a transport aircraft carrying a delegation of the Allies to a conference in Moscow. The escort party included three Tomahawks led by Major Belozerov. The party arrived successfully in the Soviet capital; however, on the way back – during the take-off from Chkalovskaya airfield, near Moscow – the engine of Belozerov's fighter failed. The aircraft fell down and burned out, together with the pilot. That was the first P-40 lost by the Soviet Air Force.

The conference to which the British and American representatives were flying was dedicated to the problem of military assistance to the USSR. The issues to be discussed included updating the amount of shipments and the types of various military aircraft to be shipped. Recommendations as prepared by the Intelligence Directorate of the General Staff and the Chief Air Force Administration mentioned the P-40 among the aircraft, shipments of which were desirable. There was a reservation: the variants earlier than the P-40E were considered obsolete; however, the situation was critical: the Soviet Air Force was experiencing huge losses and, in such conditions, was willing to receive any combat-worthy aircraft.

Initially, the shipments from the USA were arranged on a 'cash-and-carry' basis. Before 23 September, 68 P-40s of earlier modifications were purchased and the shipment began in October; before late November, 39 aircraft left the American ports. These also included a batch of P-40 fighters, with preparations of which starting in early July. Among the arrivals, there were twenty P-40s and a P-40G (a modification of the P-40, with the P-40C's wing and additional machine guns). By the end of December, as many as 76 aircraft had left the USA. In total, before the end of 1941, 230 Tomahawks had passed military acceptance in the Soviet territory. Of them, 23 aircraft were of type IIA and the majority of the rest were of type IIB; these differed (mostly) in radio equipment. There were also several aircraft of type I.

A Tomahawk IIA (s/n AH975), which came with the first batch of aircraft from Great Britain on 25 September 1941, was examined at NII VVS. Later, it passed State tests in accordance with the established procedure. In particular, it took part in training combats with the German Messerschmitt Bf 110 two-engine fighter. The Air Force Command did not quite appreciate the results: with a maximum speed of 545km/h, the aircraft was inferior to the Yak-1, LaGG-3 and the MiG-3. The Yakovlev Yak-1 considerably exceeded the American aircraft in terms of rate of climb, whereas the MiG-3 offered a better service ceiling. The absence of cannons made firing from a large distance impossible, but on the other hand, the weight of fire was rather high; it was almost thrice higher than, for example, the MiG-3's performance in the configuration with three

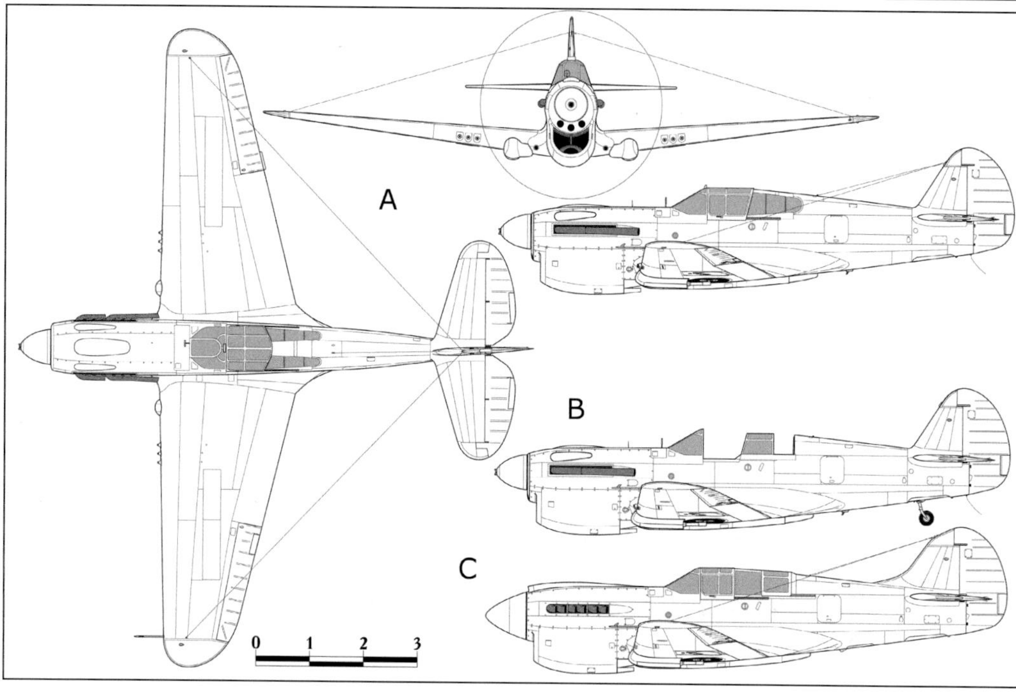

P-40

A Three-view of the P-40E, which was powered by the M-105 engine.
B Two-seat trainer versions of the P-40E, which was powered by the M-105 engine.
C The P-40EF two-seat reconnaissance version.

machine guns. The armor backrest protected the pilot only from rifle-caliber bullets. The tanks were self-sealing, but without the inert gas filling system, and the oxygen equipment was obsolete.

The reported advantages of the Tomahawk included good take-off and landing performance; a satisfactory horizontal maneuverability; and considerable (according to Soviet standards) operational range and endurance. Also, the canopy featured good transparency. The windows did not distort the image; the movable section could be secured in any intermediate position, or dropped in an emergency event. It was mentioned that the aircraft was well suited for night flying: it had a headlight, and there was good lighting for the instruments and for the sighting device. For wintertime operations, a device to dilute oil with fuel was provided.

Specialists of NII VVS recommended using the Tomahawk in the air defense forces for the escorting of bombers, and in the capacity of a light attack aircraft to combat infantry troops at the front line.

It was the air defense forces' regiments that received the first Tomahawks, and the 126th Fighter Air Regiment was the first to master the American aircraft. The regiment entered the action on 12 October and took part in the defense of Moscow, as well as acting on the Western Front and at the Kalinin Front. Within a month (before 15 November), its pilots made 685 combat sorties on the Tomahawks and shot down 17 enemy aircraft. Senior Lieutenant S.G. Ridnyy, who was flying a Tomahawk, was awarded the title of Hero of the Soviet Union.

Sometime later (in November), the 154th Fighter Air Regiment began operations in the Leningrad Front using the Tomahawks. On 28 October, the regiment received 20 disassembled fighters at Kadnikov airfield; as soon as 26 November, the first combat sortie was carried out. In December, the 159th Fighter Air Regiment joined the frontline air force; in January 1942, the 196th Fighter Air Regiment came to the front. All of these regiments constituted part of the Eastern Operations Group, whose purpose was to provide cover for transport aircraft which were bringing cargoes to the sieged Leningrad across Ladoga.

The Germans tried hard to destroy the 'air bridge', and the Tomahawks made their contribution to repelling their assaults. For example, on 17 December 1941, P.A. Pokryshev of the 154th Fighter Air Regiment (with a flight of five P-40s) engaged nine Messerschmitts in order to protect the transport aircraft. On another day, Squadron Leader Pilyutov had to escort nine PS-84 transport aircraft alone. In a battle with six Germans, he shot down two of them, but was shot down himself.

In the navy, the regiments of the Northern Fleet were the first to master the fighters of this type. The 2nd Guards Composite Air Regiment received 20 Tomahawks at Vaenga airfield.

On the whole, the Soviet pilots had a better opinion of the Tomahawk than of the Hurricane, but everybody agreed that the Tomahawk was, in many aspects, inferior to both the Soviet and German fighters. V.M. Perov (later a famous polar pilot), who had served with the 27th Backup Air Regiment, wrote in his memoirs about the Tomahawks: '... The American aircraft ... proved to be of rare clumsiness and heavy weight...'

Documents of the People's Commissariat of Aviation Industry contained this statement: 'The aircraft won approval on the part of the flight crew in respect of its take-off and landing performance, horizontal maneuverability, and piloting technique. However, in terms of maximum horizontal speeds and rate of climb, it is inferior to the Me-109F'. On the whole, this is an unbiased opinion.

The maintenance of the Tomahawks in the USSR brought a lot of trouble: electrical power generators tended to fail and were replaced with Soviet GS-650 generators. The defect revealed itself as early as during the tests in the USA and, on account of that, the Americans were not surprised when as many as 300 generators were requested from them in January 1942. Many problems were connected with engines: the V-1710 engines were fitted with bearings whose inserts were made of the so-called 'white alloy' (lead, silver and a small quantity of cadmium). Such bearings ensured a better performance at high speeds and severe loads, but were very sensitive to the quality of oil and the presence of dust in it. Besides, they required precise adjustment at installation. Furthermore, the Allison engine featured a whole set of short-time augmented power modes – and to use them, sufficient skill was required, otherwise the oil could become overheated; the bearings could be melted and jammed; and the piston-rods could be torn off. All of this often brought about accidents, and oil system defects caused fires in flight. For example, this was the case when Hero of the Soviet Union P.T. Kharitonov of the 964th Fighter Air Regiment was burning in his aircraft. At first, the V-1710 engines failed to serve out more than 35-40 percent of their lifetime in the Soviet aviation, and the situation was aggravated by a shortage of spare parts.

The Russian winter was too severe for the Tomahawks, and they proved entirely unsuited for it. Engines could only be started by means of an electric starter; however, at temperatures as low as -5°C, the starter was unable to bring the engine to rotation. Units were sending in urgent requests to fit the propellers with a claw clutch, in order to be able to connect it to the arm of the automobile starter unit. The standard coolant, which was, essentially, a mixture of Preston and distilled water, froze at -12°C, which was not an infrequent temperature for the temperate zone of middle Russia; the cold caused oil cooler cores to rupture (sometimes even in flight). A report from the 154th Fighter Air Regiment read: 'On the night of 5 December 1941 (at minus 26), nine oil coolers ruptured, in spite of having been warmed up every 1.5 to 2 hours'. The 126th Fighter Air Regiment reported a rupture in an oil line along the weld seam near the thermostatic regulator. The oil tank was located at a considerable distance from the engine; after the start, it took a significant time for the long tube to warm up. The oil, at first, was not completely drained from the line, and pilots (in a hurry to take off) attempted to warm up the engines at a high rpm. The consequences were deplorable: the weld seam failed because of a high pressure in the pipe, which was blocked with frozen oil.

The inner tubes of tires could not withstand the cold and were bursting; hydraulic fluid was getting thick – leading to problems with landing gear extension. If brakes of a grounded aircraft were left engaged, it took the wheel a long time to become released.

All these troubles were solved in different ways: drain valves were installed to fully drain oil for the night, and imported hydraulic fluid and Preston anti-freeze were replaced with Soviet (i.e. more frost-proof) equivalents.

The quantity of rounds which came for the first batches of Tomahawks was too small; as regards incendiary and tracer bullets, there were none at all. On 20 November 1941, the Chief Air Force Administration applied to the People's Commissariat for Aviation Industry with a request to attempt to re-weapon the American fighters with Soviet BS (12.7mm) and ShKAS (7.62mm) machine guns. Two options were considered: the first consisted of the installation of four ShKAS machine guns in the wing and two Berezin machine guns in the fuselage; the other option implied replacing only the wing guns. The first variant proved rather difficult to implement, as the installation of the BS machine gun required a different mount type; a more powerful timing unit; new boxes for longer rounds; and a compressed-air bolt operation mechanism. Furthermore, the Berezin machine gun was manufactured with a single-way feed; for this reason, only one BS could be installed instead of two Colts. When installed normally, the Soviet machine gun ejected empty cartridge cases sideways – thus, they might hit the stabilizer leading edge. For mounting a BS with its belt-fed mechanism directed upwards, it would be needed to modify the engine cowling by means of hammering. With the wing machine guns, the situation was simpler: it was enough to change the mounts; to replace the ammunition boxes (with narrower ones); to cut out new access holes; and to introduce the electric trigger.

Options for the rearmament of the Tomahawk were discussed until early 1942, but finally, the idea was totally discarded; however, some of the American fighters were fitted with rocket projectiles. For ground attack purposes, four rail launchers for RS-82 rocket projectiles were arranged under the wing.

In the USSR, the combat survivability of the Tomahawk was found to be insufficient. The Allies were, therefore, requested to further provide aircraft with enhanced armor and an inert gas filling system for fuel tanks.

In the beginning of the war, the Red Army was constantly retreating. Air units were frequently redeployed and not all of the airfields were duly prepared. The situation became aggravated as winter set in, when the pilots had to take off from snow and to land on it. There were not enough vehicles to tramp down the snow, so for this reason, the Soviet Air Force once again began to use skis on aircraft. There was an idea to fit the Tomahawks with a retractable ski as well; however, it turned out that this would have entailed rather serious modifications of the landing gear, and of the aircraft itself – thus, projects relating to such modifications are not known.

In spring 1942, a lot of the P-40s became grounded on account of a shortage of spare engines. On the initiative of the 154th Fighter Air Regiment Commander A.A. Matveev and Colonel Engineer P. Malikov, a modification of the Tomahawks was attempted to fit them with the Soviet engines M-105P and M-105R. The parts and assemblies for the new power plant installations were found at the facilities of the evacuated Factory No.23 in Leningrad, where the LaGG-3s had been manufactured. The M-105 engine was smaller and lighter than the Allison engine and, therefore, it did not require much effort to find room for it under the cowling. The Soviet engine was arranged somewhat higher than the American one, and the spinner of the VISh-61P propeller was much smaller than that of the original. For this reason, an adapter ring was installed, in which holes were made to supply air to the supercharger. The entire exhaust system was that of the LaGG-3. A certain quantity of aircraft in this modification was manufactured by the 1st Repair Base, and they were used at the Leningrad Front by the 196th Fighter Air Regiment.

To carry out the conversion training of pilots to fly the new fighter – and to train flight crews – several makeshift two-seater aircraft were made. Their second (rather narrow) cabin was arranged in the fuselage fairing.

The Tomahawks were still shipped to the USSR in early 1942, but in rather modest quantities (only 17 of them were received); however, the aircraft (which had arrived earlier) were used both as replacements for frontline units and to equip the new units. In January, they were received by one of the squadrons of the 20th Guards Fighter Air Regiment and, sometime later, by the entire 964th Fighter Air Regiment. By the beginning of 1943, there had already been no Tomahawks left at the front line; however, they were still operating at some locations in the rear areas. In the air defense forces, 27 Tomahawks saw the victory over Germany.

At the time when the Tomahawks were entering action in the snows of Russia, the US factories began manufacturing aircraft of new generation – namely the Hawk 87s (the British referred to it as 'Kittyhawk'). The upgraded fighter had a more advanced engine (the V-1710-39 instead of the V-1710-33), which featured better altitude performance and offered the possibility of short-time augmentation (the so-called 'War Emergency Power'). At the same time, the designers modified the entire fuselage: it became lower, and its contours were changed to provide a better view from the cockpit. The engine was shifted upwards, which allowed shortening the landing gear legs, but at the same time, it 'ousted' the machine guns from under the wing – thus, all of the machine guns were concentrated in the wing. Such a concept allowed launching mass production of the aircraft in a very short time; on the other hand, however, it was, from the very beginning, doomed to retain the drawbacks of its predecessor.

The Soviet Union received the first Kittyhawks from Great Britain. Fourteen aircraft were unloaded in Archangelsk before the end of 1941, and all of the first batches arrived via the northern ports.

The aircraft entered action in the northern segments of the Soviet-German Front as well. The first Kittyhawks were handed over to regiments which had already mastered the Tomahawk (i.e. the 126th Air Regiment and the 154th Air Regiment). The latter, by late February 1942, had already had at its disposal almost as many P-40Es as aircraft of earlier types, but the Kittyhawks were arriving in greater quantities than the Tomahawks. For this reason, more and more air units began receiving them. In spring, these aircraft arrived at some squadrons of the 258th Combined Air Division's regiments (the 19th and the 20th Guards Fighter Air Regiment). The division fought at the Karelian Front, and the first to master the new aircraft there was the 2nd Squadron of the 19th Guards Fighter Air Regiment, which was led by A.Y. Novozhilov. This took place in April; as soon as 15 May, the regiment entered action again. At approximately the same time, the first Kittyhawks were received by the 122nd Fighter Air Division of the air defense forces, which had previously been equipped with only the Hurricanes.

In the Western countries, the P-40 was used primarily as an attack aircraft and fighter bomber. Therefore, its improvements were intended to meet the application needs – and thus, the armor was strengthened; the bomb rack was introduced; and the speed (due to enhanced aerodynamics and a more powerful engine) and range were increased, but this led to an increase in the fighter's weight, which led to a considerable worsening of the climb rate and a reduction in the service ceiling. Further negative consequences included an increase in the maneuvering time; the length of the take-off run; and (especially) the landing run. All of these disadvantages manifested themselves rather clearly during the tests of the P-40E at NII VVS in July 1942. Having studied the strengths and weaknesses of the aircraft, the specialists made efforts to find suitable applications for it. At the same time, the number of Kittyhawks in the Soviet Union was growing.

From mid-1942, aircraft of this type were ferried via Iran. In autumn the same year, ferrying of the Kittyhawks via the ALSIB route began. On 11 September, US Lieutenant Andersson brought a group of twenty-two P-40Ks to Ladd Field in Alaska. Exactly a month later, on 11 October, Soviet ferry pilots – led by Captain Finogenov – took them westward. A Boston A-20B bomber was in the lead of the fighters' group. On the following day, the group landed in Uelkal. Having completed all stages of the 'ferrying relay' in the first days of November, the P-40Ks arrived in Krasnoyarsk; two fighters had been lost en route (they had become lost in fog after the departure from Uelkal). The second group took the route on 3 November. The number of P-40s ferried via the ALSIB route was not large (only 43 aircraft), and all of them were of Mk K.

The P-40K featured a more powerful V-1710-73 engine and a fillet near the root portion of the vertical stabilizer. Beginning from the K-10 series, they also had a longer tail portion of the fuselage, which led to a shift of the center of gravity in the aft direction. To countermeasure possible spin conditions, the manufacturing company recommended underfilling the aft tank with fuel. Later, the center of gravity was brought back to almost the initial position by means of the relocation of certain equipment. The next series was the P-40M with the V-1710-81 engine, which allowed increasing the maximum speed to a certain extent and improving the rate of climb. The P-40Ms were manufactured in the USA solely for export purposes. Some of the P-40M-5 aircraft, which were shipped via the southern route, were fitted with 'tropical' filters in the engine air intake.

The last mass-manufactured aircraft of this large family was the P-40N. It represented the last attempt to improve the aircraft without any drastic changes in design; however, the amount of modifications was large. For weight-saving purposes, aluminum coolers and new wheels were introduced; one of the fuel tanks was removed; and the combat stock was reduced. In the first series, even two machine guns out of six were removed. The N-5 and the subsequent series received a new cockpit canopy with a better field of view. These aircraft were also coming to the USSR in considerable quantities.

Altogether throughout 1942, 487 Kittyhawks were accepted. In November, the 2nd Guards Fighter Air Regiment of the Northern Fleet Air Force was partially equipped with them. At the end of the same month, the 46th Fighter Air Regiment, which was under the command of Major Mukhin, joined the North-Western Front. It began combat operations from Vypolzovo airfield as part of the 5th Guards Air Division. The regiment fought above the 'Demyansky Corridor', via which the encircled 16th Army of the Wehrmacht was provided with supplies from Staraya Russa. In early 1943, the 2nd Squadron of the 45th Fighter Air Regiment, which was under the command of I.M. Dzusov, was also converted to such fighters. Later, the re-equipment of the frontline units was combined with conversion training in backup regiments. The principal part here was given to the 22nd Backup Air Regiment. Throughout 1943, a still greater quantity of Kittyhawks arrived (939); accordingly, the coverage of units and formations fitted with such aircraft became larger, and more than two tenths of regiments at different times flew these aircraft.

The 191st Fighter Air Regiment fought in the Leningrad region in P-40Ms. In August 1943, it conducted active operations near the Sinyavin Heights and made a contribution to the covering of Soviet troops in the forefront by machine gunning the enemy lines. By autumn, the role of ground attack aircraft had become the principal role for the Kittyhawks. To enhance their efficiency, the aircraft were fitted with launching rails for RS-82 rocket projectiles in summer 1944. The first combat sortie with the launching rails consisted of supporting the troops cutting across the Vuoksa River. On the way, the fighters encountered a group of eight Ju 88s and four FW 190s. The fighters fired a salvo of rockets on them, but none were shot down; however, the enemy lost courage and turned back. Later, RS-82 rocket projectiles were successfully used against ground targets more than once.

Since 1943, the principal inflow of the Kittyhawks was directed to the air defense forces, and here were reasons for this: the idea was to use the advantages of the aircraft, such as powerful armaments (in spite of the fact that the P-40E was, in terms of weight of fire, somewhat inferior to the German FW 190A-3 and the British Spitfire VC, although it exceeded both the Messerschmitt Bf 109F and the American Bell P-39D); long range; high endurance; viability; and good (considering the Soviet standards at that time) radio equipment and instrumentation – thus, the following were selected as its principal areas of application: the provision of air cover for cities and important air defense locations; the escorting of bombers and torpedo bombers; unassisted bombing and strafing attacks; and air reconnaissance.

On the part of Soviet pilots, the attitude towards the Kittyhawk was dualistic. On the one hand, it was undoubtedly ranked higher than the Hurricane, but on the other hand (in practice), they felt the insufficiency of its capabilities in air battles. Here is the opinion of the already mentioned V.M. Perov: "Our combat pilots liked its vast cockpit with good back visibility, and decent navigation equipment ... On the whole, the aircraft was mediocre and considerably overweight." B.V. Veselovsky (of the 46th Fighter Air Regiment) wrote in his memoirs: '... Our Kitties ... were inferior to the Messers in many aspects. They had lower speed and a much greater weight, which made vertical fighting difficult. We tried to fight using maneuvers...'

The Kittyhawk was not quite suitable for battles with enemy fighters; however, due to its speed and powerful armament, it was efficient against enemy bombers. At altitudes higher than 4,500m, the P-40E outdistanced the Yak-1, in spite of the fact that in the West, the V-1710 engine was considered to be of low altitude. A high cruise flight endurance allowed loitering above the facility or area being guarded. The Kittyhawk had two principal disadvantages as an interceptor, with those being the low service ceiling and a poor rate of climb. Nevertheless, it was used both for day and night flights. Due to the lack of any device for target detection in darkness, the aircraft was unable to carry out unassisted searches in the absence of visibility, whereas insufficient navigation equipment prevented the fulfilment of commands from a ground control perspective because of problems with orientation in flight. These disadvantages manifested themselves in the course of repelling a German attack on an American base in Mirgorod in June 1944, when the fighters of the 310th Air Defense Forces Fighter Air Division – which took off in response to an alarm signal on a dark, moonless night – failed to detect any of the aircraft from the German detachment; however, sometimes these fighters operated rather successfully at night. To illuminate airborne targets, each Kittyhawk carried an SAB-50 bomb. The aircraft were flying in pairs, with one aircraft to approach the target from above and illuminate it, and the other to attack. On the night of 13 March 1943, eight fighters were patrolling the approaches to Murmansk. In the light of a falling bomb, Junior Lieutenant Bokiy attacked a Ju 88; the German bomber fell near Lake Kod-Yavr. Some air defense force units used special-purpose 'lamplighter' aircraft, and they carried six SAB-100 bombs each under the wing and dropped them one by one to illuminate targets for the assault team, which was flying at a lower altitude. To facilitate piloting at night and in low-visibility conditions, some of the P-40s were fitted with Soviet RPK-10 radio compasses. Its loop aerial was installed on the fuselage behind the cockpit canopy – thus, in the 309th Fighter Air Regiment of Air Defense Forces in August 1944, approximately one third of the Kittyhawks were equipped with the radio compasses. Beginning from early 1944, when a rather extensive radar observation network had already come into existence, the Kittyhawks were also fitted with SCh-1 (later, SCh-3) IFF transponders. At the end of 1944, the air defense forces had more than 900 Kittyhawks at their disposal. By the moment of the capitulation of Germany, six regiments had been flying the Kittyhawks and there were one or two such aircraft in service with other regiments.

The naval aviation was also attracted by the P-40s' high endurance. As has already been discussed, the first aircraft of this type appeared there in spring 1942. They were handed over to the 2nd Guards Composite Air Regiment of the Northern Fleet Air Force, which used them primarily for the air cover of convoys. Before summer 1942, the navy's pilots received 27 aircraft, plus 21 more during the following year, but that was enough only to make up for losses; however, in the second half of 1943, the P-40s of different modifications began arriving in the hundreds. Finally, the number of P-40s in the naval aviation exceeded that of the Hurricanes. In late 1943, the conversion of the 27th and the 78th Air Regiments of the Northern Fleet to Kittyhawks began, whereas the 2nd Guards Fighter Air Regiment (the former 2nd Guards Composite Air Regiment) exchanged its P-40Es for Airacobras.

From 1943, the Kittyhawks saw service with the Black Sea Fleet; they were handed over to the 7th and the 62nd Fighter Air Regiments. By 1 January 1944, each of the two regiments had already had ten P-40Ks at its disposal. The composition of both regiments in terms of aircraft was rather motley: the 7th Fighter Air Regiment also had in service (along with the P-40Ks) the MiG-3s, Spitfire VBs and I-15bis; the 62nd Fighter Air Regiment was flying the LaGG-3s, I-153s and I-15bis. The first operational mission assigned to the American fighters consisted of providing air cover for the Black Sea Coast of the Caucasus at the segments from Dzhubga to Gagry and from Gagry to Kobuleti. The Kittyhawk squadrons were stationed at the Myskhako, Lazarevskaya and Mikha-Tskhakaya airfields, and flew routine patrol and occasional intercept missions against German reconnaissance aircraft. The Kittyhawks took part in the repelling of a mass raid of enemy aviation on Poti on 22 April 1943. In the American fighter, Commander of the 7th Fighter Air Regiment K.D. Denisov shot down a Ju 88 near the settlement of Kulevi during the course of the operation. During 25-27 June, the aircraft of the regiment covered the passage of the *Joseph Stalin* oil carrier ship from Batumi to Tuapse and back. On 26 June, the German aviation made an attempt to sink the ship, but with no success, as the fighters repelled all of the attacks.

From summer 1944, the aircraft of the 7th Air Regiment and the 62nd Air Regiment took part in providing air cover for transport vessels and military ships in the open sea, and in the escorting of bombers and torpedo bombers. On 20 August 1944, they covered the raid of bombers and attack aircraft on Constantsa (Romania).

In the Northern Fleet, the Kittyhawks saw extensive service in the capacity of fighter bombers. For the P-40E, the standard configuration included the mounting of a single FAB-250 high-explosive bomb under the fuselage. In fact, the FAB-500 bombs were also employed (in the 78th Fighter Air Regiment), as well as combinations of a FAB-250 and two FAB-100TsKs, or a FAB-250 and two ZAB-100 incendiary bombs. On 10 May 1944, two groups of the Kittyhawks made a bombing attack on the Hebugten and Salmiyarvi airfields with no losses, but raids on Kirkenes on 13-14 May were very successful. At first, the fighters of the 78th and the 27th Fighter Air Regiments were acting as dive bombers. A FAB-100 hit a transport of 6,000t displacement; another (smaller) vessel went aground after a direct hit. On the following day, the Kittyhawks began skip bombing. The bombs were dropped close to the water and skipped over the water surface until they hit the board of a ship. One of the transport ships took fire, while another such ship and a small coasting vessel were damaged. It is interesting that the fighters demonstrated better bombing results than the Il-4 bombers did, in spite of the fact that the Kittyhawks lacked bomb sights. During the two days, the Northern Fleet regiments lost only one Kittyhawk of the 78th Fighter Air Regiment.

The skip bombing tactics were applied more than once at a later date – thus, for example, throughout the single day of 11 November 1944, a group of aircraft from the 78th Fighter Air Regiment, which was led by Captain V.P. Strelnikov, sent two barges and five motor boats to the bottom. During the battles near Petsamo, skip bombers of one of the squadrons of the 78th Air Regiment sank 13 ships – including one with the displacement of 3,000t. Skip bombing was a rather hazardous venture, since the aircraft were flying at a height of approximately 20m. Once pilot Proyavko failed to turn away in time, he ran into the mast of a minesweeper and tore off almost one third of his aircraft wing with ailerons. Luckily, he managed to get to the base. On average, the Kittyhawks spent two to five FAB-250 bombs per each sunken ship, which was much less than in the case of horizontal flight bombing.

In June 1944, the 30th Repair Works in the Northern Fleet built a two-seater version of the Kittyhawk, which was, essentially, a light bomber. A bombardier-navigator with an OPB-1 optical bomb sight occupied the second cabin, which was arranged aft of the main cockpit; however, the version never went any farther than a prototype.

The navy attempted to use the Kittyhawk to search for the enemy submarines. Search sorties were made in pairs, and at a low altitude; however, the fighters did not manage to find any of the enemy submarines. This was no surprise, given the high flight speed and the limited downward visibility.

The bomb-carrying P-40s were also used by land-based aviation. The possibility to use these aircraft in the capacity of light day bombers seemed especially vital in 1942, when, in view of a shortage of bombers at the front, the People's Commissar of Defense issued a special Order 'On Use of Fighter Aircraft as Day Bombers in the Battle Area'. In September that year, a P-40E-1 was tested at NII VVS (flown by Lieutenant Colonel A.G. Kochetkov) with standard American bomb armament. Under the fuselage, the aircraft had a single rack, which was fit for only one type of Soviet bomb: the FAB-250. In terms of load, the FAB-500 was also suitable, but its nose section was abutting on the radiator 'skirt'. The above-mentioned bomb-carrying options, which were used by the Northern Fleet Air Force, became possible only after the modification of the fighter and the installation of additional bomb racks. According to results of the tests, it was recommended that the bombing from the Kittyhawk should be carried out in a flat dive of 50-60°.

Sometimes, the capabilities of the Kittyhawk as an attack aircraft were enhanced by suspending rocket projectiles (two RS-82s per wing, like on the Tomahawk).

Fighters which carried AFA-I vertical aerial cameras also performed reconnaissance missions. In 1942, NII VVS tested a reconnaissance version of the Tomahawk. The compartment behind the cockpit accommodated a camera for oblique photographing; however, there is no data on any frontline application of such aircraft.

On the other hand, the modified Kittyhawks were rather widespread. For example, they were in operation with one of the squadrons of the 118th Composite Reconnaissance Air Regiment, where they were found most suitable for such an application (alongside the Spitfires). By the end of 1944, they had completely superseded the Hurricanes, Airacobras, Yak-1s and the LaGG-3s there. The Kittyhawks flew reconnaissance sorties both over land and sea. In particular, they made a considerable contribution to the Petsamo — Kirkenes Offensive, during which they operated from the advanced airfield of Pummanki.

In the Black Sea, active operations were carried out beginning from 1943 by the 3rd Squadron of the 3rd Independent Reconnaissance Air Regiment (under the command of Captain Y.N. Novikov), which had received seven P-40Ks. From Bugaz airfield, the squadron's aircraft flew unassisted reconnaissance missions over land and sea, and provided cover for the Bostons of the regiment, which were making flights to Myskhako – thus, the Kittyhawks took part in the simultaneous photographing of as many as 29 ports of the Black Sea and the Azov Sea in July 1943. It took only four hours to prepare a complete picture of the enemy forces' deployment for the command of the fleet. In August 1944, the aircraft took off from Central airfield (near Odessa) to take photographs of Constantsa before a massed raid of the Soviet naval aviation.

Such aircraft with AFA-I cameras also saw service with several fighter regiments of the air force. At the Leningrad Front, the 30th Repair Base built a two-seater P-40EF reconnaissance aircraft. From photographs, it can be seen that it was based on a P-40K-5, rather than on a P-40E. The aircraft was fully stripped of armaments; in the vacant compartments, additional fuel tanks were placed. The American Fairchild K-13 camera was installed in the tail portion. The camera operator-navigator had a bomb sight to point on the object to be photographed.

The aircraft successfully passed the tests at NII VVS, and flight performance remained almost unchanged; however, the customer unexpectedly updated the requirements to visibility from the aft cabin – making them unachievable for the Kittyhawk. The P-40EF was posted to the 13th Air Army, where it stayed in service for some time.

The same repair base in Leningrad modified the P-40Es in 1942 so as to make them fit to operate with Soviet M-105P and M-105R engines. In total, more than 40 fighters were modified. That was a compulsory measure, which was brought about by a temporary shortage of spare engines. The performance parameters of the aircraft with the M-105P engine and VISh-61P propeller deteriorated against the initial ones. In particular, the maximum speed dropped from 477km/h to 465km/h. The difference of the modified aircraft in its outer appearance consisted of an absence of the air intake atop of the engine cowling; a presence of ducts on the exhaust pipes; and a much smaller propeller spinner. All of the aircraft with M-105P and M-105R engines were concentrated in the 196th Fighter Air Regiment, which operated above Ladoga. Four fighters of the regiment were posted to the 12th Independent Spotter Reconnaissance Air Squadron to escort spotter reconnaissance aircraft at daytime.

The two-seater Kittyhawks were also made for the purpose of training (including conversion training) flight crews. At different locations, they were built in different configurations (with open or closed cockpits, and using the units from the Soviet Yak-7 and UTI-4 trainers). Sometimes, such modified Kittyhawks were designated P-40UCh (from *uchebniy*, or trainer).

In operation, the Kittyhawks demonstrated their strength and weaknesses: the strength and viability of all of the P-40s were their important features. This is confirmed (to a certain extent) by the many successful ram attacks which were made by pilots in this fighter. The first of them was V.A. Chirkov of the 154th Fighter Air Regiment: on 20 January 1942, he – in a Tomahawk – rammed a German aircraft near Pogostye.

In March 1943, two Kittyhawks of the 768th Fighter Air Regiment engaged 12 Messerschmitts. During the battle, Lieutenant V. Nikolaev destroyed a German fighter in a ramming attack and survived by bailing out. Hero of the Soviet Union A.S. Khlobystov performed ramming attacks thrice, and it should be noted that two such attacks took place during one and the same battle. Moreover, in both cases, he was ramming the enemy aircraft with his right wing and then returned to the base successfully. This occurred on 8 April 1942.

The Kittyhawk inherited some of the operational drawbacks from the Tomahawk: first of all, in the power plant. The 436th Fighter Air Regiment reported in late September 1942: '… Allison engines often failed because of [the] presence of chips in oil….' During a short time, the engines of 16 fighters in the regiment failed. The engines' service life at that time did not exceed 30-40 percent of the assigned lifetime; approximately one third of the engines failed after only 30 hours or so of running. The reasons were the same as before: running on Soviet oil (which was of worse quality than the Western grades); insufficient oil purity; the poor quality of fuel; and an excessive use of augmented power. This aside, the gradually accumulating experience in the maintenance of American engines yielded its results: the correct selection of oils, as well as a thorough adjustment after repair and a compliance with maintenance schedules (and prescribed optimum settings) allowed increasing the engine's service life considerably, as well as finally bringing it up to the assigned value. Apart from the engines, two types of failures were the most common ones: the failure of the connecting tube between the fuel pump and the carburetor, and the separation of the machine guns' flame damper pipes.

In winter, the pipelines on the Kittyhawks had to be heat-insulated and the oil pressure gauge had to be changed. To completely drain the oil and coolant, additional drain valves were inserted into the pipelines. The Allison engines ran on the standard Preston mixture, Soviet anti-freezes (with the replacement of the pressure relief valve) or were modified to allow hot-water filling (similar to the Hurricanes).

At the end of the war, the majority of the Kittyhawks were concentrated in the air defense units and in the naval aviation. In the air force, they were replaced with fighters of Soviet manufacture and with the Airacobras – thus, for example, the 191st Fighter Air Regiment was converted to the La-5 in early autumn 1944. The air defense forces had, at its disposal, 844 aircraft; there, the P-40s had also begun to be superseded by the P-39s, P-63s and Soviet fighters. Throughout the war, the air defense forces' regiments shot down 255 enemy aircraft (6.5 percent of the total number), but in the naval aviation, the number of Kittyhawks was also decreasing. The conversion of the 7th and the 62nd Air Regiments to up-to-date aircraft was completed as late as November 1944; by that time, Bulgaria and Romania had already joined the Allies. After the loss of bases in these countries, the enemy could not pose a threat in the Black Sea anymore. After that, the Kittyhawks stayed in service with the Black Sea Air Force for approximately two years. In the Northern Fleet, as of early 1945, the Kittyhawks were flown mostly by the 78th Fighter Air Regiment (32 aircraft). Ten aircraft were in service with the 118th Independent Reconnaissance Air Regiment, and seven of them were in service with the 3rd Training Air Regiment. Besides, fighters of this type were at the disposal of two composite regiments of the White Sea Flotilla (the 53rd Air Regiment, with 20 aircraft, and the 54th Air Regiment, with eight aircraft), which were stationed at Kholmovka airfield. These aircraft remained in service until the end of the war and even during the first post-war years – thus, in the 574th Air Regiment, the P-40s were in service until May 1946, when they were replaced with the Airacobras.

The P-40s did not take part in the war against Japan. At that location, there were only two aircraft which arrived in June 1945 with the 27th Fighter Air Regiment from the Northern Fleet, which were used as the trainers.

The manufacture of the P-40 family in the USA was discontinued in 1944. In the same year, shipments of these aircraft to the Soviet Union were terminated. According to Soviet data, a total of 247 Tomahawks and 1,887 Kittyhawks were accepted for the air force and air defense. To these figures, naval aviation should also be added. According to American reports, it turns out that the Soviet party accepted (in total) two-thousand-and-ninety-seven P-40s. The rest constituted the Tomahawks (which were re-exported from Great Britain) and unserviceable aircraft (which were shipped by the British for spare parts). The exact breakdown per modifications is not known; the only reported data states that the aircraft shipped from the USA included three-hundred-and-thirteen P-40Ks, two-hundred-and-twenty P-40Ms and nine-hundred-and-eighty P-40Ns. The Soviet naval aviation received 311 aircraft of the Curtiss P-40 family; of them, the Kittyhawks of various modifications constituted 90 percent. According to other data, the fleets received 321 American aircraft among other aircraft provided from the air force. Of those, 211 were operated in the north, whereas 109 saw service with the Black Sea Fleet.

The Soviet pilots fought the enemy courageously in the P-40s, just like in any other aircraft. For example, Major V.M. Naidenko of the 126th Fighter Air Regiment shot down 16 German aircraft before May 1942 and became a Hero of the Soviet Union – and he was not the only one: P.A. Pokryshev of the 154th Fighter Air Regiment was awarded the title of Hero twice. In his regiment, there were more than 15 pilots who were awarded this honorable distinction – including V.A. Chirkov, who has already been mentioned above. In March 1945, naval pilot Captain V.P. Strelnikov – a skip bombing ace – also became a Hero of the Soviet Union. The Northern Fleet ace B.F. Safonov flew a Kittyhawk and was killed in it. The most significant victory score among the P-40 pilots belongs to Captain S.M. Novichkov of the 67th Guards Fighter Air Regiment. In this aircraft, he claimed 19 German aircraft.

The withdrawal of the Kittyhawks and the few remaining post-war Tomahawks from operational service began in 1946. The Resolution of the Council of Ministers of 22 March 1946 required that one-thousand-and-eighty-six P-40s (i.e. all of the available ones) should be written off before the end of the year; however, the last aircraft, which were used for training purposes, survived until the end of the 1940s.

Currently, only one Kittyhawk is available in Russia on display; it's in the Northern Fleet Air Force Museum. Unfortunately, its outer appearance has been changed to a considerable extent as a result of poor-quality restoration.

A Tomahawk II during tests at NII VVS in October 1941.

A Tomahawk IIA of the 126th Fighter Air Regiment in the Moscow area during late autumn 1941. The airplane was flown by Squadron Leader S.G. Ridny.

The Tomahawk IIB of the 154th Fighter Air Regiment being prepared for take-off, Leningrad Front, December 1941.

Refueling of the fighter of the Eastern Operations Group, which provided air cover for the supply road across Lake Ladoga into the besieged Leningrad during winter 1941/1942.

The Tomahawks of the 126th Fighter Air Regiment before take-off.

Soviet pilots near a Tomahawk.

The forced landing of a Tomahawk in Karelia in 1942.

The Tomahawks of the 126th Fighter Air Regiment in temporary white winter camouflage.

A Tomahawk (in the foreground) among other foreign-made fighters in the exhibition hall of the TsAGI Bureau of New Designs.

The Northern Fleet fighter ace B.F. Safonov in the cockpit of a Kittyhawk, Vaenga airfield, May 1942.

Commander of the 154th Fighter Air Regiment A.A. Matveev near his Kittyhawk.

Captain V.I. Pokrovsky and Captain P.I. Orlov playing draughts near a hangar, with a Kittyhawk beside it; the 2nd Fighter Air Regiment of the Northern Fleet Air Force, Vaenga airfield, summer 1942.

Squadron Leader in the 20th Guards Fighter Air Regiment Major G.V. Gromov near his fighter aircraft.

The Kittyhawks of the 154th Fighter Air Regiment at an airfield in 1942.

A P-40E near a hangar; the Northern Fleet Air Force, 1942.

A Curtiss P-40E during tests at NII VVS in July 1942.

The cockpit of the P-40E fighter.

Junior Lieutenant M.E. Bychkov of the 20th Guards Fighter Air Regiment near his aircraft.

Representatives of the Command and local authorities near the fighter flown by A.S. Khlobystov (he later became a Hero of the Soviet Union; in this photo, he is sitting in the cockpit) of the 20th Guards Fighter Air Regiment. On 8 April 1942, Khlobystov carried out two ramming attacks on enemy fighters in his Tomahawk.

Hero of the Soviet Union Major A. Kovalenko (Squadron Leader of the 2nd Guards Combined Air Regiment) in front of his Kittyhawk.

Twice Hero of the Soviet Union P.A. Pokryshev, who was the Squadron Leader of the 154th Fighter Air Regiment.

Pilot Major F.A. Zhelvakov on the wing of a P-40K at the ALSIB route in autumn 1942.

A Curtiss P-40M during tests at NII VVS.

Pilots near a P-40M of the 191st Fighter Air Regiment, Leningrad Front, 1943.

P-40M fighters of the 7th Fighter Air Regiment, Black Sea Fleet Air Force at an airfield in 1943.

The Kittyhawks of the Black Sea Fleet Air Force in 1943.

The Kittyhawks of the Black Sea Fleet Air Force providing air cover for torpedo boats.

Finnish soldiers examining a P-40M of the 191st Fighter Air Regiment during early 1944. The Soviet fighter pilot lost his bearings and made a forced landing on Lake Valkjarvi. The aircraft was later repaired and put into service with the Finnish LeLv 32 Fighter Squadron, where it was used as a trainer until February 1945.

A P-40M of the 2nd Guards Fighter Air Regiment, Northern Fleet Air Force.

A group of the P-40Ms in flight, Leningrad Front, autumn 1943.

Hero of the Soviet Union Captain I.T. Tushev (Squadron Leader of the 191st Fighter Air Regiment) near his P-40M, Karelian Front, spring 1944.

A P-40N fighter of the 2nd Guards Fighter Air Corps of Air Defense Forces, Leningrad, 1945.

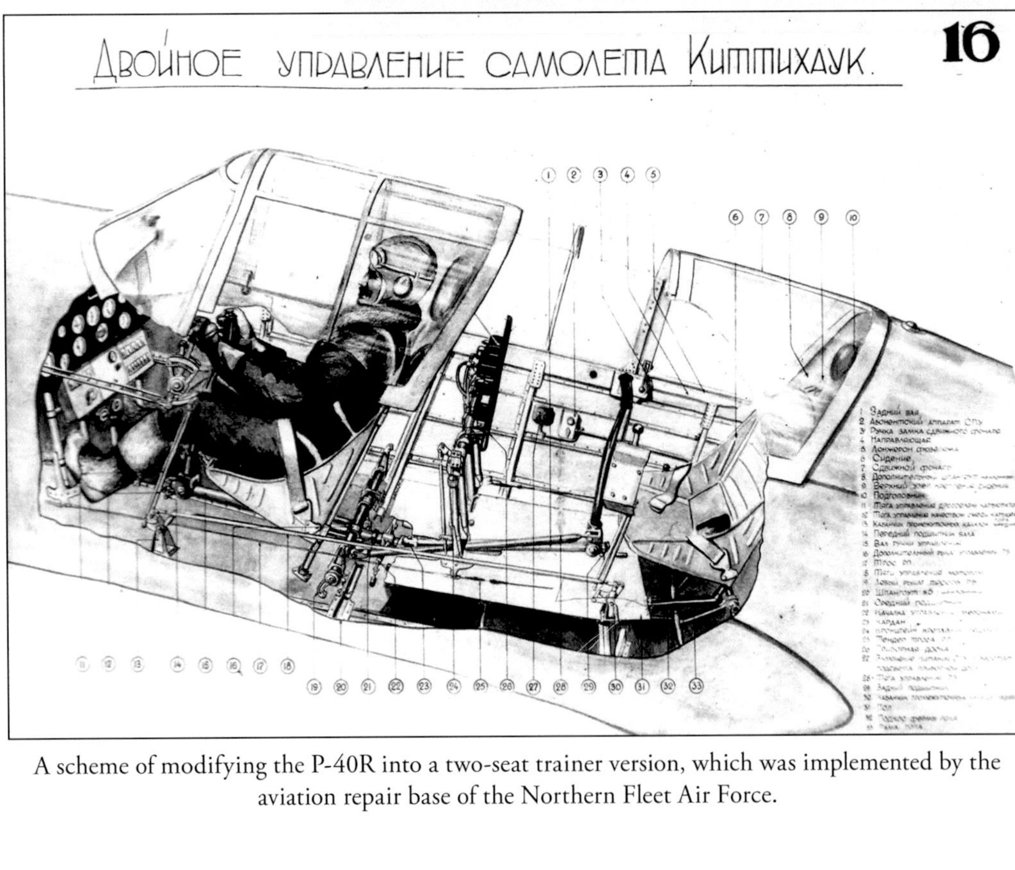

A scheme of modifying the P-40R into a two-seat trainer version, which was implemented by the aviation repair base of the Northern Fleet Air Force.

A Kittyhawk being modified into a P-40EF two-seat photo reconnaissance version.

The P-40EF two-seat photo reconnaissance aircraft, which was in service with the 191st Fighter Air Regiment in 1943.

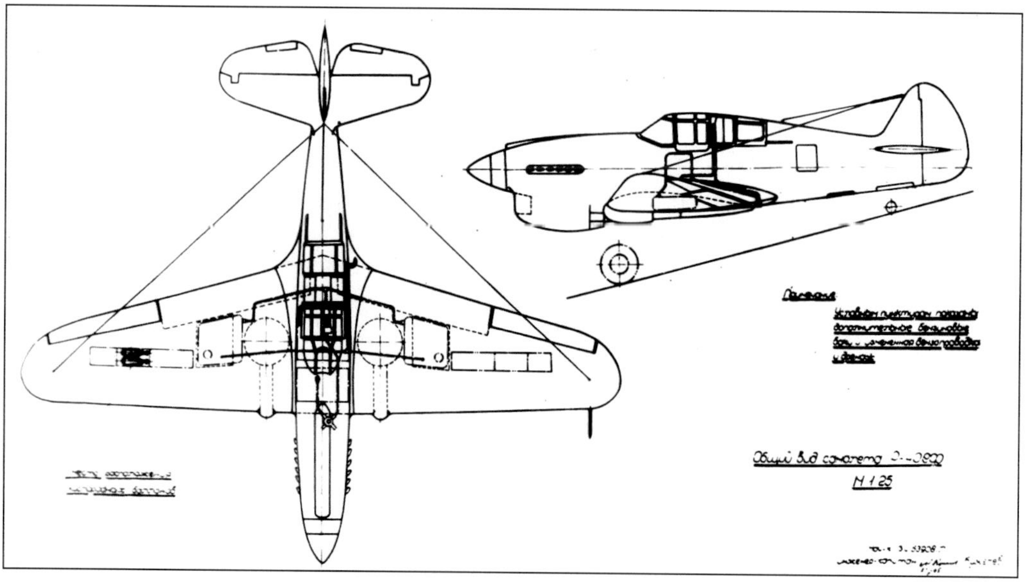

A drawing of a Kittyhawk fighter modification into a two-seat photo reconnaissance aircraft; note that the P-40K was taken as the basic version rather than the P-40E.

A P-40E modified to operate with the M-105R engine and the VISh-61P propeller in 1942; note the launchers for RS-82 rocket projectiles under the wing.

A poorly restored Kittyhawk on display in the Northern Fleet Air Force Museum in Safonovo.

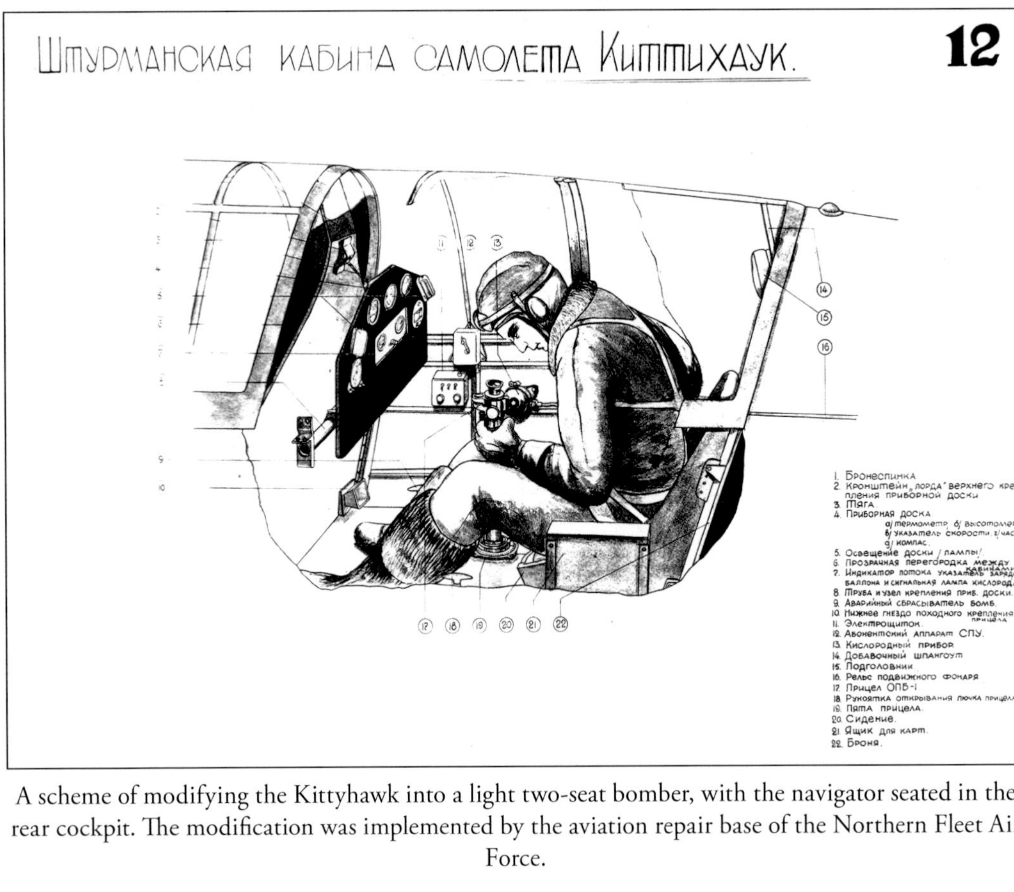

A scheme of modifying the Kittyhawk into a light two-seat bomber, with the navigator seated in the rear cockpit. The modification was implemented by the aviation repair base of the Northern Fleet Air Force.

7.4 Bell P-39 Airacobra

The Airacobra fighter is undoubtedly the most popular and the most well-known aircraft among those that were delivered to the USSR under Lend-Lease during the Second World War. The aircraft was very popular with Soviet pilots, who liked the Cobra and had a high opinion of it.

There were, of course, reasons for that: a lot of Soviet fighter aces scored a considerable quantity of their victories in Airacobras, and the best 'advertising' for the American fighter was carried out by A.I. Pokryshkin and other pilots from his division. Many of them claimed more than 20 destroyed enemy aircraft, but the record is deemed to be held by G.A. Rechkalov, who scored exactly 50 kills in a Cobra. The total number of pilots who were awarded the Soviet Union's highest decoration (the Gold Star of the Hero of the Soviet Union) for combats in the Airacobras is approximately a hundred. Some of them were honored with this award twice; as for Pokryshkin himself, he was thrice a Hero of the Soviet Union.

In the opinion of Soviet pilots, the Bell P-39 Airacobra fighter was quite compliant with the requirements of aerial warfare on the Soviet-German Front; in the West, however, the aircraft saw no extensive service.

There is a legend that the founder of the company, L. Bell – on the threshold of the war – was not successful in his attempts to find personnel for his design office and, out of despair, recruited final-year students from the Detroit Automotive College. As a result, the car designers developed a strange configuration, with the engine installed in the middle of the fuselage; a tricycle undercarriage; and side doors in the cockpit, which were similar to those of a motor car. In fact, the designing of the future Cobra was carried out under the guidance of experienced aircraft designers R. Woods and H. Poyer. Furthermore, the configuration with the propeller driven via a long shaft was not their invention. Such a layout was first attempted by the British, and then by the Dutch. This approach allowed reducing the mass distribution and achieving remarkable maneuverability; at the same time, the space in the nose portion was freed up to accommodate armament. The achievement of the American designers consisted of making such a configuration operable with the drive shaft length of approximately 3m. The operability of the configuration was accounted for by the fact that the Airacobra's shaft could 'breathe' due to a splined coupling installed in its middle. A prominent role in the development of the power plant was played by the Allison Engine Company, which manufactured an engine of special modifications, with the engine itself and the reduction gear separated by a long shaft, while also providing the possibility to mount the barrel of a powerful 37mm cannon through the reduction gear output shaft.

The lengthy period of time for the creation of the aircraft became the price paid for the numerous innovations. The aircraft was developed in 1936; however, the first prototype (XP-39) made its maiden flight as late as 6 April 1939. The mass-produced P-39Cs rolled off the production line in January 1941, and they were placed in service with the US Army Air Corps (USAAC). The manufacture of the export version for Great Britain began in August. It was the Airacobra I, with a more reliable 20mm cannon instead of the 37mm one; however, the fighter was found to be unsatisfactory by the Royal Air Force Command. The British were making efforts to bring the Airacobras up to their requirements until winter, and they really rectified some of the defects; then, however, they decided to withdraw the aircraft from service and passed them over to the Soviet Union. The decision fitted well into the already mentioned tendency to send from Great Britain to the USSR more aircraft of American origin.

In the battles above the Pacific Ocean, the P-39 did not win much success either. In horizontal flying, it was unable to compete with light and more agile Japanese fighters, plus the altitude performance was deemed to be unacceptable. The 37mm cannon, which had been returned to its place after adjustments on a later series of the P-39D modification, could, with a single round, tear a fighter into pieces or break a bomber in half; however, it was not reliable enough. The Cobra's range was insufficient for the reaches of the Pacific Ocean. Finally, in the American aviation, the P-39 was relegated to the role of a fighter bomber and an attack aircraft, but saw no extensive service. This predetermined its further evolution overall. The majority of these fighters were shipped (via various routes) to the Soviet Union. The British historian R. Jackson wrote in his book *The Red Falcons* that the Bell P-39 Airacobra and the Bell P-63 Kingcobra were shipped to the USSR (mostly) for the reason that they did not meet the operational requirements of the US Air Force.

The aircraft had quite a different destiny in the Soviet Union: it aroused interest there as early as the late 1930s. In October 1940, G.M. Gudkov was even assigned the task of building an aircraft of a similar layout using the AM-39UV (AM-41) 1,600hp engine. The aircraft was indeed designed and built, but crashed during tests in June 1943.

In September 1941, in the course of preparations for the conference in Moscow (at which the first plans for military and technical assistance from Great Britain and the USA to the Soviet Union were worked out), the P-39 was mentioned among the aircraft which were the most suitable for Soviet aviation. The report as prepared for the conference by the Intelligence Directorate of the General Staff stated that: '… the Airacobra aircraft meets the requirements to an up-to-date fighter, and can be used by the Workers' and Peasants' Red Army Air Force…' For this reason, the USSR quite willingly agreed to shipments of these aircraft.

A reply was promptly received from the Soviet representatives in the USA: 'The Company is interested in the placement of large orders, and pledges ability to ship 100 fighters to the USSR each month under the existing orders, provided that the War Department gives an appropriate permit'.

Interest in the fighter became keener after the visit of the Soviet delegation to Duxford airfield in England. There, on 7 October, a Soviet test pilot was even permitted to make two flights in an Airacobra of No.601 Squadron, which had been the first in the RAF to fly these aircraft. The pilot expressed a favorable opinion of the aircraft.

All of the first Cobras which arrived in the Soviet Union were of British origin. These were the Airacobra Is with 20mm cannons, which had been purchased by Great Britain in the USA and, after a brief period of operation, were passed over to the USSR. They were brought by the polar convoys by sea. Before the end of 1941, a total of 11 such aircraft arrived via the northern ports.

In mid-January 1942, the 6th Backup Brigade received two disassembled Airacobras. The approach to the mastering of this rather peculiar aircraft was very serious: NII VVS delegated a team of specialists, which was led by the engineer I.G. Rabkin, and the team included the test pilot V.E. Golofastov. The fighters were assembled directly in the airfield, in spite of the severe winter. British engineers and technicians who were seconded to the regiment provided assistance in the form of advice. Rabkin did not speak English, the British personnel did not speak Russian and the interpretress did not know the technical terminology; however, a way out was discovered: Rabkin and the British engineer began communicating in French.

When the first Airacobra was assembled, Golofastov started with taxiing. It was necessary, because he had never before dealt with a tricycle undercarriage. Several days later, the pilot took off. Having accumulated a certain amount of experience, the pilot began passing it on to instructor pilots of the backup regiment. Major Akulenko was the first of them to fly the P-39.

In April and May 1942, NII VVS conducted official State tests of the Airacobra. According to NII's opinion, the American fighter was, in terms of flight performance, on a level with the mass-manufactured Soviet and German aircraft of the same class. Maneuverability, take-off and landing performance, powerful armament and good equipment won approval; the aircraft even had a comfortable heated cockpit (none of the Soviet fighters could offer such luxury at that time). The 'Conclusions' section of the report by NII VVS stated that the Airacobra could be successfully used for aerial battles with all types of German aircraft, as well as for ground attack purposes.

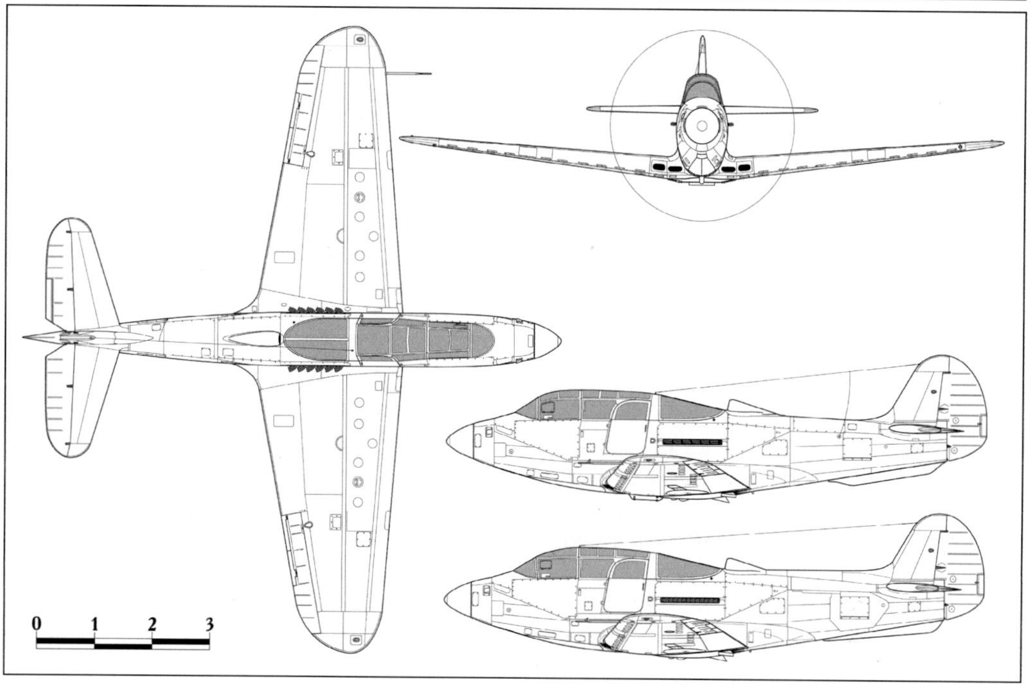

P-39

Two variants of the P-39 modification into two-seat trainers.

Concurrently with the tests, the training of pilots from combat regiments began in the Airacobras. According to the plan, a regiment had to hand over old fighters at the front to another unit, and then to arrive for training with no aircraft. Upon completion of the training course, the regiment then accepted the required number of Airacobras and flew to the destined location.

The 153rd Fighter Air Regiment, which was under the command of Major S.I. Mironov, was the first to arrive for conversion training on 25 March. In April, the 185th Air Regiment (withdrawn from the Leningrad Front) joined the training program.

Special attention was given to the techniques of take-off and landing on the aircraft with a nose wheel, which was not found on any Soviet aircraft at that time.

V.M. Perov, who had completed the training course in Ivanovo at that time, described the 'odd-looking' American fighter in his memoirs:

> The nose landing gear (leg) was long; the aircraft in the airfield resembled a big funny mosquito, with its tail up and its proboscis stuck into the ground. The nose leg seemed disproportionately thin and frail; during taxiing or after landing, one could think that it would buckle, and the aircraft would touch ground with its nose and crush the cockpit.

Indeed, making a mistake at landing and hitting soft or bumpy soil could, with considerable probability, result in damage to the nose leg.

The 19th Guards Fighter Air Regiment was the first to enter the action in the Airacobras. The pilots of the regiment mastered the new aircraft on their own – having received 16 Airacobras and 10 Kittyhawks in May 1942 at Afrikanda airfield in North Karelia. The aircraft arrived disassembled in boxes, so engineers and technicians of the regiment assembled the unfamiliar aircraft without any assistance, whereas the pilots learned to fly the aircraft using manuals (which were translated from English with the help of dictionaries, albeit in a makeshift manner). The 1st Squadron, which was under the command of Captain P.S. Kutakhov (later Air Marshal), was the first to master the Cobras. To give a personal example, on 26 April, Kutakhov made three training flights.

The conversion training of the flight crews was completed by 15 May, and with no accidents. On the same day, the Cobras flew their first combat sortie from Shongui airfield and encountered German fighters right off. Neither of the parties incurred any losses; however, on the following day, the aircraft of Senior Lieutenant I.D. Gaidayenko was damaged in a battle against eight Messerschmitts. The aircraft was wrecked in an emergency landing and discarded, but the pilot survived. That was the first loss of an Airacobra at the Soviet-German Front.

Afterwards, from Murmashi airfield, pilots of the 19th Air Regiment flew sorties to cover the Kirovsk railway and the Tulomskaya hydroelectric station, and provided assistance to the troops of the Karelian Front. Later, the Airacobras were received by the 20th Guards Fighter Air Regiment of the same division. The Soviet airmen were courageous and resolute in repelling attacks against the frontline Murmansk. For example, on 15 June 1942, six Airacobras of the 19th Guards Fighter Air Regiment intercepted six enemy bombers and 16 enemy fighters westward of the city. The battle lasted for 45 minutes, and the pilots of the regiment were led by Captain I.V. Bochkov. It was he who shot down the first Messerschmitt; in total, nine enemy aircraft were destroyed.

The 153rd Fighter Air Regiment entered the action at the Voronezh Front (as part of the 3rd Air Striking Force) in late June 1942. The hostilities began on 30 June, and the regiment operated until the end of September from airfields in Voronezh and Lipetsk. Throughout this period, the pilots of the regiment made 1,070 combat sorties, shot down 64 enemy aircraft – including 45 fighters – and lost eight aircraft. Regiment Commander (already Lieutenant Colonel) Mironov wrote: 'The small losses are accounted for, first of all, by experience of the pilots and good flight performance of the Airacobra aircraft'.

With the 185th Fighter Air Regiment, the Cobras were in service for a rather short period of time. In November 1942, the regiment was disbanded and its flight and ground crews were posted to the 1st Ferry Air Division, which was then being formed for operations along the ALSIB route. As for the 153rd Air Regiment, it was again replenished with the Airacobras in October, and redeployed to the North-Western Front. There, the regiment also fought decently and, for that reason, on 22 November, was awarded the title of the 28th Guards Fighter Air Regiment.

The naval aviation first came to know the Airacobra fighters in October 1942, when the 2nd Guards Composite Air Regiment received 10 Airacobra Is. Initially, the aircraft were used mostly to provide air cover for Murmansk – thus, on 19 April 1943, the repelling of a raid of the German aircraft on the city resulted in a multiple engagement, with 14 German fighters against 10 Cobras and six Hurricanes. The numerical advantage of the Northern Fleet pilots was not large; however, the losses ratio proved quite different – namely five to one in their favor.

The mass influx of the Airacobras to the Soviet-German Front occurred as late as 1943. At that time, more and more new P-39s kept arriving from the north (via Archangelsk and Murmansk), south (via Iran) and east (from Alaska). More and more new units were being converted to the Airacobras and joined together into divisions and corps.

In late 1942, the P-39Ds began coming via Iran. The first fighter of this type arrived in Abadan on 8 December; within five days, it was assembled and flight-tested. The D modification differed from the Airacobra I mostly in terms of equipment. The D-2 series also featured the 37mm cannon, an additional fuel tank under the fuselage and the V-1710-63 engine with a provision for short-time augmentation to 1,325hp (whereas the V-1710-E4 on the Airacobra I and P-39D-1 produced a maximum of 1,150hp). As for the P-39F modifications, these were not shipped to the USSR.

Aircraft of still more modern modifications (K, M, N and, finally, Q) were coming via the ALSIB route. The first ten P-39Ds were accepted by the Soviet mission in Fairbanks before the end of 1942 (the first of them were ferried by the Americans in November). According to the route report for December, 12 fighters were ferried to Krasnoyarsk; one aircraft crashed en route. In January 1943, the first of the aircraft was accepted by air force representatives. From the beginning of 1943, the Airacobras became the primary type of aircraft ferried via the route. The peak shipments occurred in September and, throughout the month, 288 aircraft were ferried and 106 were accepted, with only one aircraft lost. According to the Soviet statistics, a total of two-thousand-five-hundred-and-ninety-three P-39s (out of 2,618 aircraft accepted in Fairbanks) arrived in Krasnoyarsk.

The P-39Ks featured six (instead of three) exhaust pipes on each side, and new Aeroproducts propellers with hydraulic pitch control (which superseded the Curtiss Electric propellers). The first Ks arrived from Iran just before the end of 1942; the P-39Ls were again fitted with the old, electrically driven Curtiss propellers. The P-39M was a version with the V-1710-83 engine, which allowed for improving the altitude performance to a certain extent. The most mass-manufactured versions (which were almost entirely sent to the Soviet Union) were the P-39N with the V-1710-85 engine and an increased-diameter propeller, and the P-39Q with enhanced armament (a 37mm cannon and six 12.7mm machine guns). It was the latter two modifications that were the most common ones in the Soviet aviation.

By summer 1943, the Airacobras had spread over the entire Soviet-German Front, from the far north to the extreme south, and their quantity was sufficient to equip whole divisions and corps. The 258th Composite Air Division (from August, renamed the 1st Guards Composite Air Division), which was equipped with P-39s and P-40s, kept fighting at the Karelian Front. In the Leningrad region, the 102nd and the 103rd Guards Fighter Air Regiments of the air defense forces were fitted with P-39Qs. In the North-Western Front, the Airacobras were flown by three regiments of the 5th Guards Fighter Air Division, which was under the command of Colonel G.A. Ivanov; in the Central Front, the Cobras were in service with regiments of the 1st Guards Fighter Air Division, which was led by Colonel V.V. Sukhoryabov.

Quite a lot of the P-39s were concentrated in the south, where constant 'replenishments' were arriving from Iran. There, the conversion training of the pilots was carried out in the 25th Backup Air Regiment, and later by the 11th Backup Air Regiment (from September 1943) and the 26th Backup Air Regiment (from November). The 298th Fighter Air Regiment, which was under the command of Lieutenant Colonel I.A. Taranenko, received a 'mixture' of Airacobras of the D and K modifications, and was also the first to complete the conversion training course there. This regiment entered action in the Kuban region in mid-March 1943. Initially, its operations were confined to the escorting of bombers; however, from the beginning of March, the pilots began 'hunting' enemy aircraft and won their first victories. Before 20 August, they shot down 167 enemy aircraft against only 30 lost. On 24 August, the regiment was reorganized into the 104th Guards Air Regiment and, under this title, in joined the famous 216th (the 9th Guards) Air Division.

The renowned 16th Guards Fighter Air Regiment was part of the same division. Having received (after conversion training) brand-new Cobras (types D, K and L) in Tehran, the regiment arrived in the Krasnodar region in April 1943. Captain A.I. Pokryshkin's squadron was the first to arrive, which was on 8 April. On the following day, it entered severe action in Kuban; several days later, the rest of the regiment joined the squadron. The 16th Guards Fighter Air Regiment consisted of experienced flight crews which had already conducted battles in fighters of different types. Within a month, Pokryshkin shot down (in an Airacobra) 10 enemy fighters – including three of them during a single battle. Senior Lieutenant V.I. Fadeev was credited with an even greater number of victories: he claimed a dozen Messerschmitts. – and that was where the famous 'Pokryshkin's formula' ('Height, speed, maneuver, fire!') was born. To stratagems of German aces, Pokryshkin opposed his 'Kuban Air Stack' and 'Pendulum'. As soon as 22 April, six pilots of the regiment were recommended for the title of Hero of the Soviet Union.

Fierce battles were going on in the skies of Kuban until early June. After a short respite, the 16th Guards Fighter Air Regiment was, in early August, redeployed to Donbass. Later, it took part in the breaking of the front near the Mius River, in the Battles of Taganrog and Mariupol, and in the Liberation of Melitopol. The regiment was often changing airfields and made one combat sortie after another.

At the end of the year, Pokryshkin (already Major) took over command of the regiment. Throughout its long operational history, the unit was successively equipped with the P-39Ns and P-39Qs, and saw the end of the war in Prague. Among the pilots of the regiment was a thrice Hero of the Soviet Union (Pokryshkin himself, who ended the war at the post of Division Commander), two twice Heroes of the Soviet Union (G.A. Rechkalov and A.F. Klubov) and more than 15 Heroes of the Soviet Union.

The third widely known regiment of the same division was the 45th Air Regiment (later the 100th Guards Air Regiment), which was initially under the command of I.M. Dzusov. The regiment flew the Airacobras and Kittyhawks from February 1943 and, among the regiment's pilots, were such aces as the Glinka brothers (D.B. Glinka was credited with 50 victories, while B.B. Glinka scored 31 kills) and I.I. Babak (37 victories). In total, there were approximately 10 Heroes of the Soviet Union in the regiment; of those, the elder of the Glinka brothers (Boris B.) was awarded this title twice.

The Airacobras of the regiment first entered the action on 9 March. A flight of eight aircraft led by D.B. Glinka destroyed six enemy aircraft at the expense of only one lost. Glinka had his own views of how to conduct an aerial battle: he was a brilliant improvisor and developed the tactics (first and foremost) so as to make use of the best pilots' skills. The regiment's ratio between victories and losses was somewhere about four to one. The 100th Guards Air Regiment walked approximately the same path as the other units of the division did – scattering it with the wreckage of enemy aircraft.

A good reputation was also won by the 9th Guards Fighter Air Regiment – among whose pilots were four Heroes of the Soviet Union (Amet-Khan Sultan, V.D. Lavrinenkov, P.Y. Golovachev and A.V. Alelyukhin). This regiment (initially, the 69th Fighter Air Regiment) took part in the defense of Odessa in summer 1941 in the I-16s. Later, it fought at various locations in the LaGG-3s and the Yak-1s, and finally won the title of a Guards Air Regiment. Its pilots began mastering the Airacobras in March 1943, and Regiment Commander L.L. Shestakov himself took off and twice demonstrated to his subordinates the correct procedure for a spin recovery. The 9th Guards Fighter Air Regiment took part in offensive operations in the Southern (later Ukrainian) Front. Throughout summer 1943, its pilots fought 12 aerial battles and shot down 156 enemy aircraft.

In July 1943, the number of Airacobras at the front exceeded sevenfold their number as of November 1942. It is difficult to list all of the units and formations which had the P-39s at their disposal, but the Army Air Force alone sent 25 regiments equipped with such aircraft in 1942-1943 to the front.

Some units, as before, underwent conversion training directly at the front lines. From the 67th Guards Fighter Air Regiment, only the ground crews were sent to Ivanovo to be trained. As for the pilots, they 'rented' two Cobras from the 2nd Guards Fighter Air Regiment and learned to fly the American fighter on their own; they ferried their aircraft from Krasnoyarsk themselves. In May 1943, the regiment was redeployed to the North-Western Front to join the 5th Guards Fighter Air Division; in June, they were sent to the Ukrainian Front. Pilots of the 67th Guards Fighter Air Regiment performed a lot of exploits: for example, on 2 August 1943, sixteen P-39s attacked 60 enemy aircraft and shot down 13 of them, with only one P-39 lost. In total, during the day, the regiment's combat score grew by 25 enemy aircraft!

The number of Airacobras in the naval aviation grew as well. In the second half of 1943, the P-39Ns were used to equip the 2nd Guards Fighter Air Regiment of the Northern Fleet Air Force.

Sometime earlier, the 255th Fighter Air Regiment had relegated the obsolete I-153 biplanes and converted to the American fighters. As of January 1944, the Northern Fleet airmen had, altogether, approximately thirty P-39s at their disposal.

In the Black Sea, the 11th Fighter Air Regiment was converted to the Cobras in March 1943. Stationed in Vityazevskaya, Gelendzhik and (later) in Skadovsk, the regiment entered the action in July. The fighters provided air cover for Gelendzhik (where some of the Black Sea Fleet ships were moored) and the neighboring airfields. Later, they were involved in providing assistance to front-line troops, and in escorting bombers and torpedo bombers. The latter was intended to become the principal function for them, since the regiment was part of the 2nd Guards Mine-and-Torpedo Air Division. Having acquired certain experience, the pilots of the regiment began 'free-hunting' over the territory occupied by the enemy. Throughout the second half of the year, the regiment took part in 75 air battles and destroyed 92 German aircraft (60 fighters and 32 bombers/reconnaissance aircraft). The regiment's own losses, on the other hand, totaled ten P-39s. In terms of the attrition ratio, the 11th Fighter Air Regiment left behind all the other actively operating regiments of the Black Sea Fleet Air Force – including the 6th Air Regiment (in the Yak-1s); the 69th Air Regiment (in the LaGG-3s); and the 25th Air Regiment (also in LaGG-3s) – thus, for example, the 25th Air Regiment (throughout the same time period) engaged in 89 battles and shot down 73 aircraft versus 24 lost ones. From these figures, one can understand what the good mastering of aircraft and the skillful use of their advantages meant.

In the capacity of cover aircraft, the Airacobras took part in many large-scale operations. In August 1943, aircraft of the 11th Fighter Air Regiment joined the group, which was attacking an airfield in Anapa. Along with protecting the bombers and attack aircraft from enemy fighters, the Airacobras were strafing the airfield. As a result, eight German aircraft burned down and six were seriously damaged. In November, the Cobras were hovering in the sky above the foothold, which had been seized by assault forces near Odessa. Later, the regiment was redeployed to Skadovsk and, from there, its pilots flew sorties to intercept transport aircraft which were carrying cargoes and replacements to the Crimea, or evacuating the Germans from the peninsula. On 25 January 1944, Senior Lieutenant N.A. Kislyak and Lieutenant V.A. Lyubimov attacked a group of twenty-nine Ju 52/3ms and shot down four of them. By the end of 1943, the 43rd Fighter Air Regiment had also been equipped with the P-39s to a considerable extent. This regiment was used in approximately the same manner as the 11th Air Regiment, but was more active in the strafing of ground targets to support the Soviet army units on the offensive. In August 1944, both regiments were involved in a massive attack on Constantsa. Thirty-two Airacobras of the 11th Guards Fighter Air Regiment were escorting the Bostons and the Il-4s, whereas forty-three fighters of the 43rd Fighter Air Regiment covered the Pe-2 dive bombers. In November 1944, when the warfare in the Black Sea ended, the Black Sea Fleet Air Force had one-hundred-and-twenty-five P-39s in service.

In the Northern Fleet, the role of the Airacobras was also gradually becoming more important. They were most often used as 'pure' fighters to cover ships, shore facilities, bombers, attack aircraft or the Kittyhawks (when the latter were carrying bombs). For example, in this manner, the raid on Luostari airfield was organized on 17 August 1944. A flight of eight Kittyhawks released 100kg bombs on the parking areas, while the P-39Ns were blocking the airfield and firing on the aircraft which attempted to take off.

In 1943, an Airacobra which was registered as a civil aircraft appeared in the USSR, and the Civil Air Fleet used it as a trainer aircraft. This was due to the fact that ferry units (at that time) were subordinate to the Chief Administration of the Civil Air Fleet and used this P-39 for training. As soon as ferry regiments were transferred to the military domain, they had to forsake the fighter.

The year 1944 was marked by an abrupt growth in the number of Airacobras in the Air Defense Forces. In late 1943, there were only 65 of them; by early 1945, their number had reached 597. It is interesting that the P-39s were provided to regiments which were nearest to the front line; in the rear areas, the Hurricanes and Kittyhawks were deemed good enough.

For example, the 57th, the 101st and the 66th Guards Fighter Air Regiments (all of them equipped with the P-39s) were involved in providing air cover for American air bases in the Ukraine; however, they attained little success there. In June 1944, the German aviation delivered a massive night attack on Poltava and Mirgorod. Having suspected something unusual in the strengthening of the enemy air reconnaissance, the Soviet Command managed to redeploy the majority of aircraft to other airfields. The repelling of the attack, however, turned out to be quite messy and absolutely inefficient. The Airacobras began taxiing to the take-off position when the bombs were already exploding, and the Germans damaged the runway and paralyzed the operation of the fighters. The bombs destroyed 44 American and 15 Soviet aircraft.

On the following day, the enemy sent out another reconnaissance aircraft to record the results of the bombardment. When the Junkers appeared in the skies of Poltava, it was intercepted by Lieutenant Mineev in a P-39; however, the attack was not quite successful: having used up his ammunition in vain, the pilot undertook an aerial ramming and died together with the enemy crew.

At the end of the war, there were eight regiments flying the P-39s in the air defense forces (to a certain extent, they had already converted to the new P-63 fighters); altogether, they had shot down 95 German aircraft. In total, more than 50 regiments in the air force, air defense forces and naval aviation had fought in the Airacobras.

Much could be told of the combat achievements of the units and formations which flew the Airacobras. There were truly amazing phenomena of the pilots' courage, combined with brilliant piloting skills. A case worth mentioning is the engagement between a dozen P-39s of the 100th Guards Fighter Air Regiment and a group comprising fifty Ju 87s, ten Bf 109s and eight FW 190s in June 1944. The belligerents' losses included 10 Germans versus a single Airacobra. Three kills in the battle were credited to D.B. Glinka.

On 5 July 1943, during the Battle of Kursk, four Airacobras of the 27th Air Regiment, which was led by N.D. Gulaev, courageously attacked a formation of approximately a hundred German aircraft and shot down four bombers and two fighters! In total, throughout the day, these four Airacobras destroyed 16 enemy aircraft.

The Soviet aces described the Airacobras in their memoirs as follows: 'A perfect, up-to-date high-speed aircraft' [A.I. Pokryshkin]; 'A modern military aircraft, on a level with the good fighters of the war period' [V.D. Lavrinenkov]. E.Y. Savitsky, whose division had flown both the Yak-1s and P-39s, believed the Cobra to be: '... inferior, in some aspects, to the Yak-1, but undoubtedly a good aircraft...' He also noted that some pilots had preferred the P-39s. Here is the opinion of Hero of the Soviet Union F.F. Arkhipenko: 'The Airacobra was, at that time, a pilot's dream. Its principal advantages included the excellent, failure-free armament, and the steady – with only slight noise – radio communications'. Finally, there is an extract from an official document (a report of the 153rd Fighter Air Regiment): '... the Airacobra aircraft is regarded as the most dangerous opponent; the Germans dare to engage the Airacobras only when they enjoy a numerical superiority and an advantage in altitude and surprise'.

At the same time, the Americans and the British considered the Airacobra a mediocre medium-altitude fighter, which was more remarkable for its powerful armament than for flight performance, and was more suitable for ground attacks than for air combat.

Let us see what can account for the difference in opinion of the Soviet and foreign specialists: the Allies found the Cobra's altitude performance rather poor. Indeed, the P-39D developed maximum speed at an altitude of approximately 4,500m; at a higher altitude, the speed was quickly dropping. The P-39D's service ceiling totaled only 9,900m, which was lower than that of the Soviet fighters at that time; however, for the war conditions at the Soviet-German Front, altitudes below 5,000m were the most important ones – and it is at such altitudes that the majority of aerial combats took place. In terms of range, the Cobra was inferior to its 'compatriots' (the P-51B and P-47D), but was on a level with the Soviet fighters. Besides, beginning from the D-1 series, outboard jettisonable tanks were introduced, which considerably increased the range of the aircraft. In the USSR, PLGB-350 jettisonable tanks of Soviet manufacture were sometimes also installed on the British Airacobra Is, which initially had had no provisions for such an installation. PLGB-350 tanks were first introduced in April-May 1943 in the 255th Guards Air Regiment and (later) in the 2nd Guards Air Regiment in the Northern Fleet. The installation of such tanks, which were larger in capacity than the standard American ones, allowed increasing the flight endurance to 90 minutes. On 29 April, five Airacobras of the Northern Fleet engaged by surprise (for the first time) a group of the Bf 110 heavy German fighters beyond the normal Airacobra range. This offered grim prospects for the heavy (and not very maneuverable) German aircraft...

The tasks and requirements of the American and British aviation were different from those of the Soviets. In the Soviet Union, the Airacobra fitted in well: its range and speed were found acceptable, and the armament was deemed to be good. As for the equipment, the Soviet factories had never seen anything of its kind: it was space-saving, reliable and convenient to operate.

The view from the P-39's cockpit was considered to be excellent. Air Force Commander A.A. Novikov even wrote a letter to Stalin in September 1942, in which he suggested using the Airacobra's canopy as a model to be followed by designers (in terms of shape) and production engineers (in terms of transparency). Soviet fighters had nothing much to boast of as far as transparency was concerned: organic glass of Soviet manufacture was much more turbid than American Perspex acrylic glass.

The armament of the P-39 was unanimously appreciated as being very powerful. Even the firepower of the Airacobra I, which was equipped with a 20mm cannon and six machine guns – including two large-caliber ones – seemed outright smashing, let alone subsequent modifications such as the P 39Q with a 37mm cannon and four 12.7mm Browning machine guns. Soviet documents constantly admitted that the P-39's armament was rather efficient against aerial, ground and sea surface targets. For air combat, the Q's armament was deemed excessive, and two underwing machine guns were, in the majority of cases, removed. The M4 37mm cannon normally destroyed enemy aircraft in a single hit. The Cobra's cannon could bust the enemy's armored vehicles, steam locomotives, river vessels and even sea-going ships; a single round was enough to sink a small motor boat. It should also be noted that in terms of rate of fire and ballistic performance, the cannon was inferior to the Soviet-made cannons of the same caliber. Furthermore, its operation on fighters of an earlier series was not reliable enough (this coincides with the opinions of American pilots). It is interesting that the P-39D-1 with a 20mm cannon featured a greater weight of fire than the P-39D-2 with the 37mm cannon did (192kg/min versus 161kg/min); this was on account of the former's higher rate of fire.

In some aspects, the opinions of the Soviet and American specialists were convergent: the Airacobra's value against ground targets was never contested. In the second half of 1943, the P-39 began to quit the role of a 'pure' fighter – being involved more and more frequently in attacks against ground and sea surface targets. This is confirmed, for example, by the results of combat operations of the 9th Guards Fighter Air Regiment in February 1944. The score of destroyed targets included 13 aircraft, 110 motor vehicles, 100 horses, five steam locomotives and 'a lot of enemy personnel'. The 216th Air Division, during the period from 1 January through to 10 May 1943, shot down 187 aircraft in air combats, whereas the number of enemy aircraft burnt down on the ground totaled 200!

In a 'free hunt', the Cobras were directed (not infrequently) against mobile ground targets, and their role in disrupting the enemy's railway operations was especially important. The powerful cannon easily damaged a locomotive boiler with an armor-piercing round. In Dzusov's division in September 1943 (when the Germans were retreating from Mariupol), six pairs of Airacobras 'scored' 13 steam locomotives in half a day (i.e. before midday). This paralyzed the enemy's effort to evacuate various possessions from the city. Also, fighters of the 9th Guards Fighter Air Regiment successfully fired from their cannons on small vessels in the Azov Sea.

Rocket projectiles had probably been deemed an unnecessary 'luxury' by the Airacobra designers, given the high firepower of the aircraft as it was. The bombs, however, were carried by the Airacobras both in standard American bomb racks and in Soviet ones, which were attached directly in air units. For example, the Black Sea Fleet Air Force had at their disposal aircraft with additional underwing racks for bombs up to 100kg. The Airacobras used American high-explosive and incendiary bombs, as well as Soviet-made ammunition of 100-250kg. The Soviet FAB-100 and FAB-250 bombs had to be slightly modified to fit the American racks. With the FAB-250, the fighter's take-off run increased by 160-180m. The same as in the USA, the manuals imposed strict limitations on mid-air maneuvering with a bomb. The Airacobras were delivering bombing attacks either in horizontal flight, in a shallow dive (45-60°) or (at sea) in the skip bombing manner. In the latter case, a bomb was dropped close to the water and it skipped over the water surface until it hit the hull of a ship.

The same as the Americans, the Soviet Air Force made attempts to use the P-39 as a short-range reconnaissance aircraft. In spring 1943, several aircraft fitted with AFA-I vertical aerial photo cameras were in service with the 118th Independent Reconnaissance Air Regiment, but not for a long time. They were replaced with the Kittyhawks, which were found more suitable for reconnaissance missions. In October 1942, the 3rd Squadron, which was led by M.P. Konkin (later a Hero of the Soviet Union), was formed as part of the 4th Long-Range Reconnaissance Air Regiment. The squadron received six P-39Ds fitted with AFA-I or AFA-B cameras. From such aircraft, the wing machine guns were usually removed. Within five months, the aircraft flew more than 100 combat sorties. In January 1943, the squadron converted to the Yak-9Rs. AFA-I cameras were also installed on individual aircraft in fighter regiments. A fighter so fitted was in service with the 67th Guards Fighter Air Regiment, but there are no documents, however, that mention the installation of any additional armor on the reconnaissance aircraft (which was the case in the USA); on the contrary, in the Soviet Union, efforts were made to reduce their weight to the maximum extent.

It should not be concluded that the Airacobras had only advantages, as the Soviet specialists found a lot of drawbacks in the aircraft as well. In terms of speed, rate of climb and maneuverability, it was inferior to the Yak-1, Yak-9 and La-5 fighters at low and medium altitudes. This was confirmed by mock air combats conducted by expert pilots – thus, E.Y. Savitsky was 'fighting' against Commander of the 153rd Fighter Air Regiment S.I. Mironov. The former flew a Yak-1, and the latter a P-39. Savitsky won the battle…

In an attempt to improve flight performance, Soviet specialists practiced reducing the P-39's weight by stripping it of secondary equipment, certain components of the armament (especially on the Q modification) and its armor protection. For example, the armor behind the engine and the reducing gear protection were removed. In the Northern Fleet, the armor was left intact; instead, the aircraft were deprived of the wing 7.62mm machine guns; some components of the radio equipment; the oxygen bottle; code lights; and the Very pistol. The weight saving totaled 247kg and, as a result, the climb to 5,000m took 1.5 minutes less; the take-off run and landing run became shorter; and the turning time was reduced.

As early as April 1944, after the testing of a reduced-weight Airacobra, Air Force Chief Engineer Colonel General A.K. Repin concluded: "The weight-saving procedures had a favorable effect on all the maneuvers. The aircraft became less inert in maneuvering and easier to control." A Resolution was issued to remove some components of the equipment and armament from a flight of aircraft in each regiment; later, it became a widespread practice at the front.

On the other hand, weight-saving at the expense of the fuel reserve found no extensive application in the USSR. When the P-39N-1s with eight fuel tanks instead of 12 began arriving in the Soviet Union, the Red Army had already launched the offensive; a lower range would result in too frequent redeployments. The Order of the Air Force Chief Engineer stated: 'Operational experience with these aircraft has shown that such capacity of fuel tank fails to ensure proper combat performance of the aircraft'. For this reason, the full set of tanks was 'returned' to the aircraft (the four missing ones were supplied by the manufacturer with each aircraft as additional fuel tanks); however, it was not the slight inferiority in flight performance (in comparison to the most up-to-date Soviet and German fighters) that constituted the American aircraft's major drawback: the engine, which was installed in the aircraft's center of gravity, made the Airacobra respond acutely to any changes in the center of gravity position. As soon as the cannon rounds were used up, the center of gravity position changed abruptly – shifting aft and often causing the fighter to fall into a spin. In case of a half-second delay in the recovery from the spin, the P-39 passed on to a still more dangerous flat spin. A slight imprecision in a steep turn or combat maneuver – consisting of pressing the pedal with a slightly greater force than usual – immediately put the pilot in serious danger. Furthermore, the Airacobra's spin was irregular, with the 'wobbling' of the control stick and high physical loads.

On aircraft of the Q-10, Q-15 and Q-20 series, the center of gravity position was shifted still more to the aft. The NII VVS report on the tests of a P-39Q-10 (conducted by pilot K.I. Ovchinnikov) read: 'The over-pulling of the stick or overpressure on the pedals also brings the aircraft into a spin. With the center of gravity shifted aft, the tendency for the spin increases'. The situation with no ammunition on board and the oil tank full was the most dangerous of all. Such a situation was commented upon as follows: '… Performance of aerobatics on the aircraft is rather difficult … The slightest over-pulling of the stick leads to a quick drop in the speed, and to falling into a spin…' Test Pilot I.I. Shelest wrote that the Airacobra was demonstrating its 'serpentine nature' in this manner.

Spins caused a lot of accidents and crashes in combat units. In 1944, the 1st Guards Air Division alone saw two crashes and four accidents during two months. In some units, the pilots were, at first, extremely afraid of performing aerobatics on the P-39s (for example, this fact could be found in I.M. Dzusov's memoirs). It should be noted that crashes were suffered not only by pilots, who had been hastily training during wartime, but by experienced test pilots as well. At NII VVS alone, three crashes occurred: on 2 February 1943, K.A. Gruzdev was killed in an Airacobra I; on 3 January 1944, K.A. Avtonomov was killed in a P-39N; and on 27 April the same year, K.I. Ovchinnikov was killed in a P-39Q-10.

The situation was so serious that in autumn 1943, a special Bell team led by L. Rogers (Bell's claims manager) arrived in Moscow. The team also included designer Ray and two mechanics (Hawkins and Zaimbek), and they were accompanied by four Soviet officers (Colonel Gervasiy and Lieutenant Colonel Kochetkov of NII VVS, and Captain Smolyarov and Captain Vasilevsky of the Import Directorate); the Americans brought training aids and instructional films. They visited two combat regiments (the 30th Guards Fighter Air Regiment and the 67th Guards Fighter Air Regiment) and the 6th Backup Air Brigade. The films were shown to all of the units, and efficient procedures for the maintenance and repair of the aircraft were demonstrated. The American mechanics conducted training sessions on how to adjust the undercarriage, brakes and synchronizer; how to use special-purpose tools; how to disassemble the reducing gear; and how to remove the fuel tank. With the help of interpreters, they answered questions asked by pilots, technicians and engineers. In turn, Bell's representatives listened to the opinions as expressed by the flight and ground crews, and wrote down suggestions and complaints. In particular, spin conditions were discussed – including the modifications most prone to spin, and ways to recover from it.

At the time of the Americans' stay in Ivanovo, an accident with a P-39Q-5 occurred. The pilot bailed out and the fighter crashed in the woods. According to the pilot's account, he fell into a spin while performing a turn, lost his bearings and bailed out. The Americans, together with Soviet engineers, examined the wrecked Airacobra and the cause of the accident was identified very quickly: it was rooted in a violation of the instructions. The aircraft had taken off without ammunition, and with a considerable excess of oil on board (the oil tank was arranged in the aft portion of the fuselage). This had led to an excessively aft center of gravity and, finally, to the spin stall. The brigade commander was properly reprimanded, and the accident rate decreased.

It was not easy to bail out from a P-39 in a spin. The pilots abandoned the aircraft via the left door, which was jettisoned in an emergency situation. In the course of such a bailing-out, the pilots would hit against the horizontal stabilizer – and the consequences could be even fatal. Among the pilots who were seriously injured in such a situation were Heroes of the Soviet Union N.M. Iskrin (in May 1943) and B.B. Glinka (in July 1944). According to Pokryshkin: "The Cobra could not stand those who attempted to leave her in mid-air." Even if the pilot was lucky enough to recover from the spin, there was a new danger in store for him: high accelerations led to deformations of the P-39's tail unit and to the jamming of control surfaces – thus, in the first half of 1943, three Airacobras of the 6th Backup Air Brigade suffered crashes which were brought about by tail unit failure.

On 15 January, Sergeant Usachev of the 30th Guards Fighter Air Regiment was killed. At an altitude of 1,500m, he made a combat turn and then fell into a nosedive. He recovered from the nosedive, but then went into a spin and crashed into the ground with the engine running; on 28 May, Major Reznichenko was killed in an almost identical situation. On 29 July, the tail unit of Junior Lieutenant Pazyuk's Airacobra collapsed in a maneuver. The wreckage inspection report read: '...The tail unit was completely torn off in flight; the horizontal stabilizer came off at all the four attachment points ... The horizontal stabilizer broke into two parts at spar locations...' Members of the Emergency Board concluded that the horizontal stabilizer's leading edge had failed, and then had been bent upward and backward. The left portion of the stabilizer had been torn off by airflow, and had stricken and broken the vertical stabilizer. It was the sixth crash that the brigade had seen since the beginning of flights in the Airacobras.

Another accident occurred on 30 July 1943. Lieutenant Kostyakov managed to land, but with his aircraft's vertical stabilizer deformed after the performance of a barrel roll. The accident was attributed to the buffeting of the tail unit, which tended to occur in certain flight conditions. The Moscow Military District Air Force Headquarters reported: '...The flight crews have been instructed to avoid high accelerations and to change the flight condition if vibrations appear...' It was even suggested that barrel rolls, Immelmann turns, spins and abrupt pull-outs should be forbidden for the Airacobras, but this would have actually invalidated the aircraft as a fighter.

A decision was made to check the actual strength of the Airacobra's fuselage and empennage by static testing, so in mid-August 1943, a P-39N was sent to TsAGI. The tests showed that the aircraft's margins of safety were lower than those established by Soviet standards. The tail portion of the fuselage undoubtedly required reinforcement.

In March 1944, after a series of accidents and crashes in the 11th Fighter Air Regiment (which operated at the North-Western Front), an overall check of all the Airacobras in the regiment was carried out. Evident traces of deformation were found on 15 aircraft. I.G. Rabkin, who took part in the inspection, later wrote: 'We found buckles on the right and left side of the fuselage tail portion; broken horizontal stabilizer spars near the attachments to the fuselage; creases on the upper skin of the horizontal stabilizer, and on the vertical stabilizer leading edge'. The pilots were temporarily prohibited to perform Immelmann turns and spins.

The high efficiency of the control surfaces, which was a characteristic feature of the P-39s, could lead to high accelerations not only in a spin, but also during abrupt maneuvering. The results were the same: deformation of the empennage and the tail portion of the fuselage. The Senior Engineer of the 273rd Air Division reported (in September 1944): '... We have identified ... buckling in the fuselage tail portion near the radio hatch after rough evolutions in flight. Skin deformations have been found in the bottom aft portion of the fuselage ... There was a case when one of the horizontal stabilizer panels bent inward during flight...'

A comprehensive program to combat the Airacobra's major defects was implemented in the USSR. Thorough tests helped identify a pilot's actions which incited the falling into a spin. NII VVS held a training session for instructor pilots, and experienced pilots were sent to air units to demonstrate the safe piloting techniques to be used for the American aircraft; a training film, '*The Spin of the Airacobra*' was even made. All of these countermeasures contributed towards a considerable reduction of the accident rate on the front lines, but could not, of course, totally eliminate the losses.

By a Resolution of the Air Force Chief Engineer, limitations were imposed in respect of the aircraft's center of gravity; it was forbidden to put covers and tools in the aft portion during redeployment. Performing aerobatics without ammunition, or an equivalent ballast weight on board, was strictly prohibited. Sometimes, the removal of (for example) protective armor from the oil tank was practiced in order to shift the fighter's center of gravity forward, which was the case with the P-39Q-5s; however, for later versions, that was not enough. From them, armor (three steel plates and two duralumin plates) was entirely removed from the carburetor, and a ballast weight was placed in front of the storage battery.

In the course of mass manufacture, the Americans made the skin thicker and reinforced the frames around access holes; however, deformations persisted. Oblong dents kept appearing in the tail section. For this reason, Soviet specialists decided to tackle the problem of tail section reinforcement themselves. Engineer M.S. Malkov of the Air Force Central Scientific and Experimental Base suggested a procedure for the strengthening of the primary structure, and a prototype aircraft was modified and tested at NII VVS. After that, the modification of the Airacobras was carried out directly in the regiments. In the air defense forces alone, 326 aircraft were modified in such a manner. Various units introduced other reinforcements to the fighter's airframe at their own discretion – thus, for example, in the 273rd Fighter Air Division, reinforcing strips were installed to the horizontal stabilizer spars. All of these measures led to the shifting of the center of gravity in the aft direction, and caused a further search for 'something to be removed'. The most frequent practice consisted of limiting the quantity of oil in the oil tank; however, the Bell Aircraft Corporation did not stay idle either: in a later series of the Q modification, the tail portion of the fuselage was considerably reinforced, and the ballast weight was installed in the nose, but a complete victory over the spin condition was never achieved. Even after the war, pilots were killed in the Airacobras – thus, on 9 April 1947, Senior Lieutenant Moisievich of the navy's 25th Fighter Air Regiment fell into a spin and crashed into the water.

Other drawbacks of the Airacobra were also identified: the tricycle undercarriage ensured an excellent field of view during taxiing and, basically, allowed moving at a high speed in the airfield without the danger of a nose-down; however, on bumpy, unpaved airfields, the nose leg staggered and often failed, which meant limitations on the taxiing speed.

The Allison V-1710 engines were the same as on the P-40s; however, on the Airacobras, they were linked to an extended shaft which was routed through the entire aircraft to the propeller. The engines required skilled maintenance, precise adjustment, good oil and high-quality fuel. The bearings, which were made from 'white alloy', were especially vulnerable. They operated excellently at a high rpm and with loads, but with a precondition that good lubrication and a precise assembly was ensured. The precondition, however, was not always met: the engines 'retorted' with jammed crankshafts and torn-off connecting rods. It took a long time to adapt to the peculiarities of the American engines. In August 1944, the 67th Guards Fighter Air Regiment reported: '... The engine fails to attain the assigned 250 hours .... Throughout the two years in service, none of the engines has ever attained at least 60 or 70 percent of the assigned life in combat conditions...' The problem was that the 'snapping-off' of the connecting rods on the Airacobra posed a much greater danger than on the P-40 because they could easily damage the control surface cables which were routed nearby.

Inspections in air units showed that pilots tended to excessively use augmented settings and failed to take proper care of the oil system. Furthermore, the required oil and fuel grades were not always in use. In the Soviet Union, the Airacobras were initially fueled with 4B-78 fuel, which was, of course, of a lower quality than the American equivalent. In sieged Leningrad, a makeshift mixture – referred to as 'compote' – was used instead of the B-78. There was a case when an American fighter was refueled with the B-70 and it took off successfully after a forced landing!

In the second half of the war, the situation with the fuel became better, and American instructions were then complied with. The early modifications of the Airacobra required the B-95 fuel; for the later modifications, B-100 was the preferred choice. Both grades were coming from abroad. When the B-100 was unavailable, it was allowable to add tetraethyl lead to the B-95 – thus obtaining the 1B-95. This, however, led to limitations in terms of supercharging and to a strict prohibition to use the 'War Emergency Power'.

Additives in the Soviet-made fuel caused erosion of the bladder fuel tanks. To avoid erosion, the tanks were either covered from the inside (with common non-waterproof putty), or rinsed with an adhesive solution to create a thin protective film.

A similar situation existed with oil: due to the scarcity of standard American oils, they were replaced with Soviet ones and, furthermore, not only with dedicated engine oils. Instead of special oil, propeller hubs were lubricated with a mixture of engine and transformer oils; for the reducing gear, a 'cocktail' of loom oil, transformer oil and engine oil was used. The application of Soviet oils called for particular attention to the engine exhaust temperature, because when it became overheated, such oils produced a large quantity of tarry residue.

Certain modifications were connected to winter-time operations (e.g. the heat insulation of pipelines, and the installation of drain valves both in the oil system and in the cooling lines). To work with the drain valves, small access holes were cut out in the lower radiator cowling. The issue was that according to Soviet standards, coolant and oil were required to be fully drained after a flight, lest they should freeze. With the small-sized American drain valves, the process took too much time; moreover, the coolant was sometimes drained incompletely.

As the cold set in, lubrication oil in assemblies and sub-assemblies was replaced with a more frost-resistant Soviet counterpart. For example, the main bearing of the extended shaft was lubricated in winter with NK-30 oil.

The standard Preston coolant was not fit for the severe cold, since it got frozen at -17°C. Later, the Americans began exporting Zerex, which withstood temperatures down to -28°C. Attempts were made to operate the engine with more frost-resistant Soviet anti-freeze agents, but this called for modifications in the cooling system.

In severe cold, the electric starter was unable to start the engine, so for Soviet aircraft, an automobile starter was used in such situations. It was, essentially, a truck in which the torque from the engine was supplied to a crankshaft, with a cantilevered 'arm' projecting above its cabin. A system of hinges allowed setting the cantilevered arm to different positions. The arm ended with a claw clutch, which engaged with a mating part on the aircraft propeller hub; the Airacobra, however, was not fitted with a claw clutch (or, as the Americans used to put it, a 'dog clutch'). Upon a request from the Soviet Union, claw clutches were installed on several P-39Ks at the Bell Factory, and three of them were handed over to the Soviet Acceptance Board in Fairbanks in July 1943. It was intended that two of them would be subjected to operational service tests with units of the 7th Air Army; however, no traces of such tests have been found in documents.

Aircraft with claw clutches were indeed tested in the USSR in November 1943, and it was discovered that the claw clutch diameter did not fit the Soviet automobile starters. Furthermore, the setting angle was off-standard, so the use of adapters was suggested as a way out. It is not known whether such fighters were subsequently shipped to the Soviet Union.

As with the Kittyhawks, on the P-39s there were occasions of fuel system failure caused by vibrations, which led to fire in flight. In such a situation, Hero of the Soviet Union N.E. Lavitsky was killed in the course of aircraft ferrying near Gudermes. Duralumin tubes of American manufacture were replaced with annealed copper ones, and other minor modifications were also made. Soviet plastic pulleys for control cables were installed instead of aluminum ones, since such a decision allowed for reducing the cable wear. Attachments for the reduction gear were reinforced and, in view of a shortage of American instruments, Soviet KI-11 compasses and AVR clocks were installed during repairs.

More significant modifications were carried out in the Soviet Union as well. In the Northern Fleet and in the Baltic Sea Fleet, attempts were made to mount a retractable ski undercarriage on the Airacobras. In April 1944, expert workman Rakov of the White Sea Flotilla Air Force Workshops made his own version of such an undercarriage. All of the legs were retractable in flight, with the main ski protruding by 150-170mm. Rakov also suggested mounting a small forward ski to prevent the nose leg from getting stuck in the snow; it was successfully tested in April 1944. The undercarriage extension and retraction mechanisms operated normally, and the fighter was able to steadily maneuver on the airfield; however, the novelty found no application. The P-39s continued using wheels all year round.

To expedite the conversion training of flight crews, a trainer aircraft was built in the USSR. With the second cockpit forward of the main one, it was not unlike the TP-39 two-seater (which was not shipped by the Americans). The dual-cockpit aircraft were built in various units and detachments in accordance with drawings prepared by the Air Force Central Scientific and Experimental Base. These aircraft did not arouse much enthusiasm, for the reason of extreme inconvenience for the instructor pilot. For example, it was noted that: '… due to design features, spatial orientation is complicated…' V.I. Voronov, who flew such an aircraft after the war with the 6th Guards Fighter Air Regiment, wrote: 'The 'hybrid' performed its function. However, in the forward cockpit, one felt ill at ease, with the propeller rotating within some forty centimeters before the eyes. And if, in case of an unexpected situation, the pilot had to bail out, he would surely hit the propeller'; however, practice showed such a statement to be groundless. On 17 September 1947, a two-seater Airacobra of the 25th Fighter Air Regiment fell into a spin. Senior Lieutenant Petrenko (the inspecting officer), who had occupied the forward cockpit, successfully bailed out and survived, whereas Lieutenant Kovalev, who had been in the aft cockpit, failed to escape and was killed.

Except for tail portion reinforcements, the Airacobra was not subjected to major design changes. The only thing to mention is the modification of several dozen of the P-39s to fly with M-105P engines, which was due to a shortage of spare Allison engines. The work was performed in the Leningrad Front Air Workshops, but there is no precise information as to how it was done. It should be noted that the M-105 had an integrated reduction gear, on account of which the output shaft axis was positioned higher than on Allison engines. It is not known if the reduction gear was removed, or if the position of the engine on the aircraft was changed. In any case, the replacement: '… caused no violations of the aerodynamic shape of the aircraft…'

Certain minor changes were introduced directly in the air units – thus, for example, on Pokryshkin's aircraft, the control stick was modified to accommodate a single trigger switch for the cannon and for the machine guns.

In the 1st Ferry Air Division, one of the P-39s was fitted with the Soviet RPK-10 radio compass and was used as the lead aircraft during the ferrying of single-engine aircraft. On some Airacobras, radio compasses were installed in the USA. Such aircraft were also shipped to the USSR; however (probably), their quantity was not large, since their shortage was experienced even by the air defense forces. In the 4th Backup Air Brigade, at least one P-39 was fitted with an American MN-26 radio compass.

The manufacture of the P-39s at the Bell Factory in Niagara Falls was discontinued in 1944, and the last five P-39Qs came via the ALSIB route in early 1945. In total, according to different sources, 4,719 to 4,746 Airacobras of various versions were shipped from the USA. As many as 212 aircraft were re-exported from Great Britain – and of those, 158 reached their final destination. The USSR accepted 4,952 aircraft (this quantity also includes unserviceable fighters which were sent by the British instead of group spare part sets). The breakdown per versions is known solely from reports on American military assistance. According to such reports, among the shipped aircraft were one-hundred-and eight P-39Ds, forty P-39Ks, one-hundred-and-thirty-seven P-39Ls, one-hundred-and-fifty-seven P-39Ms, one-thousand-one-hundred-and-thirteen P-39Ns and three-thousand-two-hundred-and-ninety-one P-39Qs.

Many regiments and divisions of the Soviet Air Force flew the Airacobras until the end of military operations against Germany, in spite of the fact that from 1944, they were gradually replaced by modern Soviet fighters such as the Yak-3s, Yak-9Us and La-7s and, from 1945, with the American P-63s. It is in an Airacobra that G.G. Golubev shot down one of the last enemy aircraft in the European theatre of war: a Dornier Do 217 bomber in Czechoslovakia.

In May 1945, the air force and the air defense forces had, altogether, three-thousand-and-seventy-eight P-39s. Of those, the share of the air defense forces constituted 700 aircraft.

Two thirds of the above-mentioned three-thousand aircraft were of the Q version, which was the main version. At the front, their share was still greater and exceeded 90 percent. The old P-39Ds remained only in the rear districts and in the air defense forces. In total, by the end of the war, there remained only 34 of them.

The navy, by the moment of the capitulation of Germany, had received as many as 691 fighters. Of those, 324 were assigned to the Northern Fleet and 176 to the Black Sea Fleet. With both fleets, the Airacobra had become the main fighter type by the end of the war. The Northern Fleet had at its disposal three fully equipped regiments (which had 40 or more aircraft each) flying the P-39s. Those were the 2nd Guards Air Regiment, the 27th Air Regiment and the 255th Air Regiment; the 3rd Training Air Regiment also had some 10 aircraft. Among the regiments of the Black Sea Fleet, the 11th and the 43rd Air Regiments flew the Airacobras.

Approximately 150 aircraft were 'in transit' – being assigned to maritime ferry regiments. A single P-39 was at the disposal of the Stalin Training School, and five aircraft were in use with the Higher Officers' Training Courses. The 65th Special-Purpose Air Regiment in Moscow had six Airacobras in operation.

The P-39s had never seen service with the Baltic Fleet. In the Pacific, there were no Airacobras before July 1945, when (pending the commencement of a war against Japan) the 27th Fighter Air Regiment (from the Northern Fleet) and the 43rd Fighter Air Regiment (from the Black Sea Fleet) were redeployed there. The 43rd Air Regiment was stationed in Romanovka and the 27th in Nizhnee Netino. Altogether, there were exactly 100 Airacobras in service with the two regiments. In August, they were assigned the task of providing air cover for the Pacific Fleet bases; however, since the Japanese aviation stayed almost idle, the fighters saw no application there.

In total, by 1 May 1945, the Soviet Air Force had lost two-thousand-two-hundred-and-two P-39s; of them, 887 aircraft were lost in 1944 – and this quantity actually reflects their mass use at the final stages of the hostilities. By the end of the war, there had been 122 combat sorties and four destroyed enemy aircraft per lost Airacobra.

Upon the termination of warfare, the majority of imported aircraft were intended to be scrapped. On 22 March 1946, the Council of Ministers issued a Resolution prescribing the writing off of two-thousand-two-hundred-and-sixteen P-39s (that is, approximately, two thirds of the fleet) and replacing them with the Yak-3, Yak-9U and La-7 fighters. In practice, a lot of regiments converted to the American P-63s.

In spite of the fact that during the post-war years, the air force, air defense forces and the naval aviation suffered considerable reductions, the Resolution was never implemented in full. This was accounted for by the drastic decline in the production of Soviet aircraft factories, which had converted to the peacetime regime. Besides, the shortcomings of Soviet fighters which had, out of sheer necessity, been tolerated during the war, became unacceptable upon completion of the hostilities. It turned out that the re-equipment of the regiments might take a lot of time. Therefore, the imported aircraft which were still quite suitable for air combat took the stage again – thus, for example, in May 1946, pilots of the 574th Reconnaissance Air Regiment of the Northern Fleet just began conversion training from the Yak-9 and P-40 to the P-39.

The Soviet Air Force did not make much show of the presence of American aircraft in the Soviet aviation during the post-war years. The Airacobras did not take part in parades; however, they remained in service. The number of operable aircraft was gradually decreasing. Upon the termination of the war, shipments of spare parts from the USA were cut off, so the only way out was to use the remaining warehouse stock, or to manufacture some parts in a 'semi-makeshift' manner in the USSR. The situation was especially difficult with spare engines and their accessories. Strict limitations had to be imposed on full-throttle operations; for example, using emergency settings was forbidden at all times. In some units, clamps were simply screwed onto throttle levers to prevent moving the lever to a full stop. Wrecked aircraft were entirely stripped of all spare parts that could be of use.

Accidents and crashes also contributed to the reduction in the number of the P-39s. Pilots kept falling into spins and committing errors at landing. On 16 October 1946, Lieutenant Korneev died in a crash. He failed to recover from a spin and was killed in a collision with water. On 12 March 1947, two fighters of the 2nd Guards Fighter Air Regiment collided during the take-off run. Both pilots survived; however, the aircraft had to be discarded. On 12 September the same year, Lieutenant Badyuk of the 62nd Fighter Air Regiment committed an error at landing and crashed into an orchard near the airfield. Badyuk survived, but in respect of his Airacobra, the report read: 'The aircraft is wrecked beyond repair'. The same regiment saw a case when the customary speed was exceeded in a nosedive, and Lieutenant Shkutnikov's fighter simply disintegrated in flight.

In fact, the last Airacobras remained in service with regular regiments until the early 1950s; in training schools, they stayed for several years more. The whole world had already begun converting to jet fighters – and here (again), the P-39s came in useful. The new-generation aircraft had a tricycle undercarriage with a nose leg, which was just the same as the Airacobra's. The fighters that were still airworthy were then provided (as temporary equipment) to the regiments which intended to convert to the Yak-17 and MiG-9 and, later, to the Yak-23 and the MiG-15. For example, the 18th Air Defense Fighter Air Regiment in Khabarovsk flew (for a short time) the P-39s and the P-63s instead of the Yak-9Ps in June 1950.

On the whole, the Airacobra was a good and reliable combat aircraft which left a remarkable imprint in the memory of Soviet pilots, and it made a considerable contribution to aviation operations on the Soviet-German Front.

Currently, there is a single Airacobra in Russia, which is displayed as a monument to the ALSIB route in Yakutsk airport. Another former Soviet fighter can be found in Finland: a P-39Q which made an emergency landing in the Finnish territory in June 1944, and was damaged. Several years ago, it underwent restoration in order to be displayed in the Finnish Air Force Museum in Tikkakoski. Recently, the aircraft was transferred to Helsinki; however, as of today, it is not on display anywhere.

One of the first Airacobra Is, which arrived in the USSR in early 1942.

A crash landing of an Airacobra I flown by test pilot V.E. Golofastov during winter 1942.

A crash landing of Captain I.V. Bochkov's Airacobra I on 22 May 1942. The aircraft engine failed during take-off from Shonguy airfield.

Squadron Leader P.S. Kutakhov in the cockpit of an Airacobra; the 19th Guards Fighter Air Regiment.

Junior Lieutenant S.F. Bogatsky in front of his Airacobra I.

Deputy Squadron Leader of the 19th Guards Fighter Air Regiment Captain I.D. Gaydaenko near his aircraft, which features combat victory markings.

Pilots of the 153rd Fighter Air Regiment near an Airacobra in 1942.

The wreckage of an Airacobra at an airfield in Voronezh in 1942.

Junior Lieutenant V.V. Gabrinets watching the loading of ammunition belts in his Airacobra; the 19th Guards Fighter Air Regiment, spring 1942.

A P-39D-1 Airacobra, with the 'US ARMY' lettering visible on the wing's lower surface.

A demonstration of the technical features of the Airacobra at the 16th Guards Fighter Air Regiment.

Maintenance being performed on an Airacobra of the 402nd Fighter Air Regiment.

An inspection of the P-39 wheel at the 25th Backup Air Regiment.

A presentation of the Guards Banner to the 103rd Guards Fighter Air Regiment (the former 158th Fighter Air Regiment), Leningrad, 18 September 1943.

A photo of the ground crew near an Airacobra of the 26th Guards Fighter Air Regiment.

A bomb being attached to a belly mount of a P-39; the 3rd Air Army.

A P-39 of the Northern Fleet Air Force in the course of pre-flight maintenance.

Pilots of a fighter regiment near an Airacobra.

Pilots of the 3rd Squadron, 30th Guards Fighter Air Regiment, July 1943.

The P-39 fighters of the 100th Guards Fighter Air Regiment at an airfield, February 1943.

Friends congratulating Hero of the Soviet Union V.M. Drygin on the recent air victory scored on the P-39L; the 298th Fighter Air Regiment, June 1943.

Lieutenant Colonel S. Lyubimov thanking the technician Lieutenant I. Kozlov for his good job, July 1943.

Squadron Leader of the 196th Fighter Air Regiment A.D. Biryulin, who had 11 combat victories to his credit.

Squadron Leader of the 69th Guards Fighter Air Regiment Captain N.I. Proshenkov, who later became a Hero of the Soviet Union.

Personnel of the 103rd Guards Fighter Air Regiment (the former 158th Fighter Air Regiment) taking the Guards Oath, July 1943.

Lieutenant Colonel Sobolev accepts the Airacobra from the collective farmer Shumkova. The aircraft bears the inscription *Krasnoyarsky Komsomolets*, or Komsomol member of Krasnoyarsk city, with the note underneath stating that it was bought with funds collected by K.S. Shumkova.

Hero of the Soviet Union Z.A. Sorokin near his Airacobra, Vaenga airfield.

An Airacobra on a snow-covered airfield.

An Airacobra in flight.

Airacobra fighters of the Northern Fleet Air Force at Vaenga airfield.

Commander of the 129th Guards Fighter Air Regiment and Hero of the Soviet Union Major V.A. Figichev carries out a debriefing after a mission.

A.I. Pokryshkin making a note in a record book on a wing of his Airacobra.

An Airacobra of the 7th Air Army being repaired after a forced landing.

A P-39 being refueled at a frontline airfield in 1943.

Fresh newspapers received at the 69th Guards Fighter Air Regiment. In the background is the fighter flown by Captain N.I. Proshenkov (later a Hero of the Soviet Union).

Pilots of the 2nd Guards Fighter Air Regiment, Northern Fleet Air Force near a P-39.

Naval pilots dancing; an Airacobra is in the background.

Pilots of the 1st Squadron, 30th Guards Fighter Air Regiment near a P-39.

Pilots having a rest at a frontline airfield, with a P-39 in the background.

Pilots of a fighter regiment near a P-39.

During the war, the famous Soviet fighter ace A.I. Pokryshkin became a hero of American comics.

Four famous Soviet pilots who flew on Airacobras. From left to right: A.F. Klubov, G.A. Rechkalov, A.I. Trud and A.I Pokryshkin.

The refueling of P-39, which belonged to a Guards fighter air regiment.

The ground crew demonstrate maintenance of an Airacobra.

A.I. Pokryshkin near his Airacobra.

P.S. Kutakhov with pilots of the 19th Guards Fighter Air Regiment after an orders and medals awarding ceremony at an airfield near Murmansk.

An Airacobra being prepared for the next mission in one of the Black Sea Fleet Air Force regiments, June 1944.

A parachutist instructor demonstrating the correct procedure for bailing out from an Airacobra in mid-air in an emergency situation; note the jettisoned right door.

A P-39 fighter during tests in a large, full-scale wind tunnel at TsAGI.

The P-39Q fighters, with external (ferry) fuel tanks, awaiting flight to Chukotka in Alaska.

A P-39Q with a ferry fuel tank at NII VVS.

P-39Q fighters of the Northern Fleet Air Force at an airfield in 1943.

A P-39Q with an anti-spin parachute attached on a truss under the rudder, NII VVS, spring 1944.

An Airacobra being subjected to structural strength testing at TsAGI.

The tail part of an Airacobra undergoing structural testing at TsAGI.

The empennage of the P-39, in which Junior Lieutenant I.P. Pazyuk of the 21st Guards Fighter Air Regiment was killed on 29 July 1943. The aircraft empennage collapsed in flight.

Personnel of the 30th Guards Fighter Air Regiment near a P-39Q-5, Poland, autumn 1944.

The Airacobras at Alt Rosenberg airfield in Germany during early 1945.

A technician adding a victory star marking on a P-39 flown by pilot Galushkov in 1945.

One of the P-39s of the 9th Guards Fighter Air Division taking off from a motor road in Germany in 1945.

Pilots of the 9th Guards Fighter Air Division at a seized airfield in Germany in 1945.

Pilots of the 3rd Squadron, 129th Guards Fighter Air Regiment near the P-39s after the first flight over Berlin. Squadron Leader Senior Lieutenant Basenko is in the center, Germany, April 1945.

Pilots of the 101st Guards Fighter Air Regiment near a P-39 at Bromberg airfield (now Bydgoszcz) in October 1945.

A modified P-39Q with an anti-spin parachute during tests at NII VVS in April 1945.

A P-39M-1 with a radio compass during tests at NII VVS.

Maintenance of P-39 fighters at an airfield in Germany in 1945.

The installation of an MN-26Y radio compass, which was performed in the 4th Backup Air Brigade.

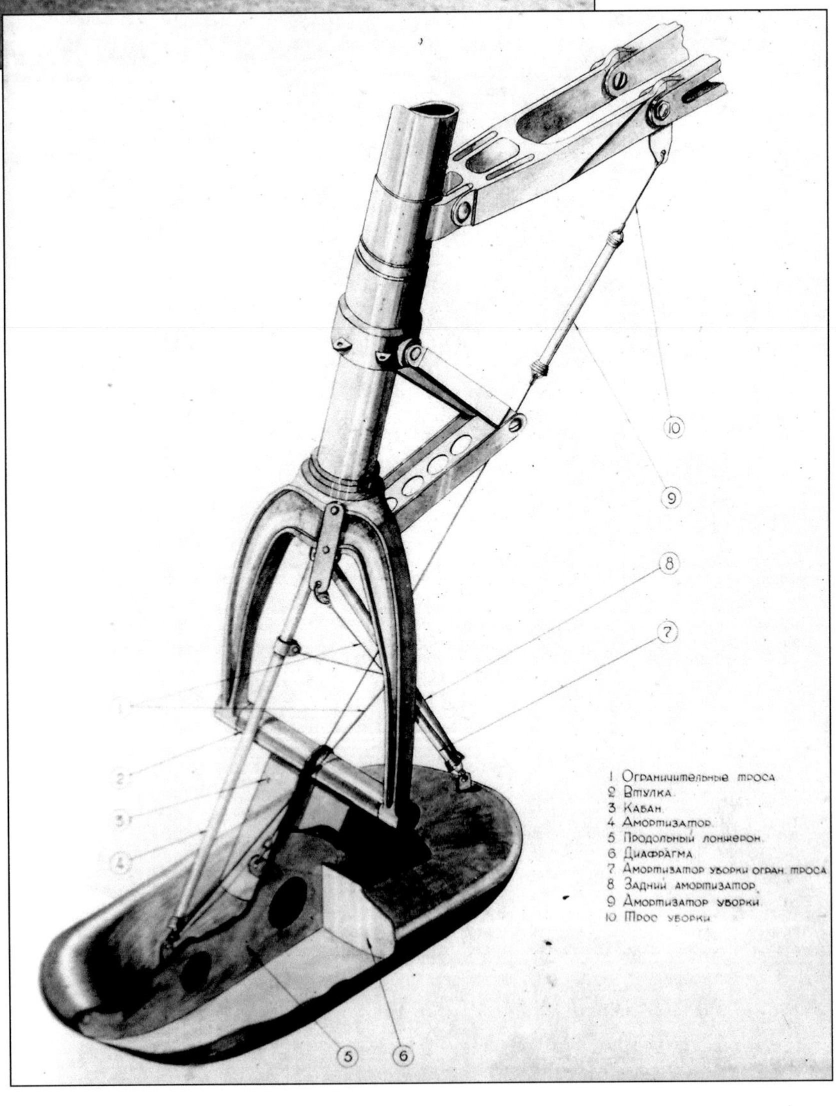

A schematic of the ski for the P-39 nose landing gear leg, which was proposed by the aircraft repair shops of the Northern Fleet.

The Soviet two-seat trainer version of the P-39.

A P-39 of the 6th Guards Fighter Air Regiment, Black Sea Fleet Air Force, Yevpatoriya, 1947.

A scaled-down flying replica of the P-39, which was on display at the MAKS air show in Zhukovsky in 1995. The aircraft markings are of the aircraft flown by Hero of the Soviet Union G.U. Dolnikov of the 100th Guards Fighter Air Regiment.

The only Airacobra which survived in Russia has been placed as a monument near Yakutsk airport – commemorating the people who had been working on the ALSIB route.

The Soviet P-39Q on display in the Finnish Air Force Museum in Tikkakoski.

The Soviet P-39Q on display in the Finnish Air Force Museum in Tikkakoski.

7.5 Bell P-63 Kingcobra

Many people believe the Kingcobra to be a version of the Airacobra. In fact, it is quite a different fighter, whose similarity to its predecessor is confined to the general layout, with the engine in the middle of the fuselage and the propeller rotated via an extended shaft. The Kingcobra was larger in size, had a different contour and, which is the most important thing, had a new wing with a laminar flow airfoil. The latter, with a tapered leading edge and the maximum height shifted back, promised a considerable reduction in drag. Therefore, the aircraft could accelerate to a higher speed. On the other hand, this led to a reduction in wing lift, which affected its take-off and landing performance.

The history of the Kingcobra began in June 1941, when the USAAF placed an order for a new fighter with Bell. It was intended that the new aircraft would differ from the existing Airacobra by a laminar flow airfoil with a larger span, and the version of the V-1710 engine with a two-stage supercharger (earlier, engines with a single-stage supercharger had been mounted). The second stage provided for an additional boost, as well as improving the engine altitude performance.

In response, a design team led by J. Strickler and D. Fabriev created the 'Model 33' design, which was given the designation P-63 by the USAAF. The first prototype fighter was built in late November 1942. On 7 December, it made its maiden flight, but it was not destined to fly for a long time: in January 1943, the aircraft was destroyed in a belly landing. The 'life' of the second prototype was shorter still, as it only lasted for three months; then, its engine stopped in flight. The pilot bailed out and survived. After that, the third prototype, which had been initially intended for static tests, was hurriedly finished. This aircraft successfully completed the entire test program.

The order for mass production had been awarded even before any of the prototypes was ready. In October 1943, the factory in Buffalo began assembling the first P-63A-1 fighters, and mass manufacture was launched in early 1944.

The number of Kingcobras was increasing: at first, the P-63A version with the Allison V-1710-93 engine was manufactured (series from A-1 through to A-10). It was constantly subjected to modifications, which expanded the ground attack capabilities of the aircraft. Underwing fuel tanks, bomb racks and removable containers with large-caliber machine guns (like on the P-39Q) were mounted; the combat stock of the 37mm cannon was increased from 30 rounds to 58 rounds; and a rack for six rockets was installed. At the same time, the armor weight was continuously increased (from 40kg on the A-1 to 121kg on the A-10).

It was quite clear that the Soviet aviation would be the main 'user' of the Kingcobras. In December 1943, Bell sent detailed information on the P-63 to Moscow. In February 1944, NII VVS representatives (the engineers A.G. Kochetkov and F.P. Suprun) were delegated to the USA and they were entrusted with the task of testing the P-63A prior to the massive influx of these aircraft to the Soviet Union.

As has already been mentioned, among the Airacobra's main problems was the excessively aft center of gravity. It occurred under certain load conditions and induced falling into a spin, which could change into a more dangerous flat spin. The second major problem consisted of an insufficient rigidity of the fuselage tail portion and empennage, which tended to buckle in conditions of abrupt maneuvering. American designers assured that the modifications which had been introduced in the P-63 had 'cured' those 'diseases' of the aircraft. This was described in detail to Lieutenant Colonel Kochetkov by designer Ray from the USA, who visited the USSR in September 1943 with the Bell delegation; however, Soviet specialists tended to doubt that.

As soon as Kochetkov and Suprun became familiar with the new fighter, they decided to prove that the defects had been rectified only partially, and that dangers for pilots were still persisting. Kochetkov, along with being an engineer, was also a pilot. Having received a brand-new P-63A-6 fighter, he (on 29 April 1944) put it into a flat spin, from which he was unable to recover. After a certain number of turns and several futile attempts to pull out and put the aircraft into a straight flight, Kochetkov, at a height of 900m, jettisoned the door and bailed out. Bell's management, which was led by the company's Vice-President Johnson, arrived at the location where Kochetkov had landed. Together, they all went to examine the wrecked Kingcobra and, instead of the expected reprimand, the Soviet pilot received a commendation for the detected defect and was invited to a restaurant to celebrate the occasion – thus, Kochetkov managed to prove to the Americans the need to enhance the anti-spin performance of the Airacobra's descendant, which had inherited the drawback of its predecessor.

Standing near the wreckage, all that were present left their signatures on the only piece of paper to be found: it was a one US dollar note, which was taken out of someone's wallet. The 'lucky dollar' was given as a keepsake to Kochetkov, who carried it with him afterwards for a long time. Later, the pilot received a commemorative (a lapel pin in the form of a golden caterpillar) from the Irvin Parachute Company. Such a commemorative was given to everybody who managed to survive using an Irvin parachute.

Kochetkov also conducted training air combats with the P-39 and P-51 fighters, and the results were determined using aerial gun camera shots. The Airacobra lost outright, and the fight with the Mustang (according to everybody's opinion) ended in a draw; then, Kochetkov destroyed another Kingcobra by subjecting it to high-g aerobatics. As a result, skin buckling and dents were found on the aircraft wing and in the tail portion of the fuselage. The manufacturer made modifications to the design to partially eliminate the defects; however, that was not done immediately and not in full.

Deliveries of the P-63s to the USSR were planned under Protocol III of the Allies' shipments for the first half of 1944. Three aircraft are listed as being brought by sea to the northern ports, while the rest were ferried by air across the Bering Strait. In June 1944, American ferry pilots brought the first Kingcobras to Fairbanks and started training Soviet pilots to fly the aircraft. Only ferry division squadron leaders were trained in Alaska; the rest of the pilots had to master the new fighters directly in their regiments. In Yakutsk, 50 pilots who had flown the A-20 bombers before completed their conversion training in 11 days. Soon, the Kingcobras took the road to Krasnoyarsk.

Not all of the Kingcobras were destined to successfully reach Fairbanks. For example, on 23 November 1944, two Kingcobras fell after take-off in the Great Falls. In January 1945, Lieutenant W. Pruddle crashed near Watson Lake and, in February the same year, two P-63s collided in mid-air during a formation flight, north of Edmonton. In total, the Americans lost 21 fighters at their segment of the route, but those were replaced by newly manufactured ones.

Acceptance was not always running smoothly either: one of the first batches was rejected entirely by the Soviet Commission in Fairbanks due to oil cooler defects, and was sent back for further work. In October 1944, all of the Kingcobras that were en route at the American segment were held back in order to carry out urgent reinforcements of the tail unit. To expedite the work, civil aviation mechanics were summoned up from all neighboring airports (including not only American airports, but also Canadian ones). In total, 233 fighters were subjected to such a modification. As for the aircraft, which had, by that time, already crossed the border, they were modified at the Soviet Air Force repair bases, in accordance with TsAGI recommendations; however, this did not lead to any major changes in the center of gravity position, because the modification also included the removal of a 16kg armor plate from behind the oil tank.

Beginning from September 1944, the P-63As were painted (directly at the factory, and according to the Soviet Air Force color scheme) with new insignias (red stars with white edging).

By the end of 1944, the number of Kingcobras being shipped had exceeded that of the P-39s. Before the end of the year, 831 aircraft were accepted in Alaska; of those, 584 managed to reach Krasnoyarsk. There were losses in the Soviet territory as well. For example, on 24 December 1944, Major N.M. Semchenko (referred to as 'Se*n*chenko' in some documents) crashed at the first Soviet

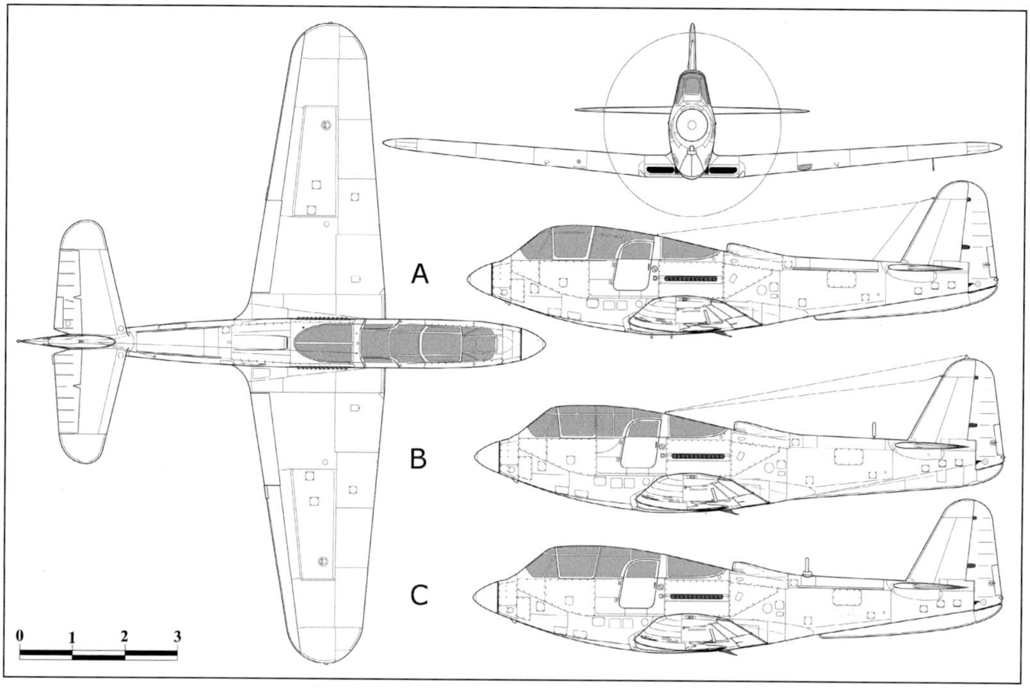

P-63

A Three-view of the P-63U two-seat trainer version, which was modified from the P-63A-8, s/n 42-69304.

B The P-63U two-seat trainer version, which was modified from the P-63C-5, s/n 43-11334.

C The P-63U two-seat trainer version, which was modified from the P63A-10, s/n 42-70503.

segment of the route, not far from Nome. In a heavy snowstorm, he lost his bearings and crashed into the ground.

The USSR was not in a hurry to introduce the new fighter to combat service, as the Soviet aviation was not suffering from an acute shortage of aircraft anymore; aircraft manufacture by Soviet factories kept growing. With the Airacobra's defects in mind, a decision was made to first study its successor thoroughly. From late 1944 through to March 1945, NII VVS and the Flight Testing Institute of the People's Commissariat of Aviation Industry (*Lyotno-Ispytatelniy Institut Narodnogo Komissariata Aviatsionnoy Promyshlennosti*, or LII NKAP) flight-tested (successively) the A-1, A-5, A-7 and A-10 versions.

On the whole, the P-63 received favorable opinions: high speed, decent maneuverability and powerful armament spoke much in its favor. The flight control system, with cables partially replaced by rigid rods, became more reliable. The convenient tricycle landing gear with efficient brakes provided for taxiing, take-off and landing with a good field of view, as well as ensuring excellent controllability on the ground. The P-63A lost in terms of speed only 9km/h (1.5 percent) at an altitude of 5,000m to the German Messerschmitt Bf 109G-4 fighter; the rate of climb lag at the same altitude was greater (2m/s, or 14 percent). On the other hand, in terms of horizontal maneuvering performance, the American fighter was superior both to the Messerschmitt and to the Focke-Wulf FW 190A-4. The latter was inferior to the Kingcobra also in speed.

Alongside that, the P-63 had considerable drawbacks: in comparison to the P-39s of the last versions, the new aircraft had a lower payload and fuel reserve, and poorer armor protection. Wing skin buckling was detected on the A-1, A-5 and A-6 versions; beginning from the A-7, the manufacturer thickened the skin and reinforced the structural members.

Insufficient stability of the aircraft at pull-out from dive – and at entering vertical aerobatic maneuvers – posed a problem as well. This was, to some extent, counteracted in the A-7 version by the installation of a counterweight in the elevator control system, and by an increased vertical stabilizer area. The problem was almost entirely eliminated in the P-63C version, which received a more powerful V-1710-117 engine and a ventral fin (i.e. an additional vertical stabilizer). Such ventral fins were also 'retroactively' mounted on the P-63As of earlier manufacture; for this purpose, ferrying via the ALSIB route was held back.

In spite of all efforts applied by American designers, the Kingcobra was also prone to falling into a spin, and the causes were the same as in the P-39. As soon as ammunition for the cannon and for the fuselage machine guns was used up, the aircraft went out of balance. This had to be immediately counteracted by adjusting the trim tabs; otherwise, the P-63 fell into a spin. The report on the Kingcobra testing as conducted by NII VVS read: 'Minor piloting mistakes, especially in vertical aerobatic maneuvers, may lead to a spin stall'; however, the spin condition was less hazardous than on the P-39: it was smooth, with no jerking or control stick 'wobbling'.

With all of the above in view, a lot of restrictions were (at first) imposed in the USSR on flying the Kingcobras. For fear of excessive accelerations, barrel-rolls, abrupt pull-outs from dives and entering vertical aerobatic maneuvers was prohibited; in general, only smooth rudder and elevator movements were permitted. Later, the restrictions were removed for aircraft with a reinforced wing and empennage; however, performing aerobatics with no ammunition or counterweight on board was strictly prohibited.

For the mentioned reasons, the supply of Kingcobras to combat air force units was delayed. First, they were sent to various workshops and repair bases; then to the 4th and 6th Backup Air Brigades for flight crew conversion training – and it was only afterward that regiments in the rear began receiving the fighters. As a result, there were 1,473 Kingcobras as of 1 May 1945, with only five of them in the combat army. The latter were probably used solely for familiarization purposes; there is no information regarding their participation in any combat sorties. On the other hand, losses were minor as well: by 1 May, only seven aircraft had been destroyed in crashes or accidents.

Beginning from spring 1945, the P-63s were sent to combat units of the air defense forces. That was no surprise, as at altitudes over 7,500m, the Kingcobra outraced both the British Supermarine Spitfire IX and the Soviet Lavochkin La-7; it offered a rather high service ceiling. Some of the P-63s were fitted with the MN-26Y radio compass, which facilitated navigation at night and in the clouds considerably. In early 1945, the Soviet Union received a P-63A-10 which was even equipped with a radar unit. The radar, however, was not a search one and it was used to provide a rear attack warning. As of 1 May, regiments of the air defense forces had as many as fifty-one P-63s at their disposal.

First and foremost, the Kingcobras were provided to units which had, up to then, been flying the P-39s. The 28th Fighter Air Regiment, which was stationed near Moscow, was the first to receive the P-63s. By August, the 17th and 821st Fighter Air Regiments of the air defense forces had received some 10 aircraft each. In autumn 1945, several aircraft arrived at the 39th Fighter Air Regiment at Malino airfield (also near Moscow).

Upon the capitulation of Germany, shipments to the USSR continued. The Kingcobras left Alaska for Chukotka in groups and, by that time, the Kingcobra had remained the only fighter on the route. The aircraft had already been rather well mastered by ferry pilots; however, crashes and accidents kept occurring occasionally – thus, on 7 July 1945, Lieutenant A.N. Terentyev was killed upon landing in Seymchan.

In summer 1945, top priority was given to the air armies in the Far East which were preparing for hostilities in Manchukuo, and the habitual ferry route via the ALSIB route changed. From

Markov, the aircraft flew to Petropavlovsk-Kamchatsky; the ferry route from Krasnoyarsk extended to Ukkurey in Transbaikalia (via Chita) to re-equip the 12th Air Army. Some of the aircraft flew there directly from Yakutsk.

Apparently, the 190th Fighter Air Division, which was under the command of Major General V.V. Fokin, was the first of the Far East air armies' units to be equipped with the P-63As; it was redeployed to Transbaikalia in June 1945. From 24 June, the division began receiving the Kingcobras and, before 2 August, conversion training was completed. In the course of the warfare in Manchukuo, the division operated from two airfields (*Ural* airfield and *Leningrad* airfield, near Choibalsan in Mongolia). After the war, the 190th Fighter Air Division was, for some time, stationed near Ulan-Ude.

The 245th Fighter Air Division, which also operated as part of the mentioned 12th Air Army at the Transbaikal Front, included two regiments (the 940th Air Regiment and the 781st Air Regiment) that flew the P-63s. The Kingcobras arrived at the 9th and 10th Air Armies as well. For them, ferry pilots laid the route to Khabarovsk – and there, by the beginning of the hostilities, ninety-seven P-63s were accumulated which had not been allocated between the regiments.

During the short campaign in the Far East, the Kingcobras were used to escort bombers and reconnaissance aircraft; to provide air cover for troops and ships; and to deliver strafing and bombing attacks on Japanese positions. On the second day of the offensive, 40 Il-4s – under the cover of fifty P-63s – bombed the fortified locality of Suzhou, from which the Japanese had been subjecting the Soviet town of Iman to fire. Units of the 190th and 245th Divisions supported the Soviet and Mongolian troops on the offensive: their aircraft operated (primarily) as fighter bombers and ground attack aircraft, and provided air cover for transport aircraft which were delivering fuel for tank units and mechanized units at the forefront. Soviet FAB-100 bombs were utilized and, for this purpose, bomb racks were modified to a certain extent; underwing large-caliber machine guns were normally not mounted.

In October 1944, the 20th Attack Air Regiment, which flew the outdated I-15bis biplanes, was redeployed to Kamchatka. In early 1945, it began receiving the Kingcobras and was renamed 'the 410th Fighter Air Regiment'. The 888th Fighter Air Regiment, which was part of the same 128th Composite Air Division, received new aircraft only five days before the beginning of the hostilities, but nevertheless, some of the regiment's aircraft were also involved in operations against the Japanese.

The 888th and 410th Regiments (from Kamchatka) delivered attacks on Japanese bases at the neighboring islands of Shumshu and Paramushir, and then supported the landing of troops to the islands. The fighters covered ships with troops on their passage, and delivered bombing and strafing attacks on enemy positions on the shore. The Japanese offered weak resistance, so therefore, the 410th Fighter Air Regiment only made nine combat sorties. In the 888th Fighter Air Regiment, seven combat sorties (including a night sortie) were flown by Captain V.A. Derkachev. On 18 August, he was killed in a collision with the slope of the Gorely Volcano. A search for the site was carried out by a crew in a U-2 biplane; however, the searchers managed to land only at a distance of several kilometers from the location and, furthermore, their biplane was destroyed at landing.

The Kingcobras also made several sorties without the application of armament to discourage the Japanese who lived in Kamchatka in Bolshevik and Oktyabrsky settlements. There, crabbing companies were operating under a concession agreement and, after the Declaration of War, all Japanese citizens were proclaimed internees; however, in spite of this, they attempted escaping on board crabbing vessels. The aircraft located them in the ocean and then returned to the port.

The Japanese aviation offered almost no resistance to the Soviet armies on the offensive, so for this reason, there was no chance of checking the Kingcobra's performance in air combats. The only successful battle was fought by Junior Lieutenant I.F. Miroshnichenko of the 17th Fighter

Air Regiment. On 15 August, he and his lead (Hero of the Soviet Union V.F. Sirotin) engaged two Japanese fighters which were making an attack on transport aircraft performing an approach near Vanemyao. One of the Japanese aircraft was shot down, while another escaped in a low-level flight in the hills. Different documents provide different information as to the type of Japanese aircraft: in some sources, they are referred to as 'I-97' (i.e. the Nakajima Ki-27), but according to other documents, those were the 'Oscars' (the American reporting name for the Ki-43). Both, however, had become obsolete a long time before, and therefore, the outcome of the battle was predetermined from the very beginning.

At the same time, the first P-63s were provided to the 7th Fighter Air Division of the Pacific Fleet Air Force. By 9 August (when the war against Japan began), the division had received 10 Kingcobras. Approximately 20 additional aircraft arrived in the course of the hostilities (before 31 August), but they did not take part in any operations against the Japanese.

Throughout the first half-year of service of the P-63 in the USSR, several design defects of the aircraft were revealed: for example, there were numerous failures of hollow duralumin rods which connected the pedal to the bellcrank, but these were replaced with steel ones. Modifications also included the reinforcement of attachment clamps for cooling system expansion tanks, and the replacement of textolite fuel tank lids with duralumin ones. Wheel doors tended to come off in flight, but this problem was counteracted by the installation of additional lock washers. There were cases of engine fuel supply cut-off, and such cases were brought about by vapor locks in the fuel line which were arranged too close to the hot tube for the anti-freeze agent feed from the engine to the cooler. To eliminate the problem, both pipelines were wound with asbestos tape.

The handover of the fighters to the Soviet mission in Fairbanks was ceased immediately after the capitulation of Japan. In total, 1,569 aircraft were accepted throughout 1945. According to various sources, the number of aircraft as shipped from the USA totaled between 2,415 and 2,421 (including one-thousand-and-ninety-three P-63Cs). According to the Soviet military acceptance data, a total of 2,400 Kingcobras out of the ordered 2,450 arrived in the USSR. Of those, 2,397 came via Alaska and only three were brought by sea, via Murmansk. It should be noted that some of the Soviet documents provide a figure of 2,640 aircraft, which were (allegedly) ferried to Krasnoyarsk; however (apparently), this figure is incorrect. Ferries via the ALSIB route continued for some time after the capitulation of Japan. The last Kingcobra was delivered to Yelizovo in Kamchatka on 29 September 1945.

After the capitulation of Japan, the collecting depots in Krasnoyarsk and Ukkurey accommodated hundreds of P-63s. Distribution of the aircraft to combat units continued until autumn 1946, with many of them sent to European Russia and to military stations in the countries of Eastern Europe.

The post-war reduction of armed forces originally implied writing off and scrapping all of the Kingcobras. The Resolution of the Council of Ministers of 22 March 1946 prescribed that two-thousand-three-hunded-and-forty-four P-63s (i.e. all the aircraft which were still operable) should be written off; later, however, intentions in respect of their fate changed.

The Soviet Kingcobras were never returned to the USA, nor were they scrapped. The fighter, which was the most up-to-date one among the Lend-Lease aircraft, occupied a strong position in the Soviet aviation after the war. It was the most widely distributed foreign aircraft – thus, in 1946, the 6th Fighter Air Division in the Ukraine converted to the P-63; the 20th Fighter Air Regiment (stationed in Zeltsy) was the first to master the new aircraft.

Units which were based abroad (in Germany, Austria and China) also received the Kingcobras – thus, they were provided to units of the 1st Guards Fighter Air Division (stationed in Neuhausen) and to the 83rd Air Corps in Port Arthur. In July 1946, 41 fighters were ferried from Krasnoyarsk to Gross-Dirnheim airfield in Germany in order to be received by the 57th Guards Fighter Air Regiment of the 5th Guards Fighter Air Division. At the same location, the 28th Guards Fighter

Air Regiment was trained (this regiment, however, was left with the P-39s until the conversion to jet aircraft). Some units were equipped with the P-63s partially. For example, the 81st Guards Fighter Air Regiment (stationed near Lvov) flew both the La-7s and Kingcobras. The conversion training of flight crews and equipping the combat units with aircraft was mainly done via the 4th and 6th Backup Air Divisions.

The navy's pilots also flew the P-63. So far, it cannot be said for certain how many aircraft of this type were handed over to the naval aviation; however, it is known that during the post-war years, regiments of the Black Sea Fleet Air Force and the Northern Fleet Air Force, which had been previously equipped with the P-39s, converted to the P-63s. In the Black Sea, the 6th and the 11th Guards Fighter Air Regiments were also equipped with the Kingcobras; the 6th Air Regiment (more precisely, one of its squadrons) kept flying the Airacobras as well. In the Baltic Fleet, the P-63s were in service with the 314th (formerly the 21st) and the 246th Guards Fighter Air Regiments.

The suitability of the P-63 for air combats with jet fighters was tested in July through to December 1947. A P-63C-1 conducted mock air combats against the MiG-9s in the Moscow region. In maneuvering combats, the Kingcobra was constantly getting the upper hand – attacking the jet aircraft from behind after one or two passes; however, the MiG pilot was always able to escape – using his speed advantage.

Soviet pilots respected the Kingcobras for their convenience in operation; their spacious and comfortable heated cockpit, with an excellent field of view; and their good instrumentation and gunsight, but after 1948, many of the aircraft began to suffer from engine wear. The use of augmented power settings was prohibited, so for this purpose, throttle lever stops were locked. The P-63s were no longer able to reach the same speed and ceiling as before. In the 6th Guards Fighter Air Regiment of the Black Sea Fleet, only one aircraft managed to climb to 10,200m during high-altitude flights. In Siberia and in the Far East, there were cases of engine failure at take-off due to a frozen-up fuel system. Air Marshal I.I. Pstygo, who was, in 1952, the deputy corps commander in Kamchatka, wrote of the P-63: '… That was a good aircraft; however, because of high wear and obsolescence of the engine, the supercharging was reduced to a minimum, and it was no longer able to perform vertical aerobatic maneuvers…'

The Kingcobras remained in service until the conversion to jet fighters, and their gradual replacement began in 1950. These aircraft had been completely withdrawn from combat units by the end of 1953. For example, the 5th Guards Reconnaissance Air Regiment in the Far East converted from the P-63 to the La-11 in March 1950; in the 241st Guards Fighter Air Regiment (the former 11th Guards Fighter Air Regiment), conversion training to the MiG-15 began in January 1951; the 246th Guards Fighter Air Regiment converted to the same MiG-15 in May 1951; and the 314th Air Regiment converted a year later, in May 1952. The Kingcobras remained in service with the 307th and 308th Fighter Air Regiments at the Kurils until 1951. The 865th (formerly the 410th) Fighter Air Regiment in Kamchatka converted to the MiG-15bis in July 1952.

Sometime later, the American fighters left service with the Pacific Fleet Air Force, and there they stayed long enough to witness the beginning of the Korean War, with all of the Soviet aviation on alert. Generally, it was deemed quite likely that the P-63s might enter action against the US aviation; however, the rapid alternation of aircraft generations left the Kingcobras on the sidelines.

In 1952, an attack by American fighter bombers occurred at the near-border airfield of Suhaya Rechka. It remains unknown whether the Americans lost their way in the skies of Korea, or if they made the assault intentionally; either way, eight retired Kingcobras (which were standing on the edge of the airfield) constituted the only loss.

Finally, the P-63s played an important role in the mass conversion of pilots to jet aircraft (the MiG-9 and, later, the MiG-15 fighters). The point was that both the P-63 and the new Soviet jet fighters had a nose-wheel undercarriage, whereas Soviet piston-engine fighters were fitted with an undercarriage of 'old' design, with a tail leg. Therefore, the Kingcobras were used for the mastering of new take-off and landing techniques. In some cases, the task was further complicated: pilots were trained to perform landing approaches without deploying ground spoilers at a speed of 400-500km/h in order to simulate the MiG-15. After the retirement of the Kingcobras from combat units, they stayed for some time with flying schools as 'conversion aircraft'; at some locations, they could be encountered as late as the mid-1950s.

Two-seater trainer versions of the Kingcobras (which were identical in design to the two-seater Airacobras) were built in the USSR. The first versions of this kind were made in a makeshift manner at different locations and, in 1948, the Air Force Central Scientific and Experimental Base suggested a typical design for the modification. There was an intention to modify a large number of aircraft to train pilots in performing take-offs and landings with the tricycle landing gear, which was becoming a characteristic feature of new jet fighters. The second cockpit was arranged in place of the armament compartment, and one of the machine guns was preserved to enable pilots to perform air-to-air gunnery exercises. A two-seater P-63 (modified at the 321st Repair Base) underwent State tests at the facilities of NII VVS, with the test flying carried out by V.E. Golofastov. Changes in the two-seater's center of gravity improved its anti-spin performance, and the test program included bailing out from the forward cabin in order to prove the possibility of a safe escape; the bailouts were performed by the famous parachute jumper V.G. Romanyuk. Afterwards, the mass modification of the fighters into the trainer version began at the repair bases of air armies and fleets. For the 3rd Air Army, aircraft so modified were tested by pilot S.Y. Tatushin. Similar modifications were also implemented at workshops in Tbilisi – and there, the modified aircraft were given the designation P-63V.

Such aircraft were provided to the regiments which were mastering jet fighters (two or three aircraft per regiment). For example, the 28th Guards Fighter Air Regiment, which was flying the MiG-9s and Yak-15s, had three UP-63s at its disposal in January 1948.

Currently, there are two restored Kingcobras in Russia. One of them is on display at the Air Force Museum in Monino, while the other can be seen in the full-scale materiel display area of the Museum of the Great Patriotic War on Poklonnaya Hill (also known as the 'Hill of Respectful Salutation') in Moscow. Both Kingcobras were assembled from the wreckage of several aircraft which had crashed on the Siberian route.

A.G. Kochetkov in the cockpit of a P-63A-10 on 29 April 1944.

The wreckage of the Kingcobra which was put into a flat spin by Kochetkov.

Brand-new P-63As awaiting acceptance at the factory airfield in Niagara Falls during the summer of 1944.

The first P-63A-1 fighter which arrived at NII VVS.

The P-63A-7 in its initial configuration during tests at NII VVS.

The P-63A-7, with its fuselage tail section reinforced as per the TsAGI method – including the installation of the outer stiffening ribs.

This P-63A-8 became the 10,000th fighter built by Bell. The man standing on the wing is the President of the Bell Aircraft Corporation (L. Bell), and in the cockpit is A.G. Kochetkov.

The P-63A-10 during tests at NII VVS in March 1945.

The aircraft bearing the inscription 'Katya from Klondike' awaits in Alaska to be ferried to the Soviet Union.

The P-63C-1 during tests at NII VVS.

The Soviet P-63C-5 on a landing approach.

A Soviet fighter pilot standing on the wing of a Kingcobra.

A P-63 being prepared for a mission; note a compressed air cylinder on the ground, and that one of the aircraft cabin doors is open.

The Kingcobras at an airfield.

Pilots having a rest after a mission (post-war photo).

Pilot N.A. Korovin at one of the Sakhalin Island airfields, where the fighter regiment equipped with the P-63 fighters was stationed.

A UTI P-63 two-seat trainer, which has been modified from a P-63A-8, during tests at NII VVS in November 1946.

A UTI P-63 modified from a P-63A-10, December 1948.

Technician P. Vikulin reporting to the flight crew about the aircraft readiness; note that this UTI P-63 two-seater was modified from a P-63C-5.

The wreckage of a Kingcobra on the outskirts of Yelizovo airfield at Kamchatka in the late 1980s.

The remains of the Kingcobras at Shumshu Island (Kuriles) in the late 1980s.

The Kingcobra at the Central Air Force Museum in Monino, near Moscow. Recently, the aircraft has been transferred to a new exhibition hall.

The Kingcobra in its initial color scheme and on display at the Museum of the Great Patriotic War on Poklonnaya Hill in Moscow.

This same aircraft – after it was repainted in 2012 – was put under a shed.

7.6 Republic P-47 Thunderbolt

By mid-1943, the American Republic P-47 Thunderbolt fighter had been holding a prominent place in the structure of the USAAF Air Fleet, which was probably the reason why it had not been shipped to other countries under Lend-Lease for a rather long time.

The development of the future Thunderbolt was launched in 1939, and the aircraft was developed as a heavy, long-range escort fighter. From the very beginning, it was designed with a certain special feature – namely the application of a turbosupercharger to improve the altitude performance of the powerful R-2800 engine.

The first prototype XP-47 made its maiden flight in May 1941; in May the following year, the mass manufacture of Thunderbolts was launched. In March 1943, the P-47Cs first entered action in Europe. At approximately the same time, the Republic Factory in Farmingdale manufactured a new version of the P-47D with the R-2800-21 engine with water injection at a war emergency power rating, as well as an improved supercharger.

On 17 July 1943, the head of the Soviet military mission in the USA – General V.I. Belyaev – asked the Americans to provide several Thunderbolts for familiarization purposes. The request was motivated by two peculiarities of the aircraft – namely long range and good altitude performance, which was accounted for by the use of the supercharger. In both respects, the Thunderbolt had no equivalent among Soviet fighters.

In response to Belyaev's request, the Americans (in September 1943) allocated three P-47D-10 fighters for the USSR. These aircraft were specially equipped with radio compasses, since they were intended to be flown a long way across the Bering Strait to Siberia. To ferry the Thunderbolts to Moscow, a special team of three pilots from the 1st Ferry Air Division was formed. The team included Senior Lieutenant D. Chulanov, Senior Lieutenant I. Burmistrov and Captain A. Bachkov. In November, the team began conversion training in Fairbanks and, after more than 20 training flights, the pilots mastered the P-47 well enough to take the road.

On 16 November, all three aircraft took off from Ladd Field and headed for Nome, but the ferrying was impeded by severe frost. Because of the cold weather, the Thunderbolts had to deviate from the main route via the 'Cold Pole' in Oimyakon, and to use the alternate route via Magadan, Nikolaevsk-on-Amur and Chita. There were some 'adventures' in store for the ferrying team as well: on 15 February 1944, the aircraft arrived at Ayan Bay (800km to the south from Magadan) and, in the night, ice drifting began; the wind was carrying the ice, together with the aircraft, to the open sea. The pilots took their places in the cockpits and lifted off promptly. The lead Douglas C-47 Skytrain, which was guiding the team along the route, was also quick enough to take to the air. It was only on 20 March that the three P-47s landed on Central airfield in Moscow.

Initially, all three aircraft were intended to be studied by specialists of the People's Commissariat of Aviation Industry; however, in November 1943, representatives of the People's Commissariat of Foreign Trade reported from the USA that the P-47 was suggested by the Americans for shipment to the USSR instead of the obsolescent P-40. Therefore, Air Force Chief Engineer Colonel General A.K. Repin requested People's Commissar of Aviation Industry A.I. Shakhurin to allocate one of the fighters for testing at NII VVS. On 2 December, Shakhurin ordered that one of the Thunderbolts should, upon arrival, be immediately ferried to NII VVS.

As a result, two aircraft were used in flight tests, which were conducted almost concurrently. One of the aircraft flew at LII (in April and May), while the other was tested by NII VVS (in April through to June). The obtained results proved somewhat lower than the figures claimed by Republic – thus, for example, NII VVS obtained a maximum speed of 661km/h and a ceiling of 11,800m.

The P-47 demonstrated decent stability performance; it behaved well at critical angles of attack; and did not display any significant tendency to fall into a spin. Ease of piloting was a considerable advantage – making the aircraft quite suitable for an average wartime pilot – plus the fighter's cockpit proved simple and comfortable. The American designers had arranged instrumentation, equipment and controls rationally, and the aircraft was fitted with an excellent radio station. Finally, it had powerful armament (eight 12.7mm machine guns) and its bomb-carrying capacity totaled 1,135kg, which was greater than that of the Soviet Petlyakov Pe-2 two-engine bomber.

On the other hand, the Thunderbolt proved rather clumsy and was considerably inferior to other fighters in its horizontal and vertical maneuvering performance. Due to its large size and weight, the aircraft demonstrated a poor response to elevator and rudder deflections. For the same reasons, the P-47 accelerated slowly, with an unusual inertness. These peculiarities of the aircraft were, in an original manner, commented upon in the memoirs of M.L. Gallay, who had flown a Thunderbolt for LII: 'This is no fighter! It is stable; it is comfortable; it has a reasonably arranged and spacious cockpit. But it is no fighter'.

After the completion of the basic test program, the LII's aircraft was destroyed in a crash near the station of Divovo in the Moscow region on 17 August 1944. The aircraft was piloted by S.F. Mashkovsky and, during the flight, he suddenly heard a popping sound; then, the engine began shaking and the cockpit was filled with smoke, so the fighter made a wheels-up landing on a plot of plough-land. At the end of the landing run, the aircraft veered across its way and turned upside down. The pilot suffered no serious injuries, but the aircraft was considerably damaged. An examination of the aircraft by an Emergency Board led to the conclusion that the valve mechanism of one of the cylinders had failed.

The third P-47D-10 was used to study its construction in the New Materiel Bureau of the People's Commissariat of Aviation Industry and TsAGI, as Soviet specialists appreciated certain solutions in the design of the American aircraft. They noted the wing construction, which was suitable for mass production and made extensive use of open sections; the convenience of the maintenance of assemblies and sub-assemblies via rationally arranged hatches; and the unique device in the form of a welded frame, which was hidden under the skin in the bottom portion of the aircraft, and which was used to protect the fuselage from damage in case of a belly landing.

Soviet engineers paid special attention to the turbosupercharger system, which differed considerably from the Soviet equivalents, and was much more reliable.

Familiarization with the Thunderbolt led to the development (at the Mikoyan Design Bureau) of an original project which combined the airframe of the MiG-9E (aka I-211) fighter interceptor (which had initially been fitted with the ASh-82FN engine) with the power plant from the P-47D-10 (i.e. the R-2800-63 engine and the C23 supercharger). According to calculations, the aircraft (which was much lighter and smaller in size than the Thunderbolt) was intended to reach 740km/h at 10,000m. The preliminary design was presented to the People's Commissariat of Aviation Industry for review on 8 April 1944; however, it did not arouse any interest and was abandoned.

By the time of the tests in the Soviet Union, the USA had already commenced mass deliveries of the P-47s via the southern route. The shipment of the fighters from the factory in Farmingdale began in late 1943 and, in total – under Protocol III – 200 Thunderbolts were to be sent to the USSR.

The batch in question included fighters of the P-47D-22 and P-47D-27 versions. The former differed from the D-10 by the presence of underwing pylons for the carrying of large-caliber bombs; by the capacity of fuel tanks; and by the broad-bladed Hamilton propeller, which improved the rate of climb at low and medium altitudes. On the D-27, the fuselage dorsal fairing was lowered and a new bubble-type round-view canopy was installed. Forward of the vertical stabilizer, a small dorsal fin was mounted to make up for the deterioration of the directional stability after lowering the fuselage fairing.

In total, a hundred D-22s and a hundred D-27s were shipped from the USA, with the majority of the aircraft sent via the southern route. Disassembled fighters in containers were delivered by sea to the Persian Gulf, and then carried to Abadan for assembly. From there, the Thunderbolts were ferried to Azerbaijan by Soviet pilots. Via the southern sea route, 196 aircraft were shipped; of those, 189 reached Abadan successfully. The Soviet Air Force accepted 188 aircraft (one of the Thunderbolts was destroyed during trial flights) and four fighters came via the northern ports – thus, in total with the first three aircraft, the Soviet aviation received one-hundred-and-ninety-five P-47s. Almost all of them were accepted in 1944 (only five aircraft were accepted in 1945).

An issue arose in respect of the rational use of the arrived fighters: the USAAF had initially used the Thunderbolt mostly as a long-range escort fighter; later, it was used as a fighter bomber and a ground attack aircraft. In the Soviet aviation, these roles were not in high demand, as the Soviet Union had no armadas of heavy multi-engine bombers to escort. The Soviet long-range aviation consisted (almost entirely) of two-engine aircraft and they operated at night. Support for frontline troops was provided by the Petlyakov Pe-2 and Tupolev Tu-2 bombers, as well as the Ilyushin Il-2 ground attack aircraft. The latter, unlike the P-47s, had cannon armament; could carry (both underwing and inside) a large number of small-caliber bombs; and was provided with good armor protection. The Thunderbolt, on the other hand, with its high bomb-carrying capacity, had only two shackles (both external) for the bombs; its gun armament included machine guns only; and finally, its armor protection was too poor to allow using it as a ground attack aircraft.

Therefore, the P-47s were initially allocated to air defense units in the rear – taking into account the good altitude performance and flight endurance. The high service ceiling, high speed and powerful armament made the American fighter efficient enough to intercept bombers and reconnaissance aircraft which attempted to penetrate deep into the Soviet territory. A large batch of Thunderbolts was sent to the South-Western Air Defense Front in the Ukraine and, in total (as of 1 May 1945), the air force held 116 fighters of this type – including 114 ones in operational units; however, all of them were stationed in rear districts and away from the front line, yet as an interceptor, the P-47 suffered from a significant drawback – namely a poor rate of climb. At low and medium altitudes, the Thunderbolts were inferior in this respect to Soviet fighters, and at high altitudes to the British Supermarine Spitfire IXs, which had begun to arrive in the USSR by that time. There are no reported cases of any combat application of the Thunderbolts in air defense regiments, and none of the P-47s are listed among the casualties.

On the other hand, with Soviet naval pilots, the P-47 saw not only operational service, but also some combat use. Pilots of the 255th Fighter Air Regiment, which was part of the 5th Mine-and-Torpedo Air Division of the Northern Fleet, pioneered the mastering of the Thunderbolts in naval aviation. In October 1944, twelve P-47D-22s were allocated to the navy, and one of them was subjected to operational service tests at Vaenga-1 airfield, near Murmansk; it was flown by Piloting Inspector Captain Bogdanov. First and foremost, the Thunderbolt's capabilities as a fighter bomber to hit shore-based and water surface targets were of interest. In the course of the tests, the aircraft carried up to three FAB-250 bombs (250kg each), or up to two FAB-500 bombs (500kg each). With two FAB-250s, the aircraft could deliver the bombs in a dive at an angle of up to 50°C, or operate as a skip bomber. The results of the tests led to the conclusion that the Thunderbolt was quite suitable for the long-range escorting of bombers and torpedo bombers; for horizontal bombing and skip bombing; and for the strafing of escorting ships.

On 15 November 1944, the commander of the Northern Fleet Air Force ordered that the 1st Squadron of the 255th Fighter Air Regiment be equipped with the P-47D-22s. By that time, 14 aircraft for the squadron had already arrived at Vaenga airfield. The order, however, was not fulfilled for the reason that the preparations for the final defeat of the Germans in the polar regions was at its terminal phase, and nobody was willing to withdraw an operational regiment from service for conversion training purposes. Consequently, the Thunderbolts were ferried to Yagodnik airfield, near Archangelsk, and left there for some time.

Later, the Command in Moscow decided to re-equip the 255th Fighter Air Regiment entirely and sent 26 more aircraft there (among them were those of the D-27 version). In mid-May 1945, when the war with Germany was already over, the ferrying of American fighters to the north began. As of 20 June, the regiment held as many as 63 aircraft – including two unserviceable ones.

It should be noted that the pilots of the 255th Air Regiment had a lot of problems mastering the Thunderbolt. According to the pilots' opinion, the conversion from the light and maneuverable Airacobras to the heavyweight P-47s was somewhat like changing a motor boat for a battleship, and local 'humorists' nicknamed the fighter 'The Dull One'. Indeed, almost all aerobatic maneuvering – including split S maneuvers, loops, barrel rolls and steep dives – were prohibited for the P-47, but nevertheless, the regiment successfully completed the conversion training and became combat-effective. In the course of service with the 255th Fighter Air Regiment, the Thunderbolts even took part in the making of the '*Bezymyanny Island*' movie, where they 'played the part' of the German Focke-Wulfs.

In the Baltic Sea, where the Thunderbolts appeared sometime later, they took part in combat sorties. Five P-47D-22s (the first of which arrived in November 1944) joined the 15th Independent Reconnaissance Air Regiment, and combat sorties began in January 1945. Four Thunderbolts were based in Palanga, and the fifth one was based in Panevezhys. From mid-January, the American aircraft were used rather intensively for reconnaissance in the western portion of the Baltic Sea; they flew either solo, or in couples.

In autumn 1944, such aircraft were also sent to the Black Sea Air Force. As of 1 November, the Black Sea Fleet held five (according to other sources, three) P-47s; however, as soon as Bulgaria and Romania joined the anti-German coalition, hostilities in the Black Sea were terminated. As for the Pacific Fleet, the Thunderbolts were never sent there.

Some of the naval aviation's heavy American fighters were concentrated in backup regiments and training institutions. There, however, their 'career' did not last long either, as the aircraft were shifted from one unit to another. Thirty Thunderbolts were, for some time, allocated to the Stalin Training School, while 20 aircraft were held by the Higher Officers' Training Courses.

Finally, all of the naval P-47s were concentrated in the north, where their existence came to an end. After the end of the war with Japan, the Soviet armed forces underwent a considerable reduction. The disbandment of many air force units and formations led to a large excess of aircraft, and the Resolution of the Council of Ministers of 22 March 1946 prescribed writing off a considerable quantity of imported aircraft – including 186 Thunderbolts (presumably, all that were available at that time). The remaining nine Thunderbolts had (probably), by that time, already been written off after crashes.

Beginning from mid-1946, the P-47s were gradually withdrawn from service – thus, for example, in the 255th Fighter Air Regiment, they were replaced with the preserved Airacobras and scrapped (crushed by a tractor). In the air defense units, the aircraft were, at first, 'mothballed', but then they were disassembled in an attempt to make use of the most valuable parts – in particular, the power plant. Afterwards, the Air Defense Forces Fighter Aviation Command kept offering the engines to various agencies – including the Chief Administration of the Civil Air Fleet – but the R-2800 engines were not utilized on other aircraft types which were in operation in the USSR. For this reason, the engines found no application.

Some of the P-47s were, for a long time (until the mid-1950s), used as non-flying training aids at the Zhukovsky Air Force Engineering Academy (Moscow); the Moscow Aviation Institute; and the Mozhaysky Military Air Academy (Leningrad).

The P-47D-10 which was tested at LII in 1944.

The P-47D-22 during tests at NII VVS in 1944.

The P-47D-27 in the USA, which is ready for ferrying to the Soviet Union.

Pilots of the 255th Fighter Air Regiment, Northern Fleet Air Force discuss the results of a mission.

The Thunderbolt R-2800 engine undergoing maintenance at the 255th Fighter Air Regiment.

7.7 North American P-51 Mustang

In spring 1942, a batch of 10 Mustang I fighters came to the Soviet Union from Great Britain, but there are no traces of these aircraft having been ordered by any Soviet agency. They were not on the lists of materiel as recommended to be purchased from the Allies, which were prepared in September 1941 by the Chief Intelligence Directorate and the Red Army Air Force Chief Administration, so it seems that the Soviet structures knew little about the Mustang at that time, and that the aircraft were accepted for the sole purpose of having a thorough look at them.

The history of the aircraft began with the suggestion to launch the manufacture of the Curtiss P-40 Kittyhawk fighters, which was made in early 1940 by the British Purchasing Commission in the USA to the North American aviation. In reply, the Americans stated that they were not willing to master the production of another company's aircraft, and would rather design and build their own – a much better one – and they did.

The NA-73 was designed by a team under the general direction of R. Rice; however, the 'first violin' in this case was played by the German immigrant E. Schmued (the only person in the team who had already been involved in fighter design efforts before); a legend ran that Schmued had once worked for Messerschmitt. The main feature of the new aircraft was the laminar flow wing. Like on the Kingcobra, such a wing design provided an advantage in speed, but at the cost of a reduction in lift, which affected the fighter's performance at take-off and landing.

The all-metal monoplane was fitted with the Allison V-1710 liquid-cooled engine (the same as on the P-40), but it also had a powerful armament and accommodated an impressive fuel load. To aid production, the construction was divided into individual sections, which were assembled separately. The prototype of the future Mustang first flew on 24 October 1940.

As early as 16 April 1941, the first mass-manufactured fighter was rolled out from the factory in Inglewood. During tests in England, one of the first aircraft showed a speed of 614km/h, so in terms of range, it was unrivalled among single-engine aircraft; however, the Allison engine's gear-driven centrifugal-type supercharger was a single-speed one, which affected the engine's performance at altitudes over 4,500m. For this reason, the RAF initially used the Mustangs mostly as high-speed reconnaissance and ground attack aircraft. Operational units began receiving them in February 1942, and a batch of 10 fighters was offered to the Soviet Union.

The first two Mustangs (of the earliest versions, probably) were shipped on 6 December 1941, with the last aircraft from the batch arriving in May. All of them were brought by sea via the northern ports. One of the first aircraft was tested by NII VVS during June-July 1942, and it was flown by V.E. Golofastov. At short-time augmented power settings (the Allison engine offered the so-called 'war' setting, which was limited to five minutes), the speed was relatively high, although the pilot (unlike his American and British colleagues) was not successful in overcoming the 600km limit: the maximum speed obtained was 587km/h. Up to the altitude of 3,700m, the Mustang lost 10-50km/h to the Yak-7B with the M-105PF engine, but at higher altitudes, the American aircraft easily outraced its Soviet rival. In terms of rate of climb within the same altitude range, the American fighter was considerably inferior to both the Soviet and German aircraft, as it took the Mustang three minutes more than the Yak-7B to climb to 5,000m. In a combat turn, the Mustang climbed on 550m, which was almost twice as little as the Yak-1, Yak-7B or the German Messerschmitt Bf 109G did. In terms of the turn time – and, especially, the radius of turn – the Mustang was inferior as well. This was brought about by a low thrust-to-weight performance. The Mustang's ability to reach high speed was due to its excellent aerodynamics, rather than to an increase in unit thrust (calculated per kilogram of take-off weight). The Yak-1 had a lower weight, whereas the Soviet M-105PF engine was even more powerful than the Allison, which was what accounted for its high rate of climb and maneuverability. The deterioration in performance of the Soviet aircraft at altitudes over 3,700m was due to the fact that the M-105PF supercharger's design altitude was lower, and that the power began decreasing earlier.

On the other hand, the American aircraft was easy to fly, and so was quite suitable for a pilot of medium skills, plus good stability made long flights not so exhausting (as was the case in Soviet airplanes). The cockpit was comfortable, spacious and heated, with the latter being of no small importance for the conditions in Russia. Finally, in terms of the weight of fire, the Mustang exceeded the Soviet fighters quite considerably; however, NII VVS noted that the absence of cannons reduced the effectiveness of attacks against armor-protected enemy aircraft. Cannons would have allowed for firing from distances, and the defensive machine guns of the German bombers would not have been able to 'reach' the attacking fighter.

The Red Army Air Force needed a frontline fighter which would have to feature both high speed and good maneuverability, and whose main task would be air combat against enemy fighters; in this regard, the Mustang was not fit for the role: a high-speed, long-range photo reconnaissance aircraft might have been of use as well. As for the bombers, the Soviet Air Force preferred to depend on their own, as they were armor-protected; they carried bombs and rocket projectiles, along with cannons and machine guns; and they were in abundance. For these reasons, the 10 Mustangs which had arrived in the USSR were used for various secondary purposes.

The majority of the received Mustangs were sent to the 6th Backup Brigade, whose headquarters were stationed in Ivanovo. As has been already noted, the brigade specialized in the conversion of flight crews to imported aircraft. For example, five Mustangs were used to train the pilots of the 1st Ferry Air Division who needed to be familiarized with the peculiarities of American aircraft. Three fighters were in service with the brigade for a rather long time, and they were based at an airfield in Ivanovo.

In August 1942, three Mustangs were sent to the Kalinin Front for operational service tests; they departed from Ivanovo on 22 August. Two aircraft joined the 5th Guards Fighter Air Regiment, which, at that time, flew the LaGG-3s only. The regiment was part of the 3rd Air Army, which was under the command (at that time) of M.M. Gromov. The American aircraft were flown mostly by Regiment Commander and twice Hero of the Soviet Union V.A. Zaitsev; they were also tried out by pilots Popkov (later, a twice Hero of the Soviet Union as well) and Onufrienko. According to Popkov's recollections, the impression of the American fighter was extremely negative: the aircraft featured high speed, but was "as heavy as a press iron." Maneuverability left much to be desired, and the lengthy take-off was not appreciated either; the Mustangs flew no combat sorties. Soon, the propellers on both aircraft became damaged and, for want of spare ones, the aircraft were sent back.

In July 1943, two Mustangs were held by the 5th Training Air Regiment of the 3rd Air Army; as of 1 August, only one remained. Perhaps the aircraft were transferred to the 3rd Air Army Administration Air Detachment, which, according to documents, held three fighters of this type (with only one of them in good order). This assumption is supported by the fact that the army had, in total, three such aircraft at its disposal.

One of the Mustangs was allocated to the Zhukovsky Air Force Academy Training Regiment, and it was in operation up until 1946. Another aircraft of this type was on display in TsAGI's New Materiel Bureau.

Some German sources claim that a couple of P-51s were shot down in Karelia in late April 1943, but this, however, is a mere confusion of aircraft types (which was not infrequent during the war).

In the Ukraine, on the other hand, the Mustangs were encountered beyond all doubt. These were not the Soviet Mustangs, but the American P-51Ds, with the Packard V-1650 engine instead of the Allison. The Packard V-1650 was a licensed version of the British Merlin engine, and fitted with American silver-lead bearings. The Packard engine's altitude performance was as good as that of the original Merlin, and the engine was first mounted some time earlier on the P-51B version. Such a combination of the British engine and the American airframe constituted the famous Mustang, which is believed to be among the best fighters of the Second World War.

In spring 1944, bases for the B-17 and B-24 heavy American bombers began to appear in the Ukraine, and the objective was to ensure efficient attacks on targets which were 'hard to reach' from England or Italy. The concept was referred to as 'shuttle operations', with the aircraft departing from the bases in the west, bombing the targets in Germany and then landing in the Soviet territory. At the Ukrainian bases, the aircraft were refueled and their ammunition replenished; then the crews took rest before flying back to their home airfields – again dropping bombs on the enemy's heads on their way. The bombers were escorted by the P-38 and P-51 fighters with drop tanks, and the fighters landed in Piryatin. During the course of the 'shuttle operations', which were carried out until mid-September, two Mustangs force-landed in the Soviet territory. On 11 September, they lost their way in thick clouds and one of the fighters landed in Belaya Tserkov; the other one, with its fuel burnt out, made a belly landing in the open field.

As the Soviet troops were advancing westward, soldiers encountered more and more abandoned Mustangs; they were located in Poland, Hungary, Romania and Czechoslovakia. In total, by May 1945, 14 aircraft of various versions – and in different states of condition – had been found.

Later, several P-51Ds were restored and ferried to LII airfield in Kratovo. No comprehensive flight tests were conducted; however, the aircraft were tried out to gain a general impression of them. The simplicity of the piloting was noted: at low and medium altitudes, the Mustang was (as before) inferior to the Soviet fighters in dynamics due to its considerably greater weight. It was also on the losing side in terms of rate of climb and its horizontal maneuvering performance, in spite of its fast acceleration and steady behavior in dive. On the other hand, at altitudes of over 5,000m, the Soviet fighters could no longer compete with it and, furthermore, it exceeded the German Messerschmitt Bf 109K as well.

In general, during the period of the conversion to jet fighters, the P-51D was of no great interest anymore, but nevertheless, individual components of its structure and equipment were thoroughly studied by specialists.

The Mustang I during tests at NII VS in June 1942.

An American P-51D at an airfield in Poltava in 1944.

7.8 Hawker Typhoon

In 1938, the designer of the Hawker Hurricane – S. Camm – embarked upon developing a new fighter: only this time, it was a special-purpose interceptor. Several versions with different engines were designed concurrently, but the Typhoon, with the powerful Napier Sabre 24-cylinder liquid-cooled engine (which was able to produce approximately 2,000hp), turned out to be the most promising version.

Mass production of the aircraft began in May 1941, and operational squadrons first received them in September. Initially, the Typhoons were used as interceptors, just as they had been intended; however, because of their poor rate of climb, they could only operate from the 'combat air patrol' condition. From late autumn 1942, the Typhoons were used primarily as ground attack aircraft and fighter bombers.

The Soviet Union first displayed an interest in the Typhoon in June 1943. Soviet representatives in London requested to the British authorities to reduce the number of Hurricanes in the shipments and to substitute them with Spitfires, Mosquitoes and Typhoons. The British Air Ministry, however, vetoed the latter two types invoking the necessity to re-equip the RAF as a reason. On 13 September, the request to provide a single example of the Typhoon was also rejected.

The first aircraft of this type were captured from the Germans. In Rechlin, which was seized by Soviet troops in May 1945, two Typhoons were found, with one of them in an almost good order; their further destiny is unknown.

A single Typhoon, however, was officially provided by the British, but it was a rather worn aircraft which had been in service with No.263 Squadron, RAF, and which had undergone an overhaul. It was preliminarily accepted in Great Britain and then flown out in the presence of the senior engineer for the Trade Representation Engineering Administration Air Department, M.M. Pashinin; then, it was disassembled and shipped by sea to the Middle East. The aircraft was handed over to Soviet representatives in Tehran on 20 July 1945; afterwards, it was studied at LII, TsAGI and NII VVS. By that time, the Typhoon had already been deemed obsolete. Specialists were primarily interested in the engine, which had no Soviet equivalents, and in its individual design solutions (in respect of assemblies and sub-assemblies).

7.9 Douglas A-20 Havoc/Boston

The American Douglas A-20 Havoc (better known in the USSR by its British name, which was 'Boston') was the most numerous foreign bomber in the Soviet aviation inventory. Throughout the Great Patriotic War, the Soviet Union had more A-20s than the USAAF, with approximately 3,000 aircraft shipped under Lend-Lease; the A-20s were used both on land and at sea. The Bostons were utilized in the capacity of short-range bombers, torpedo bombers, heavy fighters and high-speed transport aircraft. They saw rather extensive combat service with air forces of other countries as well; however, nowhere else was the scale of their application as large as it was in the Soviet Union. For several years after the end of the war, the Bostons remained in service with the Soviet Air Force, naval aviation and Civil Air Fleet.

The first drawings of the aircraft were made by the famous American aircraft designer J. Northrop as early as 1936, and on his own initiative. By 1937, when the United States Army Air Corps issued its specification for a next-generation bomber/attack aircraft, the preliminary design of the multi-purpose Model 7A (which combined the functions of a light bomber, attack and reconnaissance aircraft) had already been prepared. In the meantime, Northrop's small company was acquired by Douglas and became one of the latter's subsidiaries; the designer left it and founded another company. The aircraft design was kept by Douglas, and was passed on to the engineer Weidenheimer, who modified it in accordance with the customers' wishes; the new version was presented for review in July 1938. Model 7B was, essentially, an all-metal cantilever monoplane with two radial R-1830 engines and a tricycle landing gear. The aircraft faced competition from the Bell 9, Martin 167, Stearman X-100 and the North American NA-40.

The US Army, however, made no choice at that time, so Douglas opted to continue work at its own peril and risk. On 26 October 1938, the prototype Model 7B made its first flight, and assistance came when it was not expected: having become familiar with the prototype, French representatives signed a contract for a hundred aircraft in February 1939. In June, the USAAC Staff finally made its choice by ordering two versions: the A-20 (with turbosuperchargers) and the A-20A (without turbosuperchargers); then, the Soviet Union became interested in the aircraft as well.

In September 1939, Amtorg approached Douglas with a proposal to sell a batch of the DB-7s. The rationale for the purchase of the American bombers was set forth in a letter from the head of the Workers' and Peasants' Red Army Air Force (A.D. Loktionov) to the People's Commissar of Defense (K.E. Voroshilov): '... the aircraft is similar to our SB, but offers more powerful gun armament (six machine guns) and higher flight speed (480-507km/h). The DV-7 [*sic*] possesses a design feature, which is of special interest for us, namely, a tricycle landing gear'. Douglas agreed to sell the aircraft, but on the stipulation that a batch of at least 10 aircraft would be ordered, and that they would not be fitted with armament or any military equipment. In such a condition, the aircraft were of interest (primarily) to designers and production engineers. Military men, however, insisted that the company should be pressed to sell ten DB-7s with armament. On 29 September 1939, Soviet representative Lukashev reported from New York that Douglas had agreed to sell them, and to provide both a license and technical assistance in launching the production of the DB-7 in the Soviet Union. Concurrently, negotiations were conducted with Wright in order to obtain a license for the R-2600 engine; in October, the text of the contract was agreed upon. It seemed quite plausible that the American bomber would soon be put into service with the Workers' and Peasants' Red Army Air Force. Negotiations were ongoing until the beginning of the Winter War in November 1939, when President Roosevelt promptly imposed a 'moral embargo' on deliveries to the Soviet Union. American companies, one after another, began cancelling the already concluded contracts. Shipments of machinery, tools and instruments ceased, and any assistance in the mastering of purely military products was not to be mentioned at all. Contacts with Douglas were discontinued, among others.

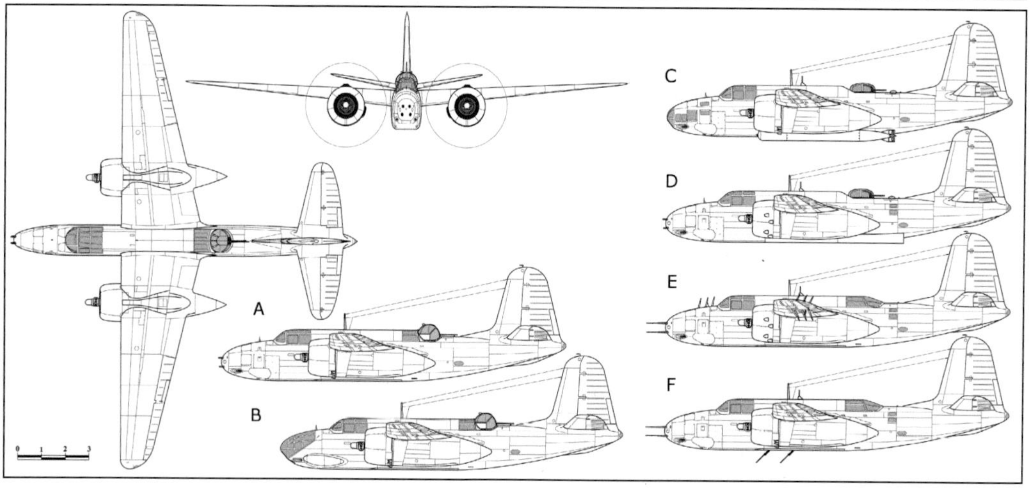

A-20

A Three-view of the A-20G-5, with a UTK-1 turret.
B A-20C, with a UTK-1 turret.
C A-20G-20 torpedo bomber, with the navigator's cabin in the fuselage nose part.
D A-20G torpedo bomber, with the navigator's cabin positioned behind the air gunner's compartment.
E A-20G-1 night interceptor, which was equipped with the Gneis-2 radar.
F A-20G-1, which was equipped with the AKAB under-fuselage gun battery (shown in a lowered position).

The Americans did not regret it: a major war had already been under way, and had brought huge orders with it. Unable to cope with the orders on its own, Douglas transferred some of them to Boeing. In total, the USA, England and France requested approximately 3,000 aircraft to be supplied by spring 1940. France received the DB-7 with the R-1830-SC3-G or R-1830-S3C4-G engines (1,100hp each), and intended to receive the DB-7A with the more powerful 1,600hp R-2600-A5B engines. The DB-7A also featured elongated engine nacelles and an oversize tail unit. For Great Britain (initially), the DB-7B version was manufactured, which was similar to the DB-7A, but had an elongated nose and a larger glazing area in the navigator compartment.

Concurrently, the A-20, A-20A and A 20B were built for the USAAF. The latter was, essentially, the A-20A with a modified bomb bay and a new 'stepped' nose glazing. The American aircraft (afterwards referred to as 'Havoc') carried different armament, and machine guns were country-specific (7,5mm in France, 7.69mm in England, and 7.62mm and 12.7mm in the USA).

The French DB-7s took part in the hostilities in summer 1940 and suffered considerable losses when strafing German tank columns. After the defeat in France, aircraft of this type which had not, by that time, been shipped from America, were diverted to the UK along with other orders. All versions of the aircraft as taken up by the RAF were given the service name 'Boston', which later became established in the Soviet aviation as well.

The Soviet authorities did not forget about the DB-7, and remembered it at the earliest opportunity. When, after the German invasion of the Soviet Union, the governments of Great Britain and the USA decided upon providing military assistance, the issue of military aircraft shipments arose at once. Several Soviet agencies prepared their requests for the conference of the Allies' delegations, which was held in September 1941 in Moscow. The A-20 was listed among the aircraft types as recommended by the People's Commissariat of Aviation Industry, air force and the Intelligence Directorate of the General Staff. In particular, the note by the Air Force Chief Administration stated: '... the Douglas DV-7A (A-20A) medium bomber should be ordered...' In the USSR, the American aircraft was categorized as a short-range bomber, rather than a ground attack aircraft. In fact, aircraft which were classified among medium-range bombers in the USA stood closer to long-range bombers in the Soviet inventory; in terms of weight, crew size and defensive armament, they were even beyond the latter category.

During the course of the meeting in September, General Chaney, who represented the USAAF, suggested shipping the A-20, A-29 and B-25 bombers. The Bostons were undoubtedly better than the slow-speed and poorly armed Lockheed A-29s, which were insistently forced upon the USSR. Air Force Commander P.F. Zhigarev wrote to People's Commissar of Trade A.I. Mikoyan: '... the DV-7V [*sic*] aircraft, which have been offered to us by the Americans, deserve attention in terms of their combat qualities, and are worth purchasing...' Initially, a shipment of five-hundred-and-eighty-four A-20s was suggested, but later, the figure grew to 828 aircraft (of those, 300 aircraft were to be taken from orders which had been placed by the British). The latter figure was included in the Moscow Protocol for shipments in 1941-1942.

In October 1941, a delegation of Soviet aviation specialists visited the USA. Test pilots who were members of the delegation were given an opportunity to try out several American bombers – including the A-20. In November, they visited the Douglas Factory, where the aircraft were built.

The shipment of the bombers from American ports began in the second half of December 1941. Before New Year's Day, 44 aircraft of this type were shipped, while only three aircraft were brought to the USSR by Arctic convoys. The rest went the long way, via Iran and Iraq.

Initially, the A-20s were taken by sea (in a semi-dismantled condition) to Basra in Iraq, and were then assembled at the nearest British airfield of Margil. The first bombers came there in early 1942, and these were the Boston IIIs, which had been manufactured for the British. A Soviet acceptance commission was delegated to Iraq and, simultaneously, the forming of ferry units began. On 14 January 1942, the air force requested that the Chief Civil Air Fleet Administration provide 10 crews 'for ferrying the B-3 aircraft from Basra'. The designation B-3 was widely used afterwards both for the British Bostons and for other versions which were similar to them. On 26 January, the civil aviation allocated six pilots, six engineers and six radio operators – and four more crews were to arrive from Kazan. They departed for the south on 3 February, and the ferry detachment was led by F.A. Khrutsky.

The first Boston was accepted by the Soviet military mission in February. Before 1 May, 92 aircraft were assembled; afterwards, the assembly activities were carried out at Shuaiba base. From there, aircraft were ferried to the 11th Backup Air Regiment in Kirovabad.

In spite of the fact that all of the aircraft were given the designation 'Boston III' (B-3), there were also the DB-7Bs and the similar A-20Cs among them. Sometimes, the DB-7Cs from the Dutch order were encountered – meaning those which had not been delivered to the Netherlands before the country was defeated by the Germans. Some of the aircraft came directly from American factories, while others arrived from Great Britain. Among the latter, there were a lot of aircraft which had already seen service, and some had even had overhauls.

Later, the bombers began arriving in an assembled condition on board converted oil carriers. After the arrangement of an intermediate base on Ascension Island, they were ferried by air from Florida via Brazil, the West Coast of Africa and the Middle East. They were handed over to Soviet acceptance specialists in Abadan or Tehran. In Abadan, Douglas built an aircraft assembly and repair factory to carry out the finalization of aircraft before its handover/acceptance.

The conversion of flight and ground crews was arranged on a wide scale from the very beginning. Regiments which had lost their aircraft in battles were withdrawn from the front lines; units from rear districts abandoned their obsolete SB bombers behind the Urals and came for conversion training; and new regiments were formed (these consisted mostly of young pilots who had completed a hurried training course in flying schools). Initially, conversion training to the Bostons was centered in Kirovabad, where the 11th Backup Air Regiment, which was under the command of Major Salomakha, was stationed.

The conversion of flight crews to the new aircraft involved certain difficulties, since the A-20 was manned by one pilot and American factories built no special trainer versions. Pilots had to study 'by watching': first, the trainee would lie on the floor in the compartment behind the instructor's head and watch the latter's actions; then, they changed places. All of the aircraft of earlier versions were fitted with a second set of controls, but these, however, were arranged not at the navigator's position, but near the gunner, who could hardly see anything in the forward direction. It was almost useless, so finally, the Americans stopped equipping the aircraft with it. At a later time, aircraft with a second set of controls in the navigator compartment were built at certain Soviet air units, and they were given the designation UA-20 or UB-3.

Two regiments completed the conversion training in May 1942, with the 794th Bomber Air Regiment being the first to master the American bombers. In March 1942, the regiment received twenty-two B-3s in Kirovabad. First, the pilots made several familiarization flights on another American bomber (the North American B-25B Mitchell), which had two side-by-side pilot seats. At the same time, the pilots were getting accustomed to the tricycle landing gear, and to the unusual units of measure (feet, pounds and miles) on the instruments; then, the crews began flying the Bostons. In May, the regiment was sent to the Southern Front (near Voroshilovgrad) and, in June, it was redeployed to the South-Western Front, where fierce battles were going on. In July, the regiment made a successful raid on Rossosh airfield. The Bostons approached by surprise from the side of the marsh, and damaged and destroyed 21 aircraft by bombing and machine gun firing (the figure was later found out by partisans). The regiment pilots attempted repeating the raid, but failed to attain surprise. Two B-3s were shot down; one more bomber was damaged, and made a forced landing. The Germans, in response, bomb-destroyed the regiment's airfield and burned down six Bostons; in August, the unit held only two operable bombers.

On 27 April, a special train with personnel of the 57th Bomber Air Regiment, which was under the command of Major Surzhin, arrived in Kirovabad. The unit had first entered action in the SB bombers near Yelnya, but by mid-November, it had lost almost all of the aircraft and had been withdrawn to the rear. Consequently, the regiment was equipped with A-20Bs. The conversion process went rather smoothly, with only one accident occurring: a wheel came off pilot Nikotin's aircraft at the end of the take-off run; however, he managed to land with a bank and performed a landing run on two wheels (it was only at the end of the run that he lowered down onto the damaged leg). In late May, the already mentioned Major Salomakha (formerly with the 57th Bomber Air Regiment) took over the command of the regiment. He introduced himself to the Command personnel and simply said: "That's all; the conversion training is over." An interesting fact is that initially, crews of the A-20B bombers consisted of three persons (as in the USA), but later, an additional gunner was included in each crew; however, there were no 'spare' gunners in the regiment, since the SB was a three-seater as well. For this reason, technicians or armourers flew (for some time) in the capacity of gunners.

In late May, there were as many as 11 regiments which had mastered the Bostons to one extent or another, and by 1 July, six of them had already reached battle readiness (the 57th, 45th, 861st, 860th, 201st and 453rd Air Regiments).

There were regiments that mastered the American aircraft on their own – thus, when the 561st Short-Range Bomber Air Regiment (which was, at that time, based in Lomonosovka, on the bank of the Northern Dvina River) lost all of its aircraft (except for three SBs and a U-2 in summer 1942), three Bostons were brought on board a barge and put in service rather promptly.

In spite of the fact that the B-3 was a 'good-tempered' aircraft, the mastering stage involved a number of accidents. A series of accidents and crashes occurred in the 11th Backup Air Regiment in Kirovabad during the course of night-flying exercises, so Senior Sergeant Oskin of the 452nd Bomber Air Regiment retracted the landing gear too early at take-off and overlooked the moment when the wing touched upon the ground; here, however, the pilot's omission was detected right away. On the other hand, cases of aircraft unexpectedly falling into a steep dive or spin remained unsolved for a rather long time. Such cases occurred not only in Kirovabad, but also in combat units. For example, in the 742nd Reconnaissance Air Regiment, Sergeant Serezhenko failed to recover from a spin. The crews were usually killed together with the aircraft, with no survivors left to clear up the situation.

In the 11th Backup Air Regiment, five crashes took place which were described by those who witnessed them in approximately identical words: in mid-air (usually, in a level flight), the aircraft stalled and fell into a vertical dive, from which they never recovered. The bombers were destroyed, along with their crews. Similar cases occurred in combat units – thus, in the 745th Bomber Air Regiment (during the course of a target practice), Senior Lieutenant Gavrilov's aircraft suddenly fell into a steep dive and crashed into the ground. The cause was discovered by Regiment Commander Lieutenant Colonel Bazulev: to check the piloting skills of one of the pilots, Bazulev lied down in the fuselage behind the pilot's seat. During the flight, the aircraft suddenly fell into a nosedive in response to an abrupt deflection of the control wheel. As a result, the pilot slipped down in his seat and pressed the control column with his body. It was only with the help of the commander that the pilot managed to regain a normal position in the seat and to pull out from dive. Further investigations showed that many pilots either failed to use their safety harnesses at all, or they used them improperly, with the straps being too loose. It turned out that there had already been such an occurrence in the regiment, and that the crew had been saved by a technician who had been taking part in the mission. It was ordered that the correctness of safety harness fastening should be monitored and, as a result, the 'epidemic' of unaccounted-for crashes waned promptly.

In July and August, large units which were equipped with only the B-3s appeared at the front (these were the 221st and 244th Air Divisions). The 221st Air Division, which was under the command of Colonel I.D. Antoshkin, was made up from units which had arrived at the South-Western Front near Voroshilovgrad (the 794th, 745th and 57th Bomber Air Regiments). The latter flew its first combat sortie on 24 June, but the sortie was not successful, so the bombers were ordered to return because there were not enough fighters to escort them. The second combat sortie, which was on the same day, also proved to be ineffective; most of the aircraft failed to release their bombs due to various malfunctions. It was only during the third sortie (on the evening of 25 June) that good luck attended the pilots. They delivered a successful bombing attack on a cluster of tanks and motor vehicles on the edge of the village of Yefremovka. Indeed, the target was so large that it would have been difficult to miss it. In reply to an intelligence man's question in respect of the situation, one of the pilots answered: "There's a whole lot to be bombed!" The bombing was done day after day, with several missions flown per day. On 26 June, the regiment suffered its first casualty: Flight Leader Lantukh's aircraft was lost during a raid on a motor convoy near Kupino, although nobody actually saw it being destroyed. The A-20B vanished in the clouds to evade German fighters, and simply never came back…

On 30 June, the Germans launched an offensive. The Red Army troops retreated to behind the Oskol River, but the enemy force-crossed the river and pursued the offensive. The 221st Bomber Air Division was tasked with bombing the enemy's lead tanks, with operations beginning at dawn and ending at sunset. The summer days were long, and the take-off time was set simply as 'when flights are ready'. Under such conditions, four to five combat sorties were flown per day.

Enemy fighters and anti-aircraft artillery offered fierce resistance to the bombers. In their combat sorties, the A-20Bs were usually escorted by the LaGG-3 fighters; however, they also

LEND-LEASE AND SOVIET AVIATION IN THE SECOND WORLD WAR

Colour profile section

Hurricane IIB – re-armed with two ShVAK machine guns and two UBT cannons – was flown by Major V. Krupsky, the 760th Fighter Air Regiment, Boyarskaya airfield (North Karelia) at the beginning of 1942.

Hurricane IIC/Trop during tests at NII VVS in August 1943.

Hurricane IID of the 246th Fighter Air Regiment, Omgovichi airfield (near Bobruisk), June 1944.

Spitfire PR.IV during tests at NII VVS.

Spitfire PR.IV, which was flown by Captain A.I. Platonov of the 118th Independent Reconnaissance Air Regiment, Northern Fleet Air Force in 1943.

Spitfire VB of an unknown Soviet regiment.

Spitfire VB of an unknown Soviet regiment.

Spitfire VB of the 2nd Fighter Air Corps, Air Defense Forces, Leningrad, 1945.

Spitfire LF.IX of the 26th Guards Fighter Air Regiment, Air Defense Forces, Leningrad, 1945.

Tomahawk IIB, which was flown by Lieutenant G.D. Shorokhov of the 126th Fighter Air Regiment in December 1941.

P-40B, which was flown by Lieutenant A.S. Khlobystov of the 20th Guards Fighter Air Regiment, Murmashi airfield (Karelian Front) in April 1942.

P-40EF photo reconnaissance version, the 191st Fighter Air Regiment, Leningrad Front.

P-40E, which was flown by Major B.F. Safonov, commander of the 2nd Guards Fighter Regiment, Northern Fleet Air Force, Vaenga airfield in May 1942.

P-40K of the 78th Fighter Air Regiment, Northern Fleet Air Force, October 1944. This airplane was used for skip bombing attacks on the German shipping in the Kirkenes area; note the FAB-250 bomb under the fuselage.

P-40M of the 7th Fighter Air Regiment, Black Sea Fleet Air Force, summer 1943. The belly-mounted fuel tanks were used for torpedo bomber escorting missions.

P-40N of the 2nd Fighter Air Corps, Air Defense Forces, Leningrad, 1945.

Airacobra I during tests at NII VVS at the beginning of 1942.

Airacobra I of the 2nd Guards Fighter Regiment, Northern Fleet Air Force, Vaenga airfield, 1942.

Airacobra I of the 19th Guards Fighter Air Regiment, Karelian Front, 1942.

Airacobra I, which was flown by Junior Lieutenant V.V. Gabrinets of the 19th Guards Fighter Air Regiment, Shongui airfield (Karelian Front) in the summer of 1942.

Airacobra I of the 2nd Guards Fighter Regiment, Northern Fleet Air Force, Vaenga airfield, winter 1942/1943.

Airacobra I, which was flown by pilot Yu. Penakov of the 6th Independent Fighter Air Squadron, Northern Fleet Air Force during the winter of 1942/1943.

P-39D-2, which was flown by Senior Lieutenant V.I. Fadeev of the 16th Guards Fighter Air Regiment in May 1943.

P-39D-2 of the 2nd Guards Fighter Regiment, Northern Fleet Air Force, Vaenga airfield, summer 1943.

P-39M-1 before ferrying along the ALSIB route, Fairbanks, Alaska during winter 1942/1943.

P-39M-1, which was flown by Junior Lieutenant E.P. Mityaev at the Shongui airfield (Karelia) in May 1944.

P-39N, which was flown by Major N.I. Proshenkov of the 69th Guards Fighter Air Regiment, Stepnoy Front during the autumn of 1943.

P-39N, which was flown by Major N.D. Gulaev of the 129th Guards Fighter Air Regiment in August 1944.

P-39N of the 191st Fighter Air Regiment, Leningrad Front, autumn 1944.

P-39N, which was flown by Colonel A.I. Pokryshkin, commander of the 9th Guards Fighter Air Division in Germany during 1945.

P-39N, which was flown by Major G.A. Rechkalov of the 16th Guards Fighter Air Regiment.

P-39Q-10 during tests at NII VVS in October 1943.

P-39Q, which was flown by Major P.S. Kutakhov, commander of the 20th Guards Fighter Air Regiment, Shongui airfield (Karelian Front) in 1943.

P-39Q of the 508th Fighter Air Regiment, 1943.

P-39Q, which was flown by Captain G. Dmitryuk of the 19th Guards Fighter Air Regiment, Shongui airfield (Karelian Front) during the autumn of 1943.

P-39Q, which was flown by Lieutenant E. Mariinsky of the 129th Guards Fighter Air Regiment in Germany during 1945.

P-39Q, which was flown by Major V.F. Sirotin of the 17th Fighter Air Regiment, Baltic Fleet Air Force.

P-39Q-10, which was flown by Captain D.V. Zyuzin of the 11th Guards Fighter Air Regiment, Black Sea Fleet Air Force in Odessa during April-May 1944.

P-39Q-15 of the 68th Guards Fighter Air Regiment, winter 1944/1945.

P-63A-9 ferrying along the ALSIB route.

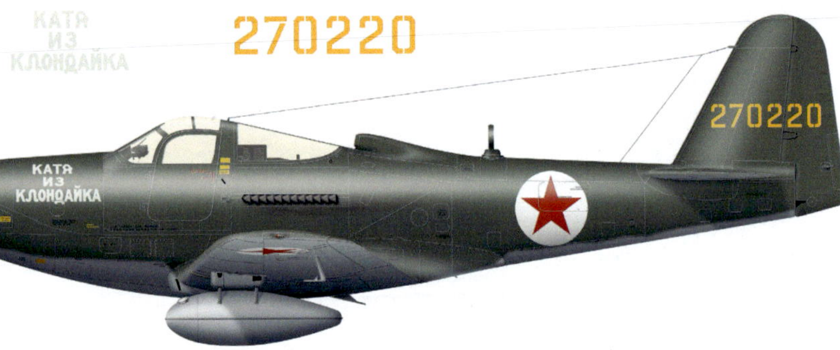

P-63A-10 ferrying along the ALSIB route, Ladd Field, Alaska.
The inscription on the nose reads: 'Katya from Klondike'.

P-63A-10 before ferrying to the USSR from Buffalo.

P-63A-10 ferrying along the ALSIB route, Fairbanks, Alaska.

P-63A-10 at the military airfield of Ashkhabad in 1947.

P-63C-5 of a fighter regiment.

P-63C-5 of the 16th Guards Fighter Air Regiment.

P-63C-5, which was flown by pilot Sukhov of the 16th Guards Fighter Air Regiment.

P-47D-10 during tests at NII VVS in the summer of 1944. The aircraft was purchased on the funds collected by US senators and received the name 'Knight of Pythias'.

P-47D-22 of the 255th Fighter Air Regiment, Northern Fleet Air Force, Vaenga-1 airfield at the end of 1944.

P-47D-22 of the 255th Fighter Air Regiment, Northern Fleet Air Force in October 1944.

P-47D-27 of the 255th Fighter Air Regiment, Northern Fleet Air Force.

P-47D-27 of the 255th Fighter Air Regiment, Northern Fleet Air Force.

P-47D-27 ferrying along to the USSR in 1944.

Mustang I, which was tested at NII VVS in June 1942.

A-20B of the 9th Guards Mine-and-Torpedo Air Regiment, Northern Fleet Air Force, winter 1943/1944.

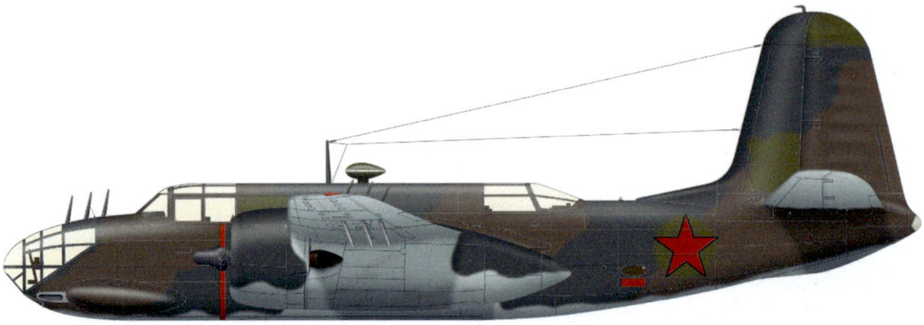

Boston III ('Pirate'), which was equipped with Soviet Gneis-2 radar during tests at NII VVS. The airplane was flown by Major Sakharov at Koltsovo airfield (near Sverdlovsk) in June 1943.

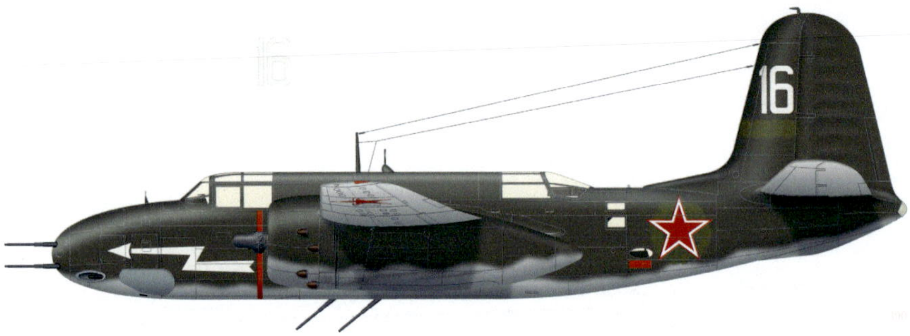

A-20G-1, which was equipped with the AKAB under-fuselage gun battery during combat tests at the 27th Guards Air Regiment of the night long-range hunter-blockers in spring 1944.

Another A-20G-1, which was equipped with the AKAB of the 27th Guards Air Regiment of the night long-range hunter-blockers in 1944.

A-20G-1, with the Gneis-2 radar of the 45th Air Regiment of the long-range fighters; Minsk, September 1944.

A-20G-30 of the 13th Guards Bomber Air Regiment, Black Sea Fleet Air Force; South Tavriya, April-May 1944.

A-20G-1 torpedo bomber of the 51st Mine-and Torpedo Air Regiment, Baltic Fleet Air Force, winter 1944/1945.

A-20G-25 torpedo bomber of the 51st Mine-and-Torpedo Air Regiment, Baltic Fleet Air Force, 1944.

B-25B before ferrying from the USA, October 1941.

B-25C of the 125th Long-Range Bomber Air Regiment, March 1943.

B-25C of the 125th Long-Range Bomber Air Regiment, January 1943.

B-25C-10, which was modified into a transport plane in the USSR.

B-25J of the 198th Bomber Air Regiment, 1946.

B-25J of a bomber air regiment; note the 'Standard 407' camouflage.

Hampden TB.I of the 3rd Squadron, 24th Mine-and-Torpedo Air Regiment, Northern Fleet Air Force, Vaenga airfield in October 1942.

Hampden TB.I of the 3rd Squadron, 24th Mine-and-Torpedo Air Regiment, Northern Fleet Air Force, Vaenga airfield in January 1943.

Hampden TB.I, which was equipped with the Soviet UTK-1 turret – which belonged to the 3rd Squadron, 24th Mine-and-Torpedo Air Regiment, Northern Fleet Air Force, Vaenga airfield – in May 1943.

Mosquito B.IV during tests at LII. The airplane was flown by test pilot N.S. Rybko at the end of April 1944.

GST of the Moscow unit of the Polar Aviation of Chief Administration of the Northern Maritime Route (GUSMP), which was assembled in Taganrog from the US-manufactured parts in August 1939.

PBN-1 of the Northern Fleet Air Force at the end of 1944.

PBN-1 of the 16th Independent Reconnaissance Air Regiment, Pacific Fleet Air Force in August 1945.

PBN-1 of the 53rd Combined Air Regiment, White Fleet Flotilla Air Force at the end of the 1940s.

PBN-1 of the 16th Independent Reconnaissance Air Regiment, Pacific Fleet Air Force, which participated in the Port Arthur landing operation in August 1945.

PBN-1 ferrying along to the Pacific, Kodiak Island, in September 1944.

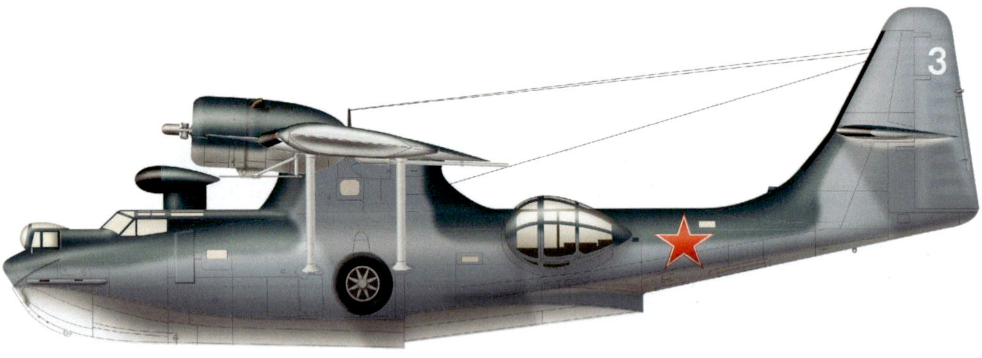

PBY-6A of the Soviet Naval Regiment.

PBY-6A of the Pacific Fleet Air Force during the winter of 1945/1946.

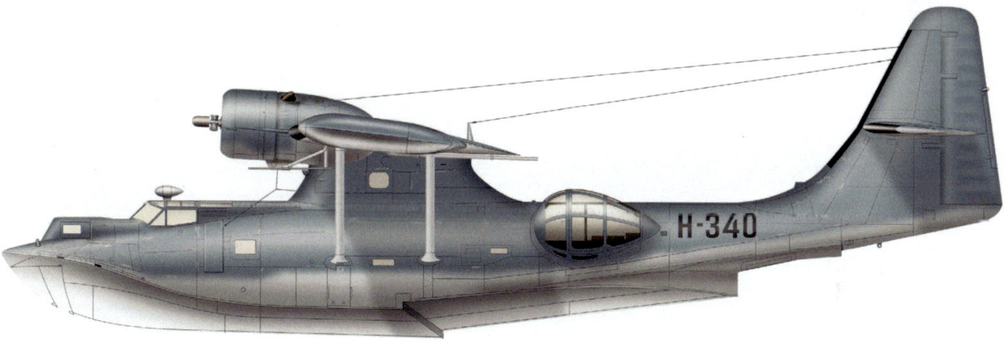

KM-1 of the Polar Aviation Department of GUSMP.

KM-1, which was flown by pilot I.S. Kotov of the Polar Aviation Department of GUSMP at Provideniya Bay in 1948.

KM-2 of the Moscow unit of the Polar Aviation Department of GUSMP; Kish Lake, Riga, September 1948.

KM-2 of the Polar Aviation Department of GUSMP.

The sole Stirling which was delivered to the USSR from Iran in the summer of 1945.

O-52 of the 22nd Backup Air Regiment; Kineshma, February 1942.

O-52 of the 22nd Backup Air Regiment; Kineshma, February 1942.

O-52, which was flown by pilot Junior Lieutenant P.K. Zhilinsky of the 12th Independent Spotter Air Squadron at Ivanovo in March 1942.

O-53 of the 13th Independent Spotter Air Squadron; Segezha airfield (Kalinin Front), May 1943.

O-52, which was flown by pilot Senior Lieutenant A.M. Orlov of the 5th Independent Aerial Survey Air Squadron at Tula in May 1945.

O-53 of the Chief Administration of Geodetic Surveying and Cartography; Syktyvkar region, at the end of the 1940s.

OS2U-3 from the *Murmansk* light cruiser, Northern Fleet, 1945.

C-47A, with a Soviet UTK-1 turret.

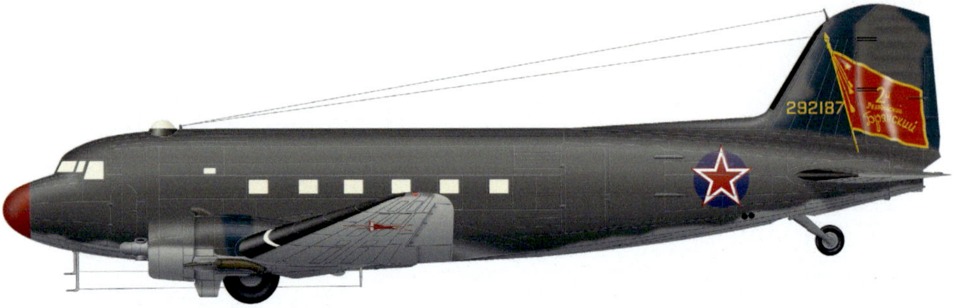

C-47A-1 – the staff airplane of General S.F. Loginov, commander of the 2nd Guards Long-Range Air Regiment at the end of 1944.

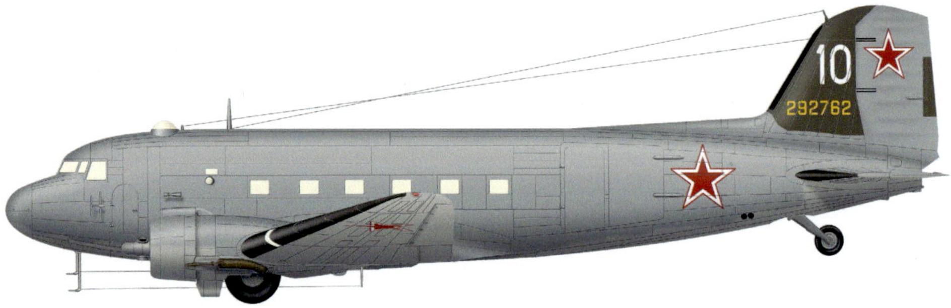

C-47A-15 of the transport squadron of the Special Purpose Air Group, which was based in Bari, Italy during July 1944.

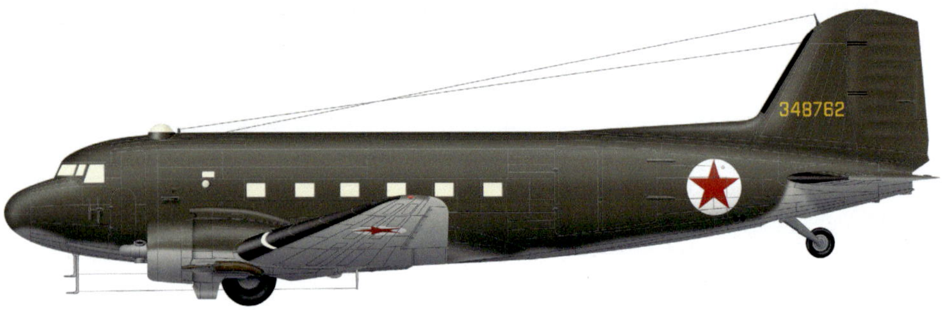

C-47B-5 ferrying along the ALSIB route.

C-47, which was used by the Soviet Polar Aviation Department. The airplane was flown by pilots L.H. Kruze and M.A. Titlov, with Valentin Akkuratov as navigator.

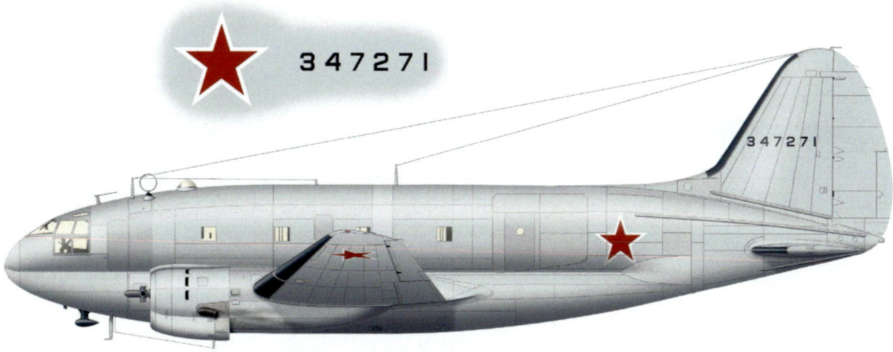

C-46A-60, which was flown by pilot P.M. Stefanovsky during tests at NII VVS in the summer of 1945.

Albemarle I(SF) of the 305th Training Unit was based in Errol, Scotland during January 1943.

Albemarle I(SF), which was flown by pilot Major V.V. Lisitsin during tests at NII VVS in the spring of 1943.

AT-6C during the acceptance at Abadan in 1943.

AT-6C during tests at NII VVS in May-June 1943.

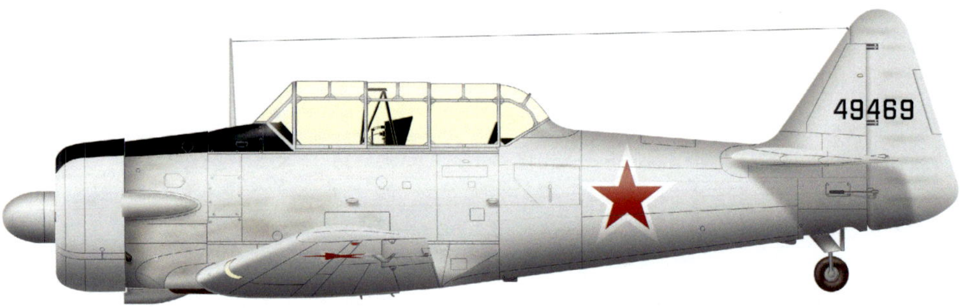

AT-6F of one of the Soviet training units.

P-38L-1, which was flown by pilot V.I. Khomyakov during tests at NII VVS in the beginning of 1947.

B-17G-40 of the 890th Heavy Bomber Air Regiment, Balbasovo airfield, May 1945.

B-17G-50 of the 890th Heavy Bomber Air Regiment, Balbasovo airfield, July 1945.

B-24H-30 of the 201st Heavy Bomber Air Regiment, Balbasovo airfield, July 1945.

B-29-5 of the 890th Heavy Bomber Air Regiment, Balbasovo airfield, July 1945.

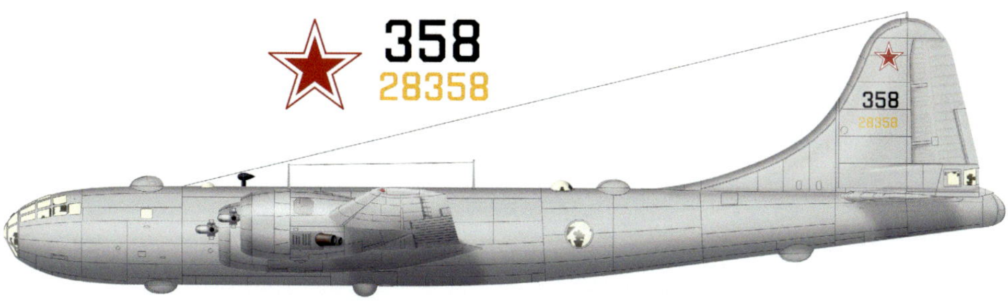

B-29-15, Izmaylovo airfield, July 1945.

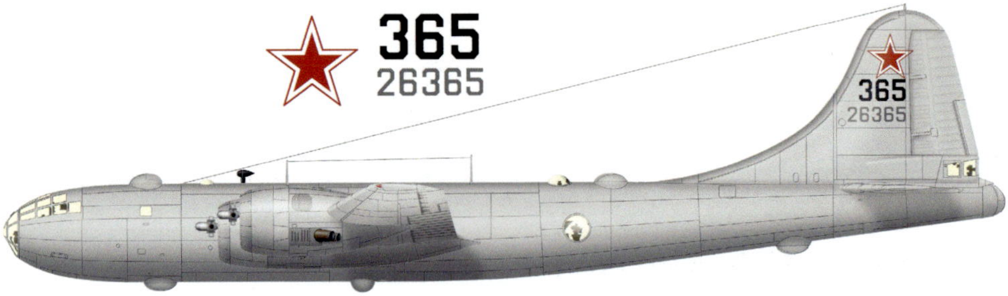

B-29-15, Moscow Central airfield, July 1945.

PV-1 during tests at NII VVS.

This Lancaster B.I was modified into a transport plane and flown by pilot I.I. Dubenets of the 16th Transport Air Detachment, White Sea Flotilla Air Force in 1945.

Walrus I of the 16th Transport Air Detachment, White Sea Flotilla Air Force.

suffered losses. When attacked by the enemy, the bombers adopted a close formation to cover each other by fire and then started climbing, whereas the escort fighters dived down onto enemy aircraft from a higher flight level.

Reconnaissance missions were usually flown by the Bostons solo. When the Messerschmitts appeared, the bomber usually climbed to a higher altitude, or turned its nose toward the enemy and fired from the forward machine guns from a suitable distance. There was a case when an A-20B withstood a battle with three two-engine Messerschmitt Bf 110s. The bomber shot down one of the enemy fighters and shook off the other two by hedgehopping in between ravines. In spite of the damaged hydraulic system and a blown wheel tire, the pilot managed to land at the home airfield. The aircraft displayed more than 50 shot holes – including those in the fuel tank.

On 8 July, pilot Mitin flew a special reconnaissance mission, with the gunner's cockpit occupied by a major of the General Staff, who wished to evaluate the situation personally. During the flight, an anti-aircraft shell tore a huge piece of skin from the fuselage left side, which was exactly where the major was sat. The officer suffered no injuries; however, the map he was holding was forced out from his hands, and then it whirled away to the depths of the bomb bay. The tactful wording in the mission report ran: 'In the second half of the mission, his observing conditions became worse'. Anyway, the combat mission was fulfilled and even the confidential map, which had become stuck in the bomb hatch, was retrieved.

A flight led by Junior Lieutenant Mikheev destroyed the Germans' temporary bridge across the Oskol River, but the enemy built a new one; however, it was destroyed again by two bombs which were dropped by pilots of Captain Osipov's squadron. Later, the bombers destroyed the third bridge as well. The Soviet troops were retreating, so therefore, flight crews were often tasked to drop their bombs at a certain location and then to fly to a new airfield in the rear.

On 20 July, an extraordinary incident occurred in the division: Sergeant N.N. Devichenko headed the burning bomber into fueling trucks which were parked in an enemy airfield; however, three crew members out of four survived, as the explosive blast flung them away into a ravine. Moreover, they even rejoined their regiment. Sergeant Devichenko was killed later, in December. The battles were extremely fierce: in two months of fighting, the regiments were left with only two or three aircraft each.

The 244th Air Division joined the 4th Air Army at the Transcaucasian Front in late August. The division was scantily equipped, as it held only twenty B-3s. In early September, the Air Force Command addressed the General Headquarters with a request to withdraw the unit and to equip it with more aircraft. Finally, both divisions were replenished and sent back to the southern section of the front in October.

In general, it was the southern segment of the Soviet-German Front where the overwhelming majority of the Bostons were initially concentrated. In late July 1942, the 860th Air Regiment joined the 244th Air Division, in addition to the three initial regiments (the 861st, 45th and 449th); by winter, the division had grown to include five regiments, with all of them flying the B-3s. Thus composed, the division entered the Battle of Stalingrad. The 132nd Air Division, which was fighting on the Caucasian foothills, had three regiments that flew the Bostons (the 63rd, 277th and 42nd). Later, one more regiment of the division (the 367th) converted from the Pe-2s to the A-20s.

The Bostons gained an excellent reputation with pilots. Commissar of the 221st Bomber Air Division S.I. Chernousov later wrote: 'The aircraft's flight performance was good for their time. They could compete with German aircraft in speed and maneuverability'. The B-3s which came to the Soviet-German Front were able to outrace the new Pe-2s. The American bomber featured good maneuverability and a high service ceiling, and it could easily perform steep turns and fly with one engine inoperative. Given the mediocre skills of the pilots, who were hastily trained in flying schools at wartime, the aircraft handling qualities were of no small importance. In this respect, the

Boston was unrivaled: it was simple and easy to fly, and manageable and reliable during turns. It was much easier for a pilot to perform take-off and landing in the Boston than in the Soviet-made Pe-2.

NII VVS provided the following opinion of the B-3: '... The Boston-3 is a first-rate bomber, manageable and easy to handle; it is quite suitable for a pilot of medium skills...' This can be complemented with phrases from surveys conducted by the Army Forming and Training Directorate: 'An undoubtedly very good aircraft'; 'A reliable, pleasant-to-fly aircraft'. From the records of NII VVS: 'When comparing the Boston-3 and the Pe-2, all test pilots agree that the Pe-2 is incommensurably more difficult to handle than the Boston-3, and requires a more skilled pilot'. In his official reply to a request from the People's Commissariat of Foreign Trade, Air Force Chief Engineer A.K. Repin wrote in July 1942: 'The aircraft offers good maximum speeds and good maneuverability, and is easy to handle'.

The engines were reliable and got started well; however, their intensive operation led to failures before the expiry of the assigned service life. This brought about the need to break the seals (which had been placed by the Americans) and to replace pistons, cylinders, piston rings and bearings. It should be noted though that the nominal lifespan of the Wright engines exceeded the lifespan of any Soviet aircraft engine twice, or sometimes even thrice.

In comparison with Soviet designers, their American colleagues paid greater attention to the crews' working conditions. The A-20 had spacious cockpits, and both the pilot and the navigator had a good field of view, as well as occupying comfortable and armor-protected seats. The cockpit was heated, which was an undreamt-of luxury after the freezing SBs and Pe-2s. The report by the Institute of Special Services of the Air Force read: 'According to subjective opinion of the flight personnel, the heating system is a very good one'. Pilots were amazed by the abundance of excellent instruments, as the Boston was fitted with a complete set of up-to-date navigation aids (except for the radio compass). The air force attempted to solicit the People's Commissariat of Aviation Industry for three-hundred-and-thirty RPK-10 radio compasses to equip the bombers; however, the request was denied, since radio compasses were in short supply. Later, some units fitted their Bostons with radio compasses (mostly of the RPK-2 type) at their own discretion. The installation guidelines were worked out at Factory No.81 under the direction of A.P. Golubkov. Some of the aircraft, which were ferried by air via the South Atlantic, were equipped with Bendix radio compasses in the USA; however, the first combat experience also revealed the weaknesses of the American aircraft. It was understood within a rather short period of time that the Boston's firepower was insufficient, so a decision was made to take steps to increase it. A draft Resolution of the State Defense Committee (as submitted to I.V. Stalin for review in September 1942) ran as follows: '... Combat operational experience of the 221st Bomber Air Division ... shows that the existing gun armament of the aircraft, which includes only the 7.7mm machine guns, cannot ensure good protection from fire of enemy fighters. For this reason, the Boston-3s suffer considerable losses in combat operations...' Indeed, the 221st Bomber Air Division lost 38 aircraft within a month of hostilities; twenty-seven of those were shot down by enemy fighters.

The urgent development of projects for the rearmament of the Boston began, and the first modifications were made directly at the front lines. Instead of the Browning machine guns, the Soviet manufactured large-caliber Berezin UB machine guns were mounted. The upper installation of twin machine guns, which had an insufficient scope of fire (not more than 30° to each side from the aircraft centerline), was replaced with the MV-3 turret with a ShKAS machine gun, or with the UTK-1 turret with a Berezin UBT machine gun. The Resolution of the State Defense Committee of 24 September approved the following rearmament design as suggested by the design bureau of Factory No.43: two stationary Berezin UBK machine guns on the sides of the navigator compartment (with a box of 120 rounds for the portside machine gun, and a box of 130 rounds for the right machine gun); the UTK-1 turret with a Berezin UBT machine gun on top (with a stock of

200 rounds); and another Berezin UBT machine gun in the hatch on a mount from the Pe-2 (with a stock of 220 rounds). The development of this variant was directed by A.I. Shulgin. All of the B-3s – including the DB-7B, DB-7C and A-20C versions – were subject to the modification. It was required that the first 30 aircraft should be rearmed in September 1942.

On 1 September, nine bombers from the 221st Air Division were ferried to Factory No.81 in Moscow for modification purposes. In the same month, the first Bostons fitted with Soviet machine guns entered action at the front line. One such aircraft, which was in service with the 221st Air Division, shot down two German Bf 109 fighters in five combat sorties. By the end of 1942, Factory No.81 had rearmed 96 Bostons; of those, 80 aircraft were the DB-7Bs. According to the schedule, 225 aircraft should have been rearmed by that time; however, the aircraft were in service at the front line, and it seemed inexpedient to withdraw them to the rear during the period of severe battles. For this reason, special kits for the rearming of the bombers in combat units were manufactured.

The modification of the armament brought about an increase in the aircraft weight and drag, which led to a loss of 10km/h of maximum speed and a reduction of the normal bomb load to 600kg. On the other hand, firing angles increased; the need to switch the dorsal mount from traveling to a combat position was eliminated; and finally, the large-caliber machine guns contributed to a dramatic increase in the effective firing distance.

Some of the aircraft were modified by means of a makeshift installation of the DAG-10 aviation grenade launcher in the tail portion of the fuselage. It was controlled by the radio operator gunner, and threw AG-2 grenades to the most dangerous zone behind the bomber's tail. The grenade was decelerated by a parachute, and exploded in front of the attacking fighter. Modifications of the Bostons' armament continued until the arrival of the A-20G-20 version, which, finally, met all of the requirements in this respect.

Concurrently, Factory No.81 performed reinforcements of the armor protection and introduced modifications for winter operations. In particular, removable face panels with controllable louvers (also referred to as 'face curtains') were suggested to protect engine cowlings. Such panels were later mass-manufactured by Factory No.2 in Kimry.

The B-3's bomb armament was also subjected to criticism. All of the early versions had low bomb capacity (780-940kg); however, it was limited rather by the number of bomb attachment points than by the aircraft thrust-to-weight ratio. The load was also restricted by the take-off run length, and by the capabilities of the landing gear, which was too weak to enable taking off from a grass airfield with a large weight.

The load figures as prescribed by the Americans were deemed too conservative. Modifications began with changes to bomb racks, which were implemented directly in the combat regiments. In the 221st Bomber Air Division, Senior Engineer D.I. Stepanov created his own design, which increased the aircraft capabilities by about one-and-a-half times.

At approximately the same time, Factory No.43 suggested a modification design which later became widely used. It was officially approved by the Order of the Air Force Chief Engineer of 20 June 1942, which read:

> In view of the fact that bomb armament of the imported Boston III aircraft does not provide for adequate attachment of Soviet bombs in the required variants of bomb load, and is different from the bomb armament control system as established for Soviet aircraft, the imported aircraft shall be provided with Soviet bomb armament including modification of the bomb armament control system on the aircraft.

Initially, the DB-7B was fitted with four bomb racks mounted inside the fuselage, with each able to carry a bomb of up to 230kg (in practice, up to 250kg); however, with bombs of a smaller caliber, the bomb load became dramatically lower, since the number of bombs remained unchanged, but each combat mission required a specific combination of calibers. After the modification, each of the aircraft bomb bays (the forward and aft ones) accommodated a KD-2-439 multiple rack for four FAB-100 bombs each. At the same time, the Soviet ESBR-3P bomb release gear and OPB-1 and NKPB-4 bomb sights (to substitute the primitive Vimperis D-8 sight) were mounted; a version so modified was tested at NIPAV in August 1942. As an alternative, four Der-19 bomb racks could be mounted to carry 250kg bombs, or KMB-Su-2 wooden box-type dispensers for small-caliber bombs.

In spring 1942, aircraft of the A-20B version began to arrive. Like all early modifications for the USAAF, these had neither armor, nor self-sealing tanks. Having acquired a certain combat experience, the Americans thought this to be a considerable disadvantage, so for this reason, some such aircraft were used in a training capacity. More than two thirds of them (a total of 665 aircraft) were sent to the Soviet Union, while on the other hand (due to lower weight), the A-20Bs offered a higher maximum speed and ceiling.

The first batches of such aircraft came via Iran, but the majority of the A-20Bs, however, were ferried to the USSR via the ALSIB route. On 14 September, the Soviet Commission in Fairbanks accepted the first batch of Bostons; on 29 September, the training of ferry pilots began; and, on the following day, a group of twelve A-20Bs – led by Major P.V. Nedosekin – headed for Nome. On account of the bad weather, the aircraft arrived in Markovo (where the crew exchange took place) as late as 7 October, and the first two bombers were handed over in Krasnoyarsk in November. By the end of 1942, a total of 50 aircraft had been ferried via the ALSIB route and only six had been handed over/accepted at the final destination. The main influx took place during the following year.

From December 1942, the Bostons were also coming via the northern ports. During December 1942-January 1943, Convoys JW 51A and JW 51B unloaded 37 aircraft in Murmansk, and six more aircraft were brought by Convoy JW 52 in late January.

The A-20B had a top-mounted large-caliber machine gun; however, it was arranged on the same swivel mount which had been used on earlier versions. The bomb armament featured only slight changes for the better and, therefore, this version was deemed unsatisfactory and thus subjected to modifications. In December 1942, a minor modification of the A-20B was presented for tests, with the standard American bomb racks (the A-20B had six internal and four external ones) simply modified to carry Soviet bombs.

In June 1943, a more in-depth modification was tested at NIPAV. The internal bomb bays of the modified aircraft accommodated Der-21 multiple bomb racks, which were intended to carry a total of sixteen FAB-100 bombs; on the outside, Der-19P racks for bombs of up to 250kg each were mounted. The Der-21 bomb racks allowed carrying (in the bomb bays) KMB-Pe-2 small-caliber bomb dispensers for AO-2.5, AO-10, AO-25 and ZAB-2.5 bombs, as well as AZh-2 capsules (usually filled with the self-inflammable fluid 'KS'). On the external surface, provisions were made for the attachment of VAP-250 chemical spray tanks for toxic agent solutions. The aircraft was also fitted with ESBR-6 bomb release gear and OPB-1R and NKPB-7 bomb sights. As a result, the maximum bomb load grew to 2,000kg. In total, more than 600 aircraft (among them, several hundred A-20Bs) underwent bomb armament modifications. The changes in the defensive armament of such aircraft were confined (mostly) to the mounting of the UTK-1 turret on the top. The turret, however, did not accommodate the Soviet Berezin UBT machine gun, but the American Colt-Browning, which was removed from the standard swivel mount. On 31 October 1942, Deputy Air Force Commander Colonel G.A. Vorozheikin addressed the People's Commissariat of Aviation Industry with a request to modify fifty-four A-20Bs in accordance with the above-described design as quickly as possible.

Such aircraft took part in the Battle of Stalingrad – and there, again, pilots of the 221st Air Division showed themselves to good advantage. When the Soviet troops sealed the ring around

Stalingrad, the Germans had nothing left to do but to try to establish an 'air bridge'. Bombers were involved in cargo-carrying missions along with transport aircraft; however, merely providing supplies to 22 divisions in the pocket was an impossible task in itself (all the more so because the Soviet party was making every effort to destroy the 'bridge').

The Bostons' role consisted (primarily) of making raids on airfields where enemy aircraft were based; attacks were delivered on Morozovsk, Millerovo and Tatsinskaya. Group and solo strikes were alternating, without giving any time to the enemy to load the aircraft, or to repair the airfield. Sometimes, bombing was complemented with low-altitude machine gun firing. G.A. Osipov, who had, at the time, been a squadron leader with the 57th Bomber Air Regiment, wrote later that finding the target had not been a difficult task due to pillars of smoke from the burning aircraft, which had revealed the airfield location from afar. The previously mentioned 57th Bomber Air Regiment burnt away 17 aircraft of various types in Tatsinskaya during a single operational day.

The Bostons also engaged the enemy in flight – thus, there was a case when a flight of five A-20Bs caught sight of a three-engine Ju 52/3m. One of the bombers took a course parallel to the German aircraft, and radio operator gunner I.I. Zelenkov opened point-blank fire on the cockpit. The transport aircraft fell into a spiral dive and crashed into the ground. The Bostons attempted to attack the well-armed He 177 and FW 200 bombers as well; they fired at the German aircraft, but failed to shoot any of them down. On the other hand, the results of raids on ground targets were impressive: they were confirmed later, as soon as the Soviet troops occupied the airfields, which proved full of maimed and burnt-down aircraft.

The Germans, though, strove to repay in kind – thus, on 15 February 1943, the Messerschmitts administered a considerable thrashing to the aircraft of the 45th and 745th Bomber Air Regiments near Stalino.

From March 1943, the number of aircraft coming via Alaska kept increasing drastically. The peak occurred in June, with one-hundred-and-ninety-five A-20s ferried along the ALSIB route. In total, throughout 1943, 682 aircraft of this type were handed over in Krasnoyarsk.

The new arrivals were mostly the A-20Cs, and this version was unified with the export DB-7B to a maximum extent. The navigator compartment transparencies were similar to those on the A-20A, as the aircraft was armed with seven 7.62mm machine guns (four stationary ones in the fuselage nose, two in the gunner's turret and one in the ventral hatch). Reinforced armor protection and self-sealing tanks made the aircraft more viable; however, additional weight did affect its flight performance to a certain extent. The A-20C utilized an additional ferry tank (a huge drop-shaped detachable tank, which was attached under the aircraft belly), and the later series were fitted with a 530L tank, which was mounted inside the bomb bay.

This version was built by two factories, which were the Douglas Factory in Santa Monica and the Boeing Factory in Seattle. The versions were designated, respectively, the A-20C-DO and the A-20C-DO, with the British referring to them as the 'Boston III' and the 'Boston IIIA'. The aircraft from Seattle were fitted with an exhaust system, electrical equipment and dust filters in engine air intakes.

Aircraft which were ferried from the USA included certain special modifications for operation in the USSR. This was connected with the fact that British and American crews consisted of three persons each, whereas Soviet crews were four-person crews (the bottom gunner was added). The modifications included the installation of a seat; oxygen equipment; Intercom connections etc. for the additional gunner; and changes in the arrangement of radio equipment. This was done not at the factories (there, aircraft were equipped in accordance with US Army standards), but at a special modification center in Tulsa, to which Soviet military acceptance specialists were attached. All later versions of the A-20 that were intended for the USSR passed through this center.

In 1943, the number of units flying the A-20s continued to grow – thus, in February, the 33rd Bomber Air Regiment began receiving the B-3s. In spring, the combat army held approximately

400 Bostons, with almost all of them in the south (108 aircraft in the South-Western Front, 101 in the North Caucasian Front, 163 in the Transcaucasian Front and 24 in the Southern Front).

The 221st Bomber Air Division, which had been replenished with manpower and materiel, arrived at the Kursk salient in early June 1943. It was there that the 57th Bomber Air Regiment was visited by the aviation adviser to the US President and famous flying ace of the First World War E. Rickenbaker. As usual, a new outfit and two packs of expensive cigarettes per pilot had been delivered to the regiment in two Li-2s before the visit. Rickenbaker saw through the trick with the clothes; however, he was happy with the American aircraft being made use of. Later, orders and medals arrived, which were awarded to Soviet pilots by the US Government.

On 14 July, combat sorties began. The 57th Air Regiment made a night raid on the German headquarters in the village of Brasovo; the target was lit by fires, which had been caused by the preceding daytime air strikes. The pilots dropped the bombs, and then – by means of machine gun fire – they destroyed two floodlights and suppressed an anti-aircraft battery.

During the course of the Battle of Kursk, a remarkable episode occurred: on 4 August, two squadrons of the 57th Bomber Air Regiment flew to bomb the retreating German troops near the village of Naryshkino. Above the target, they were subjected to anti-aircraft fire, and one of the pilots (Junior Lieutenant A.M. Pogudin) was seriously wounded. When he realized that he was no longer able to control the aircraft, he ordered the crew to abandon it and bailed out, which was witnessed by crews of other bombers. The squadron leader ordered the party to put up speed and disperse, lest the uncontrolled Boston should crash into any of the bombers. After a while, however, it became clear that Pogudin's bomber had been following the formation without the pilot. As has already been mentioned, all early A-20 versions were fitted with the second set of controls, which was mounted at the seat of the radio operator gunner, whose visibility in the forward direction was almost zero – thus, gunner M.Y. Karas took over control of the aircraft and flew it in accordance with the commands of navigator P.V. Parshutin. The situation was a classic example of 'A Blind Man Carrying a Legless Man'. Controlled by the navigator and the gunner, the aircraft successfully reached Limovoye airfield. Landing posed another challenge for the two, but they coped with it. The belly landing was so hard that a grating sound was heard, and a fire broke out; however, it was successfully suppressed. Karas and Kovalev (the second gunner) were injured. Afterwards, the navigator and the radio operator gunner were awarded Orders of the Red Banner of Military Valor for their behavior under the circumstances, while Kovalev was awarded the Medal for Courage, for the sake of encouragement. Later, Parshutin graduated from a flying school and became a pilot.

In 1943, a new version began arriving via Alaska and Iran: the A-20G. In the USSR, it was usually given the designation A-20Zh (hence one of its nicknames, *Zhuchok*, which literally means 'Beetle'), and it was the next mass-manufactured Boston version.

The A-20G was purely a ground attack version, and the nose portion accommodated a whole battery of cannons and machine guns. The aircraft of the first series (the A-20G-1s) had four 20mm M2 cannons (with a stock of 60 rounds each) and two 12.7mm machine guns in the nose – and besides, the armor protection was enhanced; the aircraft equipment was improved; the aft bomb bay was elongated; and the bomb capacity was increased dramatically (with a maximum overload of up to 1,800kg). The aircraft became heavier (the empty weight grew by more than a ton) and somewhat less speedy and maneuverable; however, its combat efficiency increased. Almost all G-1s were sent to the USSR.

The cannons in the nose were soon abandoned, so instead, six large-caliber machine guns were mounted on the G-5 and the subsequent series. The G-20 had a wider aft fuselage, which accommodated an electrified Martin 250GE turret with two 12.7mm machine guns.

Each new series of the Bostons was equipped with more and more efficient armament, as well as offering a higher bomb capacity and better armor protection; on the other hand, however, the aircraft was becoming heavier and its flight performance lowered. In terms of speed, the G version was inferior to the latest Pe-2 series, but nevertheless, the Boston remained a menacing frontline bomber.

The A-20Gs first came to the Soviet-German Front in summer 1943, and this version truly found multi-purpose application with the Soviet aviation. It was used in a number of versatile roles, such as a day and night bomber; a reconnaissance aircraft; a torpedo bomber; a minelayer; a heavy fighter; and even a transport aircraft. The only role that was in little demand was that of a ground attack aircraft, which was the role for which it had initially been intended!

The A-20G-1s that were shipped via Iraq and Iran naturally arrived first. These aircraft were tried out in bombing and strafing attacks on the enemy's positions, as well as on motor vehicles in transit, railway trains and airfields. *Zhuchok* turned out to be very vulnerable to anti-aircraft fire at low altitudes due to its large size and insufficient armor protection. Given the high efficiency of the German anti-aircraft defense, a relative safety at strafing could only be expected in case of a surprise attack. Nevertheless, Soviet pilots strafed motor convoys, trains and surface ships. Under the circumstances, crews of the 449th Bomber Air Regiment usually attacked from a height of 300-700m in a 20-25° dive. After a burst of 20-30 rounds, the aircraft left promptly at a low level. The Ilyushin Il-2 gained a firm foothold as a ground attack aircraft in the Soviet aviation, whereas the A-20G was relegated to other roles.

The opinions of crews from the 321st Bomber Air Division as received by NII VVS in September 1943 testified to the fact that pilots (in general) appreciated the new version. They noted the high firepower; the reliability of armament; the convenience of firing both during daytime and at night; and the decent flight performance. NII VVS even categorized *Zhuchok* among fighter bombers. Among the drawbacks were that combat crews mentioned the insufficient rigidity of the upper gun mount in the rear cabin, which led to a high dispersion of bullets. Also, American oxygen masks were only good enough in a warm environment, as cold-weather operations resulted in the blocking of tubes with condensate.

Technicians complained about the difficulties in removing the engine cowlings, as the procedure took up to three man-hours. With additional fuel tanks in the bomb bay, many assemblies became inaccessible, but these were only minor troubles. Sometime later, it turned out that the forward portion of the fuselage tended to buckle due to cannon recoil. Failures of the rear armament attachment brackets also occurred; however, the overall conclusion was a positive one: '... The detected defects of the A-20-Zh aircraft present no obstacle for ... frontline operation of the aircraft...'

At the same time, an emphasis was put on the need to include a navigator in the crew, but the A-20G had no navigator compartment. Without a navigator, terrain orientation posed certain difficulties, and it was not easy to take sight during bombing missions either. In the USA, the manufacture of the A-20J lead aircraft with a new fuselage nose section and an improved field of view was launched almost concurrently with the A-20G. It was expected that a group of bombers would be guided by a lead aircraft, whose navigator would do the sighting and give a command to drop the bombs to pilots in the rest of the bombers.

The USSR received only a few aircraft of this version; they came later than the Gs. An A-20J-10 was tested at NII VVS in August 1944, but the A-20Gs, on the contrary, kept coming in increasing quantities. For this reason, attempts were made to arrange navigator workstations in them.

A modification is known of which was implemented in the 244th Bomber Air Division under the direction of M.Z. Melamed: four upper machine guns were removed from the nose section; then, it was glazed and the navigator's seat – and all the required equipment – were installed. The change in the center of gravity was compensated by the mounting of steel plates in the navigator's cabin; the said plates also constituted an additional armor protection. In the aft section, coaxial UBT machine guns were mounted (the baseline aircraft belonged to a series preceding the

G-20), and bomb armament was also modernized. This modified A-20G was sent to Moscow as a prototype.

Later, similar modifications were carried out at Factory No.81 at repair bases and directly in the regiments. Aircraft so modified were flown by the 218th and the 244th Bomber Air Divisions, the 970th Bomber Air Regiment and other units and formations. Since modifications at different locations were made in a different manner, there were many versions of nose portion glazing which differed from each other. In some units, for example, the nose portion of the navigator cabin canopy from the Il-4 was used. An incompetently implemented modification could lead to a center of gravity shift in the aft direction beyond the allowable limit, which, in turn, caused a dangerous flat spin condition.

In August 1943, Factory No.89 modified one of the aircraft to accommodate the navigator in the radio operator gunner's cabin, together with the latter. The navigator's workstation was equipped with an OPB-1R sight; an instrument panel (with mostly Soviet instruments); an A-4 compass; ESBR-3 bomb release gear; and the radio compass control panel. To provide the navigator with some visibility, windows were cut in the fuselage sides and in the floor. Additionally, armaments in the aft cabin were replaced with Soviet ones. At the top, the UTK-1 turret with a UBT machine gun (with a stock of 200 rounds) was mounted; in the lower section, a hatch-mounted turret from the Pe-2, but with the same UBT machine gun (also with a stock of 200 rounds), was arranged. Soviet KD2-429 bomb racks were mounted inside the bomb bay; an emergency mechanical bomb jettisoning system was installed; and the oxygen system was modified (for the latter, the modification consisted of the installation of four oxygen bottles). To reduce the aircraft's weight, additional fuel tanks were removed from the bomb bay, together with their dedicated pipelines, valves and pumps. As a result, the modified *Zhuchok* could no longer carry additional tanks. On 4 September 1943, this aircraft was approved as a reference model for the modification of other bombers at the factory. In October, an aircraft so modified was submitted for tests to NII VVS.

The designers at Factory No.89 were not alone in their attempts to solve the problem of how to accommodate the navigator in the A-20G. A.P. Golubkov's design office was entrusted with the task of checking the possibility of arranging the navigator workstation behind the pilot, at the expense of a reduction in length of the forward bomb bay. In October 1943, Factory No.456 modified a bomber and presented it instead of the mock-up as had been requested by the assignment. The navigator was placed in the enclosure of the forward bomb bay and, for this purpose, the partition separating the enclosure from the cockpit was partially removed. The navigator's compartment turned out to be extremely narrow (approximately 70x70cm) and, on the sides, it was lined with veneer; no armor protection was provided. The navigator was to occupy a flap seat, and the seat bucket accommodated a parachute. The navigator's 'workstation' was equipped with an OPB-1 bomb sight; ESBR-6 bomb release gear; a compass; an instrument panel, with the main instruments; and a KPA-3bis oxygen regulator. Also, three windows were cut out in each side of the cabin.

Tests of the modified aircraft revealed a number of drawbacks: the undersized bomb bay could only accommodate six 100kg bombs instead of eight. Furthermore, the gap between the bomb nose and the wall was reduced, so it became impossible to insert fuses into the upper two bombs – thus, the bombs had to be fitted with fuses before any installation on the aircraft, which was prohibited by safety regulations.

Forward visibility was almost zero – especially with the torso back protective armor fully up – and when working with the bomb sight, the navigator had to stand on half-bent legs, which became tiring very quickly; however, on 24 October, the modification was approved by a commission chaired by Major General Archangelsky – and the commission even permitted suspending bombs with fuses!

On 15 November, Factory No.456 presented two reference A-20Gs with the additional navigator's cabin; a bomb armament modified to use Soviet bombs; and Soviet large-caliber machine guns.

There were other variants for the arrangement of the navigator's cabin and, in practice, each unit or formation implemented its own ideas – depending on the availability of materials, parts from other aircraft and equipment. It is difficult to determine the total share of the modified A-20Gs, since inventory records do not specify such aircraft separately; however, the percentage of the modified aircraft was rather large.

The prospects of the need to considerably modify all of the Bostons that were shipped to the USSR arose no enthusiasm either among the Air Force Command, or among the management of the People's Commissariat of Aviation Industry. On 26 November 1943, Deputy Air Force Commander A.V. Nikitin and People's Commissar of Aviation Industry A.I. Shakhurin sent a letter to People's Commissar of Foreign Trade A.I. Mikoyan requesting the latter to insist on the resumption of shipments of the A-20B version; moreover, it was stressed that the aircraft's bomb armament should be modified. Factory No.43 prepared special drawings for the minor modifications of the standard American version, which would allow increasing the internal bomb load and carrying Soviet bombs of various calibers; however, this move went unattended. The USA continued shipping the A-20Gs to the Soviet Union.

There were two approaches to the modification of the A-20G-1's armament: all of the modification variants discussed above were based on suggestions of NII VVS, which advocated the conversion to Soviet machine guns to the maximum possible extent. On the other hand, NII AV (the Research Institute of Air Armament) suggested replacing the mounts, but keeping the American machine guns. This was explained by the need to unify the spare parts and armaments supply. According to the scheme suggested by NII AV, four 20mm cannons and one of the 12.7mm Colt-Brownings were to be left in the nose. The other 12.7mm machine gun was to be removed and installed on the Pe-2 ventral mount in the lower aft cabin, whereas the top-mounted machine gun was to be relocated into the UTK-1 turret. This variant was adopted and, on 3 September, was approved by the air force's chief engineer; however, the majority of modifications continued to be implemented in accordance with the suggestions of NII VVS.

In mid-1943, the gradual replacement of the earlier A-20 versions with the G version began at the front lines; however, the earlier versions – including the B-3 – remained in service with some units. Consequently, the 221st Bomber Air Division (which has been repeatedly mentioned above) held, as of 31 December 1943, four old B-3s (one of them was an UB-3, with a dual set of controls); forty-four A-40Bs; eleven A-20Cs; and only six A-20Gs. Shortly before the end of December, one of the division's A-20Gs went missing in action, while another had crashed during take-off at night. Nevertheless, by mid-1944, the A-20G had become the most mass-used version of the Bostons (as all aircraft of the A-20 family had still usually been referred to) within the Soviet Air Force.

The delivery of the G-20s, with their swivel mount in the aft cabin replaced by the electrified Martin 250GE turret with two 12.7mm machine guns, normalized the situation as regards defensive armament, so now it was deemed to be quite adequate. In comparison to the UTK-1, the new American turret offered higher firing power and better mobility. It is worth noting that at that time, no such mounts were manufactured in the Soviet Union. One of the A-20G-20s was tested at NII VVS in October 1943 and won a high opinion.

By the end of the war, the deliveries of the A-20s were gradually decreasing. In 1943, the Soviet Union received one-thousand-three-hundred-and-sixty A-20s of various versions, while in 1944, there were only 743 of them. Finally, in 1945, only one Boston passed the Soviet military acceptance.

Together with the A-20G and the A-20J, their 'younger brothers' – the A-20H and the A-20K – took part in the war at its final stage. They were undistinguishable from the former aircraft in appearance, but had more powerful engines (the R-2600-29, which were boosted to 1,850hp), which, as a consequence, provided a slightly higher speed. Those were the last representatives of the A-20 family. In September 1944, their manufacture was discontinued and the new model of the same purpose (the A-26) was launched instead. The 'lion's share' of the Hs and Ks were sent to the Soviet Union, and an A-20K-11 was tested by NII VVS in October 1944. In should be noted though that only approximately 10 such bombers had arrived at the front before the end of the war with Germany.

In one of the A-20Ks, pilot M.A. Nyukhtikov and navigator Skorokhod led the ferry of a group of Yak-9DD fighters from the Soviet Union to Italy. The fighters were intended to provide cover for the C-47 transport aircraft which were staying at an Allies' base in Bari. On 24 August 1944, they left Moscow; then, they made an intermediate landing in Beltsy for refueling and, finally, landed in Bari with no difficulties.

In the Soviet Union, the Bostons saw successful service until the very end of the war – taking part in all of the major operations at the final stage of the hostilities (e.g. the Belorussian Offensive; the Jassy — Kishinev Offensive; the East Prussian Offensive; and many others), and fighting in the skies above Poland, Romania, Czechoslovakia and Germany. In August 1944, the 221st and the 132nd Bomber Air Divisions operated in Poland. The enemy was opposing fiercely – thus, during a raid against the Germans' strongpoint in Debe near Warsaw, the 221st Air Division lost 14 bombers and 43 men from the flight crews.

The bombs dropped by the A-20Gs helped to stifle the German counter-offensive in Hungary, with the Bostons making a considerable contribution towards the destruction of almost half of the total number of tanks by the air force. During the Vienna operation, the 244th Bomber Air Division alone destroyed 24 tanks and self-propelled guns, 13 warehouses, eight bridges and crossings, 886 motor vehicles, and a large number of personnel.

In April 1945, the Bostons appeared above Berlin. The 221st Bomber Air Division operated within the offensive sector of the 8th Army and, in particular, it supported the assault on the Seelow Heights. The 57th Bomber Air Regiment even flew in conditions of poor visibility, when aircraft from other units remained grounded. In spite of the low and continuous cloud, 23 crews bomb-destroyed artillery and mortar batteries near Gelsdorf. On 22 April, the Soviet A-20s dropped bombs on Berlin for the first time; on the following day, a flight led by Lieutenant Gadyuchko destroyed a crossing on the Spree.

As of 1 May 1945, the Soviet Air Force had 935 Bostons, and more than two thirds of them were of the G version. As for the new A-20Js and A-20Ks, there were only 65 of them. It should be noted, however, that a considerable number of the Bostons were handed over to the naval aviation, which will be described in more detail below.

Apparently, the Soviet pilots flew their last combat sortie in Europe on 13 May 1945 (i.e. already after the capitulation of Germany). On that day, aircraft of the 449th Air Regiment bombed the units of the 6th and the 8th German Armies in Austria.

During the war, the Boston became a multi-purpose aircraft in the Soviet Union – having demonstrated considerably ampler capabilities than those of the Petlyakov Pe-2. The A-20 saw little service as a reconnaissance aircraft in the West, whereas in the Soviet Union, its application in the role was rather extensive. Apparently, one of the aircraft from the 794th Bomber Air Regiment, which bore the side number '6', became the first Boston for reconnaissance purposes. It was fitted with the AFA-27 Soviet aerial camera and, according to pilots' recollections, the aircraft flew two missions to take photographs of the port in Trapezund in 1942. Later, a large number of aircraft were subjected to such a modification.

The 325th Independent Reconnaissance Air Squadron, which was under the command of Captain D.S Sherstyuk, was the first of the special-purpose reconnaissance units to begin mastering the Bostons. In July 1942, the unit received the B-3s in Kirovabad; then, the squadron was redeployed to Monino in the Moscow region, where its aircraft were fitted with Soviet small arms. In October, the 325th Independent Reconnaissance Air Squadron was sent to the Don Front, and there it operated for approximately two months – including the period of the counter-offensive at Stalingrad. The Bostons made 126 combat sorties to take photographs of positions and facilities close behind the enemy's lines. During the missions, the unit lost four aircraft: two of them were shot down by fighters, the third by anti-aircraft artillery and yet another was destroyed in a crash. In December, the squadron received new aircraft and was converted to the 16th Independent Reconnaissance Air Regiment – operating as part of the 16th Air Army.

Opinions on the suitability of the B-3s for the role of reconnaissance aircraft were, in general, favourable. For example: "The Boston III aircraft has showed itself to advantage in terms of rate of climb and level flight speed. The enemy's fighters, such as the Messerschmitt Me 109G2 and the Messerschmitts Me 109F, are unable to catch up with it provided that they are detected at a sufficient distance. The Boston outpaces them with a climb to 9,000m," but this aside, the operating radius of the aircraft was found to be insufficient for reconnaissance missions.

This drawback was eliminated by the installation of additional fuel tanks and, during the modification, they were mounted in the bomb bay. Different fuel tank types were installed, depending on what was available at the moment. Sometimes, original American additional tanks were used, but those, however, were not self-sealing. For this reason, the preference was given to the Soviet tanks which were removed from written-off aircraft. Sometimes, tanks were even tailor-made to fit the size of the bomb bay. Photographic equipment (cameras of the types AFA-1, AFA-B, NAFA-13 or NAFA-19, as well as various American cameras) was installed in the radio operator gunner's cockpit and, sometimes, in the bomb bay, where special hatches for lenses were cut out.

Initially, the B-3s were used as reconnaissance aircraft; then, the A-20B, which featured a higher speed, took over the role. Later, the A-20G, with its high defensive potential, was also not infrequently used for the purpose. In 1944-1945, some crews flew the A-20Js.

The reconnaissance Bostons were included in the 48th and the 98th Guards Long-Range Reconnaissance Air Regiments, which carried out strategic photo reconnaissance for the purposes of the General Headquarters of the Supreme Commander-in-Chief. In the 98th Air Regiment, the 2nd Squadron was equipped with the A-20Bs in 1943, and it performed urgent special tasks as set by the Command. Individual crews repositioned to advanced airfields, from which they flew deep into the enemy's rear – thus, during preparations for the advance on Kiev in May 1944, the Bostons flew their missions from Skomorokhi airfield. From there, they reached Warsaw, Lodz and Krakow; for this purpose, they had to fly distances of up to 1,600km and get 300-400km beyond the front line. In August 1944, the squadron converted to the Pe-2s and Pe-3s.

The defensive armament of the reconnaissance Bostons was not different from that of the bombers, and aircraft of earlier versions were re-equipped to carry Soviet machine guns and turrets. The only exception is the modification by 'innovators' of the 48th Long-Range Reconnaissance Air Regiment, who decided to use rocket projectiles not only for attack, but also for defense purposes. In addition to the underwing RS-82s, they mounted two launching rails under the aft portion of the fuselage. The rocket projectiles from such rails were launched in the backward direction and struck the enemy in the bomber's 'blind zone' behind the tail.

Some individually modified aircraft were also at the disposal of ordinary bomber air regiments. Hero of the Soviet Union G.I. Lashin of the 861st Bomber Air Regiment was a brilliant air scout. His Boston, with a red figure '4' on the tail, took photographs of Constantsa, Sulin, Ploesti and Bucharest. Above the latter, the aircraft was hit by anti-aircraft fire, and then attacked by fighters. The navigator was wounded by fragmentation; however, the aircraft successfully brought the films (along with the priceless photos) to the home base. In the skies of Sofia, the pilots themselves shot down an enemy aircraft. Later, Lashin credited photographs from Athens, Beograd and Budapest to his account. In Budapest, he (in passing) destroyed a bridge with a couple of 100kg bombs and returned home with only the left engine operative. On that day, the number of large holes alone in his aircraft totaled 37. During the photographing of Vienna, the pilot used his nose machine guns to set an FW 190 fighter on fire, which was attempting to attack the Soviet reconnaissance aircraft.

In 1943, the Bostons began to be used extensively by the naval aviation. In fact, they had appeared there earlier – almost simultaneously with their application by the Army Air Force. In its original configuration, neither the Boston III, nor the A-20B was fit for the role of a naval bomber. There were, essentially, two drawbacks: one of them was the comparatively small operating radius (1,380km, which was less than that of the Pe-2), and the other consisted of the impossibility to use the heavy bombs which were needed to hit ships. For these reasons, the Bostons were, initially, used as reconnaissance aircraft. In May 1942, an additional reconnaissance air squadron was formed, which received two A-20Bs, five B-3s and three Pe-2s. In November, it was given an official status and designation (the 29th Independent Reconnaissance Air Squadron) and, in May 1943, it was converted into the 30th Air Regiment, whose two squadrons flew the Bostons. In February the same year, six A-20Bs were allocated for the 1st Guards Mine-and-Torpedo Air Regiment in the Baltic Sea, and there, they were tried out and handed over to the 15th Independent Reconnaissance Air Regiment. In March, aircraft of the same version appeared in the 118th Independent Reconnaissance Air Regiment of the Northern Fleet. The reconnaissance Bostons were used by the naval aviation throughout the entire war and scored a lot of important successes – thus, for example, it was an A-20, from which on 20 May 1943, Lieutenant Colonel N.G. Pavlov took the first photographs of Narvic port. He 'sneaked in' on the target with engines muffled, and successfully left without being noticed or fired at from the ground.

Sometime later, the Boston III also began to be used as a bomber at the Black Sea. The aircraft were provided to the 36th Bomber Air Regiment, which entered the action in January 1943. The Bostons dropped bombs on ships at sea, as well as in harbors. For operations in the open sea against small-sized mobile targets, the American aircraft turned out to be less efficient than the Pe-2 dive bombers. The number of target hits from the same bombing altitude was reduced by almost one third, so to hit a high-speed invasion barge for sure with at least one bomb, a raid of 28 Bostons was required! Nevertheless, in April 1944, another regiment (the 13th Bomber Air Regiment) was equipped with a mixed composition of B-3s and A-20Gs. The bomber Bostons operated with the greatest efficiency against land-based targets and ships in ports (for example, on 1 June 1944 in Feodosiya, the 36th Air Regiment destroyed 11 vessels). Sometimes, however, they achieved success on the open sea as well – thus, on 22 April, they sent the *Ossag* tanker and the KT-26 transport ship to the bottom; two days later, the *Leo* lighter shared the same fate. The first A-20s, which were used as bombers in the north, were flown by the 24th Mine-and-Torpedo Air Regiment; however, the Bostons that were modified into torpedo bombers saw much more extensive service with the navy. For the first time, the possibility of carrying the Mk XIII American torpedo was provided for in the DB-7C version. The semi-recessed torpedo was fixed in the bomb bay, with its doors removed. Such aircraft were delivered to the USSR and, in particular, by 1 March 1943, 44 of them had been ferried via the southern route and they were registered separately as 'torpedo bombers'. Later, an identical configuration for the torpedo carrying was implemented on the A-20G; however, the US Navy aviation used its BD-1s and BD-2s solely for auxiliary purposes. RAF Coastal Command (i.e. the land-based naval aviation in Great Britain) had no Bostons at all. The A-20s of all versions found application with the Americans against combat ships and, especially, against transport vessels (for example, in the Pacific); however, they used in such cases only machine gun fire, bombs (including skip bombing) and rocket projectiles.

In the USSR, on the other hand, the Boston rather quickly became the most widely used torpedo bomber type. American torpedo racks were not suitable for Soviet 45-36A torpedoes and, furthermore, Soviet torpedoes were longer and did not fit in the bomb bay. Therefore, the development of external torpedo mounting designs was initiated. The first modifications of this kind were made to the A-20B and DB-7C bombers, and in order to make the aircraft able to carry torpedoes, so-called 'torpedo bridges' were mounted on the left side and on the right in the lower portion of the fuselage under the wings. A torpedo bridge was, essentially, an I-beam (often welded or riveted from two channel sections) with wooden fairings at the ends, which was attached to the fuselage by means of a system of braces. The hold-down beam was passed transversely to the bomb bay, so theoretically, this allowed carrying two torpedoes, which was actually done sometimes for short-range flights from hard-soil airfields; however, typically, a single torpedo was carried on the right side. Torpedo bridges were made directly at the facilities of air units in various shops or at factories and, in most cases, T-18 torpedo beams (from the Il-4) were used. In this case, the American underwing bomb racks were removed.

In March 1943, NII VVS tested a DB-7C modified by Factory No.81. The aircraft was fitted with Soviet armament, which consisted of four large-caliber machine guns. Torpedo bridges with T-18 torpedo beams manufactured by Factory No.43 were installed under the wing on the fuselage sides. Soviet ESBR-3P bomb release gear and the PTN-5 torpedo sight were mounted at the navigator's seat, and the aircraft was test-flown by Major S.B. Reidel. As compared to a non-modified bomber, the torpedo bomber was more inert; however, even with two torpedoes on board, the DB-7C proved easier to fly than the Il-4 with a single torpedo. Vibrations of the torpedo carriers were detected, but this defect, however, was successfully rectified shortly afterwards.

Sometime later, a torpedo bomber version as suggested by Factory No.89 appeared. In this case, the A-20B was modified: the internal American torpedo carrier was replaced with a 2T-18 external double bridge and, in the nose portion, two Berezin UBK machine guns were arranged, with a stock of 250 rounds each. For aiming, the pilot was provided with the K-8T sight, while the navigator received the NKPB night bomb sight and the PTK-5 torpedo sight. Small arms configuration in the aft was altered in a manner similar to the modification of an ordinary bomber (i.e. the UTK-1 turret and the ventral mount from the Pe-2, which was slightly modified by Factory No.43, were installed). The flight range was very important for naval operations, so therefore, additional fuel tanks were mounted. Standard American tanks, which were, typically, arranged in the bomb bay, were rejected for the reason that they were not self-sealing. Instead, two tanks from the Pe-2 were suspended on straps in the forward portion of the bomb bay. This version was approved as a reference model for the Northern Fleet Air Force.

The first test of the A-20 in the role of a torpedo bomber was conducted in early June 1943 in the 2nd Squadron of the 9th Guards (formerly 24th) Mine-and-Torpedo Air Regiment. The aircraft was fitted with provisions for carrying two torpedoes and the PTN-5 sight. For the Soviet 45-36AN torpedo (which was intended for low-altitude drops), the recommended release speed was 270-280km/h; however, for the Boston, such a speed proved too low, as at this speed, the aircraft behaved in an unstable manner. For this reason, the torpedo release speed was increased to 290-300km/h and the torpedo withstood it. On 24 June, participants of the tests received awarding bonuses, and the baptism of fire for the torpedo-carrying Bostons took place on 17 July 1943.

The subsequent modified aircraft were somewhat different from the reference model, with the differences being dictated by both the recommendations of flight crews, and by the presence (or, more precisely, the absence) of certain equipment items. In particular, there was a shortage of OPB-1 bomb sights and uniform fuel tanks, so the changes included a modification of the oxygen system and the introduction of the Soviet SPU-3bis intercommunication system. The final modification project was developed under the supervision of Chief Engineer for the Northern Fleet Air Force Lieutenant Colonel R.M. Sobchenko. The modifications were implemented by Aircraft Repair Shop No.85, with the assistance of a team from Factory No.22. The work began on 4

August 1943 and was performed concurrently on four bombers. The first of them was completed in five days (on 9 August), while the subsequent Bostons were handed over for acceptance at a rate of one aircraft in every one-and-a-half to two days. In total, 36 aircraft were modified.

As has already been mentioned above, the used fuel tanks were of various types, with the modified batch including six different 'sub-variants'. On them, different tanks from the Pe-2 and from the British Handley Page Hampden torpedo bombers were installed in different combinations. All of the tanks were fitted with an inert gas pressurization system which was not available on the American aircraft in their original configuration. Unlike the majority of the Soviet aircraft, the tanks were supplied with carbon dioxide instead of cooled and purified exhaust gases. The carbon dioxide bottle was placed under the navigator seat, with the tap and the pressure gauge installed near the pilot.

The bomb armament had two variants as well: in the first case, original bomb racks were preserved in the aft portion of the bomb bay, which was not occupied with additional fuel tanks; such bomb racks could be used to carry a pair of FAB-100 bombs. In the second variant, Soviet Der-21 bomb racks were installed instead of the American bomb racks, with the bomb load thus increased to 400kg. Bombs and torpedoes were released from different release gears (ESBR-3 for bombs and ESBR-6 for torpedoes) – and besides, there were mechanical release gears at the pilot's and navigator's seats; however, it was not the DB-7C or A-20C that were mostly subjected to mass modification: the most mass-modified version was the later A-20G. The 1st Guards Mine-and-Torpedo Air Regiment of the Baltic Fleet was the first to receive a *Zhuchok* with torpedo bridges.

The regiment entered the action in mid-April, and with only four torpedo-carrying Bostons at its disposal. Throughout the war, the regiment flew a mix of the A-20Gs and the Il-4s. In October the same year, the 51st Mine-and-Torpedo Air Regiment – equipped with the A-20Gs only – was raised at the Baltic Fleet. To the Northern Fleet, aircraft of this type were provided in April 1943, and there they were used to equip the 9th Guards Mine-and-Torpedo Air Regiment, which had, earlier, flown the Il-4s and the British Hampdens. In May, the Bostons began flying torpedo attack missions. The first major raid, with the participation of the A-20Gs, was made by personnel of the Northern Fleet on 20 July near Varde.

Among the units of the Black Sea Fleet, the 36th Bomber Air Regiment was the first to receive aircraft with torpedo-carrying capabilities. In spring 1944, it was fully converted from the B-3s to the A-20Gs, and turned into a mine-and-torpedo regiment; however, in this configuration, the regiment was redeployed to the Northern Fleet in April the same year. As of 1 January 1944, there were 73 Bostons altogether in service with all of the fleets – and among them, the torpedo bombers constituted the majority. In June, the 8th Mine-and-Torpedo Air Division of the Baltic Fleet alone had approximately 70 such aircraft.

The modification of the A-20G into a torpedo bomber included the installation of an additional fuel tank in the bomb bay, which was just the same for the reconnaissance version. As a result, the flight ranges of the Boston and the Il-4 became approximately equal. Sometimes, the navigator's cockpit was arranged in the nose (in the same manner as on bomber aircraft) and, in another widely used version, the navigator's seat was in the radio operator gunner's cockpit; this version was designed at Factory No.89. For the navigator, two windows were cut out in the aircraft sides, with the third window arranged above them. Overhead, there was a transparent hatch, with a dome-type blister. The navigator's equipment included an instrument panel; a short OPB-1m bomb sight; and a radio compass control panel. The aiming during the torpedo release was the pilot's responsibility and, just the same as on the A-20B, the oxygen system was modified. Oxygen bottles were, for the most part, taken from written-off Hurricanes. It should be noted that such an arrangement of the navigator's seat was not very convenient, on account of a very limited field of view, but on the other hand, such a configuration allowed preserving the standard nose of the A-20G. In an attack, such an aircraft usually flew ahead of the others in order to subdue anti-aircraft fire from ships; they carried no torpedoes. A report from the 51st Mine-and-Torpedo Air Regiment contained a special mention of the powerful fire from the nose, which was particularly efficient during group attacks. As for armor protection of the aircraft, the Baltic Fleet pilots found it expressly insufficient.

In the Northern Fleet, the striking force included an approximately equal number of both torpedo-carrying and attack Bostons, while in the Black Sea Fleet, there were three or four aircraft with a powerful nose armament per six to 10 torpedo bombers. The Black Sea Fleet flight crews supplemented the cannon and machine gun fire with the dropping of a large quantity of AO-2.5 small-caliber fragmentation bombs, which were intended to hit anti-aircraft gun personnel.

The modifications of the A-20G-1 version sometimes included additional changes to the defensive armament. The configuration of small arms was designed at Factory No.89 for the A-20B, with the only exception being that instead of the ventral mount from the Pe-2, the old American mount accommodated the 12.7mm Colt-Browning, which was removed from the top. The modified Boston had a gross weight of 11,306kg with a single torpedo, and 11,626kg with two torpedoes (in the latter case, the fuel reserve was reduced due to landing weight restrictions, because the landing gear could not take such a load).

On the A-20G-20s and later versions, the defensive armament was considered quite satisfactory and was not subjected to any modifications. When modified, such aircraft had a slightly lower weight: the gross weight was 11,303kg with a single torpedo, and 11,623kg with two torpedoes (also with limitations for the fuel reserve).

The Bostons were usually operated as low-altitude torpedo bombers, and they dropped the torpedo at a distance of 600-800m from the target from an altitude of 25-30m. The aircraft speed in such conditions was approximately 300km/h.

Such tactics was rather efficient – thus, for example, on 15 October 1944 at dawn, the aircraft of the Northern Fleet delivered a massive strike on a German convoy of 26 ships, with air cover provided by seven enemy fighters. The first attack team consisted of twelve Il-2s; an hour later, another group of 12 attack aircraft entered the action; then, a third wave of ten A-20Gs followed, who were accompanied by 15 fighters. As a result, several ships were sunk, with the task being completed by the 'fourth wave', which consisted of ten A-20Gs led by Commander of the 9th Mine-and-Torpedo Air Regiment Lieutenant Colonel B.P. Syromyatnikov. His aircraft was hit by the Germans, but Syromyatnikov – in a burning aircraft – struck a transport vessel, which soon exploded. The Soviet torpedo bomber fell into the sea, and the entire crew was posthumously awarded the title of Hero of the Soviet Union. In a similar manner, on 22 December 1944, the aircraft of V.P. Nosov from the 51st Mine-and-Torpedo Air Regiment was set on fire while running on a German ship; the heroes had chosen to make a ramming attack.

Low-altitude torpedo releasing was an efficient, but hazardous technique. On 18 December 1943, a solitary Boston, which was flown by V.V. Pirogov, attacked a convoy near Rolfsey Island. The pilot managed to sink a 7,000t transport ship, but the aircraft control cables were damaged by shell fragments, so the gunner tied the cables using straps. In spite of this, the battered aircraft managed to return to base. In a single month (from 1 April through to 1 May 1943), the 9th Guards Mine-and-Torpedo Air Regiment lost seven Bostons out of the available 11. In the wing of the aircraft piloted by Lieutenant Karabanov of the 1st Guards Mine-and-Torpedo Air Regiment, a piece of mast with the acorn button stuck, with which he returned to the base airfield! Because of heavy casualties, the 1st Air Regiment had been left with only one A-20G and an Il-4 by 1 January 1944.

Soviet naval pilots scored a lot of victories in the torpedo-carrying Bostons. The 8th Mine-and-Torpedo Air Division of the Baltic Fleet alone, from March 1944 through to the end of the war, sunk 229 enemy vessels and warships. On 24 March 1945, pilot Podyachy scored the 'milestone' 200th victory for the 1st Guards Mine-and-Torpedo Air Regiment.

Pilots noted the high combat survivability of the Bostons, and especially generous praise was given to the Wright engines. With one engine inoperative, a torpedo bomber was often able to successfully fly a distance of up to 500km.

Combat experience called for some other modifications to the aircraft equipment – thus, the magnetic compass was originally installed in the tail. The suspension of a heavy steel torpedo influenced it in the same manner as the famous piece of iron in the novel by Jules Verne influenced the ship's compass. Its indications were mercilessly false, so when above the sea and in bad weather conditions (with the sun not visible), that was extremely dangerous. For this reason, the compass was relocated to the pilot's cockpit and, near the navigator's seat, a directional indicator was installed. As for the torpedoes, they were subjected to demagnetization. The only unpleasant phenomenon was that several days later, a torpedo usually acquired its former magnetic properties again.

The torpedo bombers of this regiment were fitted with the first Soviet airborne radar stations (type *Gneis-2M*), which were intended to detect sea surface targets. At the suggestion of Senior Engineer for the Baltic Fleet Air Force A.A. Bubnov, five aircraft were equipped with radar stations as received from the fleet's warehouses. First, they were tried above the Ladoga River, and the trials demonstrated that the radar stations were able to detect the riverbank from a distance of 90km, whereas a barge with a tug boat was only identifiable from a distance of 20km. The first combat sortie was flown on 15 October 1944 by Hero of the Soviet Union Regiment Commander I.I. Borzov. In poor visibility conditions, the radar allowed finding, in the Gulf of Riga, a group of three German ships. The crew released a torpedo and sank a 15,000t transport vessel which was carrying military materiel. Later, the radars were used in several more attacks – thus, for example, on 28 April 1945, a German tanker ship was torpedoed to the west of the Rickhoft beacon.

The Bostons were also involved in high-altitude torpedo bombing. For this purpose, 45-36AVA torpedoes were used, and they were launched with parachutes. After water touchdown, such torpedoes began circling or spiraling, and they were useful against ship formations or groups of transport vessels to impede their maneuvering. It is worth noting that the armed forces of Western countries had no such armament at their disposal.

To be able to carry 45-36AVA torpedoes, the American aircraft were subjected to additional modifications. Very similar designs were developed, but independently from each other, in the Baltic Fleet and in the Northern Fleet; in the Baltic Fleet, the work began in October 1944. It took the specialists of the 1st Guards Mine-and-Torpedo Air Regiment just a single day to design a parachute container rack, which was, essentially, a truss attached in the aft bomb compartment. It was assembled in the workshops and mounted on the aircraft later that same day. On 5 October 1944, the crew, which was led by Captain Presnyakov, successfully launched a dummy torpedo during flight tests.

The version developed by Workshop No.85 of the Northern Fleet – under the supervision of D.I. Levin, with the participation of Factory No.43 designer Shulgin – was very similar to the one described above. The same standard container from the Il-4 was mounted in the aft bomb compartment, so only the truss design was slightly different. Later, Levin and Shulgin designed a rack for two parachute torpedoes. The parachutes were stowed inside the small-caliber bomb dispensers of the Pe-2, which were attached to Der-21-100 bomb racks.

Torpedo bridges could also be used to accommodate air-launched mines and large-caliber bombs. The Bostons carried and released the Soviet AMG-1 anchored mine, as well as the Soviet AMD-500 and AMD-1000 bottom mines (the latter were used beginning from September 1944) and the British A Mk.I, A Mk.IV and A Mk.V bottom mines. Typically, the mine load consisted of a pair of AMG-1 mines, which were 500kg each.

In July 1944, the A-20Gs laid 135 aerial mines in the mouth of the Daugava River and in the Gulf of Tallinn; also, similar minelaying sorties were flown near Konigsberg. In total, throughout

1944, 650 mines of various types were laid in the Baltic Sea. They brought about the explosion of two transport vessels in the port of Libau and two destroyers near the Isle of Nargen; in 1945, four German transport ships were sunk by aerial mines. In April 1944, the 36th Air Regiment laid mines in the mouth of the Danube and in the approaches to Constantsa and Sulin. The aircraft of the Northern Fleet laid a total of 167 mines throughout 1944.

The external mount was fit to carry a FAB-500 (or even a FAB-1000) bomb on each side; however, the latter version was seldom used. Typical targets for the Bostons' bombs included ships and harbor installations – thus, in August 1944, the A-20Gs of the 2nd Guards Mine-and-Torpedo Air Division took part in a raid on Constantsa. The striking force consisted of sixty-two Pe-2s and fourteen A-20Gs, and among the sunken assets were a torpedo boat; a tanker ship; three submarines; and five mosquito boats. Also, a destroyer; an auxiliary cruiser; three more submarines; a transport vessel; and a dockship were damaged. Finally, a fuel-oil depot was exploded and some repair shops were destroyed. A group of A-20Gs of the 13th Bomber Air Regiment set a smokescreen above the port – using DAP-100 smoke generators, which were carried on the underwing bomb racks – to impede the anti-aircraft fire.

In June the same year, a similar 'combination attack' was delivered by pilots of the Northern Fleet on Kirkenes port, which was a joint operation by the Il-2s, A-20Gs and fighter bombers (the Pe-2s and the Kittyhawks).

In the sea, the Bostons hunted not only for surface ships, but also submarines. In the Northern Fleet and in the Black Sea Fleet, the aircraft (beginning from 1944) were fitted with four suspended PLAB-100 bombs and then involved in anti-submarine patrolling; however, its efficiency turned out to be extremely low: a high speed and a limited downward view (especially in case of the A-20G) resulted in difficulties for the crew in searching for a submarine periscope in the waves, but nevertheless, several German U-boats were allegedly destroyed by the Bostons' attacks (the enemy does not confirm such victories). The techniques were different: A.V. Presnyakov claimed to have sunk a surfaced U-boat with a torpedo, whereas I.K. Sachko allegedly used the skip bombing method.

The latter technique (i.e. when the bombs were dropped close to the water and skipped over the water surface until they hit the hull of a ship) was mastered during the second half of the war and was used by the A-20Gs rather frequently. In the Baltic Fleet, skip bombing missions in 1944 constituted approximately 20 percent of the overall combat sorties. Typically, the aircraft began accelerating from a distance of 5-7km; then, having got closer to the target, it commenced machine gun fire and cannon fire to weaken the anti-aircraft gunners' resistance. The bomb was dropped as close as within 200-250m from the board of the ship.

In the Northern Fleet, attempts were even made to create a special skip bomber Boston, so an A-20G which had been previously modified into a torpedo bomber was used for this purpose. The navigator was seated behind the pilot, and the canopy transparencies were extended to the wing leading edge. In such a configuration, the navigator had two windows on each side of the aircraft, and a transparent section on the top. The navigator occupied a flap seat made from a sheet of armor, while from behind, he was protected with a torso back protective armor; the floor under the seat was also armored. A small table for maps and an OPB-1 optical bomb sight were installed – and the latter (when in the operative position) was 'looking out' of a hatch which was cut out in the left door of the bomb bay.

Additional installations included the traditional (for all Soviet modifications) inert gas system (also of the bottle type), as well as the SPU-3bis intercommunication system. On the other hand, the oxygen system was totally removed from this aircraft, since it was considered unnecessary for a skip bomber. To prevent interference between the external large-caliber bomb mount and the internal bomb attachment system, bomb bay door opening stops with an electrical alarm system were installed; however, ordinary torpedo bombers were used for skip bombing purposes more often, although a PTN-1 sight was sometimes mounted at the pilot's station.

Perhaps the most well-known example of a successful Soviet skip bombing operation is the sinking of the German anti-aircraft cruiser *Niobe* (originally HNLMS *Gelderland*, which had been seized and modified by the Germans). On 8 July 1944, it was staying in Kotka harbor (Finland), and the attack group consisted of a regiment of dive bombers and two pairs of skip bombing A-20Gs. Each of the Bostons carried two FAB-1000 bombs, and the dive bombers attacked first: as a result, the cruiser was hit with two bombs; then, the first pair of skip bombers entered the action. The second pair did not have to deliver a strike on the ship anymore, since the two 1,000kg bombs which were dropped by the first pair hit *Niobe's* hull and she sank. For this reason, the second pair turned on a transport ship, which was located nearby, and hit her. Apart from *Niobe*, the record of the skip bombing Bostons of the Baltic Fleet includes the auxiliary cruiser *Orion*, several destroyers and a lot of transport vessels.

A case of a skip bombing attack on a land-based target is known: in June 1944, before the offensive by the Soviet armed forces, a need arose to destroy a dam on the Svir River, which was in the Germans' rear. In a joint effort involving the skip bombing A-20Gs, Il-4s with sea mines and ground attack aircraft (whose task was to subdue anti-aircraft fire), the dam was exploded.

As torpedo bombers, reconnaissance aircraft and skip bombers, the Bostons were in service with the naval aviation until the end of the war in Europe.

With a high rate of speed and maneuverability, the A-20 could, when necessary, be used in the role of a fighter. The Soviet Union did not receive any heavy fighters from abroad; however, there was a demand for them, since the Soviet Pe-3s had been manufactured in a small quantity and their performance was mediocre. The air defense forces were in the most urgent need of such aircraft to perform as long-range night fighters.

The first B-3s were handed over to the Moscow air defense forces in October 1942 and, in January through to June the next year, NII VVS conducted tests on a B-3 in the night fighter version (and with a *Gneis-2* radar). The aircraft, which was nicknamed 'Pirate', was modified at Factory No.81. Its differences from an ordinary B-3 bomber included a cannon mount in the nose, additional fuel tanks in the bomb bay and the navigator's seat relocated to the gunners' cockpit.

Factory test flights were flown in September at Central airfield in Moscow by a crew led by Major G.A. Osipov. At the final stage of the tests, the aircraft suffered an accident: a taxiing Il-4, which was piloted by V.K. Kokkinaki, ran into it; the collision was brought about by the bomber's failed brakes. The issue was settled amicably: in a single night, Ilyushin's personnel replaced the fighter's empennage, which had been mangled by the propeller of Kokkinaki's aircraft, while Kokkinaki himself tore the accident report to pieces. The factory tests were successfully completed and, in late September, the aircraft was ferried to Koltsovo airfield, near Sverdlovsk, which was where NII VVS was located at that time.

At this location, 'Pirate' was tested by Major Sakharov's crew. The acquisition range of the *Gneis* radar was only 3.5-4km, so therefore, it was expected that the interceptor would be homed onto a target by a guidance officer in accordance with data from ground-based radars; however, on the whole, the number of Bostons in the air defense forces was not large. In May 1943, the Air Defense Forces Fighter Aviation Command requested that the People's Commissariat of Aviation Industry urgently modify seven aircraft (and later, 20 more) to the configuration of the 'Pirate', but Factory No.81 – already laden with orders – refused to undertake the task. As a result, there were only six such aircraft in use with the air defense forces as of 1 May 1945.

Strange as it may seem, the overwhelming majority of heavy night fighters were handed over to the long-range aviation and, in July 1943, the raising of the 56th Long-Range Fighter Air Division began. The division, with Colonel I.O. Kuznetsov in command, consisted of two regiments (the 45th Air Regiment and the 173rd Air Regiment). To form the division, a batch of A-20G-1s was modified at Factory No.21, and an additional 1,036L fuel tank was installed in the bomb bay. Fighter crews consisted of three persons (the pilot, the radio operator and the navigator, whose seat was in the radio operator's compartment). The radar station itself was arranged partially behind the pilot's seat, and partially near the seat of the radio operator gunner (who was, in fighter crews, referred to as the 'radio operator'). An interesting fact is that the large-caliber machine gun in the aft cockpit was retained, and antennas were installed on the top in the nose portion of the fuselage and on the wings. Because of the protruding antennas, the interceptor was nicknamed *Yorsh* ('Ruff').

Each regiment received thirty-two A-20G-1s, and the preparations for combat operations were carried out at Ryazhsk airfield, near Ryazan. As early as October 1943, one of the squadrons of the 173rd Long-Range Fighter Air Regiment was redeployed to the Konotop region to provide air cover for railways; however, the operations of the squadron proved to be extremely inefficient. A poor knowledge of the new aircraft resulted in a failure to make any successful attempt to intercept a night bomber, let alone any air victories. The squadron was sent back to continue training.

As late as May 1944, the Command found that the 173rd Air Regiment had reached combat readiness and, consequently, was sent it to the Orel region. The 45th Air Regiment was redeployed to the front line in August, and it was stationed near Minsk. At first, both day and night combat sorties were flown, but later, the aircraft only began to fly after dark.

The division was assigned the task of providing air cover for railway junctions in Minsk, Gomel, Kalinovichi, Unecha and Novozybkov; however, the *Yorshes* had no combat achievements to boast of. Throughout four months in 1944, aircraft of the 45th Air Regiment attacked the enemy only four times, but without any success – thus, for example, on 11 September, Junior Lieutenant Zenin detected a target which was approaching his aircraft on an opposite course. At the very last moment, he saw an He 111 bomber rushing head-on, and managed to open fire; however, while the A-20 was making a turn, the German aircraft left the radar's acquisition range and vanished into thin air.

The causes of the failures were multifarious, but among them were the poor performance, short range and low reliability of the *Gneis-2* radar station; an absence of an extensive network of ground-based radar stations; and the poor training of guidance operators. The Germans and the British had completed this (first) stage in the mastering of night interception tactics back in 1940; four years later, they had an excellent target acquisition system, as well as highly skilled flight crews and flight control officers. In the Soviet Union, on the other hand, all of these things were at the incipient stage; there was a lot to be learned and, as usual, people learned from their own mistakes. It should be noted that the pilots for the 56th Long-Range Fighter Air Division were recruited from the personnel of the bombardment and transport aviation; they had no experience in air combats as fighters.

Problems with guidance were also connected with the short communication range of the SCR-274N radio stations which were mounted on the A-20Gs: it was only 55-65km, whereas the *Pegmatite* ground-based guidance radar had a range of 100-120km. Specialists from NISO (the Scientific Institute of Aircraft Equipment) had worked out a project to improve the aircraft's radio equipment, so in October 1944, a NISO team modified five aircraft from the 45th Air Regiment. They replaced antennas and lead-ins, and made changes to receivers. As a result, the interceptor crews were provided with the possibility to receive instructions from a control station at a distance of up to 170-200km. The said five aircraft were regarded as reference models for the modification of all of the other aircraft; however, there is no information as to how many A-20Gs were actually modified.

A certain level of success was achieved as late as May 1945 near Breslau (currently Wroclaw in Poland), with the command of the division having been taken over by Colonel B.V. Bitsky (it was the third time that the division had received a new commander). The Germans made efforts to deliver supplies for their entrapped forces by air, and they'd had difficulties flying at daytime, since the Soviet aviation had already gained the air supremacy. Cargoes were mostly brought by assault gliders, and the latter became a target for the *Yorshes*. Their 'hunting' resulted in 246 combat sorties and, of them, 13 ended in air combats. Three gliders and two He 111H tow-planes were shot down, and both Heinkels were destroyed by the crew led by Captain I.O. Kaznov. In several cases, when attacked by night fighters, tow-planes detached the tow rope – thus leaving the gliders no other choice but to make a forced landing at the dispositions of the Soviet troops. The Breslau garrison capitulated on 7 May, and the 45th Air Regiment ended the war at the town of Brieg in Germany (currently Brzeg in Poland).

The naval aviation also wished to have its own night fighters in order to cover shore bases, and the first batch of *Gneis-2* radars was delivered to the navy in early 1944. It was decided that the radars should be mounted on the A-20Gs because the naval aviation had a lot of these aircraft at its disposal. In March 1944, the 39th Squadron of night fighters was raised within the Black Sea Fleet. Initially, it was based on the Caucasian shore, where the ships were stationed after the loss of the Crimea; however, there were no tasks for the night fighters, since the Germans, who had been forced back to the West, seldom sent their aircraft to Poti and Novorossiysk. For this reason, a decision was made to use the fighters as reconnaissance aircraft. On 6 April, a radar-equipped Boston flew the first combat sortie to perform reconnaissance in the ports of the southern portion of the Crimea. Later, several more combat sorties of this kind were flown.

In June, there was an attempt to use aircraft fitted with *Gneis* radars for submarine searches in night conditions. Late in the evening on 24 June, an aircraft flew on a mission to patrol the sea near Novorossiysk; however, because of a storm, it returned promptly. On 26-28 June, a decision was made to test whether it was physically feasible to detect a submarine from a night fighter. A surfaced M-54 submarine was moving on the route from Poti to Novorossiysk, and then to Tuapse. It took three nights to find it from an aircraft.

The Bostons kept searching for enemy submarines at night, so for this purpose, two aircraft were specially allocated; however, they attained no success. The *Gneis-2* radar, which was designed for the acquisition of aerial targets, did not allow for detecting an object against the background of reflections from the sea surface. To identify the control tower of a submarine, the pilots had to almost touch the water, as from a height of 200m, submarines were not detectable. Later, these drawbacks were partially rectified in the *Gneis-2M* radar, which was specially designed for naval aviation; however, such radars were mounted on reconnaissance aircraft and torpedo bombers, but not on fighters.

After the Liberation of the Crimea, the 39th Squadron was redeployed to Saki, where it combined air defense functions with patrolling in the western portion of the Black Sea.

More advanced *Gneis-3* and *Gneis-5* radars were also tested on the A-20G, with the aircraft of the 56th Long-Range Fighter Air Division being used (in combat conditions near Breslau) to test the RD-1 television guidance system. An image of the ground radar display – superimposed over the map of the terrain, and with the position of the interceptor aircraft and its target indicated on it – was transmitted from a ground control station to the screen in the cockpit; the RD-1 system proved to be rather reliable and efficient. In the same division, experiments were conducted which involved the guidance of night fighters from flying control centers (i.e. specially equipped C-47 transport aircraft with radio radars; there were two aircraft of such a type).

Sometimes, the Bostons from bomber air regiments were involved in fighting the enemy's night bombers. In summer 1943 near Shakhty, pilots from the 10th Guards Bomber Air Regiment were hunting German aircraft. The Bostons flew to German airfields, waited for the returning aircraft to turn on their identification lights and then attacked them from the darkness during the approach. In July and August, P. Bochin scored three air victories in his bomber in such a manner. In a similar way, air cover was arranged for Soviet troops near Kerch in January 1944 by regiments of the 123rd Bomber Air Division. On the night of 27 January, pilot Timotchenko (in a B-3) frustrated the pinpoint bombing plans of a group of He 111s. He had, however, little experience in air combats and opened fire from too great a distance. For this reason, he failed to shoot down a German aircraft, but made the enemy hastily drop their bombs and scamper.

At the sea, the Bostons partially made up for the shortage of long-range fighters. They provided air cover for convoys and individual ships in the open sea, and escorted bombers and torpedo bombers. The A-20Gs had quite sufficient speed and firepower to attach an enemy bomber or seaplane. On 10 October 1944, Lieutenant Aminyev of the Northern Fleet (in a Boston) shot down a Blohm und Voss BV 138 three-engine flying boat. In August 1943, B. Maslov of the Black Sea Fleet dived onto a FW 190 fighter and set it on fire.

A special role was played by the regiments of the 'night hunters'-long-range blockers, which were part of the long-range aviation corps; they were, essentially, the Soviet equivalent of the British intruder aircraft. The 112th (later the 26th Guards) Air Regiment of the 'night hunters'-long-range blockers flew the A-20Gs and operated near Leningrad and Brest. There, its aircraft supported the action of long-range bomber formations by blocking the airfields of night fighters. In April 1944, the regiment took part in the raid on Constantsa, and its aircraft attacked the nearby Romanian airfields – subduing the enemy's anti-aircraft fire.

In the 113th (later the 27th Guards) Air Regiment, which was under the command of Lieutenant Colonel M.P. Dedov-Dzyadushinsky, Captain N.A. Krapiva enjoyed the well-deserved reputation of an ace hunter for enemy aircraft. His well-trained crew waited for the German pilots during their landing approach and swept them with fire from all of the available guns.

During one of its combat sorties, Krapiva managed to destroy two German aircraft: one of them was shot down by a burst of fire from the nose machine guns, and then the second aircraft was engaged and set on fire by the ventral gunner.

Along with machine guns and cannons, the pilots made use of underwing RS-82 rocket projectiles. Most often, they were used against parked aircraft; however, in April 1944, they were released during strafing raids against German vessels which were taking the troops out from Sevastopol.

For ground attacks, the Bostons in the Soviet Union were equipped with the original AKAB under-fuselage gun battery; in the bomb bay, two ShVAK cannons and two UBK machine guns were installed. Their combat stock (440 rounds and 340 shells) was arranged in the former radio operator's/gunner's compartment, and the crew consisted of two persons (the pilot and the navigator). Electromechanical actuators tracked the position of the selected target and allowed for hitting it efficiently even with the aircraft moving at a high speed; six aircraft were equipped in such a manner. The AKAB tests on the A-20G-1 were conducted in spring 1944; in summer, the system was handed over to the 27th Guards Air Regiment of 'night hunters'-long-range blockers for operational trials. On the night of 28 June, this Boston, which was piloted by the already mentioned Captain Krapiva, took part in a raid on the airfield in Baranovichi. It set two German aircraft on fire before being damaged by anti-aircraft artillery.

In spite of the continuous flow of Bostons via Siberia, they did not arrive in the Far East before mid-1945. Both the Army Air Force units and the naval aviation flew, for the most part, already obsolete bomber and torpedo bomber types such as the Tupolev SB and the Ilyushin DB-3B. It is only pending the commencement of hostilities against Japan that more up-to-date aircraft began arriving in the Far East, and among them were the A-20s of the G, K, J and H versions. Besides, in July 1945, the 36th Mine-and-Torpedo Air Regiment, which consisted of fourteen A-20Gs, was redeployed from the Northern Fleet; it was stationed at Romanovka airfield.

By the time of the Declaration of War against Japan, the Pacific Fleet had received, in total, 46 torpedo-carrying Bostons and twelve A-20K reconnaissance aircraft, with the latter assigned to the 50th Independent Reconnaissance Air Regiment. During the course of the hostilities, the regiment conducted reconnaissance above the southern portion of Sakhalin; the Kuril Islands; the ports of Northern Korea; and even above Japan (Hokkaido Island).

The crews of the mine-and-torpedo regiments had not had enough time to master the A-20s by the beginning of military operations, so it is only at the very end that they did their modest bit. On 18 August, 14 Bostons of the 49th Air Regiment took part in a raid on a railway junction in Kyushu. The last bombs on the same day were dropped by the A-20Gs of the 36th Mine-and-Torpedo Air Regiment, and destroyed a bridge near Syuotsyuondzio. The naval aviation kept receiving the Bostons until 31 August and, throughout the period of the hostilities, 27 more aircraft were accepted.

Certain air force units had also converted to the Bostons by the beginning of operations in the Far East – thus, for example, the 903rd Bomber Air Regiment of the 128th Composite Air Division in Kamchatka, which had, before, been flying the Tupolev SBs, received 30 aircraft of the K-16, H-11 and H-16 versions in August. They were used in operations at the Kuril Islands in August 1945.

In the Soviet Union, the Bostons remained in service longer than they did in the USA and in Great Britain; however, in spring 1945, the air force began the conversion from the A-20Gs to the Soviet Tu-2s, which exceeded the former in terms of range, service ceiling and bomb load. A portion of the Bostons were returned to the Americans or destroyed under the supervision of the latter in 1946-1947, but not all of the aircraft of this type shared such a fate.

The A-20s were not mentioned in the Resolution of 1946, which provided for writing off the majority of the imported aircraft; it was probably connected to the fact that a full conversion to the Tu-2s had not been implemented, as was initially planned. The A-20s, as well as the Pe-2s, remained in combat service with the frontline aviation in considerable quantities until the early 1950s. Some regiments were converting from them directly to the Il-28 jet bombers – bypassing the piston-engine Tu-2s.

The night fighters 'quitted the stage' somewhat earlier. After the end of the war, the 45th Air Division was, for some time, stationed in Brzeg (Poland). The A-20Gs in its regiments were in service until 1947, but later they were replaced with the Tu-2s, which had more advanced *Gneis-5* radars. The 39th Squadron was redeployed from the Black Sea to the Baltic Sea in November 1948 and joined the air force of the 4th Fleet (the Baltic Fleet was, at that time, separated into two fleets).

The Boston was in service with the naval aviation for a rather long time and, immediately after the war, it was the principal torpedo bomber type over all of the fleets. In the Black Sea Fleet, the Baltic Fleet and the Northern Fleet, the conversion to the Bostons had taken place during the war; in the Pacific, the conversion ended in 1946, as soon as all of the three Pacific mine-and-torpedo regiments were fitted with such aircraft. Some units mastered the Bostons even later, while one of the squadrons of the 574th Independent Reconnaissance Air Regiment in the north began converting to the A-20Gs in July 1946. Meanwhile, in the Northern Fleet and in the Baltic Fleet, the A-20Gs could be encountered as late as the 1950s.

On 25 June 1950, the Korean War began. The Soviet Union did not take a direct part in it; however, it rendered assistance to North Korea in various forms. In particular, aircraft of the Soviet naval aviation which were stationed in Primorye – and on military bases on the Lyaodun Peninsula – conducted continuous reconnaissance near the Korean shore and patrolled the Yellow Sea. Data on the movements of American (and, later, British and Australian) ships were provided to the North Korean Command, but of course, the Americans were not happy with such activity. On 4 September 1950, in international waters, 11 Corsair fighters from USS *Valley Forge* attacked and shot down an A-20G from the 36th Mine-and-Torpedo Air Regiment of the 589th Air Division, which was stationed in Port Arthur. The pilot (Senior Lieutenant K. Karpol) and the entire crew were killed. Sometime later, the Americans presented official apologies and handed over the remains of the killed crew to the Soviet Union.

Seeking revenge, Soviet fighters scoured the skies above the sea in search of American aircraft and, finally, on 6 November 1951, they did indeed bring down a patrolling Lockheed PV-2. The situation between the USSR and the USA became so strained that the aviation in Primorye was placed into operational readiness, and the Bostons were equipped with live torpedoes; however, the governments of the two countries displayed prudence and the conflict was abated.

The A-20s were in service with the naval aviation until the end of the Korean War; the Tupolev Tu-2Ts, which appeared later, failed to act as substitutes for the Bostons until the time of the conversion to jet aircraft. The 9th Guards Mine-and-Torpedo Air Regiment began receiving the jet-propelled Tu-14s in August 1952; however, the regiment kept a 'mothballed' set of Bostons until 1954. A lot of the A-20s were modified into target-towing aircraft for air-to-air gunnery and anti-aircraft gunners' training. At certain locations, the Bostons were used (until 1948-1950) for auxiliary purposes (e.g. as aerial survey or liaison aircraft etc.) – thus, for example, the A-20G-31-Dos, which was fitted with Soviet photographic equipment and then disarmed, flew in 1946-1949 in the Baltic region in the 5th Independent Aerial Survey Air Squadron.

Back at the time of the war, the Bostons used to be operated in the rather unintended role of transport aircraft. In March 1944, the B-3s delivered armament, ammunition and foodstuffs to the Cavalry Mechanized Group, which was under the command of General Pliev and which had become separated from sources of supplies. In September the same year, four A-20Gs of the 449th Bomber Air Regiment (with an assault party in their bomb bays) took part in an operation to intercept a train with members of the Bulgarian Government and a German mission on the Bulgarian-Turkish border.

In the USSR during the war, transport aviation was under double jurisdiction, since the entire Civil Air Fleet had become subordinated to the air force. Civil pilots were involved in ferry units, transport regiments and frontline detachments and, in 1943, two A-20s were handed over to the Civil Air Fleet. They were probably used to train ferry pilots, or as lead aircraft for the ferrying of fighter groups. A year later, one of them was returned to the air force.

In late 1944, an idea emerged to use the A-20s as high-speed liaison aircraft to deliver couriers with important documents to the front. It was intended that the A-20s would act as a substitute for the old and worn PS-40s and PS-41s (essentially, the disarmed SBs). On 11 January 1945, a Resolution was issued to hand over twelve A-20Gs from the 559th Squadron of the Moscow Military District Air Force (which was based in Kostroma) to the 3rd Liaison Air Division of the Civil Air Fleet. In late January, two Bostons arrived at the division airfield in Myachkovo.; in late February, there were nine of them; and by mid-March, their number had reached 12.

In February, the division prepared a project for the modification of the received A-20Gs into liaison aircraft; the project was rather promptly approved by NII GVF. The aircraft could carry 1,100kg of cargo – including 200kg in the nose portion (which was made free from armament); 500kg plus two persons in the former bomb bay and a radio operator; and two more persons, as well as an additional 200kg of cargo in the aft cockpit. An additional fuel tank in the bomb bay allowed a flight range of up to 1,800km.

In February, the first four Bostons were subjected to modification and, on 1 March, they were placed in operation. In March, six more aircraft were modified, and the aircraft bore the traditional (for the Civil Air Fleet) insignia of the line service, which began with the letter 'L'.

The air force arranged the handover of another batch of bombers from the 5th Bomber Corps of the 4th Air Army. On 26 May, seven A-20Gs were sent out from there, and three more followed on 28 May. It was ordered that a regiment of the Civil Air Fleet be equipped with the Bostons; however, in view of the low efficiency of the A-20Gs in the role of transport aircraft, the Chief Administration of the Civil Air Fleet prescribed refraining from the further reception of such aircraft. The decision was connected with the work of NII GVF, whose specialists (in the first half of May) had conducted research of potential post-war operations of military aircraft of various types with civil aviation. The findings testified to an almost complete lack of prospects for the A-20 in the Civil Air Fleet: even with the armament, internal bulkheads and the fuselage fuel tank fully removed; the bomb hatch covered up; and the radio station relocated to the nose, the useful volume of the cabins could only reach 7m^3 at a load of 1,400kg. In such a configuration, one of the cargo hatches was arranged in place of the upper turret, and the ventral machine gun mount hatch was used as the other cargo hatch. The loading/unloading procedure appeared to be rather inconvenient – and as for large-sized cargoes, the hatches could not accommodate them at all, so such an aircraft was only suitable for the role of a mail-plane.

In late May, the division had twenty A-20Gs at its disposal; of them, five were based on the frontline airfield in Lodz, and served the headquarters of the 1st Belorussian Front and the 2nd Belorussian Front. With the end of the hostilities, part of the aircraft was 'mothballed'. As of 20 September, among the available twenty-nine A-20Gs and A-20Ks, 18 were in mothballs; then, the process of gradual disposal began. As of 1 January 1946, there were 27 aircraft of this type and, by December, none had been left.

All of these aircraft were handed over to the departmental aviation, and the Bostons were in service with five agencies. The Ministry of Fisheries had a single A-20G-1 at its disposal, which belonged to the *Sevryba* (North Fish) Group, and flew missions to pinpoint the locations of fish stocks; its registration number was X-578. The Ministry of Aviation Industry operated an aircraft which had been modified into a passenger model; it was based at LII. Another Boston was allocated to the Ministry of Consumer Industry, and it was used to drop anthropomorphic dummies during parachute tests.

The Chief Administration of Hydrometeorological Service (*Glavnoe Upravlenie Gidrometeosluzhby*, or GUGMS) used the A-20s for weather and ice reconnaissance. After receiving the first batch of the aircraft from the Civil Air Fleet, its stock of aircraft was replenished by those handed over by the air force. As of 1 January 1947, the meteorologists had 15 Bostons at their disposal and, as of 1 October, there were 23 of them. Later, however, the aviation of this agency was disbanded and most of the aircraft were written off.

On a much larger scale, the disarmed American bombers were used by cartographers. The Chief Administration of Geodetic Surveying and Cartography (*Glavnoe Upravlenie Geodezii i Kartografii*, or GUGK) began using them in 1946 and, in accordance with the Resolution of the Council of Ministers of 13 April 1946, GUGK was to receive forty A-20s from the air force. Before the end of the year, the cartographers accepted 20 aircraft, as well as photographic equipment, for them, and these were distributed over several air detachments. The A-20s which were in service with GUGK bore registration numbers beginning with the Russian letter *Ф*.

The Novosibirsk Air Detachment received several aircraft, as well as the accompanying task to test them; modify them into an aerial survey version at their repair shops; and then perform practical trials of the equipment. There were a lot of difficulties: the Bostons came without tools, spare parts or spare engines, plus the pilots of the air detachment were mostly fighter pilots and, as a consequence, were not familiar with two-engine aircraft. Nevertheless, the aircraft were successfully mastered.

As of 1 January 1947, GUGK's fleet totaled thirty-six A-20Gs, but by 1 October, the target figure of 40 had been reached. The 'peak' number of Bostons in this agency (76) fell on January 1949, but then, their quantity gradually diminished: as of 1 January 1950, there were only 63 of them.

In the early 1950s, GUGK continued to operate the A-20s; however, their technical state left much to be desired. In 1951, several accidents and crashes took place one after another. On 10 August, pilot Solovyov's aircraft burst into flame in flight – killing five people – and on 2 September, the right undercarriage leg on pilot Ryabkov's aircraft failed at landing. In this case, no one was injured; however, the first deputy head of the Civil Air Fleet Chief Administration ordered to cease flying all of the A-20s which had not been subjected to an overhaul. He also raised the question as regards the feasibility of the further general use of all of the remaining aircraft of this type.

Nevertheless, the last A-20s remained in service with the cartographers for another couple of years; for example, two aircraft were in operation in Yakutia until 1953. Later, a considerable number of the aircraft were written off, but there is no information as to when the last flights took place.

In total, the American factories manufactured seven-thousand-three-hundred-and-eighty-five A-20s of various versions – and of these, 3,123 were sent to the Soviet Union (3,066 from the USA and 57 from Great Britain; in total, 2,771 aircraft reached their final destination). From among these, 667 aircraft were accepted by the air force in 1942; in 1943, 1,360 were accepted; in 1944, 743 were accepted; and finally, a single (last) aircraft was accepted in 1945. Via the ALSIB route, one-thousand-three-hundred-and-sixty-three A-20s were delivered; aircraft arriving by sea via Iraq totaled 550; and 869 Bostons were ferried by air across the South Atlantic. Both of the latter came along the southern route via Iran. Finally, 126 Bostons were unloaded in the northern ports. The naval aviation received 796 aircraft; however, most of them were handed over by the air force.

A Boston which was raised from the bottom of the sea is now on display at the Northern Fleet Air Force Museum, but unfortunately, it has not been subjected to restoration. Another model is part of the museum collection in Monino, but this aircraft did not see military service, as it crashed while being ferried via the ALSIB route and, consequently, remained in the taiga for a long time. Also, the Samara State Aerospace University has separate wing and fuselage assemblies in its collection.

The Boston is remembered by Soviet pilots as being one of the best aircraft among those shipped by the Allies during the war, and it enjoys a well-deserved high reputation with both flight and ground crews.

The A-20Bs waiting for ferrying to the Soviet Union in Abadan in 1942.

A B-3 on the South-Western Front during May-June 1942. It is possible that this aircraft belonged to the 794th Bomber Air Regiment.

The A-20C-10 in Abadan before its delivery to Russia.

A B-3 (A-20C) destroyed by the Germans at the airfield in Kuban in 1942.

A B-3 of a bomber regiment at the front line; note the loop aerial of an American MN-26Y radio compass behind the radio mast.

The bomber flight crews before a mission in North Caucasus in 1942.

Technicians N. Skachkov and R. Sabatov working on a bomber propeller in 1942.

An A-20C of a bomber regiment in North Caucasus in 1942.

A B-3 at an airfield in the North Caucasian Front, October 1942.

A navigator in the cabin of a Boston.

This B-3 was brought to the workshops of the 7th Air Army for repair.

This A-20B had picturesque nose art, with a lion painted on the fuselage.

A Boston III during tests at NII VVS in July 1942.

Armament technicians preparing a bomb for lifting into the A-20 bomb bay.

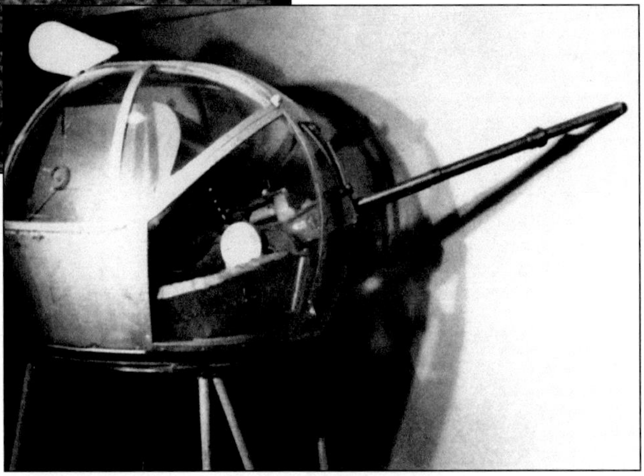

A UTK-1 turret accommodating a 12.7mm UBT machine gun.

A B-3 modified to carry Soviet armament; note the dorsal-mounted UTK-1 turret.

The 12.7mm Colt-Browning machine gun in the upper gun post was fed with a belt from compact, removable ammunition boxes.

An A-20B with a Soviet UTK-1 turret.

This A-20B, which was rearmed according to the schematics of Factory No.43, was tested at NII VVS. The UTK-1 turret accommodates the American Colt-Browning large-caliber machine gun. The aircraft was (apparently) taken from a service unit, since it bears the 'Guards' inscription behind the red star.

Bombs being suspended on external racks under the wing of an A-20B in March 1943.

The crew of Captain I.S. Petrosyan (second from left) near a reconnaissance A-20B in winter camouflage, Voronezh Front, March 1943.

This A-20C received an interesting modification, with the drop-shaped fairing of an RPK-2 radio compass antenna installed not behind the pilot's compartment, but in the nose section of the aircraft.

A pilot taking his seat in the cockpit of an A-20B in early spring 1943.

An A-20B departing for a night mission in 1943.

Bombs being prepared near a tree branch-masked Boston, North Caucasus, June 1943.

The flight crew of pilot Mileyko near an A-20B, North Caucasian Front, 1943.

This bomber, which was piloted by Lieutenant Afonin, was flown after a mission to the home airfield without half of its horizontal stabilizer. All of the crewmembers returned safe and sound.

An A-20B of the 454th Bomber Air Regiment, Voronezh Front, March 1943.

A group of B-3s in flight over Kuban, June 1943.

An instructor parachutist demonstrates the correct procedure for bailing out from the A-20 cockpit in an emergency.

Navigator P.V. Parshutin (left) and radio operator/gunner M.Y. Karas of the 57th Bomber Air Regiment, who successfully brought the Boston to its home base after the pilot was heavily wounded during a mission, Limovoe airfield, August 1943.

Commander of the 108th Separate Reconnaissance Air Squadron V.I. Donchuk, with the crew of his Boston at the Karelian Front.

A Boston after crash landing.

Senior Lieutenant N. Zastoin (on the right) being awarded the Order of the Patriotic War (1st Class) in Kuban in 1943.

An A-20B during the course of repair in 1943.

A-20G bombers at Ladd Field, Alaska in 1944.

The A-20G-1 during tests at NII VVS.

The flight crew of Senior Lieutenant I. Loborev carried out 150 combat missions in 1944.

An A-20G crew of the 260th Bomber Air Regiment near their aircraft. From left to right: Nazarov, Zakharov, an unknown technician, Arutyunov and Kuzmin.

The A-20G, with the fuselage nose section modified to accommodate the navigator's cabin, during tests at NII VVS. The transparent nose section looks to be borrowed from the Il-4 bomber.

The ground crew of the 48th Bomber Air Regiment after completing modifications on one of the unit's A-20Gs.

Two rearmed A-20G-15s at an airfield near Tula in March 1944; note the additional tail markings on the nearest aircraft.

An A-20G, with its nose section modified to accommodate the navigator's compartment.

A flight crew in front of their A-20G; note the modified nose of the bomber.

Another A-20G with a modified nose section at Kshisini airfield in September 1945.

A political officer (at the extreme right) talking to the ground crew at an airfield; note that there is an A-20G-20 in the background.

A technician and a pilot (on the right) near an A-20G bomber which was flown by the crew of Captain Mamaev of the 244th Bomber Air Regiment.

This A-20G was modified to carry four VAP-6 chemical spray tanks.

A group of A-20Bs on a mission over the Crimea in spring 1944.

A Boston torpedo bomber of the Northern Fleet Air Force carrying out a training attack on a destroyer in 1945.

A group of three A-20s in flight over Berlin in May 1945.

A group photo of the flight and ground crew in front of the A-20G, which was modified in the Soviet Union into a trainer aircraft with the installation of dual controls.

A B-3 fitted with a Soviet-made *Gneis-2* radar during tests at NII VVS, Koltsovo airfield, 1943.

An A-20G-1 with a *Gneis-3* radar installed at Factory No.81 in spring 1945.

An A-20G of the 27th Guards Blocker Air Regiment after a forced landing near Lvov in 1944.

The A-20G-1 with an AKAB under-fuselage gun battery (the gun barrels are in the stowed position) in 1944.

The same aircraft, but with the gun barrels deflected downward.

The AKAB under-fuselage gun battery in the firing position.

The crew of pilot G. Ilyushkin of the 5th Guards Mine-and-Torpedo Air Regiment, Black Sea Fleet Air Force after a successful reconnaissance mission in 1943.

An A-20B of the 13th Bomber Air Regiment, Black Sea Fleet Air Force at an airfield near Sofia in September 1944. The aircraft bears the inscription *Bogatyr*, or Mighty Warrior, on the fuselage nose part.

A group photo at an airfield in Sofia in September 1944. The A-20B in the background belongs to the 30th Separate Reconnaissance Air Regiment, Black Sea Fleet Air Force; note the nose art of the bomb-carrying seagull.

Pilots of the Black Sea Fleet Air Force, near the unit's A-20B; note the seagull emblem on the fuselage.

A modified A-20G, with two 45-36AN torpedoes mounted on torpedo-carrying beams on the fuselage sides; note the cylindrical tail covers on the torpedoes' rear parts, which are necessary to reduce the depth of the torpedoes' penetration into the water after the drop.

The aircraft flown by the crew of Hero of the Soviet Union A.M. Gagiev being prepared for flight. The fuselage nose part of this A-20G was modified to accommodate the navigator's compartment.

A 45-36AN torpedo being pushed for loading on an A-20G, Baltic Fleet, 1944; note the external torpedo mounts on the aircraft's fuselage side.

This A-20G of the 1st Guards Mine-and-Torpedo Air Regiment, Baltic Fleet Air Force had the modified fuselage nose, 1944.

The refueling of an A-20G with the modified fuselage nose; the 1st Guards Mine and Torpedo Air Regiment of the Baltic Fleet Air Force, Panevezhis, September 1944.

The navigator's compartment of this A-20G was arranged in the fuselage rear part (note the astrodome and additional side windows); the 1st Guards Mine-and-Torpedo Air Regiment, 1945.

The damaged *Schlesien* battleship after raids of the Soviet aviation in Swinemünde, 4 May 1945.

A German ship in the Baltic Sea after a torpedo hit by one of the aircraft of the 51st Mine-and-Torpedo Air Regiment.

A crew of pilot Lieutenant N.F. Bazhenov (in the center) near an A-20G-25, Baltic Fleet Air Force, 1944.

A formation of personnel of the 51st Mine-and-Torpedo Air Regiment at Grabstein airfield during March–April 1945. The man in the middle – standing with his back to the camera – is Regiment Commander I.F. Orlenko; note the three different Boston versions of the regiment and the Tu-2 bombers of the 12th Bomber Air Regiment in the background.

A 45-36AN torpedo being lifted onto the T-18 torpedo-carrying beam.

FAB-500 bombs being attached to the right-side torpedo-carrying beam.

The dam of the Svirskaya hydroelectric plant in Volkhov, which was destroyed on 21 June 1944 after an attack by a skip bombers group, which was headed by Captain Tikhomirov.

Armament technician V.K. Gosudarenko of the 51st Mine-and-Torpedo Air Regiment installing the ammunition box of the Boston nose machine gun, Palanga, January 1945.

Armament technicians Vishnevsky and Ivanov of the 2nd Squadron, 51st Mine-and-Torpedo Air Regiment lifting the bombs onto the wing racks.

Junior Lieutenant V.V. Bykov writes the slogan *Za Rodinu!* (For the Motherland!) on the bomb mounted on the torpedo-carrying beam.

One of the crews of the 51st Mine-and-Torpedo Air Regiment taking notes before a combat mission at Kolberg airfield.

Officers of the 51st Mine-and-Torpedo Air Regiment, Baltic Fleet Air Force near a modified A-20G; note the extensive nose art, with two Orders of the Red Banner and Ushakov; three ship hit marks; and a star in roundel with figure three. The inscription translates as: 'Tallinn Air Regiment'.

An A-20G-10-DO of the 1st Guards Mine-and-Torpedo Air Regiment, Kamenka Airfield, January-February 1944.

An A-20G crew of a bomber regiment, Kołomyja, 1946.

This A-20G was unarmed and modified into a cone target towing aircraft. Pilot Korobkov crash-landed the aircraft in June 1947, near the village of Knekhta (Archangelsk region), after the engine failed.

The A-20G was modified into a high-speed passenger aircraft and used for business flights of TsAGI specialists.

A group photo of specialists near a Boston which has been modified into a civil aerial survey aircraft, 1946.

The aerial survey A-20G of the Chief Administration of Geodetic Surveying and Cartography (GUGK) in Ukhta during the late 1940s.

This disarmed A-20G was used in civil aviation for carrying mail; note the aircraft's civil registration number.

The flight and ground crew near a disarmed A-20G, which was used for aerial survey purposes by GUGK; note the inscription on the nose section, which translates as: 'aerial survey of GUGK'.

The wing from the A-20 was used as a training aid at the Samara State Aerospace University in 2000.

The A-20G on display at the Russian Air Force Museum in Monino.

The A-20G on display at the Russian Air Force Museum in Monino.

7.10 North American B-25 Mitchell

During the war, a considerable share of the long-range aviation fleet was constituted by the North American B-25 two-engine bombers. This aircraft was derived from the project of the NA-40 attack bomber, which had been developed in accordance with the same specifications as the previously described A-20, and together, they took part in the bid in 1938. The NA-40 aroused greater interest on the part of the USAAC than its competitors did. Although the prototype aircraft (NA-40-2) was destroyed in a crash while undergoing testing, its demonstrated flight performance made it quite promising for the future.

The North American aviation modified the design in accordance with the USAAC's requirements and gave the aircraft a new designation: NA-62. Having become larger and heavier, the new design was beyond the class of ground attack aircraft or light bombers (according to American standards, the NA-62 was a medium bomber). On the brink of the war, the USAAC customers were in such a hurry that they ordered 184 aircraft into production as the B-25, which was before the construction of a prototype. Sometime later, the aircraft was named 'Mitchell' in honor of Major General William 'Billy' Mitchell, who was a famous advocate of air power. On 19 August 1940, the flight testing of the first B-25 began.

The aircraft had a crew of six persons (two pilots, a navigator, a bombardier, a flight engineer and a gunner), and the bomber's configuration was that of a cantilever monoplane with a twin-fin tail unit. Everything was after the latest aviation trends – including the all-metal structure with load-bearing skin; a tricycle undercarriage with a nose leg; two powerful R-2600 engines (1,350hp each); an anti-icing system; and a powerful defensive armament.

In 1941, USAAF combat units began receiving the mass-manufactured B-25As. In the Soviet Union, the aircraft was a known model; however, before the beginning of the Great Patriotic War, the bomber did not arouse much interest. It was deemed to be a 'mediocre' aircraft, with nothing much to boast of in terms of performance. Much more attention was given to its competitor, which was the Martin B-26 Marauder.

For the discussion of future military materiel shipments, which was held in Moscow in September 1941 between representatives of the USSR, the USA and Great Britain, different agencies prepared their findings as to what should be requested and in what quantities. Only the Intelligence Directorate of the General Staff listed the B-25 among potentially interesting aircraft; however, it also gave an unambiguous preference to the B-26.

The Americans, on the contrary, offered (first and foremost) a list of three bombers, which included the Douglas A-20, the Lockheed A-28 and the North American B-25. At the time when American, British and Soviet diplomats and generals held the conference in Moscow, a team of Soviet pilots, navigators and engineers had already been staying in the USA. It was led by the famous test pilot M.M. Gromov, who had been in charge of LII before the war.

It was initially planned that the Americans would hand over several Boeing B-17 Flying Fortress bombers, which would be ferried by Soviet crews to England. There, the aircraft were to be equipped with bombs and would then fly to Moscow – dropping the bombs on Berlin on their way; however, the Americans refused to give any Fortresses. For this reason, the Soviet Command had to study the aircraft which the Allies were actually willing to provide, and they began with the B-25A. Familiarization with the aircraft and their equipment took place at air bases in Spokane and Patterson. The Soviet crews were given an opportunity to thoroughly study the B-25As, as well as to fly them and to have training air combats with the P-43 fighters.

Captain E. York, who spoke Russian, acted as host. According to the American historian E. McDowell, the Russians flew the B-25s as if they were fighters, so as a result, the Mitchells' wings lost some rivets, several gunners suffered rib injuries and a P-43 crashed into the ground.

Gromov, with his vast experience as a test pilot, personally tried the A-28, the B-25A and the B-26. The Lockheed aircraft was rejected at once, on account of being utterly inconsistent with the demands of current warfare. The B-26 demonstrated high flight performance, but was difficult to fly, so the B-25 turned out to be the most reasonable choice. It had, however, some weak points, too: in Gromov's opinion, the B-25A's crew was inappropriately numerous for a frontline bomber, and its armor protection and armaments were found to be insufficient.

On 16 September, an improved B-25B was demonstrated to Gromov at Bolling Field air force base; it featured an enhanced defensive armament (dorsal and ventral turrets with twin large-caliber machine guns). Several days later, the Soviet Embassy sent in a request for three B-26s and two B-25Bs; however, on 1 October, the decision was changed in favor of five B-25Bs. The request was accepted, but the aircraft were shipped with a delay, on account of the Soviet party's requirement to equip the aircraft with deicers, which had not been initially stipulated.

On 6 November 1941, the first two B-25Bs were loaded on board the *Dekabrist* steamship, which headed with one of the convoys for the homeland shores. On 20 December, *Dekabrist* moored in Murmansk port and, in January, the bombers were assembled; however, it took some time to deliver a spare wheel for one of the Mitchells (to replace the one damaged during transportation). It was only on 5 March that both aircraft were ferried to the Moscow region.

Two more B-25Bs came to Archangelsk on board American ships. On 15 January 1942, assembly work began, which was carried out by a team led by Captain G.A. Osipov. The transport ships had become frozen in at a distance of 30-40km from the shore, so the aircraft (with their wings removed) were lifted by a crane, placed onto tractor sleds and taken to Kegostrov. On the way there, ice under one of the tractors broke and the tractor sank; however, two technicians who were escorting the cargo managed to cut the ropes and the sled did not follow the tractor. On 19 January, the assembly of the bombers began at Kegostrov. In the cabins, maintenance and flight manuals were found, but they were in English. On 21 January, a translator arrived to render assistance; later, four technicians came, who had been to America with Gromov's team. The assembly of the B-25Bs was completed in late February. The first aircraft was test-flown by Osipov, together with Major N.K. Romanov. Later, Osipov and his team were withdrawn, and the work was completed by the group of specialists who had arrived with Romanov.

None of the B-25Bs was used as combat aircraft. One of them was handed over to NII VVS, where it was tested in April 1942, and the flights were performed by Lieutenant Colonel A.I. Kabanov's crew. The aircraft produced a solid impression with its flight performance, powerful defensive armament and good equipment, but there were, of course, certain problems during the tests. For example, the retaining mechanism of the lower extendable turret was damaged, and the gun mounts failed several times. Powerful engines came with automatic propellers, which had a feathering mode, and piloting was easier than on the Pe-2 and the DB-3F (Il-4). Fully mechanized turrets, which were fully unserviceable with the electrical and hydraulic systems deactivated, seemed uncustomary.

Among the drawbacks, the impossibility to fully drain oil after a flight and the use of non-arctic rubber in the hydraulic system seals was mentioned. During the tests in flights made from unpaved surfaces, the nose landing gear struts were broken twice – thus, a conclusion was reached that the aircraft was only able to operate from level surfaces with hard pavement or solid ground. It was also advised that the armor protection should be enhanced by adding 40-45kg of armor.

All of the rest of the B-25Bs were used for training purposes. One of the aircraft was assigned to the 11th Backup Air Regiment in Kirovabad, while three went to the 6th Backup Air Brigade in Ivanovo. Of these five bombers, one of them had a chance to visit the USA again. It became I.P. Mazuruk's personal aircraft and, in September 1942, it arrived in Fairbanks as a leader of a group of PS-84 passenger aircraft which had brought the Soviet ferrying pilots there.

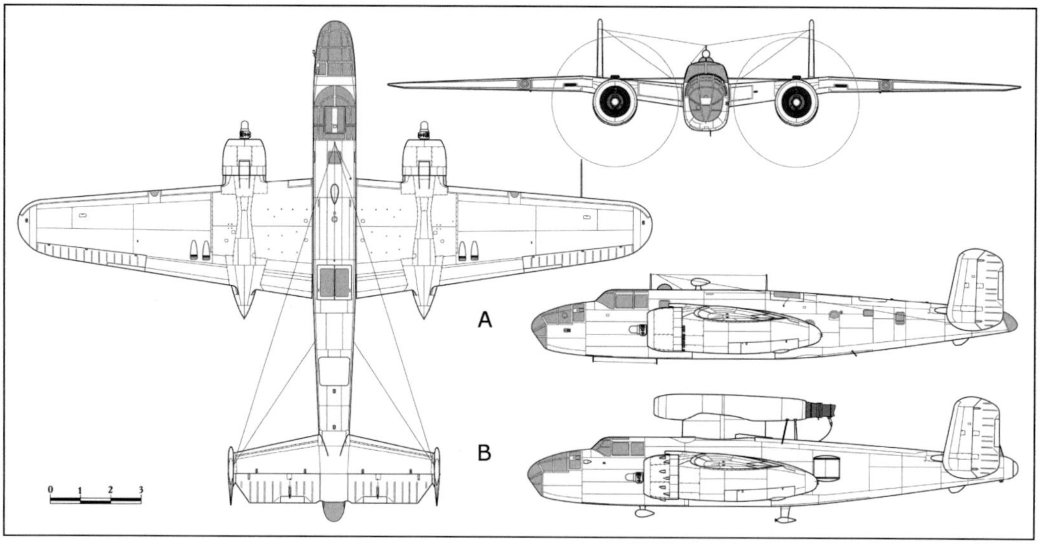

B-25

A Three-view of the B-25C-10 s/n 42-3244, which has been converted into a transport plane, with the armament removed.

B The B-25J-20, s/n 44-29347 was used as a flying test bed for testing the RD-10F turbojet engine.

In combat units of the Soviet Air Force, the Mitchells only appeared after the opening of the 'Persian Corridor', which was deemed a safer supply route via Iran. Piloted by civil Pan American crews, the aircraft came from the USA via Brazil, the Atlantic Ocean, Africa and the Middle East. The first seventy-two B-25Cs (an improved version, with new R-2600-13 1,700hp engines and several other modifications) came to Iran in March 1942. In particular, the C version bombers were fitted with pneumatic Goodrich de-icers in the wing and tail unit leading edges, and had a larger fuel reserve. Also, changes in the bomb rack structure allowed for increasing the maximum bomb load (up to 2,000kg with Soviet bombs, whereas a B-25B could carry, at most, 640kg).

Acceptance was arranged at Kwali Margi airfield in Iran and, from there, ferrying pilots delivered the bombers to Kirovabad. From Kirovabad, they were taken away by representatives of NII VVS and combat units – thus, for example, nine crews of the 222nd Bomber Air Division ferried twenty-two B-25s to Monino and Chkalovskaya via the route from Kirovabad through Astrakhan, Saratov and Kuybyshev to Tushino. Before the end of the year, one-hundred-and-two B-25s had been delivered to the Soviet Union via the southern route; in total, 118 such aircraft came through Iran.

Initially, Soviet specialists planned to use the North American aircraft in accordance with the role as intended for them by American designers (i.e. as daytime frontline bombers).

In April 1942, the first three (in accordance with other sources, four) B-25Cs were handed over to the 37th Bomber Air Regiment, which was under the command of Lieutenant Colonel Katarzhin. This unit was redeployed from the Far East to Monino airfield, near Moscow. Specialists of NII VVS (who themselves had ferried the aircraft from Basra) and TsAGI's New Materiel Bureau helped study the new aircraft, and one of the aircraft was disassembled for the purpose of better familiarization. Some of Gromov's team specialists (pilots, navigators and engineers) who had studied the B-25 in the USA had been transferred to the 37th Air Regiment.

TsAGI had an interest of their own in studying the aircraft: the Mitchell was a manifest example of the achievements in American aircraft construction technology. Detailed descriptions of the B-25 were made, and all of its main structural components were analyzed. There was a lot to be learned from the American bomber, such as its suitability for large-scale manufacture. According to TsAGI's report: '... the work breakdown structure provides for an extensive field of activities, and, apparently, its primary purpose is to ensure mass manufacture...' In June 1942, a B-25C was subjected to full-program State tests at NII VVS (first in Chkalovskaya; then, at Koltsovo airfield, near Sverdlovsk) and was met with a very high opinion. The aircraft was flown by Lieutenant Colonel Stefanovsky's crew. The performance parameters were slightly lower than those of the B-25B, on account of a higher weight; however, they were better than those of the Soviet bombers and the German Ju 88A. The test pilots and specialists were reluctant to openly admit this fact, and compared the American aircraft not only with the mass-manufactured Il-4, but also with the experimental Yermolaev Yer-2 medium bomber with AM-37 engines. The latter aircraft exceeded the American model in terms of speed and service ceiling, but was inferior to it in its rate of climb and take-off/landing performance. The unreliable engines, however, were never mass-manufactured, and the aircraft itself existed as a single example.

The bombers which arrived at Monino were subjected to modifications. American crews included both a bombardier (who occupied the nose cockpit) and a navigator (who was seated behind the pilots). In the Soviet Air Force, the navigator combined both functions, and all of the navigation instruments were relocated to the nose cockpit for him. The obsolete Vimperis bomb sights, with which the exported B-25s had been fitted, were removed and replaced by Soviet OPB-1 sights and, to enhance combat survivability, an inert gas pressurization system was installed. The modifications were made at Factory No.156 in Moscow, and at air force repair shops in Monino.

By late spring 1942, as many as three regiments (the 37th, the 125th and the 16th) had managed to convert to the Mitchells. The regiments were part of the 222nd Bomber Air Division, which, in turn, was assigned to the 1st Army, which was under the command of V.A. Sudets. First, the Command personnel were trained; then, training was arranged for the rest. Initially, there were quite a lot of forced landings, as sometimes, the pilots confused the fuel tank controls, or they simply ran out of fuel too early. The problem was that the documentation arrived later than the bombers did. Descriptions and manuals only came with the aircraft, which was the ninth to arrive and, furthermore, they were in English. In general, Division Engineer Colonel A.M. Akvilyanov had a lot of difficulties to contend with.

The name 'Mitchell' never came to be in common use in the Soviet Union; the bombers were simply referred to as 'B-25'.

Sudets' army was not sent to the front as a whole; instead, its formations were individually redeployed to different locations. After the disbandment of the army, the 222nd Bomber Air Division got to the Western Front. The 37th Air Regiment entered the action in July; the 16th entered the fray in August; and the 125th arrived in September. Remembering the unpleasant accidents with other aircraft of new types, the Command personnel took steps to preliminarily demonstrate the B-25 to fighters and anti-aircraft gunners. Beginning from 11 July, a crew led by Senior Lieutenant B.V. Nazarov of the 37th Bomber Air Regiment was performing demonstration flights at various airfields.

The bombers operated near Vyazma, Dorogobuzh and Yartsevo, and there were a lot of daytime combat sorties, which were made solo and in small groups without fighter cover. The targets included motor convoys, tank columns and fortified positions.

Almost immediately, a strange defect manifested itself: the bladder fuel tanks tended to become 'soaked through'. It turned out that Soviet 4B-78 fuel, which was rich in benzene hydrocarbon impurities, was quickly destroying the internal rubber layers. As early as 5 October, an Order of the Chief Air Force Engineer was issued, which prescribed fueling the B-25s with imported B-100 fuel. The fuel was mostly supplied from the USA in fuel cans, and the ground personnel had a lot of trouble pouring the contents of the cans into the fueling truck. On the other hand, the bladder tanks were not damaged anymore.

The Mitchells did not see service with the frontline aviation for a long time. At low altitudes, the rather clumsy B-25 was inert and proved to be a good target for German fighters and anti-aircraft artillery. Losses began to grow, and the situation was aggravated due to the fact that the aircraft were used in small groups or even solo, and without fighter cover – thus, for example, pilot Balenko was sent on a daytime mission to bomb a bridge across Volga, not far from Kalinin. His aircraft was engaged by five heavy Bf 110 fighters simultaneously; however, Balenko himself began to attack and shot down one of the fighters before hiding in the clouds. The crew managed to find the bridge and drop the bombs; however, they missed the target. On the way back, Balenko encountered enemy fighters once again, but this time there were three of them, and they were more successful: the bomber was badly damaged; the gunner was killed; and the radio operator was injured. The crew had to perform a ditching on a water reservoir and abandon the sinking aircraft in ice-cold water.

Finally, a conclusion was made that using the B-25 against tactical targets was inefficient and, furthermore, problems arose due to a shortage of spare parts. For example, in September, many bombers were grounded, as they were waiting for new wheels. On 29 September 1942, the 222nd Air Division was officially handed over to the long-range aviation.

Such an application of the B-25 at the Soviet-German Front was quite logical: whereas the Pe-2 and the A-20 were much better suited for the role of a frontline bomber, the long-range aviation offered the opportunity to fully use the B-25's high operating range; its excellent radio navigation equipment; powerful armament; and considerable bomb load. In all such parameters, it was much closer to the long-range Il-4 than to the Soviet frontline bombers. In some aspects (such as speed, defensive armament and aircraft equipment), the B-25 exceeded the Il-4; however, it was inferior to the latter in terms of service ceiling, and it required larger spaces for take-off and landing.

In order to become familiar with the aircraft's capabilities, the long-range aviation crews performed several long-range flights in the rear (at daytime and at night), and dropped bombs in the range – thus, they verified the aircraft's suitability for its future tasks.

By the moment of the handover of the 222nd Air Division, the long-range aviation had already had several B-25s at its disposal – thus, the 747th Air Regiment had received four such aircraft by June 1942.

The Mitchells began making night raids to the enemy's rear; at first, they flew either in small groups, or solo.

As of 18 November, the fleet of the 222nd Air Division totaled sixty-eight B-25s and, for night bombing attacks, the aircraft were equipped with special NKPB-7 bomb sights. To increase the range, specially designed additional U-shaped fuel tanks were mounted in the bomb bay; such tanks were used for long-range flights. The bombs in such a configuration were arranged on the external underwing racks (usually, an aircraft took two FAB-250s, which were 250kg each). Later, Factory No.156 mastered the production of disposable cardboard underwing tanks, and the first combat sortie with these tanks was flown by A.A. Skvortsov of the 16th Air Regiment to carry out night reconnaissance in the enemy's rear. Later (to check the maximum range), a flight from Kratovo to Buzuluk was performed, during which four FAB-500 bombs were dropped in the test range.

In autumn 1942, the first frost brought about a mass failure of units, flight instruments and armament. The cause consisted of the fact that the hydraulic system hoses were not frost-resistant, so ruptures appeared in the oil coolers; however, these problems were solved rather quickly, as removable winter front panels for engine cowlings were designed and manufactured at Factory

No.81. They had sector slots which opened and closed when necessary, so all of the Soviet aircraft with air-cooled engines were equipped with such a device.

Later, all of the aircraft coming from the USA were (before shipping) subjected to so-called 'winterization', which was, essentially, an adaptation for winter operations. Provisions were made for the complete drainage of fuel and oil, and the aircraft were supplied with winter lubrication greases and hydraulic fluid. The bombers were also fitted with special gaskets, hoses and wheel tires for winter operations. In general, the B-25 was well fitted for operations in cold weather, as its equipment included a system for the dilution of oil with fuel; wells for the quick heating of oil tanks; a system for the heating of cabins and armaments; devices for blowing the cabin windows with warm air; pneumatic deicers on the wing and tail unit; and provisions for washing propeller blades with alcohol.

From late 1942, the majority of the bombers were coming from America via the ALSIB route. On 28 October, the first training flight was performed by a Soviet crew in a B-25C at Ladd Field and, on 3 November, Captain P.P. Gamov began to ferry the first of the aircraft to the West. In total, eight bombers reached Krasnoyarsk in November – and of those, two were handed over to the long-range aviation representatives; one of the B-25s crashed en route.

Before the end of 1942, a maximum of 10 Mitchells had been accepted in Fairbanks; however, during the following year, their number increased considerably: each month, 10-20 aircraft passed acceptance. The peak occurred in September 1943, when 26 bombers flew from Fairbanks to Krasnoyarsk.

Deliveries via Iran continued as well. By 1 March 1943, 105 bombers had been accepted there, and 102 of them had departed for the destination location.

After the B-25Cs, the B-25Ds began to arrive. They were manufactured at a different factory (in Kansas City), and were, from the very beginning, fitted with an additional fuel tank in the bomb bay, as well as with underwing bomb racks. On the later-version B-25D-30 (in the USSR, they were referred to as B-25DP, with the 'P' standing for *Perekhodnye*, or 'Transitional version'), the lower extendable turret was removed. Soviet crews were criticizing it by right, as it had a limited field of view; it tended to become jammed when extended abruptly; and it could only be operated after a complete extension. Therefore, it was replaced with a pair of machine guns in the side mounts. This configuration of the defensive armament was preserved on the latest versions as well, and a B-25D-30 was tested at NII VVS in June 1944.

In 1943, the American factories mastered another version with a reinforced armament: the B-25J. With additional machine gun containers in the forward portion on the fuselage sides, the number of machine guns reached 11, and all were 12.7mm. Also, another member was added to the crew: in the USSR though, five-person crews continued to fly, with one and the same person combining the functions of the navigator and the bombardier, just as before. This version was equipped with more powerful R-2600-29 engines; however, the increased weight (which was brought about, inter alia, by the greater bomb load) impaired all of the performance parameters of the aircraft. In the Soviet aviation, the B-25J gradually began to replace the B-25C and the B-25D from 1944.

The number of B-25s as supplied to the long-range aviation kept growing. In 1942, the long-range aviation received only 16 aircraft of this type, while in 1943, their number reached 129; in 1944, however, it totaled 210. Before 1 May 1945, the 18th Air Army (into which the long-range aviation had been reorganized) received 128 more aircraft.

In total, under Lend-Lease, eight-hundred-and-seventy B-25s were sent to the USSR – and of those, 862 reached their place of destination, while several more aircraft were interned after forced landings in the Far East. To use these airplanes, the State Defense Committee prescribed (by the Resolution of 13 March 1943) that two additional regiments should be formed. Some of the units which had been flying the Il-4 were also converting to the B-25 and, as a result, the Mitchells were placed in service with several more long-range aviation regiments (the 337th, the 362nd, the 747th and others) during 1943-1944. The 4th (formerly the 222nd), the 5th and the 15th Guards Air Divisions were fully equipped with the B-25s. In August 1943, the 2nd Guards Air Regiment, which was under the command of Colonel I.F. Balashov, began receiving such aircraft. They were provided to the 1st Squadron, which was led by twice Hero of the Soviet Union A.I. Molodchiy. In February 1944, the regiment had as many as twenty B-25s at its disposal (mostly of the latest J version). In general, in early 1944, the B-25s constituted approximately 10 percent of the long-range aviation fleet. At the end of the same year, its entire corps (except for the 2nd Guards Air Corps) had the B-25s at their disposal; in the 4th Guards Air Corps, they were the predominant type. As of 1 January 1945, the 18th Air Army flew 320 Mitchells, which constituted approximately one fifth of all of its materiel.

As part of the long-range aviation, the American bombers were used primarily at night-time in raids on railway terminals, airfields and German defensive posts. On the night of 29 December 1942, one of the regiments of the 222nd Air Division delivered a bombing attack on troop trains in Vitebsk, with the fire lasting for more than three days. The enemy's losses totaled 24 locomotives and up to 500 railway cars. Similar raids were also made on railway hubs in Orsha, Bryansk, Velikiye Luki, Brest and other locations. In June 1943, the B-25s destroyed a German airfield in Seshcha with bombs. The Soviet troops, which were liberating the region, found the entire airfield littered with aircraft wreckage. In September, the Mitchells took part in the suppression of enemy long-range batteries near Leningrad. On the night of 5 October 1943, a raid on Minsk was made: the Government House, which accommodated the German headquarters, was the target for the four crews, and the lead aircraft hit it with a ZAB-100 incendiary bomb – thus facilitating the aiming on the fire for the rest of the crews.

A considerable number of targets were located rather close to the front line – thus, for example, on the night of 16 October 1943, 54 crews of the 4th Air Corps delivered a strike on a bunch of tanks, artillery and infantry near Valki, Bolshevik and Vyshgorod. It is noteworthy that in the above-mentioned raid, not only Soviet-made bombs, but also the captured and slightly modified German SC 250 bombs were used as well.

On the night of 21 June 1944, a very successful raid was made on Yamnitsa, near Mogilev, where enemy tank crews were stationed. Partisans marked the target with bonfires, and 29 aircraft dropped their bombs on barracks, depots and vehicles. At that time, the Germans were having a rousing celebration of the anniversary of the successful outset of hostilities against the Soviet Union. As a result, 400 men were killed and approximately 800 were injured; also, 60 motor vehicles and some depots were burned down. The data on the enemy's casualties were provided by the already mentioned partisans.

Throughout the entire second half of the war, the B-25s kept making long-range raids on Warsaw, Breslau, Konigsberg, Tilsit and Berlin, and they were also operating near Bryansk, Roslavl, Smolensk, Gomel and Sevastopol. In 1944, the 222nd Air Division destroyed the Debrecen railway junction in Hungary.

The American bomber carried a powerful defensive armament which was often used successfully against enemy fighters and bombers – thus, in a raid on Constantsa on 17 April 1944, a B-25 piloted by A.A. Gorelik engaged a two-engine Ju 88. The side of Gorelik's machine was decorated with seven stars, which indicated the number of shot-down enemy aircraft; however, the results were not always so brilliant. The bomber piloted by G.G. Fedotov was once exchanging fire with a Do 217, but it is not known whether the German aircraft was damaged in any way; at the same time, the B-25 was hit in the nacelle and its radio operator was wounded. A.V. Mansvetov encountered a German bomber of the same type on the night of 6 October 1944. The aircraft were, for some time, flying almost parallel routes above the Danube and firing on each other, but in vain.

Another B-25, which was piloted by E.A. Mukhin, was shot down by a German Messerschmitt Bf 110 night fighter near the Yugoslav-Hungarian frontier. The bomber exploded in the air – killing the entire crew.

Speedier, more maneuverable and better armed than the Il-4s, the B-25s were often used to support the strike to be delivered by the main bomber force. Their missions included searching for and identifying targets; providing illumination; suppressing ground-based air defense weapons; and blocking the night fighters' airfields. For example, the 251st Guards Bomber Air Regiment operated in such a manner in 1944 in Hungary to support the functioning of other regiments from the 15th Guards Bomber Air Division. Mass raids typically involved a selection of aircraft pairs, squads or individual crews to block the neighboring airfields. They circled above the airfield for several hours and dropped (from time to time) a bomb or a small cluster of bombs. Besides, the B-25Js (with their enhanced forward firepower) subjected aircraft parking areas and hangars to fire in a flat dive. In the 2nd Guards Bomber Air Regiment, the B-25Js (with additional machine guns) were used to deliver strafing attacks on the enemy airfields at night.

Just the same as other long-range aviation aircraft, the Mitchell was, from time to time, used in the role of a transport aircraft. It had a spacious fuselage, which, in the course of redeployment, could accommodate up to 20 persons (technicians and armament operators). Additionally, a B-25 could carry one ton of cargo to a distance of 2,240km.

The first time that the large-scale use of these bombers for cargo-carrying purposes took place was in February 1944. They carried armaments, medicines and foodstuffs for the National Liberation Army of Yugoslavia. Additional fuel tanks were installed in the bomb bays, and the cargo was placed in the cabin. Each aircraft carried up to twelve PDMM-100 parachute bags (100kg each), which were dropped through hatches. Later, a portion of the cargo was placed in the bomb bay. Initially, flights to Yugoslavia were performed by the Special Southern Group of the 15th Guards Air Division, which was under the command of Major A.P. Dudnik. It included five (or, according to other sources, six) crews of the 14th and the 22nd Long-Range Bomber Air Regiments.

The first sortie, which took place on 19 February, was a failure: the aircraft returned, and only one of them had managed to reach the home airfield; the others had landed on alternative airfields closer to the front. The first cargo dropping in Yugoslavia was made by B.I. Zhilin on the night of 14 March. On 23 March, G.G. Agamirov's aircraft was attacked by a pair of FW 190 fighters. Gunner Intezarov managed to set one of them on fire; then, the B-25 vanished in the clouds. Beginning from 3 May, the entire 4th Guards (formerly the 222nd) Air Division – consisting of 44 crews – was engaged in the cargo carrying, with the flights continuing until the Liberation of Yugoslavia. On one of the sorties, pilot A. Karakozov engaged a German bomber above the Black Sea Coast and shot it down, and then damaged the second one.

In summer 1944, the Mitchells took part in the 'air bridge' to Slovakia, and they delivered anti-tank rifles, machine guns, assault rifles, explosives and ammunition for the Slovak National Uprising. The Li-2s and C-47s landed on Tri Duby airfield, whereas the B-25s of the 4th Guards Air Division dropped cargoes by parachute. They were operating from Kalinovka, near Vinnitsa.

The B-25 was used in the Soviet Union as a long-range reconnaissance aircraft as well. It was tried out in this role for the first time in June 1942 in the 747th Long-Range Bomber Air Regiment and, later, the aircraft were assigned to special long-range reconnaissance regiments. The first three aircraft of this type were handed over to the 40th Long-Range Reconnaissance Air Regiment in November 1942, but afterwards, such aircraft were distributed to various reconnaissance regiments, air force squadrons and navy squadrons. The combination of the Mitchells' powerful defensive armament and excellent instrumentation allowed for performing flights both in the day and at night. The B-25s of the long-range aviation units were also used for reconnaissance purposes. In April 1943, Hero of the Soviet Union V.P. Dragomiretsky of the 14th Guards Air Regiment took photographs of a bridge across the Desna River at night after dropping some illumination bombs; in May, he photographed a railway terminal in Orel using the same technique.

It is no surprise that the Mitchells were also operated by training units, such as the training regiment of the Air Force Engineering Academy and the 1st Higher Officers' School for Night Crews of Long-Range Aviation.

One of the Mitchells came to the USSR in a somewhat unconventional way: this was the aircraft of the already mentioned Captain York, who had, some time before, given a hearty welcome to the Soviet pilots in his squadron. He was taking part in the famous Doolittle Raid on Tokyo. Sixteen bombers took off from the aircraft carrier USS *Hornet* and, on the Emperor of Japan's birthday, dropped their bombs on targets in Tokyo, Yokohama, Kobe and Nagoya. It was expected that the crews would either land their aircraft in China, or bail out in the area where American submarines were patrolling. Not everybody turned out lucky enough, and Captain York chose a different option: he landed near Vladivostok. York's B-25 (c/n 40-2242) had a non-standard configuration, as it featured shortened wings; an incomplete set of armament; an extra fuel tank; and no tail turret (which was replaced with a wooden dummy). The aircraft was examined and test-flown by the Pacific Fleet Air Force pilots. From Unashi, where it had landed, the aircraft was then ferried to Semyonovka airfield, and then (under an order) to the 65th Special-Purpose Air Regiment in Moscow.

In autumn 1943, several B-25Gs came from the USA via the ALSIB route, which were the heavy ground attack aircraft with a 75mm cannon in the nose. Since all of the Mitchells were, at that time, concentrated in long-range aviation units, the B-25Gs were sent there as well. The first two B-25Gs were assigned to the 15th Guards Air Regiment, and Lieutenant Colonel V.A. Gordilovsky was the first to fly such an aircraft. Operational service tests were conducted by A.V. Dudakov's crew, with the crew performing three daytime flights at the test range, and then carrying out night firing practice. It turned out that a cannon shot was dazzling the pilot in the dark.

One of the two aircraft piloted by the already mentioned Dudakov's crew saw service on the front line and, on its very first combat sortie (on 9 October), it destroyed two railway troop trains at the Mozyr — Gomel segment. The crew was strafing the targets from the cannon, the stationary nose machine guns and the forward-oriented turret. In total, Dudakov flew three combat sorties in the B-25G – including airfield strafing; however, based on the results of the tests, the B-25G was found not fit for long-range aviation. The opinion was that the absence of the nose navigator's compartment was inconvenient; charging the cannon took too much time and was too hazardous (during the tests, the deputy chief engineer of the corps was injured by the breechblock); and the forward-shifted center of gravity adversely affected controllability performance.

The received aircraft were handed over to the naval aviation, and all of them were assigned to reconnaissance regiments. Two ground attack aircraft from the 15th Guards Long-Range Air Regiment were transferred to the 118th Independent Reconnaissance Air Regiment of the Northern Fleet Air Force, and it appears that the large-caliber gun was only used by naval pilots in an operational environment on one occasion. On 25 April 1945, Major Nakonechny's crew of the 118th Air Regiment attacked a German submarine by shooting several times from the cannon, and also by dropping depth bombs; wreckage and an oil spot appeared on the surface. According to Soviet data, the submarine was damaged, and the aircraft crew was awarded orders and medals; the Germans, however, never admitted to the loss of the submarine.

Another two B-25Gs later joined the 15th Independent Reconnaissance Air Regiment in the Baltic Sea and, according to documents, their first combat sorties took place in November 1944. In the Pacific, the B-25s appeared in late 1944 and one of the aircraft was assigned to the 14th Combined Air Regiment in Vtoraya Rechka airfield, while the other was assigned to the Administration of the 2nd Mine-and-Torpedo Air Division. The aircraft from the 14th Air Regiment was later transferred to the 50th Independent Reconnaissance Air Regiment, where it was piloted by Regiment Commander Major I.V. Sidin. According to official sources, the fleet received, in total, eight B-25s of various versions.

Soviet crews noted (first and foremost) the high piloting performance of the B-25: it could be flown by a pilot of average skills, and it had no considerable drawbacks in terms of take-off or landing performance, or directional stability or maneuverability (the latter, of course, with the allowance for the aircraft's weight and size taken into account). Test pilot I.I. Shelest wrote: 'The tricycle landing gear allowed excellent visibility at taxiing and perfect maneuverability on ground; it made the B-25 behave rather dynamically during motion on concrete, at taxiing to take-off position or at taxiing out from the runway after landing'. Piloting at take-off, landing and in flight was easier in the Mitchell than it was in the Il-4. The Soviet piloting manual for the B-25 reads: 'The aircraft is stable during take-off run. It displays no tendency to turn, and obeys the rudders well'. Thanks to the powerful and reliable engines, and sturdy landing gear, the aircraft was even able to take off from rather deep snow – and with a full load.

All of this allowed for the quick conversion of pilots to the new aircraft. Conversion training often required no interruptions in combat service, but even a pilot of little experience could master the B-25 in a few days.

The aircraft was easy to control even in a flight with only one engine operative. According to the manual: 'Load on the rudders in flight with a single engine operative is fully removed by the trim tabs'. On the Il-4, such a situation resulted in the need to engage the navigator's controls, so that the latter should press the pedal to assist the pilot.

With a normal bomb load and the attachment of additional fuel tanks, the B-25 was able, with one engine inoperative, to not only maintain the altitude, but also to climb. Pilot S.M. Antonov of the 8th Long-Range Bomber Air Regiment, with one of its aircraft's engines having become inoperative soon after take-off, managed to reach the target, drop bombs on German troop trains in Orel, and then return to the base!

Unlike the unstable Il-4, where the pilot had to keep hold of the steering wheel every single moment, the American bomber did not exhaust the pilots to such an extent. The test report on the B-25D read: 'Adjusted by the trim tabs, the aircraft itself strives to maintain the selected attitude [position] or to restore it if, for some reason, it falls out of such attitude [position]'.

The cockpit was fitted with a complete set of state-of-the-art flight navigation and monitoring instruments, plus it was spacious, light and comfortable. On the Il-4, the cockpit was not heated at all, with the temperature in it sometimes reaching -30°C in winter. Instrument scales on the American aircraft were conveniently illuminated by UV lamps, and the state-of-the-art radio equipment included an automatic direction finder.

The aircraft was equipped with an excellent defensive armament, so an enemy coming from nearly any direction had to face bursts of large-scale machine gun fire. There were only two 'dead areas', which were in the form of narrow sectors at approximately 45° to the aircraft centerline in the lower semisphere. There were illustrative examples of the efficiency of the Mitchell's armament – thus, A.I. Molodchiy's crew, throughout the 18 months of flights in a B-25, shot down five enemy fighters. Throughout 1944, the relative losses of the B-25s per a battle-worthy aircraft were 2.2 times lower than those of the Il-4s; also, it should be noted that the American bombers were used more intensively than their Soviet counterparts.

The aircraft was able to carry a heavy bomb load: up to 2,000kg on the latest versions, and up to 3,000kg in the overload variant. The spacious bomb bay could accommodate any Soviet bombs (up to FAB-500), American bombs of 100lbs through to 1,000lbs, and captured 250kg and 500kg German bombs, which were also sometimes used. It should be noted that to enable the use of the 500kg bombs, some amendments were made to the safety requirements. The internal bomb bay volume was sufficient to accommodate even the jumbo RRAB-3 (RRAB-500) bomb dispenser, which the Il-4 could only carry externally, with a 20-30km/h loss in speed in a level flight. The

Il-4's internal weapon-carrying capacity was restricted to items of up to 100kg in caliber, while larger munitions had to be suspended on under-fuselage or underwing bomb racks.

The B-25 also had provisions for the external mounting of the combat load. The underwing racks were fit to carry any bombs of up to 250kg, but it should be noted that the shackles of the American underwing racks had to be slightly altered in order to enable the attachment of Soviet-made bombs without changing the position of the lifting lugs; also, 'armed-safe' mechanisms were modified; finally, the American-made bomb bay internal winch was replaced with the BL-4 winch. The modification scheme was worked out in 1942 by the OKB-43 Design Bureau, which was headed by A.I. Shulgin. Such minor modifications were implemented at Factory No.156 in Moscow, or directly at the facilities of the air units.

The arrangement of an in-flight emergency escape for the B-25 was worse than that for the Il-4, as all of the crew members in the aircraft nose section were expected to bail out one by one via the same hatch. The navigator (in such a situation) had to crawl, with his parachute donned, via a narrow and crooked tunnel to the cockpit, whereas the tail gunner had to go forward to the center of the aircraft. On the Il-4, each of the crew members bailed out independently via their own dedicated hatch or canopy.

On the other hand, crew members on the American aircraft could standby for each other, whereas a serious injury to the pilot on the Il-4 led to the loss of the aircraft.

Of course, there were certain problems in the operation of the B-25s: like all Lend-Lease aircraft, there was, initially, a lack of technical descriptions, manuals and other publications for the B-25. The incorrect selection of flight conditions resulted in the engine overheating or an inefficient fuel consumption, which sometimes led to forced landings. Nose landing gear failure was a typical problem, and there were also occasions of trim tab breakaways, engine malfunctions and ice protection system faults. Manufacturing defects were also encountered – thus, in October 1944, the Soviet acceptance in Fairbanks rejected approximately half of the shipped B-25Js due to carburetor failures.

On the whole, however, the B-25 was a reliable and convenient-to-operate aircraft, which is confirmed (at least) by the percentage of serviceable aircraft; it was rather high in air units which were equipped with the B-25s. Another convincing shred of proof is that the Mitchell was not subjected to any major modifications in the USSR.

The B-25s saw successful combat service in the Soviet Union until the very end of the hostilities. As of 1 May, the Soviet Air Force had 552 such aircraft at their disposal – including 398 at the front line. Ninety-eight aircraft were stationed in internal military districts, whereas 56 were in transit to destination locations. Losses throughout the war totaled 201 bombers.

The Mitchells took part in the last military operations against Germany – in particular, in the Battle of Berlin. On 16 April 1945, Commander of the 250th Air Regiment Lieutenant Colonel Gordilovsky dropped a bunch of multi-colored incendiary bombs to give a signal to attack the Seelow Heights, near Berlin.

On 9 May 1945, the B-25s colored the Moscow skies with flares as part of the festive illuminations, as the Soviet capital was celebrating the victory over Germany.

In August 1945, these aircraft were used in the hostilities against Japan. Among the aircraft in service in the Kurils, there were several which had been obtained via 'unofficial' channels: they were interned in 1943-1945. The first four of them landed on Yelizovo airfield, near Petropavlovsk, after the raid of the American aviation on Paramushir on 11 September 1943; all of them belonged to the USAAF 77th Squadron. Another bomber arrived a year later, on 17 September 1944; in total, twelve B-25s landed on Kamchatka. The last of them – a B-25J piloted by R. Wolbrink – was severely damaged by Japanese anti-aircraft fire and performed a belly landing on 10 June 1945. Several aircraft were successfully repaired and placed in service with the 128th Composite Air Division. As of 27 August, the division had five B-25s, with four of them assigned to the 903rd

Bomber Air Regiment. All of them were of different versions (C, D, G and J), and they were used in the trainer role (as part of the preparations for the conversion to the American-made Douglas A-20 bombers), as well as for various auxiliary purposes.

With the end of the war and the expiry of the Lend-Lease term, the Soviet Union was expected to return the aircraft to the Americans. Typically, the procedure was confined to destroying the machines under the supervision of American representatives and, in 1945-1947, some of the aircraft were indeed eliminated under the American inspectors' control. In particular, such activities were carried out near Vinnitsa, where the bombers were crushed by tractors, but such a fate, however, did not befall all of the Mitchells.

The conversion of the Soviet long-range aviation to the B-25s continued after the war – thus, for example, the 330th Bomber Air Regiment in Bobruisk had been completely equipped with such bombers by 1946, and the American aircraft remained in service with the regiment until their conversion to the Tu-4 in 1949. A similar situation existed in the 52nd Guards Heavy Bomber Air Regiment: before January 1946, the regiment pilots flew the TB-3RNs, but later they began to receive the American bombers. The conversion process to the latter was completed in January 1948, with the regiment stationed near Orsha. In summer the same year, the conversion to the Consolidated B-24 Liberator (also American-made) began.

Furthermore, during the initial post-war years, the B-25 was considered to be the main long-range aviation aircraft. The Li-2 (the most widely used aircraft in the long-range aviation) was, essentially, an ersatz bomber, which had (out of necessity) been modified from an airliner. After the war, the Li-2s resumed operations in the passenger-carrying or cargo-carrying role, or were transferred to the military transport aviation. The four-engine Pe-8s were scarce, and were prohibited to fly on account of being severely worn. The manufacture of the obsolete Il-4s was discontinued, since they failed to comply with the required standards. There was no alternative but to fly the B-25s, which had to bear their burden until the arrival of sufficient quantities of the Tu-4s.

It was after the war that Soviet crews mastered the S-1 autopilot, which was linked to the Norden M-9 high-precision bomb sight as installed on the B-25J. By the way, in late 1945, an attempt was made to replace the M-9 with the more advanced – and German-made – Lotfe-7 bomb sights. Approximately a thousand of these bomb sights were captured from Carl Zeiss warehouses, and German specialists provided assistance in adapting the Lotfe system for the installation on the B-25; however, the German bomb sights and the American autopilots turned out to be incompatible, with the system becoming prone to oscillations, which altered the bomber's attack course.

The 14th Air Division, which was near Poltava, operated the B-25s until 1950. The composite corps in Kamchatka (on their part) converted from the B-25s to the jet-powered Il-28 in 1953, but in some cases, the Mitchell was used as a transition aircraft in the process of converting to the Tu-4 – thus, in June 1951, the 444th Bomber Air Regiment began flying the B-25s; then, in August, they commenced mastering the Tu-4. On account of a shortage of spare parts (first and foremost, for engines), the battle-worthiness of the American aircraft kept decreasing, and such a situation brought about the need to return the old Il-4 to certain regiments.

In summer 1946, the B-25s were provided to the 151st Independent Aerial Photography Air Squadron in Irkutsk; in October the same year, the squadron was redeployed to Krasnoyarsk. The squadron's missions mostly included terrain mapping air photography; however, armament on the aircraft was preserved. The armament was made use of in spring 1948, when the squadron was sent out to bomb ice blocks on the Yenisei River. The American aircraft remained in service with the above-mentioned unit until 1954; then, they were replaced by the Li-2s.

From 1947, the B-25s were in service with the Navigators' Higher Military School in Ryazan. As late as 1953, the school was still operating 18 such aircraft, which were assigned to the 671st Training Air Regiment.

A small number of the Mitchells were operated by the civil aviation. They began their service there in 1943, with the handover of two B-25s to the Civil Air Fleet. A year later, nine more aircraft came; however, shortly thereafter, some of them were transferred to the long-range aviation. They were used initially as the lead aircraft during the ferrying of fighters via the ALSIB route, as well as for the training of ferrying pilots, but in early 1945, a decision was made to hand over the Mitchells to the 3rd Liaison Air Division, which was stationed at Myachkovo airfield near Moscow. Its principal task was to carry couriers and documentation to the front line and back. In February, the division engineers worked out a project for the modification of the B-25 into a liaison aircraft. In March, two aircraft (both of the G version) arrived at Myachkovo and, in the same month, one of them was modified. Later, it was tested at NII GVF, with B. Ostapchuk acting as the test pilot. From April, the two aircraft were in constant operation, but in June, the third aircraft joined them.

After the war, the Civil Air Fleet's management expected a rather extensive application of such aircraft in the civil aviation. According to the estimations of NII GVF's specialists, the disarmed B-25s – in terms of economic performance – were close to the C-47 and Li-2. Their opinion read as follows: 'The B-25 aircraft is the most cost-efficient military aircraft. It can be used by the Civil Air Fleet in the role of the cargo-carrying or passenger-and-cargo express aircraft on the main routes'.

Two modification options (the cargo version and the cargo-and-passenger version) were worked out: the first option could carry 2,700kg of cargo, whereas the second option accommodated 1,400kg of cargo, plus five to eight passengers. It was expected that the passengers would occupy the cabin behind the bomb bay, and the intention was to remove all armament items and internal bulkheads from the aircraft, as well as to install a cover plate for the bomb hatch and to relocate the radio station. The cargo hatches were planned to be cut out in the bottom nose portion and under the wing, and the passenger version was expected to be fitted with additional seats, as well as having windows in the sides; however, there were almost no comfortable conditions for the passengers at all.

Marshal F.A. Astakhov, who was, at that time, the head of the Civil Air Fleet, addressed a request to the air force's headquarters to hand over excessive B-25s to the civil aviation; however, the answer was negative. In order to 'demobilize' the required number of bombers, it would have been necessary to disband one of the long-range aviation divisions, so the Air Force Command rejected the idea. Aircraft from the 3rd Liaison Air Division were transferred to the Yakutsk Civil Air Fleet Administration and remained in service with it until November 1948.

After the war, a certain number of B-25s were in use with the so-called 'departmental aviation'. Among the Mitchells' operators were such branches and agencies as the Polar Aviation Division of the Chief Administration of the Northern Maritime Route (*Glavnoe Upravlenie Severnogo Morskogo Puti*, or GUSMP); the Chief Administration of Hydrometeorological Service; the Chief Administration of Geodetic Surveying and Cartography; the Ministry of Aviation Industry; the Ministry of Geology; the Ministry of Fisheries; the Ministry of Internal Affairs' *Dalstroi* (the 'realm of camps' in the Far East); and the Ministry of Internal Affairs' Chief Administration of Mining and Smelting Industry Camps (*Glavnoe Upravlenie Lagerey Metallurgicheskoy Promyshlennosty*, or GULGMP).

The Polar Aviation received its first B-25 (reg/n H-366) as early as 1944; however, it was not popular with polar pilots and, in January 1945, was handed over to *Dalstroi*. Later, GUSMP received another aircraft from GULGMP and, in January 1947, it performed a forced belly landing. The Polar Aviation specialists repaired it and replaced its former registration number (X-717) with H-445. The aircraft was in service with the Moscow Squad, which was stationed at Zakharkovo airfield (now the territory of Khimki), but this B-25 was written off in the first half of 1950.

The Hydrometeorological Service operated the former bombers as weather and ice reconnaissance aircraft in order to make use of their long range. The number of aircraft in operation with the Hydrometeorological Service reached its peak value (i.e. eight aircraft) in June 1947, but afterwards, their number gradually decreased as a result of wear and crashes – thus, on 6 September 1947, during the ferrying of the aircraft (reg/n M-345) which was in operation with the Main Geophysical Laboratory from Naberezhnaya airfield to Leningrad, the left engine caught fire immediately after take-off. The aircraft fell down on a house near Klyazma and burnt down. Out of the crew, only the radio operator survived, while among the passengers, a woman died; the rest were injured. In the house, a small boy was killed and his mother was injured.

The aircraft which were operated by the Ministry of Internal Affairs were pure cargo transports. One of them was in service with *Dalstroi*, while the other two were flown by GULGMP (at the detachment which served the Norilsk metallurgy plant). One of GULGMP's B-25s was written off after a crash in the first half of 1948.

The Ministry of Aviation Industry also operated its aircraft in the role of cargo transports. During the early post-war years, the Ministry had two B-25s in service. In September 1947, one of them (reg/n И-850) – during a flight to Kazan – performed an emergency landing in Vnukovo because of a fire and ran into an Il-12. All crew members and passengers of the B-25 perished in the crash.

The aircraft of the Ministry of Geology's detachments (which were part of the Aerogeologiya Group) were, for the most part, used to take photos of locations where geological parties were working. These aircraft were not numerous: as of 1 January 1950, the Ministry had only three of them at its disposal.

The Ministry of Fish Industry of the Eastern Regions attempted, in July through to September, to use the B-25s to search for fish concentrations in the Pacific. The attempt, however, was a failure, as the aircraft's speed was found to be too high. Apart from the single aircraft at Glavsakhalinrybprom's disposal, the Ministry operated two more aircraft which were based in Moscow. In February 1948, the aircraft reg/n X-686, which was being ferried from Vnukovo to Monino, experienced in-flight left engine failure. Pilot Kudin made a straight-in landing in Monino across the runway and broke the main landing gear leg, and it was later found out that a piston had burnt in one of the engine cylinders.

In November 1948, the Moscow-based aviation detachment was disbanded. One of the aircraft was written off, whereas the other was handed over to the Ministry's garage 'without the right to interfere with technical and operational activities'. This aircraft became the minister's personal 'limousine', and it had a luxury velvet-upholstered cabin for four or five passengers. Such modifications were carried out in both the civil and the military aviation. For example, such aircraft were flown by the 65th Air Regiment of the Naval Air Force, and among them were two disarmed B-25Gs and a luxury 'limousine' on the B-25J platform. In 1947, one of the B-25Gs was modified in Leningrad into a special 'headquarters aircraft' for the commander of the Naval Air Force.

Some of the aircraft were adapted for various experimental purposes, and one of the bombers was modified into a flying test bed for jet engine testing. The third engine was mounted on a pylon above the fuselage and, in particular, this aircraft was used for the testing of RD-10F turbojet engines. In 1947-1948, the B-25Js (disarmed) were used for the testing of the Soviet-made assisted take-off systems 93-I (the gunpowder type) and SU-1500 (with a liquid-propellant engine). In 1948, LII conducted tests of the '346' experimental rocket-powered vehicle and, in 1947-1948, two B-25Gs took part in the *Shchuka* ('Pike') gliding torpedo testing program in Yevpatoriya. One of the B-25Gs carried a dummy torpedo, while the other was used to try out the guidance system. For this purpose, an engineer-operator and the appropriate equipment was placed in the spacious fuselage.

In 1949, OKB-115 designed the Burlak system, which was expected to increase the range of jet fighters (which was, initially, rather short). The bomber docked with the fighter in mid-air, and then towed it on a rope. Initially, experiments were carried out with the Tu-2 and Yak-23, and later, the B-25 and Yak-25 (i.e. the first aircraft with such a designation, which was single-engine) were adapted for the purpose. The bomber deployed a cone on a rope using BLK-1 winch, while the fighter carried (in its nose portion) a hinged 'harpoon', which was expected to engage with the cone.

The testing of the Burlak system was conducted at LII facilities in June 1949 through to March 1950. The Yak-25 was piloted by S.N. Anokhin, whereas pilot Toroshchenko flew the B-25. During this time period, seven successful engagements were carried out. Testing was resumed in July, with the B-25 piloted by V.F. Khapov. At the second stage, night engagements were carried out and, for this purpose, the bomber was equipped with a red signal light; to the cone, reflectors were attached. The fighter's illumination consisted of the landing light, which was turned slightly upwards for this purpose. The Mitchell towed the fighter at a speed of 320-330km/h and could only afford to perform smooth evolutions.

Work on the Burlak system continued until 1956, but with the Tu-4 as the towing aircraft and with the MiG-15 being towed.

From 1952, the B-25s were modified into target drones. The aircraft took off with the pilot and, at the approach to the test range boundary, the pilot engaged the autopilot system and then bailed out. Further movements of the aircraft were radio-controlled. Three such targets were used, for example, in June 1951 during the testing of PROSAB-100 anti-aircraft bombs which were dropped from the MiG-17 and Il-28. The pilot bailed out at an altitude of 2,000m, but the aircraft kept moving in a straight auto-controlled flight. The target was escorted by the Tu-2 bomber, which had a camera man on board. In one of these cases, a squadron of the MiG-17 fighters attacked the escort aircraft by mistake. The bomber's pilot evaded the attack in a steep dive, whereas the B-25 remained intact and continued the flight; then, another fighter took off and intercepted and shot down the target. The wreckage of the B-25 fell down at the salt fields at Lake Baskunchak and, as a result, a certain amount of salt was spoiled. By way of compensation, the bomber wreckage was handed over to the salt mine's factory. In the mid-1950s, the B-25s were also used in the trying out of the first Soviet air defense missile system: the S-25 Berkut.

Of all the B-25s which were shipped to the USSR, only one survived; however, this aircraft did not see military service, as it made a forced landing on the ALSIB route and then stayed for a long time in the taiga. It was restored at the Novosibirsk Aircraft Factory and then handed over to the museum in Monino – and there, it can still be seen as part of the outdoor display.

Soviet and American pilots after the acceptance of one of the first B-25s during late summer 1941.

A group of G.A. Osipov's near the first assembled B-25B, Kegostrov, February 1942.

A B-25B during tests at NII VVS in May 1942.

This B-25B was flown back to the USA leading a group of the PS-84 transport aircraft which brought the Soviet mission from Krasnoyarsk to Fairbanks in Alaska in September 1942.

The B-25B which was flown by E. York, who took part in J. Doolittle's bombing raid on Japan, made a forced landing near Vladivostok.

Pilots of the 1st Ferry Air Division near a B-25C.

A B-25C of the 45th Guards Long-Range Air Division.

The warming-up of the B-25D engines before ferrying to Chukotka.

Maintenance of the B-25D which was flown by a crew of Senior Lieutenant I.A. Prokhorov of the 13th Guards Long-Range Air Regiment during winter 1943/1944.

A B-25C of the 125th Long-Range Air Regiment after a forced landing in March 1943.

Squadron personnel near a B-25C which was flown by a crew of Captain M.V. Zhuravkov of the 13th Guards Long-Range Air Regiment.

A group of the B-25 bombers in flight.

Senior Lieutenant Krapiva reporting to Squadron Leader Egorov of the 13th Guards Long-Range Regiment at Novo-Dugino airfield during winter 1943/1944.

One of the crews of the 13th Long-Range Air Regiment verifying the task before a mission.

Another aircraft of the 13th Long-Range Air Regiment.

The ground crew of the 2nd Guards Bomber Air Regiment near the B-25 which was flown by a crew of twice Hero of the Soviet Union A.I. Molodchiy, Czechoslovakia, summer 1945. The aircraft carries the inscription 'Oleg Koshevoy', who was a Soviet partisan and one of the founders of the clandestine organization 'Young Guard', which fought the Nazi forces in Krasnodon. Koshevoy was executed on 9 February 1943.

A group photo of a bomber regiment crew, with a B-25 in the background.

Pilots of the 13th Guards Long-Range Air Regiment discuss the coming mission.

A B-25D-30 during tests at NII VVS in June 1944.

Bombs being prepared for loading into a B-25DP.

Personnel of the 362nd Long-Range Air Regiment after the awarding ceremony in 1944; note the B-25D-30 with the 'yellow 20' tactical marking in the background. This aircraft was shot down by enemy fighters in October the same year.

A brand-new B-25J in the USA in 1944. The aircraft featured special 'Standard 407' camouflage and red stars with white trimming.

This B-25J bomber was flown by a crew of pilot V.V. Doveyko of the 341st Long-Range Air Regiment; note the unusual nose art with the clown's head, and the inscription, which translates as: 'For the Soviet Art', as well as the Guards' Order.

An instructor parachutist bailing out from a B-25J through the rear hatch.

A crew of Senior Lieutenant Baimurzin's near a B-25J of the 13th Guards Long-Range Air Regiment.

A line-up of the B-25Js of the 22nd Guards Long-Range Air Regiment at Tököl airfield in Hungary in May 1945.

The awarding ceremony of a reconnaissance air regiment in the 7th Air Army; note the nose of a B-25 in the background.

The famous Russian singer L.A. Ruslanova performing for the crews of long-range aviation at Kalinovka airfield in summer 1944. Some of the audience are settled down under the wing of a B-25J bomber.

A ceremonial parade of the 362nd Long-Range Air Regiment in 1944.

General B.V. Bitsky near a B-25 in Poland in 1945.

Senior Lieutenant S.N. Nakoryakov near his B-25G.

The flight crew of the 45th Air Division near a B-25D, Kazan, April 1948.

The testing of the SU-1500 booster rocket engines on the B-25 which was flown by test pilot M.L. Gallay.

This B-25 bomber was converted into a flying testbed for experiments with the RD-10F turbojet engine.

A pilot and test engineers near a disarmed B-25G during the tests of the *Shchuka* (Pike) gliding torpedo in the Crimea in 1947.

The B-25 aircraft of the *Burlak* system towing a cable with a cone.

A B-25 *Burlak* photographed from the fighter, which was approaching the cone for engagement.

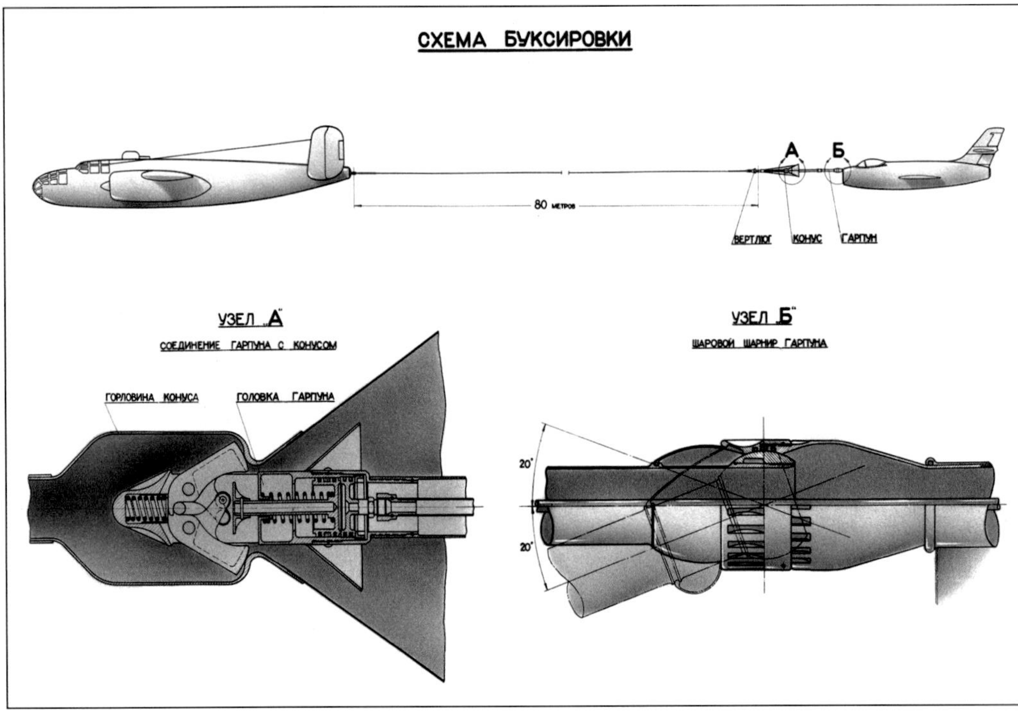

The *Burlak* system towing scheme.

A disarmed B-25 which was used as a transport aircraft.

A B-25 of GUGK which was used for aerial surveys.

A photographer changing a cassette in an aerial camera mounted inside a B-25.

A group photo, with a disarmed civil B-25 in the background, which was taken during the late 1940s.

A line-up of an air regiment of the Long-Range Aviation.

A B-25C during restoration at an aircraft factory in Novosibirsk.

The B-25C being exhibited at the Russian Air Force Museum in Monino.

7.11 Handley Page Hampden

The only British bomber type which took an active part in combat operations on the Soviet-German Front was the Handley Page Hampden. Development of the aircraft began in 1935, with four aircraft companies taking part in a bid for the order for a new day bomber.

The Handley Page designers took their time: having analyzed quite a number of options, they stayed with a cantilever monoplane which had a twin-fin tail unit and a peculiar fuselage with a narrow tail beam. The prototype HP.52 bomber was built in spring 1936, and first flew in late June. The customer was happy with the aircraft and, in summer 1938 (after a certain modification), it was put into mass production under the name 'Hampden'.

Soviet specialists first saw the HP.52 in summer 1936 at an air show in Hendon airfield, near London. Military Engineer 2nd Rank Grebenev wrote in his report: 'A monoplane; with gun posts providing good protection for it. Its horizontal speed is not high; however, the rate of climb is quite decent'.

By September 1939, as many as 10 RAF squadrons were equipped with the Hampdens. At the beginning of the war, there were attempts to use them for daytime attacks on German ships in ports, but in view of the heavy losses that followed, the bombers were 'changed over' to night sorties. During the time of the German Air Blitz in 1940, there were even attempts to operate them as 'makeshift' night fighters; however, in these roles, they did not achieve much success either. The Hampden was considerably inferior to both new British and German bombers, as it had low speed, poor maneuverability and a weak defensive armament, which included two dual 7.69mm Vickers K machine guns in the dorsal and ventral positions for the protection of the aft hemisphere, and a fixed machine gun in the fuselage nose. Specialists in the squadrons attempted to fit additional gun posts near the cabin windows, but those were of no great help.

From March 1942, the Hampdens began to be transferred to RAF Coastal Command (which dealt with maritime operations), with the role of torpedo bombers in store for them. English Electric modified the bomb bay doors and the aft gun post on 144 aircraft in order to allow attaching the standard Mk.XII British air torpedo in a half-closed position. The modified aircraft version was designated Hampden TB.I, and four squadrons were equipped with this particular aircraft.

In early autumn 1942, the British made a decision to send an air group led by Group Captain F. Hopper (according to other sources, Hopps) to support Convoy PQ 18 on its way to the Kola Peninsula from Scotland. The group included a small unit of photo reconnaissance aircraft (the Spitfires and the Mosquitoes), 10 Catalina flying boats and a wing of torpedo bombers. The latter consisted of two squadrons (No.144 and No.455), and both were manned with Australian flight personnel. Their aircraft were modified into torpedo bombers in April 1942. By the time of being sent to the Soviet Union, the squadrons had already gained a certain level of combat experience, and the wing was led by Wing Commander McLaughlin.

These squadrons were equipped with a total of 35 Hampdens which were of various years of manufacture and origin (including Canadian factories); however, during the course of modification into torpedo bombers, all of them had been brought to the uniform standard of the latest series.

On the evening of 4 September, the British crews departed one by one from the airfield in Sumburgh in the Shetland Islands (where they had made a refueling stopover) and headed for Afrikanda. Such an exotic name belonged (and still belongs) to a small settlement not far from Kandalaksha, where a military airfield was located at that time, but the torpedo bombers could also use airfields in Beloye or Gremyakha as alternate fields. The range was close to the extreme, and the normal range for a TB.I with no torpedo carried – and with an additional fuel tank in the bomb bay – totaled 1,040 miles, although an experienced pilot could 'extend' it to 1,360 miles in cruising conditions. The distance to Vaenga (the nearest airfield in the Soviet territory) amounted to 1,314 miles; however, this destination, which was exposed to incessant German raids,

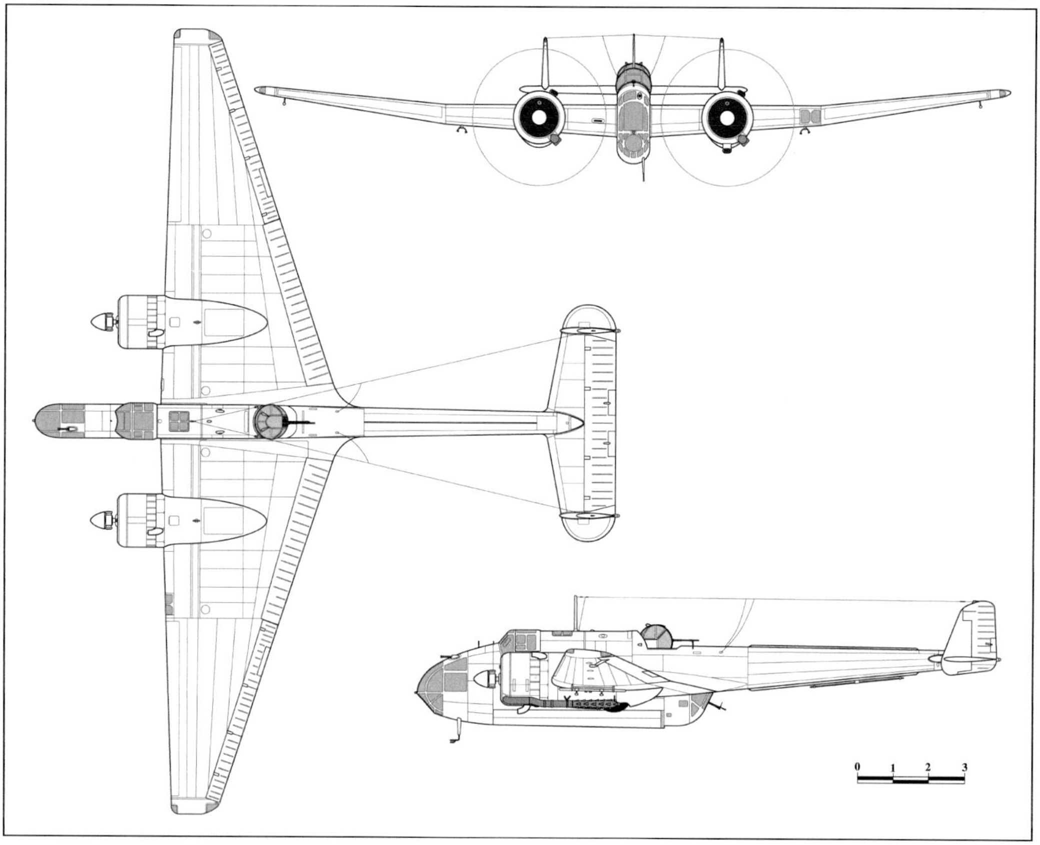

Hampden

Three-view of the Hampden TB.I, with an elongated bomb bay and a UTK-1 turret.

was deemed to be too hazardous by the British. There was an option to fly over the mountains in Norway (the range would have totaled 1,100 miles); however, in such a case, fuel would have also been required for climbing. Besides, each of the aircraft carried (in addition to its own crew) a ground crew specialist so as not to depend (for some time after arrival) on the rest of the mechanics and the engine and armament specialists who had been sent by sea.

En route, the British aircraft were under threat of being attacked by German fighters and anti-aircraft fire, while near the ground, they found a dense fog. Not all of the Hampdens were destined to reach their destination, as only 23 of them landed on Soviet airfields in Afrikanda, Kandalaksha and Murmashi. Out of the rest of the party, two aircraft made forced landings: one of them lost its way in the fog, used up its fuel and performed a successful belly landing not far from Afrikanda, while the other (with no fuel left in the tanks as well) ran into three tree stumps during its landing near Kandalaksha and was smashed to pieces. Luckily, the crew suffered no injuries. The third aircraft deviated to the north from the designated route and reached the mouth of the Kola River in the midst of a German air raid, but two Soviet fighters mistook the Hampden for a Bf 110 and promptly shot it down. The aircraft was ditched, but the crew survived except for the lower gunner Sergeant Taybor, who had been killed in flight.

Three Hampdens fell prey to German fighters while passing over Finland, and two aircraft crashed in Sweden (one because of engine failure, while the other ran into a mountain in the fog). Another Hampden lost its bearings and force-landed in the northern part of Finland – thus, approximately three fourths of the initial party reached its destination.

By 7 September, 23 battle-worthy aircraft were concentrated at Vaenga-1 airfield, near Murmansk. Ground personnel, the required equipment, spare parts and torpedoes arrived in Murmansk on board USS *Tuscaloosa*, and then also redeployed to Vaenga-1. On 14 September, the entire party of the Hampdens flew its one and only (for the British crews) combat sortie from the territory of the Soviet Union. For seven hours, they patrolled the approaches to Altafjord, where the battleship *Tirpitz* was moored at that time; however, the battleship did not leave its base and the torpedo bombers did not encounter any other German warships or aircraft either. On 22 September, Operation 'Orator' (the escorting of Convoy PQ 18) ended.

A question arose as to what to do with the torpedo bombers, as the way back was aggravated by constant head winds. Furthermore, there was a much greater probability of missing the Shetland Islands than a continental airfield, even in poor weather. On 24 September, Coastal Command suggested that the Hampdens be left at Vaenga as a gift for the Northern Fleet. While the aircraft remained grounded on the airfield and awaiting decision, the Germans delivered a powerful strike on them. Three Hampdens were destroyed, and nine more suffered minor damage.

On 1 October, the Soviet Union submitted an official request for the British torpedo bombers. On 6 October, the transfer was approved by Prime Minister W. Churchill, with the proviso that all of the equipment – including bomb sights and cameras – should be removed from the aircraft, and that the unused torpedoes should be returned to England. Eventually, good sense prevailed: on 12 October, the torpedo bombers (complete with their equipment and armament) were handed over to the Northern Fleet Air Force and, on 22 October, the personnel of the British squadrons departed for their home country on board HMS *Argonaut*.

The arrival of the new torpedo bombers allowed for the formation of the 24th Mine-and-Torpedo Air Regiment, which was the first regiment of its kind in the Northern Fleet, and the respective order was issued by the fleet's commander on 14 October. The regiment was manned with personnel from two squadrons of the famous Safonov's 2nd Guards Combined Air Regiment. The regiment's mine-and-torpedo squadron (led by Captain Popovich) became the 1st Squadron of the 24th Air Regiment, whereas the bomber squadron – which was under the command of Captain A.Z. Stoyanov – constituted the 2nd Squadron of the 24th Air Regiment. Thirteen days later, the 3rd Squadron joined the regiment. Crews for the 3rd Squadron, as well as replacements for the other two squadrons, came from the 118th Independent Reconnaissance Air Regiment (which flew seaplanes at that time) and the 35th Bomber Air Regiment of the Independent Naval Aviation Group. For some time, Captain Stoyanov was the interim regiment commander, but then his duties were taken over by Major Shipilov. Later, Lieutenant Colonel N.N. Vedmedenko arrived and he became the permanent regiment commander. The 35th Bomber Air Regiment departed for re-forming and left eight DB-3Fs, which were used to equip the 1st Squadron, whose personnel had already gained combat experience with such an aircraft. This led to ground crew 'shuffling', where mechanics of the 35th Bomber Air Regiment (who had a good knowledge of the DB-3Fs) joined the 1st Squadron, whereas specialists who had already mastered the Hampdens transferred from the 1st Squadron to the 3rd Squadron.

The first flights of Soviet crews in the British torpedo bombers began on 19 October, which was even before the 3rd Squadron was formed. Captain I.Y. Garbuz (shortly afterwards, 3rd Squadron Leader) was the first to fly a Hampden. He was followed by Captain Stoyanov, who was entrusted with the task to comprehensively test the unfamiliar aircraft. The mission was a hazardous one, and Stoyanov flew solo, so the pilot was ordered to bail out if necessary. At an altitude of 2,000m, the aircraft fell into a spin from the right turn, and the observers on the ground expected that Stoyanov would abandon the aircraft; however, the experienced pilot managed to pull the torpedo bomber out from the spin and landed safely. It turned out that the Hampden required very precise piloting, and was unforgiving when it came to even the slightest mistake made by the pilot. Moving the pedals abruptly at turns, or entering a turn at a high angle of roll was out of the question. The British aircraft lost approximately 40km/h to the Soviet-made DB-3F in terms of speed, as well as being considerably inferior in range (almost twice as) and having much poorer maneuverability. It is worth noting that the latter circumstance dramatically reduced the value of the aircraft in the role of a low-altitude torpedo bomber.

In the regiment, the Hampdens were dubbed *tarataikas*, which is Russian for a 'lightweight two-wheeled cart of simple design'. Another popular nickname was *balalaika* because of the peculiar shape of the aircraft in plain view, with a wide-at-the-root delta wing with a straight leading edge, narrow fuselage and a strange-looking twin-fin tail unit. Among the few advantages, pilots only mentioned the convenient and spacious cockpit, which had a good field of view.

Pilots of the regiment were given a month and a half to study the Hampdens and, by December, the aircraft were expected to enter service. To expedite the conversion training, the Northern Fleet workshops mounted a second set of controls in the navigator cabin on one of the torpedo bombers (spare parts from both the Kittyhawk and the DB-3F were used for this purpose). The instructor's arrangement in the navigator cabin proved to be uncomfortable, as his seat was too low, but then – at the expense of a certain reduction of the wing center section's main spar strength – the instructor's place was arranged behind the pilot's seat.

The mastering of an aircraft so demanding entailed certain losses (more so because the pilots could not wait to begin flying combat sorties), so two aircraft were damaged: one was destroyed and written off on 1 November 1942; then, almost two months later (on 21 December), another torpedo bomber suffered a severe crash during its first flight.

Lieutenant Colonel Vedmedenko never led his regiment in an attack, as he died in a crash. His post was taken over by Major F.V. Kostkin.

On 8 November, two Hampdens of the 24th Mine-and-Torpedo Air Regiment took off with a mission to conduct enemy ships reconnaissance, but came back without any results because of bad weather. The attempt to bomb Luostari airfield on the night of 14 December was a failure as well: the only Hampden which was sent to fly the sortie failed to find the target in thick clouds. Soviet pilots first dropped bombs from the British aircraft on the night of 15 December on Kirkenes port – and of the four aircraft, two released their bombs successfully. On 18 December, a pair of torpedo-carrying Hampdens first undertook a 'free hunt' sortie, and the 'hunt' ended in success: at the entry to the Tanafjord, Captain S.I. Trunov torpedoed a German transport of approximately 5,000t displacement. Until the end of December, the Hampdens kept flying combat sorties, but they were used, for the most part, as night bombers (their targets were German airfields and Kirkenes port). The raids on 29-30 December, which brought about fires in Kirkenes port, proved to be the most efficient: on 30 December, a direct bomb hit sent a transport vessel which was moored in the haven to the bottom.

In early January, the regiment began active operations against the enemy's sea communications (for the most part, using the 'free hunt' technique in pairs). On the very first day of the New Year (1943), the 24th Mine-and-Torpedo Air Regiment suffered the first combat losses and Captain Stoyanov's crew did not return from the combat sortie. Their comrades saw the aircraft take fire and fell into the sea (it is possible that the torpedo bomber was attacked by German fighters, which were escorting a convoy).

The first considerable success was achieved by the regiment's pilots in mid-January: on 14 January, crews led by Captain V.N. Kiselev and Captain A.A. Bashtyrkov torpedoed a convoy near the Norwegian Coast and they managed to sink two transport ships. Bashtyrkov's aircraft was set on fire while on the combat course, but he did not divert until the torpedo was released. The burning Hampden was subjected to point-blank anti-aircraft fire, and Bashtyrkov and his navigator – Sergeant V.N. Gavrilov – were posthumously awarded the title of Hero of the Soviet Union. It is not known whether the other two members of the crew (Master Sergeant Kuzmin and Red Navy seaman Shpuntov) were awarded any decorations.

On the following day, two more strikes were delivered on the same convoy: first, two Hampdens led by Captain S.I. Trunov and Senior Lieutenant P.N. Zaichenko secured two hits on transport vessels; then, a group led by Senior Lieutenant Agafonov (an Il-4, plus two Hampdens) hit a transport vessel and an escort ship. As a result, the convoy suffered severe losses. On 17 January, the People's Commissar of the Navy congratulated the regiment on their combat success.

The British aircraft flew reconnaissance and bombing sorties, hunted German transports and kept experiencing casualties in the course of tireless combat work. On 29 January 1943, the 24th Mine-and-Torpedo Air Regiment lost as many as three Hampdens. From among Captain Trunov's crew and Senior Lieutenant S.A. Malygin's crew, nobody survived, as their aircraft were hit by German anti-aircraft fire and fell into the sea. Captain A.I. Ostrovsky managed to reach the Rybachiy Peninsula and make a belly landing there. Allegedly, a German transport ship with a displacement of 12,000t was sunk on that day, so if this is the case, that was the biggest vessel ever sent to the bottom by the Hampdens. By 1 February, there remained 11 British aircraft in service with the 24th Mine-and-Torpedo Air Regiment.

In order to enhance the combat survivability of the Hampdens, they were equipped with an inert gas system. Cooled exhaust gases were filtered and fed into the fuel tanks and, as a result, fire hazards caused by penetration were reduced considerably. The modification proved to be quite practical: on frequent occasions, aircraft with perforated tanks safely returned to their home airfield, and the armament (which had been criticized by the British themselves) was made more powerful. For this purpose, the twin Vickers in the dorsal installation was replaced with the Soviet-made UBT large-caliber machine gun in an UTK-1 turret. The British installation was removed entirely, together with the circular guide. Taking into account the rough surface on Soviet airfields, the Navy Air Force workshops carried out a minor modification to reinforce the tail wheel retainer and lock.

In February and March, the Hampdens, for the most part, flew 'free hunt' sorties or conducted ice reconnaissance in the Barents Sea. The efficiency of the 'hunt' without the preliminary reconnaissance of enemy convoys was rather low and, on most sorties, enemy ships were simply not detected. The technical condition of the aircraft was also an influencing factor, as due to a shortage of spare parts, more than half of the aircraft lost their battle-worthiness.

From April 1943 (as has already been mentioned above), the 24th Mine-and-Torpedo Air Regiment was replenished with the American-made A-20 aircraft, and so the conversion of personnel for the new aircraft began; however, the Hampdens remained in service and continued to fly combat sorties.

In response to the growing losses, the Germans strengthened the air cover of their vessels, but on the other hand, the torpedo bombers began flying their sorties with the escort of Pe-3 two-engine fighters of the 95th Fighter Air Regiment, whose task was (inter alia) to neutralize the enemy anti-aircraft fire. With their insufficient maneuverability, the Hampdens (without the fighter cover) were easy prey for the German Bf 110 Zerstorers, which were escorting the convoys far from the coast – thus, on 10 April, the Pe-3s which were providing air cover happened to be left behind the torpedo bombers. The latter, on their way back, encountered four Messerschmitts and two of the five Soviet aircraft were shot down.

On 25 April 1943, Captain Kiselev repeated the feat of his comrade-in-arms Captain Bashtyrkov: Kiselev was leading five Hampdens to attack a convoy which had been detected by a reconnaissance aircraft near the coast. Three German fighters and a seaplane were covering 17 ships and merchant vessels, and seven Pe-3s engaged the German aircraft – forcing them aside. The torpedo bombers deployed into line formation and began the attack, with Kiselev choosing the lead transport. On the approach to the target, the left engine caught fire, but the attack continued. From a distance of 400m, the burning Hampden released the torpedo and the hit aircraft lost its maneuverability almost entirely, yet it kept flying straight at the transport. All of the anti-aircraft guns were focused on Kiselev's aircraft, but ablaze, the torpedo bomber fell at a distance of one kilometer from the sinking transport *Leesee.* The trail aircraft of Kiselev's party then managed to sink another transport and an escort ship, and Captain V.N. Kiselev – as well as his navigator, Senior Lieutenant M.F. Pokalo – were posthumously made Heroes of the Soviet Union. There is no information as to Master Sergeant Berdennikov and Sergeant Zhuchkov, who were killed together with them.

In April and May 1943, the A-20s and the Hampdens were used concurrently. Large losses of torpedo bombers impeded the decommissioning of the British aircraft (throughout April, the regiment lost seven A-20s) and, as of 1 May, the regiment had seven Hampdens; however, only one or two of them were airworthy. The others were grounded due to a lack of spark plugs for the Pegasus engines. The situation called for the adaptation of Soviet-made BG-22 spark plugs, but this brought about the need to modify the ignition system as well. The regiment also ran short of the British torpedoes, plus the Hampden's bomb bay was not fit to accommodate Soviet-made 45-36AN torpedoes, as they were more than a half-meter longer. To save the situation, modifications were made to the forward and aft bomb bay walls, and also to the bomb hatch doors in order to 'annex' part of the navigator's cabin. Such modifications were carried out jointly by the regiment's mechanics and by the Northern Fleet Air Force's aircraft repair shops.

In May 1943, the regiment was elevated to Guards status – becoming the 9th Guards Mine-and-Torpedo Air Regiment – and although the regiment's service was distinguished, the price to pay was high: by June, combat losses alone totaled 12 Hampdens. The surviving aircraft of this type were concentrated in the 3rd Squadron.

On 4 July 1943, two Hampdens, three Il-4s and two Il-2s attacked ships at Cape Kibergnes. The group was led by Regiment Commander F.V. Kostkin. The torpedo bombers sank an 8,000t transport and damaged two others; however, on the return leg, the unescorted attack aircraft and torpedo bombers (the escort P-39s had turned back half-way because of rain) were engaged by German fighters, but only the two Il-4s managed to evade. Crews of the ditched Hampdens, which were piloted by Major Shipilov and Junior Lieutenant Martynov, were rescued and that was the last combat sortie flown by the Hampdens on the Soviet-German Front.

By mid-July, there was only one Hampden left in the Northern Fleet – and furthermore, it was unserviceable. The 9th Guards Mine-and-Torpedo Air Regiment had, by that time, fully converted to the A-20s.

In England in late 1943, the Hampdens were first handed over to various auxiliary units (such as weather reconnaissance, training units etc.), and then, in spring 1944, they were scrapped.

In 1991, Hampden s/n P1344, which had, years before, force-landed en route to Russia and was then abandoned after the crash (the crew had been reported missing, and only the pilot had been taken prisoner by the Germans), was found in the Soviet territory, where it was then packed and taken to England for restoration.

Official photographs of the British torpedo bombers arriving at Vaenga airfield in 1943.

One of the British Hampdens in Vaenga before its handover to the Soviet side.

Captain A.Z. Stoyanov in the cockpit of the Hampden.

A crew of Captain S. Trunov's near the British bomber.

Captain A.Z. Stoyanov (on the right) and his crew prepare for the next mission.

A Hampden of the 24th Mine-and-Torpedo Air Regiment, Northern Fleet Air Force in flight.

The Hampdens of the 24th Mine-and-Torpedo Air Regiment being prepared for their next mission at Vaenga airfield.

The landing of a Hampden at Vaenga airfield.

A torpedo being towed on a skid to the Hampden; note the installation of a Soviet RPK-2 radio compass (a fairing of its aerial is on top of the fuselage) and an additional gun mount in the rear lower section of the aircraft.

A Hampden in flight above a gulf at a low altitude.

A technician writes the inscription 'For Kiselyov' on a torpedo being prepared for attachment to a Hampden of the 24th Mine-and-Torpedo Air Regiment, May 1943.

The same torpedo being pushed to the aircraft.

7.12 De Havilland Mosquito

No sooner had the Mosquito high-speed bomber appeared, it attracted close attention on the part of both Allies and enemies – and the Soviet Union was no exception.

The journey of the aircraft to mass production turned out to be a thorny one, so let us begin with the fact that the DH.98, which was designed under the supervision of R. Bishop, was made of wood. One might ask: "So what? In the USSR, a lot of wooden aircraft were built throughout the war," but that was a coerced choice, which was brought about by a shortage of aluminum and the unavailability of the required equipment. Typically, a wooden or mixed structure is heavier than a structure of equal strength, but made from light alloys. Furthermore, the 'lifespan' of the former is shorter. In damp conditions, wood is subject to rot, whereas a dry or hot environment causes cracking. In England, no wooden military aircraft had been built since the 1930s, so the intention to design a new wooden military aircraft was deemed to be absurd by British military men; however, Bishop's wooden design was different: the DH.98's skin was of a 'sandwich' type, and between two layers of Canadian birch, there were sheets of very light balsawood, which had been imported from Latin America. This made the airframe quite comparable to a metal one in terms of weight.

Second, the concept of a bomber without any defensive armament seemed a heresy in itself. The would-be Mosquito was intended to escape from fighters with the help of its high speed, altitude performance and maneuverability, rather than accept battle. A crew of only two men and the absence of cannons or machine guns made the aircraft a lightweight one, and a combination of excellent aerodynamic performance, the powerful Merlin engines and its low weight ensured (according to estimations) a high flight performance; however, the army men had no confidence in it. Given all of the above, the British Air Ministry tended to reject the project, but the De Havilland management supported the designers and it turned out to be the right decision!

In March 1940, the RAF ordered a prototype and 49 mass-manufactured aircraft under the name of 'Mosquito'. The prototype first flew on 25 November and it proved to be 30km/h faster than the Supermarine Spitfire fighter!

After the prototype's first flight, mass production of the aircraft was launched. Along with the high-speed bomber version, it was manufactured in the reconnaissance variant and also as a day or night heavy fighter.

Throughout the stay of the Soviet aviation delegation in Great Britain in August through to October 1941, a Mosquito in the high-speed aerial reconnaissance version was demonstrated to its members, and one of them – the famous test pilot Major General P.Y. Fedrovi – was even permitted to fly the aircraft. The delegation's report read: 'According to Comrade Fedrovi, the Mosquito aircraft features very good maneuverability, high enough to match our MiG aircraft [Author's note: here, the MiG-3 was meant]; but aileron control on the Mosquito is smoother and easier. Its take-off and landing performance is also similar to that of the MiG aircraft'.

The Soviet specialists were very impressed with the visit to the factory where the aircraft were manufactured, and the Mosquito turned out to be a unique combination of a wooden structure (which had been deemed obsolete) and a rather high flight performance.

In autumn 1942, the Soviet Union officially requested a Mosquito bomber for studying, and the British Government consented.

In July 1943, several crews from among the group of Soviet ferry pilots who were training in Scotland at the Errol air base were allocated to master the Mosquito. A Mosquito T.III with dual controls was sent to Errol for training purposes on 22 June; however, it crashed during ferrying. A substitute T.III arrived on 27 July, together with instructor pilot Raner, who was delegated from No.60 OTU.

By 9 August, Senior Lieutenant I.D. Polosukhin (formerly a squadron leader with the 1st Transport Air Division) had, together with his navigator Lieutenant Kekishev, completed the conversion training course. In September, an aircraft which was actually intended for ferrying was delivered to Errol, and that was a Mosquito B.IV s/n DK296 with the Merlin 21 engines. Manufactured in 1942, it had already seen combat service with RAF No.105 Squadron, where it had flown 15 combat sorties. During the last sortie, the aircraft suffered certain combat damage and was repaired by No.10 Maintenance (Aircraft Storage) Unit. Most probably, it was there that the aircraft was prepared for ferrying to the USSR. An additional 550L fuel tank was mounted in the bomb bay, and the bomb racks and bomb hatch door controls were removed.

Polosukhin and Kekishev studied the aircraft thoroughly to make themselves familiar with its peculiarities. By 3 October, the crew had got ready to depart for Moscow, and the aircraft was expected to fly the same route as the Albemarles. On 24 October, the aircraft had already been at the starting point when an oxygen system tube burst, and so the flight was postponed. Throughout the entire month of November, the bomber remained grounded at the airfield by reason of unfavorable weather forecasts. On 9 December, an order to depart was received; however, at midnight, a telephone message came from Moscow to the effect that the weather in the vicinity of the Soviet capital was extremely poor and that the flight should be canceled. After that, long months of waiting followed. Polosukhin and Kekishev (from time to time) flew either the B.IV or the T.III trainer, and they performed 25-minute to one-hour flights – including a night flight on 18 January 1944.

On 13 April 1944, the long-expected order to depart for the Soviet Union was finally received; this time, however, the weather took a turn for the worse in Scotland. After consultation with the British weather service, the flight was canceled again. On 16 April, the Soviet pilots performed another training flight in the bomber version; then, on the night of 18 April, the Mosquito finally departed for Moscow. The aircraft flew over the North Sea, Sweden, the Baltic Sea and the territories occupied by the Germans. Early in the morning, it landed on Vnukovo airfield, near Moscow.

The aircraft's stay in Vnukovo was short, as it did not fly there. By 25 April, it had been transferred to LII, where flight testing began, with V.S. Pankratov as the leading engineer and N.S. Rybko as the pilot. Throughout the testing, the performance data as specified by the manufacturer was confirmed: with a take-off weight of 8,850kg, the aircraft reached a speed of 580km/h (at the 'five-minute' engine operating mode) and, according to estimates by the Soviet specialists, this figure had become 10km/h lower than the initial figure due to aircraft wear. On the other hand, the speed capabilities of the Soviet prototype bombers had already exceeded 600km/h by that time. During flight testing, the Tupolev Tu-2 SDB demonstrated 633km/h, while the Petlyakov Pe-2I demonstrated 644km/h; however, the Mosquito as provided by the British was not a latest-version aircraft. By that time, British factories had already mastered the manufacture of aircraft with two-stage supercharged engines, and the high-altitude performance of such aircraft was much higher.

The controllability of this British aircraft was met with approval – in particular, the Mosquito could easily fly with one engine inoperative, as well as being able to perform (inter alia) deep banked turns in the direction of the shutdown engine.

Stability, on the other hand, was deemed to be insufficient in all aspects, so the aircraft required the pilot to have a rather high level of skill. It is worthy of special mention that in spite of the general simplicity of its landing, the Mosquito demonstrated an insistent tendency to turn to the left at the landing run. This was noted by all of the pilots who took part in the testing (apart from Rybko, Major General P.Y. Fedrovi and Major General A.I. Kabanov, who were delegated from NII VVS, were also involved in the flights). On the other hand, M.L. Gallay, in turn, expressed an opinion that such a tendency was not intrinsic to the aircraft type in question, but that it was a consequence of the imperfect repair of the tail wheel strut, which had been installed askew.

In his report, Rybko wrote: 'In terms of controllability, the Mosquito IV is very much alike the Pe-2. However, due to longitudinal instability, lower elevator and rudder loads, and a greater tendency to the left turn, it imposes heavier demands on the pilot than the Pe-2 does'.

The navigator cabin of the British aircraft was fitted with all of the required instruments, which were conveniently arranged, but the cabin itself was deemed to be somewhat incapacious – and the limited (in comparison to the Pe-2 and Tu-2) downward view was also criticized.

The Mosquito was thoroughly studied by specialists at LII, NII VVS, TsAGI and the aviation factories. Its design included a lot of features which were of extreme interest to the specialists: feathering propellers (at that time, such propellers were not installed on mass-manufactured Soviet bombers); certain power plant components; the cockpit heating system; the state-of-the-art, small-sized instruments; and flame dampers on the exhaust pipes. Unlike Soviet-made aircraft, all wooden parts were treated with an antiseptic agent on the inside to prevent rot.

In terms of ease of operation, the Mosquito went beyond praise. A lot of paper was spent on reports which described the perfect interchangeability of parts and assemblies, as well as the easy access to all of the principal components and the promptness of their replacement in case of failure. A lot of automatic devices facilitated the crew's work in flight.

On 15 May, pilot Kabanov and navigator P.I. Perevalov were ferrying the Mosquito to NII VVS airfield, where the testing was intended to be continued; however, the pilot failed to control the aircraft properly at landing. The bomber turned left and off the runway to the ground, broke its landing gear and then crawled further on its belly. The crew members were not injured, but the aircraft was damaged beyond repair and was never restored.

The thorough study of the Mosquito's design was carried out in order to check the possibility of license-manufacturing the aircraft in the USSR, and the question was raised as early as 21 April 1944 (i.e. almost immediately after the arrival of the aircraft in the Soviet Union). In terms of flight performance, the British bomber was somewhat superior to the Soviet-made Pe-2 and Tu-2 (especially at high altitude). Just the same as many Soviet aircraft, it had an all-wood airframe, which was an advantage because wood structure manufacturing techniques had, by that time, become well established at Soviet factories; however, in the opinion of TsAGI specialists, the aircraft's design and aerodynamics as it stood did not demonstrate anything conceptually new; everything had already been known for some time. The high performance was, first and foremost, due to careful manufacturing; the use of the light and strong sandwich-skin structure with the balsawood filling; and the excellent Merlin engines. The latter two circumstances were downright damning as regards the idea of manufacturing the Mosquito in the USSR.

It was not possible to ensure a large quantity of imported balsawood, nor were there any substitutes for it among the Soviet types of wood (the only considered alternative was to use an ordinary monocoque made of birch plywood). As for the engines, the Packard Motor Car Company from the USA had already had a deplorable experience with the buying of the license for the Merlin from the British. The Merlin engines were composed of parts which were manufactured with a high level of accuracy, and which were assembled and adjusted with meticulousness. The Americans, who possessed much larger resources in terms of equipment, tools and machinery, faced the need to bring over not only engineers, but also some workers from England – and it was not until then that they managed to ensure the proper level of quality. The manufacture of the Merlins in the USSR was also deemed to be impossible, and as for the engines that were imported from Great Britain, their quantities were hardly sufficient to replace those worn on the Hurricanes and the Spitfires – taking into account the fact that they steadily failed to reach the assigned lifespan.

Soviet specialists had much interest in the later Mosquito versions, with the Merlin 61 and 72; however, the Americans never provided any example of those, in spite of the fact that the question of the handover of such bombers was raised more than once (beginning from August 1943). The Soviet Union requested that such aircraft be included in Lend-Lease Protocol III, and the Resolution of the State Defense Committee of 22 May 1944 prescribed that the Mosquitoes of the latest eight versions (bombers, day fighters, night fighters and reconnaissance aircraft) should be purchased from Great Britain. Furthermore, People's Commissar of Aviation Industry A.I. Shakhurin demanded that the People's Commissariat of Foreign Trade should insist on the handover of the aircraft in a complete configuration (i.e. with the entire set of radio equipment – including radars, automatic direction finders and radar transponders; state-of-the-art aiming sights; photographic cameras; and armament). There was also an intention to receive five sets of British bombs of various types per bomber, but of course, nothing of the above was ever provided.

During the same period, there were attempts to arrange for the shipment of Mosquitoes from Canada, where a manufacturing subsidiary of De Havilland was located. The intention was to receive (beginning from July 1943) 50-100 bombers per month from the said subsidiary. At first, the Canadians agreed, but later the answer became negative, with the probable reason for this being that British and American orders were given priority.

In suggestions for Protocol IV (for 1944-1945), the Soviet party requested as many as 1,200 Mosquitoes, but this was vetoed by the British Air Ministry, which invoked an insufficient saturation of the RAF with new bombers as a reason for the veto.

The only Mosquito which happened to reach the USSR was disassembled after the crash, and the separate assemblies were handed over to various institutions for studying; however, the impact of familiarization with this aircraft on the Soviet aviation industry was considerable. The concept of a high-speed bomber without any defensive armament became very popular, and prototypes developed by V.M. Myasishchev and A.N. Tupolev (which had nothing in common with their British predecessor in terms of design) were advertised as 'Soviet Mosquitoes'.

The only Soviet Mosquito before its departure from Scotland.

The Mosquito B.IV during tests at LII.

The Mosquito after crash landing at the airfield of NII VVS on 15 May 1944.

7.13 Consolidated PBY Catalina

During the second half of the war, the Soviet hydroaviation was experiencing a severe crisis. As of 22 June 1941, the naval forces had 859 hydroplanes in service; by 1 June 1944, 588 of them had been lost. The three Western Fronts suffered the greatest damage – thus, in January 1944, there were 15 serviceable flying boats in operation at the Black Sea, whereas at the Baltic Sea, there were none. There were almost no replacements from the industry for the severe losses of the first years of the war and, throughout the entire war, the Soviet factories only built thirty-nine Che-2 and KOR-2 (Be-4) aircraft. The other 141 aircraft (for the most part, the MBR-2s) came from aviation schools and from the civil aviation.

The hydroaviation fleet lagged behind the dictates of the time in terms of quality as well. The MBR-2s, with their low speed, poor armament and insufficient range of operation and bomb load, constituted the overwhelming majority. The manufacture of the MDR-6 (Che-2) two-engine aircraft was discontinued, but the small single-engine KOR-2 (Be-4) continued to be built; however, it had been developed as a catapult-launched reconnaissance aircraft to be operated from large warships – rendering it unfit for a lot of roles. Also, the number of two-engine seaplanes in Soviet service was extremely low.

At the same time, the assumption of the strategic offensive by the Soviet Army led to an increase in the navy's demand for modern seaplanes which would be capable of successfully dealing with anti-submarine defense; long-range reconnaissance; rescue operations; and assault landings. For want of the possibility to provide the hydroaviation with Soviet-made aircraft, an appropriate request was addressed to the Allies; however, before 1944, neither Great Britain nor the USA shipped any seaplanes to Soviet Russia.

The already familiar Consolidated Model 28 flying boat became the only candidate for shipments to the USSR. The aircraft was more widely known under the name 'Catalina', which was given to it by the British. It was, essentially, a big two-engine all-metal strut-braced monoplane, and it attracted the attention of Soviet specialists almost immediately upon its adoption by the US Navy.

In March 1936, they described the Catalina as follows: "The aircraft is currently the best two-engine long-range aircraft." In essence, this was true: the advanced design; state-of-the-art manufacturing techniques; sufficiently powerful (for that time) armament; and excellent flight performance spoke very much in favor of the flying boat. In the same month, on the initiative of Head of Chief Administration of Aviation Industry M.M. Kaganovich, it was included in the list of aircraft examples to be purchased for familiarization purposes. Kaganovich suggested that the aircraft should be reverse-engineered and put into unlicensed production at Factory No.126 in Komsomolsk-on-Amur; however, Air Force Commander Y.I. Alksnis insisted on entering into a technical assistance agreement with the Americans, as this would considerably expedite launching the manufacture of the aircraft.

On 5 October 1937, the Council for Trade and Defense issued a Resolution on purchasing the license. On 9 January, the Amtorg Corporation signed a contract for the granting of a license for the cargo-passenger flying boat with Consolidated Aircraft, and a special version – designated Model 28-2 – was designed for the USSR on the base of the military PBY-1 boat; production was mastered by Factory No.31 in Taganrog. The aircraft were built under the designation GST in both civil and military versions, with the original Soviet armament. Because of process difficulties, less than 30 flying boats were assembled and their manufacture was discontinued in 1940. The aircraft were operated by the Northern Fleet's aviation; the Black Sea Fleet's aviation; and by crews of the Polar Aviation Department of GUSMP in the Arctic region. Apart from the Soviet-built aircraft, the Polar Aviation operated an American-made disarmed PBY-1. It was purchased in August 1937 from the American Natural History Museum, and was to be used in the search for S.A. Levanevsky's lost crew.

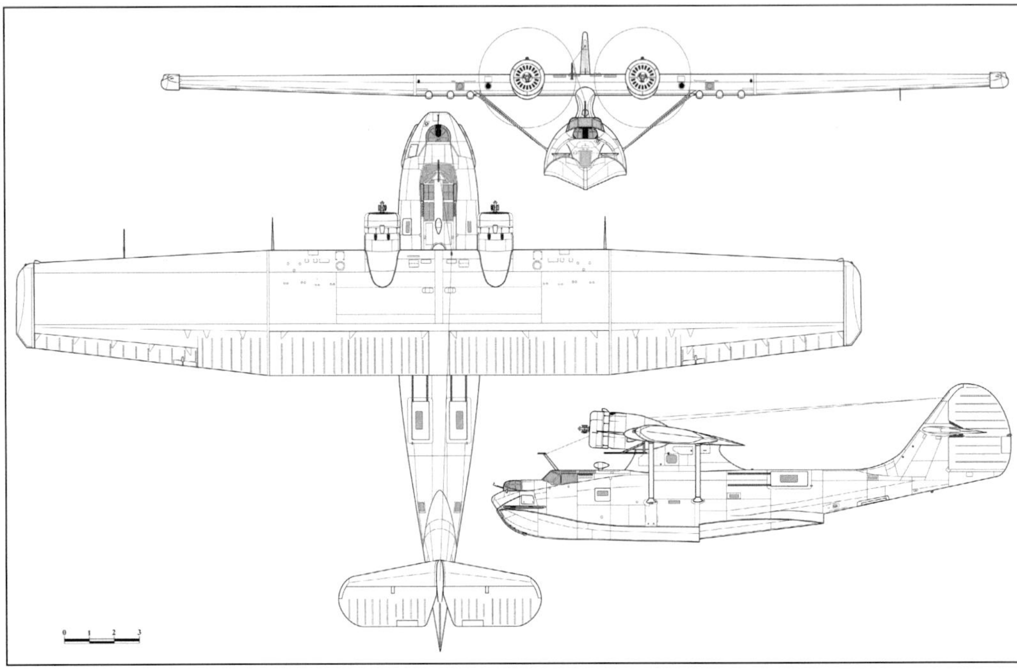

GST

Three-view of the GST flying boat, in the military version.

The GSTs (in increasingly diminishing quantities) served throughout the war, and although they were the best flying boats in service with the Soviet naval aviation, they were too few in numbers.

On the other hand, the RAF Catalinas appeared in the Russian skies repeatedly throughout the war. On 28 July 1941, one of them brought H. Hopkins (a representative of the US President) to the mouth of the Northern Dvina. In August 1942, flying boats of RAF No.422 Squadron began regular flights from Ingverdon in Scotland to Russia – carrying spare parts for the Hurricanes until the movement of Arctic convoys was resumed. In September the same year, as part of the protection for PQ 18 Convoy, ten Catalinas of RAF No.210 Squadron were arranged on Lake Krasnoe to patrol areas which were inaccessible for the MBR-2s.

The first attempt to receive the Catalinas for the Soviet Navy was made in 1942. People's Commissar of the Navy Admiral N.G. Kuznetsov twice (on 6 February and on 14 April) reported in writing to I.V. Stalin on the necessity to obtain sixty PBY-5A amphibious aircraft from the Americans (in the documents referred to as 'flying boats', for the needs of the Northern Fleet and, to a lesser extent, the Pacific Fleet). On 17 June, Stalin agreed with Kuznetsov during a face-to-face meeting, and afterwards, Kuznetsov wrote a letter to A.I. Mikoyan requesting to insist on the shipment of the aircraft by no later than March 1943. It was intended that the aircraft should be ferried across Alaska.

After the Liberation of Taganrog from the Germans, the already mentioned Admiral Kuznetsov put forward a proposal to the Central Committee of the All-Union Communist (Bolshevik) Party that seaplane manufacture should be resumed at the local aircraft factory. With the assistance of Consolidated Aircraft, the production of the modern Catalina version could be launched and it was intended that the equipment for the ruined factory should come under Lend-Lease. Restoration of the factory was commenced, but in October 1944, the

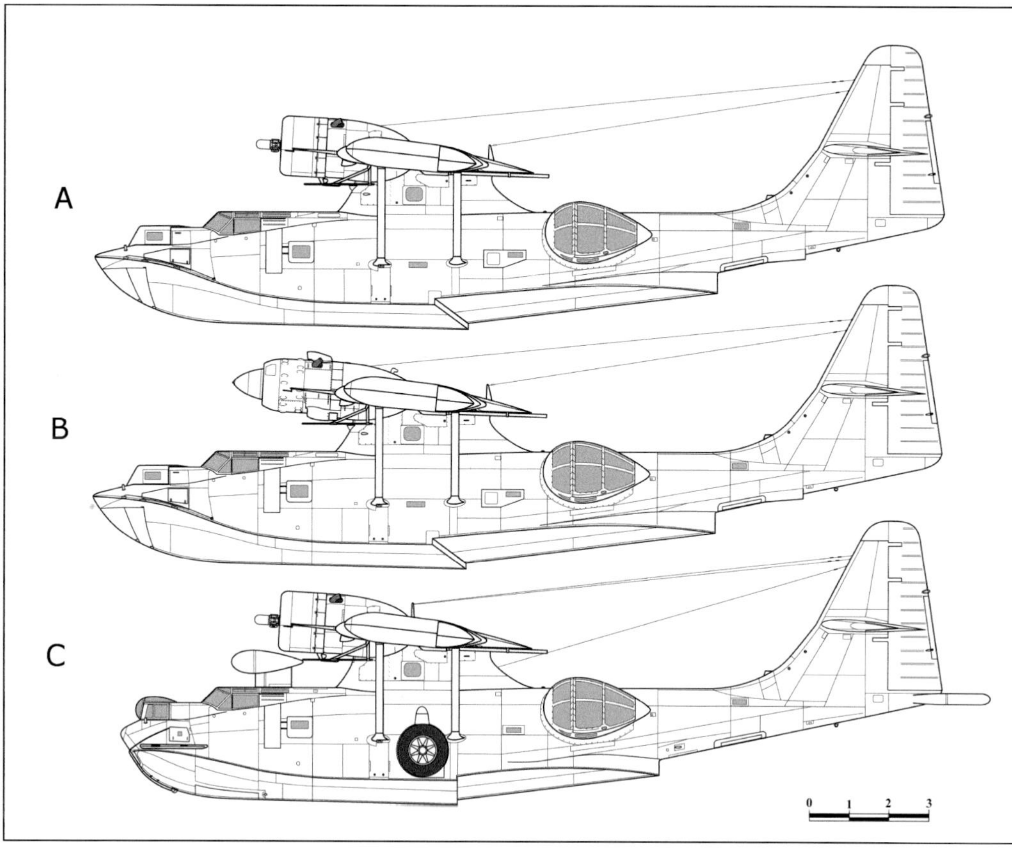

Catalina

A KM-1 flying boat.
B KM-2 flying boat.
C PBY-6A, with the *Chita* magnetometer.

decision was changed in favor of the more promising (in terms of flight performance) Beriev LL-143 (the future Be-6); however, the attempts to receive seaplanes from the USA continued. The versions which were manufactured in 1943-1944 were considerably different from the GST prototype: engines became more powerful; the armament was enhanced; the sliding side hatches were replaced by bubble-shaped blisters; and the equipment was considerably improved. For a long time, the PBY-5 and its amphibious version (the PBY-5A) were the prevailing designs. In February 1943, the Naval Aircraft Factory (NAF) in Philadelphia began building the PBN-1 Nomad, which was different from other versions, first and foremost, by the hull bottom shape. The nose was made longer and more tapered, and the louvers, which had covered the bombardier's sighting window, were replaced with hinged doors. The first step became slanted, and the second step was relocated more than a meter to the rear, with the third one installed behind it. The shape of the wing floats was changed and, as a result of all of these modifications, the flying boat's seaworthiness and take-off/landing performance became considerably better. The new tail unit helped to solve the problems with directional stability, and it was this configuration of the seaplane that was finally offered by the Americans to the USSR. Eventually, almost all of the flying boats of this version went to the Soviet Union.

For the first time, the Allies' undertakings to provide flying boats were reflected in Lend-Lease Protocol IV and, sometime later, another 50 seaplanes were included in Annex III, which covered shipments for military hostilities in the Pacific. For the same purposes, the Soviet Government requested a further 80 aircraft on 28 May 1944, and this request was also satisfied.

To ferry the aircraft from the USA, a special aviation group under the command of Colonel V.N. Vasilyev was formed in early 1944, which consisted of 10 crews from the Northern Fleet, 10 crews from the Pacific Fleet and six crews from the Black Sea Fleet. Before being sent to the USA, the pilots were trained in seaplanes because many of them (due to a shortage of hydroaviation materiel) had been flying land-based aircraft and had lost their specific skills to a certain extent.

It was intended that the handover/acceptance of the flying boats should take place at the Elizabeth City naval base near New Orleans. The Pacific Fleet pilots were the first to arrive at their destination via the ALSIB route, and they appeared in Elizabeth City on 2 April. Twenty-five PBN-1s which were ready for handover had already been waiting for them there. A special training squadron led by Lieutenant Harper was formed to carry out the conversion training of the Soviet crews, and specialists delegated by NAF (among them, factory test pilot Captain Steward) also took part in the training.

Since the PBN-1 saw almost no service in the USA, the training began with the joint testing of the aircraft with various load configurations; the Soviet Union in the testing was represented by N.F. Piskaryov.

The first group completed the training in 20 days and, in the end, each crew performed two six-hour flights over the Atlantic to train radio and navigation equipment procedures. The Pacific Fleet pilots acted as instructors for the rest of the crews, which came a month later by sea from Murmansk.

The first party of the aircraft was to fly to the north in order to join the Northern Fleet's aviation and the White Sea Flotilla. The flying boats were grouped into six squads, with four aircraft in each squad. The last (25th) flying boat took command, and since the crews had little experience in long-duration flights, they had to resort to seeking the Allies' help. The assistants were not the Americans, but the British: two British aviators (a pilot and a radio operator) joined each crew, and Piskaryov wrote in his report: '... Each of the assigned ... British pilots held a rank of at least Captain. They had vast experience in long-duration flights. Some of them have crossed the ocean up to 53 times...'

The aircraft flew the route from Elizabeth City to Murmansk via Gander Lake and Reykjavik. In spite of the elaborate training, some incidents occurred: at the approach to Iceland, the seaplanes suffered severe icing, which led to damage to the antennas. In Reykjavik, the Soviet pilots said goodbye to their British colleagues, as they were expected to fly the final segment unassisted. On 4 June 1944, the first four PBN-1s landed on Gryaznaya Bay, but one of the aircraft ran short of alcohol in its anti-icing system tanks before the end of the flight, so reluctantly, the crew refilled them with whisky and rum, which were included in the ration for the flight.

On the third day after landing, the rested ferry pilots performed a flight together with Piloting Inspector of the Northern Fleet Air Force Major Makarov. Three of the first four flying boats were then ferried to Lakhta to join the White Sea Flotilla and, on the same day, Regiment Commander S.M. Ruban's crew departed in the fourth PBN-1.

By 16 June, 24 flying boats out of the initial 25 had arrived in the Soviet Union, but a Nomad piloted by Lieutenant Colonel N.V. Romanov (with V.N. Vasilyev and lead navigator Mostsepan) turned out to be missing. Until 28 June, both Soviet and British aircraft were searching for the missing PBN-1, but without success. After the death of Vasilyev, Colonel M.N. Chibisov took over command of the group, with N.F. Piskaryov in charge of the ferrying operation.

The second party of the PBN-1s was to join the Pacific Fleet. From Elizabeth City, one could only reach Alaska from a long way around, which was via the Panama Canal Zone. The Americans did not let the Soviet pilots fly such a route, and instead ferried the flying boats to Kodiak Island themselves. For this reason, the acceptance was carried out twice (both in Elizabeth City and again on Kodiak Island). On 20 August, all of the PBN-1s were ready to depart for Chukotka and, on 25 August, the first flying boat headed for Anadyr. By the evening of 27 August, eight Nomads had arrived there, but this time the ferrying was done in accordance with a different pattern. Piskaryov's group delivered the aircraft to Magadan, where they were then taken over by crews allocated from the Pacific Fleet Air Force regiments; then they flew the PBN-1s to Vladivostok. This procedure was used for all of the aircraft except for the first four, which were brought to the Sukhodol seaplane base by mixed crews of Piskaryov's men and the Pacific Fleet pilots. These first flying boats came to Sukhodol on 4 September.

On 27 September, the entire ferrying group gathered again in Elizabeth City, with the mission to deliver the third party of the PBN-1s (for the Black Sea Fleet and for the Baltic Fleet) to the Soviet Union. This time, they had to go the longest way: Elizabeth City — San Juan (Puerto Rico) — Port of Spain (Trinidad) — Belem (Brazil) — Natal (Brazil) — Bathurst (Gambia) — Port Lyautey (Morocco) — Djerba Island (Tunisia) — Habbaniya (Iraq) — Baku — Sevastopol. The British assigned a pilot, a navigator/second radio operator and an engineer per aircraft to accompany the Soviet crews until they reach Habbania.

En route over Puerto Rico, Piskaryov's aircraft encountered a severe storm. A gust of wind made the aircraft literally stand on its tail, but the pilot managed to save the machine. On 28 October, the first PBN-1 arrived in Sevastopol, and four Nomads for the Polar Aviation came via the same route, with I.P. Mazuruk in charge of the ferrying.

Almost immediately upon arrival at the air units, the seaplanes became involved in combat operations, and the stable and 'attentive' aircraft was easily and quickly mastered by the crews. For want of hydroaviation pilots, those who had flown only wheeled aircraft before were also converted to the Nomads, but of course, there were some losses – thus, on 19 June 1944, one of the Northern Fleet flying boats crashed during a training flight; on the whole, however, the mastering of the new aircraft progressed rather smoothly. It is noteworthy that being familiar with the GST gave almost no advantages, since the PBN-1 was very different from its remote 'ancestor' in terms of behavior in flight.

In the Northern Fleet, the American flying boats were provided to the 118th Independent Reconnaissance Air Regiment (as of 1 September 1944, it had eight PBN-1s at its disposal), while in the White Sea Flotilla Air Force, the 44th Combined Air Regiment; the 53rd Combined Air Regiment; the 54th Combined Air Regiment; and the 20th Independent Naval Reconnaissance Air Squadron received several flying boats each. The aircraft flew anti-submarine patrolling and ice reconnaissance sorties. Some of the PBN-1s that came from the USA were equipped with radars, which considerably enhanced their search efficiency. In the Soviet Union, the flying boats were armed with 100kg PLAB-100 parachute-dropped anti-submarine bombs.

Almost all of the aircraft types in service with the naval aviation (Il-4s, MBR-2s, Bostons, Kittyhawks, Pe-3s, Il-2s etc.) were tried out in anti-submarine warfare during the Great Patriotic War, and all of them proved to be unsatisfactory for various reasons: some aircraft offered a poor view, while others flew with too high a speed (which resulted in damage to the PLAB-100s' parachutes), and yet others had an insufficient range. The PBN-1 turned out to be the only aircraft which was suitable in every aspect, and its numerous crew members enjoyed a good view. The aircraft had a sufficiently wide range of operating speeds, a powerful armament and a strong airframe, plus it was capable of landing (when necessary) in the open sea; finally, its equipment was superior to its Soviet counterpart.

The patrolling efficiency changed accordingly. The MBR-2s of the Northern Fleet flew 170 sorties per a detected submarine, whereas the PBN-1s only had to fly 40. Furthermore, the new seaplanes were capable of surveying the areas which the MBR-2s simply could not reach.

On 12 August, aircraft piloted by M.I. Kozlov (of the Polar Aviation) and S.M. Ruban encountered a German submarine near Bely Island. Ruban, whose aircraft was not carrying any bombs, initiated a fire duel. He machine gunned the submarine, but the latter responded with gunfire, so crews led by V.A. Gurichev and S.V. Sokol came to help their comrades-in-arms. The submarine submerged, but was attacked with depth bombs. Eventually, an oil spot spread over the water surface – and that was the first successful attack by the Soviet Nomads.

On 5 September, a flying boat, a T-116 minesweeper and a BO-206 chaser (in a joint effort) sank a U-362 near Sergei Kirov Island. On 24 October, in the same manner – and during the passage of Convoy DB-9 – pilots of the White Sea Flotilla Air Force (an MBR-2 and a PBN-1), together with the already mentioned T-116 and a BO-209 chaser, sent another enemy to the bottom. In April 1945, a Nomad of the 118th Independent Reconnaissance Air Regiment (during the course of escorting a convoy) destroyed without any assistance a U-boat by hitting it with depth bombs. As of 1 January 1945, the Northern Fleet had seven PBN-1s in the 118th Air Regiment, while another 18 American flying boats were in service with the 44th, 53rd and 54th Combined Air Regiments and the 20th Independent Naval Reconnaissance Air Squadron of the White Sea Flotilla Air Force. The Northern Fleet pilots continued to search for U-boats long after the victory over Germany and, in total, PBN-1 crews of the Northern Fleet and the White Sea Flotilla made 340 anti-submarine sorties.

In the Baltic Sea, the first PBN-1 appeared in August 1944 (it was one of the aircraft that came via the northern route) and, soon after, another one joined it. The American flying boats were handed over to the 29th Independent Anti-Submarine Air Squadron, which had, until that time, been equipped with a mixture of Il-2s and Be-4s; finally, the number of the Nomads in the squadron had reached six. The role of the PBN-1s in the squadron was the same as everywhere else, and consisted of submarine hunting, as well as rescue operations and searching for pilots from aircraft that were shot down above the sea. The seaplanes provided air cover in all of the major raids on German ports, but in March, the squadron was disbanded. Consequently, three new squadrons (the 15th, the 16th and the 17th) which only flew the PBN-1s (in total, 11 aircraft) were formed. On 22 April 1945, a flying boat saved the pilot of a torpedo bomber which was shot down east of Hela beacon.

In the Black Sea Fleet, the 18th Air Squadron was the first to master the Nomads in June 1944, with the first combat sortie being made on 7 July. Crews led by pilots Koval and Kakaurov set out on a reconnaissance flight, and the squadron was split into two groups, which were stationed in Odessa and Sevastopol. Their principal missions consisted of long-range naval reconnaissance, as well as anti-submarine patrolling and rescue operations – thus, on 19 August, Captain Koval landed on water during a moderate storm and rescued the pilot of a shot-down fighter; on the same day, Captain Kakaurov picked up another pilot. On 20 August, Major Melnikov rescued the entire crew of Lieutenant Ogorodnikov's Pe-2, while Captain Knyazev picked up the crew of another Pe-2 (piloted by Lieutenant Chelenko) and, during the same mission, shot down a fighter which had attacked his flying boat. On the following day, Kakaurov himself engaged an enemy seaplane and hit it, with the escort fighters shooting the seaplane down. One of the German airplane's crew members was rescued from the water by Captain Sedov's Nomad.

Afterwards, the PBN-1s were provided to the 11th and 82nd Air Squadrons, but the war in the Black Sea was already nearing its end. On 29 August 1944, Captain Knyazev landed in the port of Constantsa with a group led by Major General M.D. Zhelanov, which was to make the arrangements for the handover of the former Allies' property by the Romanians; on the same day, Knyazev brought parliamentaries to Sulin. On 8 September, the flying boats brought the assault troops to Varna; a PBN-1 and a GST disembarked 60 men of the 393rd Marines Battalion. The landing operation in Burgas was even greater, with five flying boats bringing 92 Marines of the 384th Battalion from Constantsa. After the loss of bases in Bulgaria and Romania, the German fleet almost terminated its actions within this basin, but nevertheless, the Black Sea Fleet aviators can boast of an impressive combat episode. Lieutenant Panichkin managed to disable, by a single bomb strike, two Kriegsmarine submarines, whose crews then yielded themselves as prisoners.

In total, before 9 May 1945, the three Western fleets received one-hundred-and-seven PBN-1s, which constituted 73 percent of their total hydroaviation. No aircraft was shot down by the enemy; however, nine machines are considered lost due to non-combat reasons.

In summer 1945, the ferrying of PBY-6A amphibians from the USA began. This version was manufactured by the factory in New Orleans and, in terms of instruments, the latest Catalina modification was superior to all of the preceding models. Fifteen aircraft were ferried from Kodiak Island, while the other 33 were accepted in Elizabeth City. At first, the pilots were unaccustomed to landing at ground airfields on a flying boat (moreover, with a tricycle landing gear), but later, they mastered the technique. In terms of behavior in mid-air, the PBY-6A was barely different from the 'pure' flying boats; the only thing was that it responded in a more inert manner to the rudder and the elevator, which was due to a greater weight. The amphibians never entered action in the West; however, they did see some combat service in the east.

As of 1 January 1945, the Pacific Fleet had twenty-eight PBN-1s and, by 9 August (the date when the Soviet Union began military operations against Japan), 49 flying boats and 21 amphibians (31 percent of the navy's hydroaviation) had already been adopted by the fleet. The 16th Independent Reconnaissance Air Regiment fully converted to the new aircraft (the regiment had both PBN-1s and PBY-6As in service), while the 48th and the 117th Independent Reconnaissance Air Regiments had just begun their conversion, and so were still flying the obsolete MBR-2s. Their conversion was completed during the course of combat activities.

The 16th Air Regiment, which was reinforced with 10 aircraft of the 117th Air Regiment and three aircraft of the Independent Weather Reconnaissance Unit, was assigned the mission of carrying out reconnaissance in the Sea of Japan. The 117th and the 48th Air Regiments were tasked with performing short-range reconnaissance in the Sea of Okhotsk; the Strait of Tartary; and the Gulf of Sakhalin. Long-range reconnaissance sorties were not actually flown, since the boundary between the operating zones of the Soviet Navy and the American Navy lay some 15-120 miles from the shore.

Flying boats entered the action during the very first days of warfare in the Pacific theater of operations. The PBN-1s of the 16th Independent Reconnaissance Air Regiment, together with torpedo boats, provided cover for Bomber Air Regiment pilots in their raids on Yuki and Rasin on the night of 8 August. Reconnaissance in the open sea yielded almost no results (due to the fact that the Japanese Navy spent all of their efforts fighting the Americans), except for a single occasion when a group of enemy ships appeared near the route of the Soviet landing party going to Seishin. The seaplanes kept watch on the Japanese ships until they returned to their ports.

In the Far East, the PBN-1s and PBY-6As were widely used for landing operations. On 21 August, two PBY-6As of the 16th Air Regiment brought 32 riflemen directly to the runway of Gensan airfield and, on 24 August, Port Arthur and Dairen landing operations followed. In the former case, 10 aircraft delivered 135 Marines, while in the latter, 90 men arrived by seven flying boats. Both in Port Arthur and Dairen, the aircraft landed on water. The Port Arthur landing party was led by Lieutenant General E.N. Preobrazhensky, who came in one of the aircraft.

Small landing parties were delivered by amphibians during the seizure of the southern part of Sakhalin and the Kuril Islands. A party that was brought by a PBY-6A of the 48th Air Regiment managed to take control of Kontoro airfield on Sakhalin and prevented it from being destroyed by the Japanese. A similar operation was prepared to be carried out in Toro; however, the swift advance of the troops rendered it unnecessary. On 27 August, amphibians piloted by A.F. Dvoryansky and P.I. Ivashin landed on one of the airfields on Iturup and disembarked a team of riflemen under the cover of aircraft machine guns.

The 16th Air Regiment, which made the largest contribution to the Far East campaign, flew 74 reconnaissance sorties, 10 ship escort sorties and 100 landing and cargo-carrying sorties during the time of military operations. Throughout the entire Far East campaign, the fleet only lost one PBN-1, which did not return from a patrolling sortie; the causes of its disappearance remain unknown.

The American flying boats put the finishing touch on the campaign by delivering (to the Tokyo Bay) a Soviet mission led by Lieutenant General K.N. Derevyanko, who signed the Act of Capitulation of Japan on behalf of the Soviet Union while on board USS *Missouri*.

With the defeat of the last of the Axis powers, the Lend-Lease Act was also terminated. Shipments of armaments and military materiel from the USA to the Soviet Union came to an end. In total, one-hundred-and-thirty-seven PBN-1s and forty-eight PBY-6As were shipped to the USSR from America, although it is also possible that several PBY-5As could have been in service with the Soviet Air Force. According to some sources, these (already not new) amphibians were handed over to the Soviet party at the Vancouver Island base in 1944; photos of a PBY-5A with a red star insignia can be deemed an indirect proof of that.

Of course, not all such aircraft joined the Navy Air Force. As has already been mentioned, four PBN-1s were accepted and ferried by the Polar Aviation using its own resources. Before 9 May 1945, 11 flying boats were handed over to various organizations, and this process was expedited in the course of the post-war armed force reduction – thus, for example, in autumn 1945, the Nomads were placed in service with the coast guard aviation. One of the aircraft was in operation with the 7th Independent Air Regiment in Khabarovsk.

After the end of the war, none of the flying boats were returned to the USA, as the American aircraft were used to fully modernize the Soviet hydroaviation. The old MBR-2s and Che-2s were scrapped and substituted for by the Nomads and Catalinas – thus, in the north, the 53rd Independent Reconnaissance Air Regiment was formed after the war (in September 1945), which was fully equipped with the PBN-1s. A year later, the 69th Independent Reconnaissance Air Regiment was raised in the Baltic Fleet, and it flew both flying boats and amphibians.

For decades, the American aircraft constituted the basis of the Soviet hydroaviation for the reason that the Soviet industry could not offer any alternative anyway. Reconnaissance regiments of all fleets had the PBN-1s and the PBY-6As in approximately equal proportion. In the late 1940s, air units modified the PBN-1s' instrumentation on the model of the more advanced PBY-6As; in particular, bearing finders were replaced with automatic direction finders.

Beginning from 1946, the Nomads were used for the training of Yeisk Aviation School students. Pilots were trained in the American aircraft until 1949 and, afterwards, the aircraft were transferred to combat units as replacements.

In 1947-1948, two flying boats of the 5th Fleet Air Force (in the Pacific) were modified into radiation reconnaissance aircraft. It was intended to use them to take air samples near the Pacific atolls, which was where the Americans were conducting nuclear tests. The cabins were pressurized and provided with filtering and ventilation equipment, and additional fuel tanks were installed to increase the flight duration to 40 hours; however, the aircraft's range was not long enough to cover the distance from the base in Sukhodol to the southern part of the Pacific Ocean. Sometime later, a decision was made to arrange for refueling from a submarine in the middle of the route; however, the flight never took place (it is possible that other ways were found to reach the objective).

It should be noted that beginning from late 1946, the expiry of an engine's lifespan became a considerable problem, and some flying boats and amphibians were, for this reason, written off. The aviators faced the need to resort to reserves and to use the spare engines which had been delivered for the C-47 transport aircraft. In terms of structure, on the other hand, the American flying boats were robust and reliable; any losses due to accidents were usually connected with piloting technique errors or unexpected circumstances. For example, on 30 August, Senior Lieutenant Livshits of the 118th Independent Reconnaissance Air Regiment ran against a sunken log and damaged the hull bottom and, as a result, the aircraft sank. On 8 August the same year, an amphibian which was in service with the Levanevsky Aviation School also went to the bottom: a poorly trained pilot landed at a high angle and the water pressed the nose wheel well doors upward, so the wheel, in turn, broke through the cockpit floor.

From 1952, the new Soviet-made Be-6 flying boats began arriving (first to the Northern Fleet, and then to other fleets). The first aircraft of this type was received by the 403rd Air Regiment of the Northern Fleet on 26 June, and this particular aircraft exceeded the PBN-1s and the PBY-6As in almost every aspect (range, speed and service ceiling), plus its armament was much more powerful. The instrumentation of the Be-6 was, to a considerable extent, a 'clone' of the Catalina's; however, naval pilots later missed the comfort, convenience, reliability and the high quality of manufacture of the American seaplanes.

In 1953, the first Soviet-made magnetometer (named *Chita*) was mounted on a PBY-6A. The device was installed on a beam behind the aft extremity of the hull, and it was developed by OKB-470 under the Order of the Council of Ministers of 21 November 1949. In November 1953, the magnetometer was factory-tested and, in spring the following year, it was subjected to State tests in Naval Aviation NII-15. The tests were conducted in Feodosiya and consisted of the search for an S-74 submarine in the Black Sea. The tests themselves were successful, and further versions of the *Chita* magnetometers were mounted on the new Be-6 flying boats.

In the north, the American flying boats remained in service until 1953. In the Baltic Fleet, the 49th Air Squadron, which was stationed in Noitis (near Kaliningrad), began its conversion from the PBY-6A to the Be-6 in September 1953 – completing it in May 1954. In the Black Sea, the PBY-6As kept flying for as long as October 1955, while in the Pacific, the amphibian stayed for longer still (the 289th Air Regiment flew them until August 1957). The aircraft had already been considerably worn and, in the middle of the month, a crash occurred – thus, flying the Catalinas was definitively prohibited.

In the civil aviation, the American flying boats appeared in 1944, which was when the navy provided the first two aircraft of this type to the Far East Civil Air Fleet Administration. Before the end of the year, the conversion training of the crews was completed and several service flights were made; during the next season, the American flying boats were operated on the Khabarovsk — Sakhalin — Kamchatka line. In 1945, the navy handed over another two aircraft, but this time from the Black Sea Fleet. They were accepted in Poti and, at the same location, the flight crews' training was conducted. The Civil Fleet Command believed that such an aircraft could find a wide application in Karelia, Siberia and the Far East. In September 1945, Head of the Civil Air Fleet Chief Administration Marshal F.A. Astakhov requested that 10-15 flying boats should be handed over, but in November, the Civil Fleet's 'appetite' rose to 20 flying boats, plus 10 amphibians. The Catalinas were too valuable for the navy and, as a result, Aeroflot had to be content with only six PBN-1s: four in service with the Far East Administration (which covered Western Siberia); the fifth with the Ural Administration; and the sixth with the Krasnoyarsk Administration. The latter was destroyed in July 1948. Upon landing in Turukhansk, the pilot made considerable porpoising and planted the nose in the water – thus, the nose broke off and the aircraft sank. From among the 16 passengers, two women and a child were killed.

As the spare parts stock was depleted, the number of unserviceable aircraft grew and, as a result, the Far East Civil Air Fleet Administration scrapped the last two Catalinas in 1957.

Their counterparts in service with the Polar Aviation flew until approximately the same time. As has already been discussed above, the polar aviation pilots accepted and ferried four flying boats in the very beginning, together with the naval aviation. Afterwards, the number of aircraft grew on account of the materiel handed over by the navy. During the summer season, there were five PBN-1s in operation in the Arctic region and, in November, the navy transferred an amphibian to the Polar Aviation. As of 1 January 1946, the Polar Aviation's fleet totaled as many as seven PBN-1s, plus one amphibian; a year later, the number grew to nine plus one. In October, GUSMP requested 10 more aircraft and received nine in the fourth quarter of 1948. The flying boats as handed over to the Polar Aviation were modified at the Krasnoyarsk Factory, where all of the military equipment was removed and various other devices were installed (e.g. original photo installations of local design). The modified aircraft were sometimes referred to as KM-1; however, the Polar Aviation also faced problems with a shortage of spare parts, and almost half of the fleet needed engine replacement. The way out was found in the form of modifying the flying boats to use Soviet-made ASh-82FN engines. The modification project appeared in 1947, and it was prepared in Krasnoyarsk by a team led by M.A. Mostovoy. The power plant of the Tu-2 bomber was taken as the basic model, and the R-1830-92 engines were replaced with the more powerful Soviet-made ASh-82FNs (1,850hp), which had four-blade AV-9-21K propellers.

The prototype of the KM-2 was tested from 4 September through to 9 October 1948, and the aircraft was piloted by Lieutenant Colonel F.S. Leshchenko's crew.

The take-off weight grew to 17,170kg, but the flight speed rose to 342km/h; the service ceiling grew to 9,000m; and the rate of climb increased. The data was taken off without engine boosting (otherwise, the results might have been better), although the flight range decreased slightly (from 6,000km to 5,820km). This was due to a higher fluid consumption by the Soviet-made engines; however, such an approach allowed for the maintaining of a lot of the serviceable Catalinas without any purchasing from the USA. The engines and spare parts were coming from manufacturers in kits, and the modification activities were carried out in Krasnoyarsk. In March 1949, there were nine aircraft at the factory which were modified simultaneously.

As of 1 January, GUSMP had as many as ten KM-2s, but by 1 July, their number had reached 14 (taking into account the fact that one flying boat had crashed in June in Khimki upon landing). Almost all of them were assigned to the Moscow Aviation Group and stationed in Khimki, and the KM-2s were successfully operated until 1957.

The American seaplanes saw service with some other Soviet agencies for a certain period of time as well. In 1947-1948, four aircraft were operated by GUGMS and they mostly flew ice reconnaissance missions in the Arctic region, as well as keeping watch on the condition of the ice. Later, both the aircraft and their functions were handed over to the Polar Aviation. Two Catalinas were in service with the Ministry of Geology's Aerogeologiya Group, and they were used to deliver supplies to remote expeditions. The Ministry of Fisheries, on the other hand, continued to make requests (for a long time) for three flying boats to conduct fish reconnaissance, but they never received them until the complete liquidation of the Ministry's aviation in the early 1950s.

On the whole, the scale of use of the Catalinas in the civil aviation was much less than in the military sphere, and the American flying boats served in exactly the same role as the one that had been envisaged by their designers (i.e. as long-range reconnaissance and anti-submarine aircraft). Becoming familiar with them gave a considerable impetus to the Soviet seaplane-building industry, and a lot of design solutions as encountered on the Catalinas were then 'copied' (in one form or another) on Soviet-made aircraft.

This disarmed PBY-1 flying boat was bought in the USA and ferried to Russia (Zakharkovo base) in July 1938.

Military GST aircraft of the 118th Separate Reconnaissance Air Regiment, Northern Fleet Air Force.

A civil GST of the Polar Aviation of Chief Administration of the Northern Maritime Route (GUSMP) moored near the shore.

Soviet aviators, together with American instructors, upon the completion of the training course in spring 1945.

A PBN-1 of the 53rd Separate Reconnaissance Air Regiment, Northern Fleet Air Force taking off.

A flying boat of the Northern Fleet Air Force Regiment in 1945.

A PBN-1 flying boat of the Northern Fleet Air Force on the shore.

A Soviet flying boat at anchorage in Port Arthur after an assault landing operation in August 1945.

A crew embarking onto a PBN-1 flying boat in Port Arthur in August 1945.

A PBN-1 of the Northern Fleet Air Force after being launched into the water from a slip.

A Soviet PBN-1 near a hangar.

A Soviet PBY-6A amphibian.

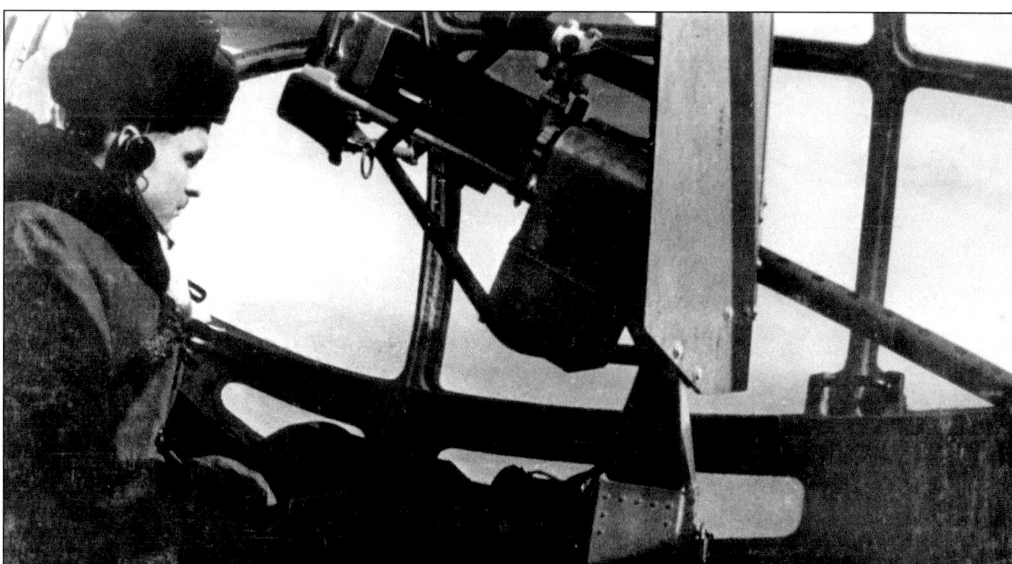

A gunner seated by the side blister, near the machine gun.

The PBN-1 flying boats at the home base of the 117th Separate Reconnaissance Air Regiment, Pacific Fleet Air Force.

A PBY-6A amphibian manufactured for the USSR.

A PBN-1 flying boat of the Pacific Fleet Air Force ashore during autumn 1945.

Air regiment crew members in front of a Catalina which brought a group of Lieutenant General K.N. Derevyanko's to Japan for the signing of the Instrument of Surrender.

A PBY-6A amphibian of the Pacific Fleet Air Force (post-war photo).

A ceremonial parade of the personnel of the 3rd Separate Reconnaissance Air Regiment on the occasion of Navy Day in July 1948.

A crew of the 53rd Separate Reconnaissance Air Regiment embarking onto an aircraft from a motor boat.

Students of the Yeysk Flying School, near a PBN-1 flying boat, are warming up the engines ashore.

Soviet military pilots near a PBY-6A amphibian.

Students of the Yeysk Flying School at an airfield, with a PBY-6A amphibian featuring in the background.

A PBY-6A amphibian fitted with a prototype of the *Chita* magnetometer during State tests in Feodosiya in spring 1954.

The mothballed PBN-1 flying boats with their engines removed.

Pilot I.S. Kotov (in the center) near a PBN-1 flying boat of the Polar Aviation at Providence Bay in 1947.

The only PBY-6A amphibian in service with the Polar Aviation Administration.

Local residents taking the cargoes, which were delivered by the polar pilots, to the shore in a boat.

A Catalina of the Polar Aviation at the port of Pevek.

A KM-2 of the Polar Aviation.

One of the modified KM-1 flying boats was operated by the Polar Aviation Administration.

A crew heaving up the anchor in a KM-1; note the absence of a turret in the fuselage nose.

The KM-2 prototype during tests in September 1948.

The KM-2 prototype during tests in September 1948.

The power plant of the KM-2 flying boat.

A KM-2 flying boat moored near the shore.

A crew preparing a KM-2 for the next flight.

A crew of the famous Soviet polar pilot I.I. Cherevichny after the flight-testing of a flying boat.

7.14 Short Stirling

In spite of the fact that at the conference in Moscow in September 1941, the Western Allies undertook the provision of heavy bombers to the USSR, only a few aircraft actually arrived. It should be noted that only one aircraft was shipped officially, and that was the British-made Short Stirling, which came after the end of the war against Germany.

The Stirling was the first four-engine bomber as adopted by the RAF after the end of the First World War. It was, essentially, an all-metal monoplane with a seemingly disproportionally long fuselage. Such a design was brought about by the fact that according to the technical assignment, the wingspan had been limited by the size of a standard hangar's gates. On the other hand, the very high landing gear legs were to ensure a sufficient angle of attack for the wing with the small lifting surface area.

The new bomber prototype first flew on 14 May 1939 and, approximately a year later, mass-production of the aircraft began to roll out from the Short Factory. Later, the Stirling was superseded by the Handley Page Halifax and the Avro Lancaster as a heavy bomber, and was relegated to the role of a transport or towing aircraft for troop-carrying gliders.

The bomber that was shipped to the USSR was the only one exported and, at the end of the war, the Stirling was not of much interest to Soviet specialists as a military aircraft; however, it could provide a certain notion as regards heavy bomber aviation development in England, as well as on British designers' approaches.

The Soviet Union requested a single aircraft for studying in 1944 and, in November that year, the RAF Command ordered to select and prepare a Stirling III for shipment to Russia. It was expected that the aircraft should be ready for ferrying in mid-December.

The intention was to deliver the indispensable spare parts in the aircraft, and all of the other things as required for the three months of operation were shipped by sea via the northern route in a container. In particular, engine oil was supplied because Soviet-made oil was not suitable for the Hercules engines, and the British crew was to ferry the aircraft to Abadan or Tehran for handover to the Soviet pilots.

Stirling III s/n LK615, which had been accepted by the RAF from Austin Motors in July 1944, was chosen for shipment to the USSR. It had been kept in reserve for some time and, for this reason, the aircraft was almost new and not worn. It was demonstrated to Soviet Embassy representatives; however, its preparation took a considerable amount of time (perhaps the aircraft was equipped for flying in a hot climate, for the reason that the intended route was over North Africa). The Stirling departed from Molton air base in England in late February 1945; in March, it arrived in Shuaiba in Iraq. It was there that the aircraft was checked again, and the British insignias were replaced with red stars. Lieutenant Weber's crew ferried the bomber to Mehrabad airfield near Tehran, where the British aircraft were stationed. On 25 March, it flew to the neighboring airfield, which was under the control of the Soviet Air Force.

Afterwards, problems began: first, it was discovered that the radio station was defective; then, the tail wheel was damaged during taxiing; finally, the tire of one of the main wheels burst on the grounded aircraft and, as a result, the doors of one of the wing bomb hatches was torn off. The Soviet side refused to accept the Stirling in such a condition, so the British ferried it back to Iraq (but to a different base). Activities continued there until 30 April, with the formal acceptance of the aircraft taking place as late as May. It should be noted that some British historians allege that the bomber which came back was not the one that had been sent for repair. This explains its long stay in Iraq, as the aviators simply waited for the arrival of a replacement from England.

The Stirling was ferried via Azerbaijan to LII airfield in Kratovo in the Moscow region, and there it was tested by G.M. Shiyanov's crew. The Soviet specialists came to the opinion that the British aircraft was of no value as a bomber: the aircraft was found to be obsolete and its performance was low, and only individual design solutions and certain items of equipment arose any interest.

When the testing was over, the aviators faced the question of what to do with the aircraft, as the military aviation did not need it, nor did the People's Commissariat of Aviation Industry; however, one of the aviation agencies agreed to accept the aircraft, and it was taken by the Polar Aviation Division of the Chief Administration of the Northern Maritime Route. Throughout the war, the Polar Aviation's fleet had considerably dwindled and had become worn out and obsolete. After the end of the hostilities, it had accepted both a lot of captured German aircraft and those received from the Allies; the Stirling was taken in among the others.

The British aircraft joined the Moscow Group of the Polar Aviation Division in spring 1946. The group was stationed at Zakharkovo airfield (currently built up with residential buildings of the expanded Khimki area) and, in May, polar pilots made several familiarization flights in the Stirling (in Soviet documents, it was also referred to as 'Sterling', 'Shirling' or simply 'Short'), with the overall duration of the flights being approximately two hours and 40 minutes. The aircraft was given the registration number H415; however, in the Polar Aviation, the aircraft was expressly found to be obsolete and its fitness for operation in the Arctic region raised considerable doubt.

Nevertheless, there were plans to modify the Stirling at the Pobezhimov Factory in Krasnoyarsk in 1947, but the aircraft never arrived there; it remained at Zakharkovo in a grounded condition. From April 1947, the aircraft was on the list of those unserviceable, and it was never restored; in fact, it was written off the same year, between September and December.

While of poor quality, this is the only known picture of the Soviet Short Stirling, which was taken at Mehrabad airfield in Iran in 1945.

7.15 Curtiss O-52 Owl

In May 1942, German photo reconnaissance aircraft spotted two machines at an airfield in Karelia, which they identified as Curtisses – and those were indeed the American-made Curtiss O-52 Owls.

The design of the aircraft, under the designation 'Model 85', was developed in 1940 and it was intended to be used as a short-range reconnaissance and spotter aircraft. Therefore, the designers focused on maneuverability, take-off and landing performance, reliability, and economic efficiency. The strut-braced high-wing pattern provided an excellent view for two crew members, plus the aircraft was light and compact, and featured a somewhat extraordinary shape, with a short barrel-contoured fuselage and a long straight wing. It is noteworthy that the low weight was achieved, to a certain extent, by abandoning its secondary role of a close-support aircraft. Unlike other short-range reconnaissance aircraft, the O-52 was not able to carry any bombs; its defensive armament consisted of only two 7.62mm machine guns.

The USAAF ordered a batch of two-hundred-and-three O-52s without even waiting for the maiden flight of the prototype, which first flew in 1941. This was followed by mass-production of the aircraft; however, the practice of combat operations in Europe showed that the very concept of a classical short-range reconnaissance aircraft (in American classification, an observation aircraft) had already become obsolete. Such an aircraft was not able to operate in conditions of counteraction on the part of a powerful anti-aircraft defense and the high concentration of enemy fighters in mid-air, and low-speed 'multi-purpose' biplanes and monoplanes with a poor defensive armament began to give way to high-speed aircraft (typically, modified fighters). The USAAF Command became rather skeptical in respect of the O-52's combat capabilities; however, something had to be done with the already built aircraft, so some of them were sent to peripheral bases in the Philippines, while others were assigned to US National Guard squadrons – and yet, some of the O-52s still awaited decision… thus, when the question of aircraft shipments to the USSR arose in July 1941, Chief of the US Army Air Force General H. Arnold decided to include a hundred O-52 reconnaissance aircraft on the list. The Americans were insistently offering these aircraft, in spite of the fact that even their own experts admitted that the Owl did not meet the warfare requirements of the Soviet-German Front. The Soviet Union was also unconditionally refusing to accept them; the Soviets requested only fighters and bombers, not short-range reconnaissance aircraft. Eventually, a compromise was reached: 30 aircraft which had already been prepared for delivery were to be shipped as 'additional' to the USA's undertakings under the Moscow Protocol.

On 14 October, the External Orders Department reported to the Air Force Chief Administration: '… 30 Curtiss O 52s (liaison and artillery spotter aircraft) are purchased and ready for shipment…'

By late November 1941, 26 aircraft left American ports on board different vessels heading for the USSR, with the remaining four aircraft following them shortly afterwards. Only 19 aircraft reached the Soviet shore, as the rest went to the bottom, together with the transports which were carrying them. Five O-52s passed Soviet military acceptance at the end of 1941, while the other 14 were accepted at the beginning of the next year.

Having avoided the hazards of the northern seas, the Owls arrived in the Soviet territory. It is noteworthy that in the Soviet Union, the aircraft was never referred to as 'Owl'; it was always either the O-52 or just the Curtiss. In January 1942, they were brought (in a disassembled condition) to the 22nd Backup Air Regiment in Kineshma, and the aircraft arrived without detailed documentation. They were assembled 'by intuition' under the supervision of Engineer A.I. Smolyarov, and the first O-52 was flown by Deputy Regiment Commander Major P.S. Akulenko. The flight observer's seat was occupied by Smolyarov, who decided to personally prove the correctness of the assembly.

To a certain extent, the new aircraft got into an ambiguous position: since they were intended to be used as artillery spotters, they were 'second rate' for aviators, but on the other hand, the aircraft itself was rather interesting, and so specialists were willing to know more details on its application. Eventually, it turned out that the data relating to the training of the aviation units in the O-52s were personally reported to Deputy Air Force Commander A.V. Nikitin. At the same time, the O-52 was probably the only imported aircraft which was not 'honored' with being tested at NII VVS, or with any serious testing at all.

On 7 February 1942, the 50th Independent Spotter Air Squadron, which was under the command of Major I.A. Kochanovsky (which had already seen action on the Leningrad Front), joined the 22nd Backup Air Regiment for conversion training purposes. Major Kochanovsky became the chairman of the commission for the testing of the O-52, which was conducted rather promptly (but somewhat superficially) in late February through to early March under the Order of the Training Section of the Chief Artillery Administration.

The results were quite satisfactory: in terms of instrumentation, view and comfort for the crew, the Curtiss was dramatically different from the old Soviet-made R-5, R-Z and SSS biplanes, which were typically used as spotter aircraft; however, the low speed, poor armament and an absence of armor constituted to a considerable 'fly in the ointment'. It was suggested that the aircraft application should be limited to gunfire spotting without entering enemy territory; otherwise, it was recommended that the armament should be enhanced and armor also installed.

Taking into account the number of received aircraft, it was planned that three squadrons would be converted to the O-52s. Therefore, two detachments were newly formed in addition to the existing 50th Independent Spotter Air Squadron: the 12th Independent Spotter Air Squadron, which was under the command of Senior Lieutenant F.A. Propp (manned with personnel of the 19th Independent Spotter Air Squadron), and the 13th Independent Spotter Air Squadron, which was under the command of Captain K.M. Myasoedov (manned with personnel of the 42nd Independent Spotter Air Squadron). The 50th Independent Spotter Air Squadron was the first to fly the O-52s on 15 February, while the other two squadrons began their flying on 27 February. The training was advancing fast – and soon, accidents began to occur, with the first of them taking place in the 12th Independent Spotter Air Squadron on 12 March. The crew of Flight Commander Junior Lieutenant D.D. Mukhar lost their bearings for some time during an en route flight and ran short of fuel before they reached the airfield and, as a result, the crew had to perform a forced landing. The O-52 was damaged to such an extent that it required an overhaul.

In the course of mastering the American aircraft, three more aircraft were made unserviceable – and all of them were from the 13th Independent Spotter Air Squadron. On 3 May, the landing gear on Sergeant P.I. Yakovlev's aircraft collapsed during taxiing and the damaged aircraft was sent to the repair shop. On 30 May and 2 June, failures occurred on aircraft piloted by Flight Commander V.S. Berezhnoy and Flight Commander F.V. Ryazanov and, as a result during the final distribution, the 50th Independent Spotter Air Squadron did not get enough aircraft (it received only two aircraft instead of the standard quantity of six).

The recommendation to install armor on the Curtisses did not remain unattended. On 13 May 1942, a commission for the flight testing of a modified O-52 was appointed, with Captain Myasoedov as the chairman. It is not known what kind of armor it was, or whether it was installed on other aircraft, but it can only be said with confidence that the aircraft of the 12th Independent Spotter Air Squadron were not subjected to any modifications. By May, the squadron had already been on the front lines – having completed the training on 29 March. With six O-52s and a U-2, the squadron had departed for the Leningrad Front. The average flying time in the new aircraft per pilot had, by that time, totaled only five hours and 35 minutes. The results of such insufficient training manifested themselves later.

The other two squadrons stayed with the backup team for a longer period of time and, consequently, received better training. The 13th Air Squadron departed for Yelets on 7 July (with an average flying time of 21 hours and 40 minutes per pilot); however, it only entered the action in October 1943 on the Kalinin Front.

The 50th Independent Spotter Air Squadron had to give away its two remaining O-52s and flew to the front in the Hurricanes. The 22nd Backup Air Regiment was left with three Curtisses (with only one of them serviceable), while the two damaged spotter aircraft were sent for repair. The last Owl survived a crash on 5 December 1943 and remained in service with the regiment until late summer 1944 – thus, 16 aircraft passed through the 22nd Backup Air Regiment, but it is not known where the other three stayed throughout that time.

With this in mind, what was the combat destiny of the O-52s? In spite of the initial gloomy forecasts, it was not bad; however, it is difficult to call the beginning of the combat experience of the 12th Independent Reconnaissance and Spotter Air Squadron successful. On 29 March, the squadron departed Ivanovo for Plekhanovo and, at an intermediate landing in Cherepovets, the aircraft of Junior Lieutenant P.T. Afonichkin toppled over with severe damage to one of the landing gear legs, as well as to the horizontal stabilizer and the engine. The five other spotters left the airfield and continued on their way and, at the approach to the destination location, the formation of the O-52s was engaged by five Messerschmitts. To save his comrades, Flight Commander Junior Lieutenant P.K. Zhilinsky undertook an aerial ramming against one of the enemy aircraft. Both aircraft crashed down to the ground and Zhilinsky was killed, whereas the German pilot bailed out and was taken prisoner. Flight Observer Junior Lieutenant S.I. Novorozhkin was thrown out of the cockpit by the impact, but he managed to draw the parachute and survived – getting off with injuries. Zhilinsky was posthumously awarded the Order of the Red Banner of Military Valor.

The four remaining aircraft flew on 1 April to Levashovo airfield and, three days later, they departed for Sosnovka. At take-off in Levashovo, Squadron Leader Propp – having climbed to 30m – lost control of the aircraft and, as a result of the left wing dropping, the aircraft crashed; the crew survived.

From Sosnovka, the considerably thinned-out squadron began combat operations for the benefit of the 23rd Army. The Curtisses adjusted artillery fire; flew visual and photo reconnaissance missions near the front line; and carried troopers to the enemy's rear under NKVD orders. The low-speed and unarmored aircraft required serious air cover at daytime; however, the fighters could not escort the American-made 'observer' on all of the sorties, so therefore, the Owls (quite reasonably) adopted nocturnal habits. Daytime sorties constituted no more than one sixth of their overall flights, and as a replacement for the losses – and to ensure daytime operations – the squadron received the Su-2s.

In early May, Junior Lieutenant D.D. Mukhar's crew did not return from a mission and, on 19 July 1942, the squadron was merged with the 50th Independent Reconnaissance and Spotter Air Squadron, with Lieutenant Colonel N.A. Kochanovsky taking over the command. Combat operations at that time were performed from Kapitolovo airfield, and the two remaining 'Americans' were mostly involved in night-time artillery adjustment missions (and, from time to time, in daytime liaison sorties).

The O-52s' flights were relatively sparse. Typically, one or two sorties were flown per day, but on rare occasions, their number reached four – thus, for example, 19 sorties were flown throughout May 1943.

After Kochanovsky, Deputy Captain K.V. Zakharov took over the command of the 12th Independent Reconnaissance and Spotter Air Squadron. In June 1943, the squadron was replenished with the Il-2KRs and received the Kittyhawks for air cover instead of the Hurricanes. In June 1944, the 12th Independent Spotter Air Squadron joined the 203rd Independent Reconnaissance and Spotter Air Regiment, and the two 'long-term survivors' became part of the latter. They were not flown anymore, and even had no crews assigned to them. On 19 September 1944, the two O-52s were written off.

As for the second squadron which was equipped with the Owls (i.e. the 13th Independent Spotter Air Squadron), it flew to Migalovo airfield on 17 October 1942 and joined the 3rd Air Army of the Kalinin Front with five O-52s and two Hurricanes. One (according to other documents, two) of the 'Americans' were lost on the way to the front lines.

Soon the squadron flew its first combat sorties, and it was losing its aircraft at a much slower rate than that of the 12th Independent Spotter Air Squadron. Perhaps the O-52s of the 13th Air Squadron were equipped with additional armor, but that was not the main thing: Squadron Leader Myasoedov insisted that the air cover should always correspond to the situation (four to six fighters per spotter aircraft).

Escorted by a pack of fighters, the O-52s suffered no losses, but there was, however, one exception: in December 1943, Sergeant P.I. Yakovlev's crew departed for its second sortie during the day to adjust fire on enemy batteries near Lake Dolgoye (20km from Nevel), along with a cover party of four Yak-7Bs. The crew had already twice transmitted the data on the coordinates of explosions in the area of enemy positions to the ground post when the aircraft shook under the influence of the explosions; then, it quaked in response to another impact and wing-dropped – making a steep dive towards the ground. It turned out that the O-52 was attacked by a Soviet La-5, which had approached (as it had been trained to) to a distance of 50 or 80 meters and then gave a cannon squirt, with the rounds piercing the spotter's left wing. The La-5's pilot made another mistake: disengaging from the attack, he struck the Curtiss with the fuselage, but Sergeant Yakovlev managed to pull his aircraft (which had lost a considerable portion of its right wing) out of the falling and wobbled to the home airfield, where he landed safely. After the landing, the aircraft was inspected: the fighter had damaged the left wing high-lift device's hydraulic actuator and the ribs, while the right wing was deformed (its panel and attachment fittings were torn off) and other parts of the aircraft were damaged as well. The aircraft was quite repairable; however, there was no spare wing panel, so a decision was made to disassemble the aircraft to spare parts.

The spotters tried to disguise themselves in clouds and to hide in sunlight – choosing routes which were not frequented by German fighters or anti-aircraft guns. In the target area, they kept at an altitude of 1,000-1,500m, while photo reconnaissance sorties were usually flown by the Owls in pairs. Photos were taken from an altitude of 2,000-2,200m and each aircraft carried a Soviet-made AFA-B aerial camera for vertical photography (from the USA, the aircraft had arrived without any photo equipment whatsoever). The technical personnel of the 13th Independent Spotter Air Squadron found a way to mount two AFA-B cameras on each aircraft. The area as photographed during a single passage increased twice, and it is clear that the number of passages was accordingly reduced twice in order to make the sorties less hazardous for the crews. Photo reconnaissance sorties were flown twice more frequently than spotting missions and, throughout 1943, 60 frontline photographing sorties were flown.

To summarize the results for 1943, Captain Myasoedov wrote: 'We have flown 162 combat sorties (36 spotting sorties; 60 frontline photographing sorties; eight reconnaissance sorties; 58 air cover sorties). As a result, 30 field artillery batteries were destroyed, and six suppressed'.

On 28 May 1943, a crew of Master Sergeant P.I. Yakovlev and Senior Lieutenant A.I. Savitsky flew the second sortie during that day upon the request of the 3rd Attack Army. No fighters were provided, so instead of them, the crew was ordered to 'operate without air cover'. The crew departed and successfully completed spotting and, at 1300 hours, they received an order to take a photo of the target. At this very moment, the aircraft was set aflame by a Bf 109, but the spotter's crew did not bail out. Another O-52 was shot down in February 1944 by anti-aircraft guns, and yet another was written off after a crash on 29 July, which was committed by Sergeant Cherepenshchikov. As of summer 1944, the 13th Independent Spotter Air Squadron had only one serviceable Curtiss at its disposal.

Only two combat losses throughout a year and a half of daytime flying (sometimes, with no air cover) is a very good figure (no worse than that for the Il-2KR), and it obviously contradicts the superficial evaluation of the O-52 and the conclusions made by the test commission long ago.

The last O-52, together with the entire 13th Independent Spotter Air Squadron, joined the 206th Independent Spotter and Reconnaissance Air Regiment, but did not stay there for long. On 14 August, it was transferred to the 5th Training Air Regiment of the 3rd Air Army.

According to documents, there were four Owls in service with the air force as of 1 May 1945. Furthermore, one of them was in operation with the combat army (i.e. on the front). Thirteen aircraft were deemed to be lost (due to both combat and non-combat causes), and three aircraft were listed as 'in transit', but where were they transferred? And again, six Owls should have been left, not three.

The 5th Independent Aerial Survey Air Squadron was based at Klyazma airfield, near Moscow. Its pilots flew old aircraft (such as the R-5s and SBs) and were subordinated to the Military Topographic Department of the Headquarters of the Moscow Military District Air Force. Squadron Leader Colonel E.P. Andryukhov requested to replace the obsolete and worn-out aircraft of his unit with something more suitable, but most of all, he wished to receive the captured German Focke-Wulf FW 189s; however, the Command did not give him any such airplanes and suggested the O-52s instead. The first aircraft arrived in August 1944, while by January 1945, the squadron had received as many as seven of them (it is probable that some of the previously damaged aircraft had been restored).

Pilots of the 5th Independent Aerial Survey Air Squadron began mastering the O-52s in October 1944; they studied the manuals and taxied over the airfield. The first 16 flights were made from Podlipki base in December. On 20 April 1945, scheduled activities began: an O-52 was flying photo survey sorties from Klyazma airfield to the Istra, Krasnogorsk and Noginsk regions and, by that time, technicians had adapted the AFA-26 cameras (which worked with 24V) to the aircraft's 12V system.

On 27 April, Junior Lieutenant Lizunov damaged the wing and horizontal stabilizer at take-off, and the repair was performed by the unit's own personnel. Two days later, Flight Commander A.M. Orlov lost control of the aircraft during a left turn at landing and experienced the same result; it took almost a month to repair his O-52.

In late May, one of the Curtisses flew to Estonia to Haapsalu airfield, while three more departed for Tula. The latter aircraft were intended to carry out surveys near Plavsk, Tambov, Michurinsk and Borisoglebsk. In July, three aircraft were redeployed to Riga, and one stayed in Haapsalu. By that time, the squadron had lost three Curtisses and Orlov 'finished off' his aircraft on 23 May in Tula. The aircraft was scrapped, whereas the pilot was transferred to light-engine aviation. Another O-52 was written off for unknown reasons, while a third one was handed over on 20 May to a unit of the Moscow Military District Air Force.

All four of the surviving planes met the end of the victory year in Riga, where the 5th Independent Aerial Survey Air Squadron (already subordinated to the 15th Air Army) was redeployed. In December 1945, Latvian leaders addressed the Air Force Command with a request to transfer the O-52s to the civil aviation, and the then Squadron Leader Lieutenant Colonel A.I. Yevseev-Sidorov agreed – writing a letter to the air force commander in which he substantiated the unsuitability of any further service of the Curtisses with the military forces in detail.

The Chief Administration of Geodetic Surveying and Cartography became the next operator of the Owls in the USSR, but it is not known when the handover took place; however, in July 1947, inspectors checking the aircraft of the agency reported that the Curtisses were 'in a good state'. As of 1 October 1947, there were three O-52s in service with GUGK.

On 20 September 1948, near the Dugovo settlement (which was then situated in the Komi Autonomous Soviet Socialist Republic), one of GUGK's aircraft crashed. On the way back to Ukhta, its engine failed and pilot P.I. Ivanov attempted to glide down onto a meadow in order to land there with the aircraft's landing gear extended; however, he failed to reach the meadow and crashed into a sand hillock slope. The pilot died and the air photographer – G.A. Ivanov – was severely injured.

Perhaps it was the crash that entailed the decision to write off the remaining American aircraft (moreover, there were no spare parts for them). As of 1 January 1949, there were no more O-52s on GUGK's aircraft inventory lists.

An O-52 during tests at the 22nd Backup Air Regiment in Kineshma in February 1942.

An O-52 of the 50th Separate Spotter Air Squadron.

The landing gear of the O-52.

The O-52 cockpit canopy, with an open side panel.8-15-9 The aerial survey O-52 of the GUGK aviation.

An aerial survey O-52 of the GUGK aviation in either Ukhta or in Syktyvkar. The Junkers W34 in the foreground was flown by the aviation detachment of the Ministry of Internal Affairs (hence the corresponding abbreviation on the fuselage nose), which serviced confined camps.

The aerial survey O-52 of the GUGK aviation.

7.16 Vought OS2U Kingfisher

These aircraft are often not listed among those shipped under Lend-Lease, in spite of the fact that they were delivered to the Soviet Union on a purely official basis. The issue is that they were itemized as 'ship-related stock' (i.e. as a 'free supplement' to the warship which was handed over to the Soviet Navy).

The Vought OS2U Kingfisher catapult-launched observation floatplane was designed in 1937 under the US Navy's specifications, and it first flew (as a landplane) on 1 March the following year. Mass-production OS2U-1s were adopted in spring 1940 and the name 'Kingfisher' was given to the aircraft by the British, who began receiving them under Lend-Lease in summer 1942.

Two such observation aircraft happened to get to the Soviet Union. In spring 1944, as part of its share during the distribution of captured Italian ships, the Americans provided the USS *Milwaukee* light cruiser to the USSR on a temporary basis. On 24 August 1944, *Milwaukee* – renamed *Murmansk*, and with a mixed Soviet-American crew on board – joined the Northern Fleet. The cruiser carried two OS2U-3s with more powerful engines, as well as self-sealing tanks and armor protection for both the pilot and the radio operator gunner. The aircraft was fitted with two machine guns and could carry up to 90kg of bombs.

The American specialist who arrived on board the cruiser briefly instructed the pilots on the Kingfisher's design and flying peculiarities – and afterwards, the Soviet pilots continued their familiarization with the new aircraft on their own. The crews studied the American observer aircraft thoroughly, and then flew them successfully. It is possible that the Kingfishers did not take part in combat operations, since *Murmansk* (for the most part of its stay in the USSR) remained moored in Archangelsk; however, the aircraft flew training and various auxiliary missions, with training flights including the catapult-launching of the aircraft.

The aircraft retained the traditional (for that time) white and gray American maritime camouflage, but red stars with white edging were painted underneath on the wing and the fuselage sides (aft of the observer's cabin). According to I.A. Platonov, who flew several sorties on a Kingfisher – including being catapult-launched from *Murmansk* – the aircraft produced a rather mediocre impression, but had no serious piloting defects.

Indeed, the OS2U-3 was inferior to the Soviet-made KOR-1 and KOR-2 (Be-4) catapult-launched reconnaissance aircraft both in terms of speed and (to the latter) its service ceiling, but on the other hand, it exceeded both of them in terms of flight range by more than twice. It was developed for ocean spaces, which the Soviet Navy was, at that time, only attempting to access.

Milwaukee, together with the aircraft, was returned to the Americans in 1947.

A Kingfisher on board the USS *Milwaukee* in August 1944.

Soviet pilots getting familiar with the cockpit of the American reconnaissance aircraft, with another Kingfisher seen in the background. The aircraft still carries American insignia.

The lifting of the Kingfisher aboard *Murmansk* after a flight.

7.17 Douglas C-47 Skytrain

In the first year of the war with Germany, the Soviet transport aviation suffered great losses. The aircraft were destroyed by the enemy on the ground and in the air, and they were left behind or burnt on their airfields during the retreat. The factories that survived the hasty evacuation to the east did not have enough time to replenish their losses, and the supply of aircraft to the frontline units and groups was mostly due to the draining of resources from the already rather depleted rear territorial administrations of the Civil Air Fleet. The aircraft were ferried to the front from Siberia, Central Asia and the Far East, but there, for the most part, the already obsolete types of aircraft were operated. The front experienced a considerable demand for aircraft with a high load-lifting capability, and the only modern 'representative' of such a type in the Soviet Union was the two-engine PS-84 (in summer 1942, it was renamed Li-2), which was, essentially, a licensed copy of the American DC-3 which was manufactured at Factory No.84 in Khimki and later in Tashkent; however, since the exact same time, the Li-2 was seen not as a pure transport, but as a dual-purpose aircraft. It was also used as a long-range night bomber and was fitted with externally mounted bomb racks and defensive machine guns. Therefore, the Li-2s (in growing quantities) were supplied to the long-range aviation regiments, which were of a higher priority. The civil aviation, which was used as a source for the raising of transport units for the front, received the remains and, as a result, the proportion of heavy aircraft in such units decreased.

The Soviet Command attempted to compensate for the lack of domestic transport aircraft by getting them from the Allies. They were requested to check the possibility of delivering such aircraft and, as a result, the Americans agreed to supply military versions of the already mentioned DC-3.

When the war began for the USA, the American military transport aviation only had a small number of converted civil aircraft and obsolete bombers, so the first thing the military did was the requisitioning (from factories) of passenger aircraft, which were, at that time, unfinished or not yet handed over to customers – including a large number of the DC-3s in various versions; then, in late 1941, the first aircraft in a special military version (the C-53 Skytrooper), which had a simplified cabin interior and more powerful R-1830-92 engines, began to come into service. Concurrently, in early 1942, American factories began to build the C-47 Skytrain with reinforced floor and swing doors which covered a large cargo hatch on the left side of the aircraft. To the United Kingdom, all of the military versions of the DC-3 were supplied under the name of Dakota.

Those that were transport aircraft were to be ferried to the Soviet Union by air via Alaska and Siberia, and the first delivery of twenty-five C-47s and four C-53s was expected in may through to June 1942; however, the first seven C-47s were delivered by the American ferry pilots to the airbase at Ladd field in Alaska only in September. On 25 September, Soviet crews arrived from Chukotka to ferry them to the Soviet Union, and it was assumed that the pilots (who were well familiar with the Li-2) would easily convert to a similar aircraft; however, the American side suspended the delivery of the aircraft until they obtained a special order at the beginning of October. On 10 October, the Soviet mission accepted six C-47s, which were then flown to the other side of the Bering Strait and then further en route to Krasnoyarsk. By the end of the month, a total of 10 such aircraft were handed over in Krasnoyarsk. Altogether, by March 1943, the Soviet Union received thirty C-47s, and afterwards, deliveries of these aircraft steadily increased.

In total, the American side allocated seven-hundred-and-nine C-47s for the USSR, but only 707 of those reached the handover point at the Ladd field base. All of them were accepted by the Soviet mission, and a total of 704 aircraft arrived in Krasnoyarsk; at least two en route crashes of the C-47 occurred (on 25 May 1943 in Krasnoyarsk and on 30 May 1944 in Uelkal). Contrary to initial intentions, the C-53s were not supplied to the Soviet Union, as only the C-47s, C-47As and C-47Bs were delivered.

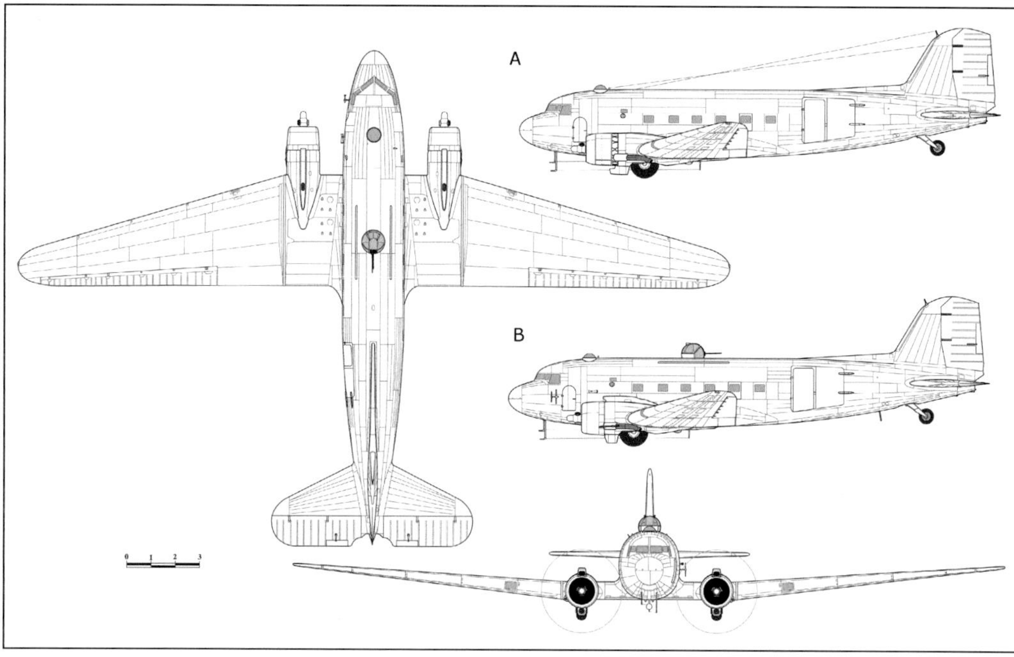

C-47

A TS-82 transport plane.
B Three-view of the C-47, which was equipped with a UTK-1 turret.

In the Soviet aviation, all of these aircraft were usually referred to as C-47s, but more often, the Li-2s and the American-made C-47s were simply called 'Douglas'. This is understandable, since it is rather difficult for even an expert to distinguish them by their external appearance. Even now, in the Russian media, photos of the C-47 are often published with the caption 'Li-2'.

The first aircraft were intended for the civil aviation, which acquired the functions of the military transport aviation during the war. Initially, it was assumed that during 1943, the Civil Air Fleet would receive twenty C-47s; in fact, however, throughout the year, a considerably greater number of the aircraft (70) was delivered. It should be noted though that part of the aircraft were handed over to the air force and the long-range aviation.

By 1 April 1943, the first two aircraft appeared on the lists of a special-purpose aviation unit in Moscow and, a month later, similar aircraft began to be used for servicing the Krasnoyarsk route. These aircraft replaced the worn-out PS-84s of pre-war manufacture, which had been operated there earlier, and the C-47s, which were handed over to service the route, constituted a transport squadron. In May 1943, the squadron had 15 aircraft, and this number considerably exceeded the one as prescribed by the Tables of Organization and Equipment. In June, it was expanded into the 8th Transport Regiment, which was under the command of V.A. Pushchinsky. His C-47s transported people and cargoes along the route; led groups of single-seat aircraft, which were not fitted with similar rich navigation equipment; and also carried out rescue operations. This regiment ensured the ferrying of other C-47s along the route. The chief of the route – the famous polar pilot I.P. Mazuruk – had his personal Douglas decorated with the image of a polar bear on the forward fuselage. In total, up to twenty-five C-47s were used to serve the Soviet portion of the ALSIB route, and they were shared between the route administration and the 8th Transport Regiment, which was part of the 1st Ferry Division.

The 1st Transport Air Division became the next to be converted to the new aircraft, which was based at the new (but non-completed) Vnukovo airport, near Moscow. By that time, the transport aviation of the civil air fleet had been reorganized, with regiments and divisions superseding squads and groups. On 17 May 1943, the commander of the 1st Transport Air Division received an order to allocate 20 crews for conversion to the C-47s, but in fact, due to a shortage of aircraft, only five crews were trained by 1 July. These aircraft were immediately put into service – leaving no time for training flights. By 1 September 1943, forty C-47s had been assigned to the Civil Air Fleet and, in the 1st Transport Air Division, there were 10 such aircraft; four more belonged to an independent transport squadron (the successor of the special-purpose squadron).

Later, the air force began to receive the new aircraft, and among the first C-47s was the one allocated to the air force's inspection regiment, which was the 'pet project' of the Soviet leader's son, V. Stalin. Both bomber and fighter regiments usually received a single transport aircraft each for various transportations; earlier, those were the PS-84s or, even more often, the obsolete TB-1, TB-3 or R-6 (KR-6) planes (the latter were referred to as 'cruisers'). At the time being described, the regiments began to strive for the new C-47s. In total, throughout the war, the air force received 218 aircraft of the type, and of those, 120 were used at the front line; seventy were used in the rear districts; and five were used in the air defense system. Another 111 aircraft were handed over to the long-range aviation, which was not subordinated to the air force (instead, it came under the direct command of the General Headquarters of the Supreme High Command); however, none of the military units whether in the air force or in the long-range aviation was fully equipped with the C-47s.

There were reasons for that: as has already been mentioned, the Li-2 in the configuration as it was manufactured during the war by Tashkent Factory No.84 was, essentially, a dual-purpose aircraft (a transport and a long-range night bomber at the same time), whereas the C-47 was purely a transport aircraft. Therefore, long-range bomber units were predominantly equipped with the Li-2s, while the transport units were fitted with the foreign-made Douglases. It should be noted though that some C-47s were given to regiments equipped with the Li-2s – thus, for example, three C-47s were allocated to the 102nd Long-Range Aviation Regiment. They were used for special missions, as well as for utility-based needs and 'technical assistance' in case of forced landings of the regiment's aircraft.

The first major operation involving the C-47s was the delivery of airborne troops to the right bank of the Dnieper in September 1943, with the objective being to seize a foothold for the subsequent force-crossing of the river. Along with the long-range aviation regiments, the 1st Transport Air Division participated in that. According to documents, along with the Li-2s, the division used nine out of 10 available C-47s for the airdrop operation.

The division's aircraft, which was based at Grayvoron airfield, delivered 5,000 soldiers of the 5th Airborne Corps into the enemy's rear. The soldiers were paradropped, and cargo gliders were used for the transportation of guns, mortars, heavy machine guns and ammunition to the operation area; the airdrop, however, turned out to be unsuccessful. Facing a strong counteraction of the anti-aircraft artillery, the aircraft dispersed and the paratroopers were spread over a large area. Sometimes, the paradropping took place directly over the enemy positions and heavy losses were already suffered in mid-air; however, most of the parachutists were able to retreat to the woods in order to get organized and to contact partisans. Later, the paratroopers made a counter-assault which contributed to the river force-crossing.

On the captured footholds on the right bank of the Dnieper, the Soviet troops arranged advanced airfields. The aviation began to deliver food, ammunition, fuel and medical supplies, as well as taking the wounded to the Soviet rear by return flights. materials to make river crossings were also delivered by air, as flights to the front line were not safe – thus, on 22 October, two C-47s which had brought fuel and ammunition from Poltava to a site near Krivoy Rog were burned on the ground by the German aviation.

The C-47, in many respects, was superior to the Soviet-made Li-2. Its powerful engines ensured reaching a higher speed and service ceiling, as well as providing for an increased load capacity; also, the engines were mounted conveniently and were easy to maintain. The replacement of one M-62IR (ASh-62IR) engine on the Li-2 took 62 man-hours, whereas on the C-47 (if the engine was removed together with the engine mount), only 10 man-hours were required! After a difficult period of the initial mastering, when the technical personnel came to know all of the nuances of servicing the American engines, they became not only able to run throughout the entire guaranteed service life, but they actually exceeded it by half or even twice as much – and it should be borne in mind that the service life of the Pratt & Whitney engines was twice as high than that of the M-62IRs!

The overhaul life of the VISh-21 propellers as utilized on the Li-2 aircraft constituted some meager 50 hours, whereas the more complex American-made Standard hydromatic propellers, which featured a very important feathering device, had the manufacturer's guarantee of 750 hours; in fact, the imported propellers ran in the Soviet Union approximately five times longer than their Soviet-made equivalents.

Higher industrial standards ensured a higher quality of airframe manufacture, and the American-made aircraft were stronger and more reliable, with its outer surfaces providing for better aerodynamic performance. It featured more refined fuel and hydraulic systems, plus American valves (to the delight of the technicians) did not leak.

The side-opening cargo door of the C-47 was much wider than the cargo door of the Li-2, which had to be moved upward to open. E.Z. Butsky wrote that his crew's aircraft was once loaded with the bodies of armored vehicles and, as a result, the crew had to get out through the upper emergency hatch in order to walk on top of the fuselage to the tail before then climbing down a ladder.

Two additional 375L soft tanks which could be placed (if necessary) in the cabin allowed for increasing the flight range to 3,400km, plus the Soviet handymen installed even more capacious non-standard tanks – thus increasing the flight duration to 24 hours. The instrumentation and radio equipment of the C-47 was far more advanced than that of the Li-2 as well, both in terms of nomenclature and in terms of accuracy, reliability and lifespan. Radio operators on the Li-2 could only sigh hopelessly when they looked at what was installed in their colleagues' American-made aircraft: three different radios; a radio altimeter; an ILS set; an automatic direction finder etc.... American radios featured five to six times greater power, as well as better stability and a lower weight and dimensions. On the C-47, the radio operator's workstation was beyond the propellers' rotation zone and was located in a special soundproof enclosure; the C-47s were shipped to the USSR with an incomplete set of equipment. The USAAF equipped their aircraft with many other instruments as evidenced by the empty stands and unnecessary placards, but even in such a configuration, the C-47s were far more superior in this respect to the Soviet transport aircraft and bombers.

The C-47s were well prepared for low-temperature operations. American designers had provided for everything – including de-icers on the wing and empennage; the flushing of the propeller blades and cockpit canopy with alcohol-based mixtures; and for the heating of the cockpit and cabin. Goodrich pneumatic de-icers were significantly more efficient than the Soviet-made thermal ones, and the hydraulically-driven wipers also won a higher opinion than the electrical ones on the Li-2 – and how the crews liked the hot-air heating! The Li-2 was equipped with a vapor-air system comprising a water boiler, and the engineer who operated it was called 'a stoker'; he did, however, have a lot of trouble making the system work reliably.

The Douglases, along with the Li-2s, were the backbone of the Soviet military transport aviation for quite a long time. Usually, a regiment included a single heavy aircraft flight (two or three Li-2s or C-47s) or a squadron, which consisted of five or six two-engine aircraft. The rest of the regiment consisted of smaller aircraft, but only one such squadron in a single sortie could deliver more cargo than all of the other aircraft in the regiment; only the regiments of the 1st Transport Air Division and some other units were fully composed of two-engine aircraft.

Although in transport aviation their number was much less than that of the single-engine biplanes U-2 and P-5 (R-5), they performed more than half (in terms of weight) of the transportations. A huge amount of cargo was carried by the C-47s during the offensive operations of the Soviet Army; for example, regiments of the 1st Transport Air Division delivered urgent cargoes to the front during the Battle of Kursk. This formation, which was renamed the 10th Guards Transport Air Division in 1944, continued to be constantly employed in the most important areas of the Soviet offensives – thus, in February through to March 1944 near Melitopol, a group of ten C-47s were operated under the command of B.K. Labutin. In the conditions of the muddy season, only aviation could help to maintain the pace of the advance. Aircraft delivered rounds, rocket projectiles, food and clothing – and on return flights, they evacuated the wounded. Those were short-range flights, with five or six sorties flown per day.

During the offensive near Leningrad in June of the same year, the C-47s of the 5th Independent Air Regiment and of one of the air force regiments provided the relocation of ground-based personnel of the 7th Air Army's regiments and headquarters, as well as delivering cargoes to the front. The same task was performed by the aircraft of the 9th and 120th guards Independent Air Regiments during the offensive in Byelorussia.

Enormous was the role of transport aviation in the Liberation of the right-Bank Ukraine, the Crimea and the Baltic region, and the high rate of advance was maintained due to the supply of the forward units by air. Sometimes, the unloading of fuel and ammunition was carried out at sites located at a distance of half a kilometer from the enemy positions, and where it was impossible to land, the cargoes were paradropped. The intensity of the flights sometimes reached eight to 10 sorties per day!

Losses were inevitable in combat missions. In 1943, the Civil Air Fleet lost eight C-47s at the front line (five of them due to combat reasons) and, in 1944, 16 aircraft were lost (eight of them were destroyed by the enemy). From among the aircraft lost in 1944, one was shot down by a German fighter; another one was destroyed on the airfield; one was burned at the partisans' site in the German rear; one was mistakenly shot down by the Soviet anti-aircraft artillery; and four were MIA. On 31 May, a pilot of the 10th guards Transport Air Division – Lieutenant Pavlov – made a mistake while landing on the partisans' site and the aircraft crashed into the trees; the entire crew and the passenger were killed. On 27 June, during a cargo paradropping operation, a C-47 piloted by Captain Bautin of the same division suffered a crash. The parachute got caught on the stabilizer and the cargo made contact with the top of a tree; the aircraft crashed to the ground. The pilots died, while the rest of the crew members were injured.

In spite of all this – thanks to the deliveries from the USA – the fleet of C-47s continued to grow. As of 1 January 1944, the Civil Air Fleet had 55 aircraft of this type, which were approximately shared equally between the frontline units and the rear administrations. By the end of the year, more than one-hundred-and-fifty-nine C-47s were received (a number three times greater than that of the Li-2s); however, some of them had to be handed over to the military. In 1944, one C-47 was handed over to the Sanitary Administration of the red Army, while five went to the Intelligence Departments of the Fronts. In the same year, the Soviet Union began to distribute C-47s among the Allies in Eastern Europe: a dozen of aircraft was provided to Yugoslavia, while six went to Poland. American aircraft were received from the Civil Aviation Fleet by the departmental aviation – thus, for example, one of the C-47s went to the people's Commissariat of Armament.

As a result, in December 1944, the Civil Air Fleet had one-hundred-and-forty C-47s. About one third of them (i.e. 59 aircraft) were concentrated in the 10th Guards Transport Air Division, while 30 were in the 1st Ferry Air Division and 17 were in the 19th Independent Air Regiment. The rest were allocated to various units in the amount of one or two aircraft; for example, the 52nd and 97th Independent Air Regiments had two aircraft each. In January 1945, the Civil Air Fleet had more C-47s than the Soviet-made Li-2s (175 versus 156), and the increase in the fleet of the modern two-engine airplanes allowed for discarding a large number of worn and obsolete aircraft; however, at the same time (on 23 July 1944), Head of the Civil Air Fleet Chief Administration F.A. Astakhov reported that the number of C-47s on which the engines had worked out their service life until the first overhaul was growing rapidly. As of 1 June, there were 24 such aircraft and, by 20 July, the number had grown by 10; it was expected that by mid-August, more aircraft would be grounded. The overhaul and repair of the American engines was complicated by a lack of special tools, spare parts and assemblies, and the average flight time went down to 50 hours per month. Astakhov asked the government to urgently purchase 100 spare engines from the USA and, while the negotiations with the Americans were in progress, the Soviet Union tried to use the aircraft in the most efficient way.

The Douglases were actively used to supply partisan units in the German rear – and of course, the main burden there fell on the unpretentious U-2s and R-5s; however, a Li-2 or a C-47 could carry as much as a dozen as these biplanes could, so for this reason (where suitable sites were available), the Douglases flew to the German rear at night (where such sites were not available, the cargo was dropped with or without a parachute). En route, they were awaited by the enemy anti-aircraft gunners and night fighters.

On 21 September 1943, Lieutenant A.T. Borovsky's aircraft departed with a cargo of ammunition to partisans in the Luben region. En route, an anti-aircraft shell exploded in the tail section of the aircraft and damaged the elevator control cables, yet the pilot was able to keep the aircraft on the route – bringing it to the point of cargo dropping. Meanwhile, the flight engineer and the air gunner tied the parachute straps to the cable ends – thus restoring the control of the aircraft – and the crew safely arrived home. After the repair, Borovsky's C-47 rejoined its military unit.

It was during a similar sortie that the 1st Transport Air Division lost the first C-47. On 13 October 1943, Lieutenant N.E. Navtsenya's aircraft went missing while delivering ammunition to the partisans.

The C-47s were involved in supplies to partisans in Karelia, Byelorussia and the Ukraine. The 120th guards Independent Air Regiment, which had been reinforced by a flight of the Li-2s and the C-47s before the beginning of the offensive in 1944, supplied ammunition to 19 partisan brigades in the forests of Byelorussia; twenty tons of explosives were delivered there by the crews of the 10th guards Transport Air Division.

Pilots of the transport aviation contributed to offensive operations in Romania, Poland, Hungary and all the way to Berlin and Prague. The Li-2s and the C-47s of the 5th Long-Range Corps became the basis for the 'air bridge' which connected the Ukraine and the insurgent Slovakia in 1944 – and it was there, at Zvolen airfield, that the C-47s of the 10th guards Transport Air Division landed. When the uprising was suppressed by the Germans, the site was evacuated and the C-47 piloted by I.I. Ryshkov of the 2rd Air Regiment was the last to depart, as it was already under mortar fire.

During the Vistula-Oder Offensive, the transport aviation enabled the rapid redeployment of fighter and attack regiments that supported the attackers, as well as also evacuating the wounded. The Berlin Strategic Offensive Operation was supported by the 62nd Guards Independent Air Regiment and the 69th and 23rd Independent Air Regiments, which were equipped (among other aircraft) with the C-47s; they all delivered urgent cargoes to the front line.

The transport operation had a lot of work to do during the brief campaign against Japan in the far East, and the pace of the offensive in Manchuria was so high that advanced tank units could only be provided with fuel from aircraft. A Li-2 usually carried eight to 10 barrels of diesel fuel, whereas a C-47 (with a higher load-lifting capacity) took 12 barrels; in addition to the fuel, ammunition was delivered in a similar manner. Groups from two to 10 aircraft transported troops to Harbin, Mukden, Jilin and Port Arthur, as well as to other locations. In the 9th Air Army, a consolidated group of seven C-47s flew such sorties, and it was in a Douglas that colonel I.G. Artemenko arrived in Changchun and handed an ultimatum to the Command of the Kwantung army; also, an aircraft of this same type brought the former Manchu monarch Pŭyí to the Soviet Union.

Since the American aircraft featured a higher flight performance than the Li-2, the former were often used for critical sorties. As early as April 1943, one of the first received aircraft was sent to Cairo to fetch a 'special cargo of the People's Commissariat of Public Health' from there. Major Monakov's crew (of the 1st Transport Air Division) brought to the USSR a batch of penicillin, which was provided by the British, as the Soviet industry was not capable of producing antibiotics at that time.

The C-47s were often used to carry reconnaissance teams beyond the front line – thus, for example, Senior Lieutenant P.A. Bystrov's crew flew five night sorties to East Prussia and delivered a total of 54 men and 5.4 tons of cargo there. Similar operations were also carried out in Byelorussia; the Ukraine; Moldavia; the Transcarpathian Region; and (later) in Slovakia and Poland.

In May 1943, the 105th Independent Night Long-Range Reconnaissance Air Squadron was raised, which was equipped with the C-47s. With three to five Douglases, the squadron flew throughout the year 131 combat sorties to the enemy's deep rear, plus 294 sorties for the delivery of people and cargoes to operational airfields. Later, the squadron (which was already part of the 2nd Special-Purpose Air Division) carried 213 agents and 90 tons of various cargoes beyond the front line before September 1944.

In summer 1944, a dozen C-47s of the 10th Guards Transport Air Division flew from the USSR to Bari in Italy, and there, an air group under the command of Major General V.I. Shchelkunov began its operations. The aircraft of the group supported the combat activities of the People's Liberation Army of Yugoslavia, and they carried ammunition, armament and medicines to Yugoslavia, as well as evacuating the wounded from Yugoslavia. The transport aircraft delivered four disassembled U-2 biplanes from the Soviet Union to Bari, and then the biplanes were handed over to the Yugoslavs. Air cover was provided by the Yak-9DD fighters, which came together with the transport aircraft. On 4 June, A.S. Shornikov's crew evacuated the Yugoslavian Supreme Headquarters, which was headed by Marshal I. Tito from the area of the city of Drvar, which was encircled by the Germans.

In September the same year, a pilot of the 2nd Air Regiment of the 10th Guards Transport Air Division – A.P. Dymov – received an order to detect and capture (in the Bulgarian territory) a special train carrying members of the Bulgarian Royal Family, ministers, and German and Italian diplomatic officials. They were attempting to escape from the advancing Soviet troops to the Turkish border, and the Douglas carried 25 troopers. The C-47 was escorted by four A-20G bombers of the 449th Bomber Air Regiment and, when the train was detected, it was approaching the Bulgarian-Turkish border. Dymov expertly landed the aircraft on a small field near the railway, and the troopers detained the train until reinforcements arrived.

In October 1944, before the defeat of the Slovak National Uprising, a C-47 crew of the 340th Long-Range Bomber Air Regiment delivered the gold and silver of the Slovak Bank to the Soviet territory and, in an aircraft of the same type, A.I. Semenkov brought the German Surrender List to Moscow in May 1945.

The Douglas' advantages could not pass unheeded by the leaders of all levels, who (apparently) preferred the C-47 to the Soviet-made Li-2. This approach was initiated by I.V. Stalin, who chose Colonel Grachev's Douglas (of the Air Force Special-Purpose Air Regiment) to fly to Tehran, in spite of the fact that five PS-84s were specially built for this mission in Tashkent. It is probable that the aircraft chosen by Stalin was one of the two Douglases which had been modified in Bykovo (their description is provided below). In 1945, the management of the Civil Air Fleet reported to the Kremlin: 'The C-47s, in terms of reliability, excel our Li-2s. For this reason, we use them to fly along the most difficult routes, to carry Government members and senior officials, and for international transport missions'.

The C-47s were flown by the Civil Air Fleet's special-purpose squad, which performed important domestic and international flights, and in July 1943, it was expanded into a squadron (with a dozen C-47s). In November 1944, the squadron was turned into the 19th Transport Air Regiment, with twenty-four C-47s and five Li-2s at its disposal. The 19th Air Regiment served the first international lines which were opened during the war, and the regiment aircraft flew to various destinations such as London, Cairo, Washington, Basra and others. For example, in October 1944, regular aerial communication with Sweden was established, and the line was rather cargo-based as opposed to being passenger-based. From Stockholm, the aircraft carried boxes with the famous SKF bearings, which were used by the defense industry. From 1944, two C-47s were operated by the Soviet airlines in Iran, and the Douglases also served the route from Tashkent to Kabul.

In September the same year, a project for establishing aerial communication with the USA via North Africa was suggested, and Soviet aircraft were expected to serve the Moscow — Ankara — Cairo segment. Furthermore, the passengers were carried by American aircraft. Ten C-47s and five C-54s were requested from the USA especially for such a mission, but the Americans refused to provide the latter – invoking the need to use them in the Pacific as the reason for the refusal – and suggested Ankara or Aleppo (Syria) as interchange locations. Eventually, Tehran was selected as the interchange terminal and 10 aircraft were delivered in excess of the Allies' previous undertakings. In January 1945, the C-47s began flying from Moscow to Tehran, where the Soviet segment of the route interfaced with the American one.

In summer 1943, two aircraft were allocated for the Soviet-Chinese Hamiata airline to serve the Alma-Ata — Hami route, which communicated the USSR to China at that time. The reception of the new C-47s by the airline allowed writing off the DC-3s which had been purchased by the Soviet Union before the war.

The growth of the fleet of modern aircraft allowed for using some of them for the most important domestic transport operations. For example, a group of the C-47s carried nickel from Vorkuta and Dudinka (the overall amount constituted approximately 1,500 tons), and aircraft of the 8th Transport Air Regiment were involved in carrying gold from Magadan.

The Northern Fleet's aviation used the C-47s to combat German submarines in the Arctic region, but the aircraft carried no bombs; however, thanks to a large fuel reserve, it was able to carry out long-time patrolling in remote regions which were inaccessible for other aircraft. Several C-47s of the long-range aviation were handed over to naval pilots for this purpose in May 1944, although the Douglases had been used from time to time during such missions in the past; for example, in November 1943, a C-47 took part in escorting Convoy AB-55 near Kolguev Island. When the Consolidated PBN-1 large flying boats arrived from the USA, they took over the long-range patrolling functions and the Douglases resumed flying their habitual transport missions. In total, the naval aviation received ten C-47s and they were operated by the 65th Independent Special-Purpose Air Regiment, which was stationed at Izmaylovo airfield in Moscow, and by transport squadrons and detachments of different fleets.

In total, throughout the war, the transport units of the Civil Air Fleet lost exactly thirty C-47s; however, it should be noted that during the final year of the war, all of the losses (a total of five aircraft) were non-combat-related. Throughout the same period, the air force lost 28 Douglases.

Shipments of the aircraft from the USA ceased after the victory over Japan, and the last C-47 left Fairbanks on 8 September 1945 with pilot P.P. Gamov and his crew on board.

During the period of service in the Soviet Union, the Douglas was subjected to different modifications which were aimed at making it fit for various special missions – thus, for example, the cargo cabin was modified for carrying senior officials. In several versions, the cabin was arranged in the same way as in the PS-84, but later, more luxurious VIP versions appeared. It is probable that the first 'executive' C-47s – with spacious, comfortable seats and an improved interior – rolled out of the NKVD air brigade repair shops in the Bykovo settlement, and there, in July 1943, two aircraft were modified for the 1st NKVD Air Regiment (they were repainted with 'light colors' instead of the traditional American olive-green). These aircraft were intended for carrying the Soviet delegation to Tehran.

In August 1944, at the Civil Air Fleet repair base in Vnukovo, another C-47 was modified. Two additional fuel tanks were installed aft of the cockpit and, on the tanks, sleeping bunks for the crew were arranged. A bulkhead separated this compartment from the passenger cabin, which accommodated 12 large-sized seats and a table; the floor was carpeted. In this aircraft, G.S. Benkunsky's crew carried the Soviet delegation to the Dumbarton Oaks conference in the USA. In 1945, a C-47 was modified into an 'executive' version for the Council of Ministers of the Uzbek Soviet Socialist Republic at Factory No.84 in Tashkent, which built the Li-2s. In the same year, VIP versions of the aircraft were provided to Air Force Commander Marshal A.A. Novikov, Deputy Marshal F.Y. Falaleev, People's Commissar of Armament D.F. Ustinov and People's Commissar of the Navy Admiral N.G. Kuznetsov. In 1947, the factory in Tashkent even designed a typical project of a personal C-47 with comfortable seats and sofas, as well as a rather rich interior.

At the same factory, the Douglases were converted into a 'headquarters' version, and their cabins accommodated seats, sofas and a table for maps and documents. In 1943, eight C-47s were subjected to such a modification and, a year later, 10 aircraft were modified in the same manner; a further five C-47s were equipped with additional tanks in the fuselage in order to use them as fuel tankers for long-range aviation units at frontline airfields. The modification of the C-47s into the 'headquarters' version continued during the following years, and it is known that such an aircraft was produced by the Tashkent Factory in both 1948 and 1949 (one aircraft per year).

For Commander of the 17th Long-Range Air Division Colonel E.F. Loginov, a C-47 was converted to the flying command center and equipped with suitable facilities such as the required means of communication. In the 45th Long-Range Air Division, two C-47s were operated as flying control posts for night fighters – being used during operations near Breslau (now Wroclaw) in spring 1945, as well as during the hunting for transport aircraft and gliders which were attempting to break through to the besieged city.

Contrary to the Li-2, the Douglas carried no defensive armament, which was typical for all American transports, since they operated (as a rule) in conditions of their domination in the air. On the Soviet-German Front, where it was necessary to act in the near-front area (and, especially, over the enemy territory), the absence of armament became a significant disadvantage. This, for example, brought about losses of the 5th Long-Range Air Corps when making the 'air bridge' in the insurgent Slovakia in 1944. In spite of the fact that the C-47s constituted only a small part of the corps' fleet, they comprised nearly half of the shot-down aircraft.

It was initially planned to arm the frontline C-47s similarly to the Li-2 which carried four machine guns: one large-caliber UBT machine gun was mounted in the UTK-1 dorsal turret; two 7.62mm ShKASes were positioned in the fuselage tail part on the side hatch mounts; and the third ShKAS was fixed in the nose section. On 2 September 1943, a corresponding order was issued by the Chief Directorate of the Civil Air Fleet and Aviation Repair Base No.400, which was located at Vnukovo, carried out modifications and the subsequent testing of one aircraft; however, due to reasons that are unclear, the mass modification of the C-47s was not performed, although there were some C-47s armed with machine guns (such an installation was occasionally done with the frontline units). Apparently, no aircraft received a full set of Li-2 armament. The 101st Long-Range

Air Regiment had several C-47s with a UTK-1 dorsal turret, while the 10th Guards Transport Air Division operated such airplanes with an additional pair of ShKAS machine guns mounted in the cabin rear windows (but not in hatches, as it was with the Li-2). At the same time, the C-47 had portholes in the cabin which allowed passengers to carry out fire using their own weapons.

In 1945, a C-47 was modified into a 'flying classroom' to train navigators in the Zhukovsky Air Force Academy, according to a project by Lieutenant Colonel A.S. Vartanyan and Major P.P. Tyurev. Ten workstations for trainees and two workstations for instructors were arranged in the cabin, and a second astrodome and extra antennas appeared above the fuselage. In January through to March 1946, the aircraft was successfully tested at NII VVS and, in September the same year, it was handed over as a model to A.P. Golubkov's OKB-30. The aircraft was used as a platform to design the UChShLi-2 (the navigator training version of the Li-2), which was adopted for service; however, other C-47s were not modified in this manner.

In June 1951, three C-47s were used during the already mentioned tests of the PROSAB-100 bombs in Akhtubinsk. The pilot took off, put the aircraft on course, switched on the autopilot and bailed out. Above the test range, the MiG-15 and the Il-28 (which were moving at a higher flight level) dropped bombs on the target, but the bombs exploded in the air. In one of the cases, the C-47 did not suffer any significant damage and performed a 'soft' belly landing in the outskirts of Akhtubinsk. The *chekists*, who came urgently to the site of the crash, reported to the headquarters: '... The crew escaped and still is not discovered...' and then, finally everything became clear...

During the last year of the war, the Soviet Administration began to think about the possible peaceful use of military transport aircraft, but the C-47 in its original configuration was poorly suited for carrying passengers. As early as July 1944, Head of the Civil Air Fleet Chief Administration F.A. Astakhov began to insist that the People's Commissariat of Aviation Industry should issue tasks for Factory No.84 in Tashkent to modify ten C-47s into the passenger version in August through to September the same year. Actually, the first such modifications were carried out there in spring 1945, and two of the modified aircraft were then handed over to the 10th Guards Transport Air Division. The folding bunks in the former cargo compartment were replaced with seats similar to those in the pre-war PS-84s – and besides, baggage compartments and a toilet were arranged; the cargo hatch was covered and only the ordinary door was left. The passenger version turned out to be 300kg heavier than the cargo equivalent, and such aircraft were referred to as the C-47P.

In June 1945, Astakhov requested that Factory No.84 should be assigned a modification plan for five aircraft per month. In a letter dated 1 November, he insisted on the modification of a total of one-hundred-and-fifty C-47s into the same version. At that time, the Tashkent Factory was converting to a similar passenger version of the Li-2 (designated Li-2P), whose assemblies were used in the modification of American aircraft; however, it was not the Tashkent Factory that was awarded the order, but Moscow Factory No.30.

In September 1945, the Douglas Aircraft Company suggested that the USSR should purchase standard sets for the modification of the C-47 into a passenger aircraft at the cost of USD 12,500 each; however, the Civil Air Fleet did not allocate the currency for that purpose.

Because of the productivity slowdown, which was caused by an industry transition to peace-time conditions, the work went quite slowly at first. On 17 January 1946, there were twenty-one C-47Ps in service with the Civil Air Fleet, which was less than 10 percent of the fleet; by 1 July, however, the number had totaled 97 and, throughout the year, 106 aircraft were modified. By 1 December 1946, more passenger-carrying Douglases had appeared than cargo-carrying ones (one-hundred-and-thirteen C-47s versus one-hundred-and-forty-five C-47Ps). Civil aviation repair bases performed modifications as well, and a total of 125 aircraft were modified there.

In the post-war period (due to a lack of spare American engines), the C-47s were modified to fly with the Soviet-made ASh-62IR engines (in addition, the Li-2 power plant assemblies were used), as well as the ASh-82FN engines. The former version was designated TS-62 (there was a majority of them), while the latter was designated TS-82. In 1950, Factory No.86 in Taganrog began to manufacture kits for modifying the C-47 into the TS-62.

Except the air force and the Civil Air Fleet Administration, the Douglases were operated by the departmental aviation as well – thus, GUSMP received two C-47s in summer 1943 from the 1st Ferry Air Division. On the night of 18 December 1945, pilot Kaminsky's aircraft crashed and burned during take-off in Tiksi. In 1946, GUSMP's aviation had six C-47s at its disposal, with Zakharkovo airfield near Moscow being their base; in summer, they were assigned to various units in the Far North.

These aircraft were rated highly by the Polar Aviation and, typically, were equipped with auxiliary large-volume fuel tanks. After the war, M.A. Titlov made a 24-hour flight in the western sector of the Arctic region! Sometimes, polar pilots attached skis from the Li-2s to the C-47s.

The Aviation of People's Commissariat (later Ministry) of Internal Affairs ranked first after the Civil Air Fleet and the air force in terms of the quantity of American heavy aircraft. A C-47 from among the first batch which had been received by the Soviet Union from America was handed over to the department under a Special Resolution. Most of them were concentrated in the 1st Independent Air Regiment in Bykovo (in July 1948, there were seven aircraft), and some aircraft were in service with local units in Siberia and in the Far East. The American transport aircraft provided the functioning of the camps as well and, as of 1 April 1947, there were four C-47s in service with GULGMP, as well as four aircraft operated by the Chief Administration of Railway Building Camps and two more which were flown by *Dalstroi*. The latter had its own Krasnoyarsk — Magadan airline, where the airplanes flew according to the schedule.

A line-up of C-47s at the factory airfield in the USA. The aircraft in the middle carries the Soviet markings, while the third one is intended for Nationalist China.

A C-47B warming up its engines at Great Falls airfield while en route to Alaska.

A Soviet star being drawn onto a C-47 before ferrying to the USSR.

A C-47B of the Soviet military service.

A Soviet C-47 at Vnukovo airfield, near Moscow.

Technical personnel of the 3rd Squadron, 2nd Regiment, the 10th Guards Air Transport Division near a C-47.

A C-47B of the 10th Guards Air Transport Division in flight above Vnukovo airfield, with more C-47Bs visible on the ground.

The loading of a C-47 of the 19th Separate Air Regiment.

The loading of fuel barrels onto a C-47; note the installation of an upper UTK-1 turret with a UBT machine gun, which is similar to the one installed on the Li-2 aircraft.

A group photo of the 101st Long-Range Air Regiment crew with paratroops at Svyatoshino airfield, near Kiev, in 1944; note the C-47B with a UTK-1 turret in the background.

Pilots of the 62nd Separate Air Regiment in front of a C-47.

A C-47A of the 10th Guards Air Transport Division at an airfield.

A C-47A of a separate transport squadron at Utti airfield in Finland, where it brought the Finnish delegation from Moscow in September 1944.

A C-47 of the 19th Separate Air Regiment at an airfield in Bucharest.

Air Marshal S.A. Krasovsky (in the center, with a moustache) and officers of the 2nd Air Army headquarters near a C-47.

The crew of pilot A.P. Dymov (the 2nd Regiment of the 10th Guards Air Transport Division) after the completion of a mission in Bulgaria in September 1944.

Soldiers of the 2nd Czechoslovak Paratrooper Brigade before boarding the C-47 at an airfield in Kiev in 1944.

A Soviet C-47B at an airfield.

The Command of the 2nd Guards Long-Range Air Corps carrying out a session right in front of the staff C-47; note the unusual tail markings of the plane – featuring the Guards' banner of the air corps.

A crew near the C-47 transport plane.

Hero of the Soviet Union B.A. Lakhtin (right), with his colleague of the 62nd Guards Separate Air Regiment of the Civil Air Fleet at Tempelhof airfield in June 1945; note the C-47 in the background.

Personnel of the French Normandie-Niémen Regiment arriving at Le Bourget airfield in June 1945. The French were taken home by the C-47s of the 19th Separate Air Regiment.

A Soviet C-47 at an airfield in Washington in 1945.

The landing party was brought to Mukden in August 1945 by the Li-2s and C-47s parked in the background.

Soldiers leaving a Li-2 in the landing attack at one of the Manchurian airfields.

A C-47 towing a G-11 assault glider.

The C-47s were often used as towing aircraft for the A-7 and G-11 assault gliders.

Some of the C-47s were handed over by the USSR to their allies. This photo shows aircraft of the 1st Czechoslovak Combined Air Division, which was formed in the Soviet Union – including the Douglas C-47 staff plane.

A scheme of modifying the C-47 into a VIP version, with an improved cabin, was developed at Factory No.84 in Tashkent.

A C-47P airliner with the Aeroflot logo.

Pilot N.I. Neyezzhaly in front of a C-47B which belonged to the Separate Syktyvkar Squad of the Civil Air Fleet.

A post-war photo showing passengers walking to board the Aeroflot C-47P airliner.

A C-47 which was in service with the civil aviation.

The Aeroflot operated C-47s on international routes until the mid-1950s.

A prototype TS-82 aircraft powered by ASh-82FN engines.

A C-47 of the GUSUMP on Wrangel Island in 1946.

A C-47A of the GUSMP in 1948.

The C-47 of the departmental aviation in flight.

7.18 Curtiss C-46 Commando

A single specimen of this military transport aircraft came to the Soviet Union for familiarization purposes.

The aircraft was designed as the CW-20 high-altitude passenger liner with a pressurized cabin, but the design complexity led to a considerable delay in its performance of work, so as a result, the prototype first flew as late as 26 March 1940. At that time, it was the world's largest two-engine passenger aircraft; however, after the beginning of the war, it was modified into a simplified military transport version without any cabin pressurization. From April 1942, mass manufacture of the aircraft began under the designation C-46 and, throughout the war, approximately one-and-a-half-thousand of them were built.

The Americans used them successfully at the Indo-Burma theater of operations (in particular, on the route through the Himalayas, which, at that time, was the only route to provide military aid to China). The C-46s were used in Europe as well (inter alia) for airborne assaults, and the high load-carrying capacity, as well as the spacious cabin and the wide openings of the hatches, allowed for carrying a variety of cargoes – including the dismantled locomotives.

As early as December 1942, the Soviet representatives tried to check the possibility of obtaining any number of the C-46s in 1943 during talks with USAAF Chief of Staff G. Arnold, but the aircraft were not allocated; the C-47s were suggested instead. Considerably later, a single Commando was handed over as a specimen for studying, and it was recorded as an additional model to the US obligations under Protocol IV. The Soviet Union received a C-46A-60-CK (s/n 43-47271), which was manufactured by the factory in Louisville in 1945. It was an aircraft of a later series and was equipped with R-2800-75 engines.

The aircraft was ferried via Alaska and, on 28 April 1945, it arrived in Fairbanks. On 15 May, it passed the Soviet military acceptance. Unlike the usual practice of the relay traffic on the route, the same crew (under the command of Senior Lieutenant Matveev) flew the Commando from Fairbanks to Moscow.

The aircraft was handed over to NII VVS, where it underwent a full program of State tests in the second half of 1945; P.M. Stefanovsky was the leading pilot during the tests. Later, in November through to December, the C-46A passed special tests for examining its stability and controllability. In particular, the boosters used by the Americans aroused much interest, and it was I.A. Stepanov's crew which performed flights in the aircraft. Representatives of the industry and the Zhukovsky Air Force Academy had an opportunity to see the aircraft as well.

Later, the C-46A was used at NII VVS as a transport aircraft, as it was superior in terms of load-carrying capacity to all existing aircraft undertaking such a role. In March-April 1946, the Commando became a mobile base for a test team which was sent to Germany to study the captured Arado Ar 234 jet bomber; the team was led by the already mentioned Stefanovsky. On 26 March, the team flew to Berlin and then to Damgarten, where the Arado had been found; then, the C-46A followed the Ar 234 from one airfield to another in Germany. It is not known when the aircraft was written off.

A C-46A during tests at NII VVS in 1945.

The cockpit of the C-46A.

7.19 Armstrong Whitworth Albemarle

In late summer 1942, the Soviet Ambassador in London – I.M. Maisky – asked the British Government about the possibility of shipping any transport aircraft to the USSR, which were in critical shortage at that time. In September, the British responded that they could share Albemarle bombers which had been modified into the transport variant.

It was an aircraft which was, initially, rather promising: it was developed as a mass bomber and long-range reconnaissance aircraft to be manufactured in war conditions, and Project AW.41 provided for the manufacture of the airframe from non-critical materials. Wood and steel pipes were expected to be widely used; however, the team of designers, which was headed by F. Barnwell, was not going to abandon various innovations: the frame in the nose portion was made of stainless steel; the wood was impregnated with an antiseptic; and the plywood skin was intended to be covered not with canvas, but with a layer of synthetic resin. The whole aircraft was divided into many assemblies that were manufactured independently, which allowed involving some non-air-industry enterprises (e.g. furniture factories and machinery works) in its manufacture.

Large orders were issued for an aircraft named 'Albemarle', which had not come into existence at that time, and contracts were concluded with more than a thousand sub-contractors. The final assembly was intended to be arranged in two factories, and was expected to reach the rate of 100 aircraft per month by the end of 1941. The Albemarle prototype first flew on 20 March 1940, but it turned out that it was extremely overweight and, as a result, its performance was far from the calculated figures – but six million UK pounds had already been spent to launch its mass manufacture!

The bombers began to be built, and changes were made to their design in the course of their mass manufacture. This slowed down production considerably, as well as significantly raising the price of the aircraft, which had been intended to be simple in design, as well as cheap. The first mass-manufactured Albemarles were distributed to squadrons of various roles and they received a negative opinion from all of them. The Albemarle proved to be unsuitable as a bomber; a long-range reconnaissance aircraft; a torpedo bomber; a naval patrol aircraft; and a training aircraft – thus, the only reasonable idea was to modify it into a transport version. Something had to be done with the already-built aircraft, whereas the factory continued to manufacture them. Therefore, the Albemarle was offered to the Soviet Union (initially, those were the hundred aircraft which could be delivered by the end of March 1943).

The bomber was presented to the Soviet representatives in Cambridge, but its problems were concealed. On 1 October, Deputy Air Force Commander G.A. Vorozheikin and Head of Civil Air Fleet Chief Administration F.A. Astakhov sent a letter to People's Commissar of Foreign Affairs V.M. Molotov with an assessment of the aircraft as a transport. Among the advantages, the modern two-engine monoplane pattern; the air-cooled engines; and the combined design were mentioned (apparently, it was decided that the repairs under Soviet conditions would be easier). The running of the engines on 100-octane fuel (there were only imported grades of such a fuel in the Soviet Union at that time); the tricycle landing gear requiring a smooth airfield surface; and the inability to carry oversized cargoes (due to the absence of a loading hatch) were considered to be disadvantages. The British suggested removing one of the fuselage fuel tanks, the turret and armor; cutting a 1,600 x 1,500mm side hatch; making hard floor; and supplementing the navigation equipment during its modification into the transport version.

The conclusion was: '... it is desirable ... to purchase 100 aircraft. It would be expedient to receive the first modified 25 aircraft as soon as possible in order to identify their flight performance and to make corrections to the modification of the rest...'

It should be noted that the Soviet specialists did not agree with the modification scheme. On 17 October, People's Commissar of Trade A.I. Mikoyan received a letter signed by Air Force

Commanders A.A. Novikov, G.A. Vorozheikin and F.A. Astakhov. The letter criticized the removal of the fuselage tank (since it led to a reduction in the flight range) and, earlier, it had been mentioned that the turret and the armor should probably not be removed because its defensive ability would be affected.

Both objections were due to the fact that the Albemarles were expected to be ferried by air – and furthermore, the ferrying route was planned to pass above the territories occupied by the Germans. The British were asked to ferry the first 15 aircraft to Kalinin, as these were intended to be used for the Soviet crews' training, and they were expected to fly back to the UK in the same Albemarles. In particular, negotiations were conducted with the delegation headed by V. Clark, who arrived in Moscow on 23 October in connection with the opening of a regular BOAC airline between Scotland and Kratovo airfield. As soon as 21 November, Maisky reported from London that the British refused to ferry the aircraft; however, they were willing to help as regards training the pilots.

The version for the USSR was designated 'type 219', although the aircraft were also referred to as Mk.I (SF) (i.e. Special Ferrying, or a Russian transport type). Negotiations began in respect of shipping as many as 200 aircraft, and information about the UK's willingness to transfer the second batch of a hundred Albemarles came on 13 January.

The first 25 aircraft were expected to have a triangular side cargo door – and furthermore, it was planned to remove one of the diagonal web elements and to introduce the appropriate reinforcements in order to provide the opportunity to make the hatch bigger, as well as rectangular in shape. Beginning from the twenty-sixth aircraft, the British promised to make changes to the unreliable propeller pitch control mechanism, and 80 aircraft were to be equipped with devices for glider towing.

On 17 December 1942, the State Defense Committee issued a Decree on the Albemarle being ferried to the USSR. The task was to deliver a hundred aircraft by 1 April 1943, and the organization of the ferrying was entrusted to the Civil Air Fleet Chief Administration (although air force personnel were also to be involved); also, the People's Commissariat of Defense and the People's Commissariat of the Navy had to ensure funding. On 17 January 1943, a decision was made to allocate 20 crews, with the intention being to train nine of them in England, while the rest were expected to be trained near Moscow. The Errol (Scotland) — Skagerrak — Norrköping — Chudovo — Bologoe — Kalyazin — Vnukovo route was chosen for the ferrying, and its total length was 2,624km; its estimated time in flight was nine hours and 25 minutes. The route ran over the North Sea; the enemy-occupied Denmark; the neutral Sweden; and the Baltic States, which was where the Germans were also staying at that time, so for this reason, a decision was made to fly at night.

Ferry pilots were mostly recruited from the 1st Transport Air Division, and among them were future Heroes of the Soviet Union A.S. Shornikov, G.A. Taran and S.A. Frolovsky. Some of the navigators and radio operators were provided by the air force, while Colonel V.M. Korotkov was appointed to command the actual ferrying. Along with the pilots, Engineer N.M. Rebrov was sent to England.

To train the crews, the 305th Training Unit was formed in January 1943 at the Errol base in Scotland. Before the departure to England, the Soviet pilots were briefly familiarized with the foreign aircraft and they were trained in the Bostons at Yoshkar-Ola to perform take-off and landing with the nose landing gear (it had not yet been used on the Soviet aircraft).

According to the plan, the first three crews (10 persons, with S.A. Gruzdin as leader) had to reach Britain on board a BOAC Liberator airliner on 10 January, while a second group of five crews (21 persons, under the command of I.Z. Kachanov) followed them with much less comfort in the Pe-8 heavy bomber.

Gruzdin's group arrived in England on 11 January in military uniform without insignia and, on the same day, the first three Soviet pilots and three flight engineers went to Scotland; then, on

13 January, the first two aircraft were ferried to Errol for them. On 21 January, the training flights began and, on 28 January, the second group of 12 men arrived from the Soviet Union; contrary to the plan, they also came from Kratovo in the Liberator. In February, at another base in Prestwick, the Soviet radio operators began their training.

The decision to train only nine crews in England was reconsidered. On 21 February, the Liberator brought another group of 12 Soviet pilots; then, one more group of the same size arrived on 6 March. A week later, a Pe-8 came from Moscow with 20 more men, which was followed by eight pilots who arrived on 23 March in the Liberator. Later still, the personnel were also transported by train to Archangelsk; then, from Lake Krasnoe, they were taken by the RAF's Catalina flying boats.

The aircraft were expected to fly a long way to Russia (and at a high altitude in order to avoid interception), so for this purpose, the Albemarles were specially modified. The modification included making changes to the power plant and to the oil coolers, since the aircraft – overloaded with fuel – had to make a long-term climb to a cruise altitude. The work was performed by No.27 Maintenance Unit in Shawbury and, to expedite the process, the Soviet side agreed to take the first 25 aircraft without any modification of the oil system.

The possibility of a long-term climb with full tanks was experimentally checked by the British test pilots. For anti-icing, they intended to use a special Vaseline-like paste, which was applied to the wing surfaces. The Soviet specialists wanted the engine cowlings to be covered with frontal shields to protect them from overcooling during the long-term altitude flight, but the British only agreed to install temporary fixed ring-type screens.

The program for the pilots' conversion training in Scotland was quite brief: it included two flights per pilot (with an instructor during the daytime), and two flights per pilot at night, plus four solo flights. Pilots tried to overcome the language barrier to the extent they could – having learned a few dozen key terms and standard phrases for communication with the instructors and control tower operators. Instructor Jan Taudy (a Czech by nationality), who had, for some time, been living in the Soviet Union and spoke Russian, provided certain help; then, the Albemarles were accepted by the Soviet Commission and assigned to the crews. There was a shortage of the aircraft, and the British proved unable to adhere to their own proposed schedule of 15 aircraft per month – thus, for example, on 20 March, the Soviet representatives stated that they were rejecting five or six Albemarles after trial flights. It was reported from London to Moscow: 'The aircraft, as a rule, have many defects, or are fully unfit for use'. There were problems with the condition of the aircraft allocated for training flights; usually, among five or six aircraft, only two or three were fully operational. The Soviet military mission reported from London: 'The British provide unserviceable aircraft for training'.

It is noteworthy that the Soviet mechanics as included in the crews were not allowed to carry out any aircraft maintenance, with the problem turning out to be with their officer rank. The mechanics came from the 1st Transport Air Division and they had graduated from civil aviation schools as Military Technicians II Rank, which was equivalent to Lieutenant. Under British standards, however, sergeants were expected to do the handiwork, whereas officers had to do the thinking. They were told to superintend the work of the British mechanics, but how could one do it without having a command of the English language?

The situation immediately attracted the attention of security officers (who were present in every unit) and, of course, aroused suspicion. An unidentified staff member of the People's Commissariat of State Security (NKGB) reported: '… The British delay aircraft acceptance on purpose … The Soviet engineers are not allowed to maintain the aircraft…'

The ferrying was expected to begin on 1 February 1943, and three aircraft were expected to be the first to depart; however, either technical problems or the weather interfered. Only on the evening of 3 March did the first crew depart from Errol, with Captain A.S. Shornikov as pilot;

Lieutenant P.N. Yakimov as navigator; Lieutenant A.A. Verderevsky as radio operator; and G.I. Galaktionov as engineer. They flew the Albemarle s/n P1567. The weather was bad and the aircraft became covered with ice, and the British paste on the wing leading edge became mixed with the ice. Over the Soviet territory, the Albemarle flew by radio beacons and, after nine hours of flight, the aircraft landed at Vnukovo. No faults were revealed during the flight, except for the fact that the illumination lamps in the cockpit had burnt out. The frontier guards and customs officers later declared a protest – stating that they had not been informed of the flight, and that the crew had not been checked in terms of smuggling.

After the landing, the aircraft was thoroughly inspected: oil leaks from the right tank and from the pipelines of the left tank were found, and the cowling of the left engine muffler had burnt through. It was also discovered that the bosses from one of the center wing section panels had broken loose.

The route was long and dangerous, as it ran over a territory occupied by the enemy and, at any moment, one might expect a fighters' attack – and not all of the Albemarles were provided with armament: often, pistols in the pockets of the crew were the only weapon on board, so in order to protect themselves from interception, the pilots climbed as high as possible, but they were the ones who suffered the greatest difficulties. On the Albemarle, there was no autopilot, but there was a second control column that was usually tilted to the side so as not to interfere with the passage to the nose compartment; however, each crew included just one pilot, with no one to take over his duties to relieve him.

On 11 March, three aircraft took off from Errol airfield; the pilots-in-command were Captains A.I. Kulikov (s/n P1455), I.Z. Kachanov (s/n P1590) and B.K. Labutin (s/n P1477). The aircraft carried tools, spare parts and special equipment – and besides, Kachanov had a female passenger on board (a certain Ms Starostina); however, some of the veterans claim that there was no passenger, as she is only mentioned in the British documents.

The aircraft took off one by one at certain time intervals. Labutin reached Vnukovo safely, but Kulikov's crew (navigator Captain A.I. Semenov, mechanic Senior Lieutenant V.S. Perelygin and radio operator Lieutenant M.I. Lobko) went missing. The last time the radio operator got in touch was at a distance of about 200 miles from the Scottish Coast and, approximately 20 miles to the east over the sea, the airplane was spotted by a British radar station, but that was all.

En route, Kachanov's Albemarle became iced so much that it fell into an uncontrolled fall and all of the antennas broke off. The pilot managed to bring the aircraft into level flight, but only near the ground and, at that moment, he saw that the aircraft was flying over the positions of the Germans, who opened fire from all weapons. Kachanov hurried away into the clouds, but having lost orientation and communication, the aircraft was flown by the magnetic compass strictly to the east. Only a few hours later did the clouds disperse and the navigator saw the Volga underneath! In addition to all of these troubles, anti-aircraft gunners sprayed the strange aircraft with machine gun fire upon landing in Kazan. The aircraft landed at Arskoe Pole airfield, which belonged to Factory No.22, but the adventures were not over: all new arrivals were arrested by airfield security, and this aircraft bore red stars as insignias, but the camouflage was of British pattern; also, the crew's overalls and helmets were British, but the pistols in their pockets were American. All of this explains why the pilots were initially mistaken for enemy spies.

On 27 March, two aircraft departed: s/n P1636, which was piloted by Captain S.A. Frolovsky's crew, and s/n P1637, which was flown by Captain F.A. Lakhno's crew. Frolovsky's crew was incomplete, so Senior Lieutenant V.V. Dryamin combined the duties of both navigator and radio operator. Both aircraft reached their destination safely and, on 4 April, Captains P.M. Rusakov (aircraft s/n P1640) and I.G. Mosalev (aircraft s/n P1647) headed for the Soviet Union. Rusakov landed safely in Vnukovo, while Mosalev returned to Errol due to the oil overheating.

The oil-cooling control was a sore point in the Albemarle, and the position of the radiator shutters could only be changed on the ground ("by one, two, three or four holes," according to M.I.

Grigoriev's recollections); in flight, the pilot could do nothing with them. The Soviet pilots did gradually get the hang of it, but it still felt uncomfortable and dangerous. The British initially refused to make the shutters controllable from the cockpit, and it was only in April 1943 that they promised to install controllable shutters (beginning from the one-hundred-and-fortieth aircraft).

Mosalev's crew departed again on 12 April, but managed to reach no further than Kalyazin, which was considered to be an alternative airfield. The second aircraft (s/n P1642), which flew on the same day, was piloted by Captain M.I. Grigoriev. Near Copenhagen, it was fired at by German anti-aircraft gunners, but the Albemarle suffered no damage. Grigoriev flew further to Vnukovo without any problems, but due to a heavy fog, landed only after the third approach.

By that time, the Albemarles' ferrying program was lagging behind the schedule considerably, and the factory had no time to modify the bombers into transports; meanwhile, the days grew longer and the nights grew shorter. On 3 April, Astakhov sent a letter to the air force commander in which he pointed out the growing danger of flying over the territory controlled by the enemy. The night-time was already barely enough for the flight of a single aircraft, but for a group which flew at intervals, such an amount of time was not sufficient at all; however, when the weather permitted, the Albemarles continued to leave the Errol base in groups. On 25 April, the crews of Captain A.V. Yakovlev (P1638), Captain A. Taran (P1595) and Senior Lieutenant P.A. Drizhenog (P1562) departed. Initially, Knyazhko was assigned as a pilot for Taran's crew; however, due to a certain fault, he was not allowed to fly the mission and was later sent home by sea. Taran's aircraft was fired at by anti-aircraft artillery above the front line, and all of the Albemarles – one after another – landed in Vnukovo in the morning.

Two days later, aircraft s/n P1645 and s/n V1598 left for the Soviet Union. The latter was piloted by Captain Frolovsky, who'd had the time to return to England after the first flight. He successfully arrived in Vnukovo, although by mistake, he had entered the restricted area near Volokolamsk and had nearly been subjected to fire by Soviet anti-aircraft gunners. Lieutenant F.F. Ilchenko, who had left 10 minutes before Frolovsky, was not so lucky: the last radiogram from his aircraft was received two and a half hours after departure, and the British radio locating stations which had spotted the transmission had determined that Ilchenko had deviated from the course. After that, Frolovsky saw a falling flash followed by an explosion. Initially, there was a theory that the Albemarle had been shot down by Swedish anti-aircraft gunners, so the missing crew was searched for by British ships and aircraft, with requests sent to the Swedish coast guard; however, no traces of the lost aircraft were found. Later, it turned out that the aircraft had been shot down by German fighters. Along with Ilchenko, the navigator V.A. Nefyodov; the engineer A.K. Matveev; and the radio operator P.S. Golovin were killed. After that, it was decided that the ferrying of the Albemarles through the danger zone was to be stopped.

By that time, 12 aircraft had arrived in the Soviet Union, but all of them were different: some of the aircraft carried no armament, while others were equipped with a twin mount, which was comprised of 7.69mm machine guns. Also, there were aircraft fitted with three or four fuel tanks, although not all of the aircraft were equipped with flame dampers. The number of oxygen bottles could be nine or 12, and several aircraft were provided with devices for glider towing; the Albemarle s/n P1477 had no cargo door.

There was an intention to ferry the rest of the Albemarles via North Africa, so in early April, the British suggested the Bristol — Casablanca — Tripoli — Cairo — Tehran — Baku — Stalingrad — Moscow route. Several variants of the Britain-Morocco segment of the route were considered – including a direct flight through the neutral (but German-friendly) Spain, as its air defense capabilities were openly neglected; also, a route via France and Italy was analyzed. To adapt the aircraft to hot climate conditions, tropic air filters were expected to be installed; mufflers were to be modified to suit the requirements of higher temperatures; and some assemblies were to be protected with dust covers.

Negotiations related to the south route took a long time. On 26 June 1943, the British reported that they were ready to support the functioning of the route, and that the aircraft were expected to be ferried in groups at daytime. The British party was responsible for fuel provision, maintenance, crew meals and tropical uniform, and it was also expected that Soviet groups with radio stations would be stationed at intermediate stops en route. The departure point was to be Hurn airfield in the UK, and the British area of responsibility ended in Tehran, as from there, the Soviet party was to ensure the ferrying of the aircraft on its own.

While the aircraft were being ferried, the Soviet specialists had already started to think about how to modify the Albemarles – and first of all, the armament was considered. The Soviet specialists deemed that even the original bomber armament was insufficiently efficient, which was to say nothing of the transport modification. Therefore, NII GVF was prescribed to develop by 1 April 1943 a new armament pattern for the Albemarle, and said pattern was intended to be used further as a model for re-equipping all of the aircraft that was to be received by the 1st Transport Air Division; in fact, the task was reassigned to designers from Factories No.456 and No.43. The installation of a 12.7mm machine gun in the aircraft nose section was quickly rejected for the reason that it would have required too many modifications, and that the navigator's area would have become incapacious. There was a suggestion to install a 7.62mm ShKAS machine gun in the ball head of the nose section; to mount a UTK-1 turret with a UBT machine gun instead of the British machine gun on the top; and to arrange another UBT on a special mount at the bottom (because it could not be installed in the tail section, since it led to undesirable changes in the CG position); finally, an option to mount a UBT on the LU-Pe-2 mount in the tail cone was considered. In case of the impossibility to implement the bottom mounting, two ShKAS machine guns were expected to be installed in the side hatches. With all of this, the firepower was the same as that of the Il-4, but the center of gravity was shifted slightly backwards.

Even earlier, a decision had been made to subject the Albemarle to thorough testing. In mid-March 1943, the Civil Air Fleet Chief Administration suggested that the air force should accept one of the aircraft at Vnukovo, as well as to perform trial flights. On 26 March, Air Force Chief Engineer Lieutenant General A.K. Repin gave the following order to Head of NII VVS Major General P.A. Losyukov: "Accept the aircraft, organize testing and provide recommendations for operation." The Civil Air Fleet Chief Administration wished to conduct joint tests, and suggested that two engineers and a pilot (Captain A.E. Dyomin) should become members of the testing commission, but the military bodies (probably) rejected the idea.

In April, Albemarle s/n P1477 was ferried to NII VVS, and the aircraft was (sort of) an intermediate result of the bomber conversion into a transport. It was deprived of all of the gun armament, but it retained its bomb-carrying capability, although there was no cargo door. The aircraft was fitted with a second fuselage fuel tank, and the floor had probably been reinforced (the Soviet report described it as a 'load platform'); also, there were differences in the radio equipment.

The aircraft s/n P1477 was flown at the NII VVS facilities by Major V.V. Lisitsyn's crew, with Colonel Kabanov, Lieutenant Colonel Nyukhtikov and Lieutenant Colonel Zhdanov also taking part in the trial flights. Dyomin was not on the list – thus, the letter from NII GVF had been ignored. In total, 48 flights were performed, and the flying time totaled and 27 hours and five minutes; the tests were completed before 19 June.

The airplane was assessed, first and foremost, as a bomber by comparing it to the Soviet-made Il-4 and Er-2, and to the American-made B-25C. The British aircraft was inferior to them in terms of speed, operational ceiling and rate of climb. With a weight of 14,500kg, its maximum speed at the rated engine power reached 396km/h; at maximum power, it was 409km/h. In terms of its take-off and landing characteristics, the aircraft was superior both to the B-25C and the Yer-2, but inferior to the Il-4. It should be noted that the Albemarle's engines were unable to reach full power, since they ran on 87-octane fuel instead of the prescribed 100 – thus, the sufficiently high boost could not be achieved. The general conclusion was: '... significantly inferior to the majority of Soviet and foreign aircraft...'

The Albemarle's take-off run was slightly longer than that of the Il-4 (565m versus 530m); however, the poor rate of climb resulted in the aircraft's dashing low above the ground for a long time, so Soviet test pilots came to the conclusion that the aircraft needed a take-off area of at least 2,000 × 2,000m. Due to its heavy weight, the tricycle landing gear and the small clearance between the propeller end tips and the ground, the aircraft could only be operated from hard-surface airfields.

The handling performance aroused no enthusiasm either, and the general opinion was that the aircraft had insufficient transverse and longitudinal stability. Furthermore, the latter became worse if the CG was shifted backwards. Nyukhtikov wrote: 'In terms of stability, it is close to the Il-4'. It was not a compliment, since before the introduction of a new wing, the Soviet bomber had been notorious for its instability, which was exhausting for the pilot. The visibility from the Albemarle's pilot seat was rather limited – especially during climb – and the approach procedure turned out to be very complicated, because at a reduced rpm, the aircraft tended to 'sink' abruptly; it was almost incapable of gliding. The landing itself was simple, but the wheel brakes were inefficient. With one of the engines shut down, the aircraft was unable to perform a level flight; it could only descend. It is interesting that the unusually gentle landing gear shock absorption was also reckoned to be among the disadvantages: the pilot sometimes did not feel the lift-off moment at night and, as a result, the Albemarle was found suitable only for pilots who had higher-than-average skills.

At the same time, its maneuverability on the ground and in flight was deemed to be satisfactory, and its cockpit and cabin were found to be comfortable and warm; however, the evacuation from the cabin in an emergency was complicated, and people – especially in winter uniform – had to squeeze through the doors with difficulty.

The power plant won high praise, which was thanks to the powerful and reliable Hercules engines, as well as the convenient arrangement of the assemblies and the efficient oil scavenge system; however, according to Soviet standards, the engine was not suitable for low-temperature operations in cold winter. As the front cowling cover was not available, the engines tended to over-cool during gliding. It was not possible to blow the oil coolers in flight because the shutter was set to a certain position so that it secured them, and the option of quick oil drainage (before the oil got cold) was impossible. Furthermore, there was no possibility to perform a complete draining of the system; in order to get to the drain valve, it was required to partially remove the cowling. The engines were started from electric starters which operated from ground storage batteries. In cold weather, their power was not always sufficient, but for this reason, it was recommended that the autostarter claw clutch should be attached to the propeller hubs.

The unreliability of the hydraulic mechanisms for the propellers' pitch control had been detected prior to the ferrying of the Albemarles, and NII VVS specialists only confirmed this point of view. The radio station and the Intercom operated quite well, but were powered from a combination of storage batteries and dry batteries. The latter (that were of a suitable type) were not available in the USSR, and the armor protection was considered appropriate for a night bomber; however, during the re-equipment (which included the hatch mount installation), a decision was made that an additional plate should be provided for the aft gunner.

It turned out that the aircraft was unable to carry Soviet bombs on the British bomb racks, so it was suggested that intermediate beams should be installed and Soviet-made racks be secured to them. With Der-21 or MD-3-40 racks, the aircraft was able to carry eighteen FAB-100 bombs; Der-19 allowed taking nine FAB-250s or six FAB-500s; with Der-20, two FAB-1000s or a FAB-2000 could be carried. The bomb sight was intended to be replaced as well (i.e. to mount the NKPB sight on the bracket from the M.9 sight).

The aircraft's combat survivability was reduced due to the fact that the British used (in the control system) not cables, but steel wire (which was easier to break, as well as being due to the weak armament and the poorly designed engine fuel feed system, which, with one of the pumps faulty, did not allow for feeding both engines).

NII VVS recommended using the Albemarle not as a bomber, but as a transport aircraft to carry people, cargoes and fuel.

Having studied the report, the Long-Range Aviation Command refused to accept the British aircraft, and Deputy Long-Range Aviation Commander Lieutenant General I.V. Markov reported: 'Due to the complexity of piloting, non-availability of stability margin, and long take-off run, the aircraft cannot be used as a night bomber'.

Concurrently (beginning from April 1943), aircraft s/n P1567 was tested at NII GVF – being assessed in the role of a transport aircraft. Specialists came to the conclusion that the high load-lifting capacity of the Albemarle could be useful solely for the transportation of compact heavy cargoes, but due to the small size of its access doors, the loading took too much time. Furthermore, the center of gravity of the fully loaded aircraft was shifted backwards considerably. The cabin could accommodate a maximum of 19 passengers, but in such conditions, they were awfully cramped for space (with only $0.4m^3$ of space per person), whereas the Li-2 offered $1.56m^3$ per person. To access the passenger cabin from the cockpit, one had to move apart the armored plates of the partition and then crawl.

NII GVF paid much attention to operation and maintenance issues, and it was found out that none of Soviet oils were suitable for the Hercules engines; special oil with tributyl phosphate was required. If the latter was not available, any other type of oil destroyed the coating of the bearing inserts, plus the reserve of the compressed air in the bottle was so small that it could be consumed during take-off.

The combined structure, which was deemed to be more repairable under Soviet conditions, fell short of all expectations; the British did the bonding and made the connections in an entirely different way. In order to repair large-sized wooden assemblies, a special tooling was required, plus leveling could bring considerable problems, since multifarious fixtures were needed for it.

The findings of NII GVF were also disappointing: the aircraft was poorly suited for cargo and passenger transportation; it required only good airfields (which were scarce in the USSR, with almost none at the front line), highly skilled personnel, and imported fuel and oil; and it was very prone to damage, plus any repairs were connected with a lot of difficulties – thus, using the British aircraft would be inefficient: '... Further purchase of the Albemarle-1 aircraft would be unpractical. Operation of the already purchased aircraft could be allowed in a cargo version, and only after elimination of all detected ... drawbacks...'

There was an attempt to use the Albemarle for the training of paratroopers; however, after a trial flight in Tushino (performed by M.I. Grigoriev's crew), the idea was rejected. The narrow fuselage, which was cluttered with trusses, did not let the paratroopers access the hatch, and the hatch itself proved to be too narrow. It is noteworthy that in the Soviet Union, there had never been any attempt to use the Albemarle in the role of a towplane for gliders.

The naval aviation was the last to get involved in the testing of the Albemarle, and it was assessed in the role of a potential torpedo bomber and a mine-laying aircraft. After the replacement of the bomb racks, the aircraft could carry (inside the bomb bay) a Soviet-made AMD-1000 bottom mine, one or two British-made A Mk.IVs or four AMD-500s. The bay size was sufficient to accommodate two 45-36AN torpedoes, but in order to arrange it there, however, one had to remove a cross girder, as well as securing the lower spars with a shaped frame instead of the girder. The middle hydraulic drives of the bay doors were also removed, and oxygen bottles were moved to the top. In such a configuration, the bay could accommodate a single 45-36AVA torpedo with a parachute system.

According to calculations, the aircraft's take-off weight with two 45-36AN torpedoes, a Soviet defensive armament and six crew members on board totaled approximately 16,000kg. The flight speed and range were nearly equal to those of the Il-4 with a single externally suspended torpedo, whereas the take-off distance (up to a height of 25m) was considerably longer.

There is no information as to which version of the aircraft was tested at NII VVS, but it is known that the aircraft was flown by Major Reidel, Captain Komarov and Captain Orlov – and here is their opinion: "In terms of handling performance... take-off, landing, longitudinal and transverse stability and maneuverability, the aircraft is superior to the Il-4." Again, however, the insufficient transverse stability was noted, as well as the impossibility to fly with one engine inoperative (even with a feathered propeller) at a weight of more than 14,200kg; also, the tendency to plunge at turns was added to the list of drawbacks. The naval aviation engineers pointed out that there would be a need to import oil and hydraulic fluid for the Albemarle because of a lack of Soviet equivalents for them.

The general conclusion was that the aircraft was suitable neither as a torpedo bomber (it was much easier to modify the American-made A-20), nor as a bomber; however, it could be used in the role of a long-range reconnaissance aircraft, or as an aircraft for navigator training purposes.

The naval pilots completed their tests in early October 1943 and, by that time, the majority of the Albemarles as ferried to the USSR had been in active operation. All of the aircraft (except s/n P1477, which was staying at NII VVS) were used to equip the 2nd Squadron of the 3rd Air Regiment (which was being raised at that time) of the 1st Transport Air Division as based in Vnukovo; Captain P.M. Rusakov was appointed as the squadron's leader. As of 1 May 1943, the squadron had 11 aircraft, and all of them were deemed to be serviceable. Since the division was subordinated to the Civil Air Fleet Chief Administration, the aircraft were assigned civil registration numbers from CCCP-Л401 through to Л411.

The crew's conversion training for the new aircraft involved certain problems: ferry pilots who had been trained in Britain were to make several flights each, and the majority of them were sent to Scotland again. Some of them stayed in the Soviet Union (for example, Taran, Kachanov and Lakhno), but on the other hand, new crews which received the unfamiliar airplanes in Vnukovo had to master them on their own. On 29 March, an order was issued on the training of 20 crews and, with the help of NII GVF specialists (headed by Engineer Kuznetsov), the technical specification, maintenance schedule and the aircraft flight manual were prepared. Everything was done with considerable haste and, in late April, the British aircraft began cargo operations on the Moscow — Kazan, Moscow — Kuibyshev and Kuibyshev — Aktyubinsk routes.

Nearly every flight involved malfunctions, and the report of Regiment Engineer Major Kolychev contained a list of the multifarious defects as detected during the early months: the break-off of the hydraulic system hoses was a constant problem, and this defect was further aggravated by failures of the hydraulic system cut-off valve, which could lead to leakages of the major portion of the hydraulic fluid; the hydraulic fluid eroded copper tubes, and the copper settled on the LG extension/retraction valve stems – resulting in their failure; the propellers could only be set to two positions, which corresponded to a high and low pitch, which restricted the pilot's freedom in the selection of the most economic flight mode; the nipples in the hydraulic control system were butt-welded to duralumin tubes and, under the action of the vibrations caused by an insufficient engine mount shock absorption, the welded joint became destroyed and the hydraulic fluid leaked away; and the propeller changed its pitch spontaneously – causing an excessive engine rpm – and there were cases when the propeller failed to set to the feathering position.

In several cases, the air compressors failed – and it was then discovered that Soviet oil was not suitable for them. The instruments and electric starters became faulty, and the landing gear well doors failed to close. The small clearance between the propeller blade tips and the ground (approximately 300mm) brought about a lot of problems – making even take-off from a dirty concrete runway difficult, which is to say nothing of unpaved runways. Tires were too thin according to Soviet standards, as they began to spin on the disks and often got burst.

In Vnukovo, the Albemarles were stationed at the airfield (not in the hangars), so the plywood gradually became soaked with water and, eventually, it cracked. Percale tapes, which were used to cover the panel joints, separated and fell off in flight.

The aircraft had quite a lot of names and nicknames in the Soviet Union! In documents, it was referred to as 'Albemale', 'Albimal', 'Albermile' and AL-1; finally, the aircraft was sarcastically nicknamed 'Abormot' (in Russian, *obormot* means 'blockhead'). Below are some opinions about the aircraft, with V.P. Yakovlev writing: '... in terms of performance, it is reckoned among [the] underdeveloped, which are gradually becoming obsolete, and are being written off...' According to Lieutenant G.P. Moiseev: 'The aircraft has poor stability; as a result, the pilot gets tired very quickly'. Lieutenant Z.I. Muromtsev echoes this sentiment: '... in flight, one gets always very tired...'

There were also complaints about the unreliable propeller control; the difficulties with the aircraft's operation from unpaved airfields; the brakes overheating during taxiing; and the unavailability of anti-icing devices. Only the engines got a definite seal of approval – thus, F.A. Lakhno wrote: 'The Bristol Hercules XI engine is wonderful'.

The multifarious defects could not help but cause accidents (and even catastrophes), with the first crash occurring during a trial flight along the Moscow — Novosibirsk route on 29 April 1943. Near Sverdlovsk, the aircraft fell into the lake and broke into halves as a result of the impact. The crew was thrown out into the water, but they survived.

Two days later, on 1 May, aircraft s/n P1595 (which was flown by G.A. Taran) made a forced landing due to a left engine failure. The aircraft was badly damaged and discarded, and the mechanic N.M. Makhalov was found guilty and brought to trial. He was accused of the careless installation of a rubber gasket, which had determined the aircraft's fate.

During the first half of the year, forced landings took place in Baku, Astrakhan and Tbilisi. During the Moscow — Baku flight on 21 June, there were two pilots on board aircraft reg/n CCCP-Л407 (Instructor Lieutenant N.V. Matveev and Lieutenant M.A. Pryshchepa, who was being checked by Matveev). Before landing at Bina airfield in Baku, it was detected that the pneumatic system had no air in it, so the pilots decided to perform the landing without the application of brakes. At the end of the landing run (in order to avoid any collision with the fighters at the parking area), Pryshchepa turned to the right, but the aircraft overran the runway and dashed toward the buildings. Navigator Sergeant S.M. Motin began to panic and jumped out of the front emergency hatch, which was a hinged window panel in the extreme nose section. Unfortunately, his jump was unsuccessful, as he got under the wheel and soon died. The aircraft then ran approximately 60m more at a speed comparable with that of a walking man, but then it caught a metal tube by the left wing, which smashed it; next, the aircraft got into a 0.5m-deep ditch, which resulted in the nose landing gear strut breaking and the 'leg' folding. The Albemarle dug its nose into a slope and stopped, but later on (while being evacuated), the aircraft bumped its tail against the towing tractor.

As a result, it was recorded that the navigator cabin framework and skin (and the left-wing bottom skin) was damaged; two ribs were broken; there were dents on the spar caps; the nose landing gear folding mechanism was broken; two blades were bent on each propeller; eight ribs and the trim tab were broken on the left elevator; and two lower ribs were broken on the left rudder.

A group headed by the leader of the 3rd Squadron – P.M. Rusakov – was delegated on 23 June to launch an investigation into the condition of the aircraft which had got 'trapped' in Astrakhan, Baku and Tbilisi. Apart from the crew, the group, which flew in aircraft reg/n CCCP-Л403 (s/n P1640), included the chief engineer for NII GVF – S.E. Kuznetsov – and Senior Flight Technician

A.G. Borisov. They visited Astrakhan, where they landed safely at Bina airfield, and it was there that they detected a leakage in the left engine oil system. While Rusakov, Kuznetsov and Borisov were taking part in the work of the Accident Investigation Commission, the mechanics were repairing the aircraft. On 26 June, the Albemarle departed for Tbilisi, and pilot F.A. Lakhno (who knew the local airfields) was on board the aircraft, together with the crew.

At a distance corresponding to five minutes of flying from Ajikabul airfield in Azerbaijan, the oil pressure in the left engine dropped again, so Rusakov performed a hasty landing in Ajikabul. Soon after landing, the personnel found an oil leakage from under the pump cover and, after a minor repair, the aircraft (during the evening of the same day) departed for Kirovabad, but after approximately 20 minutes of flight, problems with the left engine arose again; consequently, the crew shut the engine down and feathered the propeller. Rusakov attempted to reach Yevlakh airfield and almost succeeded: at the approach, the pilot started up the left engine anew, but suddenly, both engines began losing their thrust. Attempts to increase the rpm or to boost up the engines were futile, and the aircraft was descending at a rapid rate. Rusakov became aware that he would not reach the airfield, and there was no time to choose the landing location, so the pilot simply extended the landing gear. At a speed of 160-165km/h, the aircraft struck the ground with its left wing tip, and then with the left propeller. The propeller came off, together with the engine gearbox, but then (during the landing run), the left wheel got into a ditch – causing the aircraft to turn through 180° and its landing gear to collapse. The fuselage broke into two parts near the door, and its tail portion turned so that the side assumed a face-up position; the left engine broke off completely. All of the people who were on board the aircraft were either injured or wounded, and four of them had to spend some time in a hospital.

Investigations showed that both propeller controls had failed at once in flight and, after the inspection, it became clear that the Albemarle had been assembled by the British from the parts of two different aircraft (the fuselage and empennage of one aircraft, and the wing of another); this was discovered from the markings on the assemblies.

On 27 July, in aircraft reg/n CCCP-Л401 (which was piloted by Lieutenant G.P. Moiseev), one of the propellers spontaneously changed over to a low pitch and, as a result, the crew performed a forced landing near Olkhovka.

The engineering service of the regiment suggested different steps to enhance the aircraft's reliability. In the propeller pitch-adjusting mechanisms ('exactors'), aluminum tubes were replaced with ones that were made from annealed copper and had different fittings. There were also plans to modify the fuel system by introducing the cross-feeding of the engines, as well as to mount an additional 150L compressed air bottle. Soviet engine oil was mixed with an additive brought from England and, as a result, the Hercules engines ran on it without any malfunctions.

As of 1 September, the regiment had nine Albemarles, of which six were serviceable. The crews were led by V.G. Kirsanov, I.Z. Kachanov, E.T. Stepanov, F.A. Lakhno, V.P. Yakovlev, S.A. Frolovsky, A.Y. Ilyin and Z.I. Muromtsev. In view of the high accident rate, any operation of the aircraft was temporarily suspended, but by that moment, their flying time had totaled 15-112 hours. In May, the training of new crews was ceased.

On 20 July 1943, Head of the Civil Air Fleet Chief Administration F.A. Astakhov reported to People's Commissar A.I. Mikoyan: "In view of the State testing results and operational experience, I deem further acceptance and ferrying of the Albemarle aircraft impossible unless the detected design and manufacture defects are rectified." A long dispute with the British in respect of the defects began, but finally, by mid-December, the British had agreed to rectify 14 defects out of 41 for the following reasons: seven of the defects, according to the opinion of the British party, were incidental to almost any aircraft type; thirteen of the defects had not been detected during their operation in Great Britain; and the remaining seven defects were connected with operational mistakes.

On 21 September, the Soviet Embassy in London informed the British Foreign Office that as of 1 August, only 25 Albemarles out of the planned 160 had been accepted. The reason consisted of the large number of defects which had to be eliminated on a timely basis – 'otherwise, the Soviet Government sees no possibility to further accept the aircraft'. In September, the Soviet Union officially rejected 100 aircraft, and there was also a requirement to modify another 86.

Almost until spring 1944, there was a hope that the issue of the Albemarles would be settled successfully. The Soviet ferrying pilots remained at the Errol base, and training continued until 18 April 1944.

During training on 29 May 1943, A.I. Gruzdin's aircraft crashed. It fell into a spin when the pilot attempted to round a mountain during a pull-out from a dive. Together with Gruzdin, V.V. Dryamin (the navigator), A.A. Alekseev (the engineer) and the chief cook of the local canteen (who was, for some reason, on board) were killed. The commission that investigated the case came to the conclusion that the accident had occurred through the pilot's own negligence.

In April 1944, the Soviet Union rejected the last 86 Albemarles, and the aircraft which had already been accepted (but had not been ferried) were handed back. On 30 April, the training unit was disbanded and the Soviet crews came home by sea.

By that time, the 1st Transport Air Division had begun to receive the American-made C-47 transport aircraft, which considerably exceeded the Albemarles in terms of capability. A decision was made to dispose of the British ersatz transports, but the Naval Aviation Command was willing to take them and use them for navigator training purposes. In September 1943, two aircraft were transferred from the 1st Transport Air Division to the 65th Special-Purpose Air Regiment, which was stationed in Izmailovo. The unit was, at that time, involved in the testing of naval aviation airplanes – and it is probable that one of the mentioned two aircraft was tested there. Seven Albemarles stayed with the 1st Transport Air Division, but of them, only four were serviceable. In December, one more aircraft was handed over to the naval pilots.

As of 1 January 1944, there were only six Albemarles in Vnukovo, but thanks to the technical personnel's efforts, all of them could fly. Nevertheless, the transfer process continued and, during the same month, four more aircraft were handed over to the navy. The last two British aircraft were transferred much later in July.

Four aircraft were in service with the 65th Air Regiment for a rather long time, and they were used to carry high-priority cargoes in the rear. In 1944, two serviceable aircraft were handed over to the Levanevsky Higher Naval Aviation School in Bezenchuk (the Volga region), and three more aircraft came to the same school directly from Vnukovo. In the school, all of the Albemarles joined the Navigator Training Regiment. Six seats were installed for students in each aircraft's fuselage, with 'heels' for bomb sights at each seat and, besides this, the aircraft were also fitted with underwing racks for practice bombs. Together with the school, the aircraft were later redeployed to Nikolaev. As of 9 May 1945, two Albemarles were still on the list of those 'in service', but in autumn the same year, they were written off.

The aircraft, which had been tested at NII VVS, was transferred to the 4th Backup Air Brigade, which specialized in the conversion training of crews to the foreign aircraft. It was used as a trainer, but the Albemarle had a horrible reputation with the brigade; it was even referred to as 'the infernal airplane'. The regiment's instructors 'versified' it by modifying the famous stanza by Pushkin, which ended with the following line: 'And on the wreck of Albemarle our names will be inscribed'. The aircraft was destroyed in late 1943.

By early 1946, none of the Albemarles had remained in the Soviet Union.

An AW Albemarle which has been prepared for a ferried flight to the USSR. The aircraft camouflage corresponds to the RAF day bomber scheme, but it already bears the red star insignias.

The Albemarles at the Errol air base in Scotland. The aircraft in the foreground demonstrates an open polyhedral cargo hatch with two doors.

The Albemarle s/n P1477 during tests at NII VVS in spring 1943.

The Albemarle s/n P1477 during tests at NII VVS in spring 1943.

The Albemarle's bomb bay doors in an open position.

The fuselage nose, which is accommodating the navigator's cabin; note that the front emergency hatch is open.

The forced landing of the Albemarle reg/n CCCP-Л403 (s/n P1640) near Yevlakh on 26 June 1943.

7.20 North American AT-6 Texan

The entire demand of the Soviet aviation for trainer aircraft was satisfied by the domestic industry. A small number of the American-made AT-6 Texan monoplanes were shipped only at the end of the war, with this aircraft being one of the members of the large family of single-engine trainer aircraft as designed by North American; it originated from NA-16 (BT-9) in 1935. The AT-6 (NA-59) two-seater was mass-produced from 1940 and was intended for the second stage of training, with the elements of combat use. For this purpose, it was equipped with the following armament: one fixed machine gun under the engine cowling; another machine gun in the wing; and a third one on the pivot mount in the rear cockpit. Also installed were carriers for small-caliber bombs and a bomb release mechanism at the pilot's station. Several versions were manufactured, which varied in engine variants, equipment and fuselage structure; for example, some light alloys in the AT-6C's structural frame were replaced by wood to save aluminium, which was in short supply.

In terms of design, the AT-6 was much more similar to the modern warplanes than the Soviet-made UT-2. It was provided with a retractable landing gear; a variable-pitch propeller; and an enclosed cockpit, as well as more advanced equipment.

Soviet specialists showed interest in the Texan for the first time on 10 December 1942 by sending a request to the Americans about the possibility of shipping 30 aircraft.

Early in the spring of 1943, eight disassembled aircraft of the AT-6C version arrived via the northern ports, and the first six aircraft were delivered to the 6th Backup Air Brigade in Ivanovo, where they were assembled; one Texan was given to NII VVS for tests.

Flights at the Scientific Testing Institute were conducted from 21 May through to 6 June, and the commander of the 6th Backup Air Brigade – Colonel Y.I. Shumov – participated in the tests. The general opinion of the AT-6C was rather high, with the report stating: 'The aircraft is simple in terms of the piloting technique; it features satisfactory longitudinal and lateral stability, and allows performing all flight maneuvers as required for the aircraft of a fighter type such as turns, combat turns, the split 'S', rolls, Immelmann turns, loops, and dives'. The power plant was reliable, and the aircraft (as a whole) was simple and convenient to operate. The availability of armament and equipment for night flying was specifically emphasized, and it was deemed to be very useful that the cabin layout resembled the layout of the American fighters, which were numerous in the air force. The AT-6C was suited for pilot training and air gunnery training, but it was considered unfit for navigator training, since there was neither a bomb sight nor a release mechanism in the aft cockpit. A radio compass was not available either, in spite of the fact that it was installed on virtually all bombers at that time.

Another twenty-two AT-6C aircraft were sent via the southern route (across Iran), but unfortunately, two aircraft were crashed during the test flight after the assembly, so only 20 aircraft arrived in the Soviet Union; then there was a lasting break, although six-hundred AT-6 aircraft were requested by Soviet representatives in March 1945. The Americans agreed to give 225 aircraft. At that time, the Texans were sent as assembled aircraft via Alaska and all of them were of the AT-6F version, with the airframe fully made of light alloys (just like in the initial design).

The first AT-6F aircraft took the route in June, and the aircraft were ferried in batches of eight to 10. Unlike in typical cases, the ferrying was carried out without any lead aircraft, since the Texan was considerably inferior in terms of speed when compared to the A-20s, B-25s or the C-47s, which were usually used as the lead aircraft on the ALSIB route. The ceiling of the AT-6Fs was not high, so for this reason, they could not fly along the ordinary route across the Verkhoyansk Range. The aircraft flew in stages to Seymchan, with a landing for refueling in Omolon, since the fuel reserve was not enough; then to Oymyakon and, from there, to Yakutsk. The last group of the Texans departed from Fairbanks in mid-July and reached Krasnoyarsk in early August 1945.

In total, fifty-four AT-6Fs were handed over to the Soviet Union prior to the completion of shipments under Lend-Lease, and all of them completed the route successfully. On 20 August, the Texans participated in the air festival at Yakutsk, where a couple such aircraft demonstrated their aerobatic flying capabilities.

The AT-6s were mainly distributed among backup brigades and regiments which dealt with the conversion to imported aircraft, although some of them were sent to flying schools. The 4th Backup Air Brigade was the first to begin any form of familiarization with the new aircraft, but they were later supplied to the 6th Backup Air Brigade as well. The rest of the aircraft were sent to other locations, with certain combat fighter regiments receiving single specimens of them. In April 1944, three AT-6Cs were assigned to the 396th Special Operations Regiment; in December, the regiment received a fourth aircraft. In May, one of the aircraft was demonstrated at an exhibition organized for the employees of the Military Department of the Central Committee of the All-Union Communist Party (the Bolsheviks). In 1945, an AT-6 from the 4th Squadron of the 396th Air Regiment crashed and was discarded.

As of 1 May 1945, the air force had twenty-three AT-6s; of those, 22 aircraft were stationed in the rear, and one aircraft was held by the defensive air force. By that time, six aircraft had already crashed and had been written off.

The Texan, which had been tested at NII VVS, stayed at the Institute and was used during trial flights as a tracking aircraft; in such trials, a cameraman occupied the gunner's seat. Several Texans were handed over to the Air Force Inspection Regiment, and at least one aircraft went to the training regiment of the Air Force Academy, which was based in Monino.

Due to their small number, the Texans were not widely used and only saw service for a short period of time.

Acceptance of the AT-6C in Abadan in 1943.

The AT-6F aircraft intended for delivery to the USSR at the factory airfield, together with the North American P-51 Mustang fighters.

An AT-6F before a ferry flight via Canada to Alaska.

An AT-6C from an unknown unit in the Soviet Union.

An AT-6F, with red star insignias applied on its shiny metal finish.

An AT-6F undergoing maintenance in Yakutsk.

8

Those that Came by Chance

Apart from the aircraft officially shipped by the Allies to the USSR, up to 20 types of British and American designs came to the Soviet Union via different ways. Some of them were available in dozens, while others were as single specimens. They were picked up at places of emergency landings; interned under the Soviet-Japanese Neutrality Pact; and captured as 'double trophies' from the Germans. The majority of them fell into the hands of Soviet soldiers during the last months of the war.

The war in Europe hardly terminated when, on 7 May, an Order to the following effect was issued: 'Foreign aircraft, including American and British ones, which have landed in the territory occupied by our forces, shall be considered as captured. Those serviceable and field-repairable shall be sent to appropriate Air Force units. Those not repairable shall be handed over to the captured property management agencies as metal scrap or dismantled for spares', so it was done.

Strictly speaking, such aircraft are not related in any way to Lend-Lease, but still, they are an important part of the general picture of aviation ties between the USSR and the USA and Great Britain during the war. The Liberator B-24 heavy bomber belongs to such a category of aircraft. The Americans reckon that a single aircraft of this type was among those shipped to the Soviet Union under the Lend-Lease program; however, the reader will have a chance to see that this was not the case. Nobody was going to hand over the aircraft (everything happened quite spontaneously) and, furthermore, in addition to the 'official' B-24, the Soviet Union had approximately two dozen 'non-official' ones – thus, the inclusion of this aircraft in the category of 'those that came by chance' is quite reasonable.

In such a manner, the Soviet Union also received single specimens of aircraft which were shipped by the Allies in considerable quantities. I put no special emphasis on them, as the reader got acquainted with them in the previous chapter.

8.1 Lockheed P-38 Lightning

Documents of the Soviets' ex-enemies in the Great Patriotic War frequently mention the use (by the Soviet aviation) of the Lockheed P-38 Lightning heavy fighters. Finnish historian H. Valtonen describes a whole regiment of Lightnings which operated at night by Leningrad. Allegedly, the 12th Independent Spotter and Reconnaissance Air Squadron flew the P-322s (the Lightnings without turbosuperchargers, which were ordered from Great Britain). The Finnish historian states that according to pilots' reports, two such aircraft were shot down by Finnish fighters in July 1943. In fact, although the Lightnings were actually flying in the Russian skies, the P-38 was quite a rare bird.

The two-engine fighter of a twin-boom fuselage structure was designed in 1937. The prototype was built in late 1938 and first flew on 27 January the following year; however, as early as September 1938, Soviet Intelligence brought the preliminary project of the Lockheed-22 aircraft (i.e. the future Lightning) to Moscow. The package of documents included drawings of the general layout of aircraft, main assemblies, estimated performance and structural analysis. All the drawings were in the form of photocopies, together with a 'Secret' stamp. It should be noted, however, that a closer look at the drawings allows noticing that they represent not the final and conventional variant, but the intermediate one (the M-12-36). Its supercharger turbines are not arranged on top of the engine nacelles; instead, they are mounted on their outer sides. The engine nacelles have a different outline, the radiators are arranged in a different way and the cockpit canopy has a non-transparent fairing in the back. Together with the single-seater version, details of the two-seater project were brought – showing the gunner sitting back to back with the pilot at his machine gun.

All materials as available in the Soviet Union on the American fighter were handed over for study to NII VVS. The Institute's specialists became interested in the turbosuperchargers, the tricycle landing gear and the armament, which included a 37mm cannon. Military Engineer 1st Rank Znamensky of the Material-Technical Support Department wrote in his opinion of the design: '... it should be admitted that, in terms of flight performance and the power of gunnery armament, the Lockheed-22 fighter-interceptor is a breakthrough in the development of combat aircraft, and thus deserves the most thorough examination by the Workers' and Peasants' Red Army...'; however, there was actually nothing to be examined. Large-scale mass-manufacture of the already complete P-38D combat aircraft began as late as July 1941. In November, they already received a baptism of fire in the sky over the Aleutian Islands and, in the summer of 1942, were used over Europe. As fighter-bombers and long-range escort aircraft, the Lightnings fought in the Mediterranean, but their most successful service was in the Pacific, where they were flown by the best American aces.

Over the territory of the Soviet Union, they were first seen during the 'shuttle' operations of American bombers from bases in the Ukraine. In fact, the 'shuttle' flights began on 24 May 1944, with the landing of two F-5s (the unarmed modification of the Lightning as a photo reconnaissance aircraft) at the airfield in Poltava. Subsequently, the P-38s both in the reconnaissance and in the fighter version (single, in groups and in larger formations) stayed at various bases in the Soviet Union – thus, for example, during Operation 'Frantic III' in July 1944, seventy-two P-38s of the 15th US Air Army arrived in the Soviet Union; Soviet ground crews participated in their servicing. An F-5 was destroyed by German bombs during the raid of the Luftwaffe night bombers on Poltava and, after the evacuation of the base, it was abandoned there.

The pilots from the 1st Ferry Regiment could tell something about the Lightning. Some of them had a chance to look at this aircraft and even fly it during their service in Alaska, but in order to study the aircraft thoroughly, the Soviet Union had to possess it; however, requests to the American side in this respect were not successful – thus, for example, on 19 July 1943, General V.I. Belyaev requested several P-38s. The issue was under consideration for quite a long time; the refusal came in autumn, and the Soviet Union did not even attempt to get the Lightning under Lend-Lease anymore. None of the P-38s were delivered to the USSR officially.

All aircraft of this type which appeared in the Soviet Union were picked up after forced landings in Eastern Europe. It should be said that these fighters were a rare thing even there: out of 162 Allied aircraft as detected by the Soviet Army on occupied territories by mid-May 1945, there was only a single Lightning. In fact, of course, there were more of them, but only a little more – and furthermore, the condition of the aircraft left much to be desired.

For example, a P-38 made a forced landing near the city of Nagykőrös, in the Budapest area, in January 1945. This aircraft, with the inscription 'Pride of Jane', was accompanying the bombers. It was hit and made a belly landing on the field, which was covered with melted snow. The aircraft propellers were bent and the engine cowlings were crushed. The pilot was not injured and was evacuated by a team of specialists of the Soviet 5th Air Army. With him, he took a sword of the Hungarian general, which was received from Soviet infantrymen in exchange for a parachute.

There were other similar cases as well, but (probably) only a single Lightning was brought to an airworthy condition in the Soviet Union. It was an aircraft of the most readily available version (P-38L) that was involved in 'shuttle' operations, would make an emergency landing and then would be abandoned. It was a P-38L-1 s/n 42-4384, with the inscription 'Blackie' on its side. For a time, it belonged to the 173rd Air Regiment of the 56th Fighter Division, which flew the A-20Gs converted to the heavy fighters, but the Lightning was used there solely for training flights. The regiment was based near Minsk; later, it was redeployed to Częstochowa in Poland.

After the war, this Lightning was transferred to NII VVS, and the American fighter was tested there in early 1947. The leading pilot was V.I. Khomyakov, but P.M. Stefanovsky and Y.A. Antipov also took part in the trial flights. The Lightning took off without outboard fuel tanks and, first and foremost, the capabilities of the aircraft as an escort fighter were assessed in comparison with the Soviet-made aircraft Yak-9DD. The tests generally confirmed the characteristics declared by Lockheed. The only measurements that the specialists failed to conduct were those at engine maximum momentary power – and the reason for this was quite ordinary: the imported 100-octane gasoline, which was not produced by Soviet factories, was not available at the Institute.

By 1947, the Lightning had become obsolete and did not arouse much interest. In the United States, it was decommissioned in 1949.

Specialists of the 5th Air Army inspecting the P-38L-1 which made a forced landing near Nagykeresz in Hungary in early 1945.

This P-38L was tested at NII VVS in early 1947.

The Lightning airframe being subjected to structural testing at TsAGI.

The Lightning fuselage was used as a training aid at the Moscow Aviation Institute in the first half of the 1950s.

8.2 Boeing B-17 Flying Fortress

Even to a person who is poorly familiar with aviation, the name 'Flying Fortress' means the heavy bomber of the Second World War. Indeed, the B-17 is perhaps the most famous American aircraft of the class of those times. For several years, it was one of the main tools of strategic bombing attack as delivered by the USAAF.

The 'model 299' prototype first flew on 28 July 1935. At the time of its creation, the future Fortress was almost the same age as the Soviet-made TB-7 (Pe-8); in terms of design, however, the two aircraft had nothing in common. The Soviet bomber was a technological development of the ideas implemented in the TB-3, and required a lot of manual labor in its building. The American aircraft, on the other hand, featured an advanced airframe.

The Boeing Company received an order for the first small batch of thirteen Y1B-17s for operational service tests in January 1936. As soon as March, the management of the Air Force Administration addressed a memo to People's Commissar K.E. Voroshilov suggesting the inclusion of the 'four-engine Boeing' into the list of aircraft – specimens of which were to be bought in the United States. Air Force Chief of Staff V.K. Lavrov wrote: 'This aircraft provides a combination of performance parameters, which are essential for us, i.e. high speed and long range'. The March Resolution of the Council of Labor and Defense envisaged the purchase of 'the long-range four-engine Boeing bomber as an engineering model for studying the aircraft itself and its equipment and armament'. The Chief Administration of Air Industry had already found the manufacturing facilities for the Fortress (the new Factory No.124 in Kazan), and intended to master the large complex aircraft on their own (without any license), according to the model only. On the other hand, in April the same year, at a meeting of the Air Force Administration, Y.I. Alksnis suggested buying from the USA technical assistance to launch the manufacture of 'the four-engine Boeing bomber'. Negotiations with Boeing began through the mediation of Amtorg; however, the Soviet party did not succeed.

In summer 1941, when, after the German attack on the Soviet Union, the United States offered their military assistance, President Roosevelt promised to Stalin (inter alia) heavy bombers. The issue regarding the shipment of 10 heavy bombers per month by the Western Allies was discussed on 1 August by the Presidential Administration. Five aircraft were to be provided by the USA, and five by the UK. The draft with which A. Harriman arrived in Moscow stated that the USA undertook to deliver (before June 1942) 27 such aircraft. Here, undoubtedly, the B-17 was meant, since the manufacture of another similar type (i.e. the B-24) was, at that time, just being launched.

Opinions regarding the value of the Flying Fortresses differed – thus, for example, the Intelligence Directorate of the General Staff sent to the government a document to the following effect: 'The Boeing B-17, in all its versions, is an obsolete type of a four-engine bomber'. The intelligence men insisted that every effort should be made to obtain the new B-24s. On the other hand, the Air Force Chief Administration reported to People's Commissar of Air Industry A.I. Shakhurin: 'The most appropriate type of a bomber is the American-made Boeing B-17'. Apparently, the aviators' point of view won – thus, a team led by M.M. Gromov arrived via the northern maritime route by flying boats to Alaska to take the Fortresses from the United States. The team members' task was to accept the first five B-17s; then master the new aircraft quickly (among the team members were experienced test pilots who had flown many types of aircraft); and then ferry the aircraft across the Atlantic to England. It was intended that there, the aircraft would be loaded with bombs and then head for Germany. The Fortresses were expected to drop the bombs onto targets in the Reich, and to land near Moscow; however, the Americans did not give the B-17s to the USSR. The idea of providing heavy bombers to the Soviet Union was severely opposed by General Arnold, who invoked the shortage of such aircraft in the American aviation as a pretext for his opinion. Indeed, as of 1 August 1941, only forty B-17s and a single B-24 were in service with the USAAF.

The presence of secret equipment (in particular, bomb sights) on board the Fortresses was declared as the second argument, but attempts to obtain the B-17 did not cease. At the meeting of the Tripartite Commission in Moscow on 30 September 1941, where future Lend-Lease shipments were discussed, Shakhurin asked General Chaney, who represented the US Air Force: "Will it be possible to obtain the Boeing aircraft?" Chaney replied: "These cannot be shipped yet." The issue was closed for a long time.

Another attempt to get the aircraft was made in 1944, when the Soviet party sent a request for the delivery of aircraft under Military Assistance Protocol IV. An order was made for two-hundred-and-forty B-17s, but again, none were received.

By that time, the Fortress had become quite different from the 1936 version. Due to the presence of engine turbosuperchargers, the speed and ceiling grew; the bomb load increased dramatically; and the aircraft bristled up with large-caliber machine guns (the B-17G had thirteen of them). The crew and the most important assemblies were protected with armor, and the bomber was equipped with the most modern navigation and radio equipment.

Soviet specialists had a chance to see quite enough of this during the 'shuttle' operations, in which five-hundred-and-twenty-nine B-17s of the 8th US Air Army and the 15th US Air Army took part. In the Soviet Union, they landed at air bases in Poltava, Mirgorod and Piryatin. Along with American mechanics, ground crews of the Soviet 169th Special-Purpose Air Base – under the command of General A.R. Perminov – took part in equipment servicing. The first 'shuttle' raid was carried out on 2 June 1944. On that day, one-hundred-and-twenty-eight B-17Gs and 64 escort fighters landed in the Ukraine.

The Germans attempted to hinder the work of the bases. On 22 June, they made a massive night raid on Poltava; the following night, on Mirgorod. In Poltava, 44 Fortresses were destroyed, and a further two were damaged. All aircraft which were found to be non-repairable were later abandoned on the airfields. The 'shuttle' operations continued until 19 September, when the front moved far to the West, and the use of bases in the Ukraine became impractical.

The Red Army had already entered the territory of the countries of Eastern Europe. Abandoned and force-landed British and American aircraft – including the B-17s – were encountered more and more frequently. Initially, the search for (and the recovery of) such aircraft was carried out in an amateurish manner by separate detachments or units – thus, for example, the 449th Bomber Regiment dealt with the collection and restoration of the American heavy bombers in Hungary and Austria. Regiment Senior Engineer N.A. Kuzmin studied the aircraft on his own, and without any manuals. Within a few days, he figured out the design of the engines, as well as the instrumentation, units and systems, and identified procedures for their maintenance and operation. With a team of specialists, Kuzmin furbished up several bombers; then the aircraft were demonstrated to Commander of the 3rd Ukrainian Front Marshal F.I. Tolbukhin and Commander of the 17th Air Army General V.A. Sudets. It is noteworthy that one of the B-17s was demonstrated in flight.

On 10 April 1945, a Directive was issued requiring all units and divisions to report such findings to the headquarters of the 18th Air Army (the successor of Long-Range Aviation). Heavy bombers were desperately needed by the Soviet aviation. The manufactured Pe-8s were not enough for equipping even a single division, and attempts to obtain such equipment from the Allies had failed. It was decided to collect and restore the abandoned B-17 and B-24, and then to replenish them with the regiments of the 45th Long-Range Air Division (at that time, the only unit which flew four-engine bombers).

On 13 April, a B-17G (s/n 43-38902) made an emergency landing in Poland, north of Rzeszow, near the airfield of the 341st Air Regiment. On 22 April (after repairs), it was brought to Poltava. That was the first Fortress submitted to the 45th Air Division.

By mid-May – according to reports from the field in different regions of Poland, Romania, Hungary, Czechoslovakia and Yugoslavia –seventy-three B-17s of different versions were found.

The office of the American Military Attaché in Moscow knew about the collection of the abandoned equipment, but it was ordered not to interfere with it. It is interesting that according to the Americans, the number of aircraft as recovered by the Soviet Air Force was more than twice as less than it was in fact.

A practically serviceable B-17G which had landed in Yasenki (Poland) was returned to the Americans. Four Fortresses were not found at the indicated locations, and the rest of the aircraft were damaged more or less severely. Some of them had been destroyed during landing; secret equipment had been exploded by the crews, in accordance with appropriate instructions; and there were aircraft which had been plundered by local inhabitants and soldiers. Most of the B-17s were found in the territory of Poland, where Armia Krajowa troops acted; they attacked the Soviet troops. On 29 May 1945, they exploded (in Demblin) a B-17 which was being recovered by a group of specialists of the 45th Air Division.

Despite all difficulties, by 1 July, the 890th Air Regiment had been equipped with nine Pe-8s, nineteen B-25s and twelve B-17s. They were stationed at Balbasovo airfield, near Orsha. The Flying Fortresses gradually replaced the worn-out Pe-8s and the B-25 two-engine aircraft. By early October, the incoming of the four-engine bombers as collected in Europe had been terminated, with sixteen serviceable B-17s in operation with the regiment. All of them were of the G version. One aircraft of the earlier B-17F version arrived at the Flight Testing Institute, where it passed brief flight tests.

The American bombers were considered as temporary aircraft for the regiment, and to be used until the launching of the manufacture of equivalent modern Soviet aircraft. They performed flights according to the combat training schedule for long-range bombers, in order to keep the flight crews fit.

The Flying Fortresses had a good reputation among Soviet pilots. Compared to the Soviet-made Pe-8, the American bomber had a higher speed and ceiling due to turbosupercharging. Armament was more powerful, and the instrumentation was better. The aircraft were equipped with all modern navigation aids, precise bomb sights and excellent radio equipment. Designed for many hours of long-range raids, the Fortresses ensured (for the crews) a level of comfort which was unthinkable in the Soviet aircraft; pilots noted very good sealing (gaps and drafts were normal in Soviet-made aircraft at that time).

The B-17 was very simple when it came to piloting. Later, Hero of the Soviet Union S.S. Sugak wrote: 'The aircraft had excellent control, and were very responsive to the deviation of rudders. They were easier in control than our Pe-8s that I had flown a lot'. Pilots called the Fortress a 'four-engine U-2' for its ease of piloting.

Among the disadvantages, it was noted that the B-17 had a slightly worse take-off and landing performance than that of the Pe-8 (in spite of the fact that the B-17 was easier to keep straight during take-off with a greater weight), and a more limited view from the cockpit.

The 890th Air Regiment was transferred to Kazan in 1946, and several unserviceable Fortresses were shifted to Balbasovo; they stayed there until 1948. In Kazan, the aircraft was often examined by the workers of the local aircraft factory, who were just beginning to master the production of the Tu-4 (a copy of the American-made B-29). Items of equipment of the latter had much in common with those installed on board the B-17.

The regiment began to receive the first Tu-4s in summer 1947. Gradually, the B-17s were sent to the parking area, and then were scrapped. A total of twenty-one B-17Gs passed through the 890th Air Regiment.

The Flying Fortresses were used in the USSR not only in this combat regiment, but in various research institutions as well. The number of civil Fortresses increased gradually. As of 1 October 1947, the country had only one such aircraft in service with the Ministry of Aviation Industry (at the Flight Testing Institute), whereas by 1 January 1949, their number had reached two. Another B-17 s/n I-1006 was handed over to the Ministry of Aviation Industry in the third quarter the same year under a Resolution of the Council of Ministers. Five B-17s served with NII-17 as flying testbeds for radio equipment testing. In 1952, the *Sokol* radar, which was designed for the Yak-25 interceptor, was tested in one of them. A B-17 was used in 1948 by NII VVS for the testing of new parachutes; group high-altitude jumps were made from it.

It is not known when the last Soviet Fortress was written off.

This American B-17G was pictured at Tri Duby airfield in Slovakia in September 1944. In March 1945, this aircraft made a forced landing near Plzeň, but later, it was restored and ferried to the Soviet Union.

A B-17G which was abandoned at Poltava airfield after the evacuation of the American air base.

A B-17G after a forced landing in the Ukraine in 1944.

The crew of the Flying Fortress after a wheels-up landing at the Soviet territory in 1944.

The B-17G was hit above Berlin in late February 1945 and landed at the Soviet positions; note the red stars which have been painted over the American insignias.

The B-17G was hit above Berlin in late February 1945 and landed at the Soviet positions; note the red stars which have been painted over the American insignias.

This B-17G was handed over to the 45th Heavy Bomber Air Division of the 16th Air Army in May 1945.

A Soviet B-17G at an airfield.

A pilot of the 890th Heavy Bomber Air Regiment near the Flying Fortress.

Navigator V. Nedovesov near a B-17G at an airfield in Kazan.

A B-17G of the 890th Heavy Bomber Air Regiment at an airfield in Kazan in 1947.

8.3 Consolidated B-24 Liberator

The B-24 Liberator heavy bomber was much younger than the Flying Fortress. In 1938, the design office of the Consolidated Aircraft Corporation began its development. The design process was expedited by the fact that the B-24's designers, A. Ladden and D. Davis, used a lot of components from the Consolidated 31 experimental flying boat; actually, the entire wing and empennage design was taken from it. There were several re-designing efforts: the nose became stepped instead of bulbous, and the step in the rear fuselage was removed. Also, the location of the gun points was changed.

The international situation escalated quickly and, for this reason, further events developed rapidly. In March 1939, the USAAC ordered a prototype and, sometime later, the company received an order for a small batch for operational service tests. In August, thirty-four mass-manufactured B-24As were ordered.

The prototype XB-24 first flew on 29 December 1939. The last (seventh) aircraft of the trial series was accepted in January 1941; in fact, there were no operational service tests. Beginning from December 1940, the newly manufactured bombers were sent to England.

The USAAF began to receive the mass-manufactured B-24A in summer 1941. Throughout the war, approximately 18,000 Liberators were built. They saw action in the Mediterranean, the Pacific and over the Atlantic as bombers, long-distance reconnaissance aircraft, transport aircraft and anti-submarine aircraft.

The new US heavy bomber B-24 did not pass unheeded in the USSR. Soviet specialists were interested in high flight performance and individual design solutions of the aircraft; however, the attitude to the bomber was ambivalent. It was well understood that the implementation of a large number of innovations would require a long-time customization of the aircraft.

This became quite apparent in the process of the preparation for the meeting of the Tripartite Commission in Moscow in September 1941. The Air Force Chief Administration and the People's Commissariat of Aviation Industry recommended requesting the B-17, which were service-proven and reliable, and only the Investigation Directorate of the General Staff suggested taking the B-24s. Its note read: 'The B-24 became famous under the name Liberator as one of the good bombers, which are used in warfare in EUROPE. The acquisition of this aircraft is highly desirable'; however, disputes as to what was better to obtain {the Liberator or the Flying Fortress) proved groundless: the Americans gave none of them.

For the first time, the Liberators appeared in the skies of Russia in September 1941. A. Harriman, a representative of the US President, came to Moscow via England and Archangelsk with his team in two B-24As. These aircraft had been modified into transports; almost all armament in them had been removed. Later, British Prime Minister W. Churchill arrived in Moscow in a similar aircraft. Churchill's aircraft, which bore the personal name of 'Commando', had little semblance of a mass-manufactured Liberator II bomber, from which it had been modified. Specialists from BOAC workshops arranged a rather comfortable interior in the fuselage.

From October 1942, the British Liberators began to appear in the Moscow area on a regular basis. This was brought about by the opening of an airline connecting Great Britain and the Soviet Union. The BOAC aircraft flew along the route from the north of Scotland and across the North Sea; then the Skagerrak Strait, the west of Sweden and over the Baltic Sea; and then via Selizharovo and Yaroslavl to Kratovo airfield. The flights were according to schedule, and tickets were sold at a price of 3,500 rubles each. In particular, the BOAC flights were used to send Soviet ferry pilots to England with the task of accepting the Albemarle transports. The Soviet party had no aircraft at its disposal to perform reciprocal flights, so for this reason, on 24 November 1942, Stalin ordered People's Commissar of Foreign Trade A.I. Mikoyan to purchase six Liberators for the Civil Air Fleet; however, the attempt to obtain the aircraft failed again.

At the same time, in October 1942 (when the German troops rushed to the Caucasus), the Allies suggested that the Soviet Air Force in the Caucasus should be strengthened by an Anglo-American formation which was intended to include (inter alia) an American air group with the B-24s. While the parties were agreeing upon diplomatic issues, the problem ceased to be urgent. On 18 December, Stalin (in his letter to Roosevelt) advised the latter of the Soviet Union's willingness to take the aircraft, but without the crews. This option, in turn, aroused no enthusiasm on the part of the Allies; however, in November 1942, a B-24D came to the Soviet Union in a purely accidental manner. The US military delegation headed by General O. Bradley was returning home from Moscow via the recently opened Krasnoyarsk route; one of the intermediate stops was made in Yakutsk. Before take-off, the ground personnel suggested that the aircraft preparation should be carried out in accordance with Soviet regulations for the winter period in Siberia, which included a thorough pre-heating of the engines, but Feigel, the bomber pilot, refused, as he relied on the system for oil dilution with gasoline. At the same time, the ambient temperature in Yakutsk was 30°C below zero. As a result, shortly after take-off, the fourth engine stopped. Its propeller failed to become feathered, and the crew attempted to return; however, the aircraft encountered severe icing. Furthermore, upon landing, the landing gear was extending very slowly (on account of the fact that the hydraulic fluid had become too dense due to the frost) and, for the same reason, the flaps failed to operate. Consequently, the aircraft overran the runway, tore the tires and broke the right landing gear leg.

A C-47 was provided for the delegation; however, together with Bradley and his party, the Liberator crew boarded the C-47. It was surprising for the Soviet pilots that the Americans abandoned the aircraft, which still could be repaired. In reply to the question asked by Chief of the Krasnoyarsk route I.P. Mazuruk, co-pilot T. Watson (in the 1970s, he became the US Ambassador in Moscow) calmly said that the bomber had been bought by his mother and he could do whatever he wanted with it. For example, he could present it to Mazuruk. Watson was indeed a rich man, as his father was the founder of IBM. Mazuruk did not fail to grasp the opportunity: he ordered to immediately bring to the airfield a public notary, who made the gift deed in due form. Watson signed it and departed for Alaska. Afterwards, the Americans included the said B-24D s/n 41-11820 among the aircraft supplied under Lend-Lease.

Before spring 1943, the Liberator was restored to serviceable condition. Specialists of the 1st Ferry Division – D. Ostrovenko, V. Chechin and I. Kovalenko – put the aircraft in good working order. They reassembled the engines and replaced some of engine parts; however, at the first attempt to take off, the aircraft wheels began to sink in the thawed soil. To improve the situation, a P-40 fighter was sent to the runway to dry the surface with the propeller stream. After that, the Liberator could be tested in flight. In spring 1943, Mazuruk personally ferried it to Moscow.

In May, the Liberator became a part of the fleet of the Department of International Airlines (*Upravlenie Mezhdunarodnykh Vozdushnykh Liniy*, or UMVL). There were plans to use the Liberator on the intended route for ferrying aircraft from England via North Africa, Iraq and Iran. The aircraft first had to deliver Soviet specialists to the appointed places along the route, and then to ensure the return of ferry crews from the base of Ras El Ma to Hurn (England). The UMVL crew as selected for the Liberator began training in long-term flights. In June, the crew flew to Kratovo — Yegoryevsk — Saratov — Astrakhan — Makhachkala — Baku — Adjikabul — Tbilisi and back. During the flight, an unpleasant incident happened: the aircraft entered the restricted area over the Astrakhan port and was taken under fire by local anti-aircraft gunners. In October, the aircraft was subjected to a minor repair at Repair Base No.400 in Vnukovo. There existed an idea to modify it into a special aircraft for government transportation, but it is not known whether anything was actually done in this respect. Beginning from September, the Liberator was assigned to the 1st Transport Air Division, where it was operated by A.S. Shornikov's crew. The aircraft was mostly used for training, since the Soviet Union still hoped to get the Liberators from the Americans. That aircraft remained in service until spring 1945.

On 19 July 1943, General V.I. Belyaev again addressed the US Government with a request to provide several B-24s, but again without success. Nevertheless, the Liberators appeared in Russia!

In August 1943, the USAAF began to deliver strikes on Japanese bases on the northern Kuril Islands. Protection of the bases consisted of air cover (as provided by fighters) and in the use of anti-aircraft artillery. Landing in the open sea or surrendering into Japanese captivity promised nothing good, so for this reason, damaged bombers began to land on the Kamchatka Peninsula.

On 12 August (Kamchatka time; in Alaska, it was 11 August), Second Lieutenant G. Pottenger (in a B-24D) survived a combat with 11 Japanese fighters over Paramushir (he even managed to shoot down one of the fighters). There was no chance to get to the base in the Aleutian Islands, so the bomb-aimer removed the secret bomb sight and threw it overboard. The aircraft with the damaged engine belly-landed in the swampy mouth of the Avacha River. During the landing, the bomb bay doors were torn off. One of the guns fell off the carriage and wounded several people; one of them, gunner Ring, died later. All of the 11 crew members were taken to Petropavlovsk and accommodated in the House of Officers. Later, they were brought in a flying boat to Khabarovsk; then to Vladivostok and, by train, to the Tashkent area, where a special camp was located.

Under the Soviet-Japanese Neutrality Pact, which was in effect at that time, the aircraft and their crews that entered the territory of the USSR during military operations were deemed to be interned. Pilots were sent to Central Asia, from where they returned home via Iran, and they signed a pledge of secrecy for their authorities as to places they had been and the ways they had got out of there. Aircraft remained on the Kamchatka Peninsula, in the airfields of the 128th Combined Air Division.

A month later, on 12 September, two B-24Ds landed in the Soviet Union. One of the pilots (R. Pamman) found Yelizovo airfield, near Petropavlovsk, on his own and landed his aircraft with one of the engines damaged. The second bomber's pilot (K. Wagner) was led by a Soviet I-16fighter. One of those aircraft (s/n 41-23891) later became the first Liberator of the Soviet long-range bomber aviation. The number of the second aircraft is registered in the division's documents as 02355, which is obviously incorrect.

Bomber s/n 41-23891 was of the B-24D-10 version. It had been manufactured in San Diego and upgraded in the modification center in Oklahoma (the second A-6 turret – the same as in the tail – was installed in the nose). From Kamchatka to Kratovo, the aircraft was flown by a crew from the 1st Ferry Division, with Commander of the 2nd Regiment A.I. Melnikov as the pilot. On 23 October 1943, the aircraft was assigned to the 890th Air Regiment of the 45th Long-Range Air Division. That aircraft was operated intensively in the division until 5 November 1945, when it was written off and disassembled for spare parts.

Negotiations with the Americans on the purchase of the B-24s were held both on the part of the civil aviation and on the part of the air force. In December 1943, specialists of NII GVF recommended requesting the USA to supply (under Lend-Lease) the C-87 (the military transport version of the Liberator). In September 1944, the Civil Air Fleet Chief Administration was going to open a route connecting the USSR and the USA via Turkey and Africa. The Moscow — Ankara — Cairo segment was intended to be the Soviet Union's responsibility; the Americans suggested interlining in Ankara or Aleppo (Syria). The USA suggested shipping (again, under Lend-Lease) three C-87s and ten C-47s as a supplement to the previously agreed aircraft; however, the ambitions of the Aeroflot management interfered: they didn't want the C-87, but the much more modern Douglas C-54 Skymaster – and five of the latter instead of three. The USAAF had only a few such aircraft in service at that time; none at all had been provided to the civil aviation. Finally, the Soviet Union received neither of the aircraft.

On 15 March, Chairman of the Soviet Procurement Commission Lieutenant General P.G. Rudenko visited the Ford Factory at the Willow Run, where the B-24Hs were assembled at that time. He was very impressed with the aircraft. Rudenko reported to Moscow: "This aircraft can be safely recommended for the Red Army Air Force."

In the applications under the last Protocol IV on Allies' shipments in summer 1944, as many as three-hundred B-24s were requested for the Soviet Air Force. In November the same year, the Americans agreed to provide 200 aircraft to be sent via the ALSIB route (50 aircraft per month); however, the Americans wished to reserve the right to train the crews. To train the Soviet pilots in the USA, a special group flying six Liberators – and led by Colonel Moran – was formed; however, the Soviet side refused to have the training conducted in the Soviet territory, as the Soviet authorities believed that it was better to train the crews somewhere in Alaska. Finally, after a long-time correspondence, it was agreed to locate the training center in Iran.

The candidates for the trip had been selected long before. From June 1944, the 45th Air Division began the systematic training of the crews in the only available Liberator. In August, the first 10 crews began to take turns in flying the aircraft. In September, lists of pilots, navigators, radio operators and mechanics were prepared. In total, there were 20 crews to obtain the B-24s, and their personal records bore the note: 'To be sent for a business trip abroad'; however, the business trip never took place, and the Americans provided no more Liberators. The Red Army had a sufficient quantity of such aircraft; all it had to do was collect them.

In total, nine Liberators landed on the Kamchatka Peninsula by mid-May 1945 – and all of them were from No.404 Squadron. The last was W. Blake, who landed on 16 May 1945 in a B-24D with its engine failed. At different times, six bombers were staying on the airfields of the 128th Combined Air Division. The aircraft that landed in remote places were (apparently) not evacuated. The only fully serviceable bomber (except for the aircraft which was sent to Kratovo) was the one with the serial number 42-63782. It was appropriated by the Far Eastern Front Air Force Administration, but it is not known in detail how the bomber was operated there. The rest are listed with such comments as 'leakage of two fuel tanks'; 'the 1st and 3rd engines are in critical condition'; 'the 3rd engine is faulty' etc. Later, at least one Liberator from Kamchatka was transferred to the 45th Air Division.

Throughout the period of operation of American bases in the Ukraine, the B-24s appeared there only occasionally, in the role of transport aircraft. In the course of Operation 'Paravane' (a raid on the battleship *Tirpitz*), the British brought two Liberator freighters (which carried ground personnel and spare parts) to the Archangelsk region. After a short stay, they flew away safely.

During the advance of the Soviet Army deeper into Eastern Europe, the American bombers that had made forced landings were encountered with increasing frequency. By May 1945, a total of 73 airplanes of various degrees of serviceability had been found. As in the case of the Flying Fortresses, the Liberators were initially restored on the personal initiative of various regiments and divisions – thus, for example, at least one B-24 was repaired in the 17th Air Army; three in the 16th Air Army; and one in the 15th Air Army.

On 10 April 1945, the 18th Air Army was entrusted with taking care of the abandoned bombers. It should be noted that the 18th Air Army had begun searching for such aircraft in order to correct the shortage of materiel in its regiments some time before: on 30 March, three B-24Js came to Balbasovo airfield from Hungary. The bombers were gathered in Sombor airfield (Yugoslavia) and at the Kecskemét and Pech airfields in Hungary; from there, they were ferried to the Orsha area.

Not all of them reached their destination. For example, on 26 April 1945, a damaged B-24D landed on Parndorf airfield in Germany, where the 22nd Fighter Regiment was based at the time. On the ground, the crew shot at the secret radar bomb sight to destroy it; then the American pilots were sent away from the front line and the specialists from the 25th Guards Heavy Bomber Air Regiment made an attempt to restore the aircraft in good working condition. After minor repairs, they attempted to start the engines, but two engines on the left-hand side failed to start at all, whereas the third engine exploded at the starting moment and a fire began. Technician Druzhinin, with his arm injured, jumped out through the open bomb hatch. Lieutenant Kishchenko followed the technician by falling out via the cockpit window, and he suffered minor burns; the bomber, however, was burned away completely...

On 25 May, a crew under the command of Captain M.A. Kotyrev of the 890th Heavy Bomber Air Regiment had to ferry a Liberator from Baranovichi to Balbasovo. Earlier, the airplane had been ferried from Poland upon the replacement of a damaged engine; however, during the take-off in Baranovichy, the engine (which had been replaced) failed, so Captain Kotyrev had to land on a swampy meadow. When the B-24 was crawling along on the ground, the bomb hatch doors opened and soil, grass and water rushed inside. The fuselage failed and broke into halves. From among the entire crew, only the pilot hurt his left leg; the rest suffered no injuries. The aircraft was then written off.

In early June, the Liberators began to be concentrated in the 203rd Guards Air Regiment. As of 1 July, the regiment had seventeen Pe-8s, two B-25s and nineteen B-24s.

It should be noted that the attitude of pilots towards the Liberator was much worse than it was towards the Flying Fortress. Due to being inert when it came to handling, it was dubbed 'Flat-Iron', and the nickname stuck firmly to the aircraft. It accelerated at a slower rate than the B-17G, and lost speed faster after throttling down. A take-off in a B-24 had two unpleasant features: before lift-off of the nose wheel from the runway, buffeting occurred; then, during the retraction of the main landing gear, the flow about the wing changed drastically. The tricycle landing gear seemed uncustomary for those who had been flying the Pe-8.

During the mastering of the Liberator, a crash occurred in the 45th Air Division. On 25 May, one of the engines failed at take-off on pilot Kozyrev's B-24H. The aircraft landed on a plot of land behind the airfield, and the impact against the ground was severe: the fuselage split into halves, and there were victims.

By the beginning of October, the 203rd Air Regiment had been fully equipped with materiel, and had twenty-one serviceable B-24s at its disposal. Among them there were the D, H, J, L and M versions. Almost immediately upon receiving the aircraft, the insignias of their previous owners were washed off from them, or painted out. Tactical numbers (as commonly used in the Soviet aviation) were painted on the bombers' noses, and the color of the number (light blue, white or beige) depended on the squadron. Vertical fins acquired 'caps', since their tops were coated with red, green or blue paint (again, depending on the squadron).

In December 1945, pilots of the 52nd Guards Heavy Bomber Air Regiment were familiarized with the American aircraft; however, the regiment never received the Liberators (it was probably decided that there were not enough aircraft for two regiments).

The 203rd Air Regiment successfully operated B-24s for several years. Their role was to make up for the shortage of Soviet-made heavy bombers and, due to a lack of spare parts, the number of aircraft kept decreasing. A shortage of tires for nose wheels was one of the main problems: on some aircraft, the nose wheel was simply replaced with a wheel of the Il-4's main landing gear.

The B-24s were superior to the Pe-8s in terms of their operational ceiling and speed. They featured good directional stability, and were even easier to handle than the Soviet aircraft. The crews felt comfortable, and enjoyed modern navigation and radio equipment. Flying the Liberators proved to be good schooling before the conversion to the Tu-4, which was an absolute copy of the American-made B-29.

When the mastering of the Tu-4 began, the B-24s were used to train take-off and landing with the tricycle landing gear. For this purpose, several aircraft from the 203rd Air Regiment were distributed in different units of the Long-Range Aviation – thus, the already mentioned 890th Air Regiment received three aircraft, which were used as trainers until 1949.

Three airplanes were sent to Poltava, and the division which was stationed there was also preparing for the conversion to the Tu-4. One of the aircraft crashed in 1949 due to an error of the flight technician at take-off; another caught fire in mid-air in 1950, and finally burned down on the ground after an emergency landing. The third aircraft was in operation until 1951, when its engines began failing. In 1952, it was scrapped.

There are no Liberators on the list of aircraft as prepared by the People's Commissariat (later Ministry) of Aviation Industry. In January 1945, the People's Commissariat of Aviation Industry requested the air force to provide a B-24D from the 18th Air Army to be modified into a flying testbed for the Central Institute of Aviation Engine-Building (*Tsentralny Institut Aviatsionnogo Motorostroeniya*, or TsIAM), but received a flat refusal. Later, in February, Head of Civil Air Fleet Chief Administration F.A. Astakhov managed to reach an agreement with Marshal A.I. Golovanov on the allocation (by each party) of a B-24D, with an intention of assembling a serviceable aircraft from the two; however (apparently), the agreement was never implemented.

Major General A.G. Melnikov (left) near a B-24 which he was ferrying to Moscow.

This B-24D was abandoned by the Americans in Yakutsk. Later, it was returned into service with the 10th Guards Air Transport Division.

A group photo in front of the American Liberator which made a forced landing in the Crimea in 1944.

A Soviet Liberator at Balbasovo airfield in 1945.

Soviet pilots near a B-24 of the 203rd Guards Heavy Bomber Air Regiment; note the shark mouth nose art on the airplane.

A written-off B-24 of the 203rd Guards Heavy Bomber Air Regiment before scrapping.

8.4 Boeing B-29 Superfortress

Currently, the entire world knows that the first Soviet post-war Tupolev Tu-4 heavy bomber was a 'copy' of the American-made Boeing B-29 Superfortress. At the time of the Second World War, this aircraft was undoubtedly the best one in its class.

The preliminary design of the 'model 341' was presented by Boeing to the USAAC Command in 1940. The company offered a huge (under the standards of that time) bomber with a pressurized cabin and four turbosupercharged engines, which was expected to have excellent high-altitude performance. In April 1941, a full-sized mock-up was fabricated. During the finalization of the design of the aircraft (which was, at that time, referred to as XB-29), an auxiliary power unit and a remotely controlled defensive armament was added. The first XB-29 prototype first flew in September 1942, and such lateness was brought about by the great complexity of the aircraft, which required the long-time reworking of many assemblies; however, as early as May, Boeing had received an order for the mass manufacture of 250 bombers. In April 1943, mass manufacture was launched.

The first data on the new bomber was provided to Soviet specialists by the aviation adviser to President Roosevelt – E. Rickenbaker – in the course of his visit to the USSR in spring 1943. Captain Smolyarov, who was accompanying the adviser, mentioned this fact in his report on the visit. The information aroused much interest, so Captain Smolyarov was ordered to prepare a detailed report on everything he had heard about the new bomber.

On 19 July, the head of the Soviet military mission in the USA – Lieutenant General V.I. Belyaev – requested that the Americans check the possibility of providing a specimen of the B-29 to the Soviet Union. The answer was strictly negative.

The attempt was repeated two years later, but on a different scale: on 28 May 1945, the USSR requested for the delivery (under Lend-Lease) of as many as 120 such aircraft to be used in the campaign against Japan. Again, none were received from the USA; however, by that time, the Soviet Union had already gained possession of three bombers of the type in question. In total, five B-29s crossed the Soviet frontier, and all of them were taking part in American raids on Manchuria or Japan. The first of the aircraft (s/n 42-6256) landed on Tsentralnaya-Uglovaya naval aviation airfield (at a distance of 30km to the north from Vladivostok) on 29 July 1944. It belonged to the 771st Squadron and bore the nickname 'Ramp Tramp'. This B-29-5-BW was hit by Japanese anti-aircraft gunners over Anshan in Manchuria. One of the engines failed, and pilot Captain Jarrell elected to divert to the Allied base. In the Soviet airspace, the aircraft was intercepted by fighters of the Pacific Fleet and directed to the airfield.

In accordance with the Soviet-Japanese Neutrality Pact (which was then in effect), the aircraft and the crew were interned. The 'Ramp Tramp' was kept at Tsentralnaya-Uglovaya airfield, whereas Jarrell and his crew were sent to a camp in Central Asia, which was under the control of Japanese Embassy representatives. From there, the Americans later successfully 'escaped' to Iran.

On 20 August, another damaged aircraft (a B-29A-1-BN s/n 42-93829, or, according to another source, 42-9329) of the 395th Squadron crossed the Amur River. It was severely damaged during the bombing of the iron works at Yawata. Pilot McGlinn managed to pull over across the river and ordered everybody to bail out. The entire crew landed safely on their parachutes, but the uncontrollable Boeing crashed into a bald mountain near Khabarovsk. Its mangled wreckage is, for the most part, still lying in the taiga.

The next aircraft to cross the Soviet frontier was B-29-15-BW s/n 42-6365, which was piloted by Captain Price of the 794th Squadron; it was nicknamed 'General H.H. Arnold Special'. On 11 November 1944, in a raid on Japan, it met with a typhoon and was lightning-stricken. The crew lost their bearings and found themselves near the coast of the Soviet Far East. Having detected Tsentralnaya-Uglovaya airfield purely by chance, Price landed there.

The fourth aircraft, B-29-15-BW s/n 42-6358, which was piloted by Lieutenant Mikish (according to another document, Miklish), was bombing Omura. Attacked by Japanese fighters, it left with only three engines operative. Fearing to fly back, Mikish headed for Vladivostok. Near the coast, he was met by Soviet fighters and brought to the airfield. The bomber bore the name 'Ding Hao' on its fuselage.

Much later, on 29 August 1945, another B-29 appeared near Kanko airfield, where the 14th Fighter Air Regiment of the Pacific Fleet Air Force was based. It was mistakenly intercepted and subjected to fire by a pair of Yakovlev Yak-9s. The bomber's left outboard engine caught fire, and the aircraft landed in Kanko. Since it happened after the Soviet Union had declared war on Japan, this B-29 and its crew were returned to the Americans – thus, the Pacific Fleet Air Force came into possession of three B-29s, and all of them were in a different state of repair. People's Commissar of Navy Admiral N. Kuznetsov ordered that the new American aircraft should be studied. For this purpose, three pilots who were familiar with American aircraft (mostly with the Douglas A-20) were delegated to the Far East; also, local engineers were found.

As of 1 January 1945, two B-29s were assigned to the headquarters of the Pacific Fleet Air Force and the third one to the 35th Independent Long-Range Bomber Squadron, which had been specially formed for the tests; then the latter was complemented with another B-29 and a B-25, which had some time before taken part in the Doolittle Raid, and had landed in the Soviet territory. The squadron was stationed on the large airfield of Romanovka, which was not surrounded by hills and thus offered convenient approaches.

Colonel S. Reidel, a former test pilot with vast experience, was the first to master the B-29. He studied the documents, which were found in the aircraft, and then learned taxiing – continuing with short hops over the runway and (finally) getting off the ground. On 11 January, the second (V. Marunov's) crew began to fly as well. They had more difficulties with flying, since neither Marunov himself, nor his assisting engineer Chernov, read English, and had to study the aircraft with the help of a thick dictionary. Reidel decided upon acting as an instructor and made four training flights with Marunov. The tests in the Far East lasted until 21 June.

During the course of the tests, basic flight performance was assessed, piloting technique peculiarities were studied and several high-altitude flights were performed. Also, round-trip long-range flights (as well as bombing at a test range) were carried out.

Before the end of June, Reidel ferried the first aircraft to Moscow. He landed on Izmailovo airfield (currently non-existent), where the 65th Naval Aviation Regiment was based. The airstrip there was somewhat shorter than needed; however, after using up the remaining fuel, Reidel managed to land. In July, Marunov landed successfully at the same airfield. Later, the third B-29 was ferried to Moscow as well.

The 'Ramp Tramp' did not stay long in the capital. It flew to Orsha to join the 890th Regiment of the 18th Air Army, and that was done upon the urgent request of Commander of the 18th Army Marshal A.E. Golovanov.

In the 890th Regiment, the B-29 was flown by N. Ishchenko's crew. The aircraft received a Soviet insignia and number, but the pilots liked the picture of an unshaven tramp and chose to leave it intact; the bomber, however, did not stay long in the regiment. On 6 June 1945, the State Defense Committee, chaired by I.V. Stalin, adopted a Resolution to reverse-engineer the B-29. Two weeks later, the Clarifying Order of the People's Commissariat of Aviation Industry was issued, and the work was entrusted to A.N. Tupolev's design bureau. The copy (designated B-4) was intended to differ from the 'original' by the Soviet-made ASh-73TK engines, as well as by cannons instead of machine guns at all gun posts. Some differences in equipment were envisaged as well. Later, the bomber was adopted for service by the air force under the designation Tu-4.

On the evening of 10 July 1945, B-29 s/n 42-6365 was ferried to Central airfield, where it was disassembled in order to make drawings, whereas B-29 s/n 42-6256 was sent to LII in Zhukovsky for further studying and equipping, as well as testing it with the Soviet-made ASh-73TK engines. The ferrying of the bomber from Orsha to LII was carried out with the participation of the famous pilot M.L. Gallay (who was trained directly in flight); however, it was further flown by N.S. Rybko's crew. B-29 s/n 42-6358 was kept as a reserve in Izmailovo, and there it was examined by specialists of the Zhukovsky Air Force Academy.

In the USSR, all three aircraft were given registration numbers which coincided with the last three characters of the USAAF's serial numbers (i.e. 256, 365 and 358). They were painted above the old numbers in bigger black characters; the American insignias were replaced with red stars.

Later, the dismantled B-29 reg/n 365 was brought to Kazan. In 1946, its assemblies were used for the building of the prototype Tu-70 airliner (a derivative of the Tu-4). The outer wing sections, engine nacelles, flaps, main landing gear legs and tail unit were taken from the American aircraft, and the fuselage was fully manufactured 'from scratch'. In October 1947, the Tu-70 successfully completed factory tests and, in December 1948, State testing was passed, yet the aircraft never reached mass production. It was operated until 1954 in the course of various tests; besides, it was used to carry passengers and cargoes on special missions.

In Western countries, it is widely believed that the three B-29s took part in the air parade in Tushino in August 1947; however, this is a mistake. During the parade, the Tu-4s were demonstrated, which had been built by the Kazan Factory.

B-29 reg/n 256, which was in operation with LII, saw extensive service. In April 1948, it was ferried to Factory No.22 in Kazan, where it was modified to carry the '346' rocket plane created by the German designer G. Ressing. The pylon for attachment of the 346 was mounted under the right wing between the engine nacelles.

This small, swept-wing aircraft was based on the DFS 346 concept. The pilot was to fly the machine from a prone position in the nose portion; fuel tanks, oxidizing agent tanks and the 509-109 liquid-propellant engine, with a thrust of 2,000kg (based on the Walter engine), were arranged in the aft portion. To let the pilot escape, the entire nose portion was intended to be jettisoned and descended by parachute; then the pilot would eject himself, together with his 'bunk'. It was expected that the vehicle would considerably exceed the acoustic speed.

In 1948, the testing of the simplified 346-P version (without a pressurized cabin, power unit and tanks) began at Teply Stan military airfield, which today, is an area where one of Moscow's residential districts is situated. The gross weight totaled 1,800-2,180kg, depending on the ballast. The B-29 mothership was piloted by A. Yefimov's crew. The cabin of the 346-P was occupied by the German pilot W. Ziese, who was brought to the USSR among other German specialists. The escape took place at an altitude of 9,000-10,000m and at a speed of 300-350km/h. Ziese flew the 346-P four times.

The 346-1 – already a completed aircraft, but with dummy engines installed – was first flown by Ziese on 30 September 1949. The weight of the aircraft was 3,175kg, and Ziese descended in it from an altitude of 9,700m. At descent, the landing ski collapsed and the pilot struck the canopy with his head. While Ziese was being treated in hospital, the Soviet pilot P.I. Kazmin twice successfully flew the aircraft.

In summer 1951, the third version (346-3, with the engine) was completed, and it was tested at Lukhovitsy airfield. Ziese again flew the aircraft, and the first flight (on 15 August) was successful. During the second flight (on 2 September), the aircraft became uncontrollable during acceleration, at a speed of approximately 900km/h. The escape system operated excellently: the pilot bailed out and landed safely by parachute, whereas the aircraft crashed and burned out. After the accident, the 346 program was canceled.

The B-29 was returned to Zhukovsky and, for a short period of time, it was used for various studies; then, it was written off and scrapped. Apparently, throughout the entire period of its stay in the USSR, the aircraft was included among the military ones, since it was not on the aircraft lists of the Ministry of Aviation Industry.

The B-29 reg/n 358 – after being ferried to Izmailovo – never got off the ground, and it remained grounded there until it was written off.

The B-29-5 s/n 42-6256 after landing at Tsentralnaya-Uglovaya airfield, near Vladivostok, in July 1944.

The B-29-15 s/n 42-6358 at Izmailovo airfield in summer 1945.

The tail unit of a B-29 with a red star and the Soviet s/n 358.

The aircraft s/n 356 being disassembled in the hangar at the Central airfield in Moscow.

The vertical tail of the bomber is ready for copying the contours; note that s/n 356 can be clearly seen on the vertical stabilizer.

The rocket-powered 346-P aircraft suspended under the B-29 right-wing center section, Teply Stan airfield, 1948.

The B-29 carrier taking off with the 346-P rocket plane.

The B-29 carrier with the suspended 346-P test aircraft.

The Tu-70 airliner being manufactured at Factory No.156 in Moscow. Several American-made sub-assemblies taken from the B-29 (a portion of the right wing and two engine nacelles) have already been attached to the new fuselage.

The Tu-70 at the airfield.

The Tu-70 in flight at the second stage of the State tests in 1948.

The Tu-4s built by Factory No.22 are (externally) almost undistinguishable from the US-made B-29s.

8.5 Lockheed PV-1 Ventura

Formally, the PV-1s were never shipped to the Soviet Union; however, a certain number of such aircraft in 1944-1945 were interned in the Far East and were even used in military operations against Japan.

The two-engine PV-1 was, essentially, developed for military purposes from the Lockheed L-18 Lodestar high-speed passenger airliner. The PV-1 was a cantilever monoplane with twin fins and retractable landing gear. American naval aviation used it as a reconnaissance, bomber and anti-submarine aircraft, and sometimes as a heavy fighter. It could carry bombs, rockets, torpedoes and had a powerful defensive armament. This aircraft was mass-manufactured during October 1942 through to May 1944, but later, it was superseded on the assembly line by the improved PV-2. The Venturas were successfully used by American, English, Australian and New Zealand pilots in various theaters of war, but first of all in the Pacific Ocean.

In January 1944, the PV-1s (which were based at the Aleutians) began to bomb Shumshu and Paramushir (in the northern portion of the Kuril Islands). The main targets were Japanese facilities in Kataoka (currently Baikovo) and Kashiwabara (currently Severo-Kurilsk), and airfields.

Such advanced bases were well protected by anti-aircraft artillery and fighter aircraft. Many aircraft suffered damage so severe that their crews could not expect to get home in them. In such cases, the hit PV-1s (as well as aircraft of other types) headed for Kamchatka and landed at local airfields, or just in the tundra.

The first aircraft of the VB-135 Squadron landed at Yelizovo airfield on 15 June 1944 after a raid on Shumshu. Pilot R. Bon's PV-1 (with a damaged engine) was the first to land. A little bit later, an I-16 brought to the airfield the aircraft of pilot Schuette, who had wandered in search of a place for landing. Its tanks were perforated, and the fuel would not be enough for the return journey to Attu Island.

Later, the Venturas made their appearance rather frequently. On 24 July, an aircraft piloted by J. Vivian managed to reach Kamchatka with only one engine operative, while also trying to ward off Japanese fighters. The Soviet I-16s drove away the Japanese and brought the PV-1 to Yelizovo, but not everyone turned out lucky enough… On 20 July, an aircraft of VB-135 failed to reach the airfield and landed right in the forest. On 13 August, K. Lindell of VB-136 reached the landing field; however, during landing – and with only one engine operative – he missed the correct direction and crashed into trees. On 28 August, the flaps of J. Dingle's aircraft failed to be extended at landing (the reason being that bullets had pierced the hydraulic system during a fire attack by Japanese fighters over Onekotan Island), and it crashed. On 20 August, J. Coles (VB-136) – with two engines damaged and the hydraulic system perforated – made a belly landing in the tundra. At landing, the aircraft exploded, but the crew managed to escape. On 11 September, D. McDonald of VB-135 landed in Petropavlovsk in an aircraft hit by fighters; however, one of the landing gear legs collapsed and the aircraft nosed-over.

Some of the Americans chose to bail out upon reaching the Soviet shore, and this was the case, for example, with the crew led by J. Power of VPB-131 on 21 February 1945.

As has already been mentioned above, the American aircraft and their pilots were subject to internment under the Soviet-Japanese Neutrality Pact. The crews were handed over to the 60th Coast Guard Detachment of the NKVD. Furthermore, they were sent to the camp for internees in Central Asia, and then (via Iran) back home to America. The aircraft remained on the Kamchatka Peninsula.

As of December 1944, as many as eight PV-1s were staying on Kamchatka airfield, which was where the 128th Combined Air Division was stationed. From among them, only one was listed as 'recommended to be written off'; another four were fully serviceable. The rest were under repair.

In total, 11 Venturas made forced landings in Kamchatka before the end of the war. They were carefully studied by division officers and representatives of the Far Eastern Front Air Force; however, application of the Venturas went beyond simple studies. The American aircraft were used to patrol the coast and saw extensive service – thus, for example, in January through to February 1945, the Venturas flew 62 sorties. In the division documents, they are listed as the B-34s, and one of the Venturas was chosen by Commander of the 128th Combined Air Division Colonel M.A. Yeremin as his 'personal' aircraft.

Throughout the short-term campaign in the Kuril Islands, the division had seven B-34s and, among them, were five serviceable ones. One of the aircraft belonged to the divisional office; the rest (six aircraft) were assigned to the 903rd Bomber Air Regiment, which was just converting from the outdated SBs to the American-made A-20s.

After the termination of the hostilities, the Venturas quickly disappeared from the division fleet. In October, only a single aircraft of that type remained at the division's disposal; it is not yet clear what happened to the rest.

It is known that one of the PV-1s was ferried to NII VVS airfield, which was in the Moscow area. There, the aircraft underwent a full State testing program. Another aircraft was operated in 1947-1949 by a fishery scouting unit which was based in Yuzhno-Sakhalinsk. This Ventura was flown by Flight Commander N. Handozhko, who was a former fighter pilot. The aircraft armament was removed and a civil registration number was painted in black letters on its side. The aircraft had already been worn out, and spare parts were not available. For this reason, it could hardly have survived long.

The American PV-1 Ventura naval bomber during tests at NII VVS.

8.6 Avro 683 Lancaster

Another British heavy bomber in service with the Soviet naval aviation was the Avro Lancaster; officially, however, such an aircraft was never delivered to the Soviet Union.

In fact, the very coming of the aircraft into existence was, by and large, occasional. Avro was mass-manufacturing the Manchester large two-engine bomber, and the aircraft turned out to be not quite successful. The main problem was the powerful, but unreliable, Vulture engines. Things came to such a head that the British Air Ministry suggested that Avro should discontinue the manufacture of the bomber, and should launch the assembly of the Halifax four-engine aircraft which was being produced by Handley Page. In response, Avro decided to develop its own four-engine aircraft on the Manchester platform. The two Vultures were replaced with four proven Merlin engines; for this purpose, the wings had to be made longer. These – and a few more modifications – resulted in the appearance of the Lancaster, which was the best British heavy bomber of the Second World War, and the prototype first flew on 9 January 1941. From October, the Lancasters began to be manufactured in ever-growing quantities, and these aircraft became the main striking power of the Royal Air Force in the air offensive against Germany.

In September 1944, the RAF – in cooperation with the Soviets – carried out Operation 'Paravane'. The objective was to disable the German battleship *Tirpitz*, which was anchored in Kaafjord in the northern part of Norway. For this purpose, two Lancaster squadrons (No.9 Squadron and No.617 Squadron) departed for the mouth of the Northern Dvina; they carried heavy bombs and sea mines. Yagodnik airfield, which was situated on an island of the same name on a river near Archangelsk, was their assigned base; however, due to bad weather and navigational errors, some of the crews got lost and landed not on Yagodnik, but on other airfields or just where their fuel reserve came to its end.

Nineteen Lancasters landed at Yagodnik and 10 at another large airfield in Kegostrov. The rest were less fortunate: Lieutenant Camsell of No.9 Squadron was searching for Archangelsk, but in vain. When the gasoline was already running out, he decided to land in the first suitable place. In a break in the clouds, he saw a city and a small airfield; that was Belomorsk. At landing, both right engines failed; however, finally, all turned out well. Pilot Lawes of the same squadron landed on a small airfield at Vaskovo, where fighters were based. The runway there was short and planked. The heavy bomber slid along the wet planks, overran the runway and plunged into a drainage ditch, with its right landing gear leg and right-wing panel broken. Another aircraft in Vaskovo missed the runway and sank into soft soil.

On the whole, quite a lot of Lancasters were damaged. Seven of them suffered severe damage, but fortunately, there were no victims. Rescue teams were unsuccessfully trying to pick up pilot Keely's crew after a forced landing in the swamps. Finally, a parachutist was dropped to the crew's location. He led the British pilots to a lake, where a flying boat had already been waiting for them.

After a minor repair, all serviceable bombers were concentrated on Yagodnik. From there (on 14 September), they made a successful raid on *Tirpitz* and inflicted significant damage on the latter. They returned to Yagodnik and then, on 16-20 September (already without cargo), they departed for Scotland. One of the damaged Lancasters was put into operation and safely returned home.

Six aircraft remained in Russia. The British considered them to be irretrievably damaged, and wrote them off under Category 'E' (non-combat losses) after the removal of certain components and assemblies for repair of other aircraft. Before the departure of the British air group, the bombers were also stripped off some short-supply parts and the most valuable and secret equipment. Some items (such as IFF transponders) were, in certain cases, according to instructions, blasted right after the forced landings.

Immediately after the departure of the British for their home country, all the abandoned bombers were examined by the White Sea Flotilla Air Force Engineers' Commission. The commission's report stated: 'On all the aircraft, the British have removed or blasted the radars, individual units of radio equipment, bomb sights, and accessories. Furthermore, all the aircraft have been stripped off the most difficult-to-obtain engine assemblies'. After inspection of all the aircraft, members of the commission came to the conclusion that two Lancasters were repairable and, in case of acute need, one more was fit for restoring. The remaining three were suggested to be used as spare parts sources.

The White Sea Flotilla Air Force conducted operations over the White Sea, the Barents Sea and the Kara Sea. They were in desperate need of long-range aircraft; however, the Flotilla Air Force had no four-engine aircraft at their disposal. Repair of the Lancaster, which was staying in Chubalo-Navolok (Khopa Island), was deemed the top priority. Pilot Morrison's aircraft (s/n LL884) landed there on a flood plain meadow. At landing, it got into a pit and lost the left landing gear leg; the lower parts of the fins were crushed; one of the engines on the left side was smashed; and the left wing and landing flaps were damaged. That Lancaster was ordered to be restored before 7 November 1944 (the anniversary of the October Revolution).

The repair was entrusted to the 86th Aviation Repair Workshops, which were located at Yagodnik. General management was carried out by Chief Engineer of the Flotilla Air Force Major Kiryanov, whereas Major Rovinsky exercised direct supervision of the work. It was decided that the missing items – including the engine assembly – would be taken from a wrecked aircraft which was lying in Kegostrov (s/n ME559). The latter's landing gear was entirely demolished; its wing, fuselage and tail unit were badly damaged. Removal of the required items was the responsibility of Captain Danich's team.

Indeed, by early November, the Lancaster was put in good condition; the repair was carried out at the location of the forced landing. Since the aircraft was intended to be used in the role of a long-range reconnaissance and transport aircraft, rather than in the role of a bomber, all the turrets were removed and their openings were covered with duralumin sheets. Removal of the armament was carried out by Captain Bleikher's team. The damaged nose portion was modified to be terminated with a transparent dome-type fairing, which accommodated the navigator workstation.

The original British camouflage (green-and-brown top and black bottom) was retained; however, all insignias were painted over with Soviet-green enamel, which differed from the British one in tint. Red stars were painted on the top and bottom surfaces of the wing panels, and on the fuselage sides; also, the aircraft bore the number '01' on both sides.

The Lancaster was handed over to the 16th Transport Air Detachment. It was flown by E. Yevdokimov as pilot, with V. Andreev as navigator. The crew usually included one or two pilots, a navigator and two flight engineers. The 16th Detachment was formed on the basis of the 2nd Independent Air Group, which had, initially, been manned with polar pilots. In spite of the fact that the detachment was referred to as a 'Transport' one, it dealt not only with the transportation of personnel and cargo, but was also involved in convoy escorting, ice reconnaissance and patrolling over sea. Those were the roles for which the Lancaster was used. For example, on 24 January 1945, it flew an ice reconnaissance mission along the route beginning from Belushya Bay (Novaya Zemlya). The aircraft was even used to search for German submarines in remote areas; however, there is no evidence that the crew of the Lancaster managed to detect at least one submarine.

After the first airplane, the second one was going to be restored. It had performed a wheels-up landing on a swamp near Molotovsk (currently Severodvinsk). Pilot Ross' bomber (s/n EE131) was landing (with almost no fuel) at the nearest more or less suitable site. Under severe braking, the heavy Tallboy bomb, which the aircraft was carrying inside, broke through the bomb bay doors and flew far ahead. The entire lower part of the fuselage was badly mangled, the nose crushed and the screws bent. The crew destroyed the bomb sight and blasted the IFF transponder.

This aircraft was intended to be partially disassembled (the disassembly included the removal of the wing panels and tail unit) and further transported to Yagodnik. The missing parts (again) were expected to be brought from Kegostrov. The work was planned to be completed by 1 January 1945, but, in fact, no traces of the recovery of the aircraft have been found. In any case, there is no second Lancaster on the lists of naval aviation.

The third aircraft (s/n NF985) in Vaskovo was initially planned to be dismantled for spare parts. There was an order to place the aircraft on a paved area and to mothball it. Later, it was concluded that the aircraft was repairable, but that the cost of the repair would be very high. According to the Acceptance Act, the damaged assemblies on this Lancaster included the power plant, right wing, flaps, empennage and the fuselage nose. The British had stripped it of a large number of parts to repair other aircraft. Finally, a kind of 'watered-down' Resolution was adopted, with the following wording: '... repair term and possibility are to be determined after the repair of the first two aircraft...' Apparently, the third Lancaster was never repaired.

The aircraft that bore the tactical number '01' was operated in the 16th Detachment until summer 1945. It was based mostly at Yagodnik, but also made flights from Naryan-Mar and Vaenga. In July, the aircraft was ferried to Moscow and, from there, in August (in connection with the war against Japan), it was sent to the Far East; however, the Lancaster only managed to reach Krasnoyarsk. It stayed there for some time, since there was not enough fuel for the large number of aircraft being ferried to the east. While the aircraft were waiting for gasoline, the short war came to an end. Japan capitulated.

The Lancaster returned to Moscow, and then to Yagodnik – and there it stayed at least until spring 1946. During that time, it was twice subjected to minor repairs. After the disbandment of the 16th Detachment, the aircraft returned to Moscow, where it was assigned to the 65th Special-Purpose Air Regiment. The regiment was based at Izmailovo airfield (at that time, it was located in the suburbs of Moscow).

The further fate of the Lancaster is not known for sure. According to one version, the aircraft was written off after a crash landing in Izmailovo. Pilot N. Dubenets overran the runway and got stuck in a potato field. The landing gear collapsed, and the fuselage and the wing were severely damaged; repair was considered to be impractical.

According to another version, the already rather worn-out aircraft (spare parts for which were not available) was ferried to Riga in summer 1946, and there it was handed over to the Air Force Aviation and Technical School as an educational aid.

This Lancaster, which was flown by pilot L. Keely, made a forced landing in the swamps near Talagi.

The Lancaster flown by Flight Lieutenant G. Camsell after an unsuccessful landing at the wooden airstrip in Belomorsk.

The Lancaster of the RAF No.617 Squadron, which was flown by Squadron Leader Wyness, after landing at Kegostrov. Due to the low efficiency of the brakes on the wet runway, the aircraft passed the threshold, got into a pit and broke its left landing gear. Due to the heavy damage, the Lancaster was written off and used for spares.

Installation of the Lancaster engine at the Soviet workshops; note the nose section, which was modified after the aircraft's forced landing.

A Lancaster of the 16th Transport Air Detachment at an airfield in 1945.

8.7 Supermarine Walrus

Purely by chance, the Soviet Union came into the possession of a single, British-made Supermarine Walrus amphibian. That was a big biplane, whose engine was mounted in a nacelle between the upper and lower wing; the aircraft was also fitted with a pusher propeller. During a water landing, the undercarriage was not retracted; it was just pulled up and remained hanging in a tilted position under the lower wing.

By the time of the war, the Walrus had already been a rather obsolete aircraft: it was designed under the guidance of R.J. Mitchell (the very same R.J. Mitchell who had created the Spitfire) in the Supermarine design office in 1933. The Walrus, which was originally called the Seagull V, was, essentially, a Seagull flying boat that had been modified into an amphibian; the prototype was first flown on 21 July 1933. The crew consisted of two to four people, and the armament comprised two 7.69mm machine guns. The aircraft was intended to be used in the role of a shipboard catapult-launched reconnaissance and liaison aircraft.

Mass manufacture of the Seagull V began in June 1935 under the orders of the Australian Navy. Beginning from 1936, these reconnaissance aircraft (in a slightly modified version, and under the name of 'Walrus') were built for the British Admiralty. The reliable (and quite seaworthy) biplane remained in production until January 1944.

The Walrus that happened to get to the USSR was catapult-launched from the cruiser *Norfolk*, which was escorting Convoy PQ 17. Fearing a possible approach of the German battleship *Tirpitz*, the British Command ordered that the majority of the covering forces should withdraw, and that the convoy ships should disperse and proceed to Soviet ports on their own. Having completed the reconnaissance mission, the crew of the amphibian found out that the cruiser was not at the assigned location. During the search for their friends, the pilots found a group of transport vehicles which were escorted by the patrol ship *Pozarica*. The fuel was running out, and the pilots had to land on water; then the aircraft was towed and loaded on board the transport ship *Ocean Freedom*. In this manner, the aircraft reached Yokanga on 11 July 1942.

Of course, the towing along the wavy sea did not do the Walrus any good, and the aircraft needed repair. In a half-dismantled condition, it remained in the Archangelsk port for some time. Apparently, the British decided that 'the game was not worth the candle', and abandoned the aircraft as damaged beyond repair, but the unwanted aircraft attracted the attention of a certain person from the White Sea Flotilla Air Force Command. Formally, the Walrus had not been handed over to the Soviet Union under any documents; however, it was repaired and assigned to the 16th Transport Air Regiment, which was employing a motley (but mostly obsolete) fleet. The aircraft was operated there throughout 1942-1943, and it is not known when it was written off.

9

Lend-Lease and the Soviet Aviation Industry

The delivery of raw materials and equipment for the Soviet industry was another sphere of influence of the Allies' assistance on Soviet aviation. Shipments to the Soviet Union included ingot aluminum and aluminum sheets and rods; alloy steel and pipes made from such steel; copper, brass and bronze; brass nets; tin plates; aircraft cables; and wire. The deliveries from the United States, Great Britain and Canada began in autumn 1941. Shipments of aluminum were the most critical ones, since Soviet aircraft factories needed aluminum badly. Aluminum had been in short supply in the USSR since before the war. The demand of the People's Commissariat for Aviation Industry in terms of various items had been fulfilled in the percentage of 34 through to 93 percent. Meanwhile, the Soviet aviation industry had needed 90,000 tons per year. After the German invasion, the situation became much worse. According to the *History of the Great Patriotic War of the Soviet Union, 1941-1945*: 'In the beginning of the war, major aluminum smelting works and non-ferrous metal rolled stock factories got out of operation. Until the end of the war, the non-ferrous metals industry remained one of the 'bottlenecks' of the war economy in the Soviet Union'. Indeed, the Volkhovsky Aluminum Factory and the Dneprovsky Aluminum Factory, with 60 percent of total production, had fallen into the hands of the Germans. Factories which produced aluminum alloy sheets, pipes and sections (production of the latter was resumed as late as May 1942) happened to be located in the occupied territory as well.

In accordance with the Moscow Protocol, the Allies undertook to supply a monthly amount of 2,000 tons of aluminum in the form of ingots and semi-finished products. Imported aluminum alloys had a higher strength and were more corrosion-resistant when compared to the Soviet-produced alloys; the United States imported Alclad (high-quality plated sheet duralumin). One can often discern the respective brand markings on the skin of unpainted Soviet aircraft which were manufactured shortly before the end of the war (as represented in photographs).

The scale of aluminum shipments was rather large – thus, for example, in 1942, Great Britain supplied 2,000 tons of aluminum per month. In July through to September 1943, the United States and Canada shipped 6,000 tons per month. The Soviet side had applied for much more: the request under Protocol III included 80,640 tons of aluminum, but in reality, only 36,700 tons were received. Aluminum was initially delivered via Archangelsk, but later, shipments were also made along the southern route via Krasnovodsk. Pipes, sheets and rolled aluminum-alloy stock were also coming via Vladivostok. In total (throughout the war), the United States shipped 99,000 tons of aluminum, plus 35,400 tons from Great Britain and 33,600 tons from Canada. Of course, not all of those went to the aviation industry; however, it would be safe to say that the latter consumed the larger portion of the supplies. As for the domestic aluminum production, the Soviet Union managed to restore it to the pre-war level as late as 1943. In total, during the Lend-Lease deliveries, the Allies supplied 106 percent as related to the Soviet production. This raw material, some of which remained in storage, was used in the early post-war years.

By the end of the war, a complete set of equipment for a rolled aluminum stock production factory had been delivered from the USA.

The importance of other raw materials and semi-finished products was less vital. According to a number of sources, steel and rolled steel products featured low in quality. They tended to get damaged during long-distance transportation, and were used in the aviation industry mostly for auxiliary purposes. In late 1942, an attempt was made to replace Soviet steel in the undercarriage of the Il-2 ground attack aircraft with its American equivalent; however, the attempt failed due to differences in steel properties.

On the other hand, the Soviet Union received a lot of non-ferrous metals and various alloys. The USA shipped copper, zinc, molybdenum, brass and nichrome. Lead, tin, copper, zinc and cobalt were coming from Great Britain. Canada supplied copper, tin, lead, zinc, nickel and cobalt. The copper, as compared to the Soviet production, was received in a volume of 76 percent; lead was 223 percent and cobalt 123 percent. The British Empire, 'on which the sun never sets', also shipped commercial diamonds, graphite, natural rubber, jute and shellac from its colonial domains.

Organic glass, natural and artificial leather, various instruments, cameras, radio stations, navigation equipment, wires for various purposes, varnishes and paints, alcohol, acetone, glycerin, textolite and rubber hoses were also supplied from abroad. The United States shipped large, high-quality Perspex plexiglass sheets. In the USSR, the technology of large-sheet production had not yet been mastered at that time. Up to 800 tons of thin, brass 'noodle-type' tubes for radiators were delivered on a quarterly basis from the USA.

Many other items were also delivered – thus, before 16 November 1942, the Soviet Union received 100,000 finished bearings and a lot of balls and rollers for ball-bearing factories. Before the war, a shortage of such products hampered the operation of factories to a considerable extent. In late 1941, the situation became ultimately awful, with the output of bearings reduced by 21 times.

The imported parts included bolts, nuts, washers, rivets, springs, wire and steel band. Until summer 1942, the Soviet aviation industry used the imported hardware, as the domestic factories had been restarting the production after evacuation.

The Lend-Lease Act permitted providing industrial equipment for the manufacture of military products. As early as summer 1941, the Americans transferred (to the Soviet Union) some of the orders for the machinery for aircraft factories which had earlier been placed by British and French representatives. The purchase of special-purpose equipment from England and from the USA continued throughout the war – enabling to compensate (to a certain degree) for the reduced output of such equipment in the Soviet Union. Since the factories were overloaded with weapons manufacture and, due to a loss of facilities in the European portion of the USSR, the output of machines in 1942 dropped more than twice when compared to 1940. By 1945, the initial output value had not yet been restored.

As of 1 December 1941, 1,488 machines for the aviation industry had been ordered from the United States, plus 178 from England. The first batch came with the Arctic convoys in mid-autumn the same year (some of the delivered machines had been included in pre-war orders). Afterwards, the inflow of imported equipment kept growing. Convoy PQ 15 alone brought 180 different machines for the People's Commissariat for Aviation Industry. Throughout the first eight months of 1942, the Soviet aviation industry received from abroad 1,313 machines; 65 presses (while another 56 were in transit by sea at that time); seven hammers (with another nine in transit); 28 electric furnaces; 22 welding equipment sets; 10 moulding machines; four forging machines; 13 motortrucks; eight mechanical shears; and 15 bolt-and-rivet manufacturing machines. Throughout the same period, the Allies supplied inspection and cutting tools for a sum of 276,000 rubles and, for 65,000 rubles, commercial diamonds, plus 26 railcars with abrasive material (referenced here is only the equipment for the People's Commissariat for Aviation Industry).

When preparing Protocol II, the Soviet side made increases several times in its request for industrial machinery: it began with 150 million US dollars' worth of equipment, while ending with 315 million US dollars' worth. Such an increase in the machinery deliveries was personally insisted upon by I.V. Stalin. He was even ready to decrease the volume of armament importing in order to get a higher number of the up-to-date machines.

The Americans were resisting, as they quite rationally understood that the armament would be lost in combat, or would gradually wear out without the supply of spares. In contrast, the modernization of the industry was a serious step, as the factories would continue to produce arms after the end of the hostilities. The US Government also put a high level of pressure on their British colleagues – persuading them to deliver a lesser number of machinery and tools to the Soviet Union. As a result, only 20-63 percent of Soviet demand was satisfied on different items of machinery and tools; however, the resulting volume was still very high. For example, the aviation factory in Kamensk-Uralsky got 460 machines and 40km of electric cable. By 15 August 1944, the aviation industry had received 7,180 imported metal-cutting machines. Many of them were unique, and had not been in production in the Soviet Union. Presses for the moulding of products from plastics (which were not manufactured in the USSR at that time) were ordered from the USA. Besides, oxygen-generating plants and painting equipment was imported during the war.

The share of industrial equipment and tools in the foreign shipments kept growing – and at a much faster rate than the importing of armament. In 1943, the amount of aircraft and spare parts as sent by the Americans to the Soviet Union grew by 65 percent versus the previous year, whereas the amount of equipment, raw materials and semi-finished products increased by 173 percent. Machines brought in during the war remained in operation with Soviet factories for a long time afterwards.

The mass importing of equipment resulted in the rate of growth of the machinery stock being ahead of the rate of growth of the headcount at aircraft factories – thus, the Soviet industry began to adopt the modern model of 'less manual labor, more machinery operation'.

Here, again, a comparison could be made between the USA's assistance to Great Britain and to the USSR. The British were strongly dependent on external supplies of raw materials, but they received from the Americans (apart from raw materials and semi-finished products) a lot of complete items such as turrets, landing gear assemblies etc. American equipment (in particular, gyro units, radio equipment and radar sets) found a wide application with the British.

On Soviet aircraft, there were almost no foreign-manufactured assemblies. Probably the only exception was that the first series of Tupolev Tu-2 bombers were intended to be equipped with both Soviet-manufactured wheels and with Bendix wheels of American manufacture, whose tires were of a slightly smaller size; however (apparently), such aircraft were never built.

Imported radio equipment and photographic equipment was used on a somewhat wider scale. The USSR received American-manufactured SCR-269C and MN-26 radio direction finders (approximately 700 of them were shipped), as well as autopilots, SCR-274N radio stations and aerial cameras of different types (including gun cameras). For example, one of the series of the Tu-2 bombers (as manufactured by Moscow Factory No.23 in 1945) was fitted with American-made radio direction finders. After successful testing of the prototype at NII VVS, factory teams also began to mount such radio direction finders on the previously manufactured aircraft, which were in service with regiments in the Far East. The SCR-269s were also used to equip certain series of the Li-2s; the same was the case with the A-3A autopilots (250 of which came from the USA). SCR-274N radio stations were mounted on the Yakovlev Yak-9DD long-range fighters. From February 1943 through to September 1944, 950 radio stations were imported for fighters and 838 for bombers. The US-manufactured gun cameras were widely applied on Soviet fighters of all types; after the war, they were used on the La-9s and La-11s.

Soviet aircraft were equipped with imported instruments as well, and large orders for such instruments were placed in the USA. By 4 July 1944, 10,000 turn indicators and 5,000 gyro horizons were shipped from American factories. The first batch of instruments left American shores on board the *George Bancroft* transport ship on 13 February 1943. She was followed by *American Packer* on 15 August and then by *Java* on 15 October. Before 1 September 1944, the USSR received 784 gyro horizons, 3,632 turn indicators and 1,480 three-pointer indicators. The US-made instruments were more accurate than Soviet ones; they also required less frequent recalibrations and had a longer lifespan.

Not all of those instruments found actual application. The above-mentioned figures reflect the number of instruments as accepted in the Soviet territory; however, there were losses during further transportation on account of enemy actions, accidents or simply due to negligence – thus, for example, a large batch of radio equipment which had been delivered via the 'Persian Corridor' was found unserviceable. An investigation revealed that the boxes had been transferred from ships to rail cars in Baku, and had been further carried in open rail cars (even without a canvas cover).

The multi-stage structure of purchasing agencies brought about rather 'expensive' mistakes. Officers of the People's Commissariat of Foreign Trade, who were staying in the USA, had no direct communication with aviation industry experts and had only a poor notion of the latter's real needs – thus, for example, three-pointer indicators which were shipped to the Soviet Union proved to be not completely sealed; they failed to operate in sub-zero conditions and were beyond the standard dimensions as adopted in the USSR. For these reasons, they were considered unfit for military aircraft.

Electrical switches (188,767 of those were received throughout the above-mentioned period) and various-purpose wires (172km in total) were also imported.

An interesting fact about aircraft deliveries under Lend-Lease was that they caused (apart from direct influence) some indirect impact. It consisted of a mass-scale familiarization of Soviet pilots, engineers and designers with foreign equipment items (which were different from Soviet ones in terms of design concepts and engineering traditions) and featured different (sometimes much more advanced) technologies. Even before the war, the Soviet Union had been purchasing licenses which usually provided for the training of Soviet specialist teams at foreign factories, as well as sending delegations to visit aircraft exhibitions or just to get acquainted with the industry of a certain country, and buying sample aircraft; however, only a limited number of selected persons were involved in such activities. Broad communication with foreigners had always been deemed suspicious and reprehensible in the Soviet Union – and it was strictly limited by *chekists*.

During the Second World War, a large number of people had to be familiarized with 'non-Soviet-manufactured' aircraft out of sheer necessity. Those were ferry pilots, frontline pilots, repair personnel etc. They got to know the American aircraft first hand and formed their own judgment of them. It often led to undesirable questions, such as: 'If they can, why can't we? Why do they care about the pilots' comfort, whereas we don't? Why is there such a huge difference in quality and reliability?' On the one hand, it was an additional 'headache' for the Secret Service and political instructors; on the other hand, constant dropping wears away a stone. The Soviet industry had to somehow respond to the opinion of frontline pilots and technicians.

Pilots of the Northern Sea Fleet, who shared base airfields with the British, saw that the latter were servicing and repairing their aircraft in a different manner, and that flight preparations were completely different. The British Allies, in their turn, were terrified by the quality of Soviet gas and oil. They shuddered when they saw Soviet mechanics walking about the handed-over aircraft in boots rather than felt slippers. The same things happened at American bases in Poltava, Mirgorod and Piryatin, where Soviet specialists worked side by side with the Americans. A lot of methods were adopted by the ferry pilots who operated along the ALSIB route – especially those of the 1st Ferry Regiment, which was based in Fairbanks. The aircraft, which were designed for a higher operational culture, forcedly 'pulled up' Soviet flight and ground crews by making them gain new experience. That gave a huge impetus to the development of Soviet aviation in the post-war period, when the USSR often borrowed many design solutions, concepts and terminologies – and sometimes even boldly copied foreign aircraft.

All the aircraft types as delivered to Russia were thoroughly studied and tested. That was the case not only with the mass-manufactured models, but also with individual samples. Soviet specialists made trips abroad (both to the USA and to Great Britain) to get acquainted with new aircraft. Many aircraft which were offered for supply, but were rejected, passed through their hands. Also, there was (as already mentioned) the familiarization with the B-26 and A-29 bombers in the USA. In 1941, I.I. Sikorsky offered his first helicopter as adopted for service (the R-4) to the Soviet Union, and P.V. Kondratiev made a familiarization flight in it. The Grumman and Lockheed Companies sent in their proposals for the supply of naval aircraft of various types and, at the end of the war, also for the supply of passenger aircraft.

Soviet representatives were constantly visiting aircraft factories – always with the intention to be provided with a sample of some innovative product, or just to scrounge it – thus, the head of the Soviet military mission in London – Admiral N. Kharlamov – reported on 28 April 1943 that the Soviet delegation managed to obtain samples of glue (which were used to join wooden fuselage skin) at the De Havilland works, where the Mosquito was being built. A visit to the North American facilities yielded a collection of different plastic parts used in the P-51 and the B-25.

In September 1944, the Soviet military attaché Colonel Sergeev – accompanied by Colonel Shibanov, Major Marakazov and Major Lebedev – were on a trip to Los Angeles, where they visited the aircraft manufacture facilities of Lockheed and Hughes. In workshops, they were shown the process of assembly of the B-17 bombers and the C-69 transport aircraft. The Americans also showed the Soviet colleagues layout diagrams for the C-69, as well as providing its specifications. The XP-58 experimental fighter was demonstrated in flight; a dummy of the huge XH-1 flying boat, as well as drawings for XF-11 high-speed reconnaissance aircraft, were presented on ground.

A large amount of different documentation was brought from the USA – including manuals, guidelines, technical descriptions, specifications, drawings, parts catalogues and reports of military laboratories. The documents were obtained wherever possible and brought to the USSR by a diplomatic bag. Intelligence was involved in this process, along with official representatives.

Any Soviet citizen who visited a company, design office, research institute or university where military technical researches were carried out received a detailed questionnaire stating what he/she should pay attention to; what places were of particular interest; and what he/she should try to look at, touch or cajole out. After the trip, a detailed report had to be prepared, together with attached photos, diagrams and samples.

Of course, Soviet delegations were not familiarized with everything they would have liked to have been. Soviet representatives were constantly trying to obtain specimens of the latest British and American aircraft; however, in most cases, they were denied – thus, for example, the Americans flatly refused to provide (for studying purposes) a specimen of their first Bell P-59 Airacomet jet fighters (the Soviet party requested two or three specimens) and the Lockheed P-80 Shooting Star. It should be noted, however, that the company management themselves treated the respectable customers with due understanding. President of the Bell Company L. Bell invited Engineer of the Soviet Procurement Commission V. Mazurin to attend a demonstration flight of the P-59 (as arranged for the US State Committee) on 2 November 1944. At the end of the month, Mazurin sent a dimensional drawing of the fighter and a layout of its engine to the USSR.

There were also cases when the Soviet Government themselves gave up very interesting aircraft for political reasons. When the Germans made successful night raids on the American air bases in Poltava and Mirgorod, the United States suggested strengthening the local air defense forces with a squadron of the latest Northrop P-61 Black Widow night interceptors and several anti-aircraft batteries equipped with radars and up-to-date fire-control systems. Both were of interest for Soviet military men. It was intended that American flight and ground crews would come together with the materiel and, along with combat operations, would train the Soviet crews. Upon completion of the training, the Americans would depart for home – leaving the aircraft and the rest of the materiel; however, the Kremlin objected to any enlargement of the contingent as deployed at these bases, so the Widows were reluctantly rejected…

The Soviet side sometimes refused to make concessions to the Allies as well. In 1945, the British requested that the USSR provide documents for the fuel tanks' free space inert gas filling system, as they intended to use the system in the Lancaster heavy bomber. Some of the Allies' aircraft featured their own similar systems; however, they made use of nitrogen or carbon dioxide. In the USSR, such a method had already been out of date. The Soviet design utilized cooled and purified engine exhaust gases. The bottle is depleted sooner or later, but the exhaust gases are available while the engines are running. The Soviet system was especially advantageous for long-duration flights. It took a long time for politicians and military authorities to decide whether or not to provide the design to the British, but finally, they came to the conclusion that the Soviet Union was not interested in the enhancement of the defense capabilities of the British Air Force. The Allies were refused; however, the case was rather an exception: the Soviet side took a much greater amount of useful technical information from the Americans and the British than it was able to give.

The defense industries of Great Britain – and especially the USA – worked under quieter conditions and possessed far greater technological capabilities. They were not so pressed by the metal shortage, and had reserves to master the production of new aircraft types during the war. In the USSR, only two conceptually new aircraft were put into production throughout the entire war period: those were the Tu-2 bomber (designed before the war) and the Il-10 ground attack aircraft. The Yak-3 and the Yak-9 were, essentially, modifications of the Yak-1 basic aircraft, whereas the La-7 was a further development of the LaGG-3. Meanwhile, the Americans created up to 20 new fighters and bombers. The British were poorer; nevertheless, they designed the Tempest, the Mosquito, the Lancaster (and the latter's transport version named York) and the Beaufighter, let alone the Meteor (the first British jet aircraft).

All of the American combat aircraft featured an all-metal, state-of-the-art structure with stressed skin. In the USSR (on the contrary), all fighters as manufactured before the end of the war had a combined (mainly wooden) structure, which caused a heavy weight of the airframe. American factories utilized an advanced technology, which involved using large double curvature panels that were stamped and casted. Aircraft were segmented into large blocks, which were assembled separately until the wiring and equipment installation phase.

Conveyor assembly was widely spread. The Bell Company assembled fighters at a former automobile factory, which utilized the classical Ford procedure, with the only difference being that the Airacobras (unlike the Model T) were never painted in a radical black color (olive was the preferred color); also, plastics and new light alloys were made use of. The American military industry absorbed all of the achievements of the civil sectors and could afford the luxury of taking due care as regards crew comfort, ergonomics and accurate machine furnishing.

The British were in a more complicated situation, but the majority of their aircraft were also superior in technology to their Soviet peers.

During his life, the famous test pilot M.L. Gallay tried almost all types of aircraft supplied under the Lend-Lease program. The latest (oddly enough) was the Texan training aircraft, in which he had a chance to fly as late as in the 1970s during his trip to the USA. No medical certificate was asked from Gallay, in spite of the fact that the Medical Board in the Soviet Union had 'decommissioned' the pilot long before. Once, I asked him: "What was in common between all those imported aircraft?" Gallay scratched his head and gave an unexpected answer: "They could be climbed into without gloves! In our aircraft, you either run a splinter into a finger, or cut yourself by a burr..." I was also told things like that by a lot of mechanics, engine technicians and repairmen who were handling the Lend-Lease materiel during the war and after it.

Each type of aircraft which happened to get to the USSR was carefully examined by specialists in different institutions and factories. Upon completion of the test program, a list of components and assemblies (subject to scrutiny and copying) was always drawn up. The People's Commissariat of Aviation Industry identified the organizations to which it was entrusted. Often, an aircraft was stripped of all such components and assemblies, and the latter were further distributed over factories. For example, on the Mosquito, the water and oil systems' valves aroused certain interest. They were copied at LII and, in October 1944, equivalent specimens were produced.

On the Tu-2, in November 1946, engine exhaust manifolds similar to those mounted by the Boeing were implemented.

Familiarization with foreign technologies drew attention to areas where it was evident that the Soviets were lagging behind the West (i.e. metallurgy, radio engineering, instrumentation and crew life-support systems). Many specimens of British and American aircraft equipment were often straightforwardly copied by Soviet designers. Some of them were specially handed over to the Soviet side for investigation – thus, Soviet specialists received and copied (after the war) the famous Norden bomb sight and the C-1 autopilot, which were requested in December 1943. Both of them were provided by the Americans to the Soviet Union in 1944. As for the British-made H2X radar bomb sight that LII studied in the summer of 1945, it had probably been captured from the Germans.

Many American aircraft were equipped with Goodrich pneumatic de-icers. In the USSR, where the climate is colder than in the USA, attempts to create a reliable de-icer nevertheless failed. Both liquid ('sweating out') and electrothermal designs were tried; however, all of them proved to be inferior to their American counterparts. Finally, in February 1944, it was suggested that Goodrich de-icers should be copied and that the Soviet-made equivalent should be mounted on the Il-4 bomber. A month later, however, the opinion changed: it was decided to order (from Goodrich) the designing of de-icers for the Li-2 and the Yer-2, and then to receive the finished product from the USA in the amount of 250 sets of each type. The decision was reflected in the Resolution of the State Defense Committee of 13 March 1944. Goodrich agreed and asked for drawings of both aircrafts' wings and tails. For the Li-2, the task was deemed a fast-achievable one. Indeed, its design was based on an American one, so only the dimensions had to be converted into the metric format. It was believed that de-icers from the C-47 would fit well, and that there would be a possibility to begin shipping in June 1945, but here, the most interesting things began to happen... It should be remembered that in the Soviet Union, the drawings were considered to be secret! With the Li-2, one could find a way out by sending the original American metric drawings of the DC-3. As for the newest Yermolaev Yer-2 long-range bomber, the Soviet authorities strictly forbade the handing-over of the drawings. While the departments were intensively exchanging correspondence, the war came to an end, and so did the Lend-Lease program.

Soviet cannons and machine guns were valued higher than foreign ones; however, turrets of domestic manufacture were much inferior to the American ones, which had electric and hydraulic drives. On 1 December 1943, a request for five turret types was sent to the Americans, and the Soviets wished to receive them in batches of 10-12 each. At the same time, the USSR asked to check the possibility of providing specimens of the Sperry gunsight and the Fairchild synchronizer, but the matter came to a standstill. Later, however, the Soviet Union came into possession of all of the above-mentioned products, which were received together with the aircraft, whether officially or not.

Familiarization with the Lend-Lease aircraft often served as the impetus for the development of new materials and technologies. A story is widely known, which is described in a book by P.M. Stefanovsky: the appearance of the Tomahawk fighter in the Soviet Union led to the implementation of its canopy's advantages on Soviet aircraft and to the introduction of a new variety of organic glass. According to the Resolution the State Defense Committee of 15 May 1942, the People's Commissariat of Chemical Industry was obliged to carry out an analysis of the American material and to then reproduce it. The resulting Soviet-made organic glass did not, of course, become a rival to Perspex, but its performance grew much better. On the other hand, Perspex (as has already been discussed) was imported to the USSR in large quantities during the war.

The impact of this indirect effect of Anglo-American technology on the Soviet aviation can be well judged by the already mentioned fact that the first Soviet B-4 (Tu-4) strategic bomber was built on the platform of the American-manufactured B-29. Here, all due measures were taken to obtain (in America) the drawings, specifications, technical conditions, operating instructions and specimens of the materials used. Initially, it was expected that the Americans would assist in launching the production of the bomber. The Soviet Government allocated 1.5 million US dollars (at that time, it was big money) to purchase the necessary components, assemblies and materials in the USA. Negotiations continued after the completion of the Lend-Lease program until the end of 1945. In particular, a contract with Jack and Heintz was being prepared for the delivery of various electromechanical products; however, the military authorities insisted that only domestic products should be used on the bomber.

As a result, the launching of the aircraft manufacture was accompanied by considerable difficulties. The industry had to make a lot of effort to master new materials, processing methods and components of equipment for a highly complex aircraft in order to provide the Soviet Air Force with a domestic equivalent of the American-manufactured nuclear weapons carrier; on the whole, however, it should be considered a long-sighted step. In fact, the construction of this aircraft boosted to a new level (along with the aviation industry) all related industries.

After the war, there were a lot of hopes for continued cooperation with the Allies in the sphere of aviation. In July 1947, Head of the Department of Transport Aviation of the People's Commissariat of Aviation Industry Mikhin suggested purchasing a license for the Lockheed C-69 Constellation four-engine transport, but his appeal was rejected. Hopes to continue the beneficial (for the Soviet Union, at least) scientific-technical and industrial relations gradually dissipated, but for a long time after the war, specimens of aircraft and engines as shipped under Lend-Lease were used in institutes and flight schools to make students familiar with other countries' original design-based and technological solutions.

The as yet unpainted skin sheets of the Yer-2 bomber, which was built at Factory No.39 in Irkutsk. The metal sheets were imported from the US, as they still carry the marking printed by the American manufacturer.

The shop of manufacturing products from non-ferrous metals at Factory No.36 in Rybinsk in February 1945; note that name plates of various American companies can be seen on the machine tools.

Factory No.19 in Molotov (Perm) was originally fitted with American equipment. During the war, it was supplemented with new machine tools supplied under Lend-Lease.

The head of the Soviet military mission in Fairbanks Colonel M.G. Machin (in the center) visiting the facilities of Douglas Aircraft.

10

Relations with Allies in Aviation Engine Building

The same as with aircraft, the Soviet specialists had first-hand knowledge of British and American aviation engines before the beginning of the Second World War. It should be noted that such engines had always been present in the USSR, so let us begin with the fact that the first aviation engines in Russia were of foreign origin. Furthermore, the very first engine was an American-designed one! It was a four-cylinder 30hp Wright engine. The license and documentation was purchased via the Germans, and adaptation of the engine to Russian conditions was performed by two engineers (an Estonian and a Baltic German). It was assembled in Riga (as they say today, abroad); however, this Wright-Riga is considered to be the first Russian aviation engine.

Later on, French designs occupied a practically monopolistic position in Russian engine manufacture. The only exception was the Sunbeam Crusader engine (of British origin), which was manufactured at the Ilyin Factory in Moscow. The engines were also imported (mostly from France). It was only for the Ilya Muromets heavy bombers that three types of Sunbeam engines and a Beardmore engine were imported from England.

The list of foreign engines in operation in Russia became much larger during the Civil War. Engines which had not been encountered before (such as the British-manufactured Rolls-Royce Eagle and the RAF BR.2, and the American-manufactured Sturtevant) were added to the list, together with captured aircraft. The highest interest was aroused by the American-made A12-400 Ford Liberty engine. Such engines were mounted on the DH.4s and DH.9as, which were captured from the White Army. Afterwards, the Liberty was copied and its mass manufacture was launched at two factories under the Soviet designation M-5.

In the 1920s, Soviet Russia was actively purchasing engines from abroad. In 1924, the contracts were concluded for the supply of engines from the USA, England, Germany and France; in summer 1924, the People's Commissariat of Foreign Trade was given an assignment to bring in 250 Liberty engines. By 12 September, 100 engines of this type were supplied to depots. Initially, an order for 106 Liberty engines was placed in America; in January 1925, 400 more engines were ordered. The purchasing of the engines from America continued over six years. Furthermore, spare parts (in particular, crankshafts) were bought in 1928-1929 from Packard and Atlas. This led to the appearance of an engine series with mixed metric-inch configuration. From July 1925, Siddeley Puma engines were supplied (150 engines were ordered).

In 1929, Chairman of the Scientific and Technical Committee of the Air Force Administration N.M. Kharlamov suggested considering the issue of granting concessions to Curtiss for the manufacture of the Conqueror V-1650 engines in USSR. Also, to expedite preproduction, the air force agreed to purchase the engines in the initial inch configuration. The negotiations with the Curtiss Company were continued in 1930, but were not successful.

During the same period, aviation engine specimens were being actively purchased from abroad. On 22 December 1924, the Scientific and Technical Committee recommended to purchase such engines as the Packard, Wright T3, Bristol Jupiter, Rolls-Royce Condor, Bristol Cherub and Beardmore diesel engines. The majority of those engines were actually purchased and subjected to testing and intensive study – thus, in 1925, two Condor engines were delivered. Along with the above-mentioned engine types, the Aviation Trust received in 1925 (from the USA) two Curtiss D.12s and a Wright T4. During the same year, five Bristol Lucifer IIIs were imported from England; later, 15 more engines of the same model were purchased. In 1928, specimens of the American-manufactured Pratt & Whitney Hornet radial reciprocating engine were purchased.

All of those engines were studied and tested. In 1925-1926, specimens of the Liberty, Condor IV and Wright T3 engines were bench-tested at the Scientific Automotive Engine Institute (*Nauchniy Avtomotorniy Institute*, or NAMI). The Curtiss D.12 and another T3 were tested at the Ikar Factory in Moscow. In 1928, NAMI tested two types of Packard engines (the 2A-1500 and the 3A-2500).

The purpose of such tests was to get to know the world's engine-building experience and to select engine types to be purchased from abroad or to be manufactured in the Soviet Union. Many early Soviet aviation engines utilized components of the studied foreign designs – thus, in the M-13 engine as designed by NAMI, units similar to those of the Wright T3 were used; the carburetor was a copy of the Condor's one; and the gas distribution mechanism contained components of the Packard engine. Units similar to those of the Curtiss D.12 were integrated into the M-14 engine (later renamed W18), which was manufactured at the Ikar Factory.

In October 1924, an issue arose in respect of the license-free copying of the British-made Napier Lion engine, which was described by the specialists as 'one of the best European engines'. Sometime later, a new 'favorite' appeared: the American Wright T3 engine, which was deemed very promising. It is with the intention to use this engine that the first technical assignment was issued for the famous TB-3 bomber (initially referred to as T1-4RT3); neither of the engines, however, were adopted.

Head of the Air Force Administration of the Workers' and Peasants' Red Army P.I. Baranov, during his visit to America in January 1930, conducted negotiations on establishing a combined joint stock company in the Soviet Union for the manufacture of the Curtiss Conqueror V-1650 engine. In November 1929, this engine was recommended by the Scientific and Technical Committee of the Air Force Administration. B.S. Stechkin was familiarized with the engine in the USA, and expressed a favorable opinion of it. The Soviet Union purchased 12 Conqueror engines from the USA, and they were used on the first TB-3 bomber and on some other prototype aircraft. In 1934, at the TsAGI Factory of Experimental Designs, one of the Conquerors was modified. The modification included the introduction of the cooling fan drive and the replacement of the gear box. The engine was installed on an 11-EA helicopter prototype, and the helicopter was tested and modified until spring 1941.

In 1930, the American-manufactured Wright J6 Whirlwind engines were purchased for the ANT-9.

The attempt to launch the manufacture of the Packard radial diesel engine in the USSR turned out to be quite a long story: in late 1930, a 225hp engine of such a type was bought in America. It was brought to the Institute of Aviation Engine Development, and was disassembled for study. In 1931, the All-Union Aviation Association purchased four more such engines. Soviet representatives requested the Packard Company for a license and technical assistance in the mastering of production, but were refused; then, a decision was made to choose a different approach: Soviet Intelligence was entrusted with a task to get the required materials. In late June 1931, the Joint State Political Directorate (OGPU) handed over to the All-Union Aviation Association a complete set of documentation for the latest modification of the 230hp Packard diesel engine, which was dated November 1930. Approximately 1,500 drawings, specifications and process documents were delivered to Moscow. Later, however, the idea of launching the manufacture of the diesel engine was abandoned, since its design was considered poor.

The focus on the American engines was explained by the fact that those engines were easier to produce than British ones; however, during the pre-war period, an engine of British origin was manufactured in USSR: the M-22, which was, essentially, a development of the Cosmos Jupiter engine (later, Cosmos Engineering was renamed the Bristol Engine Company). The license, however, was purchased not in Great Britain, but in France, where the metric version of the engine was manufactured under the name of Gnome-Rhone 9A. These engines were successfully adopted and mass-manufactured in Zaporozhye in 1930-1935. Sometime earlier, the Soviet Union had been supplied with Jupiters of French and German manufacture.

In the early 1930s, the Soviet authorities overestimated the country's engineering capabilities and set a course for a full conversion to domestic-design engines only. A large-scale prototype engine-building program was being implemented and, in connection with it (in August 1931), the Revolutionary Military Council made a decision to discontinue purchasing engines for prototype aircraft from abroad. All new aircraft were to be developed to fly with Soviet-designed engines; however, this did not preclude the importing of foreign engines for study purposes. The resolution of the Council of Labor and Defense on prototype engine-building envisaged the purchase of 10 engines per year in 1929-1933 for such purposes – thus, in autumn 1932, a Rolls-Royce Kestrel engine was delivered to Moscow – and it aroused great interest on the part of Soviet specialists.

By April 1932, it had already become clear that the extensive plans of the Soviet engine-builders turned out to be an outright failure. Due to the incompetence of design organizations; a lack of skilled personnel; an inferiority in technology; and the general backwardness of the related industries (first and foremost, the electrical engineering industry, but also the iron and steel industry), only one Soviet-designed engine (the M-34, which was created by A.A. Mikulin) saw practical application in 1930-1931. Such a situation impeded the development of the aircraft-building industry. As for up-to-date altitude engines for fighters, the Soviet Union had none at all. A commission headed by future Marshal M.N. Tukhachevsky recommended obtaining licenses in the USA. The Wright R-1820 Cyclone and the Curtiss V-1800 Conqueror were selected for mastering in the USSR.

The licenses were purchased and, while badgering Curtiss-Wright, the Soviet side was also putting out the feelers for Pratt & Whitney; however, purchases were made from the former.

The manufacture of the Cyclone was launched in Perm under the designation M-25, and it became a predecessor for a large family of engines developed by A.D. Shvetsov. The Conqueror was intended to be manufactured at Factory No.26 in Rybinsk, but suddenly, all the works were discontinued. In France, a contract was concluded with Hispano-Suiza for obtaining a license for the new 12Ybrs engine. It was intended to be built in Moscow at Factory No.24, but the factory was overloaded with the manufacture of the M-34. For this reason, the planned Hispano production was handed over to Rybinsk. The entire V-1800 in-process stock was written off and destroyed.

In order to expedite the creation of the new aircraft generation, a batch of ready-made Cyclones were purchased in the USA; the majority of them were in the original inch configuration. Since the aircraft-building industry was somewhat ahead of the engine plants (which were lagging behind), in many cases, the imported engines were installed on mass-manufactured fighters. Some of the I-16s and all the first batches of the I-14s were equipped with such engines.

In 1935, a small batch of the British-designed 120hp De Havilland Gipsy III engines was purchased. Four of them were installed on the 'helicogyro', which was designed by Izakko. There, they were mounted on rotor blade tips. In 1936, one of the Gipsy engines was subjected to long-time bench testing at NII GVF.

Afterwards, until the Second World War, there were neither aviation engine purchases from abroad, nor any large-scale work under foreign licenses; however, this does not mean that foreign engines ceased coming to the Soviet Union at all: during that period, such engines were brought to the USSR as specimens for studying (both individually and together with aircraft), or as trophies – thus, for example, a lot of different engines were collected in September 1939 during the Red Army's advance into the territories of Western Ukraine and Western Byelorussia, which had previously belonged to Poland. The overwhelming majority of the engines were of British origin (the Jupiter VIIF; the Mercury IVS2, VS2 and VIS2; and the Pegasus IIM, VIII and XX). All of those engines had been manufactured at Polish factories. Also, a very small quantity of the original British-manufactured Pegasus XII engines was found.

In the late 1930s – considering the imminent danger of the war, and being aware of the lagging of the domestic aviation engine-building industry – the Soviet Government began to take new steps towards expanding contact with Western companies. Efforts were made to purchase engine specimens (for studying), technical publications and, in some cases, licenses.

In autumn 1937, the Soviet Trade Representation in London commenced negotiations about purchasing specimens of two Bristol engines (the Mercury and the Pegasus); however, Bristol refused to provide the two specimens, so instead, the company demanded that either a batch of at least 50 engines or a license should be bought. In December the following year, Moscow received a proposal from Napier in respect of the Dagger engines and, some time later, a proposal to purchase the Alvis Leonides engines. Whether those were purchased or not remains unknown. Concurrently, enquiries were made in July as to whether a specimen of the Bristol Blenheim Mk IV with Mercury engines could be bought. On 3 July, the Council of People's Commissars made a special decision to negotiate with the Bristol Engine Company on the issue of purchasing the Taurus, Pegasus and Hercules engines. In August, the negotiations with Bristol arrived at a stage when a draft five-year license agreement covering the three above-mentioned engine types was prepared. Apparently, the deal fell apart either after the beginning of the Second World War, or after the beginning of the Winter War, which exacerbated relations between the USSR and Great Britain.

In an attempt to overcome the lagging-behind of the Wright Company in respect of the improvement of the Cyclone engine's refinement, a new technical assistance contract for a sum total of 900,000 US dollars was prepared in January 1939. According to the contract, the company was to provide documentation for the modification of the engine series G100 and G200, as well as the R-2600 double-row radial engine. The company representatives themselves suggested including the new and powerful R-3350 engine in the contract; however, the US Department of War blocked the clause. The contract was signed, and it became effective on 29 March 1939. A group of Soviet engineers departed for America to accept the documentation. In September, there was an intention to additionally purchase specimens of the following engines: G205A (four engines); G205B (six engines); and R-2600-A5D (10 engines; later, however, the order was reduced to four); however, none of them were received. The work was impeded by the 'moral embargo' during the Soviet-Finnish War. From 26 December, Soviet specialists were not admitted to the Wright workshops; however, as soon as 8 February 1940, the first batch of drawings was sent to the USSR on board the *Mayakovsky* steamer. By 3 August, the acceptance of the entire set of documentation for the G100 had been complete. Afterwards, it was actively used in the course of improvements of the M-62 and M-63 engines. The contract with the Wright Company remained in effect until May 1941; then, the Americans suspended it for a year. During that period, the Soviet party paid an amount of 169,000 US dollars to the Wright Company. In 1942, the contract was prolonged, but only *de jure*. Until the end of the war, it remained suspended.

Information about foreign engines was coming to the USSR via other channels as well – thus, in 1940, Soviet Intelligence brought the drawings of the American-manufactured R-2600, V-3420 and V-1710 engines to Moscow. The drawings were copied and distributed among various design bureaus. During the short period of rapprochement between the USSR and Germany, Soviet delegations (which visited the latter) were familiarized (inter alia) with captured materiel. The lists of goods, as requested from the Germans, included specimens of British engines (in particular, the Hercules).

By the time of Germany's attack on the Soviet Union, both the air forces of the Workers' and Peasants' Red Army and the Civil Air Fleet had been almost fully equipped with engines of Soviet manufacture. Engines of foreign manufacture constituted a small percentage of the total fleet. Engines which had been manufactured under foreign licenses had, by that time, gone far enough from their prototypes and were deemed to be new designs in many aspects; however, the outbreak of the large-scale war again brought about a need for the mass importing of engines from abroad. During the first months of the hostilities, the Red Army lost a lot of aircraft and, correspondingly, engines. The Germans' offensive caused the necessity to evacuate engine-building factories into the depths of the country. The manufacture of aircraft dwindled drastically, and so did the manufacture of engines.

The Allies' assistance turned out a certain compensation for that: in total, throughout the war period, the Soviet Union received from England and the USA approximately 5,700 spare engines, in addition to those installed on aircraft. If the latter is also considered, the mass type of engines as shipped from abroad were the following: the Allison V-1710 (approximately 10,000 engines); the Wright R-2600 (approximately 7,500 engines); the Pratt & Whitney R-1830 (more than 2,000 engines); and the Rolls-Royce Merlin (approximately 5,000 engines). Among the engines that came in lesser quantities were the Pratt & Whitney R-2800 (approximately 250 engines); the Pratt & Whitney R-1340 (approximately 100 engines); the Bristol Pegasus (more than 60 engines); and the Bristol Hercules (more than 50 engines). The Allisons were arriving together with fighters (the Bell P-39s and P-63s; the Curtiss P-40s; and the North American P-51s), while the R-2600s were coming with the B-25 and the A-20 bombers. The Pratt & Whitney R-1830s were mounted on the C-47 transport aircraft, the PBN-1 flying boats and the PBY-6A amphibians; the Merlins were mounted on the Hawker Hurricane and the Supermarine Spitfire fighters; the Pegasus engines were used on the Hampden TB.I torpedo bombers and on the only Stirling bomber which was received by the Soviet Union; the Hercules engines were installed on the Albemarle transport aircraft; the R-2800s came together with the Republic P-47 fighters; and the R-1340s arrived with the AT-6 trainers and the O-52 observation aircraft.

Initially, there were a lot of problems with foreign engines. These problems were caused by the Soviet specialists' poor knowledge of their peculiarities and by a shortage of quality fuel and oil. The engines were deemed 'temperamental'; it was believed that they required only gentle treatment. To a certain extent, that was true, and Soviet technicians dubbed the British-manufactured Rolls-Royce *Roys, roys, kopays*, which literally translates as: 'Burrow-in, burrow-in, delve-into'. The assembly of the Merlin, with its complicated design of units, was much harder than the assembly of the M-105 or the AM-38. In fact, the overhaul and adjustment of the engines were, whenever possible, entrusted to the most experienced technicians; however, as Soviet technicians came to know the foreign engines better, they quickly found out their significant advantages – and the first advantage was quite obvious: the engines were neatly assembled, their parts were well-machined and they featured good anti-corrosion treatment and paint coating. Old men used to say that if one put a bare hand inside an imported engine, it would not result in any cuts or scratches, since all the burrs had been removed, the edges dulled and the surfaces ground. Once, I had a chance to open up an Allison engine which had been lying in the open air for half a century. Corroded on the outside, it still shone like new on the inside, but that was not the main thing: foreign engines were considerably superior in terms of fuel efficiency, as they consumed less fuel and oil. Their operating RPM range was much wider and, on the one hand, that allowed for the consumption of less fuel in a cruise flight at idle (imported engines ran steadily on lean mixtures), but on the other hand, they offered a lot of augmented time-limited settings, which provided additional power of up to

200hp in critical situations; however, the Merlin was inferior to the Soviet-made M-105P in terms of pickup (its transition from low RPM to high RPM was much slower).

Foreign engines were considerably superior to Soviet ones in terms of lifespan – thus, the time required until the first overhaul for the American engines was often equal to 600 hours; for British engines, it was 400 hours. For Soviet engines, a lifespan of 200 hours was considered to be a good performance. It should be noted, however, that due to incompetent maintenance and the use of ersatz substitutes instead of original fuel, oil and anti-freeze, foreign engines in the Soviet Union usually failed to provide the lifespan performance as stated in their data sheets – thus, for example, in 1943, the Allisons usually served out 35-40 percent of their assigned life; the British-manufactured Merlins was 50-60 percent. Anyway, that was longer than the Soviet engines could offer!

It should be noted (for the sake of truth) that engines shipped to the Soviet Union were well-proven, mass-manufactured ones. New engines, which were considered advanced and promising, were often put into mass manufacture (albeit with an extremely short lifespan) in the West as well – thus, for example, the Napier Sabre, with a nominal lifespan of 40 hours, was mounted on the Typhoon fighter, which was assigned to combat units of the RAF. In fact, the engine could hardly serve out 35 hours – and furthermore, it was deemed to be extremely flammable.

There were a lot of innovations in imported engines. One of them was, for example, friction-bearing inserts. Their casting technology was much more advanced than their Soviet counterpart, and many attempts to reproduce the American 'white alloy' coating resulted in failure; however, by the middle of the war, Factory No.36 in Rybinsk managed to master the manufacture of crankshaft-bearing liners and connecting rod liners for the Merlin and the Allison. Some other spare parts were manufactured in the Soviet Union as well.

The 'Achilles' heel' of all Soviet engines with two-speed, gear-driven centrifugal superchargers was the supercharger gear shift unit. There was a mechanism that resembled a motor vehicle clutch; torque was transmitted by friction. The linings, which were made from an asbestos containing material, tended to either crumble, or to tear off completely. At best, they just wore out quickly. On imported engines, the mechanism operated in a much more reliable manner. Soviet engineers disassembled their disks in an attempt to find out more about material composition and fabrication technology.

None of the Soviet aviation engines (as manufactured during the war) featured a two-stage, gear-driven centrifugal supercharger, but such superchargers were mounted on the Merlin engines type 60 and higher, and on later V-1710 versions. The approach in the two cases was totally different: the British designed a single assembly, with either one or both stages engaged. In combination with the two-speed drive of the supercharger, such a configuration provided for four modes and ensured proper altitude performance without any significant failures. The Americans attached the second (in fact, the first) stage to the engine as a separate unit, which was rotated by the engine's rear gear box. This allowed unifying engine versions that had different altitude performances; in both cases, however, an appropriate result was achieved. During a climb, foreign engines tended to lose less power, which was a benefit for interceptors, high-speed bombers and reconnaissance aircraft.

When the British-manufactured Hercules engines arrived in the USSR, Soviet experts got a chance to view for the first time the design and operation of the valveless tubular gas distribution system. The system offered a number of advantages in terms of smoothness of movement and ease of starting. In the USSR, work on a similar system had been conducted before the war; however, it had never reached even the prototype stage. Attempts had been made to purchase a specimen from the Bristol Engine Company. Negotiations in respect of licensing had been held, but without success. To operate seamlessly, the tubular gas distribution system required a perfect precision of manufacture and a well-adjusted process, but that was beyond the capabilities of the Soviet industry. Furthermore, that was where D. Napier & Son (Bristol's rival) had also stumbled after the introduction of a similar mechanism on the Napier Sabre engine. With the latter, Soviet specialists also familiarized themselves after the arrival of a specimen of the Typhoon fighter.

The same as in the aircraft industry, the Lend-Lease deliveries considerably influenced the manufacture of Soviet-designed engines. A lot of components for them were imported from abroad. In September 1941, an order for the manufacture of pistons, piston rings and valves for the M-105 engines, which were built at Factory No.26, was placed with Special Lloyd (England). The relevant drawings were brought to London from Moscow. Ball-and-roller bearings and balls with rollers were also imported. An unpleasant situation occurred around the ignition wires, which were ordered in the USA: a total length of 85km of wires had already been delivered when it was found out that the wires were of the wrong diameter and did not match Soviet sparking plugs. The purchasing agents had made a mistake, and it was never discovered what had finally happened to those wires.

The USA, Great Britain and Canada delivered aluminum in large quantities. That was sort of a compensation for the loss of aluminum facilities, which happened to be located in the territory occupied by the Germans. Throughout the war, the Americans supplied ignition wires, hoses, rolled non-ferrous metal products, gaskets for carburetors, brass nets, pipes and special varnishes and paints. The same as for the entire aircraft industry, the USA and Great Britain delivered a lot of various equipment items for engine-building factories. The imports included a number of special-purpose machines, which had not been manufactured in the Soviet Union at that time. The importing of sizing and cutting tools, abrasives, industrial diamonds, thermal and foundry equipment, and overhead cranes played a significant role.

Imported equipment acquired a special importance during the second half of the war, when the Soviet troops were advancing to the West and liberating more and more territories on their way. As soon as the advance began, there appeared a possibility to restore the previously evacuated facilities; however, a decision was made not to disturb the factories that had already been successfully operating at new locations. Instead, quite new factories (with new numbers) were arranged in old workshops and provided with machines, which were exported by the Allies.

For example, Factory No.29 in Omsk, which had been evacuated from Zaporozhye, received 220 machines and presses. As the same time, Factory No.36 in Rybinsk, which had been established at the workshops of the evacuated Factory No.26, was allocated 1,200 machines – including 700 foreign-made ones.

Successful solutions, which were found on foreign engines, were then implemented by Soviet design bureaus – thus, for example, suction pipes from the American-manufactured V-1710 engine were utilized on the AM-39 designed by A.A. Mikulin.

Unlike Great Britain, where American engines as shipped under Lend-Lease were often installed on British aircraft, Soviet aircraft were manufactured with domestic-made engines only; however, plans for such work existed. In May 1943, almost all aircraft design bureaus of the Soviet Union were tasked to prepare preliminary design versions of their aircraft to operate with imported engines. The Yak-1, Yak-7, Yak-9, LaGG-3 and Pe-2 were intended to be modified for the Merlin and the V-1710; the La-5 for the R-2600 and R-2800; the Il-4 for the R-2600 and R-1830-33; and the Li-2 for the R-1820-71, but calculations showed that none of the suggested versions offered advantages to justify the rearrangement of mass production. A gain in something was usually accompanied by a loss in something else – thus, the Yak-1 with the Merlin engine, according to calculations, was expected to reach a speed of 665km/h at an altitude of 6,000m; its range increased to 70km. On the other hand, its ground speed decreased by 15km/h and the take-off run grew by as much as 40 percent. The V-1710 offered a minor gain in maximum speed (15km/h) and range (130km), but made the rest of the aircraft performance worse. As for the Pe-2, the Merlin brought about improvements in almost all the aircraft performances except for the take-off run; the Allison, on the contrary, turned out quite unfit for the aircraft.

Attempts to mount American engines on the Li-2 were the most persevering ones. It seemed quite logical, since the Li-2 was a Soviet copy of the DC-3. On 15 June, the State Defense Committee decided to purchase two-thousand R-1820-G2 engines in the USA to mount them on the aircraft. The Type G2 roughly corresponded to the M-62IR, which it was expected to supersede. It was the R-1820-G2s that were installed on the DC-3s, which had been purchased before the war.

The Soviet mission in the United States requested to have two-thousand G2s supplied to them; however, the request was denied. The reason was not that the Americans had other plans for their use, but that the model was discontinued in early 1942. In the Wright Company's depots, 120 long-unsold engines of this type were found and shown to Soviet representatives. From among them, 52 engines were selected and sent to the USSR by sea. On the way, one of the steamers was sunk – taking 10 engines together with her. Apparently, the rest of the G2s were used as spare ones for the DC-3s that were still in operation with the Soviet Union.

The possibility of mounting the G100 engine type on the Li-2 began to be examined; however, this version was discontinued in early 1943. The Americans suggested an improved G202, but its installation required too many modifications on the aircraft. As a result, on 7 October 1943, the approved order for the G202s was canceled. In lieu of the G202s, the USAAF suggested shipping two-thousand R-1830-92s. Such engines were installed on the C-47s, but apart from weighing over 100kg more, such engines required a significant reinforcement of the wing, fuselage and landing gear – thus, the Li-2s had to stay until the end of their 'lives' with the initial M-62IR (ASh-62IR) engines. The R-1830-92s were initially rejected; in a few days, however, an awareness of the need for spare engines for the C-47s arose, so the Soviet side asked for 300 engines, but then, the Americans refused, since the engines had already been ordered to another place. Finally, an order for 120 engines was placed with the Americans, and those engines were actually shipped to the USSR.

In 1944, the People's Commissariat of Aviation Industry actively promoted the purchase of one-thousand-five-hundred R-985-16 engines in the USA (half of them with synchronizers) to equip new training aircraft. This idea was supported by A.S. Yakovlev, who was not only a designer, but also a Deputy People's Commissar. An official request was sent in on 18 September 1944 and, after a long-time correspondence, twenty R-985-AN1s were actually purchased. There was an intention to try them with the Shcherbakov Shche-2 transport airplane; however, only a single case of the engines' operation is known: that is, on the G-3 helicopter. For this purpose, the engine was modified (it was fitted with a forced-cooling fan and angular gearboxes).

Throughout the war, the Soviet Union kept attempting to obtain (from the Allies) specimens of the newest aircraft engines for study purposes – thus, in January 1943, the USA was requested to provide specimens of the R-2800, R-3350, V-3420 and V-1650; however, the request was denied. The first of the mentioned engine specimens was later supplied together with the Republic P-47 Thunderbolt fighters; it was thoroughly studied in the Soviet Union. It was not the engine itself, but rather the turbosupercharger (which provided excellent altitude performance) that aroused the highest interest. As has already been discussed, in 1944, A.I. Mikoyan's design bureau prepared a preliminary design for the modification of the MiG-3 to make it fit to carry the power plant of the P-47D-10-RE with the R-2800-63 engine and C-23 turbosupercharger.

The powerful eighteen-cylinder R-3350 engine aroused the highest interest, and the Soviet party had been striving to obtain it from 1940. On 31 July 1943, a special request was addressed to Chief of the US Army Air Force General H. Arnold. On 6 August, he replied that the situation was under consideration. The decision of 15 August read: 'temporarily postponed'; on 2 September, a formal refusal followed. Concurrently, negotiations with the Wright Company were conducted. Wright was willing to give a license, but only with the consent of military authorities.

In spite of all the difficulties, a specimen of the R-3350 was obtained (albeit unofficially). As has already been discussed above, four B-29 bombers fitted with such engines made forced landings near Vladivostok in July through to November 1944. Since the Soviet Union was not (at that time) at war with Japan, the aircraft were interned... and it was decided not to return them. The American bomber was copied at A.N. Tupolev's design bureau, and its mass manufacture was launched under the designation Tu-4; however, it was equipped not with the R-3350s, but with Soviet-manufactured M-73TKs (ASh-73TKs). Both types had the same predecessor (the Wright Cyclone engine), but designers of each country developed their ideas independently. Therefore, the M-73TK (the genealogy of which runs from the experimental M-25D18) differed considerably from the R-3350 engine; however, the design of the American engine had a great influence on the Soviet one: the studying of the R-3350 allowed borrowing several good solutions (in particular, bearing assemblies). The TsIAM specialists fully copied the TK-19 turbo-blower from the American specimen. Moreover, the first prototypes of the M-73TK passed bench tests with American-manufactured accessories (spark plugs, generators, starters, magnetos and bearings). Prototypes were fitted with various combinations of original Soviet assemblies, imported American ones and copies of the latter as made in the USSR.

To expedite the beginning of mass manufacture of the ASh-73TK, it was suggested that a large number of components should be purchased in the United States, so negotiations with American companies began. The Soviet party was looking for a company that would be willing to arrange the manufacture of state-of-the-art spark plugs in the USSR (in this respect, both American and British companies were considered). On 24 November 1945, Jack and Heintz sent in their proposals for supplying starters and electric power generators, but the Air Force Command insisted that the engine should fully consist of Soviet-manufactured assemblies only.

A considerable interest was shown towards British engines as well. On 27 January 1943, a request was sent to Great Britain regarding the possibility to obtain specimens of the Merlin 61; the Vulture; the Centaurus; the Dagger; and the Sabre. The Merlin 61 and the Sabre appeared in the USSR at the end of the war, together with the Spitfire IX and the Typhoon. In 1943, an issue regarding the practicability of the licensed manufacture of Merlins in the Soviet Union was discussed. The suggestion was first made by employees of the Soviet Trade Representation Pashinin and Bogomolov. They wrote: '... We believe it highly desirable to raise the issue regarding purchase of a license for the building, in the Soviet Union, of engines of the latest versions as designed in Great Britain by Rolls-Royce...' The People's Commissar of Aviation Industry A.I. Shakhurin deemed the purchase of a license a premature step, and suggested purchasing 10-15 engines for study to begin with. The issue was even discussed at a meeting of the State Defense Committee. Eventually, doubts about the possibility of the assembly and adjustment of such a complicated engine, with which Packard had already had problems, resulted in abandoning the negotiations.

Familiarization with the powerful and reliable Hercules engine (as operated in the Soviet Union on the Albemarles) led to the wish to become acquainted with its 'big brother', Centaurus. On 17 November 1943, a letter signed by Commercial Director of the Bristol Engine Company Bartlett, in which the company agreed to sell specimens of the engine, arrived in Moscow. In January 1944, the company offered a license for Centaurus. In the course of discussing the proposal in February, Shakhurin again suggested beginning with the purchase of five-10 engines of various types – including the Centaurus – and testing them in the USSR.

On 6 January 1945, several Centaurus VIIs arrived in Murmansk and, in the same month, TsIAM began to prepare the test bench. On 3 March, the engines were delivered to TsIAM and, in late March, the testing began (it was completed on 21 May). On 13 September, the British again offered a license; however, as further development of the ASh-73TK continued, the interest towards the Centaurus was dwindling and, eventually, disappeared completely. Another engine sent by Bristol, the Hercules 100 (the USSR had previously possessed the XI and XVI versions), was studied; however, it was found to be even less interesting.

After the war, Soviet engine factories manufactured piston engines of domestic design only, but there were some exceptions to the rule: when the manufacture of the B-29 American-designed bomber was launched in the USSR (as the Tu-4), its auxiliary engine (a small V-shaped, two-cylinder, four-stroke engine) was reverse-engineered as well; it rotated the shaft of an electric generator. The engine was put in production under the Soviet designation M-10.

The Civil Air Fleet had great projects in respect of post-war cooperation with companies from the USA and England. Long-term plans for 1946 and 1947 envisaged purchasing a large number of aircraft and engines (mostly in America), and negotiations had already been commenced with certain companies (in particular, Pratt & Whitney); however, a shortage of currency – followed by the beginning of the Cold War – cut the plans short.

The 30hp Wright, which was built in 1910, is deemed to be the first Russian aero engine.

The Sunbeam Crusader engines (of British origin) were manufactured at the Ilyin Factory in Moscow.

The first TB-1 bomber prototype was equipped with the British-made Napier Lion engines. There were intentions to mass-produce such engines in the USSR.

The Soviet M-5 was a copy of the American-made Liberty engine.

The M-22 engine, which was manufactured in Zaporozhye, was a Soviet copy of the French replica of the British-made Bristol Jupiter engine.

The Rolls-Royce Condor engine during the bench tests at NAMI.

The Soviet M-25 was, essentially, a metric version of the American-made Wright SR-1820-F3 engine. It became a predecessor for all Soviet engines developed at the A.D. Shvetsov Design Bureau.

The first prototype of the famous Tupolev SB bomber was equipped with the American-made Wright engines, which were intended to be replaced at a later date with the Soviet M-25 engines on series aircraft.

The Merlin XX engine of the crashed Hurricane, which was raised from the bottom of the lake, was found to be in a rather good condition.

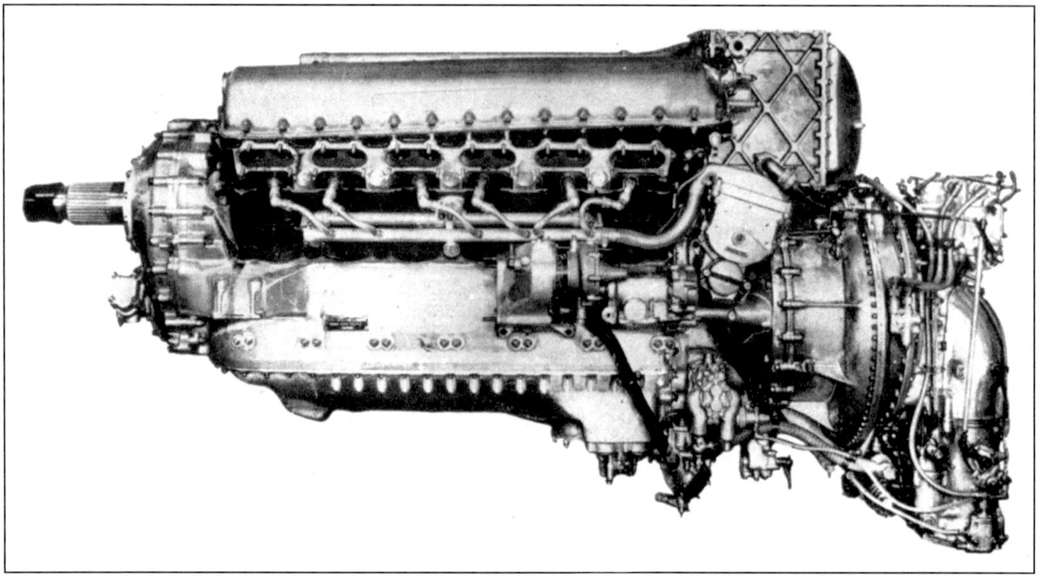

The Merlin 66 engine, with a two-stage supercharger. Such engines were coming to the USSR with the Spitfire IX fighters.

The Merlin XX in the outskirts of the Russian Air Force Museum in Monino.

The Allison V-1710-E, with a two-stage supercharger and a separately arranged reduction gear. The attachment point of the long shaft is covered with a temporary plug, and such engines were mounted on the Kingcobras.

The Allison V-1710-F engine, which was mounted on the P-40 fighters.

The V-1710 engine undergoing maintenance on an Airacobra.

The Pratt & Whitney R-985 Wasp Junior was the only foreign-made engine which was delivered to the Soviet Union under Lend-Lease for the application on aircraft other than those of American manufacture; however, such engines were also mounted on the Kingfishers from USS *Milwaukee.*

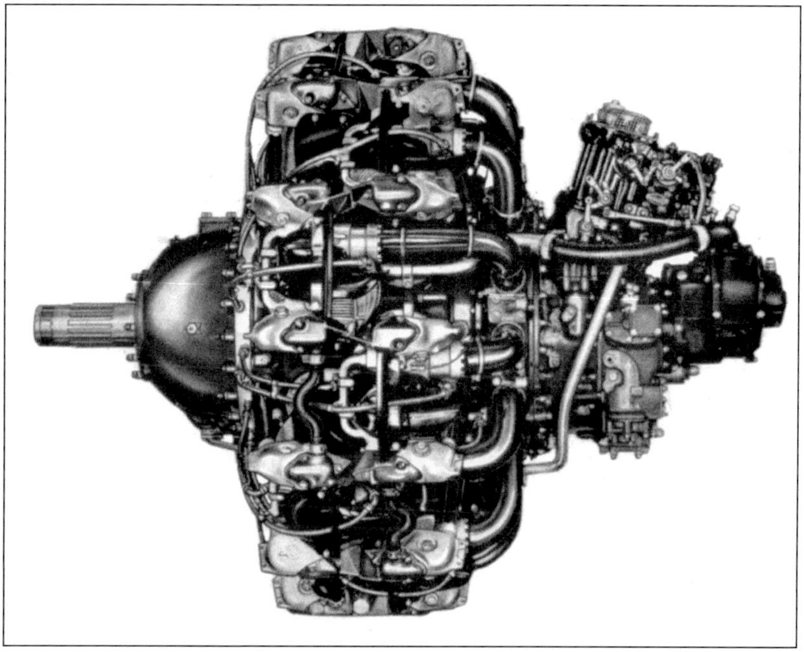

The American-made Pratt & Whitney R-1830 engine was widely used in the Soviet Union during the war. Such engines were mounted on the C-47 transport aircraft, PBN-1 flying boats and PBY-6A amphibians.

The Wright R-1820 Cyclone became a basis for the Soviet-made M-25 engine. At the time of the war, a small number of original American-manufactured engines were bought from the USA.

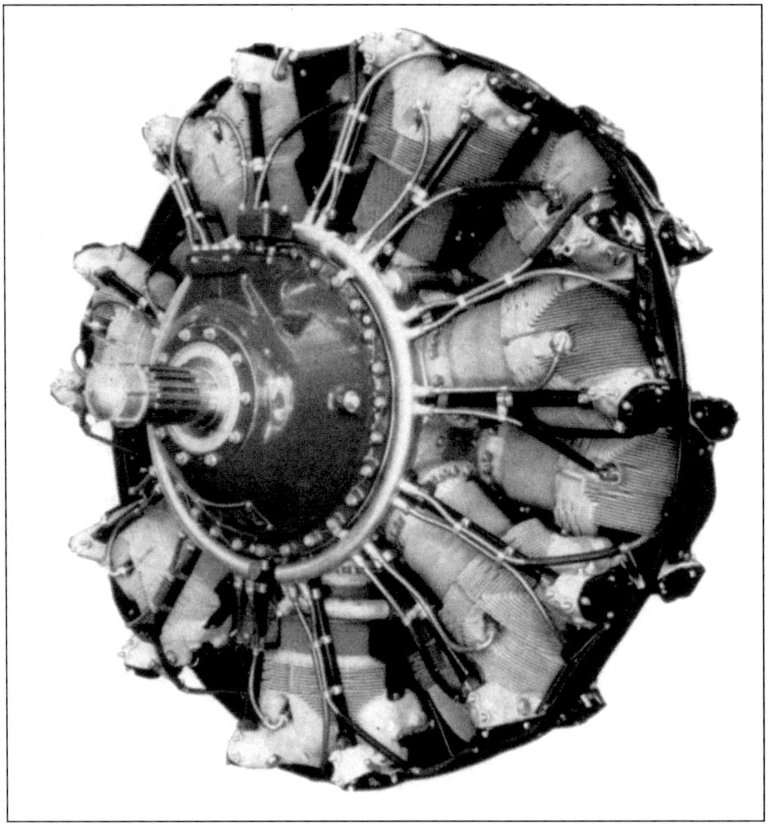

The R-2600 two-row radial engines were delivered with the A-20 and B-25 bombers.

Maintenance of the engine from the A-20 torpedo bomber of the 51st Mine-and-Torpedo Air Regiment, Baltic Fleet Air Force.

The powerful Pratt & Whitney R-2800 Double Wasp engine was mounted on the Thunderbolt fighters.

The number of Pratt & Whitney R-1340 Wasp engines shipped to the USSR was comparatively small. They were mounted on the O-52 reconnaissance aircraft and on the AT-6 trainers.

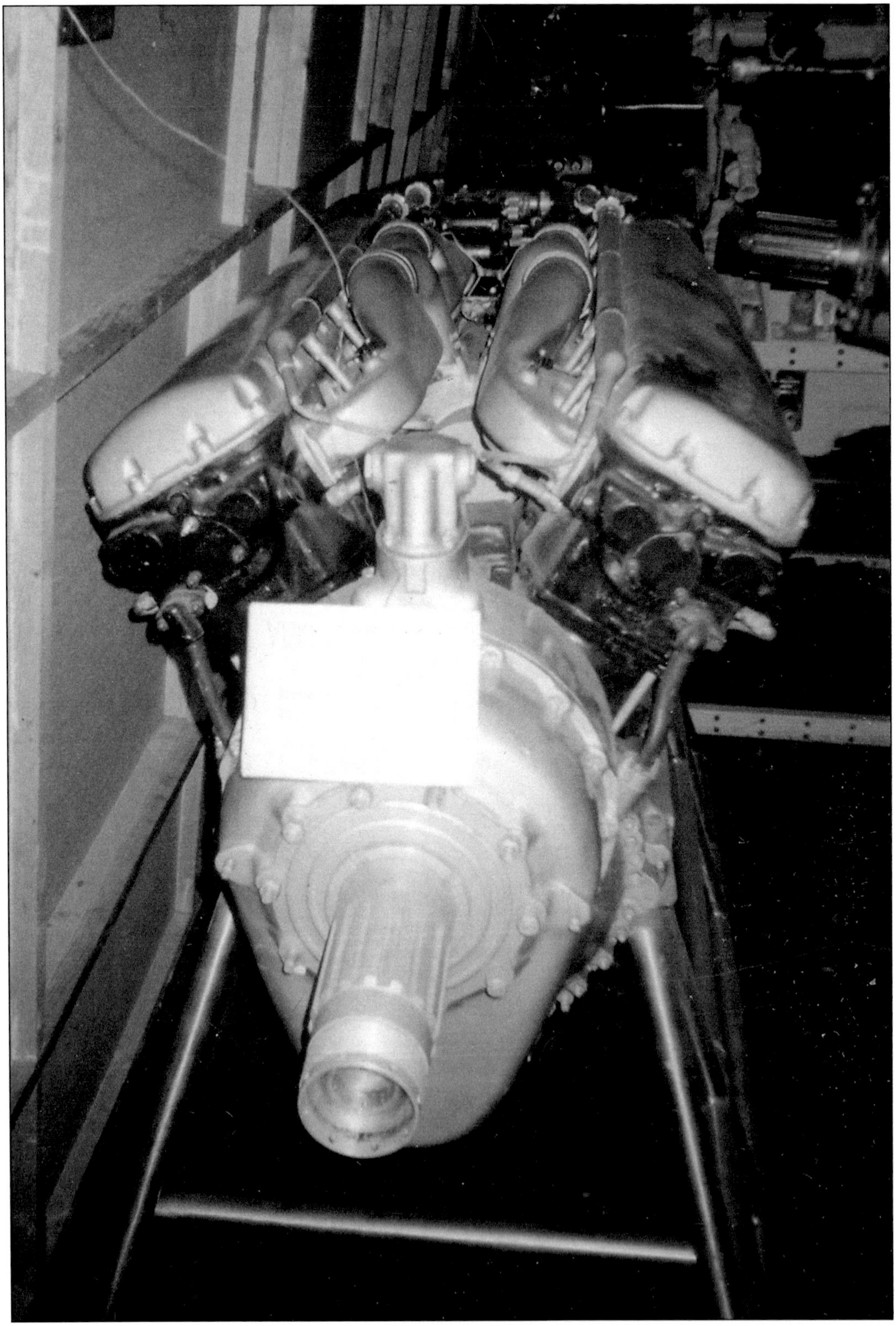

The V-1710-F engine in storage at the Russian Air Force Museum in Monino.

The Allison engine on display at the Museum of the Great Patriotic War in Moscow. This is the engine version for the Airacobra, with the attachment point of the long shaft covered with a plug.

The modified R-985 engines were used on the G-3 (AK-4) helicopter.

The Soviet M-62 engine was the further development of the M-25, which was designed using the documentation provided by the Wright Company.

The Bristol Pegasus engines were mounted on the Handley Page Hampden torpedo bombers and the only Short Stirling bomber, which were used in the USSR.

The powerful Bristol Hercules engines constituted one of the few positive features of the Albemarle.

Soviet specialists wished, for a long time, to become familiar with the Napier Sabre engine. Finally, they received it, together with the sole Typhoon fighter.

The 18-cylinder Wright R-3350 engines appeared in the USSR on the B-29 bombers.

The Soviet-made ASh-73 engine was not a copy of the R-3350, in spite of the fact that they had a common 'predecessor'; however, the Soviet engine 'borrowed' several successful design solutions from its American counterpart.

The AM-39 engine, which was designed by A.A. Mikulin, utilized suction pipes similar to the ones used in the American-made V-1710 engine.

The M-10 auxiliary power unit was copied from the American engine, together with the entire B-29 bomber. This photo represents the Soviet-made engine version used on the Tu-4.

11

The End of Lend-Lease

After Germany's surrender, the US Government terminated the Lend-Lease program in June 1945 in respect of many countries. Protocol IV for the Soviet Union also lost effect in late June, but (as has already been discussed) a special Annex to the contract was prepared for the Soviet Union. Under the Annex, everything necessary for the war with Japan was supplied – thus, after the defeat of Japan, the Annex was terminated as well.

On 15 October 1945, the USSR signed an Agreement with the USA on the continuation of the delivery of production equipment which had been ordered under the Lend-Lease program, but had not yet been supplied. The Americans allocated a loan of 240.2 million US dollars for this Agreement on the condition that it would be paid off in 50 years. The Soviet side completed its obligations by June 1975.

Another question was the armament, combat equipment and other supplied materiel which remained in the Soviet Union after the end of the hostilities. In 1946, the Resolution of the USSR Council of Ministers scheduled the mass-scale decommissioning and destruction of the majority of foreign-manufactured fighters. Some of the aircraft – including a number of bombers – were indeed destroyed under the supervision of observers from the USA; however, the majority of serviceable fighters remained in service. At first, the Americans turned a blind eye to the violations of military assistance agreements by the Soviet Union; then arose the question of payment for the Lend-Lease deliveries. On 13 June 1946, the US Government proposed to the USSR to pay for the non-military equipment and machinery which remained in the country: the merchant ships, locomotives, wagons, tractors and industrial machinery (less the depreciation).

The associated question was the performance of the inventory of all items supplied under Lend-Lease and those which had escaped destruction by the end of the war. The Soviet side evaded the answers to both questions. Therefore, the Americans made their own count: the US Government appraised the sum to be paid by the USSR at 2.6 billion US dollars, with two per cent of the annual interest.

A year later, the calculations were updated to reduce the debt down to 1.3 billion US dollars. In response, the Soviet representatives proposed 170 million US dollars. The counterproposal followed in 1948: one billion US dollars, which was later decreased to 800 million US dollars. This was related to the fact that starting from 1948, the Soviet Union began to return or destroy the warships – a process which lasted until 1955. On the other hand, the Soviet side also made a step forward by increasing the amount of the payment to 300 million US dollars; however, the development of the Cold War and the Korean War led to the abandoning of the former Allied agreements altogether. The issue remained unsettled for a long time.

In the 1970s, when relations with America had improved, Soviet military authorities (at the direction of the government) attempted to calculate the debt of the country. It should be mentioned that the cost estimate of the shipments was not the only problem for the Soviet Union: the matter was that the American military materiel had always been expensive. For instance, the Mustang was much more expensive than the Spitfire, and wages and some other components of the pricing were higher in the United States. In the agreement with Great Britain, the problem was solved by the introduction (for conversion purposes) of a special dollar exchange rate, which was approximately equalizing prices for similar products. Soviet authorities, apparently, did not attach much importance to this aspect and, as a result, the commission which was specially created for the purpose was (for a long time) unable to make head or tail of the shipments' cost estimates (here, one should also take into account that the dollar exchange rate had, by that time, undergone changes). Moreover, the prices for the same kind of products, but of different years of manufacture, were increasing or decreasing. For example, by the end of the war, the B-25 bomber cost 118 percent of its original price, while the C-47 transport plane became cheaper and its price decreased to 71 percent of the initial level. Eventually, something was determined.

In October 1972, an agreement was reached in Washington for the payment of 722 million US dollars, but under the stipulation that the Soviet Union would be granted the most favored nation treatment in trade, and would also be provided with a certain amount of loans and guarantees. By July 1973, the USSR had paid 48 million US dollars; however, the Americans failed to fulfil the stipulations. The Soviet side, in turn, ceased payments for Lend-Lease.

In June 1990, during a meeting of the countries' Presidents, an agreement was reached – indicating the amount of 674 million US dollars (the Americans decided not to charge interest), with the payment to be completed by 2030; then the matter failed to materialize again. In 2001, the US Congress was discussing a Bill of writing off the Soviet debts, but it did not gain a sufficient number of votes.

In total, the American Lend-Lease program covered 46 countries all over the world. The share of the Soviet Union amounted to 21.3 percent of the total value of the shipments; the share of Great Britain was 65.8 percent. Aircraft are expensive and, for this reason, their share turned out to be the weightiest one (approximately a quarter of the sum total) – thus, for example, I.P. Lebedev estimates the value of aircraft as shipped to the USSR at 2.4 billion US dollars. Considering other supplies for military and civil aviation (spare parts, engines, ammunition, airfield equipment, metal mats for collapsible runways, fueling trucks, mobile repair shops, flight uniforms, silk for parachutes, aviation fuel, oil etc.), the sum will grow to 3.6 billion US dollars. This figure constitutes about a third of the total expenditure of the USA on the Lend-Lease program for the USSR.

Shipments under Lend-Lease were terminated on 21 August 1945 for all countries except China; for the latter, shipments continued until 1949. The Soviet missions at acceptance centers came back home by late September and, in respect of the Soviet Union, the agreement was officially terminated by the American side in 1946.

The financial assessment in respect for British shipments is not known; however, N.I. Ryzhkov noted in his book that the loans provided by Great Britain and Canada had been almost paid off by the present time.

12

Conclusions

Now you have managed to plough through this rather thick book, what are the conclusions? The Allies' assistance to the Soviet aviation at the time of the Great Patriotic War was immense. The Soviet Union received both the aircraft and the parts, without which it would have been impossible to operate them. By the end of the war, the share of foreign materiel as in service with the air force, the air defense forces and the naval aviation had become very significant.

Furthermore, Soviet aircraft and engine factories ran, to a considerable extent, on imported equipment, raw materials and semi-finished products – thus, Soviet aircraft, to a certain extent, were also influenced by the Lend-Lease program.

If the Soviet Union had to fight Hitler alone, without assistance on the part of the British and the Americans (perhaps), the country would have withstood. After all, the first major victory in the Battle of Moscow had been won before the shipments from abroad actually developed, but the USSR would have paid a much higher price for it in the form of territories occupied by the enemy. The war would have taken a longer time, and the blood would have been shed in greater amounts.

There is no need, therefore, to either overestimate or to belittle the importance of the Allies' help. They (and, first and foremost, the Americans) did whatever they could. Politicians, of course, always pursue their own ends. At that time, the US and Great Britain were interested in a strong Soviet Union, which would be able to divert the principal forces of the enemy. Even at that time, there were a lot of foes to the Soviet Union within the ruling coterie of those countries; however, their opportunities were limited by the situation. In the Soviet Union itself, the authorities were not very eager to interact closely with foreign countries beyond purely technical issues. Political agencies and security officers tried to prevent the Soviet people from getting to know the life of the Americans and the British.

Nevertheless, there happened to be a common goal, which was apparent for people of all countries. It brought together different people who spoke different languages, and who had different traditions and social structures – and this is also, to some extent, the result of Lend-Lease.

It should be noted though that it did not last long. What followed were W. Churchill's *Sinews of Peace* (the 'Iron Curtain' speech), the Cold War and the incessant desire to mess with each other all over the globe...

Bibliography

Russian-Language Publications (in Russian alphabetical order)

Aviatory na strazhe Zapolyarya (Politotdel aviatsii KSF, 1966).
Aviatsionnye motory voennykh vozdushnykh sil inostrannykh gosudarstv (Moskva, Voenizdat, 1939).
Aviatsiya VMF v Velikoy Otechestvennoy voyne (Moskva, Voenizdat, 1983).
Akkuratov V., *Led i pepel* (Moskva, Sovremennik, 1984).
Amiryants G.A., *Letchiki-ispytateli* (Mikhail Nyukhtikov so tovarishchi, Moskva, Kulikovo pole, 2008).
Arias A., *V ognennom nebe* (Minsk, Belarus, 1988).
Badigin K.F., *Na morskikh dorogakh* (Moskva, IPL, 1978).
Baevsky G.A., *S aviatsiey cherez XX vek* (Moskva, Delta NB, 2001).
Basov A.V., *Flot v Velikoy Otechestvennoy voyne 1941 – 1945* (Moskva, Nauka, 1980).
Belyakov A.V., *V polyot skvoz gody* (Moskva, Voenizdat, 1981).
Beskorovayny A.I., *V nebe Severa* (Moskva, Izdatelstvo DOSAAF, 1986).
Bodrikhin N.G., *Stalinskie sokoly* (Moskva, NPP Delta, 1997).
Boyko V.S., *Krylya Severnogo flota* (Murmansk, Murmanskoe Izdatelstvo, 1976).
Bondarenko V.A., *Samolyoty vozvrashchayutsa na bazu* (Murmansk, Murmanskoe Izdatelstvo, 1989).
Bondarenko N.A., *V vozdukhe – ispytateli* (Moskva, Izdatelstvo DOSAAF, 1975).
Bondarchuk V., *Vozdushnye razvedchiki* (Petrozavodsk, Kareliya, 1985).
Borisov A.Yu., *SSSR i SShA: soyuzniki v gody voyny 1941 – 1945* (Moskva, Mezhdunarodnye otnosheniya, 1983).
Vayner B.A., *Severny flot v Velikoy Otechestvennoy voyne* (Moskva, Voenizdat, 1964).
Vishnyakov I.A., *Na krutykh virazhakh* (Moskva, Voenizdat, 1973).
V nebe Baltiki (Tallin, Eesti Raamat, 1974).
V nebe Stalingrada (Volgograd, Nizhne-Volzhskoe knizhnoe izdatelstvo, 1983).
Vnimanie! Vozdukh! (Murmansk, Murmanskoe knizhnoe izdatelstvo, 1990).
Voenno-vozdushnye sily Rossii. Neizvestnye dokumenty (Moskva, Vestnik vozdushnogo flota, 2005).
Volynkin N., *Nad pyatyu moryami* (Moskva, Voenizdat, 1964).
Vooruzhenie samolyota Douglas A-20B (VI NKO, Moskva, 1944).
Gelfond G.M., *Sovetsky flot v voyne s Yaponiey* (Moskva, Voenizdat, 1958).
Geroi leningradskogo neba (Leningrad, Lenizdat, 1984).
Golovko A.G., *Vmeste s flotom* (Moskva, Voenizdat, 1979).
Golubev G.G., *Na vertikalyakh* (Kharkov, Prapor, 1989).
Gornostaev N.M., *My voevali na Li-2* (Moskva, Molodaya gvardiya, 1990).
Grigorev A.B., *Albatrosy* (Moskva, Mashinostroenie, 1989).
Gromov M.M., *Cherez vsyu zhizn* (Moskva, Molodaya gvardiya, 1986).

Davtyan S.M., *Pyataya vozdushnaya* (Moskva, Voenizdat, 1990).
Denisov K.D., *Pod nami – Chyornoe more* (Moskva, Voenizdat, 1989).
Dzusov I.M., *V semye otvazhnykh* (Ordzhonikidze, Severo-Osetinskoe knizhnoe izdatelstvo, 1960).
Dolnikov G.U., *Letit stalnaya eskadrilya* (Moskva, Voenizdat, 1983).
Emelyanenko V.B., *Vozdushniy most* (Moskva, Sovetskaya Rossiya, 1998).
Efremov V.S., *Eskadriliy letyat za gorizont* (Moskva, Voenizdat, 1984).
Zhdanov N.N., *Ognevoy shchit Leningrada* (Moskva, Voenizdat, 1965).
Zhuravlyov D.A., *Ognevoy shchit Moskvy* (Moskva, Voenizdat, 1988).
Zakharov S.E., Zakharov M.N., Bagrov V.N. and Kotukhov M.P., *Tikhookeansky flot* (Moskva, Voenizdat, 1966).
Zilmanovich D.Ya., *Na krylyakh Rodiny* (Alma-Ata, Zhalyn, 1985).
Zimin G.V., *Istrebiteli* (Moskva, Voenizdat, 1988).
Zorin L.I., *Osoboe zadanie* (Moskva, IPL, 1987).
Ivanov A.L., *Byt pokhozhim* (Kiev, Molod, 1982).
——, *Skorost, manyovr, ogon* (Moskva, Izdatelstvo DOSAAF, 1974).
Ivanov P.N., *Krylya nad morem* (Moskva, Voenizdat, 1973).
Inozemtsev I.G., *Pod krylom — Leningrad* (Moskva, 1978).
——, *V nebe Zapolyarya i Karelii* (Moskva, Voenizdat, 1987).
——, *Tarany v severnom nebe* (Moskva, Voenizdat, 1981).
——, *Krylatye zashchitniki severa* (Moskva, Voenizdat, 1975).
Instruktsiya lyotchiku po ekspluatatsii samolyota Kertiss P-40E1 (Kittihawk) s motorom Allison *V-1710-39 (F3R)* (Moskva, VI NKO, 1942).
Instruktsiya lyotchiku po ekspluatatsii i tekhnike pilotirovaniya samolyota P-63 "Kingcobra" s motorom Allison *V-1710-93 (E-11)* (Moskva, VI NKO, 1945).
Instruktsiya lyotchiku po ekspluatatsii i tekhnike pilotirovaniya samolyota Spitfire LF-IX s motorom Merlin-66 (Moskva, VI NKO, 1945).
Instruktsiya po tekhnicheskomu obsluzhivaniyu samolyotov Douglas A-*20 (Boston III,* A-*20B i A-20G)* (Moskva, VI NKO, 1945).
Instruktsiya po ekspluatatsii vooruzheniya samolyota "Kittihawk" (Moskva, VI NKO, 1945).
Isaev N.V., *Etot den my priblizhali kak mogli* (Lvov, Kamenyar, 1984).
Isaenko I.F., *Vizhu protivnika!* (Kiev, IPL Ukrainy, 1981).
Istoriya aviatsii ordena Lenina Zabaykalskogo voennogo okruga (1917 – 1976 gg.) (Chita, Politotdel aviatsii Zab VO, 1977).
Istoriya Vtoroy mirovoy voyny 1939 – 1945, t. 12 (Moskva, Voenizdat, 1982).
Ikh pozvalo nebo (Moskva, Voenizdat, 1984).
Kaberov I.A., *V pritsele svastika* (Leningrad, Lenizdat, 1975).
Kazakov V.B., *Boevye aerostsepki* (Moskva, Izdatelstvo DOSAAF, 1988).
Keyssar Kh., Pozner V., *Vspominaya voynu* (Moskva, Novosti, 1990).
Kindyushev N.I., *K pobednym rassvetam* (Moskva, Voenizdat, 1978).
Kovalenko V.I., *Krylya Sevastopolya* (Kiev, IPL Ukrainy, 1988).
Kozhevnikov A.L., *Startuet muzhestvo* (Moskva, Voenizdat, 1966).
Kozhevnikova T.B. and Popovich M.L., *Pesn vysoty* (Moskva, Voenizdat, 1980).
Komissary na linii ognya. V nebe (Moskva, IPL, 1985).
Kondratev P.V., *Polyot skvoz gody* (Moskva, Moskovsky rabochiy, 1970).
Korol V.V., *Vozdushnaya gavan Peterburga* (St Petersburg, Politekhnika, 1996).
Kratkoe opisanie i rukovodstvo po ekspluatatsii bombardirovochnogo vooruzheniya samolyotov North American B-25 (Moskva, VI NKO, 1944).
Krasnoznamyonniy Tikhookeanskiy flot (Moskva, Voenizdat, 1981).

Krylya Baltiki (Kaliningrad, Kaliningradskoe knizhnoe Izdatelstvo, 1979).
Krylya nad okeanom (Moskva, Molodaya gvardiya, 1982).
Kuznetsov N.F., *Front nad zemlyoy* (Moskva, Voenizdat, 1970).
Kurzenkov S.G., *Pod nami zemlya i more* (Moskva, Voenizdat, 1967).
Lavrinenkov V.D., *Vozvrashchenie v nebo* (Moskva, Voenizdat, 1974).
Lyotno-tekhnicheskie i aerodinamicheskie kharakteristiki samolyota Boeing B-29, tekhnicheskoe opisanie No. 267 (Moskva, BNT TSAGI, 1945).
Lvov M.L., *Parol – Baltika* (Kaliningrad, Kaliningradskoe knizhnoe Izdatelstvo, 1985).
Melnikov V.A., *Stranitsy pamyati* (Kharkov, Prapor, 1989).
Minakov V.I., *O vas, boevye druzya – severyane* (Murmansk, Murmanskoe knizhnoe Izdatelstvo, 1989).
——, *Torpedonostsy atakuyut* (Leningrad, Lenizdat, 1988).
Mikhaylik Ya.D., *Sokolinaya semya* (Moskva, Voenizdat, 1971).
Mikhelson V.N. and Yalygin M.I., *Vozdushniy most* (Moskva, IPL, 1988).
Mokryak G.I., *Vysota* (Kishinyov, Kartya Moldovenyaske, 1989).
Molodchiy A.I., *Samolyot ukhodit v noch* (Moskva, Izdatelstvo DOSAAF, 1986).
Molokov V.S., *Rodnoe nebo* (Moskva, Voenizdat, 1977).
Mukhin M.Yu., *Sovetskaya aviapromyshlennost v gody Velikoy Otechestvennoy voyny.*
Na zemle, v nebesakh i na more, vyp. 3 (Moskva, Voenizdat, 1981).
Na zemle, v nebesakh i na more, vyp. 9 (Moskva, Voenizdat, 1987).
Na zemle, v nebesakh i na more, vyp. 10 (Moskva, Voenizdat, 1989).
Nebo bez granits (Krasnoyarsk, Izdatelstvo Krasnoyarskogo otdeleniya assotsiatsii "Russkaya entsiklopediya", 1995).
Nemirova M. and Avaliani Yu., *Skvoz gody na krylyakh* (Tbilisi, Sabchota Sakartvelo, 1973).
Novikov V.S., *Krylya granitsy* (Moskva, Granitsa, 2008).
*Obshchie dannye i komponovka samolyota Bell P-63*A *"Kingcobra", tekhnicheskoe opisanie No. 269* (Moskva, BNT NKAP, 1945).
Obshchie dannye i komponovka samolyota "Spitfire" IX, tekhnicheskoe opisanie No. 256, vyp. 1 (Moskva, BNT TSAGI, 1945).
Orlenko I.F., *My – "tallinnskie"* (Tallin, Eesti Raamat, 1982).
Osipov G.A., *V nebe bombardirovshchiki* (Shchelkovo, 2003).
Ot "Barbarossy" do "Terminala" (Moskva, IPL, 1988).
Papanin I.D., *Lyod i plamen* (Moskva, IPL, 1977).
Paperno A.Kh., *Lend-liz. Tikhiy ocean* (Moskva, Terra, 1998).
*Perepiska predsedatelya Soveta Ministrov SSSR s prezidentami SSh*A *i premyer-ministrami Velikobritanii vo vremya Velikoy Otechestvennoy voyny 1941 – 1945 gg.* (Moskva, IPL, 1986).
Perov V.M., *Polyarnymi trassami* (Moskva, Rusaviya, 2001).
Pokryshkin A.I., *Nebo voyny* (Moskva, Voenizdat, 1975).
Polsky A.A., *70 let sluzheniya aviatsii Rossii* (Tver, Triada, 2009).
Polynov F.P., *Boevye marshruty* (Moskva, Voenizdat, 1972).
Presnyakov A.V., *Nad volnami Baltiki* (Leningrad, Lenizdat, 1983).
Puzyryov V.P., *Belomorskaya flotiliya v Velikoy Otechestvennoy voyne* (Moskva, Voenizdat, 1981).
Pustovalov B.M., *Te trista rassvetov* (Moskva, Voenizdat, 1990).
Rabkin I.G., *Vremya, lyudi, samolyoty* (Moskva, Moskovsky rabochiy, 1985).
Reglament tekhnicheskogo obsluzhivaniya samolyota B-25 (Moskva, VI MVS, 1948).
Reymers G.K., Kamozin M.P. and Romanov A.P., *Vnimanie! V nebe Kamozin!* (Bryansk, Chitay-gorod, 2007).

Savitsky E.Ya., *Polveka s nebom* (Moskva, Voenizdat, 1988).
Samolyot Aer*ocobra* (Moskva, VI NKO, 1944).
Samolyot Boston III, A*-20*A *i* A*-20V s motorami Rayt Tsiklon GR-2600-*A*5V i GR-2600-11* (Moskva, VI NKO, 1943).
Samolyot Douglas Boston III, A*-20V i A-20G* (Moskva, VI NKO, 1945).
Samolyot Curtiss P-40E "Kittihawk" (Moskva, VI NKO, 1944).
Samolyot North-American B-25C, V-25D i B-25L (Moskva, VI MVS, 1946).
Samolyot C-47 (Moskva, VI MVS, 1948).
Samolyot "Hurricane" (Moskva, RIO Aeroflota, 1943).
Semyonov A.F., *Na vzlyote* (Moskva, Voenizdat, 1969).
Silantev V.I., *Vozdushnye razvedchiki* (Moskva, Molodaya gvardiya, 1983).
Sinikchiyants A.M., *Otechestva krylatye syny* (Moskva, Mozaika, 2002).
Sergienko A.M., *Marshrutami spetsialnykh zadaniy* (Moskva, Voenizdat, 1994).
Smirnov B.A., *Nebo moey molodsti* (Moskva, Voenizdat, 1990).
Sovetsko-amerikanskie otnosheniya vo vremya Velikoy Otechestvennoy voyny 1941 – 45 (Moskva, IPL, 1984).
Sokolov V.D., *V nebe nad Kurskoy dugoy* (Voronezh, Tsentralno-Chernozyomnoe knizhnoe Izdatelstvo, 1985).
Stepanenko I.M., *Plamennoe nebo* (Kiev, IPL Ukrainy, 1983).
Stefanovsky P.M., *Trista neizvestnykh* (Moskva, Voenizdat, 1973).
Tarasenko E., *Pod krylom samolyota* (Stavropol, Stavropolskoe knizhnoe Izdatelstvo, 1968).
Tekhnika pilotirovaniya samolyota Boston III (Moskva, VI NKO, 1943).
Timokhovich I.V., *V nebe voyny* (Moskva, Voenizdat, 1986).
Tikhomolov B.E., *Romantika neba* (Tashkent, Izdatelstvo literatury i iskusstva, 1985).
Fyodorov A.G., A*viatsiya v bitve pod Moskvoy* (Moskva, 1971).
Khametov M.I., *V nebe Zapolyarya* (Moskva, IPL, 1983).
Kharlamov N.M., *Trudnaya missiya* (Moskva, Voenizdat, 1983).
Khokhlov P.I., *Nad tremya moryami* (Leningrad, Lenizdat, 1988).
Chadaev Ya.E., *Ekonomika SSSR v gody Velikoy Otechestvennoy voyny (1941 – 1945 gg.)* (Moskva, Mysl, 1985).
Chenakal D.D., *Ognennoe nebo Povolzhya* (Saratov, Izdatelstvo Saratovskogo universiteta, 1986).
Shavrov V.B., *Istoriya konstruktsiy samolyotov v SSSR, t. 2* (Moskva, Mashinostroenie, 1978).
Shakhurin A.I., *Krylya pobedy* (Moskva, IPL, 1985).
Shelest I.I., *Krylatye lyudi* (Moskva, Moskovsky rabochiy, 1980).
——, *Lechu za mechtoy* (Moskva, Molodaya gvardiya, 1989).
Shepelev A.L., *V nebe i na zemle* (Moskva, Voenizdat, 1974).
Tsapov I.I., Konev V.N. and Myasnikov I.A., *Gvardeytsy Baltiki krylatoy* (Moskva, Delta NB, 2006).
16-ya vozdushnaya (Moskva, Voenizdat, 1973).
17-ya vozdushnaya armiya v boyakh ot Stalingrada do Veny (Moskva, Voenizdat, 1977).

Magazines

Ace
Aviatsiya
Aviatsiya i Kosmonavtika
Vestnik Protovovozdushnoy Oborony
Voenno-Istoricheskiy Zhurnal

Voprosy Istorii
Voprosy Istorii Estestvoznaniya i Tekhniki
Grazhdanskaya Aviatsiya
Krilya Rodiny
Mir Aviatsii
Morskoy Sbornik
Tekhnika Vozdushnogo Flota
Tekhnika-Molodyozhi

Non-Russian Publications

Beaumont J., *Comrades in arms* (London, 1980).
Bishop E., *Mosquito: wooden wonder* (London, 1971).
Bowers P., *Curtiss aircraft 1907 – 1947* (London, 1979).
Bowyer M., *Aircraft of the Royal Air Force* (London, 1980).
Butler P. and Hagedorn D., *Air arsenal North America* (Hincley, 2004).
Freeman R., *Thunderbolt. A document list of P-47* (London, 1978).
Golley J., *Hurricanes over Murmansk* (Wellingborough, 1978).
Green W., *Famous bombers of the Second World War* (London, 1960).
Green W. and Swanborough G., *RAF Fighters* (London, 1976).
—, *US Army Air Force Fighters* (London, 1977).
Francaglia R., *The Alaska-Siberia Aircraft Ferry Project 1942 – 1945* (New York, 1973).
Infield G., *Poltava affair* (New York, 1973).
Jackson R., *The red hawks* (London, 1970).
Kimball W., *The most unsordid act* (Baltimore, 1969).
Lucas R., *Eagles east* (Tallahassee, 1970).
McDowell E., *B-25 Mitchell in action* (Carrollton, 1978).
——, *The P-40 Kittyhawk* (New York, 1968).
Mason F., *The Hawker Hurricane* (London, 1962).
Mau H. and Stapfer H., *Unter rotem sternm* (Berlin, 1976).
Mesko J., *A-20 Havoc in action* (Carrollton, 1983).
Moyle H., *The Hampden file* (London, 1994).
Pach C., *Arming the free world* (Chapel Hill, 1991).
Price A., *The Spitfire story* (London, 1982).
Robertson B., *British military aircraft serials* (London, 1967).
——, *Spitfire – the story of famous fighter* (Letchworth, 1960).
Scarborough W., *PBY Catalina in action* (Carrollton, 1983).
Scutts J., *Hurricane in action* (Carrollton, 1986).
——, *Spitfire in action* (Carrollton, 1980).
Shofield E. and Nesbit, R., *Arctic airmen* (London, 1987).
Stettinius R., *Lend-Lease* (New York, 1944).
Swanborough F., *United States military aircraft since 1909* (London, 1963).
Vader J., *Spitfire* (London, 1972).
Wagner, R., *The Soviet Air Force in World War II* (Garden City, 1973).
Wilkinson P., *Aircraft engines of the world* (New York, 1946).

Magazines

Air Enthusiast
Air International
Cockpit
Letectvi a Kosmonautika
Journal of American Aviation Historical Society
Aviation News

Archives

Russian State Military Archive
Russian State Archive of Economics
Central Archive of the Ministry of Defense
Central Naval Archive
Scientific-Memorial Museum of N.E. Zhukovsky
Museum of the Russian Air Force
Museum of the Northern Fleet Air Force
House of Aviation and Cosmonautics